Cheltenham & Gloucester

Cricket Year

Cheltenham & Gloucester

Cricket Year

Twenty-Second Edition
September 2002 to September 2003

Edited by **Jonathan Agnew**

with additional contributions by
Qamar Ahmed
Charlie Austin
Mark Baldwin
Scyld Berry
Tony Cozier
David Fulton
Nasser Hussain
Jim Maxwell
Derek Pringle
Telford Vice
Bryan Waddle

BLOOMSBURY

Edited by Jonathan Agnew
with additional contributions by
Qamar Ahmed
Charlie Austin
Mark Baldwin
Scyld Berry
Tony Cozier
David Fulton
Nasser Hussain
Jim Maxwell
Derek Pringle
Telford Vice
Bryan Waddle
with special thanks to R. Mohan, Utpal Shuvro and Neil Manthorp

The publishers would also like to thank for the following for their kind permission
to reproduce the following photographs in this book:

Mark Baldwin (p. 46): *The Times*
David Fulton (p. 126): *Kent Messenger* Group
Scyld Berry (p. 192): *Sunday Telegraph*
Derek Pringle (p. 270): photographer Martin Pope and the *Daily Telegraph*

First published in 2003 by
Bloomsbury Publishing Plc
38 Soho Square
London W1D 3HB

www.bloomsbury.com/reference

A copy of the CIP entry for this book is available from the British Library.

ISBN 0 7475 7119 8

10 9 8 7 6 5 4 3 2 1

Project editor: Chris Hawkes
Design: Kathie Wilson at designsection
Statistics: Press Association
Pictures researched and supplied by David Munden at
Sportsline Photographic – www.sportsline.org.uk

Printed and bound in Great Britain
by Butler and Tanner, Frome and London

CONTENTS

A MESSAGE FROM CHELTENHAM & GLOUCESTER

The long, hot summer of 2003 was one which will be remembered with great affection by cricket lovers in England. It was a rollercoaster ride for the national side, culminating in the wonderful victory at The Oval in the first week of September which squared the Test series with South Africa, 2–2.

England, having been beaten yet again last winter by Australia, for the eighth successive Ashes series, and having endured a bitterly disappointing World Cup bedevilled by politics, had also bounced back to win the early-summer Tests against Zimbabwe and then both the NatWest Challenge and NatWest Series one-day tournaments.

There was drama, however, following a drawn first Test against South Africa, when Nasser Hussain suddenly announced his resignation from the Test captaincy after four passionate years at the helm. Michael Vaughan, who had already led England to their mid-summer one-day successes, was immediately named as Hussain's successor for the rest of the five-match series.

Vaughan will have learned much in the next six weeks, as he came to grips with the full time job. Numbing defeat at Lord's was followed by an uplifting victory at Trent Bridge. That, in turn, was followed by a miserable loss at Headingley, as the South Africans emerged as the clear favourites to become series winners at The Oval.

This book recalls the heroic events of that famous match, along with details of every other international game played around the globe since September 2002.

It also provides a comprehensive review of the English domestic summer, which included an historic county championship triumph for Sussex, another one-day title for Gloucestershire in the Cheltenham & Gloucester Trophy, and successes for Surrey in the National League and the newly launched and highly successful Twenty20 Cup.

At Cheltenham & Gloucester, we were delighted to have signed a new contract earlier this year with the England and Wales Cricket Board to continue our support for the Cheltenham & Gloucester Trophy until at least 2006.

As part of that long-term commitment to English cricket, we are also thrilled to have taken over from Benson and Hedges the sponsorship of *Cricket Year*, which has now reached its 22nd edition.

It offers an unmatched record of cricket's past 12 months, although regular readers will soon notice that several new features have been blended in to a tried and trusted product.

The first *Cheltenham & Gloucester Cricket Year* contains not only the identity of the winner of our inaugural Man of the Year award, Alec Stewart, but also a delightful profile of one of the greatest of England's cricketers by his successor as England captain, Nasser Hussain.

You will also find three other special, new features in this year's edition: Scyld Berry, the cricket correspondent of the *Sunday Telegraph*, writes about the Cricket World Cup; Derek Pringle, the former Essex and England all-rounder and now cricket correspondent of the *Daily Telegraph*, speaks from the heart about cricket in Zimbabwe and Kenya; and David Fulton, the captain of Kent, reflects on county cricket and a time of personal trauma.

Jonathan Agnew once again heads up a small army of regular *Cricket Year* contributors from around the world, and himself writes on all matters England, besides providing his usual forthright views in the Introduction.

We would like to express our thanks to every contributor for bringing back the memories of a busy, exciting and enjoyable year, as well as to Bloomsbury who work an autumn miracle every 12 months to ensure that *Cricket Year* is published just six weeks after the end of the English domestic season.

So what could be better, when the winter months are upon us, than to curl up by the fire with the *Cheltenham & Gloucester Cricket Year* and relive all the action from those long, hot summer days of 2003!

Chris Steele
Director of Marketing & Customer Service
Cheltenham & Gloucester

AGGERS' VIEW

Introduction
By Jonathan Agnew

The Cheltenham & Gloucester's welcome sponsorship of this long-running and popular yearbook could not have come at a more interesting time for English cricket.

Despite a successful summer on the field, with the comprehensive defeat of Zimbabwe followed by a hard-earned 2–2 draw against South Africa, a notable improvement in England's one-day performances and the great success of the Twenty20 Cup, the future of county cricket was debated with a vigour that we have not seen in a while.

Even Michael Vaughan, after only three Tests in charge, went rather hurriedly on to the offensive and suggested that county cricket is not producing enough players of international quality.

A self-styled Reform Group, including former England captains Bob Willis and Michael Atherton among others, issued a press release at The Oval calling for a root-and-branch overhaul of our domestic game. One should not forget that although neither Willis nor Atherton were ever fans of county cricket, they, like Vaughan, were nonetheless successful products of the system.

I believe that the basic structure is the right one – we must do all that we can to keep the full compliment of 18 counties, offering a geographical spread all over the country – but in the panic to produce a successful England team, the system has quickly evolved into something that caters only for the international scene and which stifles everything else.

When one analyses the problem, it is hardly surprising that county cricket often appears to be irrelevant, and finds itself under attack once again for supposedly failing to fulfil its purpose.

Happily, more people are coming round to the view that the introduction of a two-divisional championship was a mistake. The intention was for competition on the field to be increased as a result – particularly at the end of a season when the prospect of either promotion or relegation began to bite.

It is possible that there is evidence of improvement in this area, but increased competition does not necessarily improve the ability of a batsman or a bowler and, besides, if the prize money on offer in a single-tier system was increased and extended downwards, it would have the same effect.

Where the introduction of two divisions has been so damaging has been off the field where, as predicted, Division Two status – and merely the threat of it – has prompted precisely the sort of decisions that county cricket could not afford to take.

Wages for only very adequate county cricketers have spiralled because the absence of the international players has promoted their worth beyond all common sense. These are the cricketers who have no realistic prospect of playing for England: they know it and so do their employers, but they can 'do a job' in the county championship.

So, with little ambition for higher honours and with no threat of losing their place to a returning England cricketer, these players settle easily into county life, and create the 'comfort zone' that one hears so much about. Why battle away and work your socks off to improve your technique if you are already picking up £40,000 or more per summer on a cosy three-year contract?

Furthermore, in order to make these players more effective – and improve the county's chances of winning games and, therefore, gaining Division One status – the standard of pitches continues to decline well

Bob Willis and Mike Atherton set themselves up as would-be reformers of the English game.

below an acceptable level. The seam bowler is still offered far too much assistance, and is then ruthlessly exposed when called upon to perform on a Test-standard pitch. Spinners have been virtually eliminated from English cricket.

When central contracts were first introduced, the concept seemed to be a sound one. The leading England players, and particularly the fast bowlers, would be employed by the Board rather than by the counties, so the England coach could control the amount of cricket they played during the course of a summer.

However, more and more contracts have been awarded and this has, in part, led to the explosion in the amount of international cricket that is now being staged every summer. The players are indeed being protected from the rigours of county cricket, but are playing non-stop international games instead with no chance to rediscover any lost form in between.

County cricket, therefore, suffers on two fronts: the best players are not available to raise the standard of the championship and, even if there is a rare opportunity for them to appear, they are usually all rested by Duncan Fletcher.

This is hardly the fault of the county system and it is hardly surprising, then, that the counties have gone elsewhere in their search for match-winners. Their target has been foreign players who, through possession of an EU or British passport, can play county cricket as an 'Englishman'.

Theoretically, a county can put out as many of these players on the field as it wants and, at the last count, there were 22 such players appearing regularly. The most absurd case, surely, is that of Craig Spearman, who has made 70 international appearances for New Zealand, but who can play for Gloucestershire as a local because his mum was born in Wales!

Spearman, who cannot actually play for England because of his New Zealand caps, therefore takes the place of someone who can. It is a crazy situation, but one that the counties have been driven to exploit because of the absence of their best players through central contracts and international demands.

If the England and Wales Cricket Board need any further persuasion that they are embarking on a dangerous course, they should consider very seriously the enforced merger this autumn of the two regular and long-running cricket magazines in this country.

There was not enough interest to sustain both *The Cricketer* and *Wisden Cricket Monthly*, and hence *The Wisden Cricketer* was born. What with that, and

Craig Spearman, the New Zealander who plays as an Englishman because his mum was born in Wales.

Channel 4 regularly preferring to screen a down-market quiz show rather than the closing overs of a day of Test cricket, the warning bells are sounding furiously.

There is simply not the demand for the amount of cricket that the authorities are aiming for, and the current level is unsustainable in the long term, not least because of the damage it is causing to our domestic game.

Such was the level and the intensity of debate this year – and not without very good reason – it is inconceivable that this issue will simply go away. Indeed, it is in the interest of all those who love cricket and want to see it thrive in this country, that it does not. However, whether those who are responsible for the running of our game have the good sense and awareness to halt the insatiable desire to squeeze every last penny out of an English summer remains to be seen.

Jonathan Agnew
Leicestershire, September 2003

CHELTENHAM & GLOUCESTER MAN OF THE YEAR AWARD

ALEC STEWART, the inaugural winner of the Cheltenham & Gloucester Man of the Year award, is profiled here by NASSER HUSSAIN.

The 2003 season signalled the end of an era in English cricket. One of its most influential cricketers finally decided to call it a day to try to return to some kind of normality in life after 20 years of complete dedication to the game.

AJ Stewart's decision to retire from first-class cricket, after a fairytale ending at his own South London pad (The Oval Cricket Ground to everyone else!), brought an end to the career of a man who meant many things to many different people.

A winner: Alec Stewart in action.

To his team-mates and in the dressing room he was the benchmark for everything cricketing. The young and the old alike would look at him out of the corner of their eyes to see what he was doing. The reason for this, I believe, is that no other cricketer in the history of the sport has covered every single aspect of his game with such professionalism and self-discipline.

Alec left nothing to chance. He always gave himself the best possible preparation in order to be successful on the field. This included jumping off the tour bus first, so that he could get to his lucky changing spot in the dressing room, to lining up his bats and shoes in perfect numbered order, and adhering to a strict diet.

This basically consisted of a glass of milk at breakfast followed by various servings of grilled chicken throughout the day, balanced with his two treats – namely a bowl of vanilla ice-cream after lunch and a bowl of Twiglets after tea!

A training schedule passed down to him from his father Micky, which itself had evolved from the football fields of the Arsenal and the Corinthian Casuals, became part of his life. There was no such thing as a day off for Alec Stewart.

Technical days off were littered with visits to the local trendy gym – Alec is a Chelsea fan, so he doesn't do sweaty gyms! – followed by hours at the bowling machine down at his brother's indoor school. Micky would usually be there to feed him balls, essentially to groove his technique rather than ever to change it.

Team England's attempt to incorporate the philosophy of 'active rest' into the routines of contracted cricketers was never better understood than by their oldest player. He had been doing 'active rest' for over 20 years.

Andy Flower, the Zimbabwean wicketkeeper-batsman who is now my club-mate at Essex, once said to me that when he went out on to a cricket field he liked the feeling of knowing that he had done more preparation than the next man. Lucky for Andy, then, that he has never played alongside Alec.

To people in the stands Alec was the immaculate, strutting Chelsea fan who gave his all for his country. (He has always been extremely patriotic, hence the parading of the Union Jack at The Oval after the final Test against South Africa.)

They saw, too, a man who played on sheer instinct. A sweeter timer of the ball, with the exception of David Gower, there has never been. Stewart was a player who took on and won the admiration of all quick bowlers around the world. They kept running in with two men on the hook; they tested him out and time after time he would take them on and win the battle. They are not the brightest, these fast bowlers!

Alec also improved his playing of spin under the expert guidance of Duncan Fletcher, although he was never actually that bad at it. When years of opening the batting were taken away from him, learning to go in against spin first-up was never going to be that easy. He simply wasn't used to it, initially, but he worked hard to improve this aspect of his game.

His wicketkeeping, meanwhile, was nearly as immaculate as his dress. As glovemen, only Jack Russell and Keith Piper equal him over the last decade. Not bad for someone who got more than 8,000 Test runs as well! Essentially, he has been England's greatest all-rounder since Ian Botham.

To captains and selectors he was their 'joker', their trump card. Because of him you could get 16 tour players on the plane when only 15 seats were booked and 12 players on to the field!

In the early days he was virtually guaranteed a tour spot, whatever his form was like in the summer (it was invariably good), because he was the very capable second wicketkeeper who could do more than just hold a bat. In turn, that meant that selectors could fit another young player into their touring party. Indeed, his glovework probably got me on my first tour with England – enabling us to room together and make our Test match debuts together back in 1990 at Sabina Park, when we beat the West Indies. Which is proof in itself that it takes all sorts to make an international cricketer!

As England captain, picking a team on the rare occasion that you were without Alec Stewart was a lot harder. With him in the side you could balance depth in batting and also have the five bowlers needed to take the 20 wickets you require to win Test matches. His worth to England will only be truly realized now he has retired.

To the armchair cricket fan sat in front of the television he was that annoying noise, if the stump microphone was turned up too high, squeaking out 'Come on Crofty' or 'Well bowled Gilo'.

On the one hand he would be the perfect gentleman, shaking hands with opposition batsmen and putting the bails back on for the square leg umpire, but on the other hand he would be picking fights with various Sri Lankan batsmen and ex-captains. Everyone in cricket knows that Alec has to have the last word!

His last act was that incredible week at The Oval and he and his family deserved it. It was a sort of unofficial Alec Stewart testimonial week and the scenes and result were just reward for someone who has made so many sacrifices for the game of cricket.

For over 40 years now the Stewart family have been involved with first-class cricket. From Micky Stewart's many victories as Surrey captain to Micky Stewart as England manager to Alec Stewart as Surrey and England player and Surrey and England captain. Alec's mum Sheila must have gone through a few ups and downs in cricketing emotions (especially following England!). All of this, however, shows how much cricket is in the Stewart blood.

The Stewart era unfortunately now comes to an end. Alec has done the 'active rest' – 20 years of it. Anyone who has ever stepped on to a cricket field with him will now want him to go away and get some proper rest. He deserves it!

Alec Stewart is honoured by the South Africans at The Oval as he walks out to bat in his 133rd and final Test appearance.

THE YEAR IN PICTURES

NOVEMBER '02:
Glenn McGrath produces a wondrous catch to dismiss Michael Vaughan off Shane Warne as England slide to an innings defeat in the Adelaide Test.

DECEMBER '02:
The sporting theatre that is the Melbourne Cricket Ground, the traditional venue for the Boxing Day Test during the Ashes series.

JANUARY '03:
It's Sydney again, with the message at last
getting through to England ...

JANUARY '03:
... but it's Steve Waugh, and Australia,
who still end up with the Ashes.

JANUARY '03:
Ricky Ponting's batting form in
the Ashes series marked the
start of a bumper year for the
29-year-old Tasmanian.

MARCH '03:
Australia are World Cup
champions again, and this
fan leaves his allegiance in
no doubt.

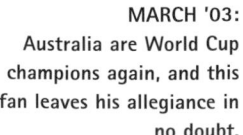

MAY '03: Bicknell lbw b Bicknell 0. It's round four of the championship and Darren falls to younger brother Martin as Surrey trounce Nottinghamshire by an innings at Trent Bridge to step up their strong defence of the county title.

MAY '03:
Head groundsman Mick Hunt (far right) and members of his staff work in harmony on a sunlit early-summer morning to get Lord's ready for England's first Test of the 2003 summer, against Zimbabwe.

JUNE '03:
Vikram Solanki, one of the successes of a new-look England one-day side which knitted together rapidly under the leadership of Michael Vaughan.

JULY '03:
It's a duck for Shaun Pollock as South Africa come off second best to England in the NatWest Series triangular tournament.

JULY '03:
Even the charms of pop band Atomic Kitten (who appeared on a boundary-edge stage during Finals Day at Trent Bridge) did not out-perform the big hit of the English domestic summer: the Twenty20 Cup.

JULY '03:
An emotional Nasser Hussain dramatically announces the end of his four-year stint as one of England's most passionate Test captains.

AUGUST '03:
Mark Boucher loses his middle stump,
but South Africa don't care: they are
about to declare on the way to a
crushing victory in the Lord's Test.

AUGUST '03:
Andrew Flintoff's century-making
defiance at the end of the Lord's
Test included this v-sign.

SEPTEMBER '03:
Flintoff's reward. After another breathtaking innings, this time in a winning cause at The Oval Test, the big lad from Lancashire celebrates England's series-levelling win – and his own elevation to the status of world-class all-rounder.

SEPTEMBER '03:
Chris Adams, the club's inspirational captain, looks to the heavens as if to say: 'Thanks for letting me be the one!' After being runners-up seven times – in 1902, 1903, 1932, 1933, 1934, 1953 and 1981 – Sussex are finally crowned as County Champions at a happy Hove.

ENGLAND

ZIMBABWE IN ENGLAND
PAKISTAN IN ENGLAND
NATWEST TRIANGULAR ONE-DAY SERIES
SOUTH AFRICA IN ENGLAND

ZIMBABWE IN ENGLAND
By Jonathan Agnew

3–5 May 2003 at Edgbaston
British Universities 146 (DT Hondo 5 for 26) and 263
(EJM Cowan 137*, AM Blignaut 4 for 89)
Zimbabweans 376 (GW Flower 130, SV Carlisle 54,
HH Streak 51, MA Vermeulen 51) and 37 for 0
Zimbabweans won by 10 wickets

This match was scheduled to last for four days, but the disappointingly poor quality of the British Universities' batting contributed to a ten-wicket victory well inside three days for the Zimbabweans at Edgbaston. Doug Hondo, the dreadlocked medium pacer, was the chief destroyer of the students' first innings, taking five cheap wickets through his consistency of line and length. The Universities side were 92 for 2 at the end of an abbreviated first day, but then collapsed to 146 all out and saw Zimbabwe build a sizeable lead of 156 by the close of play. Half-centuries from Mark Vermeulen and Stuart Carlisle were followed by a fine stand of 138 in 37 overs between Grant Flower, who made 130, and Heath Streak. That the Zimbabweans were then made to bat again was wholly down to a magnificent unbeaten 137 from Ed Cowan, a 20-year-old Australian attending Oxford Brookes. He faced only 148 balls, hitting 20 boundaries and three sixes off the spinners, Doug Marillier and Flower. It was his maiden first-class century, too, but, sadly, no one else was good enough to stay with him.

9–12 May 2003 at Worcester
Worcestershire 262 (VS Solanki 74, BF Smith 53) and
247 (AJ Hall 68, SD Peters 63)
Zimbabweans 334 (SV Carlisle 157, T Taibu 57) and
175 (Kabir Ali 5 for 48)
Match tied

A crowd of little more than 250 witnessed the climax to an exciting tie between Worcestershire and the touring Zimbabweans at New Road. In a finish worthy of a far greater audience, Kabir Ali grabbed the last two Zimbabwe wickets with the scores level to earn himself figures of 5 for 48 to underline his claims to a call-up to the senior England side. Zimbabwe's failure to clamber over the finishing line was rough on Heath Streak, their combative captain, who hit 37, despite batting with a runner because of a leg injury. Requiring 176 for victory, Zimbabwe started badly, but were rallied by Andy Blignaut's 42, which included eight fours. Streak was then well supported by a dogged Ray Price until he tried to run Kabir away for the winning single and edged to third slip. Enter last man Doug Hondo, who, two balls later, was utterly confounded by an in-swinger of full length. The tourists had looked clear favourites to win the game when, in reply to Worcestershire's first-innings 262, they reached 334 on the back of a magnificent eight-and-a-half hour 157 from Stuart Carlisle. He had made an unbeaten 139 by the close of the second day, his 31st birthday, and faced 374 balls in all. His two sixes included a superb square cut off Kabir. Worcestershire, however, battled hard to set Zimbabwe some sort of target, with Stephen Peters and Andrew Hall both compiling splendid half-centuries. In the end their efforts paid off memorably.

15–18 May 2003 at Hove
Zimbabweans 395 (MA Vermeulen 198, GW Flower 64,
SM Ervine 57*, PM Hutchison 4 for 94)
Sussex 179 for 4 (B Zuiderent 50)
Match drawn

Sussex ran into controversy at Hove when they chose to omit a clutch of regular first-team players for the visit of Zimbabwe. For a variety of reasons, not all of them as a result of injury 'niggles', the captain Chris Adams and six other first-choice men – Mushtaq Ahmed, Robin Martin-Jenkins, James Kirtley, Tony Cottey, Tim Ambrose and Matt Prior – were all stood down. Not that this mattered a jot to

Mark Vermeulen, who gratefully took the opportunity to hit a career-best 198. He scored only four of those runs on the third morning, following a second day washout, and his domination of the opening day included a six and 32 boundaries. Zimbabwe's first-innings 395 was also built around half-centuries from Grant Flower and Sean Ervine, but with only 21 overs of play possible on the third day, any chance of a result disappeared. In the time allowed on the final day, Bas Zuiderent square cut Heath Streak for six on his way to 50, while Murray Goodwin, captaining Sussex against his former Test team-mates, struck 49. History was also made on day three of this game when Hove's eight permanent floodlights, installed in 1999 at a cost of £180,000, were switched on at 2.30pm in order to keep the players on the field during a spell of poor light. It was the first time this had happened in a first-class match in England.

npower FIRST TEST
22–26 May 2003 at Lord's

The possibility of demonstrations by protestors opposed to the regime of Zimbabwe's president, Robert Mugabe, threatened to overshadow the first Test of the summer. Although there was widespread sympathy towards their cause, thankfully common sense prevailed. A group of exiled Zimbabweans and some politicians made their presence felt outside the Grace Gates, following the example of Andy Flower and Henry Olonga by wearing black armbands, and encouraging spectators to do the same. Inside the ground, two banner-waving protestors meandered quietly and peacefully onto the outfield and were gently led away by security staff. Their point was made, and the fact the game was taking place at all gave them the perfect vehicle to do so.

Zimbabwe's cricketers, therefore, had plenty on their minds as they arrived at cricket's headquarters. They must be getting used to this, and ignoring the politics while preparing for important

matches is clearly not easy. However, they would not want the distractions to be used as an excuse for their woefully inadequate display at Lord's, which confirmed their lowly status in the ICC Test Championship.

England, meanwhile, had injuries to consider. So often is this the case that it really is starting to become utterly tedious. The main drama this time focussed on the all-rounders. For a variety of reasons, Andrew Flintoff, Paul Collingwood and Craig White were all ruled out, so a surprising SOS was sent to Yorkshire's Anthony McGrath, and the Sussex fast bowler, James Kirtley, was omitted on the morning of the Test.

The first day was cloudy and overcast: a seam bowler's dream. England's decision to prefer Ashley Giles to Kirtley provoked some criticism in the

Mark Butcher was England's centurion in the first Test against Zimbabwe at Lord's.

Five-wicket hero: James Anderson marks his Test debut in style at Lord's.

FIRST TEST – ENGLAND v. ZIMBABWE
22–26 May 2003 at Lord's

ENGLAND

	First Innings	
ME Trescothick	c Ervine b Blignaut	59
MP Vaughan	b Streak	8
MA Butcher	c Vermeulen b Price	137
N Hussain (capt)	c Hondo b Friend	19
RWT Key	c Taibu b Streak	18
*AJ Stewart	c Taibu b Streak	26
A McGrath	b Ervine	69
AF Giles	b Blignaut	52
SJ Harmison	c Ebrahim b Ervine	0
MJ Hoggard	c Ebrahim b Blignaut	19
JM Anderson	not out	4
Extras	b 14, lb 27, w 3, nb 17	61
		472

	First Innings			
	O	M	R	W
Streak	37	9	99	3
Blignaut	26.1	4	96	3
Hondo	14	4	45	0
Ervine	22	5	95	2
Friend	13	2	49	1
Price	20	6	44	1
Flower	1	0	3	0

Fall of Wickets
1-45, 2-121, 3-165, 4-204, 5-274, 6-342, 7-408, 8-408, 9-465

ZIMBABWE

	First Innings		Second Innings	
DD Ebrahim	c McGrath b Butcher	68	c Key b Harmison	6
MA Vermeulen	b Anderson	1	c Trescothick b Butcher	61
SV Carlisle	c Trescothick b Hoggard	11	lbw b Butcher	24
GW Flower	c Key b Hoggard	3	c Trescothick b Harmison	26
*T Taibu	c Hoggard b Harmison	25	c Butcher b McGrath	16
SM Ervine	lbw b Hoggard	4	c Trescothick b McGrath	4
HH Streak (capt)	b Anderson	10	lbw b McGrath	11
AM Blignaut	c Butcher b Anderson	3	b Butcher	6
TJ Friend	b Anderson	0	c Giles b Butcher	43
RW Price	not out	7	c Trescothick b Giles	26
DT Hondo	b Anderson	0	not out	0
Extras	b 5, lb 1, w 1, nb 8	15	b 1, lb 6, w 3	10
		147		**233**

	First Innings				Second Innings			
	O	M	R	W	O	M	R	W
Hoggard	18	8	24	3	15	5	35	0
Anderson	16	4	73	5	15	4	65	0
Harmison	16	5	36	1	12	4	35	2
Butcher	5	2	8	1	12.5	0	60	4
Giles	-	-	-	-	8	2	15	1
McGrath	-	-	-	-	6	1	16	3

Fall of Wickets
1-20, 2-64, 3-79, 4-104, 5-109, 6-129, 7-133, 8-133, 9-147
1-11, 2-91, 3-95, 4-128, 5-132, 6-150, 7-158, 8-168, 9-219

Umpires: SA Bucknor & DL Orchard
Toss: Zimbabwe

England won by an innings and 92 runs

commentary boxes, but Nasser Hussain was mindful not only of his seam attack's inexperience – 23 caps in total of which Matthew Hoggard's contribution was 18 – but also the length of England's tail.

As it was, the argument quickly lost its intensity when Heath Streak won the toss and decided to bowl first. Michael Vaughan, recently elevated to No. 1 in the world rankings, made a tortuous eight from 42 balls and when he departed, bowled behind his legs by Streak, it was a blessing. That was to be Zimbabwe's last success for a while as Trescothick celebrated a return to form, making 59. Butcher was dropped on 36, but then dominated the innings, becoming increasingly more fluent. He reached his seventh Test century – and his second at Lord's – on the second morning in the company of Stewart, who many thought should have been pensioned off, and when Butcher was brilliantly caught by Vermeulen at short midwicket for 137, he had faced 256 balls and hit 21 fours and a six. Vermeulen promptly dropped Giles at slip off the suffering Streak, and this enabled Giles and McGrath to add 66 precious runs for the seventh wicket. Giles made 52 and just as the pundits were beginning speculatively to look up England's last centurion on debut, McGrath was defeated for length and bowled by Ervine for 69. Hoggard played a few shots for his 19, and when England were dismissed for 472, with 20 overs remaining in the second day. Zimbabwe already had their backs to the wall, needing 273 to avoid the follow-on, and this was compounded by the loss of Vermeulen to James Anderson for one before the close.

The third – and final day – was still conducive to swing bowling, but Zimbabwe's feeble technique against the moving ball was exposed to such an extent that, of the 19 wickets to fall in the day, eight were to the very part-time medium pace of McGrath and Butcher. Ebrahim scored 68 in the first innings before slicing Butcher to gully, and Anderson ran through the tail to take 5 for 73 in his first Test match. He bowled with plenty of spirit, and more than confirmed the very high hopes that English followers have in him.

Zimbabwe fared slightly better at the start of the second innings. This time it was Vermeulen who passed 50, but wickets fell steadily at the other end, with McGrath claiming three in successive overs. Flower's grotesque edge to slip with no trace of foot movement will remain a graphic illustration of Zimbabwe's shortcomings, and the match was wrapped up when Hussain claimed the extra half-hour and Butcher, the Man of the Match for his century and five wickets, snared the hard-hitting Travis Friend for 43.

30 May–2 June 2003 at Shenley
Middlesex 516 for 6 dec. (RMS Weston 129, PN Weekes 102*, MJ Brown 98, EC Joyce 80, OA Shah 68) and 222 for 2 dec. (OA Shah 101*)
Zimbabweans 401 for 4 dec. (SV Carlisle 137, GW Flower 65, MA Vermeulen 59) and 221 for 5 (DD Ebrahim 64)
Match drawn

Batsmen from both sides enjoyed the friendly surface at Shenley, with only 17 wickets falling in four days as Middlesex and the Zimbabweans shared a draw. Robin Weston and Paul Weekes both hit hundreds at the Denis Compton Oval as Middlesex ran up 516 for 6 declared in their first innings. Owais Shah and Ed

Joyce also flourished against a flimsy attack, while 23-year-old wicketkeeper Michael Brown made 98. Stuart Carlisle spearheaded the confident Zimbabwean reply of 401 for 4 declared, and Shah then blasted an 80-ball, second-innings century containing four sixes and 15 fours to set up a third declaration. For a moment, at 140 for 5, the Zimbabweans looked in a bit of bother – but then Tatendu Taibu and Grant Flower snuffed out any late possibility of a positive result by adding an unbroken 81.

npower SECOND TEST
5–9 June 2003 at Chester-le-Street

Another feeble batting performance by the visitors in their first innings condemned Chester-le-Street's inaugural Test match to a three-day affair. In the event, Durham County Cricket Club did well to persuade a total of 30,000 spectators into the pretty Riverside ground for the special occasion, but, as proud as they were of their achievement, the local

Surprise package: Anthony McGrath enjoyed instant success – with both bat and ball – after his sudden call-up in place of the injured Andrew Flintoff.

Worth the wait: eight years on from his first England selection, Richard Johnson at last makes a Test debut ... and takes 6 for 33.

authorities who worked so hard must have been left quietly wondering if the staging of Test cricket these days is really what it is cracked up to be.

Once again the match ended with more discussions about the viability of Test cricket in its present form. Zimbabwe and Bangladesh, who were both awarded Test status prematurely and for political reasons rather than sound cricketing sense, are so far removed from the others that one wonders what sort of image of the game is presented when they are involved. This Test match was utterly tedious and devoid of anything remotely resembling the cut and thrust that makes cricket such a wonderfully unpredictable sport. With so much international cricket being staged now, something will have to give and it may very well be that broadcasters and spectators simply refuse to have anything to do with what is a second-class product when there are other options available.

South Africa were at Headingley later in the summer: given a choice and limited funds, it is pretty clear which of the two games on offer would attract northern cricket fans.

As usual, injuries affected the selection of England's team. This time it was Matthew Hoggard who was unavailable with a leg injury and he was replaced by Somerset's Richard Johnson who, as a young Middlesex bowler, had been chosen to tour South Africa in 1995–96. Curiously, Andrew Flintoff was ruled unfit one day, and scored a rip-roaring 150 for Lancashire the next. With Anthony McGrath also unable to bowl because of the side strain he picked up at Lord's, there was an argument – heard regularly during the build-up to the game – that Flintoff could have played for England as a batsman. That was soon forgotten when McGrath, for the second time, came within touching distance of a century.

An unchanged Zimbabwe found themselves in the field and, in the 51st over, had England floundering a little on 156 for 5. On a slow pitch, it was Doug Hondo who had picked up the credit for some casual strokes by England's middle order, and he picked up three wickets with his medium pace. Vaughan and Trescothick both missed out in this mini-series, with Vaughan slipping to No. 2 in the world rankings as a result. He edged to slip for 20, while Trescothick was a little unlucky as he gloved a sweep straight into the waiting Taibu's gloves for 43. Butcher again looked in good touch but, on 47, he started the slide when he edged Hondo onto his stumps as he tried to cut a ball that was too close to his body. Key, whose place began to look under threat, made just four – although that backfoot force was one of the shots of the match – before being caught low down at midwicket and Hussain did little to silence his own critics by scoring 18 from 54 balls.

From that position of uncertainty, Stewart and McGrath pulled England around. Stewart overtook David Gower to become England's second highest run scorer in Test cricket on the way to his 68, while McGrath, who scored 81, appeared to have taken to Test cricket like a duck to water. That statement carries the obvious caveat that it is extremely difficult to judge anyone's performance against a team as weak as Zimbabwe, but up to this point he had looked most assured and played very strongly off his legs, in particular. They put on 149 together, and were both dropped along the way, which effectively ended Zimbabwe's hopes of taking control of the match.

After Giles had completed his second successive half-century, Zimbabwe were left 17 overs in which

SECOND TEST – ENGLAND v. ZIMBABWE
5–9 June 2003 at Chester-le-Street

SERIES AVERAGES
England v. Zimbabwe

ENGLAND

First Innings

ME Trescothick	c Taibu b Price		43
MP Vaughan	c Ervine b Streak		20
MA Butcher	b Hondo		47
N Hussain (capt)	c Taibu b Hondo		18
RWT Key	c Flower b Hondo		4
*AJ Stewart	lbw b Streak		68
A McGrath	c Taibu b Blignaut		81
AF Giles	c Ervine b Streak		50
RL Johnson	c Streak b Blignaut		24
SJ Harmison	c Vermeulen b Streak		11
JM Anderson	not out		12
Extras	b 1, lb 5, w 7, nb 25		38
			416

	O	M	R	W
Streak	34.1	11	64	4
Blignaut	23	4	95	2
Hondo	22	1	98	3
Ervine	3	0	17	0
Price	40	9	105	1
Friend	4	0	26	0
Flower	1	0	5	0

Fall of Wickets
1-49, 2-109, 3-146, 4-152, 5-156, 6-305, 7-324, 8-356, 9-390

ZIMBABWE

	First Innings			Second Innings		
DD Ebrahim	lbw b Anderson		6	lbw b Harmison		55
MA Vermeulen	lbw b Johnson		0	c McGrath b Anderson		0
SV Carlisle	lbw b Johnson		0	c Key b Anderson		28
GW Flower	c Trescothick b Anderson		8	b Anderson		16
*T Taibu	lbw b Johnson		31	c Butcher b Giles		14
SM Ervine	c Stewart b Johnson		0	b Harmison		34
TJ Friend	lbw b Johnson		0	not out		65
HH Streak (capt)	lbw b Johnson		4	run out		3
AM Blignaut	c Anderson b Harmison		13	c Hussain b Anderson		12
RW Price	lbw b Harmison		17	c Stewart b Harmison		6
DT Hondo	not out		5	b Harmison		4
Extras	b 5, lb 3, nb 2		10	b 6, lb 10		16
			94			**253**

	First Innings				Second Innings			
	O	M	R	W	O	M	R	W
Anderson	10	2	30	2	23	8	55	4
Johnson	12	4	33	6	22	7	67	0
Harmison	9.1	3	22	2	21.4	4	55	4
Giles	1	0	1	0	25	9	51	1
Butcher	-	-	-	-	2	0	9	0

Fall of Wickets
1-3, 2-3, 3-11, 4-18, 5-23, 6-31, 7-35, 8-48, 9-73
1-5, 2-65, 3-102, 4-113, 5-131, 6-185, 7-202, 8-223, 9-244

Umpires: DB Hair & DL Orchard
Toss: England

England won by an innings and 69 runs

ENGLAND

Batting	M	Inns	NO	Runs	HS	Av	100	50	c/st
MA Butcher	2	2	0	184	137	92.00	1	-	3/-
A McGrath	2	2	0	150	81	75.00	-	2	2/-
AF Giles	2	2	0	102	52	51.00	-	2	1/-
ME Trescothick	2	2	0	102	59	51.00	-	1	6/-
AJ Stewart	2	2	0	94	68	47.00	-	1	2/-
RL Johnson	1	1	0	24	24	24.00	-	-	-/-
MJ Hoggard	1	1	0	19	19	19.00	-	-	1/-
N Hussain	2	2	0	37	19	18.50	-	-	1/-
MP Vaughan	2	2	0	28	20	14.00	-	-	-/-
RWT Key	2	2	0	22	18	11.00	-	-	3/-
SJ Harmison	2	2	0	11	11	5.50	-	-	-/-
JM Anderson	2	2	2	16	12*	-	-	-	1/-

Bowling	Overs	Mds	Runs	Wkts	Av	Best	5/inn	10m
A McGrath	6	1	16	3	5.33	3-16	-	-
MA Butcher	19.5	2	77	5	15.40	4-60	-	-
SJ Harmison	58.5	16	148	9	16.44	4-55	-	-
RL Johnson	34	11	100	6	16.66	6-33	1	-
MJ Hoggard	33	13	59	3	19.66	3-24	-	-
JM Anderson	64	18	223	11	20.27	5-73	1	-
AF Giles	34	11	67	2	33.50	1-15	-	-

ZIMBABWE

Batting	M	Inns	NO	Runs	HS	Av	100	50	c/st
TJ Friend	2	4	1	108	65*	36.00	-	1	1/-
DD Ebrahim	2	4	0	135	68	33.75	-	2	2/-
T Taibu	2	4	0	86	31	21.50	-	-	5/-
RW Price	2	4	1	56	26	18.66	-	-	-/-
SV Carlisle	2	4	0	63	28	15.75	-	-	2/-
MA Vermeulen	2	4	0	62	61	15.50	-	1	2/-
GW Flower	2	4	0	53	26	13.25	-	-	1/-
SM Ervine	2	4	0	42	34	10.50	-	-	3/-
AM Blignaut	2	4	0	34	13	8.50	-	-	-/-
HH Streak	2	4	0	28	11	7.00	-	-	1/-
DT Hondo	2	4	2	9	5*	4.50	-	-	1/-

Bowling	Overs	Mds	Runs	Wkts	Av	Best	5/inn	10m
HH Streak	71.1	20	163	7	23.28	4-64	-	-
AM Blignaut	49.1	8	191	5	38.20	3-96	-	-
DT Hondo	36	5	143	3	47.66	3-98	-	-
SM Ervine	25	5	112	2	56.00	2-95	-	-
RW Price	60	15	149	2	74.50	1-44	-	-
TJ Friend	17	2	75	1	75.00	1-49	-	-

Also bowled: GW Flower 2-0-8-0

to bat before tea on the second day. At the interval they were 35 for 7, and already facing certain defeat.

The destroyer was Johnson, who became the second bowler in the series to take five wickets on his debut (the same caveat as above applies). Bowling into the breeze, he did little more than bowl straight and on a full length. Showing a complete disregard for the basics of batsmanship – and falling foul of a couple of generous lbw decisions – Zimbabwe's batsmen managed to play the ball with their pads rather than with their bats and of his six victims for 33, Johnson picked up five of them leg before wicket. Taibu scored a gutsy 31 and demonstrated why he is so highly regarded, but from the moment Johnson picked up two wickets with consecutive balls in his first over, Zimbabwe were on the slide. Taibu apart, only two made double figures – Blignaut and Price, who helped Zimbabwe to add 59 runs for the last three wickets.

Following on, Zimbabwe fared a little better and, interestingly, Johnson failed to pick up a single wicket. Ebrahim made 55 and Friend 65 not out, but Anderson and Harmison chipped away in front of a full house of 12,000 and, fittingly, it was the local boy who splattered Hondo's stumps to end the game shortly after tea.

13 June 2003 at Belfast
Zimbabweans 182 (49.5 overs) (DD Ebrahim 52, S Matsikenyeri 50)
Ireland 183 for 0 (33.4 overs) (JAM Molins 107*, JP Bray 67*)
Ireland won by 10 wickets

15 June 2003 at Eglinton
Ireland 196 (48.4 overs) (PG Gillespie 56)
Zimbabweans 199 for 2 (40.1 overs) (DD Ebrahim 81*)
Zimbabweans won by 8 wickets

17 June 2003 at Taunton
Zimbabweans 285 for 9 (50 overs) (SV Carlisle 119, S Matsikenyeri 66)
Somerset 282 for 7 (50 overs) (KP Dutch 93, PD Bowler 93)
Zimbabweans won by 3 runs

The Zimbabweans finally achieved their first meaningful victory on tour when they beat Somerset at Taunton by just three runs in a high-scoring contest. They did well to hold their nerve at the end, moreover, as they prevented Somerset from scoring the 18 they required from the last two overs, with five wickets in hand. Eleven was needed from the final over, and then six from the last two balls – a task which proved beyond the inexperienced pair of Wes Durston and Gareth Andrew. Zimbabwe totalled 285 for 9 from their 50 overs, by no means an intimidating score on a fine Taunton pitch, with Stuart Carlisle making his third century of the tour and adding 134 in 20 overs with the hard-hitting Stuart Matsikenyeri. The same number of runs, in 22 overs, had been put on by Somerset's joint top scorers Peter Bowler and Keith Dutch, who each scored 93.

19 June 2003 at Southampton
Hampshire 262 for 5 (50 overs) (DA Kenway 120*, AD Mascarenhas 50*)
Zimbabweans 246 (49.1 overs) (DA Marillier 54, ESH Giddins 4 for 33)
Hampshire won by 16 runs

Defeat to Hampshire at the Rose Bowl was perhaps not quite so demoralizing as the ten-wicket beating by Ireland the previous week, but this was another bad day for the Zimbabweans. After learning before the game that Stuart Carlisle, their leading batsman, had in fact suffered a broken thumb at Taunton, they then failed by 16 runs to chase down a Hampshire total of 262 for 5 that was built upon an unbeaten one-day best 120 by Derek Kenway. There were too many soft dismissals and, despite Doug Marillier's 54, they were in some bother at 203 for 8 before Andy Blignaut gave the tourists at least a chance of victory with a bold 44. But, in the end, Ed Giddins returned to thwart the Zimbabwean attempt to score 20 from the last three overs.

22 June 2003 at Chelmsford
Essex 189 for 9 (50 overs) (A Flower 52)
Zimbabweans 193 for 5 (39 overs) (GW Flower 60*)
Zimbabweans won by 5 wickets

A morale-boosting victory against Essex enabled the Zimbabweans to approach the NatWest Series matches with more confidence than had seemed likely. With a tidy bowling performance, in which Ray Price and Heath Streak stood out, Zimbabwe held an Essex side containing both Nasser Hussain and Andy Flower to 189 for 9, with Flower scoring 52 after being made captain against his fellow countrymen. It was Andy's brother Grant, however, who played the decisive innings of 60 not out from 79 balls. Travis Friend also played some eye-catching strokes in his 44, after being promoted to No. 3, and victory for the Zimbabweans came with 11 overs to spare.

PAKISTAN IN ENGLAND – NATWEST CHALLENGE SERIES
By Jonathan Agnew

17 June 2003 at Old Trafford
England 204 for 9 (50 overs)
Pakistan 208 for 8 (49.2 overs) (Mohammad Hafeez 69)
Pakistan won by 2 wickets

20 June 2003 at The Oval
Pakistan 185 (44 overs) (Yousuf Youhana 75*,
JM Anderson 4 for 27)
England 189 for 3 (22 overs) (ME Trescothick 86)
England won by 7 wickets

22 June 2003 at Lord's
Pakistan 229 for 7 (50 overs) (Abdul Razzaq 64, Younis
Khan 63, A Flintoff 4 for 32)
England 231 for 6 (48.2 overs) (ME Trescothick 108*)
England won by 4 wickets

For both teams, this was an early test of the clear-outs
that had followed their premature departures from
the World Cup. Pakistan had regrouped under
Rashid Latif's leadership, and had already played
tournaments in Sharjah and Sri Lanka, while Michael
Vaughan was handed the reins of England's one-day
team after Nasser Hussain's resignation in
March. Much of the pre-tournament debate had
centred on Darren Gough – and whether, or
not, he was finally fit to return to the fold. In the
end, public opinion helped sway the selectors in
Gough's favour, and he was also handed the
added responsibility of having to help the young
seam bowlers at the end of the innings.

The opening match at Old Trafford was won
in the last over by the visitors. England chose to
bat first on a pitch that helped the spinners, and
struggled to 204 for 9 in their 50 overs. It was
hardly gripping stuff, but Shoaib Malik's off spin
(he took 3 for 26) was difficult to get away and
after Solanki's run-a-ball 36, the only
contributions of note came from Flintoff (39)
and McGrath, who scored 33. Pakistan would
have been made to work much harder for their
runs had Giles bowled round the wicket rather
than over, and they reached their target with two
wickets and four balls remaining.

Three days later, the teams reconvened at The

Oval where Pakistan were duly thrashed in an entirely
one-sided game. Anderson took the first wicket, and
then the last three in recording the first hat-trick by
an Englishman in a one-day international, to finish
with figures of 4 for 27. Set 186 to win, England got
away to a flier, with Trescothick in masterful form.
His 86 came from only 55 balls, Solanki scored 40
from 49 and, although Troughton failed for a second
time, England coasted home with 28 overs to spare.

So, the last match of the mini-series was, effectively,
a final and a packed Lord's played host to the best
game of the three-match series. Floundering on 117
for 5, Pakistan seemed destined for another small
total, but they were then rescued by Younis Khan and
Abdul Razzaq. Khan's 63 came from 87 balls while
Razzaq's 64 was a more belligerent affair and set
England 230 to win.

Trescothick was again in blistering form, but he
lacked support throughout the innings – until, that is,
Read joined him with 76 still needed. In poor light,
Read demonstrated a remarkably calm head while
Trescothick reached a magnificent hundred. With ten
balls to go, Trescothick launched a six into the Grand
Stand to clinch the game, and in one fell swoop
buried the memory of a similar attempt two years
earlier that contributed to England's defeat on the
same ground against the same opponents.

The finishers: Marcus Trescothick and Chris Read
see England home at Lord's, as Pakistan are
defeated 2–1 in the NatWest Challenge.

NATWEST TRIANGULAR ONE-DAY SERIES
(England, South Africa and Zimbabwe)
By Jonathan Agnew

England's first look at South Africa – who would be their Test opponents later in the summer – proved misleading. Thrashed in the final by Vaughan's new team, South Africa regrouped and quickly turned the tables on England in the Test series only a fortnight later.

However, England's crushing victory in the Lord's final of the triangular one-day series ushered in a much-needed 'feel-good factor' about English cricket that, while only lasting for two weeks, was very welcome at the time.

The only surprising result in the tournament was in the opening game when England produced a startlingly lacklustre performance against Zimbabwe. Perhaps it was due to complacency, having dealt with the Zimbabweans so convincingly in the Test series, but Grant Flower did not complain and he rescued his team, taking them from a worrying 15 for 4 and leading them to victory with an innings of 96 not out.

An outstanding maiden century by Solanki against South Africa restored the balance, despite 107 from Kallis. This time it was Trescothick's turn to play second fiddle as his young partner raced to 106 from 107 balls. Trescothick's unbeaten 114 came from 125 deliveries.

From The Oval, England slipped up only once against South Africa – a day-night game at Old Trafford – and Zimbabwe could not muster another victory, which all added up to the Lord's crowd getting what it wanted: England against South Africa in the final.

What the supporters had not bargained for, however, was such a short game. South Africa were never in the contest after Vaughan sent them in to bat and, with Kallis despatched by Gough for a duck, they were floundering on 43 for 4. The seamers all chipped away, but it was Giles who claimed the wicket of the last recognized batsman, van Jaarsveld, to leave the visitors with nowhere to

Vikram Solanki pulls powerfully during his maiden one-day international century against South Africa.

Opposite: James Anderson ... flying high.

go on 102 for 7 in the 28th over. A pathetic batting display was sealed when Pollock gave Flintoff his second wicket, and England were set 108 to win.

Trescothick made things interesting when he edged Ntini to Hall to first slip for a duck in the second over of England's reply. All it needed, however, was one sizeable partnership and this was provided by Solanki and Vaughan. Solanki's typically wristy half-century came from 58 balls and when his dismissal followed that of Vaughan (who made 30) in the 17th over, England were only 19 runs short of victory. McGrath and Flintoff finished off the job in the 21st over – which meant that the packed crowd of 29,000 people saw the equivalent of just one innings!

Match One
26 June 2003 at Trent Bridge
England 191 for 8 (50 overs)
(A Flintoff 53)
Zimbabwe 195 for 6
(48 overs) (GW Flower 96*)
Zimbabwe (5pts) beat England (1pt) by 4 wickets

Match Two
28 June 2003 at The Oval
South Africa 264 for 6
(50 overs) (JH Kallis 107,
MV Boucher 55)
England 265 for 4 (45.5 overs) (ME Trescothick 114*,
VS Solanki 106)
England (5pts) beat South Africa (1pt) by 6 wickets

Match Three
29 June at Canterbury
South Africa 272 for 5
(50 overs) (JH Kallis 125*,
AJ Hall 56)
Zimbabwe 226 for 9
(50 overs) (TJ Friend 82)
South Africa (5pts) beat Zimbabwe (1pt) by 46 runs

Match Four
1 July at Headingley
England 81 for 4 (17 overs)
Zimbabwe did not bat
*No result. England (3pts) Zimbabwe (3pts)
Match abandoned due to rain*

Match Five
4 July at Old Trafford
England 223 for 7 (50 overs) (ME Trescothick 60,
A McGrath 52)

South Africa 227 for 3 (47.3 overs) (JH Kallis 82*, JA Rudolph 71*)
England (5pts) beat South Africa (1pt) by 7 wickets

Match Six
5 July at Sophia Gardens
Zimbabwe 174 for 8 (50 overs) (HH Streak 54)
South Africa 175 for 1 (34.2 overs) (HH Gibbs 93*, GC Smith 58)
South Africa (6pts) won by 9 wickets

Match Seven
6 July at Bristol
Zimbabwe 92 (24.5 overs) (D Gough 4 for 26)
England 95 for 4 (17.5 overs) (HH Streak 4 for 21)
England (6pts) won by 6 wickets

Match Eight
9 July at Edgbaston
South Africa 198 for 9 (50 overs) (JM Anderson 4 for 38)
England 199 for 6 (39 overs) (MP Vaughan 83, A Flintoff 54)
England (6pts) won by 4 wickets

Match Nine
10 July at The Rose Bowl
Zimbabwe 173 for 8 (50 overs) (HH Streak 50*, M Ntini 4 for 45)
South Africa 174 for 3 (35.2 overs) (JA Rudolph 69*, GC Smith 69)
South Africa (6pts) won by 7 wickets

	P	W	L	T	NR	R/R	Pts
South Africa	6	4	2	0	0	0.48	23
England	6	3	2	0	1	0.83	22
Zimbabwe	6	1	4	0	1	-1.37	9

Opposite: To the victor, the spoils.
Michael Vaughan, England's new one-day captain, displays the NatWest Series silverware.

NATWEST SERIES FINAL – ENGLAND v. SOUTH AFRICA
12 July 2003 at Lord's

SOUTH AFRICA

GC Smith (capt)	c Trescothick b Anderson	7
HH Gibbs	c Read b Gough	9
MN van Wyk	b Anderson	17
JH Kallis	c Read b Gough	0
JA Rudolph	c Read b Flintoff	19
*MV Boucher	c Read b Johnson	11
M van Jaarsveld	c and b Giles	11
SM Pollock	c Read b Flintoff	18
AJ Hall	c Vaughan b Anderson	0
A Nel	lbw b Giles	1
M Ntini	not out	0
Extras	lb 1, w 10, nb 3	14
	(32.1 overs)	107

	O	M	R	W
Anderson	10	0	50	3
Gough	7	2	9	2
Flintoff	6.1	0	18	2
Johnson	6	1	26	1
Giles	3	2	3	2

Fall of Wickets
1-10, 2-30, 3-39, 4-43, 5-75, 6-75, 7-102, 8-103, 9-107

ENGLAND

ME Trescothick	c Hall b Ntini	0
VS Solanki	b Hall	50
MP Vaughan (capt)	c Ntini b Nel	30
A McGrath	not out	15
A Flintoff	not out	6
R Clarke		
*CMW Read		
AF Giles		
RL Johnson		
D Gough		
JM Anderson		
Extras	lb 1, w 7, nb 2	10
	(3 wkts, 20.2 overs)	111

	O	M	R	W
Pollock	5	1	17	0
Ntini	5	1	24	1
Kallis	3	0	33	0
Nel	5	0	22	1
Hall	2.2	0	14	1

Fall of Wickets
1-1, 2-88, 3-89

Umpires: NA Mallender & SJA Taufel
Toss: England

England won by 7 wickets

SOUTH AFRICA IN ENGLAND
By Jonathan Agnew

20 June 2003 at Hove
South Africa 267 for 7 (50 overs) (HH Dippenaar 101*)
Sussex 114 (30.5 overs)
South Africa won by 153 runs

Sussex intended their one-day fixture against the
South Africans at Hove to be a day-night affair. The
lights, however, were not needed as the home side
were thrashed by 153 runs on a glorious day (and
late afternoon). After totalling 267 for 7 from their
50 overs, with Boeta Dippenaar hitting 101 not out
from 90 balls, the South Africans shot out Sussex for
114, with Charl Langeveldt and Paul Adams taking
three wickets apiece and Andrew Hall and Makhaya
Ntini two each.

22 June 2003 at Northampton
South Africa 229 for 6 (50 overs) (MV Boucher 69,
SM Pollock 53)
Northamptonshire 45 for 1 (15 overs)
No result

Heavy rain caused the abandonment of
Northamptonshire's one-day match against the
South Africans at Wantage Road … just when it was
getting interesting. Tight opening spells from
Damien Wright and Mike Cawdron had restricted
the tourists early on, and only Mark Boucher (69)
and Shaun Pollock (53) broke the shackles in a 50-
over total of 229 for 6. Northants were 45 for 1 from
15 overs in reply, with Mike Hussey looking well set
on 27 not out, when the rain arrived.

25 June 2003 at Worcester
South Africa 261 for 4 (50 overs) (JH Kallis 66,
GC Smith 65)
Worcestershire 192 (45 overs) (JM Kemp 77,
AC Dawson 4 for 26)
South Africa won by 69 runs

The South Africans recorded a convincing 69-run
victory over Worcestershire at New Road, despite
an 87-ball 77 from their fellow countryman Justin
Kemp, who struck left-arm spinner Nicky Boje for
four sixes. Kemp was the county side's overseas
replacement for Andrew Hall, now with the
tourists and taking 2 for 30 from his eight overs
against his county team-mates. Shaun Pollock also
impressed with 1 for 18 from eight overs as
Worcestershire were bowled out for 192 in reply to

a South African total of 261 for 4 that was based
on half-centuries by Graeme Smith and Jacques
Kallis, plus an unbeaten 48 from 58 balls by
Jacques Rudolph.

15–17 July 2003 at Taunton
South Africa 326 for 4 dec. (GC Smith 152,
ND McKenzie 66*, G Kirsten 66) and 245 for 4 dec.
(ND McKenzie 82*, HH Dippenaar 68)
Somerset 245 for 7 dec. (MJ Wood 55, M Zondeki
5 for 64) and 109 for 3
Match drawn

A rain-delayed third and final day at Taunton
allowed Somerset to emerge with a draw against
the South Africans. The tourists twice declared
after scoring freely against the county's bowlers,
with skipper Graeme Smith reaching 152 in the
first innings and Neil McKenzie enjoying unbeaten
knocks of 66 and 82. In between, Monde Zondeki
bowled at a good pace to pick up 5 for 64 from
11 overs in a Somerset first innings of 245 for 7
declared, and the county finished on 109 for 3
when time finally ran out on the last evening.

19–21 July 2003 at Arundel
India A 319 (W Jaffer 90, G Gambhir 64,
SM Pollock 4 for 46) and 160 for 3 (HK Badani 58*,
W Jaffer 54)
South Africa 463 (JA Rudolph 83, HH Gibbs 79,
GC Smith 79, G Kirsten 75, AM Salvi 4 for 92)
Match drawn

A three-day fixture at lovely Arundel was treated
as nothing more than a chance for practice by the
South Africans, who chose to continue batting on
the third morning rather than to make a game of
it. India A batted solidly enough on the opening
day to score 319, with Wasim Jaffer underlining
the class that had already won him seven Test caps
with 90 and the promising Gautam Gambhir
hitting 64. Shaun Pollock, with four wickets, and
Dewald Pretorius were the pick of the South
African attack, while Graeme Smith and
Herschelle Gibbs both made 79 as they replied
with a 150-run opening stand. Gary Kirsten then
scored 75, and Jacques Rudolph a delightful 83,
as the South Africans reached 342 for 5 by the
close of the second day. In the morning they
batted on to reach 463, but any chance of a result
disappeared as Jaffer and Badani both scored
half-centuries to guide India A to 160 for 3 and
the draw.

npower FIRST TEST
24–28 July 2003 at Edgbaston

On an extraordinary final afternoon – after the match had petered out into a draw – Nasser Hussain dramatically, and without any warning, resigned as England's captain with immediate effect. Pundits and supporters alike were left to ponder the motive behind his decision, but it was clear that Hussain no longer felt he had the full support of his team. This stemmed from England's successful run in the NatWest Series under Michael Vaughan's leadership, and Hussain did little to improve his own standing by writing a rather bizarre piece in the *Sunday Telegraph* before the match in which he not only appeared to forget Graeme Smith's name, but also claimed that South Africa were ready for the taking. When the ball was disappearing all over Edgbaston – with Smith the main protagonist – during the early part of South Africa's first innings, it might simply have been that Hussain believed he had made himself look foolish. Whatever the reason for his resignation – and it may be that we never really fully get to the bottom of it – the series began in a most unusual way.

The manner in which South Africa regrouped after their humiliating defeat in the NatWest Series final was astonishing and, because of Hussain's headline-grabbing decision, Smith and his team did not receive all the credit they deserved. Had the second day not been lost to rain, South Africa would most probably have won … in which case, somewhat bizarrely, Hussain suggested he would not have gone.

Not many teams choose to bat first at Edgbaston these days, but Smith decided to have first use of a docile pitch which appeared to offer little to the bowlers. Mind you, the way England bowled on that first day it was difficult to tell quite what help there might have been. James Anderson, in particular, had a terrible day and it made a mockery of Duncan Fletcher's decision to give the youngster the best part of a fortnight off before the match. Anderson's fragile confidence was dealt a cruel blow that day, and he never fully recovered from it. He took the first over – ahead of Gough who returned to play his first Test for two years – and the youngster's waywardness set the tone for the home side's thoroughly ill-disciplined and insipid bowling performance.

That said, Smith strikes a commanding figure at the crease and, in all my dealings with him throughout the summer, I still found it hard to convince myself that he was only 22 years old and had played in only nine Tests before this one. His elevation to the

South African captain Graeme Smith gave leading from the front a new meaning with his great innings of 277 and 259 in the opening two Tests of the series.

captaincy had not been overwhelmingly supported back in South Africa and even such luminaries as Bob Woolmer were suggesting that he should have been made to wait. So his superb innings of 277 – the highest score by a South African in Test cricket – was the most emphatic way possible of stamping his own mark on the job.

The first day was dominated by his opening partnership of 338 with Herschelle Gibbs. The rate of scoring was so high that this record stand was posted in only 75 overs, and ended when Gibbs, who was dropped on 94 when he offered a return chance to Anderson, holed out to Butcher on the deep-midwicket boundary off Vaughan's off spin for a typically free-scoring 179. He struck one six and 29 fours and, as always, his innings was a pleasure to watch. Smith, who survived a close lbw decision off

Giles when he was on 127, matched him run for run, but had already demonstrated to those of us who had not seen him bat in Test cricket before that he possessed an admirable capacity for concentration.

He was still at the crease by Saturday lunchtime, having sat and watched the rain fall throughout the previous day, and finally, after a stay of nine hours and 277 runs he, too, aimed a slog sweep into the legside and was taken in the deep by Anderson.

Three further wickets were lost in the pursuit of quick runs and Smith was able to declare half an hour before tea with the score on 594 for 5. Bad light again helped England's cause and Trescothick and Vaughan were still together at the close, but England still needed 370 more runs to avoid the follow-on.

Ntini rattled Trescothick's stumps early on the fourth morning for 31, and soon trapped Butcher leg before for 13. England were 132 for 2 and, only one run later, Hussain gave the first indication that all was not well when he offered no stroke and fell lbw to Pollock.

At the other end, Vaughan was ignoring the pressure and batted serenely. He was later to say that it was his best innings for England – personally, I enjoyed his New Year century at Sydney more – but this was certainly as valuable an innings as he has played for his country. McGrath with 34 and Stewart, 38, gave support and after Vaughan was caught behind as he drove at Pretorius for 156, Flintoff made a belligerent 40. However, in the final over of the day and with 21 runs still needed to avoid the follow-on, Giles took an unwise single, which

needlessly exposed Flintoff – and he fell lbw to Pretorius. This set up the prospect of a fascinating final morning – but, as it happened, Giles hit five fours in eight balls to see England to relative safety.

South Africa, however, were not finished, and after

Nasser Hussain announces his resignation as England's Test captain after the drawn first Test at Edgbaston.

FIRST TEST – ENGLAND v. SOUTH AFRICA
24–28 July 2003 at Edgbaston

SOUTH AFRICA

	First Innings		Second Innings	
GC Smith (capt)	c Anderson b Giles	277	b Giles	85
HH Gibbs	c Butcher b Vaughan	179		
G Kirsten	c Stewart b Giles	44		
HH Dippenaar	c Butcher b Gough	22		
JA Rudolph	c Gough b Harmison	10		
*MV Boucher	not out	15		
SM Pollock	not out	24		
R J Peterson			(2) b Anderson	9
D Pretorius			(3) c McGrath b Harmison	1
M Ntini			(4) not out	28
C M Willoughby			(5) st Stewart b Giles	8
Extras	b 8, lb 11, nb 4	23	lb 2, nb 1	3
	(5 wkts dec.)	594	(4 wkts dec.)	134

	First Innings				Second Innings			
	O	M	R	W	O	M	R	W
Anderson	16	2	92	0	10	1	37	1
Gough	25	6	88	1	-	-	-	-
Flintoff	25	6	97	0	2	0	16	0
Harmison	27	2	104	1	6	0	34	1
Giles	42	2	153	2	8	0	45	2
Butcher	2	0	15	0	-	-	-	-
Vaughan	8	0	26	1	-	-	-	-

Fall of Wickets
1-338, 2-438, 3-514, 4-552, 5-556
1-30, 2-32, 3-114, 4-134

ENGLAND

	First Innings		Second Innings	
ME Trescothick	b Ntini	31	not out	52
MP Vaughan	c Boucher b Pretorius	156	c Pollock b Peterson	22
MA Butcher	lbw b Ntini	13		
N Hussain (capt)	lbw b Pollock	1	(3) not out	23
A McGrath	c Rudolph b Pretorius	34		
*AJ Stewart	b Pretorius	38		
A Flintoff	lbw b Pretorius	40		
AF Giles	b Pollock	41		
D Gough	c Rudolph b Ntini	1		
SJ Harmison	b Ntini	0		
JM Anderson	not out	0		
Extras	b 19, lb 6, w 11, nb 17	53	b 8, lb 5	13
		408	(1 wkt)	110

	First Innings				Second Innings			
	O	M	R	W	O	M	R	W
Pollock	27.4	10	51	2	7	3	6	0
Ntini	28	8	114	4	4	0	38	0
Willoughby	20	7	46	0	-	-	-	-
Pretorius	25	2	115	4	10	6	20	0
Peterson	22	9	57	0	13	3	33	1

Fall of Wickets
1-66, 2-132, 3-133, 4-222, 5-306, 6-311, 7-374, 8-398, 9-398
1-72

Umpires: DJ Harper & S Venkataraghavan
Toss: South Africa

Match Drawn

Ntini had polished off the innings, Smith led the charge for quick runs by hammering 85 from only 70 balls. His declaration left England with 65 overs to survive and, after 34 of them, the rain returned. This miserable scene provided the perfect backdrop for Hussain's emotional and dramatic exit.

npower SECOND TEST
31 July–3 August 2003 at Lord's

The second Test followed only three days after the end of the first, and Michael Vaughan – England's new captain – could hardly have had time to catch his breath. Increasingly, the opinion in the press box was that Hussain's bolt-from-the-blue decision to resign had left England in a real mess, but Vaughan, at least, had the good grace and sense to say that he did not feel as if he had been 'bumped' into the job even if, in truth, he had been. Hussain, meanwhile, was still emotional and it seemed by no means certain that he would see out the series as a player.

It seemed unlikely that England's shell-shocked team would put up much of a fight – there was simply too much uncertainty around for that – and

More runs ... Graeme Smith in full flow at Lord's.

they played some pretty dreadful cricket. Bundled out for only 173 on the first day, it is worth noting that the final stand between Anderson and Gough was worth 55. Ntini profited more than anyone from England's woeful batting display, and finished with 5 for 75 from 17 overs. The fast bowler is invariably expensive, but he does have the happy knack of picking up wickets with his skiddy trajectory.

Trescothick was dropped on two by Smith at slip, but made only nine more runs before inside-edging Ntini onto his stumps. Butcher eased to 19 from only 17 balls before Hall caught him at third slip off Pollock – and then we all waited in anticipation to gauge the reaction of the Lord's full house to Hussain's appearance from the pavilion. To a man, woman and child, the crowd rose as one and warmly applauded the former skipper all the way to the middle. It was a special moment, and one that must have gone some way to easing Hussain's doubts about his decision. However, he was soon the third wicket to fall when he drove at Hall, the ball flicked his inside edge and bowled him for 14. Four balls later, McGrath was caught off the leading edge and a shocking morning was completed when, in the following over, Vaughan pulled Ntini straight to long leg for 33. England took lunch on 94 for 5, but the interval did nothing to ease their predicament. Stewart – who had announced before the first Test that this series would be his last – was another victim of the pull shot: 96 for 6. The tail then submitted meekly to leave England on a scarcely believable 118 for 9 when Anderson and Gough resisted for three-quarters of an hour.

To say that South Africa put that feeble performance into perspective is something of an understatement: they went on to make 682 for 6! Once again it was their captain, Smith, who rubbed England's faces in the dirt with another colossal innings of 259. He joined Don Bradman as the only man ever to score successive double centuries against England, but his score beat the Don's 254 to become the highest score by a visitor to Lord's. However, horror of horrors, Smith had been dropped in the fourth over when he was on just eight – by Hussain at cover point. It was as if it all happened in slow motion, and was a catch a focussed Hussain would take nine times out of ten. It only underlined the feeling that he could not go on.

Smith seized on his opponents' weakness as ruthlessly as one would have imagined. He did not offer another chance throughout his stay of 574 minutes – 33 more than his Edgbaston marathon – and was only dismissed after South Africa had

Andrew Flintoff's second-innings assault at Lord's was so savage that it even broke his bat.

SECOND TEST – ENGLAND v. SOUTH AFRICA
31 July–3 August 2003 at Lord's

ENGLAND

	First Innings		Second Innings	
ME Trescothick	b Ntini	6	c Adams b Ntini	23
MP Vaughan (capt)	c sub b Ntini	33	c Pollock b Hall	29
MA Butcher	c Hall b Pollock	19	c Kirsten b Hall	70
N Hussain	b Hall	14	c Boucher b Ntini	61
A McGrath	c Kirsten b Hall	4	c Boucher b Pollock	13
*AJ Stewart	c Adams b Ntini	7	c Hall b Ntini	0
A Flintoff	c Adams b Ntini	11	st Boucher b Adams	142
AF Giles	c Pollock b Hall	7	c Pollock b Ntini	23
D Gough	c Adams b Pollock	34	c Adams b Pollock	14
SJ Harmison	b Ntini	0	c Hall b Ntini	7
JM Anderson	not out	21	not out	4
Extras	b 5, lb 3, w 1, nb 3, pen 5	17	b 6, lb 5, w 3, nb 17	31
		173		417

	First Innings				Second Innings			
	O	M	R	W	O	M	R	W
Pollock	14.4	5	28	2	29	7	105	2
Ntini	17	3	75	5	31	5	145	5
Pretorius	4	0	20	0	3	0	16	0
Hall	10	4	18	3	24	6	66	2
Adams	3	0	19	0	20.1	1	74	1

Fall of Wickets
1-11, 2-35, 3-73, 4-77, 5-85, 6-96, 7-109, 8-112, 9-118
1-52, 2-60, 3-186, 4-208, 5-208, 6-208, 7-297, 8-344, 9-371

SOUTH AFRICA

	First Innings	
GC Smith (capt)	b Anderson	259
HH Gibbs	b Harmison	49
G Kirsten	b McGrath	108
HH Dippenaar	c Butcher b Giles	92
JA Rudolph	c Stewart b Flintoff	26
*MV Boucher	b Anderson	68
SM Pollock	not out	10
AJ Hall	not out	6
PR Adams		
D Pretorius		
M Ntini		
Extras	b 25, lb 21, w 5, nb 13	64
	(6 wkts dec.)	682

	First Innings			
	O	M	R	W
Gough	28	3	127	0
Anderson	27	6	90	2
Harmison	22	3	103	1
Flintoff	40	10	115	1
Giles	43	5	142	1
Butcher	6	1	19	0
McGrath	11	0	40	1

Fall of Wickets
1-133, 2-390, 3-513, 4-580, 5-630, 6-672

Umpires: SA Bucknor & DB Hair
Toss: South Africa

South Africa won by an innings and 92 runs

passed 500. England's fielding was well below par: Kirsten was dropped on 54 on the way to his calm, unfussy 108. Dippenaar was missed on 15 and scored 92, while Rudolph was dropped by Stewart when he was on 18. It was shabby, frankly. Understandable to a degree, but shabby nonetheless, and such was the rate of scoring that Smith's declaration left England with 36 overs to face on the third day.

At 208 for 3, England were making a better fist of their second innings. The result was never really in doubt, but at least there was a chance of the game going into the fifth day. Hussain and Butcher had resumed on 129 for 2, with both openers having been dismissed, and put on 122 before Butcher casually flicked Hall to midwicket for 70. Five minutes before lunch, Hussain – who had been battling away grimly – aimed an ambitious pull stroke against Ntini, completely lost his balance, and Boucher took an easy catch. It was the hammer blow and, with no further addition, McGrath and Stewart – who was out second ball – were both dispatched back to the pavilion. The end was nigh, but this fuelled a wonderful display of big hitting from Flintoff that no one at Lord's that afternoon would ever forget. Although the hopelessness of the situation was all too evident, Flintoff spectacularly dismembered the South African attack to the extent that the legacy of this bruising innings lived on through the rest of the series. He struck 18 fours and five sixes in all from the 146 balls he faced for his 142 runs – the highest score by an England No. 7 at Lord's. Finally, Flintoff was stumped off Adams to bring the curtain down on the glorious highlight of an otherwise lamentable England display. The following day, Darren Gough announced the end of his Test career, in which he claimed 229 wickets from 58 matches at an average of 28.39.

7–9 August 2003 at Canterbury
South Africa 325 for 4 dec. (ND McKenzie 105*, JA Rudolph 92, JH Kallis 77) and 243 for 7 dec. (HH Dippenaar 69, JA Rudolph 65)
Kent 235 (AGR Loudon 63, GO Jones 50) and 232 (MA Carberry 75, PR Adams 9 for 79)
South Africa won by 101 runs

A sustained spell of 22.5 overs from Paul Adams, the seemingly double-jointed left-arm spinner, earned him the memorable figures of 9 for 79 as the South Africans bowled out Kent for 232 on the third and final day to win by 101 runs. The Canterbury pitch was dry and dusting, in gloriously hot sunshine, and Adams took full advantage to underline his value to the tourists' attack. England's discarded batsman, Rob Key, scored 47 and 49 in the game, but ended up frustrated at his continuing inability to turn promising starts into innings of real substance. Geraint Jones did his own England ambitions no harm with a fighting 50 in Kent's first innings of 235, while youngster Alex Loudon took his opportunity to impress against illustrious opponents with cultured knocks of 63 and 30 not out. That he stood firm while Adams wrought havoc around him on the last day spoke well of both his temperament and his ability. Michael Carberry's 75 also stood out, before Adams got to work, while Martin Saggers caught the eye by bowling both Herschelle Gibbs and Jacques Kallis during a fine new-ball spell at the start of the South African second innings. Otherwise, the tourists' batting had

few problems against the county attack: Neil McKenzie made an excellent, unbeaten, first-innings hundred, while Jacques Rudolph pressed his own Test claims with innings of 92 and 65 and both Kallis and Boeta Dippenaar made runs.

npower THIRD TEST
14–18 August 2003 at Trent Bridge

An uncharacteristically poor Trent Bridge pitch produced a thrilling finale, and an England victory that enabled them to level the series. Graeme Smith made it clear throughout that this was not so much a Test match but a lottery, in which the toss played far too important a role, and he was right. However, after the trauma of the previous fortnight, Michael Vaughan was justifiably delighted with his first win as England captain.

The pitch at Trent Bridge had been monitored with suspicion throughout the course of the season. County games there were ending spectacularly early with reports of the surface having broken up due to 'root break' – a phenomenon that prevents the grass from binding the pitch together. Bowlers of all types were benefiting and, in the wake of Gough's retirement, the selectors chose just about every

Back in the ranks, and back in the runs: Nasser Hussain's first-innings 116 set up England's victory at Trent Bridge.

option imaginable, including a second spinner in Gareth Batty and a first call-up for Glen Chapple, the Lancashire all-rounder, in their squad of 13. In the event, neither of them played, but Ed Smith came into the team at McGrath's expense, having scored six centuries for Kent during the course of the championship summer.

That the South African captain called wrongly at the toss did have an important bearing on the game but, even so, England produced a disciplined batting display that had been so obviously missing in the previous Tests at Lord's and Edgbaston. Ironically, it was Hussain who, with Butcher, provided the backbone to England's total of 445, which was enough to win the match. With the ball skimming through ridiculously low at times, batting was always a perilous occupation, but coming together at 29 for 2, and faced with the real threat of another collapse, the two former captains put on 189 for the third wicket, which ended when Butcher was caught behind off Ntini for 106. The reception for Hussain's century seemed as if it would never end: it is rare for Hussain not to celebrate these landmarks enthusiastically, but even he seemed increasingly embarrassed as the crowd stayed on its feet, cheering and applauding. Ed Smith played some attractive shots into the second day, after 50

Hero of the shires: James Kirtley of Sussex takes 6 for 34 on his long-awaited Test debut.

fours had been struck on the first, and he was out for a thoroughly promising 64 after Hussain's departure, lbw to Pollock, for 116.

England needed every run in these conditions, and Stewart produced a typically bright 72 to take England past 400, and they were dismissed on the stroke of tea on the second day.

Gibbs soon played on to Harmison for 19, but it was the wicket of Smith for less than 200 that delighted England. It was a freakish dismissal – the powerfully built opener slipped and trod on his wicket as he played a ball from Flintoff – but that did not matter at all to Vaughan and his team, and at 84 for 2 at the close of the day, South Africa were under pressure.

Wickets tumbled the following morning, with Kirtley and Anderson enjoying the unpredictable bounce. McKenzie scored a resolute 90, but it was Pollock's brilliant 62 that galvanized the visitors. When he strode to the crease, South Africa were 262 for 6 and, with the lower order, Pollock added 101 priceless runs. Anderson finished up with the flattering figures of 5 for 102, and England had a handy lead of 83 that, in these conditions, was worth double. One over was to be faced on the third evening and, first ball, Trescothick found himself on the receiving end of one of the roughest umpiring decisions of the summer. Given out caught at short leg off the bowling of Pollock, it really was a desperate blunder, and England's second innings floundered from that moment. Pollock finished with 6 for 39 as only Hussain with 30, Flintoff, 30, and Giles, 21, reached double figures. Shot out for 118 in only 46 overs, England now had to defend South Africa's target of 202 to win.

It was no easier for the visitors. Kirtley found some fiendishly low bounce from the Pavilion End and removed Smith for five and Rudolph for a duck, both lbw. Gibbs carelessly pulled Harmison to mid-on for 28 and when Kallis, the danger man, played Anderson onto his stumps shortly before the close, South Africa were reeling on 50 for 5.

On the final morning, a near full house gathered to watch a gripping morning. South Africa needed 139 more runs to win, with Boucher and McKenzie – who had both batted so bravely in the first innings – at the crease. However, happily for England, Kirtley bowled McKenzie for the addition of only eight runs and when Pollock was bowled by a cruel scuttler in Flintoff's next over, the tail was exposed. Boucher continued to make life difficult, but once Kirtley ripped out Hall, first ball, and the obdurate Adams for 15, even Boucher knew he was attempting the

THIRD TEST – ENGLAND v. SOUTH AFRICA
14–18 August 2003 at Trent Bridge

ENGLAND

	First Innings		Second Innings	
ME Trescothick	c Boucher b Hall	24	c Adams b Pollock	0
MP Vaughan (capt)	c Gibbs b Pollock	1	c Boucher b Pollock	5
MA Butcher	c Boucher b Ntini	106	b Hall	8
N Hussain	lbw b Pollock	116	lbw b Pollock	30
ET Smith	c Boucher b Kallis	64	lbw b Hall	0
*AJ Stewart	c Smith b Adams	72	c Boucher b Kallis	5
A Flintoff	c Pollock b Hall	0	c Gibbs b Pollock	30
AF Giles	b Hall	22	c Boucher b Pollock	21
RJ Kirtley	c Smith b Ntini	1	c Boucher b Ntini	3
SJ Harmison	c Pollock b Adams	14	not out	2
JM Anderson	not out	0	lbw b Pollock	2
Extras	b 9, lb 8, w 4, nb 4	25	b 4, lb 5, nb 3	12
		445		**118**

	First Innings				Second Innings			
	O	M	R	W	O	M	R	W
Pollock	36	18	65	2	17.4	4	39	6
Ntini	33	3	137	2	13	5	28	1
Hall	24	6	88	3	6	2	6	2
Kallis	27	7	92	1	10	2	36	1
Adams	26.3	7	46	2	-	-	-	-

Fall of Wickets
1-7 2-29, 3-218, 4-322, 5-334, 6-347, 7-388, 8-408, 9-440
1-0, 2-17, 3-39, 4-39, 5-44, 6-76, 7-91, 8-114, 9-114

SOUTH AFRICA

	First Innings		Second Innings	
GC Smith (capt)	hit wicket b Flintoff	35	lbw b Kirtley	5
HH Gibbs	b Harmison	19	c Giles b Harmison	28
JA Rudolph	c Stewart b Kirtley	15	lbw b Kirtley	0
JH Kallis	b Anderson	27	b Anderson	13
HH Dippenaar	lbw b Kirtley	0	c Smith b Anderson	1
ND McKenzie	c Trescothick b Anderson	90	b Kirtley	11
*MV Boucher	lbw b Flintoff	48	c Stewart b Kirtley	52
SM Pollock	c Kirtley b Anderson	62	b Flintoff	0
AJ Hall	b Anderson	15	c Trescothick b Kirtley	0
PR Adams	b Anderson	13	c & b Kirtley	15
M Ntini	not out	4	not out	3
Extras	b 4, lb 19, w 3, nb 8	34	lb 2, nb 1	3
		362		**131**

	First Innings				Second Innings			
	O	M	R	W	O	M	R	W
Anderson	27.5	4	102	5	12	4	17	2
Kirtley	31	8	80	2	16.2	7	34	6
Flintoff	33	8	91	2	17	4	54	1
Harmison	17	3	42	1	11	2	24	1
Giles	10	3	24	0	-	-	-	-
Vaughan	1	1	0	0	-	-	-	-

Fall of Wickets
1-56, 2-66, 3-88, 4-88, 5-132, 6-261, 7-284, 8-309, 9-337
1-22, 2-28, 3-40, 4-41, 5-50, 6-71, 7-80, 8-81, 9-126

Umpires: DB Hair & DI Harper
Toss: England

England won by 70 runs

impossible. He was finally caught behind for 52 to give Kirtley figures of 6 for 34 and, thanks to the absurd *Big Brother*-style viewer-voting method of the adjudicating Channel 4, the Man of the Match award. Well as Kirtley had bowled in these helpful conditions, the rightful winner should have been Hussain, whose aggregate of 146 runs in the game made all the difference. There was a time when these awards meant something both to the players and the person whose often difficult job it was to single out the most meaningful contribution in the game. It will not be long before television viewers are asked to vote a commentator out of the box!

npower FOURTH TEST
21–25 2003 August at Headingley

When England had reduced South Africa to 21 for 4 and then 142 for 7 on the first day, it seemed utterly inconceivable that they could lose the match – let alone by the punishing margin of 191 runs. This was, indeed, England's lowest point of the summer and the one that made the difference, in the end, between them winning the series and drawing it.

As always, the Headingley pitch was an unknown quantity. At times – largely when England were bowling – it appeared benign. Then, when South Africa's bowlers hit the required spot, the ball either reared or shot along the ground. Generally, batting was an uncomfortable business, which makes Kirsten's first-innings century – his second of the series – all the more creditable.

England pulled off a considerable surprise by selecting Martin Bicknell for only the third Test of his career. A seam bowler who has been a stalwart in county cricket for as long as anyone can remember, he has continually been overlooked since his last appearance, against Australia in 1993. However, there is no doubt that for Headingley he was an ideal choice, and he confirmed that by claiming a wicket with only his second ball when Gibbs edged to Stewart. Smith had already uncharacteristically chased a wide one in the first over of the day, so South Africa were 2 for 2. Kallis drove Bicknell to mid-off: 16 for 3 and it was 21 for 4 when McKenzie edged Kabir Ali's fifth delivery in Test cricket to Stewart for four.

It was at this point that Kirsten dug in and, with help from the stylish Rudolph, took the score to 116, when Rudolph was lbw to Kabir for 55. Boucher and Hall fell to Flintoff either side of tea and South Africa were 142 for 7.

Surely the least likely partnership of the summer was then formed: Kirsten and the fast-bowling

Mr Dependable: the Headingley Test provided another showcase for the unsung talents of Gary Kirsten.

debutant, Monde Zondeki, who put on the small matter of 150 for the eighth wicket! Zondeki's previous highest score in first-class cricket was 27, and he seemed positively embarrassed when he reached his half-century. By the time he was finally dismissed on the second morning for a remarkable 59, South Africa were back in the game. Kirsten was caught at mid-on for 130, but even Ntini got in on the act – his 32 not out taking South Africa to 342 all out.

England's batsmen dominated the rest of the second day, with Butcher and Trescothick in complete control. It was, therefore, astonishing that they should accept an offer for bad light shortly before the close of play when they had just scored 23 runs from the previous 17 balls. All momentum was lost and while they were off the field, the South Africans were able to regroup. As soon as the clouds blew away, and play resumed, both batsmen were dismissed by Kallis: Trescothick for 59 and Butcher for 77. 164 for 1 had become 193 for 3 and, suddenly, the game was in the balance again. One was left seriously to question the common sense, and the approach, of both the England team and its management.

Ed Smith fell in the third over of the third day for a duck, Stewart pulled a long hop to square leg for 15, but the real blow was struck when Rudolph, with his second ball in Test cricket, persuaded Hussain to drive back a return catch to a gentle leg break, two overs before the new ball was due. The former captain had made 42, and he departed in an obvious rage.

Flintoff was cheered to the middle by the noisy occupants of the West Stand, and duly clobbered four fours and three sixes in his innings of 55 that took England to within 35 of South Africa's total before he was last man out to Ntini, who finished with figures of 3 for 62.

It was clear that England were going to have to bowl well on a pitch that was becoming increasingly untrustworthy. A target of 250 would be the most anyone would want to score in the fourth innings and when both openers had fallen cheaply to leave South Africa on 31 for 2, England were still in the hunt. After tea on the third day, Kirsten and Kallis featured in a key partnership of 97, but perished within seven overs of each other, and when Anderson returned to remove Rudolph for ten, South Africa closed the day with a lead of 199 and five wickets in hand. The result of the game was in the balance.

However, what followed on the fourth morning was as grotesque a bowling effort by England that there can ever have been. Even the experienced Bicknell lost every shred of control, and none of the bowlers showed any suggestion that they were anything but last-minute stand-ins, pressed into action from a local league. Unbelievably, South Africa added 201 runs at five runs per over, as Hall masterminded some brilliant tail-end resistance. He provided the big blows that made such a mockery of the helpful bowling conditions, and only failed by one to score a well-deserved century because Kirtley finally found a delivery straight enough to bowl the last man, Pretorius. When the dust had settled, England were out of the game, needing the small matter of 401 to win. By the end of the fourth day, they had already lost five wickets for 165, but the one hope was that Flintoff, who strode out to bat on the final morning on 45 not out, might

FOURTH TEST – ENGLAND v. SOUTH AFRICA
21–25 August 2003 at Headingley

SOUTH AFRICA

	First Innings		Second Innings	
GC Smith (capt)	c Stewart b Kirtley	2	lbw b Bicknell	14
HH Gibbs	c Stewart b Bicknell	0	lbw b Kirtley	2
G Kirsten	c Bicknell b Kabir Ali	130	lbw b Kabir Ali	60
JH Kallis	c Vaughan b Bicknell	6	c Stewart b Kirtley	41
ND McKenzie	c Stewart b Kabir Ali	4	c Bicknell b Flintoff	38
JA Rudolph	lbw b Kabir Ali	55	c Smith b Anderson	10
*MV Boucher	c Vaughan b Flintoff	16	c Stewart b Flintoff	39
AJ Hall	c Smith b Flintoff	0	not out	99
M Zondeki	c Butcher b Anderson	59	b Bicknell	7
M Ntini	not out	32	lbw b Kabir Ali	8
D Pretorius	c Stewart b Kirtley	9	b Kirtley	8
Extras	lb 20, w 2, nb 7	29	b 7, lb 24, nb 8	39
		342		**365**

	First Innings				Second Innings			
	O	M	R	W	O	M	R	W
Kirtley	29.4	10	74	2	21.5	7	71	3
Bicknell	27	11	50	2	22	3	75	2
Kabir Ali	22	3	80	3	14	2	56	2
Anderson	18	7	63	1	16	4	56	1
Flintoff	18	5	55	2	22	5	63	2
Vaughan	-	-	-	-	5	1	13	0

Fall of Wickets
1-2, 2-2, 3-16, 4-21, 5-116, 6-142, 7-142, 8-292, 9-316
1-9, 2-31, 3-128, 4-139, 5-160, 6-219, 7-232, 8-281, 9-311

ENGLAND

	First Innings		Second Innings	
ME Trescothick	c & b Kallis	59	c Gibbs b Ntini	4
MP Vaughan (capt)	b Ntini	15	c Gibbs b Kallis	21
MA Butcher	c Boucher b Kallis	77	c Hall b Kallis	61
N Hussain	c & b Rudolph	42	lbw b Kallis	6
ET Smith	c Boucher b Kallis	0	c Smith b Hall	7
*AJ Stewart	c Hall b Pretorius	15	c Boucher b Ntini	7
A Flintoff	b Ntini	55	c Hall b Kallis	50
MP Bicknell	b Ntini	4	c Boucher b Kallis	15
Kabir Ali	c Boucher b Hall	1	c Kirsten b Kallis	9
RJ Kirtley	c Boucher b Hall	1	c Kirsten b Hall	11
JM Anderson	not out	0	not out	0
Extras	b 2, lb 17, w 6, nb 13	38	lb 9, w 2, nb 7	18
		307		**209**

	First Innings				Second Innings			
	O	M	R	W	O	M	R	W
Pretorius	19	1	100	1	9	3	27	0
Ntini	20.2	4	62	3	11	2	40	2
Hall	24	3	77	2	21.4	3	64	2
Zondeki	1.5	0	10	0	3	0	15	0
Kallis	20.1	7	38	3	17	4	54	6
Rudolph	2	1	1	1	-	-	-	-

Fall of Wickets
1-27, 2-169, 3-193, 4-197, 5-239, 6-261, 7-289, 8-293, 9-307
1-11, 2-44, 3-62, 4-81, 5-95, 6-169, 7-182, 8-189, 9-206

Umpires: BF Bowden & SJA Taufel
Toss: South Africa

South Africa won by 191 runs

Jacques Kallis ... South Africa's best bowler at Headingley.

conjure up something remarkable. But it was not to be as Kallis cut down the lower order – including Flintoff for 50 – to finish with his Test-best figures of 6 for 54, and 9 for 92 in the match. South Africa thoroughly deserved their win, and Vaughan was to show his first trace of frustration in his new job by rounding on county cricket in his post-match press conference.

28–30 August 2003 at Derby
South Africa 460 for 7 dec. (JH Kallis 200, TL Tsolekile 90, MV Boucher 89, PMR Havell 4 for 129)
Derbyshire 136 for 4 dec.
Match drawn

South Africa's three-day fixture against Derbyshire at Derby became merely an exercise in batting and bowling practice after a first-day washout. Jacques Kallis made 200, but the on-field action was overshadowed by the latest outbreak of internecine politicking in and around the Derbyshire committee and dressing rooms. Dominic Cork, the captain, was upset at being told – following a meeting of the club's committee – that his position was not certain for 2004. Dave Houghton, the former Zimbabwe captain and coach, was announced as the club's future director of cricket – and Cork learned that he would need to have his captaincy ratified by Houghton before he was asked to carry on in the job. Adrian Pierson, the coach, was sacked.

npower FIFTH TEST
4–8 September 2003 at The Oval

Every now and then, Test cricket provides a timely reminder that there is no better sport in the world, and the final Test of the summer was a classic. For unpredictability alone, this match has few peers, and South Africa's players must still be wondering how they managed to lose so heavily having scored nearly 500 runs in their first innings.

Opposite: balance, timing, placement, style ... Graham Thorpe shows England just what they have been missing during his brilliant comeback century.

At 2–1 down, England had to win in order to level the series. When Smith won the toss and chose to make first use of the best pitch of the summer, it seemed that England were doomed. This was merely confirmed by tea when South Africa were on 230 for 1, with Gibbs going like a train on 122.

In fact, the only wicket had been a run out when Gibbs called his captain for an impossible single and Vaughan's underarm throw enabled Stewart – in his farewell match – to do the rest. Smith made 18 and, frankly, a run out was the only way England seemed likely to break through. However, three wickets fell in the final session to leave the game more finely balanced. The gravest culprit was Gibbs, who had dominated the bowling so absolutely that 146 of his 183 runs had come in either fours or sixes. In the

Marcus Trescothick swings away yet another boundary as England's fightback at The Oval gathers pace. Rumours that the Somerset opener might be contemplating a move down the order looked absurd as he marched relentlessly to a magnificent 219 – the first double-hundred of his first-class career.

last over before the second new ball, he carelessly aimed a wild slog at Giles, and was bowled. Giles had already trapped Kirsten lbw for 90 as he aimed a premeditated paddle to leg, and many observers agreed that Giles had never bowled better in a Test match. In the last over of the day, McKenzie edged Anderson to Stewart for nine and the visitors were in danger of squandering their excellent start.

On the second morning, Bicknell swung the ball at will. He trapped Rudolph lbw with the fifth ball of the day for nought and, 20 minutes later, had Boucher – possibly unluckily – given out caught behind for eight. England were chipping away, and they had a huge slice of luck when Kallis was run out backing up for 66. That made it 419 for 7, but an impressive feature of this South African team has been the resilience of their lower order – and Pollock came to their rescue once again with a fine 66. Ninety-nine runs were added while he was at the crease and when South Africa were finally dismissed at a quarter past two on the second day, their total of 484 seemed to be enough at least to guarantee the draw they needed to take the series.

Vaughan was caught at third slip for 23 to give a little more ammunition to those who worried that the captaincy would affect his form, and Hall removed Butcher lbw for 32 to leave England on 78 for 2. By the close of the day, however, Trescothick and Thorpe – in his first Test for more than a year – had taken England to within 120 of avoiding the follow-on. A draw still seemed to be the most likely outcome and, given that they were still 319 behind, an England win remained unthinkable.

The pair were still together at lunch the next day, with Trescothick making a welcome hundred – his first since May 2002. (There had been talk of him dropping down the order, but this innings seemed to be laying that plan to rest.) Thorpe, meanwhile, was batting as if he had never been away. He reached his century shortly after the break and, later, called the innings 'a life-changing experience'. A huge state-ment indeed from a normally quiet, reserved man.

Thorpe was eventually bowled off his pads by the persevering Kallis for 124 after a stand of 268 with Trescothick – the largest third-wicket partnership on this ground. Poor Smith, who was desperately playing for a tour place, had an impossible act to follow, and played across his pads to fall lbw to Hall for 18.

Stewart, meanwhile, had walked out on to a sun-drenched Oval to a standing ovation and a guard of honour by the South Africans. There was no problem with misty eyes for 'The Gaffer', however,

and although it took him 17 balls to get off the mark he played a typically breezy knock of 38 before Trescothick's marathon came to an end. Having reached 200 for the first time in first-class cricket, the Somerset left-hander moved to 219, having batted for nine-and-a-half hours, before hooking Ntini to Rudolph at fine leg. It was a fine innings, but England were still only five runs in the lead with four wickets in hand. There was some justification for Vaughan to have declared at this stage – England had to keep the game moving after all – but Flintoff and Giles saw it through to the close of the third day with England on 502 for 7 – a lead of 18 runs.

It was now that Flintoff's demolition of South Africa at Lord's paid dividends. The only way, it seemed, that England could produce a miracle would be as a result of Flintoff hammering the opposition into submission. This he did, to great effect, and Smith could see his precious lead in the series evaporating before his eyes. The onslaught began with a rasping cover drive to the Bedser Stand, and although Bicknell was dismissed early, Harmison provided great support. To illustrate Flintoff's domination, you need look no further than to the partnership between the two great friends that was worth 99, of which Harmison made precisely three! Flintoff thrashed 85 from 77 balls in the morning, including four sixes, and it was clear that the bowlers remained intimidated by the beating he had handed out to them at Lord's. He is unselfish, too, with no thought of patiently easing his way through the 90s – another huge swing across the line proved to be his downfall on 95, but the damage had long since been done.

All the pressure was now on the South Africans. Faced with a deficit of 120, they went into bat again with two overs remaining before lunch on the fourth day: they had to bat for their lives.

At 150 for 6, an England victory – for the first time – became a serious possibility. Their bowling had been much more focussed and mature with Harmison, for the first time, really looking Test class. The main danger men had been dismissed and when the teams met up for the final day of the series, South Africa were effectively 65 for 6.

Pollock made 43, but England claimed the last four wickets for only 44 runs, with Bicknell and Harmison finishing with four wickets apiece, and although Vaughan again fell cheaply, Butcher and Trescothick were cheered every inch of the way by a near full house, and reached the 110 needed for victory in only 22 overs.

FIFTH TEST – ENGLAND v. SOUTH AFRICA
4–8 September 2003 at The Oval

SERIES AVERAGES
England v. South Africa

SOUTH AFRICA

	First Innings		Second Innings	
GC Smith (capt)	run out	18	lbw b Bicknell	19
HH Gibbs	b Giles	183	c Stewart b Anderson	9
G Kirsten	lbw b Giles	90	c Trescothick b Harmison	29
JH Kallis	run out	66	lbw b Harmison	35
ND McKenzie	c Stewart b Anderson	9	lbw b Flintoff	38
JA Rudolph	lbw b Bicknell	0	b Bicknell	8
*MV Boucher	c Stewart b Bicknell	8	c Stewart b Bicknell	25
SM Pollock	not out	66	c Thorpe b Harmison	43
AJ Hall	lbw b Flintoff	1	c Smith b Bicknell	0
PR Adams	run out	1	not out	13
M Ntini	b Anderson	11	c Smith b Harmison	1
Extras	b 12, lb 10, w 4, nb 5	31	b 1, lb 7, nb 1	9
		484		**229**

	First Innings				Second Innings			
	O	M	R	W	O	M	R	W
Bicknell	20	3	71	2	24	5	84	4
Anderson	25	6	86	2	10	1	55	1
Harmison	27	8	73	0	19.2	8	33	4
Giles	29	3	102	2	10	2	36	0
Flintoff	19	4	88	1	6	2	13	1
Vaughan	5	0	24	0	–	–	–	–
Butcher	3	0	18	0	–	–	–	–

Fall of Wickets
1-63, 2-290, 3-345, 4-362, 5-365, 6-385, 7-419, 8-421, 9-432
1-24, 2-34, 3-92, 4-93, 5-118, 6-150, 7-193, 8-193, 9-215

ENGLAND

	First Innings		Second Innings	
ME Trescothick	c Rudolph b Ntini	219	not out	69
MP Vaughan (capt)	c Gibbs b Pollock	23	c Boucher b Kallis	13
MA Butcher	lbw b Hall	32	not out	20
GP Thorpe	b Kallis	124		
ET Smith	lbw b Hall	16		
*AJ Stewart	lbw b Pollock	38		
A Flintoff	b Adams	95		
AF Giles	c Hall b Kallis	2		
MP Bicknell	lbw b Pollock	0		
SJ Harmison	not out	6		
JM Anderson	not out	0		
Extras	b 11, lb 18, w 9, nb 11	49	lb 4, nb 4	8
	(9 wkts dec.)	**604**	(1 wkt)	**110**

	First Innings				Second Innings			
	O	M	R	W	O	M	R	W
Pollock	39	10	111	3	6	0	15	0
Ntini	31	4	129	1	8	0	46	0
Hall	35	5	111	2	–	–	–	–
Kallis	34	5	117	2	5.2	0	25	1
Adams	17	2	79	1	3	0	20	0
Rudolph	6	1	28	0				

Fall of Wickets
1-28, 2-78, 3-346, 4-379, 5-480, 6-489, 7-502, 8-502, 9-601
1-47

Umpires: SJA Taufel & S Venkataraghavan
Toss: South Africa

England won by 9 wickets

ENGLAND

Batting	M	Inns	NO	Runs	HS	Av	100	50	c/st
GP Thorpe	1	1	0	124	124	124.00	1	–	1/-
ME Trescothick	5	10	2	487	219	60.87	1	3	3/-
A Flintoff	5	8	0	423	142	52.87	1	3	-/-
MA Butcher	5	9	1	406	106	50.75	1	3	4/-
N Hussain	4	8	1	293	116	41.85	1	1	-/-
MP Vaughan	5	10	0	318	156	31.80	1	–	2/-
JM Anderson	5	8	7	27	21*	27.00	–	–	1/-
AJ Stewart	5	8	0	182	72	22.75	–	1	14/1
AF Giles	4	6	0	116	41	19.33	–	–	1/-
ET Smith	3	5	0	87	64	17.40	–	1	5/-
A McGrath	2	3	0	51	34	17.00	–	–	1/-
D Gough	2	3	0	49	34	16.33	–	–	1/-
SJ Harmison	4	6	2	29	14	7.25	–	–	-/-
MP Bicknell	2	3	0	19	15	6.33	–	–	2/-
Kabir Ali	1	2	0	10	9	5.00	–	–	-/-
RJ Kirtley	2	4	0	16	11	4.00	–	–	2/-

Bowling	Overs	Mds	Runs	Wkts	Av	Best	5/inn	10m
RJ Kirtley	98.5	32	259	13	19.92	6-34	1	–
Kabir Ali	36	5	136	5	27.20	3-80	–	–
MP Bicknell	93	22	280	10	28.00	4-84	–	–
JM Anderson	161.5	35	598	15	39.86	5-102	1	–
A McGrath	11	0	40	1	40.00	1-40	–	–
SJ Harmison	129.2	26	413	9	45.88	4-33	–	–
A Flintoff	182	44	592	10	59.20	2-55	–	–
MP Vaughan	19	2	63	1	63.00	1-26	–	–
AF Giles	142	15	502	7	71.71	2-45	–	–
D Gough	53	9	215	1	215.00	1-88	–	–

Also bowled: MA Butcher 11-1-52-0

SOUTH AFRICA

Batting	M	Inns	NO	Runs	HS	Av	100	50	c/st
GC Smith	5	9	0	714	277	79.33	2	1	3/-
SM Pollock	4	6	3	205	66*	68.33	–	2	6/-
G Kirsten	4	7	0	462	130	66.00	2	2	4/-
HH Gibbs	5	9	0	478	183	53.11	2	–	5/-
MV Boucher	5	8	1	271	68	38.71	–	2	17/1
HH Dippenaar	3	5	1	143	92	35.75	–	1	-/-
M Zondeki	1	2	0	66	59	33.00	–	1	-/-
ND McKenzie	3	6	0	190	90	31.66	–	1	1/-
JH Kallis	3	6	0	188	66	31.33	–	1	1/-
AJ Hall	4	7	2	121	99*	24.20	–	1	7/-
M Ntini	5	6	3	59	32*	19.66	–	–	-/-
JA Rudolph	5	9	0	132	55	14.66	–	1	4/-
PR Adams	3	4	1	42	15	14.00	–	–	6/-
D Pretorius	3	2	0	17	9	8.50	–	–	-/-

Also batted: RJ Peterson and CM Willoughby played in one Test but did not bat

Bowling	Overs	Mds	Runs	Wkts	Av	Best	10m	5/inn
SM Pollock	177	57	420	17	24.70	6-39	1	–
JH Kallis	113.3	25	362	14	25.85	6-54	1	–
AJ Hall	144.4	29	430	16	26.87	3-18	–	–
JA Rudolph	8	2	29	1	29.00	1-1	–	–
M Ntini	196.2	34	814	23	35.39	5-75	2	1
PR Adams	69.4	10	238	4	59.50	2-46	–	–
D Pretorius	70	12	298	5	59.60	4-115	–	–
RJ Peterson	35	12	90	1	90.00	1-33	–	–

Also bowled: M Zondeki 4.5-0-25-0; CM Willoughby 20-7-46-0

ENGLAND DOMESTIC SEASON INTRODUCTION
By Mark Baldwin

The summer of 2003, in terms both of cricket deeds and of how the sun just kept on shining, was sweet indeed. Sweeter still, however, was the absolutely perfect timing of England's great victory in The Oval Test and the magnificent, romantic, championship triumph of Sussex ten days later.

To put into context the narrow, rather ideological 'aims' of the so-called Cricket Reform Group – ironically revealed 24 hours before South Africa were gloriously beaten at Kennington – these events could not have been bettered.

Yes, English cricket is far from ideally structured. Yes, we may not possess the very best national team in the world. And yes, we may indeed require certain 'reforms' before we give ourselves the best chance of gunning down Australia and, in the words of the England and Wales Cricket Board's mission statement, 'be the best in the world by 2007'.

The problem with the constant sniping of the 'reformers', however, is that it doesn't do the overall image of English cricket any good – especially when the evidence of The Oval Test in fact suggests that we do seem to be getting some things right. They also do not seem to realize the long-term and deep damage their simplistic window-dressing would do to the development side of the game, which all 18 counties heavily sponsor.

The facile changes to 'the system' proposed by the Reform Group, which includes former England captains Bob Willis and Mike Atherton, are based on their belief that there should be a reduced county programme of fewer full-time professional teams, so as to achieve a better concentration of the best English-qualified players to improve the standard of first-class domestic cricket.

That, they argue, would then lead to a redistribution of cricket's income in which both the top end, the England team, and an improved system of regional club premier leagues feeding county cricket from the bottom end, would benefit. The need for radical change is drastic, they add, because there is evidence to suggest that the monies raised by a new television deal due in 2005 will be somewhat less than the current £147 million three-year contract that began in 2003.

So, let's address those core issues: the fear of a drop in television revenues; the debate about the number of counties, and players; and the debate about the amount of cricket played, and the standard of it.

First, English cricket is in a market place when it comes to media deals – and must stand or fall on the realities of the moment when a new contract is negotiated. How many TV companies will be interested in buying the product in 2005? How much, in the climate of that time, will the product be worth?

Crystal ball-gazing is all very well, of course, but no one can truly predict what will happen in terms of English cricket's marketability between now and 2005 – any more than anyone could have predicted, after the first day's play at The Oval, that England would actually manage to beat South Africa with a fightback which gripped the nation. Or, for that matter, that a rotund and supposedly washed-up Pakistani leg spinner would help to propel a county that had never before won the championship to glory.

Channel 4, meanwhile, attracted 3.2 million viewers to the Sunday of The Oval Test and, despite the far too high number of ridiculously late highlights packages, has brought a fresh and bright approach to the job of broadcasting cricket. Sky's coverage of England matches overseas has, for more than a decade, done a great service to the game – and its competition with Channel 4 has helped to sharpen technological aids to viewers as well as general quality of coverage.

The ECB must urgently address, however, the current policy of allowing high-summer one-day internationals to be out of reach of terrestrial television viewers, together with the new Twenty20 Cup competition.

Cricket made clear gains in popularity this summer, as the level of attendances at both international and county matches affirms. Can a challenge to Channel 4 – by the BBC, for instance – be ruled out when its cricket contract is up at the end of 2005? And what would the television deal situation be if, in 2005 itself, an England team based around the very real talents of Vaughan, Trescothick, Thorpe, Flintoff, Anderson, Harmison and Simon Jones slugged it out toe-to-toe in that summer's Ashes series against an ageing Australia?

County cricket, meanwhile, the breeding ground for the Vaughans and Flintoffs and Andersons (and, of course, the Athertons and Willises and hundreds more world-class cricketers over the years) is indeed still not as intense as it needs to be.

As Jonathan Agnew outlined earlier in this book, however, this is as much due to the almost complete absence of centrally contracted England players from the domestic game as it is to the structure and the number of counties.

There used to be a natural structure in England that had evolved over decades: a lengthy championship programme of three-day games, two knock-out one-day cups and a fun Sunday afternoon fling called the John Player League. That may not have been perfect, either, but England cricketers of the time did make regular appearances for their counties because they played only five or six Test matches per summer, plus a handful of one-day internationals to whet the appetite for the Tests.

The top players perhaps thought they played too much then, as well, but they did have their 'rest' periods (at least mentally) between internationals. Now, the likes of Vaughan and Flintoff and Anderson get no rest at all (mentally as much as physically) from mid-May until the second week of September. It is fanciful in the extreme for 'reformers' to claim that a reduced and more 'elite' championship would result in England's best being able to join in and therefore help to increase standards.

If Vaughan and Flintoff, Anderson, Trescothick and the like don't get to play for their counties now, then they won't in whatever system is put into place. Like it or lump it, county cricket must be allowed to run its game, in the same way that the England management team must be allowed to run theirs.

The trick is to achieve in cricket what England has already achieved in the sport of rugby. There, despite hiccups and rows along the way, the England management has increasingly worked with the feeder English clubs to make sure that a culture of excellence is created right through their system.

Many people in cricket are currently bleating about the number of overseas players in the county game, for instance, as if the 18 county clubs are in some way being unpatriotic. Certainly, big money is being spent on non-English cricketers but – if the general standard of the game is thus increased – then this should be seen as part of the investment that needs to be made at every level of the 'pyramid' in order for the whole to grow.

In English rugby, each Premiership club fields teams that regularly contain (percentage-wise) far more 'foreign players' than an English county cricket team (don't forget, in rugby there are also Welsh, Scottish and Irish players to come into the equation). This, however, has not prevented the standard of the England national team from rising. Far from it, as England have never been stronger internationally.

In club rugby, it is true that much money has been drained from club coffers by employing scores of non-English players, but, because overall standards (and crowds, and international and club revenue) have gone up, the club system has effectively done much of the England management's selection process for them.

In other words, if you are not good enough as a young English rugby player to get into the Gloucester, Leicester or Wasps team, for instance, then you haven't got much of a prayer of going that big step further and playing for England itself.

Interestingly, too, a further result of rugby's domestic policy of embracing foreign players has been that the general pool of English talent has increased and not decreased, even though there are far fewer places now available in the top club sides for Englishmen than ever before. Indeed, England could now field two or maybe three world-class rugby teams, and not just one. Would that the England cricket management could do the same.

In short, it is the job of the 18 first-class counties, and the 18 county academies, to produce the talent to make England's national team the world's best. But, like the rugby clubs of England, it is also their job to entertain their own public in a way that is commercially viable.

The two things can be done together – as rugby has shown – but it needs co-operation and not a constant criticism or tearing-apart of the system.

County cricket's structure has been jiggled about for too long already, and it is time for wise old heads (over to you, David Morgan?) to sit down with the counties and decide, once and for all, what is best for everyone.

For what it's worth, here are a few suggestions to be going on with:

• A one-division championship of 17 four-day matches (or a conference system, if fewer games are thought to be in everyone's best interests).

• The scrapping of the National Cricket League. It has been a great servant, but has now run its course – as no current sponsor for it reveals – and just jams up an indecipherable and overcrowded fixture list.

• An extended Twenty20 Cup competition of two nine-team groups, and then a Finals Day, played in two mid-summer 'blocks' to take advantage of (a) long evenings and (b) the start of the school holidays.

• An extended Cheltenham & Gloucester Trophy, again with two initial groups of nine counties, from which the top two in each group go straight into semi-finals. A Lord's final to be played as now.

In this way, each county would play a maximum of 68 championship days, a minimum of eight Twenty20 days (and maximum of nine), and a minimum of eight (maximum of ten) days of 50-overs one-day cricket.

The maximum number of days each cricketer would have to perform, under this structure, is 87. Currently, it is 93, which might not seem much of a saving until you calculate in the fewer number of travelling days that the culling of the National League would ensure.

It is also worth remembering, to use the 2003 summer

as an example, that the length of a cricket season is 157 days: so, somewhere between 84–87 days on, and up to 70 off, seems to me to be a perfectly workable calendar into which to find some of the extra practice or rest time which county cricketers keep saying they need.

Until the next time, then, congratulations to Sussex, and to Gloucestershire and to Surrey for their 2003 successes. They were well earned in a cricketing environment which is already more 'intense' than the critics accept it to be. However, it does need to get still more intense, and that's why everyone needs to work with what exists, and not with what their own particular prejudices might create.

John Bracewell, before he left Gloucestershire in September (after six titles in five years) to coach New Zealand, urged English cricket to leave behind 'the excuse environment', in which county cricket has been constantly used as an easy target for those playing the blame game.'Leave excuses at the door and do not blame others for your own inadequacies,' added Bracewell. It is a philosophy which English rugby and the England rugby team, working for the main part in tandem, decided to adopt several years ago. It hasn't done them much harm.

Mark Baldwin, a former cricket correspondent of the Press Association, has covered county cricket for The Times *since 1998.*

FRIZZELL COUNTY CHAMPIONSHIP
By Mark Baldwin

ROUND ONE: 18–21 APRIL 2003

Division One

The happy combination of sunny skies, warmer-than-average temperatures and the Easter weekend attracted spectators in their thousands to the opening day of the 2003 county championship. Funny, isn't it, how county cricket can suddenly belie its popular image as a sport watched by few when it is (a) staged on days when most of the population are not at work and (b) the weather is kind. Guaranteeing the weather is, of course, beyond any mortal – but the attendances for this opening round of championship matches underline how the absence of cricket from so many summer Saturdays in recent seasons, for example, has been an administrative cock-up of significant proportions.

The sunshine, however, did not make champions Surrey feel any better on the first day of the defence of their title. Lancashire, the visitors to The Oval, ended the opening day on 391 for 2 and went on to pile up a massive 599. The new opening partnership of Iain Sutcliffe and Alec Swann gave Lancashire their solid base with a stand of 108, but it was Mal

---

Round One: 18–21 April 2003 Division One

SURREY v. LANCASHIRE – at The Oval

LANCASHIRE	First Innings				
AJ Swann	run out	57			
IJ Sutcliffe	lbw b Saqlain Mushtaq	70			
MB Loye	lbw b Clarke	126			
SG Law	b Clarke	169			
MJ Chilton	lbw b Salisbury	28			
A Flintoff	c Batty b Salisbury	43			
G Chapple	c and b Salisbury	32			
CP Schofield	c Batty b Tudor	1			
*WK Hegg (capt)	b Murtagh	14			
KW Hogg	c Hollioake b Salisbury	16			
JM Anderson	not out	3			
Extras	lb 4, nb 36	40			
	(151.4 overs)	599			

Bowling
Tudor 37-7-137-1. Murtagh 21.4-2-100-1. Hollioake 8-0-27-0. Clarke 21-0-137-2. Saqlain Mushtaq 22-5-78-1. Salisbury 42-10-116-4.
Fall of Wickets 1-108, 2-169, 3-451, 4-460, 5-523, 6-534, 7-565, 8-565, 9-593, 10-599

SURREY	First Innings		Second Innings	
IJ Ward	c Hegg b Anderson	49	c Sutcliffe b Anderson	158
*JN Batty	b Anderson	13	c Swann b Chapple	4
MR Ramprakash	c Hegg b Anderson	50	c Hegg b Flintoff	13
GP Thorpe	c Loye b Anderson	35	c Anderson b Flintoff	35
AD Brown	lbw b Anderson	2	run out	0
R Clarke	c Chilton b Schofield	38	(7) not out	127
AJ Hollioake (capt)	c Flintoff b Chapple	42	(6) c Chilton b Hogg	10
AJ Tudor	c Chilton b Schofield	9	not out	11
IDK Salisbury	c Hegg b Flintoff	18		
Saqlain Mushtaq	c Anderson b Schofield	23		
TJ Murtagh	not out	0		
Extras	b 4, lb 5, nb 12	21	b 11, lb 6, w 2, nb 2	21
	(67.4 overs)	280	(6 wkts, 100 overs)	379

Bowling
Anderson 13-2-61-5. Chapple 15-2-52-1. Flintoff 13-2-42-1. Hogg 9-1-39-0. Schofield 17.4-4-77-3.
Anderson 22-7-72-1. Chapple 20-1-100-1. Flintoff 19-5-47-2. Schofield 25-8-86-0. Hogg 12-3-46-1. Swann 2-0-11-0.
Fall of Wickets 1-35, 2-106, 3-123, 4-129, 5-140, 6-204, 7-227, 8-230, 9-268, 10-280
1-8, 2-48, 3-124, 4-131, 5-150, 6-294

Match drawn – Surrey (7pts), Lancashire (12pts)

NOTTINGHAMSHIRE v. WARWICKSHIRE – at Trent Bridge

WARWICKSHIRE	First Innings		Second Innings	
NV Knight	c Read b Smith	1	c Bicknell b Elworthy	41
*T Frost	c Pietersen b Franks	17	c Cairns b Smith	0
MA Wagh	c Read b Elworthy	73	c Pietersen b Smith	14
IR Bell	c Cairns b Elworthy	32	b Shreck	11
JO Troughton	c Gallian b Franks	16	c Bicknell b Shreck	24
DP Ostler	b Elworthy	0	b Smith	58
DR Brown	c and b Shreck	7	b Smith	52
AF Giles (capt)	c Elworthy b Shreck	38	c Pietersen b Elworthy	94
MM Betts	c Read b Shreck	5	not out	56
MW Clark	not out	2	c Read b Smith	2
A Richardson	c Pietersen b Shreck	0	c Gallian b Franks	13
Extras	b 1, lb 8, w 6, nb 16	31	b 1, lb 14, nb 10	25
	(58.4 overs)	222	(79.2 overs)	390

Bowling
Elworthy 19-5-68-3. Smith 13-2-55-1. Franks 17-6-57-2. Shreck 9.4-1-33-4.
Elworthy 29-0-117-2. Smith 26-6-98-5. Franks 8.2-1-65-1. Shreck 14-1-76-2. Pietersen 2-0-19-0.
Fall of Wickets 1-1, 2-72, 3-125, 4-153, 5-153, 6-157, 7-188, 8-208, 9-218, 10-222
1-2, 2-54, 3-58, 4-81, 5-140, 6-170, 7-299, 8-341, 9-356, 10-390

NOTTS	First Innings		Second Innings	
DJ Bicknell	c Read b Brown	61	c sub b Betts	81
JER Gallian (capt)	lbw b Betts	2	lbw b Richardson	9
IJ Afzaal	c Frost b Clark	1	c Bell b Giles	43
KP Pietersen	c Ostler b Clark	0	(5) lbw b Betts	54
CL Cairns	b Richardson	44	(6) b Betts	7
BM Shafayat	c Frost b Brown	97	(7) c Brown b Betts	1
*CMW Read	c Frost b Richardson	49	(8) not out	20
PJ Franks	not out	39	(9) not out	25
S Elworthy	c Frost b Brown	4	(4) c Brown b Clark	0
GJ Smith	c Brown b Richardson	35		
CE Shreck	b Richardson	0		
Extras	b 1, lb 9, w 1, nb 6	17	b 6, lb 10, w 6, nb 2	24
	(84.5 overs)	349	(7 wkts, 100.2 overs)	264

Bowling
Betts 16-3-76-1. Clark 15-2-71-2. Richardson 22.5-8-85-4. Brown 19-4-61-3.
Giles 12-1-46-0.
Clark 18-5-39-1. Betts 16.2-2-49-4. Richardson 24-7-59-1. Brown 16-1-42-0.
Giles 26-11-59-1.
Fall of Wickets 1-9, 2-15, 3-15, 4-94, 5-121, 6-227, 7-291, 8-295, 9-349, 10-349
1-14, 2-109, 3-110, 4-209, 5-210, 6-216, 7-219

Nottinghamshire beat Warwickshire by 3 wickets – Nottinghamshire (20pts), Warwickshire (4pts)

ESSEX v. MIDDLESEX – at Chelmsford

MIDDLESEX	First Innings		Second Innings	
AJ Strauss (capt)	c Robinson b Dakin	1	lbw b Middlebrook	40
SG Koenig	c Foster b Irani	42	c Foster b Dakin	94
OA Shah	run out	13	c Habib b Grayson	46
*DC Nash	lbw b Dakin	0	c Robinson b Grayson	42
EC Joyce	lbw b Dakin	28	b Robinson	117
Abdul Razzaq	c Foster b Irani	0	c Habib b Middlebrook	81
PN Weekes	lbw b Brant	31	lbw b Brant	0
BL Hutton	not out	45	c Flower b Middlebrook	23
SJ Cook	lbw b Dakin	22	lbw b Middlebrook	0
CB Keegan	st Foster b Middlebrook	24	c Grayson b Middlebrook	0
JH Dawes	c Jefferson b Middlebrook	2	not out	32
Extras	lb 4, nb 2	6	b6, lb 4, w 6, nb 4	20
	(59 overs)	214	(172.5 overs)	495

Bowling
Brant 13-2-50-1. Dakin 18-3-57-4. McGarry 9-1-48-0. Irani 14-4-43-2. Middlebrook 5-0-12-2.
Brant 23-6-60-1. Dakin 26-11-56-1. Irani 13-4-39-0. Middlebrook 57-11-172-5. Grayson 34-5-107-2. McGarry 16.3-2-41-0. Flower 1.3-0-3-0. Robinson 1.5-0-7-1.
Fall of Wickets 1-1, 2-24, 3-24, 4-82, 5-84, 6-86, 7-124, 8-169, 9-206, 10-214
1-65, 2-174, 3-191, 4-233, 5-384, 6-385, 7-422, 8-422, 9-427, 10-495

ESSEX	First Innings		Second Innings	
DDJ Robinson	b Cook	83	not out	23
WI Jefferson	b Dawes	56	not out	18
A Flower	c Shah b Cook	7		
JD Middlebrook	c Weekes b Keegan	36		
A Habib	lbw b Weekes	34		
RC Irani (capt)	lbw b Razzaq	69		
*JS Foster	b Keegan	52		
JM Dakin	c Dawes b Razzaq	52		
SA Brant	lbw b Keegan	4		
AC McGarry	not out	4		
Extras	lb 10, nb 12	22		
	(107.3 overs)	402	(no wkt, 9 overs)	41

Bowling
Dawes 22-6-69-1. Keegan 23-3-106-3. Cook 22-3-105-2. Weekes 16-3-39-1. Razzaq 23.3-5-69-3. Joyce 1-0-4-0.
Dawes 4-0-10-0. Keegan 4-1-16-0. Strauss 1-0-15-0.
Fall of Wickets 1-104, 2-128, 3-148, 4-163, 5-215, 6-291, 7-320, 8-356, 9-356, 10-402

Match drawn – Essex (12pts), Middlesex (8pts)

Stuart Law puts a disappointing winter with Queensland behind him by hitting champions Surrey for a brilliant 169 in the championship opener at The Oval.

Loye and Stuart Law who ran the Surrey attack ragged. The Australian Law's 169 was merely reconfirmation of his class following what, for him, had been a disappointing winter with Queensland, while Loye's 126 was immediate justification of his decision to leave his native Northamptonshire for pastures north. Loye, at 30, had joined Lancashire in a bid to give fresh impetus to a career which, following England A recognition in the mid-1990s, was threatening to settle into underachievement. Ian Salisbury was the only Surrey bowler to escape the carnage with anything like respectability, but worse was to come for the champions as their first innings plunged from 106 for 1 to 280 all out. The dismissals of Ian Ward and Mark Ramprakash, and some formidable pace bowling from James Anderson, initiated a collapse which led to Surrey being asked to follow on. His haul of 5 for 61 took Anderson to 51

championship wickets at 19 runs apiece in a fledgling career which also boasted at this point a strike rate of a scalp every 33 balls. The balmy weather of the opening day had by now given way to some drizzle and bad light – costing 80 overs in all. This, plus the excellence of the pitch and the second-innings performances of both Ward and Rikki Clarke, resulted in Surrey's escape with a draw. Ward swung Chris Schofield for three legside sixes, and also hit 24 fours, in his superb 158; Clarke, who had come in at 140 for 5, finished unbeaten on 127 from 139 balls – his second championship hundred. When Ward finally fell to a weary stroke, Alex Tudor kept Clarke company until the draw was confirmed.

Nottinghamshire, newly promoted, signalled their intentions of mixing it with the so-called elite by beating Warwickshire, the 2002 runners-up, by three wickets at Trent Bridge. In the end, Notts were steered home by a coolly constructed unbeaten stand of 45 for the eighth wicket between Chris Read and Paul Franks, after Warwickshire had fought back tigerishly from 140 for 5 in their second innings – a lead of just 13. Ashley Giles, the visiting captain, led the way with 94 and both Dougie Brown and Mel Betts produced supporting half-centuries as Warwickshire reached 390 in their second innings. Betts then undermined the Notts victory dash with a spell of 4 for 0 in 15 balls, but Kevin Pietersen's 54 was another important factor in the home side's ultimate success. On the opening day, it was the six-foot-seven-inches tall pace bowler signed from Cornwall, 25-year-old Charlie Shreck, who put Notts in command by taking 4 for 33 as Warwickshire were bowled out cheaply. The experience of Darren Bicknell and Chris Cairns then rallied Notts from 15 for 3 in reply, before the prodigious talent of 18-year-old Bilal Shafayat ensured a sizeable first-innings lead. Shafayat's disappointment, after gloving a hook at Brown when just three short of his century, was indicative of the high standards he had already begun to set himself after a highly successful winter captaining England Under 19s in Australia. Read helped Shafayat to add 106 for the sixth wicket, while both Franks and the powerful Greg Smith contributed valuable runs in a ninth-wicket stand of 54.

A fourth-wicket partnership of 151 between the talented Ed Joyce and Pakistani all-rounder Abdul Razzaq did much to earn Middlesex a hard-fought draw against Essex at Chelmsford. Joyce, an Irishman ineligible for England, scored 117 as Essex battled through 172.5 overs to total 495 and overcome a first-innings deficit of 188. Jon Dakin was the most successful home bowler as Middlesex were tumbled out for 214 on the opening day, but the Essex decision to go off for bad light on 356 for 7, with 49 overs of the second day still undelivered, came back to haunt them. Darren Robinson, Will Jefferson, Ronnie Irani and Dakin all topped 50 as Essex eventually reached 402, while Sven Koenig's 94 offered the initial resistance on which Middlesex's fightback was based.

Division Two

Relegated Yorkshire signalled their intent to bounce straight back up to the top flight by hammering Northamptonshire by an innings and 343 runs at Headingley. The visitors were condemned by the end of the first day, in which they were bowled out for 184 and then saw Yorkshire cruise to 210 for 2 in reply. The home side's total eventually reached the mammoth proportions of 673 for 8 declared – topping the previous highest total conceded by Northants (670 for 9 by Sussex in 1921). The visitors' bowling and fielding standards were distinctly shoddy, but much credit is still due to Matthew Wood (157) and Richard Blakey, whose career-best 223 not out occupied only 206 balls and contained 35 fours. Blakey was enjoying something of a renaissance with the bat: in 2002 he had passed 1,000 runs for the season for the first time since 1994. At 36, too, his innings recalled some of the glories of his youth: it was at Bulawayo against

Zimbabwe, when on tour for England A in the early months of 1990, that Blakey had scored his previous career-best score of 221. Darren Gough, making a high-profile return to action following a hard winter of rehabilitation on his problematic knee, removed Rob White just before the close of day two. Northants, resuming the next morning on 20 for 1, had only a powerful half-century from Phil Jaques to offer as they subsided to 146 all out, with Gough taking three wickets and the impressive Chris Silverwood 4 for 39. The result was a fillip both for Gough, making his first championship appearance for nine months and only his 11th since 1998, and for new Yorkshire captain Anthony McGrath – but made chilling viewing for Kepler Wessels, the no-nonsense new coach of Northamptonshire.

Gloucestershire won a famous local derby victory against Somerset at Bristol to give their supporters the perfect curtain-raiser for the season. And it was a thrilling contest, too, stretching well into the fourth and final day before Roger Sillence induced a mishit drive by Simon Francis to Phil Weston at mid-off with just nine runs required. Overall, indeed, this was a great advert for the see-sawing nature of the best championship encounters, and a timely advertisement for the genuine and matchless excitement that the first-class game can provide.

Round One: 18–21 April 2003 Division Two

YORKSHIRE v. NORTHAMPTONSHIRE – at Headingley

NORTHANTS	First Innings		Second Innings	
RA White	c Wood b Silverwood	2	c Taylor b Gough	0
MJ Powell	c Blakey b Gough	0	c Lumb b Silverwood	4
PA Jaques	lbw b Silverwood	9	c and b Sidebottom	60
JW Cook	c Wood b Dawson	74	c Blakey b Silverwood	28
DJG Sales (capt)	lbw b Gough	12	lbw b McGrath	1
GL Brophy	lbw b Gough	2	lbw b McGrath	0
GP Swann	lbw b Sidebottom	10	b Silverwood	0
*TMB Bailey	lbw b Silverwood	31	lbw b Silverwood	0
CG Greenidge	c Blakey b Hoggard	1	not out	9
A Nel	b Sidebottom	17	b Gough	8
JAR Blain	not out	1	lbw b Gough	5
Extras	b 1, lb 10, w 2, nb 12	25	b 18, lb 7, nb 6	31
	(48.1 overs)	184	(40.4 overs)	146

Bowling
Gough 12–1–40–3. Silverwood 10–2–45–3. Hoggard 14–3–37–1. Sidebottom 5.1–1–14–2. McGrath 3–0–10–0. Dawson 4–1–27–1.
Gough 11.4–1–41–3. Silverwood 13–4–39–4. Sidebottom 7–1–28–1. McGrath 7–3–9–2. Fellows 2–0–4–0.
Fall of Wickets 1–2, 2–8, 3–15, 4–45, 5–53, 6–101, 7–147, 8–163, 9–181, 10–184
1–0, 2–36, 3–84, 4–85, 5–85, 6–86, 7–86, 8–123, 9–132, 10–146

YORKSHIRE	First Innings	
CR Taylor	c Brophy b Greenidge	16
MJ Wood	c White b Swann	157
A McGrath (capt)	run out	35
MJ Lumb	c Bailey b Blain	42
*RJ Blakey	not out	223
GM Fellows	b Nel	30
RKJ Dawson	c Sales b Blain	38
CEW Silverwood	c Brophy b White	53
D Gough	c Sales b Blain	3
RJ Sidebottom	not out	24
M J Hoggard		
Extras	b 4, lb 10, w 3, nb 35	52
	(8 wkts, 134.2 overs)	673

Bowling
Nel 29–3–120–1. Blain 26.2–3–153–3. Greenidge 27–1–164–1. Cook 22–3–79–0. Swann 26–1–108–1. White 4–0–35–1.
Fall of Wickets 1–46, 2–99, 3–230, 4–330, 5–405, 6–489, 7–604, 8–621

Yorkshire beat Northamptonshire by an innings and 343 runs – Yorkshire (22pts), Northamptonshire (2pts)

GLOUCESTERSHIRE v. SOMERSET – at Bristol

GLOS	First Innings		Second Innings	
CM Spearman	c Burns b McLean	8	(2) c Turner b Johnson	8
WPC Weston	lbw b Lewis	12	(1) b McLean	12
THC Hancock	b McLean	33	c Turner b McLean	44
JN Rhodes	c Bowler b Johnson	42	b Blackwell	55
MGN Windows	c Bowler b Francis	20	c Burns b McLean	78
MW Alleyne (capt)	c Turner b Francis	19	lbw b McLean	0
*RC Russell	c Blackwell b Francis	14	not out	78
ID Fisher	c Bowler b Burns	25	c Trescothick b McLean	18
RJ Sillence	b Johnson	42	b Laraman	40
J Lewis	not out	1	c sub b Laraman	8
AM Smith	c Turner b Johnson	0	c Bryant b Laraman	1
Extras	lb 2, w 1, nb 2	10	b 12, lb 10, nb 4	26
	(62.2 overs)	203	(133 overs)	368

Bowling
McLean 13–1–43–2. Johnson 13.2–3–27–3. Francis 20–7–65–3. Laraman 13–4–54–1. Blackwell 1–1–0–0. Burns 2–0–7–1.
McLean 35–9–87–5. Johnson 33–8–84–1. Francis 22–2–79–0. Laraman 21–7–45–3. Blackwell 19–7–46–1. Burns 3–1–5–0.
Fall of Wickets 1–16, 2–25, 3–92, 4–108, 5–117, 6–138, 7–143, 8–198, 9–202, 10–203
1–20, 2–28, 3–113, 4–147, 5–155, 6–258, 7–282, 8–348, 9–360, 10–368

SOMERSET	First Innings		Second Innings	
PD Bowler	lbw b Smith	0	lbw b Smith	50
ME Trescothick	b Smith	0	c Russell b Smith	10
M Burns (capt)	b Lewis	14	lbw b Lewis	25
J Cox	c Russell b Lewis	11	lbw b Alleyne	67
JDC Bryant	c Russell b Lewis	19	c Russell b Alleyne	31
*RJ Turner	not out	59	(7) c Alleyne b Sillence	15
AW Laraman	c Russell b Lewis	0	(8) b Sillence	23
RL Johnson	b Lewis	118	(9) not out	11
ID Blackwell	b Smith	31	(6) c Russell b Alleyne	0
NAM McLean	c Spearman b Fisher	9	c Russell b Smith	3
SRG Francis	c Fisher b Sillence	34	c Weston b Sillence	1
Extras	lb 5, nb 2	7	b 10, lb 10, w 4, nb 14	38
	(65.2 overs)	289	(102 overs)	274

Bowling
Lewis 21–4–58–6. Smith 16–1–64–2. Alleyne 6–3–37–0. Sillence 6.2–0–54–1. Fisher 16–6–71–1.
Lewis 23–8–40–1. Smith 28–8–69–3. Sillence 18–2–55–3. Alleyne 27–4–77–3. Fisher 22–6–13–0.
Fall of Wickets 1–0, 2–0, 3–8, 4–17, 5–36, 6–36, 7–192, 8–236, 9–247, 10–289
1–18, 2–74, 3–124, 4–204, 5–204, 6–229, 7–237, 8–262, 9–271, 10–274

Gloucestershire beat Somerset by 8 runs – Gloucestershire (18pts), Somerset (5pts)

WORCESTERSHIRE v. HAMPSHIRE – at Worcester

WORCS	First Innings		Second Innings	
SD Peters	c Smith b Mullally	52	c Pothas b Wasim Akram	24
A Singh	lbw b Wasim Akram	8	c Adams b Wasim Akram	8
GA Hick	c Crawley b Mullally	72	lbw b Giddins	82
BF Smith (capt)	lbw b Giddins	104	c Pothas b Mullally	46
VS Solanki	c and b Udal	22	c Kenway b Mascarenhas	45
DA Leatherdale	b Giddins	4	c Kenway b Wasim Akram	12
GJ Batty	lbw b Wasim Akram	12	c sub b Mullally	14
*SJ Rhodes	c Mullally b Giddins	22	not out	20
Kabir Ali	b Giddins	40	b Udal	25
M Hayward	c Mullally b Wasim Akram	22	c sub b Udal	6
MA Harrity	not out	2	not out	0
Extras	b 5, lb 6, w 7, nb 18	36	lb 7, nb 17	24
	(119 overs)	386	(9 wkts, 78.5 overs)	264

Bowling
Wasim Akram 26.5–5–102–3. Mullally 23–6–61–2. Mascarenhas 22–11–40–0. Giddins 24.5–3–88–4. Udal 20.3–2–80–1. Kendall 3–1–14–0.
Wasim Akram 18.5–4–53–3. Giddins 12–2–48–1. Mullally 21–6–69–2. Mascarenhas 17–4–47–1. Udal 11–1–48–2.
Fall of Wickets 1–15, 2–92, 3–165, 4–234, 5–257, 6–279, 7–289, 8–335, 9–359, 10–386
1–29, 2–34, 3–78, 4–175, 5–185, 6–204, 7–210, 8–257, 9–263

HAMPSHIRE	First Innings		Second Innings	
DA Kenway	b Hayward	5	c Rhodes b Hayward	1
JHK Adams	c Rhodes b Kabir Ali	11	b Hayward	4
JP Crawley (capt)	lbw b Batty	93	c Rhodes b Kabir Ali	67
RA Smith	lbw b Kabir Ali	22	lbw b Leatherdale	8
WS Kendall	c Rhodes b Hayward	16	b Batty	13
*N Pothas	not out	146	c Leatherdale b Hayward	48
AD Mascarenhas	c Batty b Kabir Ali	20	c Rhodes b Hayward	38
Wasim Akram	c Solanki b Kabir Ali	5	c Solanki b Batty	4
SD Udal	c Rhodes b Hayward	1	lbw b Hayward	4
AD Mullally	lbw b Hayward	7	not out	0
ESH Giddins	b Harrity	11	lb 2, w 1, nb 6	9
Extras	lb 1, w 2, nb 8	11		
	(119.4 overs)	347	(9 wkts, 74 overs)	276

Bowling
Hayward 31–9–95–4. Kabir Ali 26–8–74–4. Harrity 24.4–7–90–1. Leatherdale 13–1–47–0. Batty 25–9–40–1.
Kabir Ali 17–1–78–1. Hayward 18–2–70–5. Harrity 12–3–32–0. Batty 22–4–71–2. Leatherdale 5–0–23–1.
Fall of Wickets 1–10, 2–24, 3–60, 4–81, 5–263, 6–305, 7–311, 8–312, 9–326, 10–347
1–5, 2–13, 3–135, 4–160, 5–186, 6–246, 7–262, 8–267, 9–276

Match drawn – Worcestershire (11pts), Hampshire (10pts)

Francis and Richard Johnson, Somerset's last pair, came together with 12 needed after both Aaron Laraman and Nixon McLean had perished trying to slog. Johnson, moreover, had been the man who initially put Somerset in charge with a first-innings score of 118 from No. 8 – a tremendously powerful maiden hundred that took him just 75 balls, and all the more remarkable for the fact that he came to the crease with his team on 36 for 6 in reply to Gloucestershire's first-innings total of 203. Rob Turner, with an unbeaten half-century, and Francis, with a career-best 34 from No. 11, helped in the dramatic drive to an 86-run lead, while Jon Lewis' six wickets made him the pick of the home attack. Gloucestershire's own second-innings fightback was just as courageous, on a pitch now offering variable bounce. Jonty Rhodes marked his county debut with 55 off 64 balls, and Matt Windows hit 78, but it was the unbeaten 78 from Jack Russell, spread over 252 balls and five-and-a-half hours of typically cussed resistance, which most frustrated Somerset. Sillence was also a valuable partner for Russell in an ultimately match-winning stand of 66 for the eighth wicket – and Somerset were left to contemplate that the last time they scored more than the 283 they now needed to win a West Country derby was in 1938. Jamie Cox and Peter Bowler, however, looked capable of steering their side home, as both compiled determined half-

centuries as the Gloucestershire seamers wheeled away. With a touch more composure at the end, Somerset would have done it. To Gloucestershire, though, the reward for holding their nerve was victory.

There was an equally exciting finish at New Road, where the unlikely last-wicket Hampshire pairing of Alan Mullally and Ed Giddins survived the final eight balls of the match to snatch a draw against Worcestershire. Set 314 to win in 74 overs, Hampshire still required 181 from 35 overs at tea and an exciting final session ended with them on 276 for 9. John Crawley batted beautifully for the second time in the match and added 122 for the third wicket with Robin Smith, while Nic Pothas also had a match to remember. The South African wicketkeeper with a Greek passport scored his first hundred for Hampshire in the first innings, joining Crawley in a fifth-wicket partnership of 182 which rallied them from 81 for 4 in reply to Worcestershire's first-innings total of 386. Pothas then made 48 in the valiant

At the age of 36, Richard Blakey scores a career-best 223 not out as Yorkshire thump Northamptonshire at Headingley.

DERBYSHIRE v. GLAMORGAN – at Derby

DERBYSHIRE	First Innings		Second Innings	
AI Gait	c James b Wharf	0	(2) b Wharf	6
MJ Di Venuto	c Wallace b Thomas	121	(1) lbw b Croft	61
CWG Bassano	b Wharf	0	c Dale b Croft	52
SA Selwood	c Wallace b Thomas	20	lbw b Croft	10
Shahid Afridi	c Kasprowicz b Thomas	14	c Maynard b Croft	1
DG Cork (capt)	c Kasprowicz b Croft	37	b Wharf	31
*LD Sutton	c Dale b Croft	120	not out	37
G Welch	c Dale b Thomas	37	not out	25
Mohammad Ali	b Croft	31		
KJ Dean	b Wharf	20		
LJ Wharton	not out	8		
Extras	b 5, lb 7	12	b 7, lb 4, w 5, nb 6	22
	(135.4 overs)	420	(6 wkts, 78 overs)	245

Bowling
Kasprowicz 32.2–13–94–0. Wharf 23–2–83–3. Davies 4–2–23–0. Thomas 19.4–4–69–4. Croft 52.4–11–128–3. Dale 4–1–11–0.
Kasprowicz 11–1–39–0. Wharf 26–4–87–2. Davies 10–0–47–0. Croft 31–10–61–4.
Fall of Wickets 1–9, 2–9, 3–56, 4–72, 5–165, 6–204, 7–284, 8–337, 9–382, 10–420
1–32, 2–108, 3–130, 4–144, 5–149, 6–193

GLAMORGAN	First Innings		Second Innings	
SP James (capt)	lbw b Dean	1	lbw b Cork	14
A Dale	c Cork b Mohammad Ali	13	c Dean b Wharton	92
DL Hemp	b Dean	7	c sub b Welch	7
MJ Powell	b Mohammad Ali	12	lbw b Cork	37
MP Maynard	c Gait b Mohammad Ali	142	c Di Venuto b Afridi	9
*MA Wallace	lbw b Wharton	6	c Di Venuto b Afridi	16
RDB Croft	c Wharton b Mohammad Ali	79	b Cork	6
MS Kasprowicz	c Di Venuto b Cork	41	not out	10
AU Wharf	b Afridi	16	not out	19
AP Davies	c Cork b Afridi	9		
SD Thomas	not out	9		
Extras	lb 5, nb 12	17	b 9, lb 3, nb 28	40
	(90.2 overs)	352	(7 wkts, 68.4 overs)	253

Bowling
Cork 24.2–5–83–2. Dean 17–3–65–2. Mohammad Ali 17–3–79–4. Welch 16–3–66–0. Wharton 6–0–25–1. Afridi 10–2–29–2.
Cork 14–1–61–3. Dean 6–2–22–0. Welch 8–4–10–1. Mohammad Ali 8–0–56–0. Afridi 22.4–6–69–2. Wharton 10–3–23–1.
Fall of Wickets 1–3, 2–19, 3–25, 4–38, 5–71, 6–253, 7–291, 8–332, 9–342, 10–352
1–32, 2–52, 3–119, 4–154, 5–201, 6–201, 7–216

Match drawn – Derbyshire (12pts), Glamorgan (11pts)

second-innings run chase, the ultimate failure of which was in large part due to the fast bowling of his fellow South African, Nantie Hayward. His nine-wicket match haul was early evidence of the cutting edge his signing would provide for the Worcestershire attack, in which Kabir Ali and Gareth Batty also impressed. Apart from the frustration of not being quite able to force the win, the match also represented an excellent start in the job of Worcestershire captain for Ben Smith, who top scored in each innings with 104 in the first and 82 in the second.

The match between Derbyshire and Glamorgan could also have gone either way on a tense final day before ending in a draw. Here, it was fast bowlers Mike Kasprowicz and Alex Wharf who batted out the last 11 overs to take Glamorgan to safety at 253 for 7 in their second innings, having been set 314 in 69 overs by Dominic Cork. Earlier, Adrian Dale's 92 had given the Welsh county a sniff of victory. Matthew Maynard's 52nd first-class hundred, and his 47th for Glamorgan, was the highlight of their first innings. He hit 23 boundaries and was joined in a fierce stand of 182 in 30 overs by Robert Croft, which enabled Glamorgan to rally from 71 for 5 to reach 352 in reply to Derbyshire's first-innings score of 420. Michael Di Venuto was another batsman in form, scoring 121 and 61 in the match, while Luke Sutton's 120 was his first century for two years.

ROUND TWO: 23–26 APRIL 2003

Division One

Just eight balls of the match remained at Edgbaston when Graham Napier gave Ashley Giles the charge and was yorked by the England left-arm spinner – a dismissal which confirmed the first tie in the championship for ten years. The result was a triumph for the initiative of the two captains, Warwickshire's Giles and Ronnie Irani of Essex, who conjured up such a thrilling finish out of a contest which had lost its third day and all but ten overs of its second day to bad weather.

Warwickshire had reached 411 for 7 on the opening day, thanks in the main to a counter-attacking sixth-wicket stand of 201 between Jim Troughton and Dougie Brown. It was the first hundred for 21 months for Brown, whose 120 occupied just 157 balls, while Troughton took his overnight 107 to an unbeaten 129 during the small passage of play possible on day two. The two captains did their deal on the final morning, however, with Warwickshire immediately declaring their first innings closed and forfeiting their second innings after Essex themselves had rattled up 66 for 0 declared. That left Essex requiring 381 from 90 overs, and when Andy Flower was joined by Irani

Round Two: 23–26 April 2003 Division One

WARWICKSHIRE v. ESSEX – at Edgbaston

WARWICKSHIRE	First Innings	
NV Knight	lbw b Irani	26
*T Frost	c Foster b Brant	59
MA Wagh	c Foster b Brant	32
IR Bell	lbw b Brant	18
JO Troughton	not out	129
DP Ostler	lbw b Dakin	18
DR Brown	lbw b Napier	120
AF Giles (capt)	b Irani	1
MA Sheikh	not out	28
M M Betts		
A Richardson		
Extras	b 5, lb 6, nb 4	15
	(7 wkts, 114.1 overs)	446

Bowling
Brant 30.1–5–133–3. Dakin 23–5–79–1. Irani 19.5–5–51–2. Napier 13–1–62–1. Middlebrook 19–4–62–0. Grayson 10–1–48–0.
Fall of Wickets 1–44, 2–122, 3–135, 4–154, 5–176, 6–377, 7–386

ESSEX	First Innings		Second Innings	
DDJ Robinson	not out	42	c Frost b Betts	56
WI Jefferson	not out	20	lbw b Sheikh	49
AP Grayson			b Betts	28
A Flower			c Betts b Giles	55
A Habib			lbw b Giles	0
RC Irani (capt)			lbw b Giles	87
*JS Foster			c Frost b Betts	24
JM Dakin			lbw b Richardson	23
JD Middlebrook			lbw b Giles	25
GR Napier			b Giles	9
SA Brant			not out	1
Extras	nb 4	4	b 9, lb 6, w 6, nb 2	23
	(no wkt, 4 overs)	66	(89.5 overs)	380

Bowling
Ostler 2–0–13–0. Knight 2–0–33–0.
Betts 20–2–82–3. Richardson 17–0–70–1. Sheikh 18–5–54–1. Brown 7–0–44–0. Giles 27.5–3–115–5.
Fall of Wickets
1–88, 2–128, 3–147, 4–148, 5–280, 6–300, 7–330, 8–365, 9–379, 10–380

Match tied – Warwickshire (12pts),
Essex (9pts)

MIDDLESEX v. SUSSEX – at Lord's

SUSSEX	First Innings		Second Innings	
RR Montgomerie	c Nash b Keegan	20	(2) b Keegan	2
MW Goodwin	c Shah b Dawes	16	(1) lbw b Dawes	23
PA Cottey	lbw b Dawes	0	b Cook	38
CJ Adams (capt)	c and b Weekes	26	lbw b Razzaq	12
TR Ambrose	b Cook	51	lbw b Dawes	35
RSC M-Jenkins	c Hutton b Dawes	13	lbw b Weekes	50
*MJ Prior	c Razzaq b Weekes	11	lbw b Keegan	4
KJ Innes	st Nash b Weekes	15	c Hutton b Keegan	1
M Ahmed	c Nash b Keegan	9	c Nash b Keegan	2
RJ Kirtley	not out	20	not out	25
JD Lewry	c Hutton b Razzaq	45	c Nash b Dawes	8
Extras	lb 11, nb 2	13	lb 4	4
	(73.1 overs)	239	(62.1 overs)	204

Bowling
Dawes 22–4–58–3. Keegan 19–4–49–2. Cook 13–2–42–1. Razzaq 9.1–0–43–1. Weekes 10–1–36–3.
Dawes 15.1–3–47–3. Keegan 21–8–36–4. Razzaq 11–0–55–1. Cook 10–0–45–1. Hutton 2–0–10–0. Weekes 3–1–7–1.
Fall of Wickets 1–37, 2–41, 3–41, 4–92, 5–132, 6–138, 7–154, 8–168, 9–172, 10–239
1–24, 2–28, 3–63, 4–79, 5–123, 6–132, 7–136, 8–146, 9–186, 10–204

MIDDLESEX	First Innings		Second Innings	
AJ Strauss (capt)	c Prior b Kirtley	10	lbw b Kirtley	83
SG Koenig	lbw b Kirtley	43	c Prior b Lewry	7
OA Shah	b Lewry	1	lbw b Innes	61
*DC Nash	b M-Jenkins	17	b M Ahmed	29
SJ Cook	b M Ahmed	5	(9) not out	22
EC Joyce	b Kirtley	8	(5) lbw b Kirtley	49
Abdul Razzaq	lbw b Lewry	3	(6) lbw b Kirtley	11
PN Weekes	lbw b Kirtley	0	(7) lbw b Kirtley	33
BL Hutton	lbw b M Ahmed	2	(8) not out	11
CB Keegan	c Prior b M Ahmed	8		
JH Dawes	not out	3		
Extras	b 1, lb 4, w 1, nb 10	16	b 8, lb 11, w 1, nb 4	24
	(48.3 overs)	116	(7 wkts, 106.4 overs)	330

Bowling
Lewry 17–8–34–2. Kirtley 16–3–51–3. M Ahmed 10.3–4–16–3. M-Jenkins 5–2–10–1.
Lewry 25–4–50–1. Kirtley 33–10–87–4. M Ahmed 28.4–6–97–1. M-Jenkins 10–2–42–0. Innes 10–2–35–1.
Fall of Wickets 1–24, 2–29, 3–69, 4–74, 5–92, 6–97, 7–97, 8–98, 9–109, 10–116
1–19, 2–136, 3–165, 4–200, 5–225, 6–287, 7–288

Middlesex beat Sussex by 3 wickets –
Middlesex (17pts), Sussex (4pts)

KENT v. LEICESTERSHIRE – at Canterbury

KENT	First Innings		Second Innings	
MA Carberry	c Snape b Dagnall	55	c Nixon b Brignull	36
RWT Key	lbw b Dagnall	25	c Nixon b DeFreitas	18
ET Smith	run out	3	lbw b DeFreitas	0
GS Blewett	c Nixon b Dagnall	57	c Nixon b DeFreitas	0
MJ Walker	lbw b Brignull	1	lbw b DeFreitas	38
MA Ealham (capt)	run out	17	b Brignull	82
*GO Jones	lbw b Maddy	38	c Maddy b Snape	104
JC Tredwell	c Stevens b Brignull	9	c Sadler b Dagnall	31
A Khan	c Snape b Masters	23	c Snape b Snape	2
MJ Saggers	b Maddy	9	c Stevens b Snape	47
A Sheriyar	not out	0	not out	9
Extras	b 1, lb 5, nb 2	8	b 10, lb 14, w 2, nb 2	28
	(68.2 overs)	245	(121.2 overs)	411

Bowling
DeFreitas 13–1–60–0. Masters 17–5–47–1. Dagnall 14–4–43–3. Brignull 11–4–30–2. Maddy 13.2–2–59–2.
Masters 16–4–83–0. Dagnall 27–4–95–2. Brignull 17–3–42–2. DeFreitas 28–7–69–4. Maddy 20–4–63–0. Stevens 4–0–9–0. Snape 9.2–2–52–2.
Fall of Wickets 1–43, 2–52, 3–100, 4–103, 5–158, 6–170, 7–205, 8–227, 9–245, 10–245
1–54, 2–64, 3–66, 4–68, 5–169, 6–233, 7–291, 8–309, 9–397, 10–411

LEICESTERSHIRE	First Innings		Second Innings	
TR Ward	c Tredwell b Ealham	29	c Ealham b Khan	22
JL Sadler	c Key b Blewett	4	lbw b Saggers	0
DL Maddy	b Saggers	63	lbw b Khan	4
DI Stevens	lbw b Ealham	4	lbw b Sheriyar	45
*PA Nixon	not out	113	c Walker b Saggers	53
DG Brandy	c Jones b Khan	9	c Ealham b Sheriyar	52
JN Snape	c Jones b Saggers	5	not out	26
PAJ DeFreitas (capt)	c Jones b Saggers	5	not out	34
DD Masters	c Sheriyar b Tredwell	0		
CE Dagnall	lbw b Sheriyar	0		
DS Brignull	lbw b Saggers	1		
Extras	b 6, lb 11, nb 10	27	b 5, lb 4, nb 10	19
	(93 overs)	270	(6 wkts, 70 overs)	255

Bowling
Saggers 24–4–75–4. Sheriyar 20–4–72–1. Ealham 20–9–36–2. Khan 17–4–61–1. Blewett 8–5–6–1. Tredwell 4–2–3–1.
Saggers 17–3–60–2. Sheriyar 14–1–77–2. Ealham 8–1–28–0. Sheriyar 14–3–44–2. Tredwell 12–7–21–0. Blewett 5–2–16–0.
Fall of Wickets 1–40, 2–40, 3–48, 4–169, 5–196, 6–199, 7–211, 8–259, 9–259, 10–270
1–1, 2–14, 3–27, 4–102, 5–154, 6–202

Match drawn – Kent (8pts), Leicestershire (9pts)

in a fifth-wicket partnership of 132 the target looked well within reach. Irani, indeed, went on to score a belligerent 87 from 91 balls, with four sixes, but Giles then added his opposite number's scalp to that of Flower before, later, bringing himself back with dramatic effect. First he had James Middlebrook lbw, and then earned himself figures of 5 for 115 by bowling Napier. Essex lost their last three wickets for 15 runs, but Giles' tenacity had ultimately found a reward equal to that of Irani.

A stirring fightback by Middlesex, on a Lord's pitch which seemed to get better with age, brought them a morale-boosting three-wicket victory over Sussex. When they were bowled out for 116 in their first innings, a deficit of 123, all looked lost for the home side with the ball still swinging and the faster bowlers also finding enough help off the seam to make batting a difficult proposition. Robin Martin-Jenkins' second-innings half-century then appeared to extend the Sussex lead beyond the reach of Middlesex. Needing 328, however, they found inspiration, initially in a second-wicket stand between Owais Shah and Andy Strauss, the captain, which took them to 136 for 2 before the early close of the third day. Improved weather on the final day also helped Middlesex, who battled hard through Ed Joyce and Paul Weekes after Strauss had taken his overnight unbeaten 64 to 83. James Kirtley bowled his heart out for Sussex in an effort to deny

the Middlesex middle order, finishing with 4 for 87 from 33 overs, but towards the end he was visibly flagging when Simon Cook took three boundaries off him to settle a tense contest. It was a hard result for Kirtley to take, especially as on the first day he had also hung around gamely to help his new-ball partner Jason Lewry (45) add an unlikely 67 for the Sussex first-innings' last wicket.

Bad weather cost Kent dearly at Canterbury, where an under-strength Leicestershire side battled gamely for a draw in a match which featured an intriguing sub-plot involving rival wicketkeepers Paul Nixon and Geraint Jones. Rain washed out the third day's final session and the first 26 overs of the fourth, allowing Leicestershire to recover from being 27 for 3 and see out time quite comfortably through the efforts of Nixon and Damien Brandy, who both made half-centuries. For Nixon, in particular, it was a sweet return to the county who chose to release him the previous autumn, because his second-innings score of 53 followed a fighting 113 not out on the second day which even saw the Kent crowd stand to afford him prolonged applause. Nixon's hundred, however, which earned Leicestershire a slender lead, was but the curtain-raiser for a century of even greater significance by Jones, the 26-year-old, Australia-raised Welshman who had been controversially preferred to Nixon by the Kent committee. It was a maiden ton from Jones and, together with Mark Ealham's excellent 82 and a tail-end cameo from Martin Saggers (47), should have been enough to earn Kent victory.

A third day washout, and severe interruptions on two other days, condemned the match between Lancashire and Nottinghamshire at Old Trafford to a draw … but not before Andrew Flintoff had demonstrated the benefits of his pre-season diet of vegetable soup and cranberry juice. The England all-rounder, who had shed half a stone from his intimidating frame in the week before the start of hostilities, proved that his calorie-counting had not cost him any lessening of power by including a six and 15 fours in a 130-ball innings of 97 on the opening day. Mal Loye earned himself headlines, too, by becoming the first Lancashire batsman to score a hundred in each of his first two first-class appearances for the club but – after that explosive start – the rain turned the game into a damp squib. Peter Martin matched the five-wicket haul of Steve Elworthy, who was returning to his former county as Notts' temporary overseas player, and there were also good half-centuries for both Chris Cairns and Chris Read on a shortened final day.

LANCASHIRE v. NOTTINGHAMSHIRE – at Old Trafford

LANCASHIRE	First Innings		Second Innings	
AJ Swann	c Read b Elworthy	15	lbw b Smith	7
IJ Sutcliffe	c and b Elworthy	42	not out	17
MB Loye	c Afzaal b Elworthy	113	c Cairns b Smith	7
SG Law	c Shafayat b Franks	6	not out	8
MJ Chilton	c Gallian b Elworthy	14		
A Flintoff	c Read b Pietersen	97		
G Chapple	b Smith	28		
CP Schofield	b Smith	3		
*WK Hegg (capt)	b Elworthy	0		
PJ Martin	lbw b Smith	1		
JM Anderson	not out	0		
Extras	b 1, lb 9, w 7, nb 18	35	nb 2	2
	(102.1 overs)	**354**	(2 wkts, 18.4 overs)	**41**

Bowling
Smith 19-4-50-3. Harris 25-5-87-0. Elworthy 24.1-6-71-5. Franks 16-1-74-1. Gallian 7-3-17-0. Pietersen 9-0-33-1. Shafayat 2-0-12-0.
Elworthy 6-0-13-0. Harris 4.4-0-20-0. Smith 8-4-8-2.
Fall of Wickets 1-54, 2-77, 3-104, 4-156, 5-293, 6-340, 7-351, 8-353, 9-354, 10-354.
1-17, 2-31

NOTTS	First Innings	
DJ Bicknell	c Hegg b Martin	30
JER Gallian (capt)	lbw b Anderson	0
U Afzaal	c Hegg b Chapple	6
KP Pietersen	lbw b Martin	19
CL Cairns	c Hegg b Martin	57
BM Shafayat	c and b Martin	18
*CMW Read	lbw b Martin	57
PJ Franks	c Chilton b Flintoff	5
S Elworthy	c Martin b Anderson	30
GJ Smith	c Swann b Chapple	19
AJ Harris	not out	16
Extras	b 11, lb 5, w 2	18
	(82.3 overs)	**275**

Bowling
Anderson 20-2-76-2. Chapple 18.3-3-51-2. Martin 19-3-54-5. Flintoff 11-4-23-1. Schofield 13-0-52-0. Law 1-0-3-0.
Fall of Wickets 1-1, 2-11, 3-44, 4-113, 5-126, 6-155, 7-173, 8-238, 9-240, 10-275.

Match drawn – Lancashire (11pts),
Nottinghamshire (9pts)

Division Two

Brave batting by Jon Lewis, their captain, could not prevent Durham from slipping to a six-wicket defeat at the hands of Somerset in a rare low-scoring affair at Taunton. Lewis scored 78 and 50 in the match, but it was the home team's Peter Bowler who played the decisive innings of the game on the final day to guide Somerset to victory. James Bryant also contributed a half-century, in support of Bowler's unbeaten 67, after Marcus Trescothick had launched the run chase on the third evening with a short but aggressive innings featuring just seven boundaries. Trescothick had also included 13 fours in his first-innings, 81-ball 60, while the pick of the seamers who dominated the game was Somerset's Richard Johnson.

The poor weather, which bit large chunks of playing time out of both the second and third days at Northampton, ruined what could have been a fascinating contest on a pitch plainly tailor-made for spin. Kepler Wessels, the Northants coach, made no apology for that fact, saying that his side would be intending to play to their strength during the season. Chris Broad, on his first day as an ECB pitch inspector, said: 'It is turning too much for the first day, but it is not turning unduly and good batsmen will score runs on it.' Better spinners than Gloucestershire's Martyn Ball would, undoubtedly, have taken more than 5 for 104 as Northants racked up 352 in little over a day, but the visitors' reply was then badly disrupted by rain delays and, on the fourth day, there was little interest left in the match but for the statement of Jonty Rhodes, with 128, that his commitment to his new county was total.

A barnstorming, unbeaten 100 by Dimitri Mascarenhas, in which his second 50 took just 20 balls, provided the highlight of another match – between Glamorgan and Hampshire at Cardiff – in which weather intrusions had too much of a say. Mascarenhas' hitting followed fine innings from John Crawley, Robin Smith and the in-form Nic Pothas and

Dimitri Mascarenhas of Hampshire: a ferocious hundred at Sophia Gardens.

Round Two: 23–26 April 2003 Division Two

SOMERSET v. DURHAM – at Taunton

DURHAM	First Innings			Second Innings	
JJB Lewis (capt)	c Turner b Francis	78		b Francis	50
MA Gough	c Turner b Johnson	14		c Burns b Johnson	4
GJ Pratt	lbw b Johnson	8		b Johnson	21
VJ Wells	c Trescothick b McLean	7		c Turner b Francis	9
N Peng	c Turner b Johnson	15		c Turner b McLean	4
DR Law	c Turner b Johnson	4		b McLean	35
*A Pratt	b Johnson	23		c Burns b Johnson	27
NC Phillips	c Trescothick b Laraman	6		c Dutch b McLean	4
N Killeen	c Laraman b Francis	20		c Turner b Francis	0
J Srinath	not out	0		not out	13
SJ Harmison	c Bryant b Francis	0		c Turner b Francis	2
Extras	lb 2, nb 8	10		lb 1, nb 10	11
	(59 overs)	185		(58.4 overs)	180

Bowling
McLean 17–4–44–1. Johnson 16–1–64–5. Francis 15–4–49–3. Laraman 11–2–26–1.
McLean 14–4–53–2. Johnson 19–5–52–4. Francis 12.4–3–41–3. Burns 6–3–13–0.
Laraman 2–1–3–0. Dutch 5–0–20–0.
Fall of Wickets 1–24, 2–40, 3–66, 4–96, 5–100, 6–134, 7–147, 8–180, 9–185, 10–185
1–6, 2–36, 3–53, 4–66, 5–112, 6–153, 7–165, 8–165, 9–165, 10–180

SOMERSET	First Innings			Second Innings	
PD Bowler	c Srinath b Killeen	25		not out	67
ME Trescothick	c Phillips b Wells	60		c A Pratt b Killeen	28
M Burns (capt)	lbw b Wells	17		b Killeen	0
J Cox	lbw b Srinath	0		c A Pratt b Harmison	10
JDC Bryant	b Srinath	13		c A Pratt b Phillips	51
SRG Francis	b Wells	4			
*RJ Turner	not out	27			
KP Dutch	b Harmison	4			
AW Laraman	c A Pratt b Harmison	1			
RL Johnson	run out	7		(6) not out	23
NAM McLean	b Harmison	0			
Extras	b 5, lb 5, w 1, nb 6	17		lb 1, lb 6, w 1, nb 10	18
	(60.4 overs)	171		(4 wkts, 55.4 overs)	197

Bowling
Srinath 17–4–46–2. Harmison 20.4–7–49–3. Killeen 12–4–31–1. Wells 11–0–35–3.
Srinath 16–4–46–0. Harmison 15–8–25–1. Killeen 14–2–57–2. Wells 5–1–19–0.
Phillips 5.4–1–43–1.
Fall of Wickets 1–91, 2–100, 3–100, 4–125, 5–125, 6–130, 7–151, 8–153, 9–169, 10–171
1–50, 2–54, 3–82, 4–171

Somerset beat Durham by 6 wickets – Somerset (17pts), Durham (3pts)

NORTHAMPTONSHIRE v. GLOUCESTERSHIRE – at Northampton

NORTHANTS	First Innings			Second Innings	
MJ Powell	c Russell b Ball	60		c Russell b Ball	13
DE Paynter	lbw b Fisher	50		b Averis	2
PA Jaques	c Hancock b Fisher	14		c and b Ball	11
JW Cook	lbw b Ball	10		not out	21
DJG Sales (capt)	c Russell b Alleyne	59			
GL Brophy	c Hancock b Fisher	32		(5) not out	10
GP Swann	c Hancock b Ball	1			
*TMB Bailey	b Rhodes b Averis	38			
RSG Anderson	b Ball	13			
A Nel	c Russell b Ball	39			
MS Panesar	not out	5			
Extras	b 2, lb 7, nb 22	31		b 3, lb 1, nb 8	12
	(112.2 overs)	352		(3 wkts, 24 overs)	69

Bowling
Averis 19.2–5–46–1. Sillence 9–1–60–0. Alleyne 8–3–12–1. Fisher 36–6–121–3.
Ball 40–9–104–5.
Averis 5–1–22–1. Sillence 5–1–18–0. Ball 8–6–4–2. Fisher 5–0–19–0.
Hancock 1–0–2–0.
Fall of Wickets 1–126, 2–144, 3–148, 4–164, 5–253, 6–253, 7–257, 8–275, 9–338, 10–352
1–3, 2–27, 3–44

GLOS	First Innings		
CM Spearman	c Swann b Nel	69	
WPC Weston	c Powell b Panesar	13	
THC Hancock	b Swann	59	
JN Rhodes	c Cook b Swann	128	
MGN Windows	c Powell b Panesar	35	
MW Alleyne (capt)	not out	32	
*RC Russell	not out	31	
I D Fisher			
M C J Ball			
R J Sillence			
J M M Averis			
Extras	b 14, lb 10, nb 12	36	
	(5 wkts, 107 overs)	403	

Bowling
Nel 30–7–84–1. Anderson 10–1–67–0. Panesar 45–9–135–2. Swann 21–2–76–2.
Jaques 1–0–17–0.
Fall of Wickets 1–52, 2–128, 3–173, 4–330, 5–331

Match drawn – Northamptonshire (9pts), Gloucestershire (12pts)

GLAMORGAN v. HAMPSHIRE – at Cardiff

HAMPSHIRE	First Innings		
DA Kenway	c Cosker b Wharf	19	
JP Crawley (capt)	b Wharf	65	
RA Smith	c Wallace b Harrison	92	
WS Kendall	lbw b Harrison	32	
AC Morris	c Harrison b Davies	46	
*N Pothas	c Wallace b Wharf	87	
AD Mascarenhas	not out	100	
Wasim Akram	c Davies b Harrison	23	
SD Udal	not out	32	
C T Tremlett			
A D Mullally			
Extras	b 7, lb 11, w 1, nb 16	35	
	(7 wkts, 121.5 overs)	531	

Bowling
Wharf 28–4–134–3. Davies 17–3–96–1. Cosker 21–1–63–0. Harrison 20–4–87–3.
Croft 30.5–5–119–0. Dale 5–3–14–0.
Fall of Wickets 1–24, 2–147, 3–210, 4–223, 5–345, 6–387, 7–426

GLAMORGAN	First Innings		
U Thomas	c Kendall b Mascarenhas	41	
A Dale	c Pothas b Tremlett	16	
DL Hemp	b Mullally	57	
MJ Powell	b Wasim Akram	85	
MP Maynard	c Udal b Tremlett	112	
*MA Wallace	lbw b Tremlett	37	
RDB Croft (capt)	not out	15	
DS Harrison	not out	6	
A G Wharf			
A P Davies			
D A Cosker			
Extras	b 2, lb 8, w 1, nb 32	43	
	(6 wkts, 110.3 overs)	412	

Bowling
Wasim Akram 20–4–82–1. Mullally 22–5–81–1. Tremlett 22–7–101–3.
Udal 27–5–93–0. Mascarenhas 19.3–9–45–1.
Fall of Wickets 1–40, 2–109, 3–159, 4–325, 5–367, 6–400

*Match drawn – Glamorgan (11pts),
Hampshire (11pts)*

enabled Hampshire to declare on an intimidating 531 for 7. But Glamorgan's batsmen, led by Matthew Maynard and Mike Powell, were not inhibited at all. Maynard's 112 occupied only 119 balls and a high-scoring draw ensued.

ROUND THREE: 30 APRIL–3 MAY 2003

Division One

James Kirtley took nine wickets, including a second-innings haul of 6 for 26, as Sussex enjoyed an emphatic 133-run victory over Kent at Hove. Fast bowler Kirtley, however, was quick to praise the contributions of overseas stars Murray Goodwin and Mushtaq Ahmed, and underlined the extra potency that the Pakistan leg spinner Mushtaq in particular was bringing to the county attack. 'This is a massive win for us,' Kirtley said, 'especially as this game looked for long periods to be following a similar pattern to the one at Lord's last week which we lost. Murray's second-innings performance was the best batting of the match, and Mushy has already made a big difference.' The Pakistani's 39-ball 37, towards the end of a Sussex first innings which eventually reached 279, also helped the home cause after Chris Adams, Tim Ambrose and Matt Prior had all batted usefully. Alamgir Sheriyar was Kent's best bowler,

taking five wickets, but the visitors also heard dispiriting news on the opening day regarding their absent captain, David Fulton, who was told by specialists that he would never regain full vision in his injured right eye. Forties from Greg Blewett and Matthew Walker proved Kent's best as they struggled to a first-innings all-out total of 185, with Kirtley and Mushtaq taking three wickets apiece, and, at 166 for 4 in their second innings, Sussex looked to be in complete command. Then, though, towards the end of the second day, Mark Ealham and James Tredwell engineered a startling collapse which brought the loss of five wickets for eight runs inside ten overs. Goodwin's 96, after this, took on significant importance – even if, on the third day, no Kent batsman could resist the pace of Kirtley or the spin of Mushtaq for long.

The technical excellence of Mark Wagh, and the grit of his team-mate Nick Knight, was sufficient to earn Warwickshire a draw against Surrey at The Oval in a weather-affected match. Both Wagh and Knight made centuries, with Wagh's first-innings knock of 136 hauling Warwickshire to 413 and Knight's unbeaten, second-innings 103 ensuring that there were no final afternoon dramas, despite testing bowling from both Saqlain Mushtaq and Alex Tudor. Surrey all-rounder Tudor had also impressed with the ball during a first-day spell of 3 for 20 in

James Kirtley takes 6 for 26 to spearhead Sussex's final push towards victory against Kent at Hove.

nine overs, while his 55 from 72 balls added to a solid first-innings batting effort by the home team. Mark Butcher's first nine scoring shots were all boundaries, and there were 14 fours in all in his 64. Mark Ramprakash and Alec Stewart also batted attractively, but the real fireworks were provided by Adam Hollioake, whose 122 came at a run a ball. However, it was Knight, adding to a first-innings half-century, in which he had helped Tony Frost post 153 for the first wicket, who had the final word.

Constant interruptions by the weather prevented a tense, low-scoring affair at Chelmsford from reaching an exciting conclusion. Seam bowlers dominated throughout, with John Stephenson's 50 from No. 9 on the opening day and Darren Stevens' 65 being the only half-centuries of the match. Jon Dakin and Scott Brant were Essex's most effective bowlers, with Charlie Dagnall's second-innings haul of 5 for 66 the pick of the Leicestershire effort in the field.

Division Two

Poor weather condemned all four Division Two matches as draws, with no play being possible at all on the last two days at Southampton, where Yorkshire looked to be getting the better of Hampshire. Yorkshire's first-innings total of 293 owed almost everything to an eighth-wicket stand of 126 between Michael Lumb and Darren Gough. At 128 for 7, after Alan Mullally had done much of the early damage, the visitors were on the back foot, but in the next 30 overs Gough thumped 72 from 96 balls, while Lumb stayed to remain unbeaten and achieve his third first-class hundred. None of Hampshire's batsmen, however, could match either Lumb's skill and application or Gough's ebullience – although Nic Pothas did end up unbeaten on 44 in an all-out total of 175.

There were blank third days at Derby, Chester-le-Street and Worcester, besides other interruptions from the elements. The nearest anyone got to forcing a positive result was at Derby, where Somerset were thwarted by bad light and rain in the final session. Derbyshire, having been bowled out on day one for 190 by Andy Caddick and Richard Johnson, were still ten runs behind at 197 for 6 in their second innings when the weather closed in. Without an opening stand of 80 by Andrew Gait and Michael Di Venuto, however, they would not have been able to stave off the likes of Caddick even then. Somerset's first-innings total of 397 was achieved despite some fine seam and swing bowling from Dominic Cork, who took 5 for 74 in 37 overs, and was built on an aggressive 69 by Marcus Trescothick and a five-and-a-half hour 126 from Jamie Cox, his first first-class hundred for almost 12 months.

Durham also had a final-day scare at Chester-le-Street before holding off the challenge of Gloucestershire, and left-arm seamer Mike Smith in particular. An opening stand of 118 between Jon Lewis and Michael Gough was the rock on which their eventually shaky rearguard action was founded, after they had followed on. Lewis, the Durham captain, also made an excellent 50 in his side's first-innings score of 183, which was a feeble reply to a Gloucestershire total of 341 which was based on characterful half-centuries from Tim Hancock, Jonty Rhodes and Jack Russell.

Northamptonshire had the best of their much-interrupted draw at Worcester, with Phil Jaques celebrating his 24th birthday with a powerful unbeaten 149 on the final day. He had sat through the washed-out third day on 86 not out, but then made the most of the 31 overs possible as the game petered out. It was also a first first-class hundred for the Australian with a British passport courtesy of parents born in Manchester and Sheffield, who had made only two appearances for New South Wales before deciding to try his luck

in English county cricket. On the first day, Northants had also bowled Worcestershire out for 236, with John Blain returning the strange figures of 15–0–84–5 and Ben Phillips taking 4 for 45 in his first championship match for five years. Former Kent all-rounder Phillips was attempting to resurrect his county career after several years of chronic injury problems.

Round Three: 30 April–3 May 2003 Division Two

New face, new star: Phil Jaques of Northamptonshire, an Aussie strokemaker of English parentage.

HAMPSHIRE v. YORKSHIRE – at Southampton

YORKSHIRE	First Innings		Second Innings	
MJ Wood	c Pothas b Mullally	5	not out	8
MP Vaughan	b Wasim Akram	1	not out	10
A McGrath (capt)	c Udal b Tremlett	15		
MJ Lumb	not out	115		
*RJ Blakey	c Pothas b Mullally	24		
GM Fellows	c Kenway b Mullally	0		
RKJ Dawson	lbw b Udal	10		
CEW Silverwood	c Smith b Udal	0		
D Gough	c Pothas b Katich	72		
RJ Sidebottom	lbw b Wasim Akram	9		
SP Kirby	lbw b Wasim Akram	0		
Extras	b 1, lb 15, nb 26	42	lb 1, nb 4	5
	(92.1 overs)	293	(no wkt, 8 overs)	23

Bowling
Wasim Akram 19.1–6–64–3. Mullally 22–5–31–3. Mascarenhas 13–3–41–0. Tremlett 16–2–71–1. Udal 13–2–47–2. Katich 9–2–23–1. Wasim Akram 4–2–7–0. Mullally 4–1–15–0.
Fall of Wickets 1–1, 2–15, 3–49, 4–82, 5–84, 6–128, 7–128, 8–254, 9–289, 10–293

HAMPSHIRE	First Innings	
DA Kenway	b Kirby	10
JP Crawley (capt)	b Silverwood	1
SM Katich	run out	17
RA Smith	c Blakey b Kirby	30
WS Kendall	c Lumb b Sidebottom	1
*N Pothas	not out	44
AD Mascarenhas	lbw b Kirby	1
Wasim Akram	b Sidebottom	18
SD Udal	c Lumb b Dawson	31
CT Tremlett	c Vaughan b Dawson	2
AD Mullally	c Blakey b McGrath	8
Extras	b 6, lb 2, nb 4	12
	(59.5 overs)	175

Bowling
Gough 14–5–28–0. Silverwood 9–2–34–1. Kirby 11–3–19–3. Sidebottom 14–3–44–2. Dawson 7–2–23–2. McGrath 4.5–0–19–1.
Fall of Wickets 1–2, 2–21, 3–53, 4–60, 5–60, 6–64, 7–107, 8–154, 9–162, 10–175

Match drawn – Hampshire (7pts), Yorkshire (9pts)

DERBYSHIRE v. SOMERSET – at Derby

DERBYSHIRE	First Innings		Second Innings	
AI Gait	c Turner b Caddick	41	(2) lbw b Caddick	63
MJ Di Venuto	b Johnson	17	(1) lbw b Caddick	36
CWG Bassano	c Dutch b Johnson	0	c Bryant b Dutch	0
SA Selwood	c Turner b Johnson	0	c Turner b McLean	18
DR Hewson	c Cox b Caddick	37	c Dutch b McLean	13
Shahid Afridi	b McLean	4	c Trescothick b Caddick	6
*LD Sutton	c Trescothick b Laraman	38	not out	23
DG Cork (capt)	c Turner b Johnson	25	retired hurt	6
G Welch	c Dutch b Caddick	14	not out	9
Mohammad Ali	c Trescothick b Caddick	0		
KJ Dean	not out	1		
Extras	lb 7, nb 6	13	b 4, lb 12, w 1, nb 6	23
	(52.1 overs)	190	(6 wkts, 64.1 overs)	197

Bowling
McLean 14.5–5–32–1. Johnson 15–4–47–4. Caddick 17–1–66–4. Laraman 6.1–0–38–1.
McLean 19–4–66–2. Johnson 10.1–3–25–0. Caddick 21–7–44–3. Dutch 9–1–29–1. Laraman 4–0–15–0. Bowler 1–0–2–0.
Fall of Wickets 1–20, 2–20, 3–22, 4–94, 5–101, 6–105, 7–151, 8–188, 9–188, 10–190
1–80, 2–81, 3–115, 4–139, 5–150, 6–154

SOMERSET	First Innings	
PD Bowler	c Sutton b Dean	1
ME Trescothick	c and b Welch	69
M Burns (capt)	lbw b Cork	10
J Cox	c Sutton b Cork	126
JDC Bryant	c Welch b Cork	26
AW Laraman	c Dean b Cork	24
*RJ Turner	not out	32
KP Dutch	c Gait b Cork	4
RL Johnson	c Gait b Mohammad Ali	1
NAM McLean	b Welch	15
AR Caddick	b Mohammad Ali	4
Extras	b 12, lb 17, w 3, nb 26	58
	(112.1 overs)	397

Bowling
Cork 37–11–74–5. Dean 21–6–90–1. Welch 24.1–7–64–2. Mohammad Ali 18–1–118–2. Afridi 12.5–2–22–0.
Fall of Wickets 1–1, 2–60, 3–154, 4–240, 5–330, 6–337, 7–340, 8–342, 9–347, 10–397

Match drawn – Derbyshire (7pts), Somerset (11pts)

DURHAM v. GLOUCESTERSHIRE – at Chester-le-Street

GLOS	First Innings	
CM Spearman	lbw b Srinath	4
WPC Weston	c Lewis b Law	40
THC Hancock	c A Pratt b Law	59
JN Rhodes	c A Pratt b Pretorius	60
MGN Windows	c GJ Pratt b Wells	44
MW Alleyne (capt)	lbw b Law	21
*RC Russell	b Law	65
ID Fisher	lbw b Phillips	0
RJ Sillence	b Phillips	0
J Lewis	b Harmison	10
AM Smith	not out	17
Extras	b 4, lb 13, w 2, nb 2	21
	(119.2 overs)	341

Bowling
Harmison 30–11–58–1. Srinath 24–6–64–1. Pretorius 20–5–94–1. Law 18.2–5–30–4. Wells 13–3–28–1. Phillips 14–4–50–2.
Fall of Wickets 1–10, 2–65, 3–148, 4–194, 5–234, 6–240, 7–243, 8–243, 9–276, 10–341

DURHAM	First Innings		Second Innings	
JJB Lewis (capt)	c Spearman b Smith	54	c Weston b Sillence	55
MA Gough	c Fisher b Lewis	2	c Weston b Smith	73
GJ Pratt	c Alleyne b Smith	0	c Weston b Smith	0
VJ Wells	b Lewis	0	c Russell b Smith	1
N Peng	c and b Alleyne	37	c Sub b Sillence	10
DR Law	c Sillence b Alleyne	2	b Lewis	4
*A Pratt	b Smith	13	not out	8
J Srinath	b Lewis	10	not out	0
NC Phillips	c Russell b Sillence	27		
D Pretorius	lbw b Sillence	16		
SJ Harmison	not out	7		
Extras	lb 5, nb 10	15	b 1, lb 1, nb 8	10
	(64.3 overs)	183	(6 wkts, 65.5 overs)	159

Bowling
Lewis 22–5–64–3. Smith 24.5–8–43–3. Sillence 15.3–2–52–2. Alleyne 8–1–30–2.
Lewis 17.5–6–48–1. Smith 12–7–14–3. Sillence 17–4–46–2. Alleyne 7–1–38–0. Fisher 12–8–11–0.
Fall of Wickets 1–3, 2–3, 3–5, 4–80, 5–84, 6–118, 7–123, 8–129, 9–166, 10–183
1–118, 2–118, 3–130, 4–143, 5–149, 6–155

Match drawn – Durham (7pts), Gloucestershire (10pts)

WORCESTERSHIRE v. NORTHAMPTONSHIRE – at Worcester

WORCS	First Innings	
SD Peters	b Blain	17
A Singh	b Blain	6
GA Hick	c Hussey b Phillips	37
BF Smith (capt)	lbw b Cook	50
VS Solanki	c Bailey b Blain	79
DA Leatherdale	c Bailey b Phillips	2
GJ Batty	lbw b Phillips	0
*SJ Rhodes	c Cook b Blain	4
Kabir Ali	c Brophy b Blain	6
M Hayward	c Bailey b Phillips	6
MS Mason	not out	0
Extras	b 4, lb 1, nb 24	29
	(57.3 overs)	236

Bowling
Nel 21–7–46–0. Blain 15–0–84–5. Phillips 14.3–6–45–4. Cook 8–1–37–1. Panesar 3–0–19–0.
Fall of Wickets 1–27, 2–36, 3–99, 4–142, 5–156, 6–164, 7–191, 8–221, 9–236, 10–236

NORTHANTS	First Innings	
MEK Hussey (capt)	c Rhodes b Mason	45
MJ Powell	run out	31
PA Jaques	not out	149
JW Cook	b Kabir Ali	2
DJG Sales	b Kabir Ali	33
GL Brophy	st Rhodes b Batty	6
*TMB Bailey	not out	12
BJ Phillips		
A Nel		
JAR Blain		
MS Panesar		
Extras	lb 16, nb 18	34
	(5 wkts, 94 overs)	312

Bowling
Kabir Ali 25–6–65–2. Hayward 19–2–81–0. Mason 26–5–80–1. Leatherdale 9–0–43–0. Batty 15–2–27–1.
Fall of Wickets 1–57, 2–133, 3–140, 4–248, 5–284

Match drawn – Worcestershire (6pts), Northamptonshire (10pts)

ROUND FOUR: 9–12 MAY 2003

Division One

Jonathan Trott, a 22-year-old former South Africa Under 19 batsman with a British passport, became the first Warwickshire player since Brian Lara nine years earlier to score a century on his championship debut. Trott, believed to be related to Albert Trott, the legendary Anglo-Australian hitter who is still the only batsman to date to strike a ball over the Lord's pavilion, made 134 at Edgbaston in a Warwickshire first innings boosted late on by Mo Sheikh's unbeaten 57. Two other highly promising young Warwickshire batsmen, Ian Bell and Jim Troughton, also struck centuries in a stand of 182 in 37 overs which set up a second-innings declaration. Troughton struck four sixes, while Bell reached his ton with a straight six off Mushtaq Ahmed. Sussex saw two of their finest young cricketers, Tim Ambrose and Matt Prior, add 125 for the seventh wicket in a first-innings score of 367, but were scuppered by the seam and swing of Mel Betts (5 for 43) and Dougie Brown (4 for 17) as they were tumbled out for 106 to lose by 234 runs on the final day.

Surrey's seamers proved too potent for the Nottinghamshire batsmen in an innings victory at Trent Bridge, although home skipper Jason Gallian carried his bat for 112 in a first-innings total of 211. Both Alec Stewart, who faced just 70 balls, and Azhar Mahmood hit 98 in a Surrey reply of 393 before Jimmy Ormond, who had taken 5 for 45 on the first day, combined with Martin Bicknell to leave Notts reeling on a hopeless 94 for 6 by the close of the second day. Mahmood picked up two wickets the following morning, as did Bicknell (5 for 83) as Notts were dismissed for 176, despite a gutsy 50 from Steve Elworthy.

The 58th first-class hundred of his career by Stuart Law, then converted into 198, looked as if it might be the basis of a crushing victory for Lancashire against Middlesex at Lord's when Gary Keedy's 6 for 68 forced the home team to follow on. Mark Chilton and the impressive Andrew Flintoff, whose 111 took the same number of balls and contained four sixes and 12 fours, were the other Lancashire centurions in a mammoth total of 565 for 7 declared, and Keedy's steady left-arm spinners reduced Middlesex to 304 all out in reply. Poor weather, however, then plagued the third and fourth days, leaving time only for Middlesex openers Andy Strauss and Sven Koenig to grab the opportunity of making some welcome early-season runs.

Round Four: 9–12 May 2003 Division One

WARWICKSHIRE v. SUSSEX – at Edgbaston

WARWICKSHIRE

First Innings			Second Innings		
*T Frost	b Kirtley	37	(2) c Prior b Lewry	0
IJL Trott	c Montgomerie b M Ahmed	134	(1) lbw b Lewry	5
MA Wagh	b M Ahmed	43	lbw b M-Jenkins	38
IR Bell	c Prior b M Ahmed	3	lbw b Davis	107
JO Troughton	c Prior b Kirtley	41	c sub b Davis	105
DP Ostler	lbw b M Ahmed	1	b M-Jenkins	7
DR Brown	c Ambrose b M Ahmed	0	c Montgomerie b M-Jenkins	0
AF Giles (capt)	lbw b M Ahmed	22	not out	13
MA Sheikh	not out	57		
MM Betts	c Cottey b Kirtley	20		
A Richardson	b M-Jenkins	47		
Extras	b 6, lb 7, nb 4	17	b 8, lb 2	10
	(117.3 overs)	422	(7 wkts, 58 overs)	285

Bowling
Lewry 11–2–41–0. Kirtley 30–4–107–3. M-Jenkins 6.3–1–46–1. M Ahmed 48–7–157–6. Davis 22–7–58–0.
Kirtley 14–2–48–0. Lewry 9–1–51–2. M Ahmed 13–0–69–0. M-Jenkins 13–3–57–3. Davis 9–0–50–2.
Fall of Wickets 1–86, 2–194, 3–198, 4–233, 5–239, 6–239, 7–269, 8–307, 9–348, 10–422
1–5, 2–18, 3–64, 4–246, 5–271, 6–271, 7–285

SUSSEX

First Innings			Second Innings		
RR Montgomerie	lbw b Sheikh	41	(2) lbw b Betts	0
MW Goodwin	c Troughton b Sheikh	28	(1) lbw b Betts	10
PA Cottey	c Frost b Richardson	41	lbw b Brown	55
CJ Adams (capt)	b Sheikh	22	b Betts	0
RJ Kirtley	c Brown b Giles	31	(9) c Frost b Richardson	6
TR Ambrose	lbw b Sheikh	85	(5) lbw b Betts	0
RSC M-Jenkins	c Frost b Brown	7	(6) b Betts	11
*MJ Prior	c Ostler b Betts	84	(7) b Brown	5
MJG Davis	c Frost b Betts	1	(8) lbw b Brown	0
M Ahmed	not out	2	not out	7
JD Lewry	b Betts	0	b Brown	0
Extras	b 4, lb 17, w 1, nb 2	24	b 5, lb 7	12
	(128.4 overs)	367	(43 overs)	106

Bowling
Betts 23.4–2–83–3. Richardson 29–12–65–1. Brown 23–7–76–1. Sheikh 28–11–60–4. Giles 23–5–60–1. Wagh 2–1–2–0.
Betts 13–2–43–5. Richardson 13–6–19–1. Sheikh 6–2–15–0. Brown 9–4–17–4. Giles 2–2–0–0.
Fall of Wickets 1–67, 2–74, 3–116, 4–165, 5–216, 6–235, 7–360, 8–364, 9–364, 10–367
1–12, 2–17, 3–21, 4–21, 5–37, 6–43, 7–43, 8–82, 9–106, 10–106

Warwickshire beat Sussex by 234 runs – Warwickshire (22pts), Sussex (7pts)

NOTTINGHAMSHIRE v. SURREY – at Trent Bridge

NOTTS

First Innings			Second Innings		
DJ Bicknell	c Butcher b Azhar Mahmood	29	lbw b Bicknell	0
JER Gallian (capt)	not out	112	lbw b Bicknell	28
GE Welton	c Butcher b Azhar Mahmood	0	c Bicknell b Ormond	4
U Afzaal	b Butcher	16	c Butcher b Ormond	0
BM Shafayat	c Ramprakash b Azhar Mahmood	8	c Stewart b Ormond	10
*CMW Read	b Ormond	22	c Azhar Mahmood b Bicknell	26
PJ Franks	c Stewart b Ormond	0	c Brown b Azhar Mahmood	25
S Elworthy	c Stewart b Tudor	0	c Azhar Mahmood b Bicknell	52
GJ Smith	c Azhar Mahmood b Ormond	1	c Ramprakash b Bicknell	2
AJ Harris	c Stewart b Ormond	0	lbw b Azhar Mahmood	0
CE Shreck	c Stewart b Ormond	5	not out	16
Extras	b 4, lb 9, w 5	18	Lb 4, nb 6	10
	(68.4 overs)	211	(50.5 overs)	176

Bowling
Bicknell 16–4–41–0. Tudor 16–1–58–1. Azhar Mahmood 16–4–46–3. Ormond 18.4–5–45–5.
Bicknell 25.5–8–83–5. Ormond 8–0–26–3. Azhar Mahmood 16–3–59–2. Butcher 1–0–4–0.
Fall of Wickets 1–42, 2–48, 3–83, 4–96, 5–155, 6–177, 7–178, 8–179, 9–185, 10–211
1–0, 2–15, 3–15, 4–35, 5–71, 6–76, 7–128, 8–131, 9–138, 10–176

SURREY

First Innings		
MA Butcher	c Read b Elworthy	0
IJ Ward	c Franks b Smith	3
MR Ramprakash	c Smith b Shreck	38
*AJ Stewart	b Smith	98
AD Brown	c Elworthy b Smith	9
Saqlain Mushtaq	c Read b Harris	24
AJ Hollioake (capt)	b Elworthy	35
Azhar Mahmood	c Read b Elworthy	98
AJ Tudor	c Read b Gallian	27
MP Bicknell	not out	33
J Ormond	b Brown	5
Extras	b 5, lb 8, nb 10	23
	(72.1 overs)	393

Bowling
Elworthy 25.2–2–136–3. Smith 22.1–4–81–4. Shreck 12–1–81–1. Harris 12–1–75–1. Gallian 5–0–7–1.
Fall of Wickets 1–0, 2–4, 3–147, 4–157, 5–157, 6–202, 7–251, 8–333, 9–365, 10–393

Surrey beat Nottinghamshire by an innings and 6 runs – Surrey (21pts), Nottinghamshire (4pts)

MIDDLESEX v. LANCASHIRE – at Lord's

LANCASHIRE

First Innings		
AJ Swann	c Nash b Dawes	45
IJ Sutcliffe	lbw b Keegan	27
MB Loye	c Hutton b Tahir	30
SG Law	c and b Bloomfield	198
A Flintoff	b Weekes	111
MJ Chilton	lbw b Dawes	119
G Chapple	not out	7
*WK Hegg	c Shah b Dawes	9
JM Anderson		
PJ Martin		
G Keedy		
Extras	b 7, lb 9, w 1, nb 2	19
	(7 wkts, 152.3 overs)	565

Bowling
Dawes 30.3–5–82–3. Keegan 27–4–120–1. Bloomfield 21–2–101–1. Tahir 39–8–128–1. Weekes 27–0–91–1. Hutton 6–0–13–0. Joyce 2–0–14–0.
Fall of Wickets 1–38, 2–97, 3–120, 4–384, 5–519, 6–556, 7–565

MIDDLESEX

First Innings			Second Innings		
AJ Strauss (capt)	c Flintoff b Anderson	6	not out	100
SG Koenig	c Hegg b Keedy	34	not out	71
OA Shah	c Chilton b Flintoff	81		
*DC Nash	lbw b Anderson	13		
EC Joyce	c Flintoff b Chapple	53		
PN Weekes	c Swann b Keedy	39		
BL Hutton	c Flintoff b Keedy	33		
Imran Tahir	c Chapple b Keedy	0		
CB Keegan	lbw b Keedy	21		
JH Dawes	not out	1		
TF Bloomfield	c Chilton b Keedy	1		
Extras	b 4, lb 10, w 2, nb 6	22	b 5	5
	(77.2 overs)	304	(no wkt, 60 overs)	176

Bowling
Anderson 19–3–90–2. Martin 16–3–52–0. Chapple 17–2–63–1. Flintoff 3–0–17–1. Keedy 22.2–5–68–6.
Martin 12–3–25–0. Chapple 10–4–24–0. Flintoff 4–2–6–0. Keedy 23–2–82–0. Anderson 11–1–34–0.
Fall of Wickets 1–13, 2–94, 3–137, 4–147, 5–225, 6–253, 7–253, 8–299, 9–300, 10–304

Match drawn – Middlesex (8pts), Lancashire (12pts)

Luke Sutton, the Derbyshire wicketkeeper-batsman, who made quite an impression against Yorkshire.

Division Two

For only the ninth time in 100 visits to Yorkshire, there was a famous Derbyshire victory for Dominic Cork and his men to celebrate following a tense final day at Headingley. Rain in the morning had delayed the start with Yorkshire 12 without loss overnight, but when Graeme Welch bowled Michael Vaughan just before the lunch interval, Derbyshire sensed they could win. Michael Lumb, however, scored a gritty 86 and the last wicket did not fall until 5pm. Welch took 4 for 74 to add to his first-innings haul of 4 for 39, Mohammad Ali picked up three valuable scalps and Derbyshire, with maximum points, performed like a team capable of mounting a promotion challenge. Cork, though not at his best with the ball, scored a first-innings 92 from 149 deliveries as he and the impressive Luke Sutton added 159 for the sixth wicket. Wicketkeeper Sutton's 127 was a determined effort that spanned six hours and 20 minutes, and he not only built upon the base laid by half-centuries from Michael Di Venuto and Dominic Hewson but also repulsed the danger provided by Ryan Sidebottom, who eventually finished the innings with career-best figures of 7 for 97. Welch and Kevin Dean then dismissed Yorkshire for almost 200 less than Derbyshire's 422, but Cork chose not to enforce the follow-on. Di Venuto, with a run-a-ball 77, and Chris Bassano, with an unbeaten 53, profited before the declaration.

A second-innings ninth-wicket stand of 140 between David Harrison and Michael Kasprowicz made Gloucestershire work harder than they might have expected for victory against Glamorgan in Cardiff. The Welsh county, put in on a grassy pitch, had subsided to 139 all out in their first innings, with Jon Lewis (5 for 61) the chief destroyer. Craig Spearman and Matt Windows then led a solid Gloucestershire reply of 400 for 8 declared, before Lewis struck again on the third evening with two new-ball successes to leave Glamorgan on 70 for 3 overnight.

Round Four: 9–12 May 2003 Division Two

YORKSHIRE v. DERBYSHIRE – at Headingley

DERBYSHIRE	First Innings		Second Innings	
AI Gait	b Sidebottom	32	(2) lbw b Dawson	25
MJ Di Venuto	c Blakey b Sidebottom	50	(1) c McGrath b Dawson	77
CWG Bassano	c Richardson b Sidebottom	23	not out	53
SA Selwood	c Blakey b Sidebottom	2	c Blakey b Sidebottom	14
DR Hewson	run out	57	lbw b Sidebottom	3
*LD Sutton	b Dawson	127	not out	22
DG Cork (capt)	lbw b McGrath	92		
T Lungley	lbw b Sidebottom	7		
G Welch	lbw b Sidebottom	0		
Mohammad Ali	c Richardson b Sidebottom	5		
KJ Dean	not out	0		
Extras	b 3, lb 18, w 2, nb 4	27	b 7, lb 3, w 6, nb 4	20
	(132.4 overs)	422	(4 wkts, 64.2 overs)	214

Bowling
Silverwood 23–3–75–0. Hoggard 27–4–80–0. Kirby 24–4–90–0. Sidebottom 31–3–97–7. Dawson 17.4–3–38–1. McGrath 10.3–3–21–1.
Hoggard 9–2–26–0. Silverwood 6–0–23–0. Kirby 7–0–37–0. Sidebottom 10–2–24–2. Dawson 25.2–4–72–2. McGrath 6–1–15–0. Lumb 1–0–7–0.
Fall of Wickets 1–75, 2–84, 3–86, 4–116, 5–217, 6–376, 7–408, 8–408, 9–416, 10–422
1–109, 2–120, 3–147, 4–155

YORKSHIRE	First Innings		Second Innings	
MJ Wood	c Sutton b Dean	9	lbw b Mohammad Ali	32
MP Vaughan	c Cork b Welch	47	b Welch	38
A McGrath (capt)	c Hewson b Cork	61	lbw b Welch	4
MJ Lumb	lbw b Cork	38	lbw b Mohammad Ali	86
*RJ Blakey	c Gait b Welch	29	run out	11
SA Richardson	c Bassano b Welch	10	c Sutton b Welch	6
RKJ Dawson	c Di Venuto b Dean	0	lbw b Dean	13
CEW Silverwood	c Sutton b Dean	2	c Selwood b Dean	2
RJ Sidebottom	lbw b Welch	9	c Di Venuto b Welch	4
MJ Hoggard	not out	14	not out	13
SP Kirby	c Di Venuto b Dean	0	lbw b Mohammad Ali	4
Extras	lb 4, w 2, nb 20	24	b 5, lb 2, nb 20	27
	(65.3 overs)	230	(71.4 overs)	240

Bowling
Cork 21–5–69–2. Dean 12.3–1–39–4. Welch 16–4–39–4. Mohammad Ali 8–0–48–0. Lungley 8–2–33–0.
Cork 16–3–44–0. Dean 23–8–63–2. Welch 20–3–74–4. Lungley 5–0–26–0. Mohammad Ali 7.4–0–26–3.
Fall of Wickets 1–15, 2–97, 3–152, 4–155, 5–204, 6–205, 7–209, 8–229, 9–229, 10–230
1–58, 2–66, 3–103, 4–124, 5–148, 6–163, 7–165, 8–196, 9–236, 10–240

Derbyshire beat Yorkshire by 166 runs –
Derbyshire (22pts), Yorkshire (4pts)

GLAMORGAN v. GLOUCESTERSHIRE – at Cardiff

GLAMORGAN	First Innings		Second Innings	
IJ Thomas	b Smith	1	c Russell b Butler	13
A Dale	b Butler	8	c Alleyne b Lewis	17
DL Hemp	c Russell b Smith	1	c Russell b Lewis	34
MJ Powell	c Spearman b Lewis	4	lbw b Lewis	19
MP Maynard	run out	31	(6) c Windows b Butler	43
*MA Wallace	c Russell b Lewis	0	(7) b Smith	31
RDB Croft (capt)	lbw b Butler	4	(8) c and b Alleyne	14
DS Harrison	c Alleyne b Lewis	16	(9) c Russell b Smith	66
MS Kasprowicz	c Smith b Lewis	22	(10) b Lewis	78
AG Wharf	c Windows b Lewis	25	(11) not out	0
AP Davies	not out	19	(5) b Butler	4
Extras	lb 2, nb 6	8	b 1, lb 12, w 7, nb 16	36
	(42.2 overs)	139	(89.5 overs)	355

Bowling
Lewis 19.2–4–61–5. Smith 9–4–24–2. Butler 12–1–45–2. Alleyne 2–1–7–0.
Smith 19.5–2–91–2. Butler 25–7–90–3. Lewis 29–11–88–4. Alleyne 9–0–44–1. Fisher 7–2–29–0.
Fall of Wickets 1–5, 2–9, 3–16, 4–18, 5–19, 6–30, 7–57, 8–87, 9–102, 10–139
1–30, 2–41, 3–69, 4–103, 5–103, 6–173, 7–196, 8–203, 9–343, 10–355

GLOS	First Innings		Second Innings	
CM Spearman	c Thomas b Harrison	75	c Kasprowicz b Wharf	39
WPC Weston	lbw b Harrison	49	c Thomas b Wharf	17
THC Hancock	c Powell b Kasprowicz	24	c Dale b Wharf	13
JN Rhodes	lbw b Harrison	47	not out	14
IG Butler	b Harrison	13		
MGN Windows	c Wallace b Harrison	63	(5) c Maynard b Davies	0
MW Alleyne (capt)	lbw b Wharf	20	(6) not out	6
*RC Russell	c Maynard b Kasprowicz	16		
ID Fisher	not out	7		
J Lewis	not out	37		
A M Smith				
Extras	b 5, lb 23, w 5, nb 16	49	lb 2, nb 4	6
	(8 wkts, 115.4 overs)	400	(4 wkts, 15 overs)	95

Bowling
Kasprowicz 29–3–111–2. Harrison 24.4–4–80–5. Davies 12–3–37–0. Wharf 28–4–93–1. Dale 3–0–11–0. Croft 19–5–40–0.
Kasprowicz 3–0–24–0. Harrison 4–0–19–0. Wharf 5–0–28–3. Davies 3–0–22–1.
Fall of Wickets 1–137, 2–145, 3–207, 4–227, 5–264, 6–311, 7–349, 8–351
1–33, 2–71, 3–78, 4–84

Gloucestershire beat Glamorgan by 6 wickets –
Gloucestershire (22pts), Glamorgan (2pts)

ROUND FIVE: 14–17 MAY 2003

Division One

There were three rain-affected draws in this round of matches, with Surrey coming closest to forcing a win in their game against Leicestershire at The Oval. Appalling batting by Leicestershire on the opening day saw the visitors dismissed for 200, a total only reached because of a 58-ball 65 from their captain Phil DeFreitas, which hauled them up from 70 for 7. At 182 for 2, Surrey were in control by the close of the first day – with Mark Ramprakash hitting Virender Sehwag for six over long on and Alec Stewart striking three fours in an over off his fellow 40-year-old, Devon Malcolm. Ramprakash converted his overnight 59 into 152 the following day, treating spectators to a technical masterclass, and although Stewart was out for 71, adding just 13 more runs, Alistair Brown entered to thrash 73 and Adam Hollioake plundered 41 from only 25 balls. To cap it all, Ian Salisbury – who came in at 423 for 7 – hit his second championship hundred, reaching three figures with a six off Jeremy Snape. Hollioake immediately declared, with the score on 560 for 8, and by the close Leicestershire were in trouble at 14 for 2 in their second innings. Martin Bicknell, operating with six slips, had overnight figures of 4–4–0–2, but Surrey's players grew a little anxious

when rain allowed just five overs on day three. Then, on the final afternoon, more rain arrived at tea to save a Leicestershire team who by then were hanging on at 185 for 8. Sehwag hit 81, and Darren Maddy and Brad Hodge also did their best to hold up Surrey's victory march. In the end, Saqlain Mushtaq's 5 for 46 – his 28th return of five wickets or more for the county – deserved far more than the draw.

Kent forced Middlesex to follow on at Canterbury, after a first-innings total of 472 built around Ed Smith's 103 and half-centuries from Michael Carberry, Greg Blewett and Geraint Jones. The swing and seam of Martin Saggers, who took 4 for 48, then reduced Middlesex to 221, but weather interruptions on the third and fourth days helped the visitors to hold out following an opening stand of 176 between Andy Strauss and Sven Koenig.

James Anderson included Nasser Hussain as the middle victim in the first hat-trick of his burgeoning career, as Lancashire had the better of Essex in another rain-affected match at Old Trafford. Essex, dismissed for 215 on the opening day, slipped to 35 for 3 when Anderson had Darren Robinson caught in the gully, Hussain lbw and Will Jefferson caught at the wicket. It was the first time Anderson had bowled to Hussain in a competitive match, and he said later: 'The fact that it was the England captain first ball made it even more pleasurable!' Anderson also became the youngest Lancashire bowler to take

---

Round Five: 14–17 May 2003 Division One

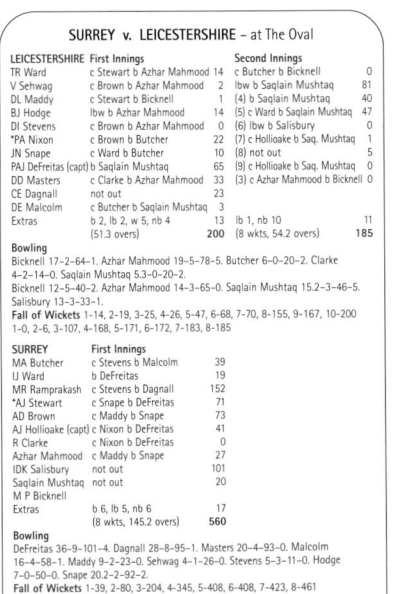

SURREY v. LEICESTERSHIRE – at The Oval

LEICESTERSHIRE First Innings

			Second Innings	
TR Ward	c Stewart b Azhar Mahmood	14	c Butcher b Bicknell	0
V Sehwag	c Brown b Azhar Mahmood	2	lbw b Saqlain Mushtaq	81
DL Maddy	c Stewart b Bicknell	1	(4) c Saqlain Mushtaq	40
BJ Hodge	lbw b Azhar Mahmood	14	(5) c Ward b Saqlain Mushtaq	47
DI Stevens	c Brown b Azhar Mahmood	0	(6) lbw b Salisbury	0
*PA Nixon	c Brown b Butcher	22	(7) c Hollioake b Saq. Mushtaq	1
JN Snape	c Ward b Butcher	10	(8) not out	5
PAJ DeFreitas (capt)	c Saqlain Mushtaq	65	(9) c Hollioake b Saq. Mushtaq	1
DD Masters	c Clarke b Azhar Mahmood	33	(3) c Azhar Mahmood b Bicknell	0
CE Dagnall	not out	23		
DE Malcolm	c Butcher b Saqlain Mushtaq	3		
Extras	b 2, lb 2, w 5, nb 4	13	lb 1, nb 10	11
	(51.3 overs)	200	(8 wkts, 54.2 overs)	185

Bowling
Azhar Mahmood 17–2–64–1. Azhar Mahmood 19–5–78–5. Butcher 6–0–20–2. Clarke 4–2–14–0. Saqlain Mushtaq 5.3–0–20–2.
Bicknell 15–5–40–2. Azhar Mahmood 14–3–65–0. Saqlain Mushtaq 15.2–3–46–5. Salisbury 13–3–33–1.
Fall of Wickets 1–14, 2–19, 3–25, 4–26, 5–47, 6–68, 7–70, 8–155, 9–167, 10–200
1–0, 2–6, 3–107, 4–168, 5–171, 6–172, 7–183, 8–185

SURREY First Innings

MA Butcher	c Stevens b Malcolm	39
IJ Ward	b DeFreitas	19
MR Ramprakash	c Stevens b Dagnall	152
*AJ Stewart	c Snape b DeFreitas	71
AD Brown	c Maddy b Snape	73
AJ Hollioake (capt)	c Nixon b DeFreitas	41
R Clarke	c Nixon b DeFreitas	0
Azhar Mahmood	c Maddy b Snape	27
IDK Salisbury	not out	101
Saqlain Mushtaq	not out	20
M P Bicknell		
Extras	b 6, lb 5, nb 6	17
	(8 wkts, 145.2 overs)	560

Bowling
DeFreitas 36–9–101–4. Dagnall 28–8–95–1. Masters 20–4–93–0. Malcolm 16–4–58–1. Maddy 9–2–23–0. Sehwag 4–1–26–0. Stevens 5–3–11–0. Hodge 7–0–50–0. Snape 20.2–2–92–2.
Fall of Wickets 1–39, 2–80, 3–204, 4–345, 5–408, 6–408, 7–423, 8–461

Match drawn – Surrey (12pts), Leicestershire (7pts)

KENT v. MIDDLESEX – at Canterbury

KENT First Innings

MA Carberry	c Nash b Keegan	53
RWT Key	lbw b Dawes	36
ET Smith	c Hutton b Dawes	103
GS Blewett	c Koenig b Dawes	60
MJ Walker	c Hutton b Dawes	32
MA Ealham (capt)	lbw b Keegan	32
*GO Jones	c Hutton b Weekes	52
JC Tredwell	c and b Weekes	36
MJ Saggers	c Hutton b Weekes	16
A Sheriyar	not out	12
BJ Trott	b Weekes	2
Extras	b 13, lb 12, w 4, nb 9	38
	(134 overs)	472

Bowling
Dawes 28–2–90–4. Keegan 28–8–72–2. Gannon 23–4–102–0. Hutton 7–1–45–0. Tahir 20–5–68–0. Weekes 28–6–70–4.
Fall of Wickets 1–66, 2–132, 3–270, 4–274, 5–319, 6–380, 7–412, 8–452, 9–455, 10–472

MIDDLESEX First Innings

			Second Innings	
AJ Strauss (capt)	run out	3	c Ealham b Tredwell	93
SG Koenig	b Saggers	42	c Walker b Trott	96
OA Shah	c Walker b Trott	5	c Walker b Tredwell	21
BL Hutton	c Sheriyar b Saggers	74	c Blewett b Trott	5
EC Joyce	b Saggers	0	not out	15
PN Weekes	lbw b Trott	3	not out	1
*DC Nash	lbw b Saggers	12		
CB Keegan	c Tredwell b Ealham	19		
Imran Tahir	c Key b Ealham	29		
JH Dawes	b Tredwell	16		
BW Gannon	not out	1		
Extras	b 5, lb 7, w 1, nb 4	17	b 1, lb 13, nb 4	18
	(71.4 overs)	221	(4 wkts, 71.3 overs)	249

Bowling
Saggers 23–9–48–4. Trott 20–4–68–2. Sheriyar 14–0–69–0. Ealham 11–4–21–2. Tredwell 2.4–0–2–1. Blewett 1–0–1–0.
Saggers 12–2–42–0. Trott 16.3–3–52–2. Tredwell 24–6–70–2. Sheriyar 11–0–31–0. Ealham 4–0–18–0. Carberry 4–1–22–0.
Fall of Wickets 1–3, 2–8, 3–105, 4–119, 5–122, 6–150, 7–154, 8–203, 9–212, 10–221
1–176, 2–212, 3–230, 4–245

Match drawn – Kent (12pts), Middlesex (8pts)

LANCASHIRE v. ESSEX – at Old Trafford

ESSEX First Innings

			Second Innings	
DDJ Robinson	c Swann b Anderson	11	c Hegg b Anderson	8
WI Jefferson	c Hegg b Anderson	19	b Martin	3
N Hussain	lbw b Anderson	0	not out	13
A Flower	lbw b Martin	25	b Chapple	16
AP Grayson	c Sutcliffe b Martin	13	not out	1
RC Irani (capt)	c Swann b Martin	0		
*JS Foster	c Anderson b Hooper	57		
JD Middlebrook	lbw b Keedy	12		
GR Napier	b Martin	40		
SA Brant	c Chilton b Hooper	23		
JB Grant	not out	2		
Extras	b 2, lb 6, nb 5	13	lb 1	1
	(57.5 overs)	215	(3 wkts, 19.3 overs)	42

Bowling
Anderson 15–1–67–4. Martin 12–3–32–3. Chapple 13–3–40–0. Chilton 4–0–10–0. Keedy 5–0–24–1. Hooper 8.5–3–34–2.
Anderson 7–3–11–1. Martin 7–2–12–1. Chapple 4.3–0–18–1. Keedy 1–1–0–0.
Fall of Wickets 1–34, 2–34, 3–35, 4–67, 5–67, 6–82, 7–95, 8–152, 9–194, 10–215
1–12, 2–14, 3–41

LANCASHIRE First Innings

AJ Swann	lbw b Irani	33
IJ Sutcliffe	lbw b Middlebrook	109
MB Loye	lbw b Irani	33
SG Law	c and b Irani	6
MJ Chilton	c Napier b Middlebrook	106
CL Hooper	c Middlebrook b Grayson	8
G Chapple	c Foster b Middlebrook	1
*WK Hegg (capt)	c Napier b Irani	23
PJ Martin	c Middlebrook b Grant	23
G Keedy	c Foster b Grant	0
JM Anderson	not out	9
Extras	b 3, lb 6, w 3, nb 12	24
	(133.1 overs)	375

Bowling
Brant 11–3–36–0. Napier 16–1–73–0. Irani 32–13–59–4. Middlebrook 40.1–11–86–3. Grant 10–0–44–2. Grayson 24–6–68–1.
Fall of Wickets 1–44, 2–128, 3–146, 4–229, 5–245, 6–255, 7–303, 8–338, 9–343, 10–375

Match drawn – Lancashire (11pts), Essex (8pts)

a first-class hat-trick and the first since Mike Watkinson in 1992. Iain Sutcliffe and Mark Chilton both made hundreds as Lancashire then secured a sizeable first-innings lead, and the second day was notable for the sight of coach Graham Gooch fielding again for Essex, as an emergency substitute, just two months short of his 50th birthday. There was no play at all on day three, however, and only 20 minutes were possible on the final day.

Division Two

The only positive result in Division Two came at Taunton, where Somerset overwhelmed Glamorgan by an innings and 143 runs after dismissing their visitors for 200 on day one. Nixon McLean led the way with 5 for 43 on a dampish, green-tinged surface, and by the close of play Somerset were only 39 runs behind for the loss of just Marcus Trescothick. The England opener had done some damage by then, however, striking two sixes in a 74-ball 70 and dominating an opening stand of 121 with Peter Bowler. The evergreen Bowler then figured in a 128-run partnership for the second wicket with Mike Burns, before falling eight runs short of what would have been a well-deserved century. Fierce hitting from both Ian Blackwell and Aaron Laraman then swept Somerset to 476 for 6 declared, before three wickets apiece for McLean, Richard Johnson and Laraman left Glamorgan down and out at 133 all out.

A superb 222 by Phil Jaques, a New South Wales batsman recommended to Northamptonshire by the county's fellow Anglo-Aussie Jeff Cook, was the highlight of a rain-affected draw against Yorkshire at Wantage Road. Jaques, who has a Yorkshire mother and a Lancastrian father, added 189 for the second wicket with Mike Hussey as Northants responded strongly to

Somerset's new spearhead, the former West Indies paceman Nixon McLean.

Yorkshire's first-innings total of 399. Michael Vaughan passed both 50 and 100 with sixes, and later added an unbeaten 64 in the second innings as the game petered out following a washout on the third day.

There was no play either on the third day at Stockton, where Durham and Worcestershire drew despite an attempt at a contrived finish. A career-best 84 not out from Kabir Ali was the highlight of Worcestershire's first-innings total of 395, while Ben Smith twice hit Nicky Phillips for six in his innings of 81.

Prolonged rain at Bristol meant that the last two days were lost after Gloucestershire had seen Craig Spearman (103) lead a spirited reply to Hampshire's first innings 369, in which John Crawley and Simon Katich added 142 for the second wicket and Will Kendall and Nic Pothas put on a further 103 for the fifth.

Round Five: 14–17 May 2003 Division Two

SOMERSET v. GLAMORGAN – at Taunton

GLAMORGAN	First Innings		Second Innings	
IJ Thomas	c Trescothick b McLean	0	(2) c Turner b Johnson	1
A Dale	c Bryant b McLean	40	(1) c Burns b McLean	15
DL Hemp	c Cox b McLean	2	c Turner b McLean	36
MJ Powell	c Trescothick b Laraman	7	lbw b Laraman	16
MP Maynard	lbw b McLean	34	(6) c Bowler b Francis	30
J Hughes	c Turner b Francis	2	(5) c Turner b McLean	5
*MA Wallace	b Blackwell	26	b Laraman	4
RDB Croft (capt)	lbw b Laraman	46	c Blackwell b Laraman	0
DS Harrison	c Turner b Johnson	0	c Turner b Johnson	11
MS Kasprowicz	c Turner b McLean	13	not out	0
AG Wharf	not out	8	c Turner b Johnson	2
Extras	b 8, nb 14	22	b 4, lb 2, w 1	7
	(63 overs)	200	(44 overs)	133

Bowling
McLean 17–6–43–5. Johnson 17–7–23–1. Laraman 10–2–46–2. Francis 14–2–61–1. Blackwell 5–0–19–1.
McLean 12–4–38–3. Johnson 14–3–36–3. Francis 12–5–33–1. Laraman 6–2–20–3.
Fall of Wickets 1–0, 2–6, 3–15, 4–70, 5–95, 6–99, 7–140, 8–141, 9–182, 10–200
1–2, 2–41, 3–58, 4–64, 5–80, 6–88, 7–92, 8–111, 9–127, 10–133

SOMERSET	First Innings	
PD Bowler	c Wharf b Dale	92
ME Trescothick	c Dale b Wharf	70
M Burns (capt)	b Dale	82
J Cox	lbw b Wharf	29
JDC Bryant	lbw b Dale	30
ID Blackwell	b Harrison	42
*RJ Turner	not out	32
AW Laraman	not out	61
R L Johnson		
N A M McLean		
S R G Francis		
Extras	b 6, lb 17, w 1, nb 14	38
	(6 wkts, 114 overs)	476

Bowling
Kasprowicz 30–9–103–0. Wharf 22–3–113–2. Harrison 27–3–116–1. Croft 23–5–92–0. Dale 12–2–29–3.
Fall of Wickets 1–121, 2–249, 3–290, 4–316, 5–373, 6–390

*Somerset beat Glamorgan by an innings and 143 runs –
Somerset (22pts), Glamorgan (3pts)*

Round Six: 21–24 May 2003

Division One

Kevin Innes became the first 12th man in the history of the county championship to score a century as Sussex beat Nottinghamshire by ten wickets at Horsham. This remarkable occurrence was made possible by James Kirtley's omission from the England Test squad on the morning of their first match against Zimbabwe at Lord's, 24 hours after the start of this championship round. New ECB rules allowed for counties to nominate a player from their original line-up, before the start of the game, who would then be replaced if the omitted Test player became available. Innes, at the crease overnight after Sussex had reached 330 for 5 on the opening day, due in no small part to Richard

---

NORTHAMPTONSHIRE v. YORKSHIRE – at Northampton

YORKSHIRE	First Innings		Second Innings	
MJ Wood	c Hussey b Blain	15	lbw b Panesar	33
MP Vaughan	lbw b Brown	103	not out	64
A McGrath (capt)	c and b Panesar	51	not out	0
MJ Lumb	c Nel b Panesar	46		
*RJ Blakey	b Brown	8		
GM Fellows	lbw b Brown	18		
TT Bresnan	lbw b Brown	7		
RKJ Dawson	b Panesar	77		
AKD Gray	lbw b Blain	25		
RJ Sidebottom	c Bailey b Nel	0		
MJ Hoggard	not out	21		
Extras	lb 2, nb 26	28	nb 12	12
	(127.1 overs)	399	(1 wkt, 19.1 overs)	109

Bowling
Nel 26–7–84–1. Blain 13–0–75–2. Penberthy 11–4–26–0. Brown 46–18–99–4. Panesar 31.1–6–113–3.
Blain 8–0–54–0. Cook 5–2–11–0. Hussey 3–0–32–0. Powell 2–0–12–0. Panesar 1.1–1–0–1.
Fall of Wickets 1–31, 2–173, 3–189, 4–207, 5–249, 6–271, 7–273, 8–339, 9–345, 10–399
1–105

NORTHANTS	First Innings	
MEK Hussey (capt)	c Lumb b Gray	65
MJ Powell	c Bresnan b Hoggard	5
PA Jaques	lbw b Hoggard	222
JW Cook	c and b Sidebottom	29
DJG Sales	c Dawson b Hoggard	2
AL Penberthy	not out	32
*TMB Bailey	lbw b Sidebottom	7
MS Panesar	not out	3
A Nel		
J A R Blain		
J F Brown		
Extras	b 15, lb 6, nb 16	37
	(6 wkts, 120.2 overs)	402

Bowling
Hoggard 29–6–74–3. Sidebottom 23–4–66–2. Bresnan 12.2–3–43–0. Dawson 27–3–105–0. Gray 24–4–66–1. McGrath 4–0–22–0. Vaughan 1–0–5–0.
Fall of Wickets 1–23, 2–212, 3–346, 4–353, 5–366, 6–382

Match drawn – Northamptonshire (12pts), Yorkshire (10pts)

DURHAM v. WORCESTERSHIRE – at Stockton

WORCS	First Innings	
SD Peters	lbw b Harmison	62
A Singh	run out	16
GA Hick	c Phillips b Law	30
BF Smith (capt)	c Harmison b Srinath	81
VS Solanki	c A Pratt b Srinath	52
AJ Hall	b Srinath	0
GJ Batty	c Muchall b Wells	18
*SJ Rhodes	lbw b Harmison	1
Kabir Ali	not out	84
MS Mason	b Wells	0
M Hayward	b Harmison	28
Extras	lb 18, w 1, nb 4	23
	(107 overs)	395

Bowling
Harmison 29–14–69–3. Srinath 27–10–70–3. Wells 14–2–58–2. Law 22–2–100–1. Phillips 15–0–80–0.
Fall of Wickets 1–18, 2–70, 3–149, 4–250, 5–254, 6–255, 7–258, 8–334, 9–346, 10–395

DURHAM	First Innings		Second Innings	
JJB Lewis (capt)	not out	66	lbw b Hall	43
MA Gough	b Hayward	22	c Hick b Kabir Ali	1
GJ Muchall	c Rhodes b Hayward	0	c Singh b Hall	74
GJ Pratt	c Hick b Batty	38	c Rhodes b Batty	4
NC Phillips	not out	1		
J Srinath			(5) c Peters b Batty	1
VJ Wells			(6) st Rhodes b Batty	0
N Peng			(7) lbw b Hall	0
DR Law			(8) not out	0
*A Pratt			(9) not out	0
S J Harmison				
Extras	b 2, lb 1, nb 16	19	b 8, lb 11, w 1, nb 8	28
	(3 wkts, 41 overs)	146	(7 wkts, 40 overs)	151

Bowling
Hayward 10–1–34–2. Kabir Ali 9–0–44–0. Hall 3–0–21–0. Mason 8–4–21–0. Batty 11–5–23–1.
Hayward 5–0–32–0. Kabir Ali 8–0–37–1. Batty 16–6–34–3. Mason 5–0–19–0. Hall 2–0–13–0.
Fall of Wickets 1–41, 2–41, 3–140
1–3, 2–135, 3–148, 4–150, 5–150, 6–151, 7–151

Match drawn – Durham (7pts), Worcestershire (9pts)

GLOUCESTERSHIRE v. HAMPSHIRE – at Bristol

HAMPSHIRE	First Innings	
DA Kenway	c Weston b Smith	8
JP Crawley (capt)	c Alleyne b Butler	69
SM Katich	b Fisher	96
RA Smith	c Windows b Lewis	0
WS Kendall	c Russell b Butler	69
*N Pothas	c Russell b Lewis	63
AD Mascarenhas	c Spearman b Butler	14
SD Udal	retired hurt	6
CT Tremlett	not out	10
AD Mullally	b Lewis	0
JA Tomlinson	c Russell b Lewis	6
Extras	b 4, lb 10, w 2, nb 12	28
	(112.5 overs)	369

Bowling
Lewis 29.5–12–80–4. Smith 19–4–50–1. Butler 23–7–80–3. Alleyne 19–5–58–0. Fisher 22–2–87–1.
Fall of Wickets 1–11, 2–153, 3–168, 4–213, 5–316, 6–342, 7–352, 8–353, 9–369

GLOS	First Innings	
WPC Weston	c Katich b Mascarenhas	61
CM Spearman	c Kenway b Katich	103
THC Hancock	run out	47
JN Rhodes	not out	57
MGN Windows	c Kenway b Katich	21
MW Alleyne (capt)	not out	18
*R C Russell		
I D Fisher		
I G Butler		
J Lewis		
A M Smith		
Extras	lb 5, nb 4	9
	(4 wkts, 83 overs)	316

Bowling
Mullally 22–5–67–0. Tremlett 12–3–35–0. Mascarenhas 20–5–74–1. Tomlinson 9–0–62–0. Katich 20–2–73–2.
Fall of Wickets 1–141, 2–216, 3–217, 4–253

Match drawn – Gloucestershire (10pts), Hampshire (9pts)

Montgomerie's third successive hundred at Cricketfield Road, continued his burgeoning partnership with Matthew Prior the following morning while Kirtley was driving south from London. On and on they went, finally adding 157 in 27 overs. Prior made 133, a superb performance containing six sixes and 15 fours, yet even that was overshadowed by Innes, who fought off an attack of nerves and eventually pulled a ball from Kevin Pietersen for four to reach the historic three figures. 'It was very strange for me in the 90s,' admitted Innes afterwards. 'My emotions were a mixture of excitement and nervousness. And then to get there … well, what a great feeling. If I could bottle how I felt and sell it, I would be a rich man!' Sussex declared after Innes had reached his landmark, at which point Kirtley took over from him. Inevitably, it was then Mushtaq Ahmed who took centre stage, his match figures of 12 for 244 making him the first Sussex spinner since Ian Salisbury in 1996 to take more than ten wickets in a championship game. Kirtley did contribute, taking 4 for 74 as Notts were dismissed for 247 second time around, having been forced to follow on, but it was Mushtaq who struck the two most important blows on the final day after Notts had begun it on 103 without loss following a fine opening stand between Darren Bicknell and Jason Gallian. Kevin Pietersen and Bilal Shafayat, who had added 193 in 26 overs together on the

previous day, fell to 'Mushy' for one and nought respectively. In Nottinghamshire's first innings, Pietersen had belted 166 from just 137 balls, with four sixes and 17 fours, winning a thrilling joust

Round Six: 21–24 May 2003 Division One

SUSSEX v. NOTTINGHAMSHIRE – at Horsham

SUSSEX	First Innings		Second Innings	
RR Montgomerie	c Gallian b MacGill	105	(2) not out	25
MW Goodwin	c Pietersen b Elworthy	38	(1) not out	23
PA Cottey	lbw b MacGill	58		
CJ Adams (capt)	c Gallian b MacGill	9		
*TR Ambrose	c Read b Elworthy	55		
RSC M-Jenkins	c Welton b Harris	49		
MJ Prior	c sub b Elworthy	133		
KJ Innes†	not out	103		
MJG Davis	not out	32		
M Ahmed				
B V Taylor				
Extras	b 2, lb 20, w 1, nb 14	37	lb 2, nb 2	4
	(7 wkts, 147 overs)	619	(no wkt, 10.2 overs)	52

Bowling
Smith 24-2-97-0. Harris 20-2-102-1. Gallian 12-2-45-0. Elworthy 30-3-107-3. MacGill 50-12-172-3. Shafayat 4-0-39-0. Pietersen 1-0-9-0.
Elworthy 5-1-22-0. MacGill 4-1-13-0. Pietersen 1-0-9-0. Harris 0.2-0-6-0.
Fall of Wickets 1-87, 2-210, 3-227, 4-232, 5-312, 6-378, 7-535

NOTTS	First Innings		Second Innings	
GE Welton	lbw b M Ahmed	50	(3) st Ambrose b M Ahmed	12
JER Gallian (capt)	c Prior b Taylor	36	c Montgomerie b M Ahmed	44
U Afzaal	c Ambrose b Kirtley	35	(4) c Ambrose b Kirtley	18
DJ Bicknell	lbw b Kirtley	0	(1) c and b Kirtley	61
KP Pietersen	st Ambrose b M Ahmed	166	c Cottey b M Ahmed	1
BM Shafayat	lbw b M Ahmed	71	b M Ahmed	0
*CMW Read	lbw b M Ahmed	0	lbw b Kirtley	42
S Elworthy	c Ambrose b M-Jenkins	28	c Ambrose b M Ahmed	45
GJ Smith	b M Ahmed	9	not out	5
AJ Harris	b M Ahmed	0	st Ambrose b M Ahmed	1
SCG MacGill	not out	0	c sub b Kirtley	2
Extras	b 1, lb 1, nb 6	8	lb 5, w 1, nb 10	16
	(93.1 overs)	421	(82.2 overs)	247

Bowling
Kirtley 21-7-85-2. M-Jenkins 17-0-87-1. M Ahmed 37.1-3-163-6. Taylor 11-3-32-1. Davis 7-0-52-0.
Kirtley 24.2-4-74-4. Taylor 13-3-36-0. Davis 9-1-26-0. M-Jenkins 6-1-25-0. M Ahmed 30-9-81-6.
Fall of Wickets 1-71, 2-109, 3-126, 4-139, 5-332, 6-332, 7-369, 8-390, 9-398, 10-421
1-103, 2-111, 3-132, 4-133, 5-142, 6-143, 7-237, 8-239, 9-242, 10-247

Sussex beat Nottinghamshire by 10 wickets – Sussex (22pts), Nottinghamshire (7pts)

† Nominated 12th man, replaced by RJ Kirtley

ESSEX v. SURREY – at Chelmsford

SURREY	First Innings		Second Innings	
IJ Ward	lbw b Brant	0	b Dakin	49
*JN Batty	c Foster b Dakin	7	not out	168
MR Ramprakash	c Foster b Napier	10	c Flower b Napier	1
GP Thorpe	c Foster b Napier	52	c Foster b Napier	8
AD Brown	lbw b Napier	4	c Jefferson b Middlebrook	64
AJ Hollioake (capt)	lbw b Napier	10	c Robinson b Middlebrook	51
Azhar Mahmood	b Brant	77	c sub b Napier	16
MP Bicknell	c and b Dakin	141	c Foster b Napier	13
IDK Salisbury	run out	30	not out	1
Saqlain Mushtaq	b Brant	30		
J Ormond	not out	9		
Extras	lb 4, nb 2	6	lb 7	7
	(99.3 overs)	376	(7 wkts, 87 overs)	381

Bowling
Brant 29-4-94-3. Dakin 20.3-5-96-2. Napier 24-4-82-4. Irani 9-2-31-0. Middlebrook 9-0-38-0. Grayson 8-1-31-0.
Brant 19-5-62-0. Dakin 17-2-55-1. Napier 21-0-124-4. Middlebrook 26-0-117-2. Grayson 4-0-16-0.
Fall of Wickets 1-0, 2-8, 3-17, 4-17, 5-99, 6-132, 7-179, 8-243, 9-252, 10-376
1-102, 2-120, 3-124, 4-209, 5-303, 6-339, 7-368

ESSEX	First Innings		Second Innings	
DDJ Robinson	lbw b Ormond	5	lbw b Ormond	41
WI Jefferson	c Batty b Bicknell	11	lbw b Ormond	4
AP Grayson	c Batty b Bicknell	1	c Batty b Ormond	19
A Flower	c sub b Azhar Mahmood	51	c Batty b Azhar Mahmood	6
A Habib	lbw b Bicknell	0	c Batty b Ormond	61
RC Irani (capt)	c Ramprakash b Azhar Mahmood	47	(7) c sub b Saqlain Mushtaq	9
*JS Foster	c Azhar Mahmood b Bicknell	38	(6) lbw b Ormond	42
JM Dakin	c Azhar Mahmood b Ormond	59	c Az. Mahmood b S. Mushtaq	15
JD Middlebrook	c Batty b Ormond	29	b Salisbury	13
GR Napier	c Saqlain Mushtaq b Salisbury	5	not out	15
SA Brant	not out	0	c sub b Salisbury	0
Extras	lb 6, nb 6	11	lb 11, nb 12	23
	(71.1 overs)	252	(62.2 overs)	247

Bowling
Bicknell 19-5-67-4. Ormond 19-3-68-3. Saqlain Mushtaq 19-2-65-0. Azhar Mahmood 11-2-39-2. Salisbury 3.1-1-8-1.
Bicknell 15-6-37-0. Ormond 22-3-82-5. Azhar Mahmood 12-1-72-1. Saqlain Mushtaq 11-2-42-2. Salisbury 2.2-1-3-2.
Fall of Wickets 1-7, 2-8, 3-17, 4-17, 5-99, 6-132, 7-179, 8-243, 9-252, 10-252
1-16, 2-44, 3-69, 4-69, 5-188, 6-197, 7-205, 8-225, 9-247, 10-247

Surrey beat Essex by 258 runs – Surrey (21pts), Essex (5pts)

WARWICKSHIRE v. KENT – at Edgbaston

WARWICKSHIRE	First Innings		Second Innings	
MJ Powell (capt)	c Jones b Saggers	50	c Jones b Ealham	30
*T Frost	c Tredwell b Trott	6		
MA Wagh	c Ealham b Saggers	0	not out	50
IR Bell	c Blewett b Sheriyar	31	not out	12
JO Troughton	c Tredwell b Sheriyar	120		
IJL Trott	run out	9	(2) c Ealham b Trego	31
DR Brown	c Blewett b Saggers	18		
MA Sheikh	c Walker b Saggers	5		
NMK Smith	c Tredwell b Saggers	57		
MM Betts	c and b Trego	46		
A Richardson	not out	10		
Extras	b 1, lb 1, w 1, nb 4	9	w 1	1
	(78 overs)	311	(2 wkts, 30 overs)	124

Bowling
Saggers 23-5-62-5. Trott 17-2-90-1. Sheriyar 17-2-66-2. Ealham 12-2-39-0. Trego 8-0-43-1. Tredwell 1-0-7-0.
Walker 4-0-25-0. Ealham 9-3-35-1. Blewett 6-0-27-0. Carberry 6-1-11-0. Trego 5-0-26-1.
Fall of Wickets 1-4, 2-6, 3-6, 4-77, 5-113, 6-170, 7-193, 8-195, 9-275, 10-311
1-50, 2-98

KENT	First Innings	
MA Carberry	c Smith b Sheikh	58
JC Tredwell	lbw b Betts	10
ET Smith	lbw b Sheikh	43
GS Blewett	lbw b Brown	71
MJ Walker	b Richardson	106
MA Ealham (capt)	c Sheikh b Brown	0
*GO Jones	c Frost b Brown	12
PD Trego	c Wagh b Sheikh	13
MJ Saggers	not out	24
A Sheriyar	b Brown	2
BJ Trott	c Powell b Brown	0
Extras	lb 9, w 5, nb 14	28
	(106.5 overs)	376

Bowling
Betts 15-2-55-1. Richardson 23-3-91-1. Sheikh 36-4-110-3. Bell 3-0-10-0. Brown 19.5-6-72-5. Smith 8-2-26-0. Wagh 2-1-3-0.
Fall of Wickets 1-13, 2-102, 3-129, 4-273, 5-295, 6-308, 7-327, 8-371, 9-374, 10-376

Match drawn – Warwickshire (10pts), Kent (11pts)

LEICESTERSHIRE v. MIDDLESEX – at Leicester

MIDDLESEX	First Innings		Second Innings	
AJ Strauss (capt)	c Snape b DeFreitas	28	c DeFreitas b Brignull	25
SG Koenig	lbw b Masters	18	b Maddy	18
OA Shah	c Nixon b Masters	28	c Nixon b DeFreitas	9
BL Hutton	lbw b Maddy	3	not out	41
EC Joyce	lbw b Maddy	0	c Masters b Stevens	23
PN Weekes	lbw b Whiley	29	lbw b Masters	6
*DC Nash	c Stevens b Maddy	3	not out	11
SJ Cook	c Schwag b Maddy	2		
AA Noffke	c Nixon b Masters	40		
CB Keegan	lbw b Maddy	32		
Imran Tahir	not out	1		
Extras	b 2, lb 4, w 5, nb 6	17	lb 6, w 1, nb 2	9
	(54.1 overs)	201	(5 wkts, 49.5 overs)	142

Bowling
DeFreitas 14-4-37-1. Whiley 6-0-54-1. Brignull 11-3-22-0. Maddy 13.1-1-49-5. Masters 10-3-28-3.
DeFreitas 16-7-35-1. Brignull 8-1-28-1. Maddy 10-2-29-1. Masters 6-1-12-1. Stevens 3-1-5-1. Whiley 6.5-2-27-0.
Fall of Wickets 1-33, 2-66, 3-81, 4-82, 5-83, 6-89, 7-93, 8-146, 9-195, 10-201
1-39, 2-56, 3-56, 4-99, 5-115

LEICESTERSHIRE	First Innings	
V Sehwag	c Strauss b Keegan	10
RJ Cunliffe	b Nash b Noffke	0
DL Maddy	c Nash b Keegan	0
BJ Hodge	b Keegan	22
DI Stevens	c Weekes b Cook	29
*PA Nixon	c Nash b Cook	17
JN Snape	c Cook b Keegan	54
PAJ DeFreitas (capt)	lbw b Cook	9
DD Masters	c Weekes b Cook	4
DS Brignull	b Keegan	46
MJA Whiley	not out	0
Extras	lb 6, w 1, nb 4	11
	(60 overs)	198

Bowling
Noffke 24-4-89-1. Keegan 18-4-61-5. Cook 18-4-42-4.
Fall of Wickets 1-1, 2-2, 3-15, 4-63, 5-71, 6-86, 7-112, 8-112, 9-185, 10-198

Match drawn – Leicestershire (7pts), Middlesex (8pts)

Jon Batty of Surrey ... a career-best 168 not out.

with Kirtley by hitting the fast bowler for a six and three boundaries in one six-ball barrage and reaching his hundred from just 75 deliveries. Shafayat's 71, from 74 balls, included three sixes off Mushtaq – but it was the Pakistani leg spinner who enjoyed the last laugh with his match-clinching second-innings haul of 6 for 81.

Career-best hundreds from Martin Bicknell and Jon Batty, by no means the leading lights in Surrey's galaxy of batting stars, inspired the champions' 258-run win against Essex at Chelmsford. Bicknell, who reached 99 with a six that just eluded long on, scored 141 in Surrey's first-innings total of 376 and in stands of 90 with Ian Salisbury and 102 with Saqlain Mushtaq rallied the lower order to such an extent that it made a mockery of earlier positions of 51 for 5 and 168 for 7. Graham Thorpe's 52 was also a worthy effort in initially helpful conditions for the seamers, while Azhar Mahmood also played a notable part in the recovery by hitting a fierce 77. Bicknell then took 4 for 67 as Essex replied with a below-par 252, before Batty took over the leading role with an unbeaten 168 in the second innings. He lofted James Middlebrook's off spin for six, and also struck 23 fours in the perfect anchor innings. Aggressive half-centuries from Alistair Brown and Adam Hollioake helped take Surrey into an unassailable position, but skipper Hollioake still decided not to declare at tea on the third day, at which stage the lead was 426. Bad light and rain then scuppered his plans to have a bowl at the Essex top order before the close, but fears of a missed chance evaporated when a pessimistic final day weather forecast failed to materialize and Jimmy Ormond's five wickets proved too much for the home resistance.

Constant weather interruptions blighted Warwickshire's draw with Kent at Edgbaston, although Jim Troughton's 95-ball 120 – 82 of which came in boundaries – did illuminate an opening day in which the home side struggled to 195 for 8 from the 51.5 overs of play that were possible. Neil Smith and Mel Betts then added 80 for the ninth wicket, but Kent responded with half-centuries from

Michael Carberry and Greg Blewett, while Matthew Walker, facing the expiry of his current contract at the end of the season, completed his first championship hundred for two years on the last day.

A similar, rain-ravaged pattern of on-off cricket afflicted proceedings at Grace Road, where the seamers dominated a low-scoring draw between Leicestershire and Middlesex. Chad Keegan took 5 for 61 – his first 'five-for' in first-class competition, and Darren Maddy's opening day haul of 5 for 49 underlined the all-round strides he has made in recent times. Jeremy Snape and tail-ender Dave Brignull also deserved praise for rallying Leicestershire from 112 for 8.

Division Two

Durham won a championship match for the first time since July 2002, holding their nerve in the field to pip Derbyshire by 30 runs at Chester-le-Street. Dewald Pretorius and Vince Wells were the last-innings heroes with the ball, as the home side withstood attacking

Vince Wells: his all-round skills helped to make the difference for Durham against Derbyshire.

knocks from both Shahid Afridi, who struck four sixes in his 67, and Dominic Cork, who included three sixes in reaching an unbeaten 48 on the third evening to take his side to 159 for 6, but who then fell the next morning after adding just four more runs to his overnight score. Derbyshire's eventual defeat, however, was more down to their first-innings failure to support Michael Di Venuto. The Australian left-hander hit a magnificent 150, but 20s from Steve Selwood and Graeme Welch were the best that his team-mates could produce in support and a total of 244 was massively inadequate. Durham had totalled 317 in their first innings, with Jon Lewis scoring his sixth 50 in seven innings, Martin Love hitting ten fours in his 54, and both Gary Pratt and Wells reaching the 60s. Lewis and Love also briefly threatened in the second innings, but Welch's 5 for 60 reduced them to 149 all out, and set up the exciting finish.

Nixon McLean took four wickets in each innings to spearhead Somerset's eventual six-wicket victory over his former club Hampshire at Southampton. McLean's new-ball partner Simon Francis was also taking on his previous county, and his 3 for 24 helped the West Indian to scatter Hampshire for 129 in reply to a Somerset first innings of 308 that had been built upon an unbeaten 127 from Jamie Cox. Gareth Andrew, a 19-year-old seamer, picked up 3 for 20 on his first-class debut, and Somerset were held up on the third day only by a six-hour unbeaten 94 from Derek Kenway and 55 from Robin Smith. McLean, however,

immediately ended Kenway's resistance when Hampshire resumed at 239 for 6 on the fourth day, and although Somerset initially slid to 59 for 4, they then suffered no further alarms as James Bryant and Ian Blackwell sped them to their modest victory target.

Round Six: 21–24 May 2003 Division Two

DURHAM v. DERBYSHIRE – at Chester-le-Street

DURHAM	First Innings		Second Innings	
JJB Lewis (capt)	b Wharton	52	b Welch	32
MA Gough	c Sutton b Smith	12	c sub b Dean	17
ML Love	c Pratt b Welch	54	c Wharton b Mohammad Ali	41
GJ Muchall	b Welch	0	c Selwood b Mohammad Ali	9
GJ Pratt	lbw b Welch	62	c Sutton b Welch	4
VJ Wells	c Gait b Dean	61	c Cork b Welch	15
DR Law	c Wharton b Mohammad Ali	3	b Cork	7
*A Pratt	not out	5	lbw b Cork	3
NC Phillips	b Dean	15	c Wharton b Welch	4
N Killeen	not out	0	lbw b Welch	0
D Pretorius			not out	1
Extras	lb 29, w 1, nb 23	53	lb 14, nb 4	18
	(103.4 overs)	317	(66.4 overs)	149

Bowling
Cork 19-2-65-0. Dean 20.4-11-41-4. Welch 21-10-53-3. Mohammad Ali 14-2-49-2. Afridi 10-2-27-0. Wharton 16-3-48-1. Di Venuto 2-0-7-0. Cork 23-8-49-2. Dean 10-5-19-1. Welch 26.4-6-60-5. Wharton 3-1-5-0. Mohammad Ali 4-3-2-2.
Fall of Wickets 1-34, 2-137, 3-137, 4-137, 5-263, 6-279, 7-301, 8-312, 9-317, 10-317 1-22, 2-70, 3-106, 4-108, 5-110, 6-132, 7-136, 8-146, 9-146, 10-149

DERBYSHIRE	First Innings		Second Innings	
AI Gait	c A Pratt b Killeen	5	(7) b Phillips	10
MJ Di Venuto	lbw b Law	150	(1) lbw b Pretorius	4
SA Selwood	c A Pratt b Pretorius	20	c Love b Wells	8
DR Hewson	b Pretorius	9	c Love b Wells	10
*LD Sutton	b Phillips	9	c A Pratt b Law	10
Shahid Afridi	c GJ Pratt b Phillips	0	(2) c Phillips b Wells	67
DG Cork (capt)	c Love b Phillips	0	(6) c A Pratt b Pretorius	52
G Welch	c Wells b Pretorius	20	(9) not out	23
Mohammad Ali	c Lewis b Pretorius	1	(10) c Love b Pretorius	0
KJ Dean	run out	15	(8) c A Pratt b Phillips	1
LJ Wharton	not out	0	c Gough b Pretorius	1
Extras	b 2, lb 2, nb 11	15	lb 1, w 1	2
	(77.3 overs)	244	(44.2 overs)	192

Bowling
Pretorius 17-2-96-4. Killeen 20-5-49-1. Law 9.3-1-35-1. Phillips 31-8-60-3. Pretorius 12.2-1-49-4. Killeen 9-1-60-0. Wells 6-1-13-3. Phillips 13-0-49-2. Law 4-0-20-1.
Fall of Wickets 1-11, 2-81, 3-97, 4-130, 5-130, 6-131, 7-174, 8-182, 9-236, 10-244 1-4, 2-49, 3-61, 4-92, 5-130, 6-151, 7-164, 8-164, 9-172, 10-192

Durham beat Derbyshire by 30 runs – Durham (20pts), Derbyshire (4pts)

HAMPSHIRE v. SOMERSET – at Southampton

SOMERSET	First Innings		Second Innings	
PD Bowler	b Tremlett	3		
MJ Wood	lbw b Tremlett	18	(1) lbw b Mascarenhas	4
M Burns (capt)	c Kendall b Mullally	7	(5) c Pothas b Bruce	17
J Cox	not out	127	lbw b Bruce	8
JDC Bryant	run out	18	(3) not out	39
ID Blackwell	c and b Udal	19	not out	41
*RJ Turner	b Katich	11	(2) c Pothas b Mascarenhas	13
KP Dutch	c Katich b Mascarenhas	61		
GM Andrew	lbw b Katich	7		
NAM McLean	c and b Mascarenhas	16		
SRG Francis	c Kendall b Katich	0		
Extras	b 1, lb 14, nb 6	21	b 2, nb 4	6
	(116.5 overs)	308	(4 wkts, 39.5 overs)	128

Bowling
Mullally 30-11-67-1. Tremlett 12-2-28-2. Udal 15-3-36-1. Mascarenhas 32-11-75-2. Bruce 15-3-39-0. Katich 12.5-1-48-3. Mullally 7-2-13-0. Mascarenhas 11-3-37-2. Bruce 11-3-32-2. Udal 7-2-17-0. Katich 3.5-0-27-0.
Fall of Wickets 1-7, 2-18, 3-30, 4-82, 5-137, 6-162, 7-277, 8-288, 9-307, 10-308 1-17, 2-20, 3-35, 4-59

HAMPSHIRE	First Innings		Second Innings	
DA Kenway	lbw b McLean	3	(1) c Turner b McLean	94
JP Crawley	lbw b McLean	0	c Turner b Francis	2
SM Katich	lbw b Francis	24	c Turner b Burns	4
RA Smith	b Andrew	0	b Andrew	55
WS Kendall	c Dutch b Andrew	49	c Dutch b McLean	33
*N Pothas	c Bowler b Andrew	34	lbw b Burns	13
AD Mascarenhas	c McLean b Andrew	10	c Dutch b Burns	24
SD Udal	b McLean	6	c Blackwell b Francis	34
CT Tremlett	c Bowler b Francis	4	b McLean	43
AD Mullally	not out	4	lbw b McLean	0
JTA Bruce	c Burns b Francis	0	not out	5
Extras	lb 6	6	b 1, lb 6, nb 6	13
	(55.5 overs)	129	(114.5 overs)	306

Bowling
McLean 15-7-31-4. Francis 17.5-11-24-3. Andrew 9-1-30-3. Blackwell 10-4-27-0. Burns 4-1-11-0. McLean 28.5-7-64-4. Francis 30-12-81-2. Andrew 17-5-55-1. Burns 25-4-64-3. Blackwell 9-6-19-0. Dutch 6-1-16-0.
Fall of Wickets 1-1, 2-6, 3-6, 4-38, 5-114, 6-115, 7-116, 8-125, 9-125, 10-129 1-10, 2-18, 3-107, 4-171, 5-188, 6-202, 7-239, 8-270, 9-271, 10-306

Somerset beat Hampshire by 6 wickets – Somerset (20pts), Hampshire (3pts)

WORCESTERSHIRE v. GLOUCESTERSHIRE – at Worcester

WORCS	First Innings		Second Innings	
SD Peters	c Rhodes b Lewis	8	c Alleyne b Butler	20
A Singh	c Spearman b Smith	26	not out	83
GA Hick	c Hancock b Lewis	20	c Spearman b Alleyne	5
BF Smith (capt)	lbw b Butler	1	b Smith	15
VS Solanki	c Russell b Smith	34	b Smith	15
AJ Hall	c Russell b Smith	4	(7) c Windows b Butler	35
GJ Batty	not out	32	(8) b Butler	5
*SJ Rhodes	lbw b Smith	3	(9) c Fisher b Smith	9
Kabir Ali	c Spearman b Smith	0	(6) lbw b Smith	0
MS Mason	b Butler	30	c Rhodes b Lewis	29
M Hayward	b Lewis	2	b Butler	1
Extras	lb 9, nb 6	15	lb 10	10
	(56.3 overs)	175	(74 overs)	212

Bowling
Lewis 18.3-8-37-3. Smith 22-4-70-5. Butler 16-4-59-2. Lewis 23-7-64-1. Smith 18-5-41-4. Butler 20-3-74-4. Alleyne 13-6-23-1.
Fall of Wickets 1-26, 2-40, 3-41, 4-70, 5-83, 6-112, 7-124, 8-126, 9-172, 10-175 1-33, 2-38, 3-57, 4-75, 5-75, 6-135, 7-136, 8-174, 9-211, 10-212

GLOS	First Innings		Second Innings	
WPC Weston	b Hayward	42	(2) c Solanki b Hayward	6
CM Spearman	b Hayward	19	(1) c Solanki b Kabir Ali	24
THC Hancock	lbw b Hayward	0	c Rhodes b Hayward	0
JN Rhodes	lbw b Mason	14	run out	13
MGN Windows	c Hall b Mason	14	lbw b Hall	3
MW Alleyne (capt)	lbw b Batty	19	b Mason	11
*RC Russell	lbw b Kabir Ali	38	lbw b Hall	1
ID Fisher	c Batty b Kabir Ali	15	not out	1
J Lewis	b Hayward	0	b Hall	5
IG Butler	lbw b Kabir Ali	0	c Rhodes b Kabir Ali	0
AM Smith	not out	0	b Kabir Ali	2
Extras	lb 9, w 4, nb 4	17	lb 4, lb 5, w 6, nb 8	23
	(72.1 overs)	178	(32 overs)	98

Bowling
Hayward 21.1-5-58-4. Kabir Ali 14-3-51-3. Mason 22-9-31-2. Hall 10-4-18-0. Batty 5-1-11-1. Hayward 9-3-30-2. Kabir Ali 13-5-39-4. Hall 7-1-15-2. Mason 3-1-5-1.
Fall of Wickets 1-37, 2-37, 3-62, 4-93, 5-75, 6-133, 7-171, 8-178, 9-178, 10-178 1-15, 2-19, 3-52, 4-52, 5-60, 6-60, 7-75, 8-96, 9-96, 10-98

Worcestershire beat Gloucestershire by 111 runs – Worcestershire (17pts), Gloucestershire (3pts)

YORKSHIRE v. GLAMORGAN – at Headingley

YORKSHIRE	First Innings		Second Innings	
MJ Wood (capt)	c Dale b Harrison	9	not out	73
SA Richardson	c and b Harrison	1	c Wallace b Harrison	50
Yuvraj Singh	c Powell b Kasprowicz	11	not out	25
MJ Lumb	b Kasprowicz	39		
*RJ Blakey	c Powell b Wharf	1		
GM Fellows	c Wallace b Wharf	53		
TT Bresnan	c Maynard b Kasprowicz	3		
RKJ Dawson	c and b Kasprowicz	20		
CEW Silverwood	c Powell b Harrison	10		
RJ Sidebottom	b Wharf	21		
SP Kirby	not out	13		
Extras	b 1, lb 9, w 1, nb 10	21	lb 3, nb 8	11
	(69.4 overs)	209	(1 wkt, 41 overs)	159

Bowling
Kasprowicz 21-7-51-4. Harrison 22-8-58-3. Wharf 15.4-4-63-3. Croft 9-3-21-0. Dale 2-0-6-0. Kasprowicz 6-0-23-0. Harrison 12-5-32-1. Croft 15-2-50-0. Wharf 6-0-39-0. Dale 2-0-12-0.
Fall of Wickets 1-4, 2-19, 3-43, 4-46, 5-85, 6-90, 7-126, 8-141, 9-183, 10-209 1-105

GLAMORGAN	First Innings		
A Dale	c Blakey b Silverwood	0	
IJ Thomas	c Blakey b Silverwood	25	
DL Hemp	c Blakey b Silverwood	0	
MJ Powell	c Lumb b Kirby	5	
MP Maynard	c Yuvraj Singh b Sidebottom	51	
J Hughes	c Blakey b Kirby	10	
*MA Wallace	c Sidebottom b Bresnan	94	
RDB Croft (capt)	lbw b Kirby	9	
DS Harrison	c Blakey b Sidebottom	1	
MS Kasprowicz	c Blakey b Dawson	36	
AG Wharf	not out	29	
Extras	b 8, lb 12, w 3, nb 26	49	
	(81.4 overs)	315	

Bowling
Silverwood 20-4-57-4. Sidebottom 16-3-51-2. Bresnan 11.4-0-51-1. Kirby 22-3-89-3. Dawson 10-1-47-1.
Fall of Wickets 1-4, 2-6, 3-35, 4-57, 5-95, 6-141, 7-152, 8-157, 9-251, 10-315

Match drawn – Yorkshire (8pts), Glamorgan (10pts)

Uncharacteristic sloppiness in the field cost Gloucestershire dear in a low-scoring battle against Worcestershire at New Road. Having gained a slender first-innings advantage, on a pitch on which the quicker bowlers held sway, the visitors then dropped home opener Anurag Singh four times as he carried his bat for 83 in an innings which ultimately decided the game. Mike Smith's nine wickets in the match were in vain as Kabir Ali, supported by Nantie Hayward and Andrew Hall, tumbled out Gloucestershire for 98.

No play was possible on day two at Headingley, where Yorkshire's meeting with Glamorgan meandered to a watery draw. Mark Wallace's 94 was the best individual performance of a non-event which finally ended with the Yorkshire top order accepting the chance of batting practice.

ROUND SEVEN: 30 MAY–2 JUNE 2003

Division One

The heroics of Mike Yardy could not, in the end, prevent Sussex from suffering a 113-run defeat at The Oval. Surrey, having dominated the game, were almost denied victory by the stubbornness, and skill, of the batsman only called up because of an injury to Tony Cottey. In his first championship appearance since July 2002, Yardy hung on for 241 balls to make 69 before finally being dismissed when he went back to a ball from Jimmy Ormond and edged to second slip with just five-and-a-half overs remaining. Earlier, Yardy had made only 18 in a fifth-wicket stand of 113 with Robin Martin-Jenkins, who stroked 14 fours in a fluent 88 from 92 balls, before being joined in the final session by Mushtaq Ahmed in a ninth-wicket partnership worth 51. Mushtaq scored 36, once being bounced in frustration by his Pakistani compatriot Saqlain Mushtaq!

The eventual result, however, was a fine reward for Surrey's perseverance in a game played in such heat that Adam Hollioake had decided not to enforce the follow-on after Sussex had been bowled out for 307 in reply to the home side's first-innings 480. Graham Thorpe's 156 was a superlative innings which had begun in tense opening exchanges, while Alistair Brown and Hollioake both included a six and 11 fours in calculated, aggressive knocks which took the match away from their opponents. Ian Salisbury and Saqlain then added a further 75 for the ninth wicket on the second morning, before Ormond noticeably outbowled James Kirtley to undermine the Sussex reply. Murray Goodwin, Tim Ambrose and Martin-Jenkins all made half-centuries, but Surrey were in the ascendancy, and

Round Seven: 30 May–2 June 2003 Division One

SURREY v. SUSSEX – at The Oval

SURREY	First Innings		Second Innings	
IJ Ward	c Ambrose b Kirtley	9	c Goodwin b Innes	135
*JN Batty	c Adams b Taylor	12	b M Ahmed	56
MR Ramprakash	c Yardy b M Ahmed	37	c Prior b Innes	23
GP Thorpe	c Adams b M Ahmed	156	not out	18
AD Brown	c Goodwin b Kirtley	74	not out	1
AJ Hollioake (capt)	lbw b M-Jenkins	77		
Azhar Mahmood	c Adams b Kirtley	0		
MP Bicknell	b M-Jenkins	11		
IDK Salisbury	c Ambrose b M Ahmed	45		
Saqlain Mushtaq	c Montgomerie b M-Jenkins	52		
J Ormond	not out	1		
Extras	b 4, lb 17, w 1, nb 4	26		
	(119.5 overs)	480	(3 wkts, 60 overs)	233

Bowling
Kirtley 33–5–122–3. Taylor 7.2–2–15–1. M-Jenkins 23.4–8–86–3. Innes 12–4–59–0. M Ahmed 36.5–1–159–3. Yardy 7–1–18–0.
Kirtley 14–3–49–0. M-Jenkins 19–3–66–0. M Ahmed 11–1–47–1. Innes 11–1–64–2. Yardy 2–0–7–0.
Fall of Wickets 1–22, 2–22, 3–132, 4–263, 5–359, 6–360, 7–379, 8–394, 9–469, 10–480
1–137, 2–192, 3–219

SUSSEX	First Innings		Second Innings	
RR Montgomerie	c Ward b Ormond	5	(2) c sub b Saqlain Mushtaq	31
MW Goodwin	b Saqlain Mushtaq	60	(1) b Azhar Mahmood	26
MH Yardy	c Thorpe b Ormond	0	c A Mahmood b Ormond	69
CJ Adams (capt)	c Batty b Azhar Mahmood	5	b Saqlain Mushtaq	0
TR Ambrose	c Ramprakash b Ormond	75	b Saqlain Mushtaq	1
RSC M-Jenkins	lbw b Azhar Mahmood	61	b Azhar Mahmood	88
*MJ Prior	b Saqlain Mushtaq	6	c Ramprakash b Az. Mahmood	14
KJ Innes	b Salisbury	2	(10) lbw b Saqlain Mushtaq	36
M Ahmed	lbw b Ormond	41	(9) c sub b Salisbury	7
RJ Kirtley	run out	21	(9) c sub b Salisbury	7
BV Taylor	not out	4	not out	0
Extras	lb 9, w 2, nb 16	27	b 9, lb 3, w 2, nb 6	20
	(73.1 overs)	307	(95.4 overs)	293

Bowling
Bicknell 3–1–9–0. Ormond 15.1–2–81–4. Azhar Mahmood 16–1–57–2. Salisbury 14–1–67–1. Saqlain Mushtaq 21–4–68–2. Hollioake 4–0–16–0.
Ormond 19.4–3–65–1. Azhar Mahmood 21–4–76–3. Salisbury 21–5–67–1. Saqlain Mushtaq 34–15–73–5.
Fall of Wickets 1–5, 2–13, 3–24, 4–98, 5–189, 6–217, 7–220, 8–279, 9–282, 10–307
1–45, 2–83, 3–83, 4–85, 5–198, 6–218, 7–221, 8–242, 9–293, 10–293

Surrey beat Sussex by 113 runs – Surrey (22pts), Sussex (6pts)

KENT v. LANCASHIRE – at Canterbury

LANCASHIRE	First Innings		Second Innings	
AJ Swann	lbw b Saggers	8	(2) c Walker b Saggers	4
MJ Chilton	c Tredwell b Ealham	10	(1) b Trott	5
MB Loye	c Jones b Ealham	27	c Smith b Sheriyar	86
SG Law	c Jones b Ealham	0	c Carberry b Saggers	67
CL Hooper	lbw b Ealham	1	c Smith b Tredwell	48
A Flintoff	c Tredwell b Ealham	154	c Smith b Tredwell	43
G Chapple	run out	66	c and b Trott	3
*WK Hegg (capt)	not out	37	c Trott b Tredwell	35
PJ Martin	c and b Tredwell	2	c Jones b Tredwell	14
SI Mahmood	lbw b Sheriyar	34	run out	4
G Keedy	c Blewett b Sheriyar	0	not out	4
Extras	b 2, lb 5, nb 2	9	b 4, lb 9, nb 2	15
	(97.2 overs)	347	(91.5 overs)	334

Bowling
Saggers 22–3–100–1. Trott 9–3–35–0. Sheriyar 20.2–6–70–2. Ealham 23–8–54–5. Tredwell 16–3–48–1. Blewett 7–0–33–0.
Saggers 13–2–36–2. Trott 16–1–67–2. Sheriyar 19–3–58–1. Ealham 15–3–44–0. Tredwell 26.5–4–112–4. Carberry 2–0–4–0.
Fall of Wickets 1–8, 2–43, 3–43, 4–43, 5–52, 6–231, 7–284, 8–295, 9–347, 10–347
1–5, 2–19, 3–155, 4–188, 5–252, 6–257, 7–269, 8–295, 9–322, 10–334

KENT	First Innings		Second Innings	
DP Fulton (capt)	lbw b Martin	11	c Hooper b Mahmood	7
MA Carberry	c Hooper b Mahmood	38	c Chilton b Chapple	0
ET Smith	b Chapple	26	c and b Keedy	56
GS Blewett	b Keedy	0	c Flintoff b Keedy	7
MJ Walker	b Keedy	11	b Keedy	52
MA Ealham	b Keedy	43	(7) c Hooper b Martin	79
*GO Jones	c Martin b Mahmood	92	(8) c Flintoff b Keedy	31
JC Tredwell	c Hegg b Martin	16	(9) lbw b Chapple	16
MJ Saggers	b Keedy	12	(6) lbw b Chapple	14
A Sheriyar	c Chapple b Keedy	4	c Hegg b Chapple	5
BJ Trott	not out	0	not out	2
Extras	lb 9, w 1, nb 4	14	b 14, lb 10, w 2, nb 4	30
	(77.1 overs)	267	(103.2 overs)	339

Bowling
Martin 20–8–52–2. Chapple 15–4–43–1. Mahmood 12–1–40–2. Keedy 23.1–4–99–5. Hooper 7–1–24–0.
Martin 23–3–95–1. Chapple 21.2–5–66–4. Keedy 29–5–79–4. Mahmood 6–0–20–1. Hooper 19–2–55–0.
Fall of Wickets 1–26, 2–56, 3–57, 4–85, 5–91, 6–219, 7–241, 8–262, 9–266, 10–267
1–15, 2–79, 3–92, 4–121, 5–156, 6–200, 7–279, 8–319, 9–324, 10–339

Lancashire beat Kent by 75 runs – Lancashire (20pts), Kent (5pts)

NOTTINGHAMSHIRE v. ESSEX – at Trent Bridge

ESSEX	First Innings		Second Innings	
DDJ Robinson	c Gallian b Smith	9	c Noon b Malik	4
WI Jefferson	c Noon b Smith	0	lbw b Harris	10
AP Grayson (capt)	c Pietersen b Harris	27	b Smith	20
A Flower	lbw b Smith	4	(5) lbw b Malik	32
A Habib	c Gallian b MacGill	31	(6) lbw b MacGill	151
*JS Foster	lbw b Smith	12	(7) lbw b Pietersen	85
RS Bopara	run out	9	(8) not out	15
JD Middlebrook	lbw b MacGill	0	(4) lbw b MacGill	3
GR Napier	c Noon b Smith	57	c Welton b MacGill	15
SA Brant	b Smith	0	c Cairns b MacGill	0
Extras	b 1, lb 2, w 1, nb 6	10	lb 12, nb 8	20
	(68 overs)	203	(91.2 overs)	359

Bowling
Smith 18–6–42–5. Harris 20–2–68–1. Malik 15–3–43–0. MacGill 13–3–41–2. Gallian 2–1–6–0.
Smith 16–2–79–1. Malik 18–3–58–2. Harris 16–1–75–1. MacGill 30.2–3–118–5. Pietersen 11–5–17–1.
Fall of Wickets 1–1, 2–10, 3–20, 4–64, 5–82, 6–94, 7–114, 8–115, 9–203, 10–203
1–5, 2–23, 3–26, 4–47, 5–125, 6–303, 7–331, 8–337, 9–359, 10–359

NOTTS	First Innings		Second Innings	
GE Welton	c Foster b Brant	1	lbw b Dakin	11
JER Gallian (capt)	c Flower b Dakin	0	lbw b Brant	42
U Afzaal	lbw b Dakin	3	lbw b Napier	22
KP Pietersen	b Dakin	0	c Grayson b Middlebrook	18
BM Shafayat	lbw b Brant	1	c Bopara b Napier	21
CL Cairns	lbw b Brant	39	b Middlebrook	39
*WM Noon	c Grayson b Dakin	0	lbw b Napier	5
GJ Smith	b Brant	0	c Robinson b Middlebrook	0
MN Malik	not out	30	(10) c Foster b Napier	15
AJ Harris	b Brant	0	(9) lbw b Napier	4
SCG MacGill	c Middlebrook b Brant	27	not out	8
Extras	b 9, lb 3	12	b 9, lb 2	11
	(16.5 overs)	79	(72 overs)	215

Bowling
Brant 8.5–3–45–6. Dakin 8–2–22–4.
Brant 16–7–30–1. Dakin 19–8–42–1. Middlebrook 16–2–64–3. Napier 18–5–66–5. Bopara 3–2–2–0.
Fall of Wickets 1–2, 2–2, 3–2, 4–7, 5–7, 6–7, 7–8, 8–15, 9–19, 10–79
1–31, 2–90, 3–96, 4–116, 5–150, 6–184, 7–184, 8–188, 9–200, 10–215

Essex beat Nottinghamshire by 268 runs – Essex (18pts), Nottinghamshire (3pts)

Andrew Flintoff ... a century of awesome power against Kent, and the hint of better things to come for England?

even more so when Ian Ward and Jon Batty began their second innings by putting on 137. Ward went on to 135, from 166 balls and with 18 fours and a six, before the declaration.

Lancashire moved into second place in the table after recording their first win of the championship season at Canterbury, and their first at Kent's headquarters since 1936. Kent fought hard in their second innings, on a pitch beginning to turn and which had also started to produce uneven bounce, with Mark Ealham leading the resistance against Glen Chapple and Gary Keedy. In truth, however, the home side never really recovered from the battering they took on day one from Andrew Flintoff. Lancashire were struggling on 52 for 5 at one stage, and Ealham went on to pick up 5 for 54, but that the visitors rallied to 347 was due to Flintoff. Displaying awesome power, and supported in a sixth-wicket stand with Chapple which produced 179 runs, Flintoff smote a breathtaking

154 from 158 balls. He got off the mark with a six to long on off Ealham which seemed a mere push, and proceeded to add seven more sixes and 17 fours to his collection of boundary hits. Officially not fit enough to play for England in the second Test against Zimbabwe, because of a shoulder injury that meant he could not bowl, Flintoff showed that his current Test batting average of 19 was one of the major underachievements in world cricket. Geraint Jones, the Kent wicketkeeper, added to his growing reputation by hitting three sixes and 13 fours in an exhilarating 92, and his 128-run stand for the sixth wicket with Ealham rescued the home side who had slid to 91 for 5. Keedy took five wickets with his left-arm spin, but, at 19 for 2 in their second innings, Lancashire were not yet in total command. That came as a result of a third-wicket stand of 136 between Mal Loye (86) and Stuart Law (67), before Flintoff and Carl Hooper made sure of a winning lead. David Fulton, in his first game since suffering an horrific pre-season eye injury, made a gritty 37 in Kent's second innings ... batting on bravely with a broken thumb! All in all, this was clearly not going to be Kent's match.

Peter Walker, the ECB pitch inspector, viewed events on the opening day at Trent Bridge – when 23 wickets fell in bizarre fashion – and said: 'The pitch is definitely up to speed, but I am not allowed to comment on the quality of the batting!' Quite. Essex, having fallen to 115 for 8, rallied to 203 as Graham Napier and Jon Dakin hit out strongly. Then, when Nottinghamshire replied, they soon found themselves at a scarcely believable 19 for 9. Swinging the new ball to dramatic effect, Dakin (4 for 22) and Scott Brant (6 for 45) were mastered only when Nadeem Malik and Stuart MacGill reacted to the crisis by adding a riotous 60 for the last wicket in a mere six overs. Notts' total of 79 took them just 16.5 overs. This was crazy cricket, which continued apace when Essex slid to 39 for 3 by the close. Mercifully, normal service was resumed on the second day as Aftab Habib hit 151, his highest score for Essex with 26 fours, and James Foster made 85. Notts, needing the small matter of 184 to win, at least managed to take the contest into its third day before bowing to the bowling of Napier (5 for 66) and James Middlebrook. 'This victory is a huge boost for us,' said Napier afterwards. 'We don't have a mystery spinner or a super-quick bowler, so it means the rest of us have to take extra responsibility.' Notts coach Mick Newell, reviewing a match in which his side were 8 for 7 at one stage in their first innings, added: 'The pitch was pretty good and Essex played the better cricket. The last session on the first day was the most bizarre I have ever seen, and it was always going to be difficult for us to come back after that.'

Division Two

The 122nd first-class century of Graeme Hick's career put Worcestershire on course for a crushing nine-wicket victory against Derbyshire at Derby, propelling them into Division Two's top three. Stephen Peters and Anurag Singh set the scene with an opening partnership worth 106, and then Hick took over with a brilliant 155. His increasing dominance is illustrated by the decreasing number of balls it took him to complete each of the three separate 50s that made up his innings: 71, 51 and 36. Mohammad Ali, though taking four wickets, felt much of the force of Hick's strokeplay as he conceded 124 runs from his 12 overs. Tom Graveney, the Worcestershire president and former England batsman, was on the ground to see Hick draw level with his own 122-hundred mark. Hick is now equal 12th on the all-time list, with Denis Compton just one century away. In reply to Worcestershire's 374, Derbyshire crumbled from 83 without loss to 179 all out in the face of some excellent pace bowling from Nantie Hayward, Matt

Mason and Andrew Hall, and by the close of the second day were hanging on at 185 for 6 only because of a stubborn seventh-wicket stand between Dominic Cork and Graeme Welch. They eventually added 92, with both of them scoring half-centuries after they had come together with the score on 111 for 6, but Hayward took his second four-wicket haul of the match and Worcestershire had soon knocked off the few runs they needed to complete victory.

A youthful Durham side earned themselves a famous triumph at Headingley, beating Yorkshire by 167 runs when they dismissed them for a second-innings 93 on the third afternoon. Only two home batsmen reached double figures as the pace of Dewald Pretorius, who took 4 for 15, and the medium pace of Gordon Muchall wreaked havoc on a dubious surface. In the conditions, the batting of Durham captain Jon Lewis proved the real difference between the two teams. Lewis made 124 and 66, in the process becoming the leading run-scorer in the county's first-class history when he moved past John Morris' mark of 5,670. Ian Pattison, a young all-rounder, helped Lewis to add 132 for the fifth wicket on the opening day, but his highly promising 62 was followed by an unfortunate dislocation of his shoulder on the second day when he fell awkwardly in his follow-through when bowling his sixth over. Of the six batsmen in the Durham order for this game,

Round Seven: 30 May–2 June 2003 Division Two

DERBYSHIRE v. WORCESTERSHIRE – at Derby

WORCS	First Innings		Second Innings	
SD Peters	b Mohammad Ali	47	not out	25
A Singh	b Cork	50	c Dean b Mohammad Ali	21
GA Hick	c Khan b Mohammad Ali	155	not out	1
BF Smith (capt)	lbw b Mohammad Ali	0		
VS Solanki	c Hewson b Dean	6		
AJ Hall	lbw b Dean	0		
GJ Batty	c Dumelow b Dean	4		
*SJ Rhodes	c Sutton b Welch	29		
Kabir Ali	not out	19		
MS Mason	c Dumelow b Mohammad Ali	4		
M Hayward	b Cork	1		
Extras	b 4, lb 13, w 10, nb 32	59	nb 4	4
	(92.1 overs)	374	(1 wkt, 7.5 overs)	51

Bowling
Cork 24.1–9–70–2. Dean 21–7–41–3. Welch 26–6–81–1. Mohammad Ali 12–0–124–4. Dumelow 9–1–41–0.
Cork 3–0–22–0. Dean 2–0–16–0. Mohammad Ali 1.5–0–10–1. Dumelow 1–0–3–0.
Fall of Wickets 1–106, 2–125, 3–125, 4–172, 5–172, 6–222, 7–332, 8–348, 9–367, 10–374
1–50

DERBYSHIRE	First Innings		Second Innings	
AI Gait	c Rhodes b Mason	50	(2) b Batty	18
MJ Di Venuto	c Smith b Mason	54	(1) lbw b Kabir Ali	4
RM Khan	c Hayward b Mason	2	c Kabir Ali b Hayward	32
SA Selwood	b Hayward	17	lbw b Kabir Ali	11
DR Hewson	c Rhodes b Hall	0	c Hick b Kabir Ali	4
*LD Sutton	c Rhodes b Hall	3	lbw b Dean	25
DG Cork (capt)	c Pretorius b Hayward	24	b Hayward	52
G Welch	c Singh b Hall	9	not out	51
NRC Dumelow	b Hayward	5	c Rhodes b Hayward	6
Mohammad Ali	not out	3	c Solanki b Mason	5
KJ Dean	b Hayward	0	b Hayward	21
Extras	b 1, lb 4, w 3, nb 4	16	b 5, w 1, nb 4	16
	(56.5 overs)	179	(63 overs)	245

Bowling
Hayward 16.5–4–53–4. Kabir Ali 9–3–35–0. Mason 10–1–27–3. Batty 9–2–31–0. Hall 12–0–28–3.
Kabir Ali 11–0–60–3. Mason 19–4–54–1. Batty 9–1–29–1. Hall 10–3–24–1. Hayward 14–1–67–4.
Fall of Wickets 1–83, 2–93, 3–113, 4–114, 5–118, 6–159, 7–170, 8–171, 9–179, 10–179
1–5, 2–48, 3–71, 4–75, 5–82, 6–111, 7–203, 8–211, 9–216, 10–245

Worcestershire beat Derbyshire by 9 wickets –
Worcestershire (21pts), Derbyshire (3pts)

YORKSHIRE v. DURHAM – at Headingley

DURHAM	First Innings		Second Innings	
JJB Lewis (capt)	lbw b Silverwood	124	c Lumb b Silverwood	66
MA Gough	c Blakey b Gough	10	lbw b Lumb	43
GJ Muchall	c Blakey b Kirby	10	c and b Swanepoel	4
GJ Pratt	c Blakey b Swanepoel	4	c Blakey b Silverwood	0
N Peng	c Richardson b Gough	2	(6) st Blakey b Dawson	29
I Pattison	lbw b Fellows	62	absent hurt	
*P Mustard	c Blakey b Dawson	23	c Yuvraj Singh b Silverwood	20
LE Plunkett	lbw b Kirby	4	(5) lbw b Gough	0
NC Phillips	c Blakey b Silverwood	19	(5) lbw b Swanepoel	9
N Killeen	lbw b Silverwood	0	(9) not out	2
D Pretorius	not out	1	(10) c Yuvraj Singh b Silverwood	1
Extras	b 1, lb 12, nb 8	21	b 7, lb 3, w 1, nb 14	25
	(111.3 overs)	280	(9 wkts, 66 overs)	200

Bowling
Gough 23–5–55–2. Silverwood 21.3–1–80–3. Kirby 20–4–40–2. Swanepoel 18–9–30–1. Dawson 16–7–27–1. Fellows 10–1–20–1. Lumb 3–0–15–0.
Gough 15–2–36–1. Silverwood 15–2–40–4. Kirby 12–5–29–0. Swanepoel 16–2–40–2. Lumb 6–0–29–1. Dawson 2–0–16–1.
Fall of Wickets 1–29, 2–41, 3–46, 4–55, 5–183, 6–220, 7–230, 8–275, 9–279, 10–280
1–79, 2–84, 3–99, 4–117, 5–169, 6–191, 7–192, 8–194, 9–200

YORKSHIRE	First Innings		Second Innings	
MJ Wood (capt)	lbw b Pretorius	0	b Pretorius	0
SA Richardson	b Pattison	18	lbw b Killeen	18
Yuvraj Singh	c Mustard b Pretorius	56	b Plunkett	9
MJ Lumb	b Phillips	105	c Gough b Pretorius	9
*RJ Blakey	c Mustard b Plunkett	3	lbw b Muchall	4
GM Fellows	c Killeen b Plunkett	9	c Pretorius b Muchall	4
RKJ Dawson	c Phillips b Plunkett	0	lbw b Muchall	21
D Gough	c Pretorius b Plunkett	4	b Pretorius	9
CEW Silverwood	b Plunkett	0	b Pretorius	2
PJ Swanepoel	c and b Pretorius	17	b Plunkett	2
SP Kirby	not out	0	not out	1
Extras	lb 5, w 1, nb 2	8	b 1, lb 8, nb 4	13
	(60.4 overs)	220	(30.4 overs)	93

Bowling
Pretorius 16–2–54–3. Plunkett 12–1–53–5. Killeen 15–2–46–0. Pattison 5.4–3–7–1. Muchall 4.2–0–13–0. Phillips 7.4–0–42–1.
Pretorius 9.4–1–15–4. Plunkett 7–1–21–2. Killeen 6–1–22–1. Muchall 8–2–26–3.
Fall of Wickets 1–29, 2–41, 3–46, 4–49, 5–111, 6–111, 7–115, 8–115, 9–194, 10–220
1–4, 2–39, 3–18, 4–39, 5–39, 6–52, 7–71, 8–85, 9–91, 10–93

Durham beat Yorkshire by 167 runs –
Durham (19pts), Yorkshire (4pts)

NORTHAMPTONSHIRE v. GLAMORGAN – at Northampton

GLAMORGAN	First Innings		Second Innings	
A Dale	c Powell b Nel	37	c Hussey b Greenidge	2
J Hughes	b Nel	24	lbw b Greenidge	73
DL Hemp	c Jaques b Phillips	4	lbw b Nel	9
MJ Powell	b Phillips	29	b Phillips	8
MP Maynard	c Greenidge b Brown	26	(6) c Powell b Phillips	11
*MA Wallace	lbw b Brown	32	(7) lbw b Nel	3
RDB Croft (capt)	c Nel b Phillips	34	(8) not out	50
DS Harrison	c Brown b Cook	33	(5) st Bailey b Brown	1
MS Kasprowicz	c Sales b Brown	21	(10) c Bailey b Nel	23
AG Wharf	c Bailey b Phillips	4	(11) c Sales b Nel	17
DA Cosker	not out	1	(9) c Powell b Croft	0
Extras	lb 11, w 2, nb 10	23	lb 4, w 2, nb 17	23
	(85.3 overs)	269	(66 overs)	220

Bowling
Nel 24–4–86–2. Greenidge 15–3–65–0. Phillips 15.3–7–33–3. Cook 8–1–22–1. Brown 23–7–52–4.
Nel 25–8–57–4. Greenidge 12–0–72–2. Cook 4–1–10–0. Phillips 18–4–59–3. Brown 7–3–18–1.
Fall of Wickets 1–48, 2–57, 3–112, 4–114, 5–173, 6–174, 7–225, 8–259, 9–263, 10–269
1–13, 2–22, 3–62, 4–65, 5–93, 6–101, 7–139, 8–140, 9–190, 10–220

NORTHANTS	First Innings		Second Innings	
MEK Hussey (capt)	c Wallace b Kasprowicz	39	c Cosker b Kasprowicz	14
RA White	c Croft b Wharf	55	b Kasprowicz	14
PA Jaques	c Hemp b Kasprowicz	0	c Wallace b Kasprowicz	59
JW Cook	lbw b Kasprowicz	0	c Powell b Croft	6
DJG Sales	c Wallace b Harrison	23	c Wallace b Harrison	6
MJ Powell	lbw b Cosker	55	run out	15
*TMB Bailey	c Hemp b Harrison	2	lbw b Kasprowicz	2
BJ Phillips	c Dale b Croft	23	b Kasprowicz	16
CG Greenidge	b Harrison	13	c Hughes b Kasprowicz	0
A Nel	c Hughes b Harrison	24	c Wharf b Harrison	14
JF Brown	not out	1	not out	12
Extras	b 4, lb 8, w 2, nb 14	28	b 4, nb 10	14
	(95.3 overs)	262	(53.1 overs)	172

Bowling
Kasprowicz 24–4–77–3. Harrison 24.3–8–64–4. Wharf 16–4–44–1. Croft 18–4–32–1. Dale 3–0–16–0. Cosker 10–4–17–1.
Kasprowicz 23–3–72–6. Harrison 6.1–0–19–2. Wharf 8–2–41–0. Croft 15–5–34–1. Cosker 1–0–2–0.
Fall of Wickets 1–97, 2–101, 3–101, 4–113, 5–161, 6–169, 7–224, 8–224, 9–255, 10–262
1–37, 2–40, 3–70, 4–85, 5–120, 6–126, 7–137, 8–137, 9–152, 10–172

Glamorgan beat Northamptonshire by 55 runs –
Glamorgan (19pts), Northamptonshire (5pts)

Poor batting was the root cause of Northamptonshire's 55-run defeat against Glamorgan at Wantage Road. First they failed to gain a first-innings lead, after bowling out their visitors for 269 and reaching 97 for 0 in reply. Then, after Ben Phillips had taken his match wicket haul to six and Andre Nel had chipped in with 4 for 57 to bowl out Glamorgan again for 220, the home batsmen flashed too often. Mike Kasprowicz finished with figures of 6 for 72, and only Phil Jaques, with 59, made any significant headway in a disappointing team performance.

ROUND EIGHT: 4–7 JUNE 2003

Division One

Sussex bounced back from their disappointment at The Oval by beating Kent convincingly at the traditional local derby venue of Tunbridge Wells. The Nevil Ground rhododendrons made for a fitting backdrop of imperious purple as Mushtaq Ahmed bamboozled the Kent batsmen, despite feeling unwell for much of the game. The Pakistan leg spinner took 5 for 70 and 4 for 56, and also hit a vital quick-fire 43 to boost the Sussex first innings up to 311. Chris Adams and Robin Martin-Jenkins played their parts with the bat, too, with 62 and 67 respectively after Alamgir Sheriyar had made early strikes with the new ball to reduce Sussex to 142 for 5 by the close of a weather-shortened opening day.

The turning point of the match may have come towards the end of day two when Kent, moving along nicely, saw Andy Symonds hole out to long off for 54. Mushtaq, the successful bowler, then got into the Kent lower order the next morning and, despite a fine unbeaten 46 from Geraint Jones, Sussex had won themselves a first-innings cushion. Murray Goodwin and Tony Cottey then reached half-centuries, during a second-wicket stand of 111, and the in-form Martin-Jenkins' 84, supported by Matthew Prior's 45, ensured that the visitors remained on top. Kent did make it to 65 for 1 on the final afternoon, but then collapsed to 131 all out as Mushtaq spun his web and both Martin-Jenkins and Jason Lewry picked up three wickets.

Mr Relentless: Graeme Hick collects his 122nd first-class century as Worcestershire trounced Derbyshire.

below Lewis and his opening partner Michael Gough, the oldest was Gary Pratt at 21 years and five months. Moreover, all except Liam Plunkett were born and raised within 20 miles of the River Tyne, and the 18-year-old from Middlesbrough included four wickets in nine balls as he took 5 for 24 in an inspired second spell to hasten Yorkshire's first-innings decline. Michael Lumb played exceptionally well for his 105, after coming in at 66 for 2, and Yorkshire needed Lumb's ninth-wicket stand of 79 with Pieter Swanepoel to reach 220. An opening partnership of 79 between Lewis and Gough then built on Durham's first-innings advantage.

Lancashire trounced Leicestershire at Liverpool, all but completing an innings win as spin duo Carl Hooper (5 for 52) and Gary Keedy (4 for 61) cleaned up on the fourth morning. Keedy had also taken three scalps as Leicestershire could reply only with 314 to Lancashire's own first innings of 503.

Round Eight: 4–7 June 2003 Division One

```
          KENT v. SUSSEX – at Tunbridge Wells

SUSSEX         First Innings            Second Innings
RR Montgomerie b Sheriyar           13  (2) lbw b Saggers        0
MW Goodwin     run out              35  (1) run out             58
PA Cottey      lbw b Sheriyar        0  lbw b Symonds           52
CJ Adams (capt) c Ealham b Sheriyar  62 lbw b Sheriyar          4
TR Ambrose     c Walker b Blewett    11  lbw b Symonds          17
RSC M-Jenkins  c Tredwell b Symonds  67  c Jones b Sheriyar     84
PM Hutchison   b Ealham             18
*MJ Prior      c Symonds b Saggers  23  c and b Tredwell        45
KJ Innes       c and b Sheriyar     30  b Tredwell              0
M Ahmed        c Jones b Saggers    43  c Loudon b Sheriyar     9
JD Lewry       not out               0  (11) not out            9
RJ Kirtley                              (10) c Jones b Sheriyar 0
Extras         b 2, lb 5, w 2        9  b 3, lb 12, w 1         16
                                   311  (95.1 overs)           286

Bowling
Saggers 24.1–6–76–2. Sheriyar 24–6–49–4. Ealham 20–8–63–1. Blewett 5–0–21–1.
Tredwell 12–0–65–0. Symonds 10–2–30–1.
Saggers 20–4–62–1. Sheriyar 23.5–1–93–4. Ealham 10–2–37–0. Symonds
10–1–25–2. Tredwell 10–2–37–2. Blewett 2–0–17–0.
Fall of Wickets 1–21, 2–25, 3–79, 4–104, 5–136, 6–174, 7–205, 8–249, 9–311, 10–311
1–1, 2–112, 3–117, 4–131, 5–184, 6–273, 7–273, 8–284, 9–275, 10–286

KENT           First Innings            Second Innings
MA Carberry    c Cottey b Kirtley   23  b M Ahmed               40
GS Blewett     b Innes              46  c Prior b Lewry         0
ET Smith       lbw b Kirtley        13  c Montgomerie b Lewry   40
A Symonds      c Innes b M Ahmed    54  lbw b M Ahmed           1
MJ Walker      c Ambrose b M Ahmed  30  c Prior b Lewry         7
AGR Loudon     c Ambrose b M Ahmed   0  (8) lbw b M-Jenkins     0
MA Ealham (capt) c M-Jenkins b M Ahmed 9 lbw b M-Jenkins        0
*GO Jones      not out              46  (6) c Lewry b M-Jenkins 22
JC Tredwell    lbw b Kirtley        16  c Montgomerie b M Ahmed 11
MJ Saggers     b Kirtley             2  not out                 0
A Sheriyar     lbw b M Ahmed         7  c Goodwin b M Ahmed     4
Extras         b 11, lb 10          21  lb 1, w 2              3
               (73.2 overs)        275  (47.4 overs)          131

Bowling
Lewry 11–4–19–0. Hutchison 5–0–27–0. M-Jenkins 10–3–26–0. Kirtley 21–4–84–4.
Innes 9–1–28–1. Mushtaq Ahmed 17.2–3–70–5
Kirtley 9–2–29–0. Lewry 11–2–36–3. M Ahmed 20.4–7–56–4. M-Jenkins 7–3–9–3.
Fall of Wickets 1–74, 2–84, 3–90, 4–180, 5–180, 6–198, 7–203, 8–238, 9–250, 10–275
1–0, 2–65, 3–66, 4–83, 5–99, 6–110, 7–110, 8–127, 9–127, 10–131
```
Sussex beat Kent by 191 runs – Sussex (20pts), Kent (5pts)

```
       LANCASHIRE v. LEICESTERSHIRE – at Liverpool

LANCASHIRE     First Innings            Second Innings
MJ Chilton     lbw b Brignull      108  not out                16
IJ Sutcliffe   c Maddy b Masters    55  not out                5
MB Loye        c Grayson b Keedy    54
SG Law         c Nixon b Maddy      82
CL Hooper      c Stevens b Dagnall  74
A Flintoff     not out              71
G Chapple      c Masters b Brignull 15
*WK Hegg (capt) not out             23
P J Martin
G Keedy
S I Mahmood
Extras         b 5, lb 5, w 5, nb 6 21  b 1, lb 2              3
               (6 wkts, 127.4 overs) 503 (no wkt, 8.2 overs)  24

Bowling
DeFreitas 31–9–73–0. Dagnall 28–8–81–1. Masters 17–3–68–1. Brignull
21.4–3–113–2. Maddy 15–1–84–2. Sehwag 1–0–1–0. Snape 11–1–48–0. Hodge
2–0–10–0. Stevens 1–0–15–0.
Sehwag 4.2–0–10–0. Snape 4–0–11–0.
Fall of Wickets 1–104, 2–211, 3–254, 4–377, 5–394, 6–436

LEICESTERSHIRE First Innings            Second Innings
JK Maunders    c Flintoff b Mahmood 16  (2) c Hegg b Hooper    39
V Sehwag       c Hooper b Chapple   30  (4) run out            5
DL Maddy       c Law b Keedy        85  st Hegg b Hooper       48
BJ Hodge       lbw b Martin         26  (5) lbw b Hooper       14
DD Masters     c Sutcliffe b Martin  0  (6) c Loye b Hooper    0
DI Stevens     c Law b Chapple      65  (7) c Law b Keedy      6
JN Snape       b Keedy              31  (8) c Sutcliffe b Keedy 26
*PA Nixon      c Hegg b Chapple      0  (1) b Keedy            32
PAJ DeFreitas (capt) c Chilton b Mahmood 16 c Martin b Keedy   9
DS Brignull    c Chapple b Keedy     5  b Hooper               6
CE Dagnall     not out               5  not out               0
Extras         b 4, lb 5, w 5, nb 21 35 b 10, lb 5, nb 12      27
               (93.4 overs)        314  (72.4 overs)         212

Bowling
Martin 20–2–71–2. Chapple 21–4–66–3. Mahmood 19–3–91–2. Keedy 24.4–12–43–3.
Hooper 9–1–34–0.
Chapple 12–1–57–0. Mahmood 4–1–21–0. Hooper 26.4–7–52–5. Martin 1–0–6–0.
Keedy 29–7–61–4.
Fall of Wickets 1–41, 2–59, 3–105, 4–116, 5–238, 6–246, 7–246, 8–294, 9–303, 10–314
1–81, 2–83, 3–99, 4–126, 5–130, 6–147, 7–191, 8–199, 9–208, 10–212
```
Lancashire beat Leicestershire by 10 wickets – Lancashire (22pts), Leicestershire (5pts)

Darren Maddy and Darren Stevens were the only visiting batsmen to hold up the effectiveness of Lancashire's powerful top order on days one and two. Mark Chilton began it all by hitting 108 and figuring in stands of 104 for the first wicket with Iain Sutcliffe and then another 107 for the second with Mal Loye. Then came Stuart Law (82), Hooper (74) and Andrew Flintoff who, still 'unfit' for England, smashed 71 not out from only 55 balls.

The highly promising teenager, Ravinder Bopara, batted throughout the tense final session at Lord's to score an unbeaten 40 and claim a draw for Essex against Middlesex. At 165 for 7, after being forced to follow on, Essex looked down and out, but Bopara was joined by James Middlebrook in an eighth-wicket stand of 100, and hung on after Middlebrook finally fell for 52. Middlesex were left frustrated, especially as the match had been interrupted more than once by bad weather, but Simon Cook's bowling was a major positive for them to take out of the fixture. They had done well on the opening day, too, recovering from 23 for 3 to reach the heights of 363 after an initial rally from Ben Hutton (107) and Ed Joyce, who added 128 for the fourth wicket, and then attractive half-centuries from Abdul Razzaq and Paul Weekes. Jon Dakin's 5 for 86 from 35 overs, meanwhile, was his first five-wicket analysis in championship cricket.

A high-scoring affair at Edgbaston ended with Nottinghamshire just running out of time in a

```
          MIDDLESEX v. ESSEX – at Lord's

MIDDLESEX      First Innings
AJ Strauss (capt) b Dakin         11
SG Koenig      c Foster b Dakin     0
OA Shah        c Jefferson b Dakin  4
BL Hutton      c Foster b Dakin   107
EC Joyce       c and b Bopara      69
Abdul Razzaq   b Dakin             54
PN Weekes      not out             51
*DC Nash       b Brant              1
AA Noffke      lbw b Brant          8
SJ Cook        b Napier            20
CB Keegan      b Middlebrook       21
Extras         lb 12, w 5          17
               (121.1 overs)      363

Bowling
Brant 31–10–67–2. Dakin 35–10–86–5. Napier 24–5–74–1. Bopara 15–1–61–1.
Middlebrook 16.1–1–63–1.
Fall of Wickets 1–4, 2–8, 3–23, 4–151, 5–254, 6–261, 7–272, 8–282, 9–324, 10–363

ESSEX          First Innings            Second Innings
DDJ Robinson   c Nash b Keegan      7  b Keegan               13
WI Jefferson   c Nash b Noffke     22  lbw b Abdul Razzaq     30
AP Grayson (capt) c Nash b Keegan   0  c Nash b Cook          69
A Flower       c Nash b Keegan     11  c Nash b Cook          2
A Habib        lbw b Noffke        15  b Abdul Razzaq         15
*JS Foster     c Shah b Cook       11  c Weekes b Noffke      15
RS Bopara      run out             48  not out                40
JM Dakin       lbw b Cook           5  c Joyce b Cook         24
JD Middlebrook c Strauss b Cook     1  lbw b Cook             52
GR Napier      c Keegan b Noffke   44  not out                0
SA Brant       not out              0
Extras         lb 2                 2  b 5, lb 9, nb 4        18
               (65.1 overs)       166  (8 wkts, 95 overs)   269

Bowling
Noffke 18–6–39–3. Keegan 16.1–3–56–2. Cook 16–7–33–3. Abdul Razzaq
13–0–34–1. Weekes 2–1–2–0.
Noffke 25–5–81–1. Keegan 20–4–52–1. Cook 18–4–54–4. Abdul Razzaq 20–3–40–2.
Hutton 3–1–18–0. Weekes 6–2–14–0. Joyce 3–0–13–0.
Fall of Wickets 1–29, 2–29, 3–37, 4–46, 5–62, 6–70, 7–76, 8–78, 9–157, 10–166
1–21, 2–65, 3–70, 4–75, 5–129, 6–137, 7–165, 8–265
```
Match drawn – Middlesex (11pts), Essex (7pts)

```
      WARWICKSHIRE v. NOTTINGHAMSHIRE – at Edgbaston

WARWICKSHIRE   First Innings            Second Innings
NV Knight      c Noon b Smith      33  lbw b MacGill         146
IJL Trott      c Franks b Smith    63  b Pietersen           28
MA Wagh        b Smith             58  lbw b MacGill         39
IR Bell        c Noon b Franks     21  b MacGill             64
*JO Troughton  c Shafayat b Franks  0  lbw b Pietersen       5
A Habib        c Noon b Smith      15  c Gallian b MacGill   15
DR Brown (capt) c Pietersen b MacGill 40 c Welton b Smith    20
MA Sheikh      c Noon b Pietersen  13  b MacGill             8
CO Obuya       c Noon b Smith      55  not out               30
MM Betts       c Smith b Malik      6  b Pietersen           11
Waqar Younis   not out             15  lbw b MacGill         8
Extras         b 2, lb 13, w 1, nb 20 36 b 13, lb 6, nb 12   31
               (87.3 overs)       351  (117.4 overs)        405

Bowling
Smith 15.3–4–60–4. Malik 19–1–102–1. Franks 20–2–80–2. MacGill 28–4–75–1.
Pietersen 5–2–19–1.
Smith 21–4–85–1. Malik 5–0–24–0. MacGill 47.4–10–117–6. Franks 13–1–57–0.
Pietersen 29–3–95–3. Shafayat 2–0–8–0.
Fall of Wickets 1–104, 2–109, 3–184, 4–184, 5–198, 6–216, 7–238, 8–298, 9–309, 10–351
1–113, 2–198, 3–270, 4–297, 5–312, 6–317, 7–329, 8–350, 9–385, 10–405

NOTTS          First Innings            Second Innings
GE Welton      c Knight b Bell     99  (2) b Waqar Younis    11
JER Gallian (capt) c Wagh b Betts   6  (5) not out           6
U Afzaal       b Wagh              72  (1) c Troughton b Waqar Younis 28
KP Pietersen   c and b Obuya      221  (3) c sub b Waqar Younis 9
CL Cairns      c Frost b Sheikh   104
BM Shafayat    b Waqar Younis      11  c Waqar Younis        8
PJ Franks      not out             62  (4) c Frost b Sheikh  0
*WM Noon       c Frost b Bell      25  (7) not out           0
MN Malik       c Knight b Obuya    10
GJ Smith       c Knight b Obuya     9
SCG MacGill    c Sheikh 4–0–30–1. Wagh 1–0–1–0.
Extras         b 12, lb 5, w 4, nb 15 36 b 5, lb 1, w 1     7
               (154.3 overs)      646  (5 wkts, 11 overs)   67

Bowling
Waqar Younis 25–3–84–1. Betts 4–1–7–1. Sheikh 36–9–94–1. Brown 25–2–127–0.
Obuya 17–1–91–3. Wagh 21–3–93–1. Bell 14.3–1–79–3. Trott 12–0–54–0.
Waqar Younis 6–1–30–4. Sheikh 4–0–30–1. Wagh 1–0–1–0.
Fall of Wickets 1–14, 2–160, 3–244, 4–517, 5–536, 6–564, 7–616, 8–639, 9–639,
10–646
1–25, 2–52, 3–52, 4–55, 5–66
```
Match drawn – Warwickshire (9pts), Nottinghamshire (12pts)

Mushtaq Ahmed was feeling under the weather at Tunbridge Wells, but still managed to rout Kent.

desperate effort to beat Warwickshire. Needing 111 from 12 overs, they raced to 49 for 1 from six before Waqar Younis took 4 for 30 to halt them in their tracks. It was hard to take for Notts, who had built a mammoth first innings total of 646 – the seventh highest in their history – to take control of the match after first bowling out Warwickshire for 351. Greg Smith took four good wickets, including that of Collins Obuya, the Kenyan leg spinner, who made 55 on his championship debut. Guy Welton and Usman Afzaal then laid the base for Notts' huge score by adding 146 for the second wicket, and although Welton was out an agonizing one run short of a century the visitors were on a commanding 389 for 3 by the close of the second day. Kevin Pietersen, on 140 overnight, powered on to 221 and with Chris Cairns added 273 for the fourth wicket in 58 overs of rich entertainment. Pietersen struck four sixes and 27 fours, while Cairns' 104 was followed by

bright unbeaten 62 from Paul Franks. Warwickshire, however, were far from beaten, and Nick Knight led the fightback by reaching 85 not out by the end of the third day. He went on to score 146, after Warwickshire had resumed on the fourth morning at 138 for 1. Staying positive, the home batsmen kept the scoreboard ticking as Notts were forced to attack. Ian Bell's 64 also held up Notts, for whom Stuart MacGill finally finished with 6 for 117 and Pietersen 3 for 95. By reaching 405, Warwickshire had succeeded in buying themselves enough time, just, to force the draw.

Division Two

Mike Hussey, the Northamptonshire captain, batted for more than ten hours at Archdeacon Meadow, Gloucester, to set up a much-needed victory for his team. The Australian left-hander, who also made 310 against Gloucestershire's bowlers at Bristol in 2002, hit two sixes and 35 fours and added 126 for the second wicket with Phil Jaques (75 from 101 balls) before teaming up with Gerard Brophy in the partnership which broke the home side's spirit. Hussey and Brophy put on 260 for the sixth wicket, and when the declaration to the first innings finally came at 622 for 8, South African-raised Brophy remained unbeaten on 152. Initially, at least, Gloucestershire seemed to be making a fight of things with openers Chris Taylor and Tim Hancock raising 96, but by the close of day two they were 109 for 4. Andre Nel finished with a season's best 5 for 47 as Gloucestershire were bowled out for 230 the next day and, following on, the home side battled to 338 thanks to a determined stand between Matt Windows (150) and Jack Russell. Jason Brown, the off spinner, at last removed Russell for 63 to earn figures of 4 for 106, while Nel grabbed 3 for 87 from 32.1, big-hearted overs to help to wrap up victory by an innings and 54 runs.

Stephen Peters, his first scoring shot a six off Nixon McLean, was the central figure in Worcestershire's eventual nine-wicket win over Somerset at Bath. Peters went on to an assured 165 on the opening day of this much-loved festival, putting on 201 for the first wicket with Anurag Singh (105) and then a further 119 for the second wicket with Graeme Hick, who made 71. Andrew Hall then swashed and buckled his way to 104, hitting six sixes and 11 fours and boosting the Worcestershire total to 538. Somerset were 300 runs behind after their own first innings, but at least Jamie Cox showed some fight second time around with a fine 160 to take the game into the final day. Mike Burns stayed long enough to help Cox add 179 for the fourth wicket, but the Somerset tail then folded miserably against Gareth Batty's off spin. Batty picked up 6 for 88 and then Hick enjoyed knocking off the runs for victory.

Round Eight: 4–7 June 2003 Division Two

The scheduled opening day at Swansea was washed out by rain, but Glamorgan were still able to brush aside Derbyshire by an innings and 70 runs. First, the home side totalled 395, thanks largely to Robert Croft's 84 batting from No. 7 and his 81-run stand for the final wicket with fellow spinner Dean Cosker. Croft and Cosker then teamed up with the ball, taking 6 for 71 and 3 for 49 respectively as Derbyshire's first innings was wrapped up for 209. Following on, the visitors crumbled to 116 all out, Mike Kasprowicz and Alex Wharf reducing them to a hopeless 15 for 5 with the new ball and then the Welsh spin twins sharing the remaining four wickets. Dominic Cork, the Derbyshire captain, was unable to bat in the second innings.

Hampshire were denied a certain victory at the Rose Bowl by the Durham tail – and the weather. John Crawley's team were left cursing the rain that had washed out the third day, as it allowed the visitors to cling on for a draw at the end of a final day in which they had lost 17 wickets. Nicky Phillips' 31 not out – at the end of the second innings with his side struggling on 137 for 9 – ultimately frustrated Hampshire, who had run up 456 on the first couple of days and then bowled out Durham for 235. Simon Katich provided the best batting of the match with 135, but Dimitri Mascarenhas also entertained with 92 and, for Durham, debutant James Lowe took advantage of some good fortune to make a valuable 80.

GLOUCESTERSHIRE v. NORTHAMPTONSHIRE – at Gloucester

NORTHANTS	First Innings	
MEK Hussey (capt)	c Hancock b Lewis	264
DE Paynter	b Butler	5
PA Jaques	lbw b Ball	75
JW Cook	b Smith	1
DJG Sales	c Russell b Butler	46
MJ Powell	c Russell b Butler	19
*GL Brophy	not out	152
BJ Phillips	b Ball	3
A Nel	b Ball	0
CG Greenidge	not out	3
J F Brown		
Extras	b 13, lb 6, w 6, nb 29	54
	(8 wkts, 158.5 overs)	**622**

Bowling
Lewis 35.5–6–145–1. Smith 25–5–63–1. Butler 28–2–130–3. Ball 44–6–149–3. Gidman 17–1–76–0. Taylor 9–0–40–0.
Fall of Wickets 1-32, 2-158, 3-172, 4-286, 5-328, 6-588, 7-612, 8-612

GLOS	First Innings		Second Innings	
CG Taylor	b Nel	45	run out	31
THC Hancock	lbw b Greenidge	44	c Brophy b Nel	18
MGN Windows	lbw b Greenidge	0	(4) c Hussey b Brown	150
JN Rhodes	lbw b Nel	24	(5) b Brown	4
MW Alleyne (capt)	c Brophy b Nel	0	(6) c Sales b Brown	8
APR Gidman	c Powell b Phillips	20	(7) c Sales b Brown	8
*RC Russell	lbw b Nel	22	(8) c Brophy b Phillips	63
MCJ Ball	b Brown	53	(9) b Nel	1
J Lewis	c Greenidge b Nel	5	(10) not out	11
IG Butler	run out	0	(3) c Powell b Brown	7
AM Smith	not out	0	c Brophy b Nel	4
Extras	b 3, lb 3, w 3, nb 8	17	b 12, lb 6, w 5, nb 10	33
	(86.1 overs)	**230**	(123.1 overs)	**338**

Bowling
Nel 28.1–11–47–5. Greenidge 19–1–80–2. Brown 26–8–63–1. Phillips 13–4–34–1. Nel 32.1–6–87–3. Greenidge 14–1–59–1. Phillips 16–5–32–1. Brown 49–20–106–4. Cook 6–4–10–0. Paynter 1–1–0–0.
Fall of Wickets 1-96, 2-96, 3-96, 4-96, 5-146, 6-146, 7-218, 8-222, 9-225, 10-230
1-61, 2-66, 3-93, 4-97, 5-126, 6-147, 7-322, 8-322, 9-324, 10-338

*Northamptonshire beat Gloucestershire by an innings and 54 runs –
Northamptonshire (22pts), Gloucestershire (2pts)*

SOMERSET v. WORCESTERSHIRE – at Bath

WORCS	First Innings		Second Innings	
SD Peters	b Francis	165		
A Singh	c Cox b Dutch	105	c Bryant b Francis	15
GA Hick	c Parsons b Blackwell	71	not out	29
BF Smith (capt)	st Turner b Blackwell	2		
VS Solanki	b McLean	10	(1) not out	20
AJ Hall	lbw b Parsons	104		
GJ Batty	b Francis	26		
*SJ Rhodes	lbw b Blackwell	22		
Kabir Ali	c Turner b Blackwell	0		
MA Harrity	not out	2		
M Hayward	c Turner b Parsons	4		
Extras	lb 17, w 2, nb 8	27	nb 4	4
	(133.4 overs)	**538**	(1 wkt, 7.1 overs)	**68**

Bowling
McLean 21–1–105–1. Francis 30–5–112–2. Parsons 14.4–3–63–2. Burns 8–0–25–0. Blackwell 45–8–131–4. Dutch 15–1–85–1. Francis 4–0–40–1. Blackwell 3.1–0–28–0.
Fall of Wickets 1-201, 2-320, 3-326, 4-353, 5-383, 6-432, 7-524, 8-532, 9-533, 10-538
1-21

SOMERSET	First Innings		Second Innings	
PCL Holloway	c Rhodes b Kabir Ali	30	lbw b Kabir Ali	11
MJ Wood	c Singh b Hayward	8	c Solanki b Batty	32
JDC Bryant	c Smith b Batty	28	c Rhodes b Harrity	12
J Cox	lbw b Hall	37	lbw b Hall	160
M Burns (capt)	c Hick b Batty	6	c Solanki b Hall	57
ID Blackwell	lbw b Batty	28	c sub b Batty	10
*RJ Turner	c Smith b Batty	23	lbw b Batty	10
KA Parsons	c Hick b Hayward	4	c Singh b Batty	6
KP Dutch	c Rhodes b Kabir Ali	17	c Hick b Batty	1
NAM McLean	not out	35	not out	9
SRG Francis	lbw b Kabir Ali	4	c sub b Batty	1
Extras	lb 1, w 1, nb 16	18	b 4, lb 14, w 9, nb 26, p 5	58
	(65.4 overs)	**238**	(116.1 overs)	**367**

Bowling
Kabir Ali 13.4–1–68–3. Hayward 15–5–56–2. Harrity 8–3–20–0. Batty 22–8–66–3. Hall 7–1–27–2.
Hayward 15–2–49–0. Kabir Ali 19–4–75–1. Batty 39.1–8–88–6. Harrity 20–2–69–1. Hall 23–7–63–2.
Fall of Wickets 1-40, 2-42, 3-115, 4-123, 5-138, 6-169, 7-182, 8-188, 9-220, 10-238
1-37, 2-66, 3-68, 4-247, 5-282, 6-334, 7-356, 8-363, 9-365, 10-367

*Worcestershire beat Somerset by 9 wickets –
Worcestershire (22pts), Somerset (3pts)*

GLAMORGAN v. DERBYSHIRE – at Swansea

GLAMORGAN	First Innings	
A Dale	lbw b Lungley	43
J Hughes	c and b Cork	69
DL Hemp	c Sutton b Lungley	9
MJ Powell	lbw b Lungley	23
MP Maynard	c Hewson b Lungley	35
*MA Wallace	c Sutton b Dean	35
RDB Croft (capt)	c Lungley b Dean	84
DS Harrison	c Gait b Welch	4
MS Kasprowicz	b Dean	19
AG Wharf	c Sutton b Cork	15
DA Cosker	not out	12
Extras	b 4, lb 17, nb 26	47
	(97.5 overs)	**395**

Bowling
Cork 21–5–71–2. Dean 22.5–4–84–3. Welch 25–7–78–1. Lungley 20–3–101–4. Wharton 9–2–40–0.
Fall of Wickets 1-82, 2-92, 3-126, 4-176, 5-216, 6-258, 7-263, 8-282, 9-314, 10-395

DERBYSHIRE	First Innings		Second Innings	
AI Gait	b Croft	23	(2) c Wallace b Wharf	0
MJ Di Venuto	c Maynard b Croft	29	(1) lbw b Kasprowicz	0
CWG Bassano	lbw b Croft	8	c Wallace b Kasprowicz	0
M Kaif	c Dale b Cosker	13	lbw b Wharf	6
DR Hewson	c Hughes b Croft	18	c Wallace b Wharf	3
*LD Sutton	lbw b Kasprowicz	28	b Cosker	29
G Welch	c Wallace b Croft	16	c Dale b Croft	31
T Lungley	c Cosker b Croft	20	b Cosker	29
DG Cork (capt)	c Powell b Cosker	18	(11) absent injured	
KJ Dean	lbw b Cosker	15	(9) c Wallace b Croft	5
LJ Wharton	not out	0	(10) not out	0
Extras	b 8, lb 5, nb 8	21	b 6, lb 2, w 1, nb 4	13
	(75.3 overs)	**209**	(9 wkts, 50.5 overs)	**116**

Bowling
Kasprowicz 15–4–43–1. Croft 30.3–9–71–6. Wharf 7–2–21–0. Harrison 4–0–12–0. Cosker 19–3–49–3.
Kasprowicz 9–1–29–2. Wharf 7–3–12–3. Harrison 4–1–5–0. Croft 18–5–39–2. Cosker 14.5–5–38–2.
Fall of Wickets 1-19, 2-57, 3-78, 4-89, 5-107, 6-131, 7-159, 8-181, 9-209, 10-209
1-0, 2-2, 3-2, 4-8, 5-15, 6-68, 7-98, 8-116, 9-116

*Glamorgan beat Derbyshire by an innings and 70 runs –
Glamorgan (21pts), Derbyshire (4pts)*

HAMPSHIRE v. DURHAM – at Southampton

HAMPSHIRE	First Innings	
DA Kenway	c Mustard b Law	8
JP Crawley (capt)	b Law	29
SM Katich	b Phillips	135
RA Smith	c Muchall b Law	5
WS Kendall	run out	33
*N Pothas	c sub b Plunkett	79
AD Mascarenhas	lbw b Phillips	92
Wasim Akram	b Phillips	0
SD Udal	not out	60
AD Mullally	c sub b Phillips	0
ESH Giddins	c Mustard b Law	0
Extras	b 4, lb 7, nb 4	15
	(136.4 overs)	**456**

Bowling
Pretorius 4–2–9–0. Plunkett 28–7–109–1. Killeen 28–7–57–0. Law 22.4–2–71–4. Muchall 18–3–70–0. Phillips 36–7–129–4.
Fall of Wickets 1-36, 2-45, 3-61, 4-151, 5-284, 6-330, 7-332, 8-455, 9-455, 10-456

DURHAM	First Innings		Second Innings	
JJB Lewis (capt)	c Pothas b Giddins	44	c Katich b Mascarenhas	8
JA Lowe	lbw b Wasim Akram	80	c Smith b Giddins	0
GJ Muchall	lbw b Udal	0	lbw b Katich	16
GJ Pratt	lbw b Mullally	43	st Pothas b Katich	30
N Peng	b Mullally	0	c Smith b Katich	7
DR Law	c Pothas b Mullally	0	lbw b Wasim Akram	0
*P Mustard	b Wasim Akram	0	c Kendall b Udal	30
LE Plunkett	not out	10	lbw b Wasim Akram	0
NC Phillips	b Wasim Akram	10	not out	31
N Killeen	c Kendall b Giddins	0	c Smith b Wasim Akram	10
D Pretorius	b Giddins	12	not out	0
Extras	b 1, lb 12, nb 8	21	lb 5	5
	(88 overs)	**235**	(9 wkts, 52 overs)	**137**

Bowling
Wasim Akram 25–7–53–3. Giddins 17–4–51–3. Mullally 21–4–57–3. Mascarenhas 4–1–9–0. Udal 19–3–40–1. Katich 2–0–12–0.
Mascarenhas 6–1–13–1. Giddins 10–2–29–1. Katich 16–9–39–3. Wasim Akram 14–2–44–3. Mullally 2–0–3–0. Udal 4–2–4–1.
Fall of Wickets 1-79, 2-80, 3-175, 4-175, 5-175, 6-179, 7-194, 8-208, 9-223, 10-235
1-0, 2-14, 3-52, 4-59, 5-62, 6-73, 7-63, 8-107, 9-136

Match drawn – Hampshire (12pts), Durham (7pts)

The prolific Mike Hussey: a ten-hour epic 264 at Gloucester.

ROUND NINE: 27–30 JUNE 2003

Division One

Sussex made up ground on the rest of the division at Hove, moving into second place after beating Warwickshire by the thumping margin of an innings and 59 runs while the other three matches in this round all ended in draws. Once again it was Mushtaq Ahmed who was at the heart of their effort in the field, combining effectively with James Kirtley as Warwickshire were tumbled out for 201 in their first innings, in reply to Sussex's intimidating 545, and then virtually running through the visiting batting order himself to take 7 for 85 as the visitors ended up on 285 following on. Mark Davis, the off spinner, did his support act job well with two of the other three wickets, but Mushtaq's performance in taking his match wicket tally to 11 was all the more commendable because Michael Powell and Nick Knight had launched the Warwickshire second innings by compiling an opening stand of 135. Once they were both

removed, however, with Powell adding 80 to his first-innings 60, only Ian Bell's two-hour 37 held up the leg-spinning maestro for long. The match was also a triumph for Tony Cottey, the 37-year-old in the final summer of the five-year contract he signed when arriving at Sussex from his native Glamorgan. Cottey went some way towards clinching a new deal by hitting 31 boundaries in a magnificent 276-ball 188. Richard Montgomerie and Tim Ambrose scored valuable 50s, Matthew Prior continued to build his reputation with a well-judged 100 from 133 balls on the second morning, and Kirtley played a canny tail-end hand with 40 not out.

Leaders Surrey were so frustrated by Middlesex's stern resistance at Lord's that the match ended with Adam Hollioake being removed from the attack by umpire Graham Burgess for continually bowling bouncers in the last over of the match! It made for an amusing end to a contest that finished tamely because of poor weather on the final day. In the 38.3 overs bowled Middlesex, 198 behind on first innings, advanced from their overnight 74 without loss to 218 for 2 on the back of an opening partnership of 186 between Andy Strauss and Sven Koenig. Days two and three, however, had seen a dogged effort in the field by a Middlesex attack clearly outclassed by a Surrey top six of stellar quality. Ian Ward made 104, Mark Butcher 44, Graham Thorpe 46 and Alec Stewart 87. Even nightwatchman Saqlain Mushtaq chipped in with 69, although pride of place most certainly went to Mark Ramprakash, whose 110 on his former home ground made him the first batsman to score championship hundreds against all 18 counties. Surrey, however, scored at little more than three runs per over as they put together their 568, with Abdul Razzaq and Paul Weekes both claiming three wickets as a tangible reward for their unstinting efforts. Earlier, Ben Hutton had included four sixes and ten fours in 101, his second successive hundred, while Martin Bicknell picked up yet another five-wicket haul as Middlesex made 370 – their highest first-innings total of the summer to that date.

A chanceless and calculated innings of 206 by Nasser Hussain, in seven hours and 40 minutes at the crease, gave Essex the upper hand for a while against Kent at Chelmsford. It was Hussain's best score for his county since he made 197 against Surrey in 1990, and his first championship hundred for Essex in four years. With Aftab Habib hitting 77, it meant that Essex were able to reach 514 in reply to a Kent first innings of 381 that was based on an opening partnership of 138 between David Fulton and Michael Carberry. Fulton went on to make 93, including 14 fours, and Geraint Jones then appeared to flick Justin Bishop over midwicket for

six and also strike 14 boundaries in an 81-ball 84. James Middlebrook took six Kent first-innings wickets, but the off spinner could not take advantage of the visitors' initial struggle to 108 for 4 second time around. In the end, on a still-dependable batting surface, Kent recovered to 416 for 8 declared to earn the draw. A fifth-wicket stand of 127 between Matthew Walker and Mark Ealham rallied them on the third evening, and four brief stoppages for rain and one for bad light all added up to 40 overs being lost on the final day, which Kent had begun on 278 for 5. Ealham converted his overnight 85 into 101, his seventh first-class hundred, while Jones cashed in on some friendly bowling late on to romp to an unbeaten 108. Habib and Andy Flower enjoyed the closing overs, too: they each took a rare first-class wicket!

Nottinghamshire's hopes of forcing victory over Leicestershire at Grace Road were washed away with the rain that ruled out any play at all on the final day. There were only 40.5 overs possible on the opening day, too, with Phil DeFreitas restricting Notts to 90 for 3 with a spell of 12–6–20–2. However, not even the evergreen DeFreitas, who took his overall figures to 4 for 68 from 30 overs, could prevent Kevin Pietersen (88) and Paul Franks, with a superb unbeaten 123, from accelerating on day two. Virender Sehwag then blasted 137 from 157 balls, with 25 fours, before being caught at third man, but the Notts bowlers held their nerve in the face of the Indian's assault and, with Greg

Round Nine: 27–30 June 2003 Division One

SUSSEX v. WARWICKSHIRE – at Hove

SUSSEX

	First Innings		
RR Montgomerie	c Frost b Brown	66	
MW Goodwin	c Frost b Waqar Younis	0	
PA Cottey	c Frost b Richardson	188	
CJ Adams (capt)	c Bell b Waqar Younis	31	
*TR Ambrose	b Richardson	50	
RSC M-Jenkins	b Waqar Younis	28	
MJ Prior	c Frost b Brown	100	
MJG Davis	b Waqar Younis	6	
M Ahmed	c Trott b Waqar Younis	2	
RJ Kirtley	not out	40	
JD Lewry	b Brown	6	
Extras	b 1, lb 9, nb 18	28	
	(147.1 overs)	545	

Bowling

Waqar Younis 24–2–99–5. Betts 20–1–91–0. Brown 31.1–8–95–3. Richardson 34–6–92–2. Bell 3–0–24–0. Obuya 19–1–89–0. Wagh 14–1–40–0. Trott 2–1–5–0.
Fall of Wickets 1–3, 2–168, 3–239, 4–342, 5–357, 6–407, 7–431, 8–439, 9–519, 10–545

WARWICKSHIRE

	First Innings		Second Innings	
MJ Powell (capt)	c Ambrose b M-Jenkins	60	c Adams b M Ahmed	80
NV Knight	lbw b Lewry	11	c Prior b M Ahmed	64
MA Wagh	c Prior b M Ahmed	39	c Prior b M Ahmed	2
IR Bell	lbw b M Ahmed	0	c M-Jenkins b M Ahmed	37
IJL Trott	c Goodwin b Kirtley	6	lbw b Davis	31
*T Frost	run out	1	b Davis	4
DR Brown	not out	42	c Adams b M Ahmed	20
CO Obuya	lbw b Kirtley	2	(9) not out	8
MM Betts	c Davis b M Ahmed	21	(8) c Adams b Lewry	15
Waqar Younis	c Ambrose b Kirtley	8	c Kirtley b M Ahmed	14
A Richardson	b M Ahmed	0	c Ambrose b M Ahmed	0
Extras	b 1, lb 9, w 1	11	b 2, lb 7, w 1	10
	(59.5 overs)	201	(92.4 overs)	285

Bowling

Kirtley 15–2–57–3. Lewry 10–2–35–1. M Ahmed 22.5–6–55–4. M-Jenkins 10–1–40–1. Davis 2–1–4–0.
Kirtley 16–2–62–0. Lewry 9–2–41–1. M Ahmed 32.4–9–85–7. M-Jenkins 12–4–38–0. Davis 23–6–50–2.
Fall of Wickets 1–22, 2–104, 3–105, 4–122, 5–124, 6–131, 7–140, 8–171, 9–198, 10–201
1–135, 2–139, 3–146, 4–185, 5–196, 6–236, 7–249, 8–267, 9–284, 10–285

Sussex beat Warwickshire by an innings and 59 runs – Sussex (22pts), Warwickshire (3pts)

MIDDLESEX v. SURREY – at Lord's

MIDDLESEX

	First Innings		Second Innings	
AJ Strauss (capt)	c Hollioake b Saqlain Mushtaq	47	c Butcher b Salisbury	95
SG Koenig	c Saqlain Mushtaq b Bicknell	22	c Thorpe b Hollioake	89
OA Shah	c Stewart b Bicknell	31	not out	7
BL Hutton	b Salisbury	101	not out	5
EC Joyce	lbw b Bicknell	0		
Abdul Razzaq	c Stewart b Bicknell	29		
PN Weekes	c Stewart b Bicknell	39		
*DC Nash	not out	36		
AA Noffke	b Ormond	23		
SJ Cook	lbw b Ormond	0		
CB Keegan	b Ormond	20		
Extras	b 8, lb 7, w 7	22	b 10, nb 12	22
	(115.2 overs)	370	(2 wkts, 58 overs)	218

Bowling

Bicknell 35–7–92–5. Ormond 28.2–3–103–3. Tudor 13–5–43–0. Saqlain Mushtaq 24–5–66–1. Salisbury 9–2–21–1. Butcher 2–0–12–0. Hollioake 4–0–18–0.
Bicknell 8–0–33–0. Ormond 12–2–53–0. Tudor 12–2–45–0. Salisbury 17–2–60–1. Saqlain Mushtaq 2–1–1–0. Hollioake 6.3–1–15–1. Ward 0.3–0–1–0.
Fall of Wickets 1–59, 2–92, 3–110, 4–110, 5–148, 6–256, 7–305, 8–340, 9–340, 10–370
1–186, 2–202

SURREY

	First Innings	
IJ Ward	c Shah b Weekes	104
MA Butcher	c Koenig b Abdul Razzaq	44
MR Ramprakash	c Hutton b Cook	110
GP Thorpe	c Nash b Abdul Razzaq	46
Saqlain Mushtaq	c Keegan b Weekes	69
*AJ Stewart	c Joyce b Weekes	87
AJ Hollioake (capt)	b Noffke	10
AJ Tudor	b Abdul Razzaq	30
MP Bicknell	c Nash b Joyce	10
IDK Salisbury	b Cook	17
J Ormond	not out	1
Extras	lb 23, w 3, nb 14	40
	(131.4 overs)	568

Bowling

Noffke 37–5–134–1. Keegan 31–6–102–0. Abdul Razzaq 29–4–95–3. Joyce 11–3–25–1. Cook 28–4–101–2. Weekes 32.2–7–88–3.
Fall of Wickets 1–89, 2–193, 3–270, 4–352, 5–413, 6–444, 7–497, 8–535, 9–562, 10–568

Match drawn – Middlesex (10pts), Surrey (12pts)

ESSEX v. KENT – at Chelmsford

KENT

	First Innings		Second Innings	
DP Fulton (capt)	b Middlebrook	93	c Flower b Middlebrook	33
MA Carberry	lbw b Brant	50	c Flower b Middlebrook	8
ET Smith	lbw b Brant	0	c Habib b Napier	0
A Symonds	c Brant b Middlebrook	37	b Napier	39
MJ Walker	c Habib b Middlebrook	20	lbw b Bishop	65
MA Ealham	c Hussain b Middlebrook	34	c Brant b Napier	101
*GO Jones	run out	84	not out	108
JC Tredwell	c Habib b Middlebrook	16	c Brant b Flower	20
Mohammad Sami	c sub b Middlebrook	2	c Flower b Habib	1
A Sheriyar	not out	18		
BJ Trott	b Brant	12		
Extras	lb 6, w 1, nb 8	15	b 17, lb 17, w 3, nb 4	41
	(93 overs)	381	(8 wkts, 123.4 overs)	416

Bowling

Brant 24.4–2–107–3. Napier 21–3–79–0. Grant 4.2–1–13–0. Bishop 9–1–53–0. Middlebrook 34–8–123–6.
Brant 20–0–75–0. Napier 27–4–90–3. Middlebrook 47–7–138–2. Bishop 20–3–48–1. Flower 7–0–21–1. Habib 2.4–0–10–1.
Fall of Wickets 1–138, 2–138, 3–191, 4–214, 5–215, 6–278, 7–302, 8–340, 9–351, 10–381
1–27, 2–28, 3–72, 4–108, 5–235, 6–335, 7–402, 8–416

ESSEX

	First Innings	
DDJ Robinson	lbw b Ealham	47
N Hussain	lbw b Ealham	206
*JS Foster	c Jones b Sheriyar	44
A Flower	c Smith b Tredwell	13
A Habib	b Sheriyar	77
RC Irani (capt)	b Sheriyar	0
JD Middlebrook	c Jones b Sheriyar	39
GR Napier	lbw b Tredwell	19
JE Bishop	b Mohammmad Sami	21
SA Brant	not out	6
JB Grant	c Ealham b Mohammmad Sami	4
Extras	b 1, lb 3, w 2, nb 32	38
	(131.4 overs)	514

Bowling

Mohammmad Sami 28.4–3–150–2. Sheriyar 30–5–73–4. Tredwell 34–4–119–2. Trott 14–3–60–0. Symonds 6–0–31–0. Ealham 16–2–65–2. Carberry 12–0–52–0.
Fall of Wickets 1–114, 2–189, 3–202, 4–376, 5–376, 6–458, 7–460, 8–487, 9–510, 10–514

Match drawn – Essex (12pts), Kent (10pts)

LEICESTERSHIRE v. NOTTINGHAMSHIRE – at Leicester

NOTTS

	First Innings		Second Innings	
GE Welton	b Masters	41	(2) c Stevens b Dagnall	86
JER Gallian (capt)	c Hodge b DeFreitas	7	(3) b Dagnall	5
DJ Bicknell	c Maddy b DeFreitas	1	c Nixon b Maddy	38
*RJ Warren	c Maunders b Masters	40	(6) c Nixon b Dagnall	11
KP Pietersen	lbw b Amin	88	(4) c Nixon b Dagnall	95
CL Cairns	b DeFreitas	5	(5) not out	41
PJ Franks	not out	123	c DeFreitas b Masters	21
GD Clough	c Maddy b Hodge	0	not out	1
GJ Smith	b DeFreitas	2		
AJ Harris	c Hodge b Maddy	3		
SCG MacGill	c Snape b Maddy	5		
Extras	b 8, lb 7, w 1	16	b 6, lb 9, w 3, nb 2	20
	(109.5 overs)	326	(6 wkts, 67 overs)	318

Bowling

DeFreitas 30.9–68–4. Dagnall 19–5–69–0. Maddy 17.5–7–52–2. Masters 20–7–58–2. Amin 14–3–40–1. Snape 4–0–11–0. Stevens 1–0–1–0. Hodge 4–0–12–1.
DeFreitas 10.3–2–33–0. Dagnall 16–4–61–4. Amin 13–1–90–0. Masters 12–2–62–1. Maddy 7–2–15–1. Snape 6–2–22–0. Sehwag 3–1–30–0.
Fall of Wickets 1–9, 2–11, 3–89, 4–104, 5–123, 6–272, 7–277, 8–291, 9–310, 10–326
1–5, 2–62, 3–211, 4–270, 5–290, 6–311

LEICESTERSHIRE

	First Innings		Second Innings	
JK Maunders	b Smith	4	(2) not out	0
V Sehwag	c Smith b Harris	137		
DL Maddy	lbw b Franks	23		
BJ Hodge	b Smith	13		
DI Stevens	c Warren b Smith	4		
*PA Nixon	st Warren b MacGill	5		
JN Snape	b Smith	0		
PAJ DeFreitas (capt)	c Warren b MacGill	5		
DD Masters	not out	25	(1) lbw b Harris	5
CE Dagnall	c Warren b Franks	0		
RM Amin	lbw b MacGill	0		
Extras	b 7, lb 17, w 1, nb 2	27		
	(66 overs)	243	(1 wkt, 3.5 overs)	5

Bowling

Smith 20–8–40–4. Harris 18–2–64–1. Franks 11–0–47–2. Clough 4–0–20–0. MacGill 12–2–44–3. Pietersen 1–0–4–0. Smith 2–0–3–0. Harris 1.5–1–2–1.
Fall of Wickets 1–30, 2–114, 3–188, 4–193, 5–196, 6–196, 7–201, 8–217, 9–220, 10–243
1–5

Match drawn – Leicestershire (8pts), Nottinghamshire (10pts)

Plunder in the shires: England captain Nasser Hussain enjoyed making championship runs by the hundred (or, in this case, by the double-hundred) in his return to Essex colours.

Smith and Stuart MacGill to the fore, they eventually bowled Leicestershire out for 243. Notts then built on their first-innings lead with relish, Pietersen taking his season's first-class run aggregate to 668 at an average of 60 by hitting 95 from 89 deliveries and Guy Welton anchoring the second innings with 86. At the close of day three, Leicestershire were already one wicket down, having been set an unlikely target of 402 for victory, but the weather then had the last say.

Division Two

There was a pitch controversy at Northampton, with 30 wickets falling on the first two days and Derbyshire plummeting to 106 all out early on the third to lose by 180 runs. Umpires Tony Clarkson and Mike Harris reported the surface to Lord's on day one, but a pitch panel of David Hughes and Mike Denness ruled that the pitch was merely 'below average' at the end of the second day's play, a rating which meant no penalty points would be given to Northamptonshire. Derbyshire clearly thought their opponents had been let off the hook: Why? Kepler Wessels, the Northants director of cricket, had been quoted before the game saying that he hoped 'that the pitch will perform as we want it to'. Dry, and giving much assistance to the spinners from the start, it helped Derbyshire's young off spinner, Nathan Dumelow, to career-best match figures of 10 for 160. Northants' Jason Brown took seven wickets at negligible cost with his off breaks, while Graeme Swann's off spin proved the chief destroyer of the Derbyshire second innings. After seeing Swann return career-best figures of 7 for 33, the Derbyshire coach Adrian Pierson said: 'The pitch panel was a complete joke. This pitch was basically unfit, and there is total inequity from one panel to the next. It is unfair to everyone in our division.' Alan Fordham, the ECB cricket operations manager, countered: 'This pitch was borderline, not poor.' Whatever, Northants batted with greater assurance throughout – in large part due to innings of 60 and 57 from the powerful and prolific Phil Jaques. Only Dumelow, who added to the impression he made with the ball by thumping an unbeaten first-innings 52 from No. 9, took the fight to the Northants bowlers.

Yorkshire had the irrepressible fast bowler Steve Kirby to thank for their crushing ten-wicket win against Somerset at Taunton, their first championship success since April. Kirby, still uncapped by his county, took 5 for 74 and then an heroic 8 for 80 to make himself the proud possessor of the best match figures by a Yorkshire bowler since Raymond Illingworth claimed 14 for 64 against Gloucestershire at Harrogate 36 years previously.

On a blameless pitch, Kirby kicked things off by taking three early wickets with the new ball on the opening day – undermining the Somerset first innings by striking with the first, second and fifth balls of his third over. In Somerset's second innings, it was his burst of three wickets in 13 balls late on the third evening that kept Yorkshire on course for a morale-boosting win. Kirby's pace, bustling style and fiery temperament have sometimes incurred the wrath of opponents and umpires alike, but after completing his match haul of 13 for 154 Kirby said: 'I am not going to change. A lot of the time I don't say anything to batsmen. I just glare. Well, I'm not going to make a complete chop of myself!' Somerset only reached 275 in their first innings because Rob Turner dug in with an unbeaten 81 and was given fine late support by Steffan Jones (39) and last man Simon Francis, who contributed 44 to a tenth-wicket stand of 71.

Yorkshire, however, then amassed 512, with Matthew Wood making a career-best 207 and New Zealand captain Stephen Fleming joining him in an opening partnership of 165 while scoring a classy 98 himself. Andrew Gray helped Wood add a further 116 for the seventh wicket before accelerating on to 104, a maiden first-class hundred. At the end, after Wood and Fleming had dashed off the runs required for victory, the only irritant for Yorkshire was the docking of a quarter of a point for a slow over rate!

Gloucestershire might well have beaten Hampshire on a wearing pitch of increasingly uneven bounce at Southampton, but for the loss to the weather of the last day's morning session. As it was, Shaun Udal held on for more than an hour to guide Hampshire to a draw at 161 for 7, after they had been set 283 in 55 overs. It was rough luck on

The inimitable Steve Kirby winds it up again for Yorkshire.

Gloucestershire, who had fought back strongly in their second innings, through centuries from Phil Weston and Jonty Rhodes, after being bowled out on day one for just 185 and then seeing Hampshire move into a 145-run first-innings lead. High-class swing bowling by Wasim Akram and Dimitri Mascarenhas, who shared six wickets, proved Gloucestershire's undoing first time around, but Weston's first ton for the county and Rhodes' unbeaten 151 (he reached his century with a pull for six off Ed Giddins) stood the match on its head. Derek Kenway's first championship hundred for two years underpinned Hampshire's first-innings 330, with Simon Katich and Robin Smith both contributing worthy half-centuries. Ian Harvey, with four wickets in each innings, was Gloucestershire's most incisive bowler. One other incident of note: umpire Allan Jones found himself locked in the Rose Bowl on the second evening after deciding to share a fish and chip supper with his colleague, Alan Whitehead, who was sleeping in his mobile home inside the ground!

There was a draw, too, at Cardiff where Worcestershire were grateful for the loss of ten overs to the weather in the final session of the match. A hard-fought affair ended with Glamorgan reducing the visitors to 175 for 6 in their second innings after bouncing back from conceding a first-innings deficit of 58 to total 366 for 9 declared and set a target of 309. Michael Powell was the Glamorgan hero, scoring

two hundreds in a match for the first time in his career. His 125, which kept the first innings afloat, and 142 were his 12th and 13th first-class centuries, and he timed the ball far better than anyone else on view, despite the slowness of the surface.

Round Nine: 27–30 June 2003 Division Two

NORTHAMPTONSHIRE v. DERBYSHIRE – at Northampton

NORTHANTS	First Innings		Second Innings	
MEK Hussey (capt)	st Sutton b Dumelow	59	c Sutton b Dumelow	28
MJ Powell	b Dean	6	st Sutton b Welch	5
PA Jaques	c Di Venuto b Dumelow	60	lbw b Kaif	57
JW Cook	c Di Venuto b Dumelow	10	c Di Venuto b Dumelow	21
DJG Sales	c Di Venuto b Dumelow	20	lbw b Dumelow	33
GP Swann	b Wharton	0	c Cork b Welch	19
BJ Phillips	c Cork b Dumelow	4	lbw b Dumelow	4
*TMB Bailey	lbw b Wharton	9	run out	40
A Nel	not out	23	c Dean b Welch	23
MS Panesar	c Cork b Wharton	0	b Dumelow	1
JF Brown	b Dumelow	2	not out	2
Extras	b 8, lb 2	10	b 6, lb 4	10
	(64.4 overs)	203	(69 overs)	243

Bowling
Welch 7–3–23–0. Dean 8–2–18–1. Lungley 0–15–0. Wharton 24–7–50–4. Dumelow 23.4–4–82–5.
Welch 17–3–55–3. Wharton 20–4–70–0. Dumelow 23–2–78–5. Dean 5–2–9–0. Kaif 4–1–21–1.
Fall of Wickets 1–36, 2–116, 3–127, 4–161, 5–161, 6–161, 7–172, 8–180, 9–184, 10–203
1–19, 2–60, 3–100, 4–124, 5–168, 6–174, 7–174, 8–204, 9–209, 10–243

DERBYSHIRE	First Innings		Second Innings	
AI Gait	run out	7	(2) c Swann b Brown	29
MJ Di Venuto	c Powell b Nel	10	(1) lbw b Brown	29
CWG Bassano	lbw b Brown	1	not out	17
M Kaif	c Swann b Nel	28	c Sales b Swann	0
*LD Sutton	c St Bailey b Panesar	25	lbw b Brown	2
DG Cork (capt)	b Brown	16	c Jaques b Swann	3
G Welch	st Bailey b Brown	0	c Hussey b Swann	7
T Lungley	c Swann b Brown	7	c Bailey b Swann	0
NRC Dumelow	not out	52	b Swann	11
KJ Dean	c Jaques b Nel	3	c Panesar b Swann	3
LJ Wharton	b Nel	1	c Panesar b Swann	1
Extras	b 4, lb 6	10	b 1, lb 4	5
	(53 overs)	160	(47.1 overs)	106

Bowling
Nel 17–1–52–4. Phillips 3–1–8–0. Brown 23–6–39–4. Panesar 10–2–51–1.
Nel 6–1–19–0. Phillips 5–0–19–0. Brown 21–5–30–3. Swann 15.1–2–33–7.
Fall of Wickets 1–13, 2–18, 3–22, 4–60, 5–81, 6–87, 7–97, 8–141, 9–150, 10–160
1–57, 2–58, 3–61, 4–72, 5–75, 6–85, 7–85, 8–99, 9–103, 10–106

*Northamptonshire beat Derbyshire by 180 runs –
Northamptonshire (18pts), Derbyshire (3pts)*

SOMERSET v. YORKSHIRE – at Taunton

SOMERSET	First Innings		Second Innings	
PD Bowler	c Fleming b Silverwood	0	c Yuvraj Singh b Kirby	58
MI Wood	c Yuvraj Singh b Kirby	16	c White b Silverwood	1
JDC Bryant	b Kirby	7	c Fleming b Yuvraj Singh	45
J Cox	lbw b Kirby	0	lbw b Kirby	39
M Burns (capt)	lbw b Kirby	0	c White b Kirby	39
ID Blackwell	c Guy b Silverwood	19	c Guy b Kirby	23
*RJ Turner	not out	81	c Yuvraj Singh b Kirby	4
AW Laraman	b Sidebottom	36	not out	39
NAM McLean	c Yuvraj Singh b Silverwood	5	c Gray b Kirby	35
PS Jones	b Kirby	39	b Kirby	0
SRG Francis	c Wood b Sidebottom	44	c Yuvraj Singh b Kirby	6
Extras	lb 11, w 1, nb 16	28	lb 8, w 4, w 2, nb 6	17
	(67 overs)	275	(83.4 overs)	306

Bowling
Silverwood 14–3–46–3. Sidebottom 18–3–74–2. Gray 8–1–34–0. White 9–1–21–0. Lumb 2–0–15–0.
Silverwood 15–6–76–1. Kirby 24.4–5–80–8. White 5–0–27–0. Sidebottom 18–3–49–0. Gray 10–3–22–0. Yuvraj Singh 11–1–43–1.
Fall of Wickets 1–70, 2–19, 3–19, 4–19, 5–40, 6–64, 7–137, 8–144, 9–204, 10–275
1–11, 2–98, 3–128, 4–191, 5–194, 6–210, 7–236, 8–296, 9–296, 10–306

YORKSHIRE	First Innings		Second Innings	
MJ Wood (capt)	c Bowler b Francis	207	not out	30
SP Fleming	c Jones b Blackwell	98	not out	40
Yuvraj Singh	c Burns b McLean	5		
MJ Lumb	c Turner b McLean	5		
RJ Blakey	c Turner b Francis	13		
C White	run out	6		
*SM Guy	c Bowler b McLean	16		
AKD Gray	c Cox b Francis	104		
CEW Silverwood	b Jones	22		
RJ Sidebottom	b Blackwell	16		
SP Kirby	not out	0		
Extras	lb 10, w 2, nb 8	20	lb 1	1
	(128.2 overs)	512	(no wkt, 13 overs)	71

Bowling
McLean 25–5–87–3. Francis 28.2–3–111–3. Laraman 23–4–82–0. Jones 22–1–135–1. Burns 3–1–14–0. Blackwell 3–0–27–0.
McLean 4–1–22–0. Francis 6–2–18–0. Jones 3–0–30–0.
Fall of Wickets 1–165, 2–176, 3–188, 4–219, 5–254, 6–297, 7–413, 8–483, 9–512, 10–512

*Yorkshire beat Somerset by 10 wickets – Yorkshire (22pts),
Somerset (5pts)*

HAMPSHIRE v. GLOUCESTERSHIRE – at Southampton

GLOS	First Innings		Second Innings	
CM Spearman (capt)	b Wasim Akram	4	(2) c Pothas b Giddins	20
WPC Weston	c Pothas b Mascarenhas	39	(1) c Pothas b Giddins	100
CG Taylor	lbw b Giddins	24	(4) c Smith b Udal	31
JN Rhodes	lbw b Giddins	11	(5) not out	151
MGN Windows	c Pothas b Wasim Akram	3	(6) lbw b Mascarenhas	40
APR Gidman	b Mullally	16	(7) c Pothas b Mascarenhas	17
IJ Harvey	c Katich b Mascarenhas	20	(8) b Udal	10
MCJ Ball	b Mullally	4	(9) st Pothas b Katich	7
*SP Pope	c Smith b Wasim Akram	14	(10) run out	14
J Lewis	c Smith b Mascarenhas	14	(11) c Pothas b Wasim Akram	26
AM Smith	not out	7	(3) b Mascarenhas	0
Extras	b 4, lb 16, w 1, nb 8	29	b 3, lb 9, w 5	17
	(66.5 overs)	185	(129.4 overs)	427

Bowling
Wasim Akram 16.5–8–31–3. Giddins 14–2–41–2. Mascarenhas 19–7–48–3. Mullally 17–6–45–2.
Wasim Akram 24.3–5–71–1. Giddins 21–5–79–2. Mullally 9.1–1–34–0. Mascarenhas 29–12–79–3. Udal 25–6–84–2. Katich 16–4–44–1. Kendall 5 1 20 0.
Fall of Wickets 1–14, 2–70, 3–90, 4–99, 5–99, 6–140, 7–144, 8–146, 9–177, 10–185
1–41, 2–50, 3–112, 4–208, 5–283, 6–314, 7–345, 8–372, 9–382, 10–427

HAMPSHIRE	First Innings		Second Innings	
DA Kenway	b Ball	115	c Taylor b Harvey	12
JP Crawley (capt)	b Lewis	15	b Harvey	5
SM Katich	b Gidman	61	c Pope b Harvey	52
RA Smith	b Gidman	50	lbw b Ball	16
WS Kendall	lbw b Harvey	22	c Windows b Harvey	2
*N Pothas	b Lewis	21	c Windows b Ball	14
AD Mascarenhas	c Pope b Harvey	21	c Taylor b Ball	29
SD Udal	c Rhodes b Smith	5	not out	16
Wasim Akram	b Harvey	0	not out	4
AD Mullally	b Harvey	0		
ESH Giddins	b Harvey	0		
Extras	b 6, lb 16, w 4	26	b 1, lb 7, w 1, nb 2	11
	(96.2 overs)	330	(7 wkts, 55 overs)	161

Bowling
Lewis 25–7–86–2. Smith 21–12–44–1. Harvey 18.2–2–73–4. Ball 17–2–65–1.
Lewis 12–1–49–0. Harvey 16–8–43–4. Smith 8–3–25–0. Gidman 1–0–12–0. Ball 18–9–24–3.
Fall of Wickets 1–29, 2–162, 3–247, 4–260, 5–299, 6–311, 7–330, 8–330, 9–330, 10–330
1–10, 2–31, 3–58, 4–87, 5–110, 6–112, 7–149

Match drawn – Hampshire (10pts), Gloucestershire (7pts)

GLAMORGAN v. WORCESTERSHIRE – at Cardiff

GLAMORGAN	First Innings		Second Innings	
A Dale	lbw b Hayward	10	c Batty b Mason	1
J Hughes	lbw b Mason	1	c Kadeer Ali b Batty	41
DL Hemp	c Adshead b Mason	15	run out	63
MJ Powell	b Hayward	125	c Adshead b Kemp	142
MP Maynard	c Kemp b Mason	9	b Kemp	0
*MA Wallace	c Moore b Kemp	9	c Adshead b Kemp	3
RDB Croft (capt)	run out	36	b Khalid	17
DS Harrison	c Moore b Hayward	11	lbw b Kemp	4
MS Kasprowicz	b Mason	19	b Kemp	35
AG Wharf	not out	17	not out	32
DA Cosker	not out	2	not out	1
Extras	b 2, lb 21, w 1, nb 2	26	b 14, lb 7, w 2, nb 4	27
	(78.2 overs)	270	(9 wkts, 108 overs)	366

Bowling
Hayward 21.2–4–71–4. Mason 21–7–69–4. Kemp 13–2–40–1. Batty 17–4–47–0. Khalid 6–0–20–0.
Hayward 19–2–74–0. Mason 20–4–69–1. Kemp 17–0–48–5. Batty 30 6–100–1. Khalid 22–7–54–1.
Fall of Wickets 1–3, 2–31, 4–75, 5–103, 6–187, 7–210, 8–251, 9–251, 10–270
1–9, 2–60, 3–208, 4–209, 5–217, 6–281, 7–291, 8–300, 9–364

WORCS	First Innings		Second Innings	
SD Peters	c Wallace b Kasprowicz	2	c Hughes b Croft	32
A Singh	c Hemp b Kasprowicz	38	lbw b Kasprowicz	0
Kadeer Ali	b Kasprowicz	15	b Kasprowicz	53
BF Smith (capt)	c Cosker	32	c and b Cosker	44
JR Kemp	b Wharf	14	lbw b Kasprowicz	3
SC Moore	c Hemp b Harrison	24	not out	28
GJ Batty	c Hughes b Croft	49	st Wallace b Cosker	2
*SJ Adshead	c Kasprowicz b Wharf	63	not out	3
MS Mason	b Cosker	52		
SA Khalid	lbw b Wharf	13		
M Hayward	not out	0		
Extras	b 2, lb 8, w 5, nb 6	21	b 5, lb 2, w 1, nb 2	10
	(97.5 overs)	328	(6 wkts, 79.4 overs)	175

Bowling
Kasprowicz 21–5–38–3. Wharf 16.5–1–76–3. Harrison 10–3–23–1. Cosker 19–1–56–2. Croft 28–4–99–1. Batty 6–0–20–0.
Kasprowicz 16–4–35–3. Harrison 11–2–32–0. Croft 23.4–9–54–1. Cosker 19.7–3–42–2. Wharf 10–4–13–0.
Fall of Wickets 1–12, 2–58, 3–59, 4–85, 5–135, 6–135, 7–207, 8–291, 9–323, 10–328
1–3, 2–53, 3–104, 4–110, 5–153, 6–165

Match drawn – Glamorgan (9pts), Worcestershire (10pts)

ROUND TEN: 2–5 JULY 2003

Division One

Surrey went 26 points clear at the top of the Division One table when Kent gambled and lost at The Oval. Much to the disgust of Sussex and Lancashire, the main challengers for Surrey's crown, Kent captain David Fulton gave up a position of strength on day three to allow Surrey back into a game in which they were being batted out of. In short, Fulton decided that the best way his side could win was to do a deal with Surrey that would ultimately leave his own team needing to score 301 in 90 overs on the final day. Instead, they were bowled out for just 114, with Jimmy Ormond striking twice with the new ball before spinners Saqlain Mushtaq, taking 4 for 27 to move past 700 first-class victims, and Ian Salisbury (3 for 11) wrapped things up. Fulton defended his decision, citing the fact that Kent were second from bottom in the table and that they needed to be proactive in their quest to preserve their Division One status. He also said that his side aimed 'to play with no fear'. Yet Kent were rolling along comfortably on 352 for 5 when Fulton declared their first innings just 49 runs behind Surrey. They had Matthew Walker unbeaten on 82 and Geraint Jones equally secure on 38 and they still had plenty of time

to build a sizeable lead and then put pressure on the Surrey batsmen on the final afternoon. Kent, too, were only nine points adrift of sixth-placed Middlesex, and would have surely gained a fifth and final batting bonus point, as well as guaranteeing themselves the four points available for a draw, if they had batted on. All in all, it was a little puzzling – and tended to overshadow the fine batting earlier in the game by Surrey's Mark Butcher and Graham Thorpe – who added 138 together for the third wicket in the home side's total of 401 – and the Kent trio of Ed Smith, Walker and Andrew Symonds. Butcher, captaining Surrey in the absence of Adam Hollioake, whose father John had been taken ill, made 144. Smith, continuing his dazzling mid-summer form, stroked 135 from 177 balls. Kent's Rob Ferley and Ben Trott also deserved praise for sharing eight of Surrey's first-innings wickets.

A nip-and-tuck encounter at Grace Road ended with Leicestershire and Warwickshire sharing an honourable draw. The home side gained the early advantage, despite Waqar Younis hitting out from No. 10 to score 52 and lift Warwickshire's first innings from 167 for 8 to an all-out total of 253. Darren Maddy then joined John Maunders in a second-wicket partnership of 156 in 41 overs, with the left-handed Maunders' 64 being a maiden championship 50. Maddy went on to 98, while

---

Round Ten: 2–5 July 2003 Division One

SURREY v. KENT – at The Oval

SURREY	First Innings		Second Innings	
IJ Ward	c Fulton b Trott	33		
MA Butcher (capt)	c Jones b Trott	144	(1) c Smith b Carberry	90
MR Ramprakash	c Ealham b M Sami	6	(2) c Symonds b Trott	22
GP Thorpe	c Jones b Ferley	68	(3) c Jones b Ferley	46
AD Brown	c Symonds b Ferley	27	(4) not out	64
*AJ Stewart	c and b Ealham	1	(5) not out	25
AJ Tudor	c Ealham b Trott	18		
MP Bicknell	c Jones b Ferley	22		
IDK Salisbury	not out	34		
Saqlain Mushtaq	b Trott	4		
J Ormond	c Tredwell b Ferley	15		
Extras	b 5, lb 10, w 2, nb 12	29	b 2, lb 2	4
	(95.2 overs)	401	(3 wkts, 47.2 overs)	251

Bowling
M Sami 22-3-83-1. Trott 18-5-73-4. Ealham 21-3-67-1. Symonds 10-0-55-0. Tredwell 8-1-32-0. Ferley 16.2-0-76-4.
M Sami 3-0-10-0. Trott 7-0-37-1. Tredwell 6-2-35-0. Ferley 11.2-2-53-1. Carberry 8-0-45-1. Symonds 5-0-28-0. Walker 4-0-25-0. Smith 3-1-14-0.
Fall of Wickets 1-73, 2-105, 3-243, 4-293, 5-305, 6-305, 7-336, 8-355, 9-359, 10-401
1-72, 2-130, 3-208

KENT	First Innings		Second Innings	
DP Fulton (capt)	lbw b Bicknell	14	b Ormond	11
MA Carberry	c Stewart b Saqlain Mushtaq	16	c Stewart b Saqlain Mushtaq	24
ET Smith	c Brown b Salisbury	135	c Butcher b Ormond	0
A Symonds	c Butcher b Bicknell	53	c Salisbury b Tudor	30
MJ Walker	not out	82	c Stewart b Saqlain Mushtaq	7
MA Ealham	c Thorpe b Ormond	5	c Butcher b Saqlain Mushtaq	5
*GO Jones	not out	38	c Saqlain Mushtaq b Salisbury	8
JC Tredwell			lbw b Salisbury	2
RS Ferley			b Saqlain Mushtaq	0
M Sami			lbw b Salisbury	0
BJ Trott			not out	9
Extras	b 1, lb 5, w 1, nb 2	9	lb 1	1
	(5 wkts, 95 overs)	352	(49.4 overs)	114

Bowling
Bicknell 18-4-65-2. Ormond 16-4-60-1. Saqlain Mushtaq 23-5-63-1. Salisbury 29-5-111-1. Tudor 8-1-47-0. Butcher 1-1-0-0.
Bicknell 11-5-26-0. Ormond 9-3-23-2. Tudor 10-2-26-1. Saqlain Mushtaq 14-5-27-4. Salisbury 5.4-1-11-3.
Fall of Wickets 1-25, 2-40, 3-151, 4-275, 5-286
1-21, 2-21, 3-61, 4-67, 5-73, 6-78, 7-92, 8-94, 9-95, 10-114

Surrey beat Kent by 186 runs –
Surrey (20pts), Kent (7pts)

LEICESTERSHIRE v. WARWICKSHIRE – at Leicester

WARWICKSHIRE	First Innings		Second Innings	
MJ Powell (capt)	b DeFreitas	0	lbw b DeFreitas	11
NV Knight	b Whiley	66	(5) c Sehwag b DeFreitas	33
MA Wagh	c Sehwag b Masters	35	c Nixon b DeFreitas	138
IR Bell	lbw b Masters	0	run out	93
IJL Trott	b Maddy	23	(2) lbw b Dagnall	9
*T Frost	c Nixon b Masters	11	c DeFreitas b Masters	17
DR Brown	c Sehwag b Whiley	5	lbw b DeFreitas	5
NMK Smith	c Hodge b Masters	4	c Stevens b DeFreitas	8
MM Betts	c Hodge b Masters	20	not out	16
Waqar Younis	c Stevens b Snape	52	b DeFreitas	0
A Richardson	not out	16	c Snape b Masters	10
Extras	b 6, lb 8, w 1, nb 6	21	b 4, lb 8, w 3, nb 6	21
	(75 overs)	253	(99.5 overs)	361

Bowling
DeFreitas 13-9-22-1. Dagnall 12-3-46-0. Whiley 17-3-76-2. Masters 17-4-53-5. Maddy 12-3-36-1. Snape 3-0-5-1. Sehwag 1-0-1-0.
DeFreitas 31-10-78-6. Dagnall 19-5-60-1. Masters 14.5-3-60-2. Maddy 9-1-32-0. Whiley 10-1-49-0. Maunders 3-1-10-0. Stevens 3-0-15-0. Snape 4-1-20-0. Hodge 3-0-19-0. Sehwag 3-1-9-0.
Fall of Wickets 1-0, 2-78, 3-78, 4-120, 5-142, 6-146, 7-154, 8-167, 9-193, 10-253
1-16, 2-20, 3-244, 4-300, 5-305, 6-317, 7-331, 8-336, 9-336, 10-361

LEICESTERSHIRE	First Innings		Second Innings	
JK Maunders	c Frost b Betts	64	b Waqar Younis	2
V Sehwag	b Betts	30	b Richardson	40
DL Maddy	lbw b Waqar Younis	98	st Frost b Waqar Younis	80
BJ Hodge	lbw b Bell	7	b Richardson	128
DI Stevens	b Betts	7	lbw b Richardson	4
*PA Nixon	c sub b Brown	11	run out	36
JN Snape	lbw b Brown	4	not out	5
PAJ DeFreitas (capt)	c Wagh b Betts	45	not out	6
DD Masters	lbw b Brown	0		
CE Dagnall	run out	23		
MJA Whiley	not out	0		
Extras	b 7, lb 15, nb 17	39	b 2, lb 13, nb 6	21
	(88.2 overs)	328	(6 wkts, 60.3 overs)	241

Bowling
Waqar Younis 22-2-75-1. Betts 21.2-1-88-4. Richardson 21-6-44-0. Brown 18-3-53-3. Smith 4-0-36-0. Bell 2-1-10-1.
Waqar Younis 9-1-60-2. Betts 12-2-53-0. Brown 13-2-47-0. Richardson 17-5-29-3. Bell 8-0-33-0. Smith 1.3-0-4-0.
Fall of Wickets 1-42, 2-198, 3-215, 4-232, 5-234, 6-244, 7-259, 8-267, 9-328, 10-328
1-2, 2-20, 3-77, 4-93, 5-223, 6-230

Match drawn – Leicestershire (10pts), Warwickshire (9pts)

ESSEX v. LANCASHIRE – at Chelmsford

LANCASHIRE	First Innings		Second Innings	
JJ Haynes	b Brant	12	c Foster b Brant	0
AJ Swann	lbw b Brant	7	lbw b Napier	16
MB Loye	c Grayson b Dakin	5	b Brant	0
SG Law	c ten Doeschate b Brant	80	c Foster b Brant	4
MJ Chilton	c Foster b Brant	0	c Foster b Middlebrook	70
CL Hooper	b Dakin	18	c Grayson b Middlebrook	50
G Chapple	lbw b Middlebrook	31	not out	132
CP Schofield	not out	35	c Middlebrook b Dakin	38
*WK Hegg (capt)	lbw b Dakin	6	not out	61
PJ Martin	lbw b Middlebrook	12		
SI Mahmood	b Middlebrook	3		
Extras	lb 6, w 1	7	lb 8, w 2, nb 2	12
	(67.2 overs)	218	(7 wkts, 100 overs)	383

Bowling
Brant 18-7-39-4. Dakin 16-2-55-3. Napier 12-3-40-0. ten Doeschate 5-1-27-0. Middlebrook 15.2-2-47-3. Grayson 1-0-4-0.
Brant 18-3-67-3. Dakin 27-6-97-1. Napier 14-2-43-1. ten Doeschate 9-1-42-0. Middlebrook 28-3-93-2. Grayson 9-0-33-0.
Fall of Wickets 1-11, 2-22, 3-30, 4-34, 5-66, 6-148, 7-168, 8-179, 9-212, 10-218
1-1, 2-3, 3-13, 4-30, 5-109, 6-188, 7-252

ESSEX	First Innings		Second Innings	
AP Grayson	b Martin	0	lbw b Mahmood	17
N Hussain	c Haynes b Chapple	54	lbw b Hooper	31
*JS Foster	c Haynes b Martin	0	c Martin b Hooper	5
A Flower	lbw b Hooper	46	c Law b Hooper	49
A Habib	b Chapple	19	c Law b Hooper	69
RC Irani (capt)	b Martin	19	b Chapple	9
JD Middlebrook	c and b Schofield	9	c Hegg b Hooper	21
JM Dakin	c Schofield b Martin	18	lbw b Schofield	3
GR Napier	c Hegg b Hooper	5	not out	0
RN ten Doeschate	st Hegg b Hooper	6	c Swann b Hooper	5
SA Brant	not out	1	not out	1
Extras	b 2, lb 4, w 1, nb 24	31	b 7, lb 1, nb 18	26
	(61.5 overs)	208	(9 wkts, 88 overs)	236

Bowling
Martin 21-8-60-4. Chapple 13-3-44-2. Mahmood 10-1-67-0. Hooper 16.5-7-30-3. Schofield 1-0-1-1.
Martin 18-4-50-0. Chapple 19-3-58-1. Mahmood 9-2-39-1. Hooper 32-13-51-6. Schofield 10-2-30-1.
Fall of Wickets 1-0, 2-90, 3-128, 4-128, 5-162, 6-170, 7-177, 8-196, 9-202, 10-208
1-29, 2-56, 3-57, 4-170, 5-195, 6-219, 7-230, 8-230, 9-235

Match drawn – Essex (8pts),
Lancashire (8pts)

Ed Smith of Kent: his dazzling summer form continued with an innings of 135 against Surrey.

Phil DeFreitas' late fling boosted Leicestershire's reply to 328. Then came the Warwickshire fightback, however, with Mark Wagh anchoring the second innings with a determined 138 and Ian Bell including two sixes to midwicket off Jeremy Snape in an innings cut short on 93 only when he was run out by a direct hit from Virender Sehwag. Wagh and Bell put on 224 for the third wicket, but DeFreitas in particular was not giving up. The veteran seamer's 6 for 78 left Leicestershire needing 287 from what turned out to be 61 overs, and much depended on the explosive Sehwag. The Indian Test star, though, first had to see Leicestershire past a tricky start after they had fallen to 20 for 2, and was then dismissed for 40 before he could do any real damage. Brad Hodge did his best to maintain the chase, hitting a superb 128 and being joined by Paul Nixon in a fifth-wicket stand of 130. Victory, however, remained tantalizingly out of reach.

At Chelmsford, there was only one team to blame for Lancashire's failure to see off Essex … and that was Lancashire. Bewilderingly, they batted on pointlessly for fully 50 minutes on the final morning before declaring their second innings at 383 for 7. That set Essex 394 to win in 88 overs, yet their overnight lead had already been 337. As it was, Essex declined to 236 for 9, despite a fourth-wicket alliance of 113 between Andy Flower and Aftab Habib, before last pair Graham Napier and Scott Brant held on for a draw. It was all a great shame for Lancashire, who had earned themselves a narrow ten-run first-innings advantage by bowling out Essex for 208 – largely through the efforts of Peter Martin and Carl Hooper – and then recovering spiritedly from 30 for 4 in their second innings to reach their position of great strength on the final day. Mark Chilton, with 70, led that recovery alongside

Hooper, before Glen Chapple underlined his mid-career elevation to all-rounder status by completing a fluent hundred just before the close of the third day. Warren Hegg's decision on the fourth morning to bat on allowed himself to reach an unbeaten 61, and Chapple 132 not out, but to come away with just four extra points for the draw, rather than the 14 available for winning, would have made the Lancashire captain curse more than once on the long journey home. Stuart Law, meanwhile, in his first championship appearance back at Chelmsford since his acrimonious departure from Essex, hit 80 on the first day. James Foster, dismissed for a duck just before the end of play on that opening day, was later fined £400 by Essex, and reprimanded for verbally abusing a spectator as he left the field.

Division Two

Durham's brave effort to beat high-flying Worcestershire on their own New Road patch was undone when Gary Pratt was given out caught at the wicket off Matt Mason for a superb 85. It proved the beginning of the end for Durham who, before that decision, were cruising along on 229 for 5 in search of a victory target of 297. With Mason going on to take career-best figures of 6 for 68, and Gareth Batty also bowling well to return 4 for 78, Worcestershire could even afford to watch last pair Steve Harmison and Liam Plunkett add a defiant 22 at the end before wrapping up a 31-run win. The home side also owed a big debt of gratitude to the batting of their skipper, Ben Smith, whose innings of 73 and 60 did much to counter the twin pace threat of Harmison and Shoaib Akhtar, Pakistan's 'Rawalpindi Express' who was making his championship debut for Durham. Harmison, released from England's one-day squad, responded to the chance of actually playing some cricket by picking up four good wickets in Worcestershire's first-innings total of 218. Only Vince Wells, however, held up the Worcestershire attack for long as Durham collapsed in reply to 120, and despite two wickets apiece for Harmison and Shoaib the home side's second innings of 198 meant that Durham faced a difficult task as they set out to make by far the highest total of the match to win. Jon Lewis kicked them off with a gutsy half-century and the promising Pratt took up the baton with relish until the umpire's fateful finger went up to end his, and Durham's, quest for glory.

Craig White and Ryan Sidebottom, with a little bit of help from Steve Kirby and Michael Lumb, spearheaded Yorkshire's ten-wicket victory over Derbyshire at Derby. Lumb was joined at the crease by White with Yorkshire wobbling on 78 for 4 on the first morning, but their partnership of 195 set the tone for the match. When Lumb departed for 93, the stage was White's alone until the end of the innings at 444. Last man Kirby had by then scored 33, too, to help White add a further 96 and take his own individual tally to a brilliant unbeaten 173. Graeme Welch battled hard with the ball to take 6 for 102, but Derbyshire's brittleness with the bat was fully exposed by Sidebottom. Kirby's three wickets in eight balls hastened the home team's decline to 80 for 8 by the close of the second day, and only a defiant 60 not out by Nathan Dumelow – which included three sixes – enabled them to reach 128 the following morning. Sidebottom, though, took the last two wickets to finish with 6 for 38, and the long-haired, left-arm paceman then added three more second-innings wickets. So did Kirby, although Derbyshire did at least display considerably more fight after they had been asked to follow on. Michael Di Venuto, Mohammad Kaif and Welch all passed the half-century mark to take the match well into the final day. An unbeaten 30 from No. 11 Kevin Dean, and more resistance from Dumelow, forced Yorkshire to bat again, but their second win on the trot took them into second place in the division.

A career-best 38 from Jason Brown, one of the game's natural No. 11s, proved the crucial contribution to Northamptonshire's eventual seven-wicket win over Hampshire at Northampton. Brown lifted his first-class batting average above seven as he figured in a remarkable last-wicket stand of 77 with

Round Ten: 2–5 July 2003 Division Two

WORCESTERSHIRE v. DURHAM – at Worcester

WORCS	First Innings		Second Innings	
SD Peters	c Mustard b Harmison	0	run out	0
A Singh	b Harmison	15	c Mustard b Shoaib Akhtar	8
Kadeer Ali	b Harmison	35	b Harmison	13
BF Smith (capt)	b Phillips	73	c Pratt b Plunkett	60
JM Kemp	c Mustard b Shoaib Akhtar	32	lbw b Harmison	5
SC Moore	c Mustard b Harmison	28	b Plunkett	17
GJ Batty	c Wells b Plunkett	11	lbw b Shoaib Akhtar	16
*SJ Adshead	c and b Phillips	5	c Mustard b Plunkett	31
MS Mason	c Mustard b Harmison	0	c Mustard b Phillips	27
MA Harrity	not out	0	not out	5
M Hayward	c Love b Phillips	2	c Wells b Phillips	0
Extras	b 5, lb 5, w 5, nb 2	17	b 8, lb 3, nb 6	17
	(56 overs)	218	(51.5 overs)	198

Bowling
Shoaib Akhtar 13-5-28-1. Harmison 13-3-50-4. Wells 6-1-35-0. Plunkett 13-4-55-2. Phillips 11-1-40-3.
Shoaib Akhtar 13-2-33-2. Harmison 14-3-53-2. Plunkett 13-0-61-3. Phillips 11.5-2-40-2.
Fall of Wickets 1-7, 2-16, 3-93, 4-135, 5-188, 6-207, 7-212, 8-212, 9-216, 10-218
1-5, 2-17, 3-21, 4-41, 5-86, 6-110, 7-127, 8-188, 9-198, 10-198

DURHAM	First Innings		Second Innings	
JJB Lewis (capt)	lbw b Hayward	0	b Batty	53
MA Gough	c Adshead b Mason	4	c Adshead b Mason	26
ML Love	c Adshead b Mason	28	c Peters b Mason	0
GJ Pratt	b Harrity	23	c Adshead b Mason	85
GJ Muchall	b Harrity	3	c Peters b Mason	11
VJ Wells	c Adshead b Mason	36	b Batty	18
*P Mustard	c Batty b Harrity	7	b Batty	20
LE Plunkett	c Peters b Kemp	3	(9) not out	15
NC Phillips	b Kemp	0	(10) c Kemp b Mason	8
Shoaib Akhtar	c Kemp b Harrity	6	(8) c Kemp b Batty	2
SJ Harmison	not out	5	c Batty b Mason	10
Extras	lb 1, w 1, nb 4	6	b 1, lb 9, w 1, nb 6	17
	(45.1 overs)	120	(85.4 overs)	265

Bowling
Hayward 4.5-2-10-1. Mason 16-3-48-3. Kemp 8.1-2-15-2. Harrity 11.1-2-39-4. Batty 5-1-7-0.
Mason 30.4-6-68-6. Kemp 15-5-41-0. Harrity 14-1-68-0. Batty 26-4-78-4.
Fall of Wickets 1-0, 2-6, 3-42, 4-50, 5-84, 6-100, 7-106, 8-108, 9-114, 10-120
1-53, 2-53, 3-120, 4-149, 5-195, 6-229, 7-229, 8-234, 9-243, 10-265

Worcestershire beat Durham by 31 runs – Worcestershire (18pts), Durham (3pts)

DERBYSHIRE v. YORKSHIRE – at Derby

YORKSHIRE	First Innings		Second Innings	
MJ Wood (capt)	c Bassano b Welch	35	not out	21
SP Fleming	lbw b Welch	13	not out	42
Yuvraj Singh	lbw b Cork	6		
MJ Lumb	c Kaif b Welch	93		
RJ Blakey	lbw b Dean	0		
C White	not out	173		
*SM Guy	lbw b Welch	0		
AKD Gray	c Sutton b Welch	14		
TT Bresnan	c Sutton b Welch	19		
RJ Sidebottom	c Bassano b Dean	2		
SP Kirby	c Di Venuto b Lungley	33		
Extras	b 5, lb 14, w 3, nb 34	56	lb 3, nb 2	5
	(130.4 overs)	444	(no wkt, 20.3 overs)	68

Bowling
Dean 36-7-113-2. Welch 41-13-102-6. Cork 15-5-34-1. Lungley 16.4-1-84-1.
Dumelow 21-3-90-0. Hewson 1-0-2-0.
Cork 7-0-20-0. Dean 7-3-12-0. Welch 3.3-0-20-0. Dumelow 3-0-13-0.
Fall of Wickets 1-25, 2-44, 3-75, 4-78, 5-273, 6-273, 7-299, 8-339, 9-348, 10-444

DERBYSHIRE	First Innings		Second Innings	
AI Gait	c Guy b Sidebottom	17	(2) c Gray b Bresnan	6
MJ Di Venuto	c Guy b Sidebottom	27	(1) c Yuvraj Singh b Sidebottom	74
CWG Bassano	lbw b Kirby	0	c White b Kirby	7
M Kaif	b Kirby	0	c Gray b Kirby	87
DR Hewson	c Fleming b Sidebottom	0	c sub b Gray	14
*LD Sutton	c Guy b Sidebottom	5	run out	35
DG Cork (capt)	lbw b Bresnan	1	c Sidebottom b Kirby	35
T Lungley	lbw b Sidebottom	6	lbw b Bresnan	1
G Welch	b Sidebottom	0	c Guy b Sidebottom	54
NRC Dumelow	not out	60	b Sidebottom	25
KJ Dean	b Sidebottom	0	not out	30
Extras	b 1, lb 9, nb 2	12	b 5, lb 11, p 5	21
	(42.4 overs)	128	(128.3 overs)	383

Bowling
Kirby 12-5-31-3. Sidebottom 13.4-6-38-6. Bresnan 9-4-21-1. Gray 7-1-25-0.
Yuvraj Singh 1-0-10-0.
Kirby 30-5-85-3. Sidebottom 22.3-5-73-3. Bresnan 25-5-63-2. Gray 43-10-125-1. White 7-2-16-0. Yuvraj Singh 1-1-0-0.
Fall of Wickets 1-33, 2-33, 3-35, 4-47, 5-52, 6-55, 7-55, 8-55, 9-128, 10-128
1-38, 2-71, 3-106, 4-115, 5-201, 6-250, 7-257, 8-263, 9-315, 10-383

Yorkshire beat Derbyshire by 10 wickets – Yorkshire (22pts), Derbyshire (3pts)

NORTHAMPTONSHIRE v. HAMPSHIRE – at Northampton

HAMPSHIRE	First Innings		Second Innings	
DA Kenway	c Wright b Cawdron	0	c Sales b Cawdron	3
JP Crawley (capt)	c Sales b Cawdron	21	lbw b Wright	16
SM Katich	c Jaques b Cawdron	11	lbw b Brown	36
RA Smith	c Bailey b Phillips	41	b Wright	28
JD Francis	c Bailey b Swann	8	c Powell b Cawdron	36
WS Kendall	c Kenway b Mascarenhas	4	lbw b Phillips	3
*N Pothas	c Sales b Wright	0	lbw b Swann	5
AD Mascarenhas	c Hussey b Swann	11	c Cook b Swann	14
SD Udal	c Bailey b Swann	12	c Bailey b Wright	6
JTA Bruce	c Powell b Brown	4	not out	1
JA Tomlinson	not out	0	b 2, lb 1	
Extras	lb 2, nb 6	8	b 2, lb 1	3
	(69.4 overs)	125	(72.2 overs)	179

Bowling
Wright 16-6-33-2. Cawdron 13-5-25-3. Phillips 6-2-27-1. Brown 15-5-27-1. Swann 3.1-0-11-3.
Wright 16.2-5-38-3. Cawdron 19-7-58-3. Phillips 10-6-15-2. Swann 12-3-24-1. Brown 15-3-41-1.
Fall of Wickets 1-7, 2-23, 3-83, 4-84, 5-94, 6-94, 7-107, 8-114, 9-125, 10-125
1-19, 2-19, 3-71, 4-89, 5-92, 6-100, 7-151, 8-171, 9-174, 10-179

NORTHANTS	First Innings		Second Innings	
MEK Hussey (capt)	c Pothas b Bruce	4	(2) lbw b Tomlinson	18
MJ Powell	c Kendall b Bruce	0	(1) not out	38
PA Jaques	lbw b Mascarenhas	15	c Pothas b Tomlinson	0
JW Cook	c Kenway b Mascarenhas	1	c Katich b Tomlinson	25
MJ Cawdron	c Pothas b Mascarenhas	24		
DJG Sales	c Pothas b Mascarenhas	6	(5) not out	5
GP Swann	c Katich b Mascarenhas	10		
DG Wright	c Pothas b Mascarenhas	46		
*TMB Bailey	lbw b Bruce	11		
BJ Phillips	not out	48		
JF Brown	lbw b Udal	38		
Extras	b 2, lb 4, nb 10	16	lb 1	1
	(91.4 overs)	218	(3 wkts, 20.4 overs)	87

Bowling
Mascarenhas 25-6-55-6. Bruce 21-6-72-3. Udal 16.4-4-49-1. Tomlinson 6-1-35-0. Katich 1-0-1-0.
Mascarenhas 6-1-18-0. Bruce 5-0-24-0. Tomlinson 5-0-37-3. Udal 4.4-0-7-0.
Fall of Wickets 1-0, 2-5, 3-8, 4-21, 5-35, 6-51, 7-72, 8-116, 9-141, 10-218
1-44, 2-44, 3-72

Northamptonshire beat Hampshire by 7 wickets – Northamptonshire (18pts), Hampshire (3pts)

SOMERSET v. GLOUCESTERSHIRE – at Taunton

GLOS	First Innings		Second Innings	
CM Spearman	b McLean	54	(2) lbw b McLean	3
WPC Weston	c Gazzard b Laraman	19	(1) b Laraman	179
CG Taylor	c Turner b Francis	23	c Cox b McLean	0
JN Rhodes	c Turner b Laraman	50	c Turner b Burns	49
MGN Windows	c Turner b Laraman	19	c Turner b Laraman	89
MW Alleyne (capt)	b Burns	10	(7) lbw b McLean	29
IJ Harvey	c Gazzard b McLean	28	(6) not out	128
MCJ Ball	lbw b Burns	0	c Dutch b Suppiah	6
*SP Pope	c Turner b Burns	8	c Cox b Dutch	7
J Lewis	c Cox b McLean	5	st Turner b Dutch	14
AM Smith	not out	0	not out	8
Extras	lb 8, nb 2	12	b 6, lb 8, w 2, nb 14	30
	(61.4 overs)	228	(9 wkts, 158 overs)	611

Bowling
McLean 16-2-68-3. Francis 16-2-73-1. Laraman 18-8-44-3. Burns 11.4-4-35-3.
Francis 32-2-147-1. Burns 31-7-105-1. Dutch 28-7-60-2. McLean 30-2-139-3. Laraman 26-3-102-2. Suppiah 11-1-44-1.
Fall of Wickets 1-57, 2-83, 3-127, 4-172, 5-175, 6-197, 7-209, 8-213, 9-222, 10-228
1-37, 2-41, 3-117, 4-315, 5-368, 6-436, 7-576, 8-584, 9-600

SOMERSET	First Innings		Second Innings	
MJ Wood	c Ball b Harvey	10	not out	49
CM Gazzard	b Smith	2	b Smith	4
JDC Bryant	c Pope b Smith	29	lbw b Smith	15
J Cox	c Pope b Harvey	69	c Lewis b Alleyne	28
M Burns (capt)	b Smith	66	not out	6
*RJ Turner	lbw b Smith	7		
AW Laraman	not out	148		
KP Dutch	c Harvey b Lewis	15		
AV Suppiah	c Alleyne b Lewis	16		
NAM McLean	c Windows b Ball	7		
SRG Francis	c Windows b Lewis	19		
Extras	b 7, lb 7, w 2, nb 4	20	lb 3, nb 10	13
	(133 overs)	477	(3 wkts, 43 overs)	115

Bowling
Lewis 28-6-107-3. Smith 31-10-67-4. Harvey 27-6-103-2. Alleyne 28-6-116-0. Ball 19-2-90-1.
Lewis 9-2-37-0. Smith 11-5-19-2. Ball 13-5-20-0. Alleyne 6-2-18-1. Weston 2-0-10-0. Taylor 2-0-8-0.
Fall of Wickets 1-10, 2-12, 3-101, 4-113, 5-136, 6-244, 7-259, 8-331, 9-432, 10-477
1-6, 2-38, 3-76

Match drawn – Somerset (12pts), Gloucestershire (8pts)

A brilliant unbeaten 173 by Craig White was the inspiration behind Yorkshire's victory against Derbyshire.

Ben Phillips, who remained unbeaten on 48. Northants, replying to Hampshire's feeble first-innings 125, were themselves 72 for 7 before Damien Wright, a Tasmanian all-rounder making his championship debut as a temporary replacement for Andre Nel, hit out to make a well-judged 46. Phillips and Brown, who faced 56 balls and played some strokes which even he might not have realized he possessed, then pushed the lead up to almost three figures – which was particularly rough on Dimitri Mascarenhas, the Hampshire swing bowler, who had displayed great stamina and skill to take 6 for 43 from 20 overs. Wright then snatched three second-innings wickets, while Mike Cawdron marked his Northants championship debut by also adding three more scalps to his first-innings haul of 3 for 25 as Hampshire were dismissed for 179. Mark Powell anchored the pursuit of a small victory target with an unbeaten 38 – but no one in this rather strange match topped 50.

A maiden hundred from Aaron Laraman, who came in at 136 for 5 and finished up on 148 not out, seemed to have put Somerset in complete command against Gloucestershire at Taunton. Laraman hit a six and 24 fours, from 222 balls, and was joined in a ninth-wicket stand of 101 by Nixon McLean, whose 76 took him just 65 deliveries. But Gloucestershire, facing a first-innings deficit of 249, fought back so tigerishly that, in the end, Somerset were probably content that there was not a fifth day. Phil Weston led the second-innings charge to an eventual 611 for 9 declared by striking 28 fours in a fine 179, Matt Windows made 89, and then Ian Harvey laid into some tiring home bowlers to score an unbeaten 128 and put on 140 for the seventh wicket with Martyn Ball, whose 75 was a career-best score.

ROUND 11: 9–12 JULY 2003

Division One

Nasser Hussain and Mushtaq Ahmed fought out one of the great duels of the championship season at Arundel, illuminating an opening day of a classic four-day contest that was claimed, finally, late on the last afternoon, by Sussex. But Hussain, relishing the chance to test himself against the country's leading wicket-taker, kept Essex afloat almost single-handedly in the first two sessions of the match. The England captain used his feet in an exemplary fashion to deal with the threat of Mushtaq, and had made it to 95 before the Pakistani leg spinner at last got his man. Graham Napier, however, going in far too low at No. 9, rallied Essex with an unbeaten 89 of controlled aggression. Ryan ten Doeschate hung around determinedly while 116 were added for the ninth wicket, and Essex's 340 looked an excellent total once Sussex had declined to 53 for 3 in reply. Tony Cottey, however, was in the form of his life and in the equally diminutive Tim Ambrose he found a partner determined to launch a counter-attack. They put on 178, until Ambrose fell for 88 trying to turn Paul Grayson's left-arm spin from out of the rough outside his leg stump and being caught at slip off a leading edge. Cottey went on to reach 107, and Sussex eventually earned themselves a slender first-innings lead when Mushtaq, James Kirtley and Jason Lewry fashioned 79 more runs from the last two wickets.

Essex, mainly through Grayson, Andy Flower and Aftab Habib, then fought hard to get back on top and initially Sussex were grateful for the three wickets picked up by off spinner Mark Davis. Lewry, however, grabbed a vital wicket just before the close of the third day and, the following morning, polished off the Essex tail to finish with figures of 5 for 52. Needing 256 from 82 overs for victory, Sussex slid to 32 for 3 before, again, Cottey and Ambrose – referred to in one newspaper as being like two petit pois in a pod – resuscitated the innings. This time Cottey fell just short of his hundred, by two runs, but Ambrose went on to finish the job with 93 not out after their fourth-wicket stand had realized 172 in 56 overs. Victory, which kept Sussex within 26 points of Surrey with a game in hand, was achieved with 4.5 overs to spare.

Earlier in the day, Surrey had wrapped up a win of their own against Warwickshire at Edgbaston, with the home side ultimately paying the price for a woeful first-innings batting display. Replying to Surrey's 355, they reached a promising 85 for 1 by the close of the opening day, but then crumbled to 245 all out with Azhar Mahmood and Martin Bicknell doing much of the damage. Surrey needed no second invitation to move into a position of total dominance. Mark Butcher sped to a century in 102 balls and, overall, hit two sixes and 20 fours in his innings of 118 while adding 187 for the second wicket with Mark Ramprakash. When Surrey declared at 450 for 5 early on the third day, Ramprakash was 182 not out – the 18th time in his career that he had passed 150. Mahmood's 50 not out from just 25 balls underlined Surrey's command, but at least Warwickshire showed some spine after setting off in pursuit of a distant 561. Mike Powell, the captain, led the way with 91 and four other players topped 50 as Surrey were made to work for every wicket. Eventually, with Saqlain Mushtaq

Round 11: 9–12 July 2003 Division One

SUSSEX v. ESSEX – at Arundel

ESSEX	First Innings		Second Innings	
AP Grayson	c Ambrose b Kirtley	0	b Davis	71
N Hussain	c Montgomerie b M Ahmed	95	c M Ahmed b Lewry	22
*JS Foster	c Montgomerie b Lewry	12	run out	1
A Flower	lbw b Kirtley	37	lbw b Davis	54
A Habib	c Ambrose b Lewry	0	c Ambrose b Lewry	53
RC Irani (capt)	c Adams b Lewry	15	c Adams b Davis	6
JD Middlebrook	lbw b Martin-Jenkins	0	c Adams b Lewry	23
JM Dakin	c Kirtley b Lewry	35	(9) b Lewry	0
GR Napier	not out	89	(10) not out	10
RN ten Doeschate	b Lewry	31	(8) lbw b M Ahmed	6
SA Brant	c Prior b M Ahmed	3	b Lewry	2
Extras	b 2, lb 7	9	lb 19, w 5, nb 2	26
	(114.5 overs)	340	(93.4 overs)	274

Bowling
Kirtley 24–4–88–2. Lewry 29–7–72–5. M Ahmed 36.5–10–102–2. Martin-Jenkins 17–3–44–1. Davis 8–0–25–0.
Kirtley 17–2–48–0. Lewry 19.4–6–52–5. M Ahmed 30–4–92–1. Martin-Jenkins 8–3–19–0. Davis 19–3–44–3.
Fall of Wickets 1–0, 2–23, 3–95, 4–97, 5–115, 6–149, 7–203, 8–215, 9–331, 10–340
1–49, 2–50, 3–140, 4–187, 5–193, 6–243, 7–258, 8–262, 9–262, 10–274

SUSSEX	First Innings		Second Innings	
MW Goodwin	b Brant	11	(2) b Dakin	18
RR Montgomerie	c Hussain b Brant	1	(1) c Foster b Dakin	1
PA Cottey	c Middlebrook b Dakin	107	c Foster b Dakin	98
CJ Adams (capt)	c Foster b Napier	20	c Habib b Middlebrook	0
*TR Ambrose	c Flower b Grayson	88	not out	93
RSC Martin-Jenkins	lbw b Grayson	6	not out	21
MJ Prior	lbw b Brant	13		
MJG Davis	c Habib b Grayson	12		
M Ahmed	c Dakin b Grayson	34		
RJ Kirtley	not out	35		
JD Lewry	c Flower b Middlebrook	22		
Extras	lb 3, w 3, nb 4	10	b 7, lb 4, w 15	26
	(110.5 overs)	359	(4 wkts, 77.1 overs)	257

Bowling
Dakin 25–5–67–1. Brant 25–4–90–3. ten Doeschate 10–1–53–0. Napier 16–2–45–1. Middlebrook 17.5–1–54–1. Grayson 17–2–47–4.
Brant 7–0–27–0. Dakin 16–2–54–3. Middlebrook 23.1–1–78–1. Napier 7–0–24–0. Grayson 24–7–63–0.
Fall of Wickets 1–4, 2–13, 3–53, 4–231, 5–233, 6–250, 7–254, 8–280, 9–323, 10–359
1–1, 2–31, 3–32, 4–204

Sussex beat Essex by 6 wickets – Sussex (21pts), Essex (6pts)

WARWICKSHIRE v. SURREY – at Edgbaston

SURREY	First Innings		Second Innings	
IJ Ward	c Knight b Wagg	23	c Frost b Waqar Younis	9
MA Butcher	c Trott b Waqar Younis	28	c Frost b Smith	118
MR Ramprakash	c Frost b Carter	18	not out	182
GP Thorpe	lbw b Carter	30	c and b Smith	4
*AJ Stewart	c Frost b Carter	74	b Brown	45
AJ Hollioake (capt)	c Wagh b Brown	88	lbw b Wagg	30
Azhar Mahmood	c Frost b Wagg	13	not out	50
MP Bicknell	not out	25		
IDK Salisbury	c Frost b Carter	0		
Saqlain Mushtaq	c Trott b Carter	0		
J Ormond	b Brown	33		
Extras	b 4, lb 3, w 4, nb 12	23	b 3, lb 7, nb 2	12
	(79.2 overs)	355	(5 wkts, 82 overs)	450

Bowling
Waqar Younis 17–7–65–1. Carter 17–0–75–5. Wagg 18–2–101–2. Brown 17.2–4–59–2. Smith 7–0–34–0. Bell 3–0–14–0.
Waqar Younis 14–1–81–1. Wagg 13–0–88–1. Carter 20–3–81–0. Brown 12–0–74–1. Smith 22–1–111–2. Bell 1–0–5–0.
Fall of Wickets 1–47, 2–56, 3–102, 4–103, 5–253, 6–288, 7–288, 8–288, 9–288, 10–355
1–20, 2–207, 3–219, 4–319, 5–364

WARWICKSHIRE	First Innings		Second Innings	
MJ Powell (capt)	c Azhar Mahmood b Salisbury	27	b Ormond	91
NV Knight	c Ormond b Azhar Mahmood	42	lbw b Bicknell	51
MA Wagh	lbw b Azhar Mahmood	34	c Stewart b Hollioake	71
IR Bell	c Stewart b Bicknell	1	c Salisbury b Saqlain Mushtaq	71
IJL Trott	lbw b Azhar Mahmood	0	b Hollioake	0
*T Frost	c Butcher b Azhar Mahmood	24	b Saqlain Mushtaq	12
DR Brown	lbw b Ormond	61	c Thorpe b Saqlain Mushtaq	56
GG Wagg	c Stewart b Bicknell	11	c sub b Saqlain Mushtaq	16
NMK Smith	c sub b Bicknell	1	c Salisbury b Saqlain Mushtaq	8
NM Carter	c Thorpe b Ormond	20	lbw b Salisbury	11
Waqar Younis	not out	0	not out	10
Extras	lb 4, w 5, nb 14	23	b 8, lb 14, nb 10	32
	(68.2 overs)	245	(113.1 overs)	425

Bowling
Bicknell 21.2–4–62–3. Ormond 15–3–57–2. Azhar Mahmood 16–4–61–4. Salisbury 6–2–20–1. Saqlain Mushtaq 10–0–41–0.
Bicknell 11–5–31–1. Ormond 17–3–83–1. Hollioake 11–2–32–2. Azhar Mahmood 10–0–53–0. Salisbury 29–2–70–1. Saqlain Mushtaq 35.1–3–134–5.
Fall of Wickets 1–62, 2–114, 3–116, 4–120, 5–120, 6–195, 7–224, 8–224, 9–245, 10–245
1–39, 2–138, 3–188, 4–293, 5–296, 6–321, 7–327, 8–351, 9–387, 10–425

Surrey beat Warwickshire by 135 runs – Surrey (21pts), Warwickshire (4pts)

KENT v. NOTTINGHAMSHIRE – at Maidstone

KENT	First Innings		Second Innings	
DP Fulton (capt)	c Warren b Harris	6	c Warren b Smith	18
RWT Key	run out	31	st Warren b Vettori	140
ET Smith	c Pietersen b Franks	149	c Vettori b Cairns	113
A Symonds	c Warren b Vettori	8	not out	103
MJ Walker	c Welton b Vettori	0	not out	11
MA Ealham	c Gallian b Vettori	5		
*GO Jones	c Gallian b Franks	82		
JC Tredwell	b Smith	16		
RS Ferley	not out	14		
M Sami	c Franks b Smith	16		
A Sheriyar	c Franks b Vettori	0		
Extras	b 5, lb 3, w 1, nb 26	35	b 6, lb 11, w 2, nb 14	33
	(61.3 overs)	362	(3 wkts, 80.3 overs)	418

Bowling
Smith 13–0–58–2. Harris 9–0–55–1. Franks 10–0–51–2. Logan 6–0–48–0. Vettori 14.3–2–74–4. Pietersen 6–0–39–0. Cairns 3–0–29–0.
Smith 12–0–55–1. Harris 14–4–62–0. Cairns 12–2–43–1. Franks 12–1–53–0. Vettori 20–0–124–1. Pietersen 7.3–0–48–0. Gallian 3–0–16–0.
Fall of Wickets 1–11, 2–98, 3–112, 4–112, 5–121, 6–299, 7–312, 8–336, 9–360, 10–362
1–22, 2–255, 3–375

NOTTS	First Innings		Second Innings	
JER Gallian (capt)	c Jones b Ferley	51	(2) c Tredwell b M Sami	106
GE Welton	c Symonds b Ferley	17	(1) lbw b M Sami	15
DJ Bicknell	not out	37	b M Sami	0
*RJ Warren	c Jones b M Sami	1	lbw b Tredwell	23
AJ Harris	lbw b M Sami	0	(11) b M Sami	0
KP Pietersen	c Key b M Sami	6	(5) c Smith b Symonds	32
CL Cairns	b M Sami	19	(6) b Ealham	58
PJ Franks	b M Sami	0	(7) b M Sami	45
DL Vettori	c Jones b M Sami	0	(8) c Walker b M Sami	3
RJ Logan	c Tredwell b M Sami	4	(10) not out	5
GJ Smith	b M Sami	1	(9) c Jones b M Sami	2
Extras	b 1, lb 9, nb 10	20	b 1, lb 11, w 7, nb 2	21
	(49.1 overs)	156	(101.2 overs)	337

Bowling
M Sami 14.1–3–64–8. Sheriyar 6–3–17–0. Ferley 19–6–39–2. Ealham 5–1–17–0. Tredwell 1–0–9–0.
M Sami 21.2–8–50–7. Sheriyar 13–2–40–0. Ferley 21–6–70–0. Ealham 14–3–39–1. Tredwell 21–5–84–1. Symonds 12–0–42–1.
Fall of Wickets 1–63, 2–106, 3–113, 4–113, 5–121, 6–146, 7–146, 8–146, 9–150, 10–156
1–27, 2–29, 3–80, 4–158, 5–249, 6–330, 7–330, 8–331, 9–333, 10–337

Kent beat Nottinghamshire by 287 runs – Kent (21pts), Nottinghamshire (3pts)

MIDDLESEX v. LEICESTERSHIRE – at Southgate

MIDDLESEX	First Innings		Second Innings	
AJ Strauss (capt)	c Nixon b Amin	147	(2) not out	73
SG Koenig	c Maddy b Masters	20		
OA Shah	c Nixon b Masters	16	st Nixon b Amin	20
BL Hutton	b Hodge	40		
EC Joyce	b Snape	102	(4) not out	29
Abdul Razzaq	c Nixon b Masters	25		
PN Weekes	c Maddy b DeFreitas	75	(1) b Whiley	29
*DC Nash	not out	103		
JWM Dalrymple	not out	33		
A A Noffke	(did not bat)			
C B Keegan	(did not bat)			
Extras	b 7, lb 3, w 15, nb 34	59	lb 12, w 3	15
	(7 wkts, 160.4 overs)	620	(2 wkts, 24 overs)	166

Bowling
DeFreitas 24–5–75–1. Masters 26–6–81–3. Whiley 27.4–4–118–0. Maddy 11–1–32–0. Amin 34–8–137–1. Snape 17–0–83–1. Hodge 5–2–18–1. Sehwag 16–1–66–0.
DeFreitas 3–0–19–0. Masters 3–0–17–0. Whiley 5–0–33–1. Amin 8–0–49–1. Sehwag 2–0–10–0. Snape 2–0–17–0. Maddy 1–0–10–0.
Fall of Wickets 1–33, 2–96, 3–185, 4–277, 5–324, 6–432, 7–523
1–51, 2–84

LEICESTERSHIRE	First Innings		Second Innings	
JK Maunders	c and b Keegan	55	c Nash b Noffke	0
V Sehwag	c Koenig b Keegan	130	c Nash b Keegan	13
DL Maddy	c and b Keegan	4	b Weekes	94
DD Masters	c Weekes b Keegan	23	(9) b Dalrymple	4
BJ Hodge	c Nash b Keegan	52	(4) b Noffke	112
DI Stevens	lbw b Abdul Razzaq	0	(5) c Shah b Weekes	0
*PA Nixon	not out	52	(6) b Weekes	34
JN Snape	c Hutton b Dalrymple	3	(7) not out	40
PAJ DeFreitas (capt)	lbw b Keegan	46	(8) c Hutton b Keegan	0
RM Amin	c Weekes b Noffke	11	b Abdul Razzaq	11
MJA Whiley	c Joyce b Weekes	6	lbw b Keegan	3
Extras	lb 7, nb 39	46	b 7, lb 9, nb 8	24
	(118 overs)	447	(100 overs)	335

Bowling
Noffke 29–7–74–1. Keegan 29–4–114–6. Weekes 11–65–1. Abdul Razzaq 27–6–113–1. Dalrymple 14–1–73–1. Joyce 1–0–1–0.
Noffke 20–5–48–3. Abdul Razzaq 15–2–54–1. Dalrymple 15–3–45–1. Keegan 23–10–66–3. Weekes 25–2–98–2. Hutton 2–0–8–0.
Fall of Wickets 1–197, 2–206, 3–209, 4–296, 5–297, 6–332, 7–337, 8–413, 9–422, 10–447
1–0, 2–31, 3–207, 4–207, 5–247, 6–292, 7–292, 8–294, 9–326, 10–335

Middlesex beat Leicestershire by 8 wickets – Middlesex (22pts), Leicestershire (7pts)

taking 5 for 134, Warwickshire reached 425 before their resistance ran out.

Mohammad Sami, the Pakistan fast bowler, produced the quickest and most destructive display of sustained hostility of the county summer to propel Kent to a morale-boosting victory against Nottinghamshire at Maidstone. The pitch at The Mote is traditionally pacy, but nothing had prepared the Notts batsmen for the threat of Sami. The Kent faithful could hardly believe their eyes, either, as Sami's heroics topped the entertainment of a remarkable match. Almost 500 runs were scored on the opening day, with Kent flying to 362 as Ed Smith (149 from 143 balls) and Geraint Jones (82 from 78 balls) added 178 in a mere 24 overs. Then, in the final session, Notts declined to 137 for 5 as Sami, initially expensive, returned to take three wickets in an over.

The next morning saw Sami blow away the tail to finish with 8 for 64, a career best and the best figures of the championship season to date. Sami, however, had not finished. By the close of the second day he had also shot out Guy Welton and Darren Bicknell as Notts slipped to 29 for 2 in their second innings. In between, Kent's batsmen had made hay again in the blissful conditions: Rob Key returned to form with 140, Smith made two hundreds in a match for the first time in his career, and Andrew Symonds blasted an unbeaten 103 from 81 balls, with 15 fours and a six, as Kent raced to 418 for 3 declared. Had any first-class team ever been set 625 in the fourth innings before the end of a second day? Almost certainly not, and no wonder Notts looked shell-shocked as Sami fixed them in his sights once again. To their credit, Jason Gallian, the Notts captain, battled to a brave, six-hour 106 on the third day, while Kevin Pietersen and Chris Cairns also hit half-centuries, but Sami earned himself yet another standing ovation from the home crowd after blasting out the last five Notts batsmen in the space of just 14 balls to complete a 287-run win for Kent. His second-innings 7 for 50 gave him match figures of 15 for 114, the best for Kent since Doug Wright took 16 Somerset wickets in 1939, and it was a quite astonishing achievement on such a batsman-friendly surface.

Durham's Gary Pratt turned his maiden first-class hundred into 150 against Northamptonshire.

The highest match run aggregate in Middlesex's history occurred at Southgate, with Chad Keegan adding to his growing reputation by proving himself the most tenacious and effective bowler on view. Keegan's career-best figures of 6 for 114 were the reason Leicestershire were forced to follow on despite an opening stand of 197 between Virender Sehwag (130 from 111 balls) and John Maunders, and the fast bowler still had the energy in the blazing heat to pick up three more wickets second time around as the visitors were bowled out again for 335. Brad Hodge (112) and Darren Maddy (94) held up Middlesex with a determined third-wicket partnership of 176, but Andy Strauss's 67-ball 73 not out ensured that a victory chase in the final session did not falter. Strauss had struck 147 on the opening day, too, to launch his Middlesex side towards a mammoth first-innings total of 620 for 7 declared. Ed Joyce and David Nash also scored hundreds and no fewer than eight Leicestershire bowlers were slow-roasted in the sunshine.

Division Two

The resignation of Bill Midgeley, their chairman, followed Durham's eight-wicket defeat to Northamptonshire at Chester-le-Street. It was the off spin of Jason Brown that separated the two sides after the honours had been shared after the first two days. Brown's career-best figures of 7 for 69

destroyed the Durham second innings and, after the early loss of Mark Powell, the visitors were swept home on the back of a second-wicket stand of 156 between Mike Hussey and Phil Jaques. Hussey remained unbeaten on 72, content to watch Jeff Cook strike a succession of meaty blows after Jaques had fallen for 81 to add to his first-innings 109. Mike Cawdron, who took 6 for 87 on the opening day, was the other Northants player to shine. But 21-year-old Gary Pratt, of Durham, will at least be able to look back on the match with pride: his superb 150 on day one was his maiden first-class hundred.

A sixth consecutive defeat, their worst losing sequence in 81 years, was the sorry epitaph to Derbyshire's struggles against Gloucestershire at Derby. Jon Lewis (6 for 48) and Ian Harvey, with three wickets, were the destroyers on the first morning when Derbyshire plunged to 89 all out. Craig Spearman then launched himself at the home attack with 85, and Gloucestershire reached 277 in reply, despite Dominic Cork's four wickets. At 39 for 3 second time around, Derbyshire looked doomed to humiliation, but at least Michael Di Venuto, in century stands first with Dominic Hewson and then Luke Sutton, regained some pride. Di Venuto hit 148 and Sutton remained 81 not out when the innings closed at 356. Gloucestershire were a shaky 15 for 2 and then 52

for 4 before Jonty Rhodes, with ten boundaries in his 93-ball unbeaten 62, saw the visitors home for their first championship success in six matches following a good fifth-wicket stand of 69 with Alex Gidman.

Glamorgan were 203 for 8 on the opening afternoon of their match against Somerset at Cardiff when Robert Croft was joined by Alex Wharf in the ninth-wicket partnership that was, ultimately, going to decide the outcome. Croft went on to make 122, adding some more important runs for the final wicket, but it was the 104 he put on with Wharf (who made 45) which made all the difference. Somerset, in reply, could only manage 233 – despite Ian Blackwell's 82 – as Mike Kasprowicz produced a telling mid-afternoon burst of 3 for 0 in 11 balls on the second day. Matthew Maynard then showed just why the county had awarded the veteran batsman another two-year contract by hitting the 54th century of his career and Somerset were soon left requiring 424 for victory. They made a decent stab at it, with Mike Burns battling to 106, but Wharf grabbed two wickets before lunch on the final day and then another couple with the second new ball immediately after the interval to settle matters. The final victory margin was 110 runs, underlining the worth of that Croft-Wharf alliance three days previously.

Round 11: 9–12 July 2003 Division Two

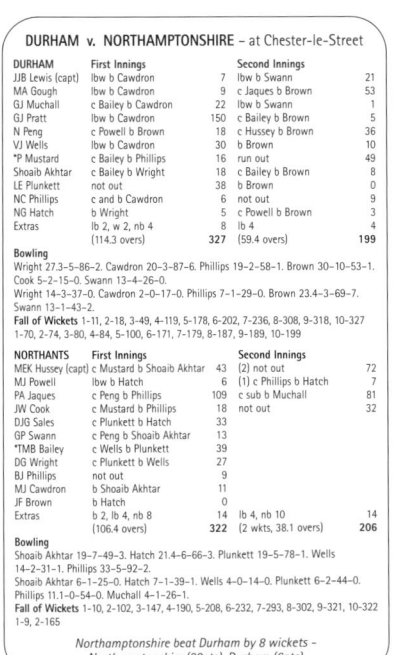

DURHAM v. NORTHAMPTONSHIRE – at Chester-le-Street

DURHAM	First Innings		Second Innings	
JJB Lewis (capt)	lbw b Cawdron	7	lbw b Swann	21
MA Gough	lbw b Cawdron	9	c Jaques b Brown	53
GJ Muchall	c Bailey b Cawdron	22	lbw b Swann	1
GJ Pratt	lbw b Cawdron	150	c Bailey b Brown	5
N Peng	c Powell b Brown	18	c Hussey b Brown	36
VJ Wells	lbw b Cawdron	30	b Brown	10
*P Mustard	c Bailey b Phillips	16	run out	49
Shoaib Akhtar	c Bailey b Wright	18	c Bailey b Brown	8
LE Plunkett	not out	38	b Brown	0
NC Phillips	c and b Cawdron	6	not out	9
NG Hatch	b Wright	5	c Powell b Brown	3
Extras	lb 2, w 2, nb 4	8	lb 4	4
	(114.3 overs)	327	(59.4 overs)	199

Bowling
Wright 27.3–5–86–2. Cawdron 20–3–87–6. Phillips 19–2–58–1. Brown 30–10–53–1. Cook 5–2–15–0. Swann 13–4–26–0.
Wright 14–3–37–0. Cawdron 2–0–17–0. Phillips 7–1–29–0. Brown 23.4–3–69–7. Swann 13–1–43–2.
Fall of Wickets 1-11, 2-18, 3-49, 4-119, 5-178, 6-202, 7-236, 8-308, 9-318, 10-327
1-70, 2-74, 3-80, 4-84, 5-100, 6-171, 7-179, 8-187, 9-189, 10-199

NORTHANTS	First Innings		Second Innings	
MEK Hussey	c Mustard b Shoaib Akhtar	43	(2) not out	72
MJ Powell	lbw b Hatch	6	(1) c Phillips b Hatch	7
PA Jaques	c Peng b Phillips	109	c sub b Muchall	81
JW Cook	c Mustard b Phillips	18	not out	32
DJG Sales	c Plunkett b Hatch	33		
GP Swann	c Peng b Shoaib Akhtar	13		
*TMB Bailey	c Wells b Plunkett	39		
DG Wright	c Plunkett b Wells	27		
BJ Phillips	not out	9		
MJ Cawdron	b Shoaib Akhtar	11		
JF Brown	b Hatch	0		
Extras	b 2, lb 4, nb 8	14	lb 4, nb 10	14
	(106.4 overs)	322	(2 wkts, 38.1 overs)	206

Bowling
Shoaib Akhtar 19–7–49–3. Hatch 21.4–6–66–3. Plunkett 19–5–78–1. Wells 14–2–31–1. Phillips 33–5–92–2.
Shoaib Akhtar 6–1–25–0. Hatch 7–1–39–1. Wells 4–0–14–0. Plunkett 6–2–44–0. Phillips 11.1–0–54–0. Muchall 4–1–26–1.
Fall of Wickets 1-10, 2-102, 3-147, 4-190, 5-208, 6-232, 7-293, 8-302, 9-321, 10-322
1-9, 2-165

Northamptonshire beat Durham by 8 wickets –
Northamptonshire (20pts), Durham (6pts)

DERBYSHIRE v. GLOUCESTERSHIRE – at Derby

DERBYSHIRE	First Innings		Second Innings	
AI Gait	c Taylor b Lewis	12	(2) c Windows b Smith	3
MJ Di Venuto	b Lewis	17	(1) c and b Ball	148
CWG Bassano	c Ball b Lewis	3	lbw b Harvey	3
M Kaif	c Pope b Harvey	12	lbw b Harvey	6
DR Hewson	c Pope b Gidman	8	lbw b Harvey	39
*LD Sutton	c Gidman b Harvey	5	not out	81
G Welch	lbw b Lewis	3	lbw b Ball	0
DG Cork (capt)	b Lewis	0	b Ball	39
NRC Dumelow	c Bailey b Harvey	0	c Spearman b Ball	5
KJ Dean	c Spearman b Lewis	6	lbw b Smith	1
Mohammad Ali	not out	14	run out	2
Extras	b 4, lb 5	9	b 17, lb 9, w 3	29
	(36 overs)	89	(122 overs)	356

Bowling
Lewis 11–0–48–6. Smith 11–6–14–0. Harvey 13–6–18–3. Gidman 1–1–0–1.
Lewis 29–7–91–0. Smith 25–5–72–2. Ball 34–11–65–4. Harvey 24–7–58–3. Gidman 10–1–44–0.
Fall of Wickets 1-16, 2-28, 3-37, 4-51, 5-57, 6-69, 7-69, 8-69, 9-73, 10-89
1-21, 2-24, 3-39, 4-145, 5-264, 6-268, 7-318, 8-342, 9-349, 10-356

GLOS	First Innings		Second Innings	
CM Spearman (capt)	c Gait b Dean	85	(2) lbw b Dean	0
WPC Weston	b Welch	28	(1) c Di Venuto b Dean	6
CG Taylor	c Sutton b Mohammad Ali	1	c Hewson b Welch	6
JN Rhodes	lbw b Cork	6	not out	62
MGN Windows	lbw b Cork	20	lbw b Welch	0
APR Gidman	c Sutton b Dean	25	b Cork	41
IJ Harvey	c Di Venuto b Mohammad Ali	27	not out	21
MCJ Ball	not out	34		
*SP Pope	b Cork	1		
J Lewis	b Cork	13		
AM Smith	b Cork	0		
Extras	b 5, lb 6, w 1, nb 10	22	b 14, nb 11	25
	(86.2 overs)	277	(5 wkts, 39.4 overs)	171

Bowling
Cork 27–3–75–4. Dean 22–4–85–2. Welch 19–2–64–5–2. Mohammad Ali 16–2–60–2. Dumelow 2–1–1–0.
Cork 13–3–47–1. Dean 8.4–2–42–2. Welch 11–1–36–2. Mohammad Ali 7–0–32–0.
Fall of Wickets 1-53, 2-60, 3-101, 4-158, 5-158, 6-202, 7-230, 8-231, 9-257, 10-277
1-4, 2-15, 3-52, 4-52, 5-121

Gloucestershire beat Derbyshire by 5 wickets –
Gloucestershire (19pts), Derbyshire (3pts)

GLAMORGAN v. SOMERSET – at Cardiff

GLAMORGAN	First Innings		Second Innings	
JP Maher	c and b Blackwell	21	c Bowler b Dutch	62
J Hughes	lbw b McLean	7	lbw b Burns	16
A Dale	c Turner b Blackwell	13	c Burns b Dutch	0
MJ Wood	c Turner b Blackwell	14	c Bowler b Dutch	1
MP Maynard	lbw b McLean	37	lbw b Burns	101
*MA Wallace	c Bowler b McLean	20	c Turner b McLean	26
RDB Croft (capt)	c Bryant b McLean	122	c Turner b McLean	17
SD Thomas	c Dutch b Laraman	25	b McLean	4
MS Kasprowicz	c Cox b Dutch	24	c Turner b McLean	5
AG Wharf	c sub b McLean	45	lbw b Laraman	39
DS Harrison	not out	18	not out	12
Extras	lb 6, w 1, nb 2	9	b 8, lb 3, w 1, nb 10	22
	(109.1 overs)	349	(82.4 overs)	307

Bowling
McLean 23.1–4–79–5. Francis 5.5–1–20–0. Dutch 31.1–9–100–1. Blackwell 35–6–93–3. Laraman 12–4–43–1. Burns 2–0–8–0.
McLean 25–4–84–4. Burns 18–3–61–2. Dutch 16–3–56–3. Blackwell 19–6–65–0. Laraman 4.4–0–30–1.
Fall of Wickets 1-9, 2-34, 3-35, 4-52, 5-93, 6-114, 7-163, 8-203, 9-307, 10-349
1-39, 2-56, 3-68, 4-164, 5-223, 6-233, 7-251, 8-251, 9-260, 10-307

SOMERSET	First Innings		Second Innings	
PD Bowler	c Wallace b Wharf	5	c Wallace b Thomas	49
MJ Wood	c Powell b Thomas	5	lbw b Croft	26
JDC Bryant	lbw b Thomas	20	b Kasprowicz	7
J Cox	c Hughes b Kasprowicz	24	c Maynard b Wharf	24
M Burns (capt)	c Wallace b Kasprowicz	50	run out	106
ID Blackwell	c Wallace b Harrison	82	b Wharf	10
AW Laraman	lbw b Kasprowicz	0	c Wallace b Wharf	21
*RJ Turner	c Croft b Kasprowicz	9	c Wallace b Kasprowicz	9
KP Dutch	b Wharf	22	c Thomas b Croft	30
NAM McLean	b Wharf	0	lbw b Wharf	18
SRG Francis	not out	0	not out	2
Extras	b 4, lb 4, w 4, nb 12	24	b 6, lb 1, nb 4	11
	(59.4 overs)	233	(109.5 overs)	313

Bowling
Kasprowicz 19–6–53–4. Wharf 15–3–55–2. Thomas 12–0–41–2. Harrison 10.4–1–52–2. Croft 3–0–24–0.
Kasprowicz 35–11–91–2. Wharf 26–5–90–4. Thomas 13–3–36–1. Croft 28.5–5–74–2. Harrison 7–1–15–0.
Fall of Wickets 1-7, 2-37, 3-38, 4-102, 5-163, 6-163, 7-169, 8-205, 9-206, 10-233
1-44, 2-81, 3-102, 4-144, 5-164, 6-228, 7-247, 8-263, 9-294, 10-313

Glamorgan beat Somerset by 110 runs –
Glamorgan (20pts), Somerset (4pts)

Round 12: 15–18 July 2003

Division One

Breathlessly, at Grace Road, Sussex won a fourth successive victory to move to within five points of leaders Surrey. Victory, by five wickets over Leicestershire, came at 4.45pm on the final afternoon after Tony Cottey, with 58 to add to his first-innings knock of 147, took his run tally for his past six innings to more than 650. Matt Prior, with 96, had helped Cottey to add 155 for the sixth wicket as Sussex won a first-innings lead close to the three-figure mark, despite Phil DeFreitas holding them up on day one with a belligerent 103 batting from No. 8. DeFreitas hooked Robin Martin-Jenkins for consecutive sixes to reach his tenth first-class hundred from just 116 balls, and also took 5 for 55 in the Sussex reply. Amongst all these heroics, however, Pakistan leg spinner Mushtaq Ahmed again stood out. With five-wicket hauls in both Leicestershire innings – boosting his season's tally to 65 – Mushtaq was once more the architect behind Sussex's success.

The man to frustrate Kent at Blackpool was their former favourite, Carl Hooper. The former West Indies captain, who scored 22 first-class hundreds in 85 matches for Kent and averaged more than 50 for them, hit a maiden championship century for his new

Tony Cottey: more runs for Sussex in his golden summer.

Round 12: 15–18 July 2003 Division One

LEICESTERSHIRE v. SUSSEX – at Leicester

LEICESTERSHIRE	First Innings		Second Innings	
JK Maunders	lbw b Kirtley	0	lbw b M Ahmed	27
DI Stevens	st Ambrose b M Ahmed	51	lbw b M Ahmed	50
DL Maddy	lbw b M Ahmed	30	c M-Jenkins b Innes	40
BJ Hodge	c Montgomerie b M Ahmed	47	lbw b Kirtley	18
TR Ward	lbw b M Ahmed	4	c Prior b M Ahmed	50
*PA Nixon	lbw b M Ahmed	4	lbw b M Ahmed	11
JN Snape	b Kirtley	36	run out	20
PAJ DeFreitas (capt)	b M-Jenkins	103	b M-Jenkins	8
DD Masters	run out	0	c Ambrose b M-Jenkins	4
CE Dagnall	not out	15	c Cottey b M Ahmed	15
RM Amin	b M-Jenkins	0	not out	6
Extras	b 1, lb 22, w 5, nb 2	30	b 1, lb 9, w 3	13
	(85.5 overs)	320	(95.5 overs)	258

Bowling
Kirtley 21–6–68–2. Lewry 6–1–18–0. M-Jenkins 13.5–1–66–2. M Ahmed 33–4–93–5. Innes 12–1–52–0.
Kirtley 22–7–72–1. M-Jenkins 25–9–53–2. M Ahmed 41.5–18–96–5. Innes 7–1–27–1
Fall of Wickets 1-0, 2-60, 3-107, 4-123, 5-127, 6-154, 7-250, 8-251, 9-320, 10-320
1-70, 2-93, 3-128, 4-150, 5-162, 6-225, 7-234, 8-234, 9-237, 10-258

SUSSEX	First Innings		Second Innings	
MW Goodwin	lbw b DeFreitas	34	(2) b Masters	11
RR Montgomerie	b DeFreitas	52	(1) b Amin	28
PA Cottey	lbw b DeFreitas	147	b Amin	58
CJ Adams (capt)	lbw b DeFreitas	0	lbw b Maddy	16
*TR Ambrose	b Dagnall	2	b Snape	25
RSC M-Jenkins	lbw b Dagnall	7	not out	6
MJ Prior	c Hodge b Maddy	96	not out	4
KJ Innes	not out	14		
M Ahmed	st Nixon b Amin	21		
RJ Kirtley	c Maunders b Amin	0		
JD Lewry	c Snape b DeFreitas	0		
Extras	b 15, lb 16, w 2, nb 10	43	b 10, lb 2, w 2, nb 4	18
	(137.5 overs)	416	(5 wkts, 38.5 overs)	166

Bowling
Dagnall 30–10–87–2. Masters 27–5–89–0. Amin 19–5–50–2. Maddy 17–1–70–1. Hodge 1–0–1–0.
DeFreitas 24–0–5–0. Dagnall 2–0–20–0. Masters 8–2–41–1. Amin 11–1–41–2.
Maddy 7–0–23–1. Hodge 6–0–28–0. Snape 1.5–0–6–1.
Fall of Wickets 1-58, 2-161, 3-161, 4-187, 5-215, 6-370, 7-382, 8-415, 9-415, 10-416
1-30, 2-48, 3-96, 4-156, 5-158

Sussex beat Leicestershire by 5 wickets –
Sussex (21pts), Leicestershire (5pts)

LANCASHIRE v. KENT – at Blackpool

KENT	First Innings	
DP Fulton (capt)	c Swann b Hooper	47
RWT Key	c Hegg b Martin	1
ET Smith	b Hooper	203
A Symonds	c Hegg b Chapple	10
MJ Walker	c Chapple b Hooper	150
MA Ealham	c Schofield b Loye	95
*GO Jones	not out	66
JC Tredwell	not out	3
R S Ferley	(did not bat)	
M J Saggers	(did not bat)	
A Sheriyar	(did not bat)	
Extras	b 1, lb 13, w 5, nb 8	27
	(6 wkts, 169 overs)	602

Bowling
Martin 26–4–82–1. Chapple 27–8–64–1. Wood 21–1–101–0. Hooper 51–10–147–3. Mahmood 11–1–53–0. Schofield 15–1–86–0. Chilton 13–2–36–0. Swann 3–0–11–0. Loye 2–0–8–1.
Fall of Wickets 1-5, 2-127, 3-150, 4-346, 5-488, 6-586

LANCASHIRE	First Innings		Second Innings	
MJ Chilton	c Key b Tredwell	114	(2) c Jones b Saggers	2
AJ Swann	lbw b Ferley	2	c Jones b Saggers	1
MB Loye	c Key b Ferley	13	lbw b Ealham	33
CL Hooper	c Smith b Saggers	60	(5) not out	128
SG Law	b Tredwell	29	(4) lbw b Saggers	0
CP Schofield	b Saggers	66	c Smith b Symonds	40
G Chapple	c Jones b Sheriyar	33	c Jones b Tredwell	9
*WK Hegg (capt)	not out	10	not out	10
PJ Martin	lbw b Sheriyar	18		
J Wood	lbw b Saggers	0		
SI Mahmood	hit wkt b Sheriyar	2		
Extras	b 8, lb 10	18	b 4, lb 7, nb 4	15
	(105 overs)	365	(6 wkts, 84 overs)	244

Bowling
Saggers 20–1–93–3. Sheriyar 19–6–63–3. Ferley 14–4–51–2. Ealham 14–4–46–0. Symonds 13–3–30–0. Tredwell 13–2–35–0.
Saggers 12–3–31–3. Sheriyar 12–2–35–0. Ealham 12–4–31–1. Ferley 16–7–30–0. Tredwell 18–4–64–1. Symonds 13–4–42–1.
Fall of Wickets 1-6, 2-30, 3-143, 4-203, 5-256, 6-330, 7-334, 8-361, 9-362, 10-365
1-3, 2-4, 3-12, 4-55, 5-127, 6-163

Match drawn – Lancashire (9pts),
Kent (12pts)

MIDDLESEX v. WARWICKSHIRE – at Southgate

WARWICKSHIRE	First Innings	
MJ Powell (capt)	b Hutton	8
NV Knight	b Keegan	11
MA Wagh	c Joyce b Noffke	0
IR Bell	c Shah b Abdul Razzaq	31
JO Troughton	c and b Noffke	37
*T Frost	c Nash b Noffke	84
DR Brown	b Keegan	113
AF Giles	c Abdul Razzaq b Keegan	96
NMK Smith	c Weekes b Hutton	30
MM Betts	c Nash b Weekes	38
A Richardson	not out	9
Extras	lb 20, nb 19	39
	(144.4 overs)	496

Bowling
Noffke 32–8–92–3. Keegan 34.4–9–125–3. Hutton 15–3–53–2. Abdul Razzaq 21–6–71–1. Dalrymple 16–2–53–0. Weekes 23–6–60–1. Joyce 4–0–17–0. Shah 1–0–5–0.
Fall of Wickets 1-14, 2-15, 3-45, 4-67, 5-100, 6-309, 7-309, 8-386, 9-476, 10-496

MIDDLESEX	First Innings		Second Innings	
AJ Strauss (capt)	c Troughton b Giles	37	c Wagh b Betts	23
SG Koenig	c Powell b Richardson	35	b Giles	96
JWM Dalrymple	lbw b Brown	0	c Brown b Betts	0
OA Shah	b Richardson	31		
BL Hutton	c Frost b Smith	38	(4) not out	102
EC Joyce	b Giles	29	(5) not out	22
Abdul Razzaq	c Betts b Giles	0		
PN Weekes	lbw b Giles	18		
*DC Nash	not out	44		
AA Noffke	c Knight b Richardson	7		
CB Keegan	c Wagh b Richardson	0		
Extras	b 12, lb 5, w 2, nb 12	31	lb 9, nb 29	38
	(89.1 overs)	260	(3 wkts, 80 overs)	281

Bowling
Betts 15–2–63–0. Richardson 19.1–5–37–4. Brown 5–2–8–1. Giles 30–7–90–4. Smith 20–5–47–1.
Richardson 12–1–52–0. Betts 12–2–44–2. Brown 19–5–45–0. Giles 28–4–78–1. Troughton 5–0–47–0. Knight 4–3–6–0.
Fall of Wickets 1-51, 2-52, 3-110, 4-123, 5-177, 6-177, 7-201, 8-211, 9-252, 10-260
1-50, 2-56, 3-215

Match drawn – Middlesex (8pts),
Warwickshire (12pts)

county Lancashire after they had been forced to follow on. Hooper also made 60 in the first innings, in support of Mark Chilton's 114, but he saved his best for when Lancashire crumbled to 12 for 3 on the final morning as Martin Saggers caused havoc with the new ball. In the end, Hooper was 128 not out and all Kent's efforts to force victory on a fine batting pitch were in vain. The 46 overs lost to showers on the third day did not help them either, after they had put themselves into an impregnable position by reaching 602 for 6 declared on the first day and a half. Ed Smith, having had three ducks as well as four hundreds in his previous seven innings, continued his extraordinary progress through the 2003 summer by hitting 203 – his maiden double-hundred – and in the process became the first man to pass 1,000 first-class runs for the season. He struck a six and 35 fours in his 257-ball epic, while Matthew Walker was also in fine touch as he racked up 150. Mark Ealham and Geraint Jones also enjoyed themselves in the conditions, although the Kent batsmen might not have had things all their own way if England coach Duncan Fletcher had released both Andy Flintoff and James Anderson for the game. Jack Simmons, the Lancashire chairman, pronounced himself 'flabbergasted' when the England hierarchy insisted that the players needed a rest instead.

Middlesex eventually held on with few alarms for a draw against Warwickshire at Southgate, but the home side may have found life a little more difficult had bad weather not caused the loss of 42 overs early on the third day. Middlesex, replying to a Warwickshire first innings of 496, were 58 for 2 by the close of the second day and subsided further to 244 for 8 in the play that was possible on the shortened third. Dismissed at the start of the final day for 260, with four wickets for both Ashley Giles and Alan Richardson, they were then indebted to Sven Koenig with 96 and Ben Hutton, whose unbeaten 102 was his third hundred in four matches. Earlier, Warwickshire's position of strength had been built upon the success of their lower-middle order. From 100 for 5, Dougie Brown joined Tony Frost in a sixth-wicket partnership worth 209 – Brown including 17 boundaries in his 113 – before Giles hit out profitably for 96.

Division Two

Durham completed a memorable double over their 'big brother' northern rivals Yorkshire by securing a thrilling three-wicket victory at Chester-le-Street. Shoaib Akhtar, their charismatic Pakistan fast bowler, pulled Darren Gough for six and then drove

him back over his head for four to sweep Durham gloriously over the finishing line with 7.3 overs to spare. It capped a gutsy batting effort in which almost everyone had chipped in, but in which no one had played a big innings. Nevertheless, rejoicing in the North East was boundless after the way in which Yorkshire and Gough – whose match figures of 2 for 145 also produced much gnashing of teeth in the Broad Acres – had been seen off. All this, too, after Durham had conceded a first-innings deficit of 121 and had seen a follow-on averted only by a brave 50 from Graeme Bridge. Anthony McGrath had scored an effortless 86 on the opening day,

Eight-wicket hero: Kabir Ali routed Derbyshire's batsmen in the visitor's second innings at Worcester.

before slapping a long hop to cover, but Craig White's unbeaten 135 and a determined 60 by Andrew Gray put Yorkshire in control. Shoaib, however, had taken three late first-innings wickets and it seemed as if this sharpened him up for a second-innings assault. Steaming in, he took 4 for 38 and, with Steve Harmison picking up 3 for 45, Yorkshire slid to an all-out total of 129 against the pacemen. Vince Wells, mind you, nipped out White for 30 as he also took 3 for 20 with his medium-pace seamers, and his contribution was a vital part of Durham's success. Scoring 251 in 87 overs to win might have been hard work, too, but it ended with Shoaib's flourish.

Another candidate for the championship's 'match of the summer' came at the Rose Bowl, with Hampshire remarkably beating Glamorgan after being forced to follow on. Only twice before in their history, in 1895 and 1922, had a Hampshire team performed such a feat; Glamorgan, predictably, were left shattered. Centuries from Adrian Dale and Matthew Maynard put the Welsh county in command after the first day, and it all looked up for Hampshire when they were bowled out for just 185 in reply, with Mike Kasprowicz bowling with genuine hostility in taking 5 for 48. Robert Croft then took four wickets with his off breaks to leave the home side struggling on 114 for

4 by the close of the second day. Simon Katich, moreover, had given his wicket away for 53 in the day's final over, senselessly swiping to deep square leg. The third day, however, witnessed one of those turnabouts in fortune that cricket, thankfully, specializes in. Led by Nic Pothas – who made a heroic 121 despite pulling a hamstring when he was on 52 and needing a runner thereafter – the Hampshire lower-middle order counter-attacked against tiring bowlers. Dimitri Mascarenhas made 75 and added 149 in 30 overs with Pothas, and then most romantically of all came an unbeaten 68 from Richard Hindley. A 28-year-old journeyman off spinner and loyal servant of the Havant club, Hindley had been called into the Hampshire team as an emergency replacement for the injured Shaun Udal. His bowling had been mercilessly exposed by Maynard, but now – in what was likely to be his only first-class appearance – he grabbed his chance of a place in the sun. Temporarily unemployed, too, he turned up for the game fresh from doing a painting job for his mother … but now he did a job on the Glamorgan attack. Going boldly for his shots, he struck 11 fours and made his runs from just 70 balls. Soon he had run out of partners, but the Hampshire membership gave him a deserved standing ovation at the end of the innings. He had pushed their lead up to 197, and it emerged later

Round 12: 15–18 July 2003 Division Two

DURHAM v. YORKSHIRE – at Chester-le-Street

YORKSHIRE	First Innings		Second Innings	
MJ Wood	c Peng b Harmison	18	lbw b Harmison	10
SP Fleming	c and b Harmison	10	c Mustard b Wells	38
A McGrath (capt)	c Pratt b Wells	86	c Pratt b Shoaib Akhtar	3
MJ Lumb	c and b Bridge	43	c Pratt b Shoaib Akhtar	5
Yuvraj Singh	c Mustard b Hatch	7	c Mustard b Shoaib Akhtar	0
C White	not out	135	lbw b Wells	30
*SM Guy	c Mustard b Wells	3	b Harmison	7
AKD Gray	c Gough b Shoaib Akhtar	60	c Mustard b Shoaib Akhtar	11
D Gough	c Mustard b Shoaib Akhtar	4	c Gough b Wells	0
RJ Sidebottom	c Peng b Shoaib Akhtar	12	not out	18
SP Kirby	c Peng b Bridge	25	c Gough b Harmison	1
Extras	b 12, lb 28, w 1, nb 12	53	b 4, lb 2	6
	(129 overs)	448	(36.3 overs)	129

Bowling

Shoaib Akhtar 25–6–87–3. Harmison 29–7–92–2. Hatch 21–3–79–1. Wells 20–10–41–2. Bridge 34.9–9–109–2.

Harmison 10.3–2–45–3. Wells 9 3 20 3. Shoaib Akhtar 10–2–38–4. Hatch 6–1–20–0. Bridge 1–1–0–0.

Fall of Wickets 1-11, 2-39, 3-160, 4-167, 5-191, 6-197, 7-340, 8-346, 9-382, 10-448
1–11, 2-32, 3-40, 4-40, 5-72, 6-86, 7-104, 8-104, 9-128, 10-129

DURHAM	First Innings		Second Innings	
JJB Lewis (capt)	lbw b Kirby	7	c Fleming b Sidebottom	41
MA Gough	c Yuvraj Singh b Gough	54	c Yuvraj Singh b Gough	8
GJ Muchall	c Guy b Kirby	8	c Fleming b Sidebottom	30
GJ Pratt	c Gray b Sidebottom	51	b Kirby	14
VI Wells	c Fleming b Gray	42	(6) b Gough	17
N Peng	c Guy b Sidebottom	8	(5) b Gray	30
*P Mustard	c Guy b McGrath	32	run out	34
GD Bridge	lbw b Kirby	0	not out	1
Shoaib Akhtar	c Wood b Kirby	25	not out	14
NG Hatch	b Gray	4		
SJ Harmison	not out	14		
Extras	b 9, lb 5, nb 18	32	b 13, lb 11, nb 8	32
	(72 overs)	327	(7 wkts, 79.3 overs)	251

Bowling

Gough 18–2–77–1. Kirby 20–3–93–4. Sidebottom 17–0–67–2. McGrath 8–3–31–1. Gray 9–1–45–2.

Gough 19.3–6–68–1. Kirby 20–5–54–2. Sidebottom 16–2–57–2. McGrath 11–1–18–0. Gray 12–2–30–1.

Fall of Wickets 1-13, 2-27, 3-102, 4-175, 5-177, 6-210, 7-240, 8-284, 9-300, 10-327
1-57, 2-97, 3-117, 4-172, 5-172, 6-229, 7-232

Durham beat Yorkshire by 3 wickets –
Durham (20pts), Yorkshire (8pts)

HAMPSHIRE v. GLAMORGAN – at Southampton

GLAMORGAN	First Innings		Second Innings	
JP Maher	hit wkt b Tomlinson	30	c Crawley b Tremlett	9
J Hughes	c and b Mascarenhas	4	c Crawley b Tremlett	7
A Dale	c Kenway b Katich	123	(9) c Katich b Tremlett	8
MJ Powell	c Kenway b Katich	44	(5) c sub b Bruce	4
MP Maynard	c Pothas b Tremlett	129	(6) b Tremlett	3
*MA Wallace	b Katich	0	(3) b Bruce	0
RDB Croft (capt)	c Francis b Mascarenhas	28	(8) c Katich b Mascarenhas	14
MS Kasprowicz	c Pothas b Tremlett	24	(10) c Katich b Mascarenhas	14
AG Wharf	not out	16	(11) not out	10
DS Harrison	c Pothas b Tremlett	0	(7) c sub b Tremlett	15
DA Cosker	c Katich b Mascarenhas	1	(4) lbw b Bruce	4
Extras	b 3, lb 4, w 3, nb 22	32	nb 16	16
	(105.1 overs)	437	(31.2 overs)	104

Bowling

Mascarenhas 20.1–4–50–3. Tremlett 22.5–5–72–3. Tomlinson 20–2–89–1. Bruce 17–3–86–0. Hindley 9–0–46–0. Katich 17–2–87–3.

Tremlett 16–3–51–6. Mascarenhas 5.2–2–11–1. Bruce 10–1–42–3.

Fall of Wickets 1-7, 2-69, 3-158, 4-287, 5-287, 6-360, 7-407, 8-424, 9-430, 10-437
1-16, 2-21, 3-33, 4-39, 5-46, 6-50, 7-74, 8-79, 9-94, 10-104

HAMPSHIRE	First Innings		Second Innings	
DA Kenway	b Wharf	26	b Croft	24
JHK Adams	c Wallace b Kasprowicz	21	c Wallace b Croft	21
SM Katich	c Wallace b Kasprowicz	53	b Wharf b Croft	53
JP Crawley (capt)	c Hughes b Croft	24	st Wallace b Croft	4
JD Francis	c Wallace b Croft	27	c Wallace b Wharf	40
*N Pothas	lbw b Kasprowicz	2	c Croft b Harrison	121
AD Mascarenhas	c Maher b Harrison	0	lbw b Kasprowicz	75
RJE Hindley	c Wallace b Harrison	8	not out	68
CT Tremlett	c Wharf b Kasprowicz	22	c Maher b Kasprowicz	6
JTA Bruce	not out	21	c Wallace b Kasprowicz	5
JA Tomlinson	b Kasprowicz	0	c Wallace b Croft	1
Extras	lb 4, w 2, nb 8	14	b 9, lb 6, nb 6	21
	(73.5 overs)	185	(107.3 overs)	449

Bowling

Kasprowicz 22.5–10–48–5. Wharf 10–1–31–1. Harrison 15–3–51–2. Croft 26–8–51–2.

Kasprowicz 28–8–103–3. Wharf 17–4–68–1. Harrison 10–0–81–1. Cosker 14–1–65–0. Croft 38.3–9–117–5.

Fall of Wickets 1-40, 2-48, 3-58, 4-93, 5-102, 6-126, 7-137, 8-140, 9-169, 10-185
1-40, 2-55, 3-75, 4-114, 5-194, 6-343, 7-394, 8-420, 9-442, 10-449

Hampshire beat Glamorgan by 93 runs –
Hampshire (17pts), Glamorgan (8pts)

WORCESTERSHIRE v. DERBYSHIRE – at Worcester

DERBYSHIRE	First Innings		Second Innings	
CWG Bassano	c Rhodes b Mason	16	(2) lbw b Kabir Ali	4
MJ Di Venuto	c Rhodes b Kabir Ali	12	(1) lbw b Kabir Ali	2
RM Khan	b Peters b Mason	15	lbw b Kabir Ali	6
M Kaif	lbw b Mason	31	lbw b Mason	30
SA Selwood	c Peters b Mason	0	c Rhodes b Hayward	7
DG Cork (capt)	c Solanki b Hall	12	c Rhodes b Hayward	7
G Welch	c Batty b Mason	28	not out	0
*KM Krikken	c Rhodes b Hall	14	b Kabir Ali	1
KJ Dean	c Solanki b Hayward	4	b Kabir Ali	0
Mohammad Ali	b Hayward	11	c Rhodes b Kabir Ali	0
LJ Wharton	not out	5	b Kabir Ali	30
Extras	b 4, lb 7, w 2, nb 2	15	lb 3, nb 8	11
	(44.2 overs)	163	(32.4 overs)	96

Bowling

Kabir Ali 7–1–25–1. Hayward 11.2–4–46–2. Mason 14–4–43–5. Hall 12–3–38–2. Kabir Ali 15.4–3–58–8. Mason 12–7–16–0. Hayward 3–0–10–2. Batty 1–1–0–0.

Kabir Ali 15.4–3–58–8. Mason 12–7–16–0. Hayward 3–0–10–2. Batty 1–1–0–0.

Fall of Wickets 1-33, 2-41, 3-56, 4-56, 5-86, 6-121, 7-130, 8-142, 9-155, 10 163
1-2, 2-4, 3-19, 4-27, 5-39, 6-56, 7-58, 8-58, 9-58, 10-96

WORCS	First Innings	
SD Peters	c Di Venuto b Cork	5
A Singh	c Di Venuto b Cork	8
Kadeer Ali	lbw b Cork	18
BF Smith (capt)	c Selwood b Welch	22
VS Solanki	b Welch	24
AJ Hall	c Mohammad Ali b Dean	6
GI Batty	lbw b Dean	37
*SJ Rhodes	not out	81
Kabir Ali	c Krikken b Mohammad Ali	68
MS Mason	b Mohammad Ali	0
M Hayward	b Cork	0
Extras	b 5, lb 9, nb 14	28
	(102 overs)	301

Bowling

Cork 26.2–6–60–4. Dean 30–8–95–2. Welch 28–7–81–2. Mohammad Ali 18–6–51–2.

Fall of Wickets 1-21, 2-26, 3-58, 4-83, 5-98, 6-104, 7-190, 8-294, 9-294, 10-301

Worcestershire beat Derbyshire by an innings and 42 runs –
Worcestershire (20pts), Derbyshire (3pts)

that the gloved single off Kasprowicz which brought up his half-century had actually broken a finger. Hindley's bowling was not required, though, as Glamorgan were further buffeted by a tide that had so dramatically turned against them. By the close they were 33 for 3 against rejuvenated opponents. Chris Tremlett, with two of those early successes to his name, made it a career-best 6 for 51 on the final morning to complete Glamorgan's destruction. James Bruce supported him well taking 3 for 42, and Croft was top scorer with just 12 as the visitors plunged to a sorry 104 all out.

Derbyshire's worst run of defeats in the championship was confirmed at Worcester, where they suffered their seventh consecutive loss. The sad run was complete when Kabir Ali took a career-best 8 for 58 to hustle them out for only 96 in their second innings. Poor weather dragged the game into its final day, but Derbyshire only batted for 77 overs in all. On the first day they had been tumbled out for 163, with Matt Mason taking 5 for 43, and rain became their only realistic hope of survival once Kabir had struck an uninhibited 68 to help Steve Rhodes add 104 for the eighth wicket – to haul Worcestershire up beyond 300 – and then make three rapid new-ball strikes as Derbyshire declined again to 27 for 4 before a cloudburst cut short day two.

ROUND 13: 23–28 JULY 2003

Division One

Bad weather interrupted a glorious summer to play havoc with this round of matches, with only one fixture from the two divisions ending with a positive result. No play at all on the third day at Guildford, for instance, frustrated Surrey in what was developing into a hard-fought affair with Middlesex. After two days, Middlesex were 346 for 8 in reply to Surrey's first-innings 411 – with both teams staging fine recoveries. First Surrey fought back from 131 for 5, initially through Rikki Clarke's 110-ball 85 and an equally forthright 40 by Ian Salisbury, and then thanks to a superb last-wicket stand of 89 between Saqlain Mushtaq and Jimmy Ormond. Saqlain ended up unbeaten with 61, while Ormond followed up his 47 with a remarkable piece of bowling to rip open the Middlesex innings. At 163 for 1, with Andy Strauss on 87, the visitors were cruising. Suddenly, however, they were 165 for 6. Ormond took four wickets in an over, including a hat-trick, and Martin Bicknell then removed Owais Shah in

the very next over. Ormond's four victims were all, curiously, left-handers: Strauss, Ben Hutton, Ed Joyce and Paul Weekes. Strauss fell lbw to the first ball of the over, and Hutton gloved a bouncer from the fourth delivery. The next saw Joyce lbw to a ball which nipped back, and finally Weekes was bowled off stump to complete the hat-trick. Abdul Razzaq and David Nash then restored some order, with Nash ending up just four runs short of a deserved century when, eventually, the Middlesex first innings was wound up on a final day which was also bedevilled by rain.

Sussex suffered a first day washout at Trent Bridge and, ultimately, it was the time lost to the weather which prevented them from putting more pressure on Nottinghamshire's batsmen after running up 497 for 6 declared on the back of centuries from Murray Goodwin and Robin Martin-Jenkins. Kevin Pietersen, twice sweeping Mushtaq Ahmed for six, kept the Notts ship afloat with a classy 139 in a first-innings reply of 296, but a slow pitch prevented James Kirtley from adding substantially to his first-innings haul of 5 for 60 when the follow-on was enforced on the last day. In the end, with Darren Bicknell (75) and Russell Warren (114 not out) putting on 110 to offset an initial slide to 34 for 2, and Pietersen hitting 81 in a further stand of 131 with Warren, Sussex could not stop the home side from making it to safety as time ran out.

There was a similar pattern to the match at Old Trafford, where a third-day washout enabled Warwickshire to bat out time against Lancashire. The home side took charge when Stuart Law's wonderful unbeaten 236, an innings occupying just 257 balls and featuring two sixes and 27 fours, took them to the heights of 575 for 6 declared. Iain Sutcliffe made 86 and Glen Chapple then followed a terrific 132 (two sixes, 20 fours) by snapping up 4 for 43 as Warwickshire were reduced to 192 for 8 by the end of day two. Down came the rain, however, and Lancashire were left to curse the weather – not for the first time in their watery history at Manchester – when Mark Wagh and Nick Knight prevented the follow-on from becoming a headlong rout.

Essex were also aided by the weather as they emerged with a draw against Leicestershire at Southend. A youthful home attack, in which 26-year-old James Middlebrook was the senior citizen, was savaged by Darren Stevens, Brad Hodge and Trevor Ward as Leicestershire raced to 600 for 7 declared. Stevens reached a career-best 149 and Ward, who made it to three figures in only 88 balls, eventually scored 168. Andy Flower and James Foster steadied Essex from 97 for 4, but their task of saving the game was made a lot easier by the fact that just 16 overs were possible on day three.

Round 13: 23–28 July 2003 Division One

```
          SURREY v. MIDDLESEX – at Guildford
SURREY             First Innings              Second Innings
IJ Ward (capt)     b Noffke            10     not out            33
*JN Batty          b Keegan             2     retired hurt       25
MR Ramprakash      c Nash b Cook       33     not out            28
GP Thorpe          c Weekes b Cook     51
AD Brown           c Strauss b Cook     8
R Clarke           b Noffke            85
AJ Tudor           c Strauss b Keegan  27
MP Bicknell        b Keegan            11
IDK Salisbury      c Nash b Noffke     40
Saqlain Mushtaq    not out             61
J Ormond           c Weekes b Keegan   47
Extras             b 7, lb 15, nb 14   36     nb 8                8
                   (101.5 overs)      411     (no wkt, 26 overs) 94
Bowling
Noffke 24-3-91-3. Keegan 28.5-3-114-4. Abdul Razzaq 5-1-17-0. Cook
22-4-77-3. Hutton 3-0-18-0. Weekes 19-3-72-0.
Noffke 6-1-21-0. Keegan 8-1-29-0. Cook 6-1-21-0. Hutton 5-0-20-0. Joyce
1-0-3-0.
Fall of Wickets 1-16, 2-20, 3-113, 4-126, 5-131, 6-210, 7-232, 8-283, 9-322,
10-411

MIDDLESEX          First Innings
AJ Strauss (capt)  lbw b Ormond        87
SG Koenig          c Batty b Tudor     42
OA Shah            c Batty b Bicknell  22
BL Hutton          c Batty b Ormond     2
EC Joyce           lbw b Ormond         0
PN Weekes          b Ormond             0
Abdul Razzaq       c Ward b Bicknell   78
*DC Nash           not out             96
AA Noffke          c and b Saqlain Mushtaq 18
SJ Cook            lbw b Bicknell       4
CB Keegan          b Bicknell           4
Extras             b 8, lb 10, nb 14   32
                   (104.3 overs)      385
Bowling
Bicknell 29.3-3-102-4. Ormond 26.5-5-106-4. Tudor 11-4-28-1. Clarke 17-2-74-0.
Saqlain Mushtaq 16-3-33-1. Salisbury 5-0-24-0.
Fall of Wickets 1-101, 2-163, 3-165, 4-165, 5-165, 6-165, 7-320, 8-343, 9-377,
10-385
```

Match drawn – Surrey (12pts),
Middlesex (11pts)

The final day was affected by the weather as well, with Flower adding an unbeaten 39 to his first-innings 127 when Leicestershire were at last able to enforce the follow-on. Middlebrook's unbeaten 82 had boosted the Essex first-innings total up to 351, and Will Jefferson then eagerly joined Flower in batting out time.

Division Two

A spineless Somerset performance at Northampton condemned them to a fourth defeat in five matches. Northamptonshire won by an innings and 61 runs to record their fifth successive victory after taking 18 Somerset wickets on the second day. The quick-fire kill, accomplished comfortably inside two days, also enabled Northants to become the only team to beat the weather in this round of matches and get a positive result. Peter Walker, the ECB pitch officer, passed the surface on which Somerset subsided for 96 and 168 and added: 'It is below average, but you cannot condemn one side for bad batting by the other.' Jamie Cox top scored with 22 in the Somerset first innings, with left-arm seamer Adam Shantry taking 3 for 8 in five overs on his championship debut and Andre Nel also picking up three wickets. The only real resistance second time around came from Mike Burns and Ian Blackwell, who put on 83 for the fifth wicket.

```
      NOTTINGHAMSHIRE v. SUSSEX – at Trent Bridge
SUSSEX             First Innings
MW Goodwin         b Clough           148
RR Montgomerie     c Read b Cairns     32
PA Cottey          c Harris b Franks   53
CJ Adams (capt)    c Franks b Harris   46
MH Yardy           c Read b Harris     47
RSC M-Jenkins      not out            121
*MJ Prior          c Clough b Franks   17
KJ Innes           not out              6
M Ahmed
R J Kirtley
P M Hutchison
Extras             lb 6, w 5, nb 16    27
                   (6 wkts, 113 overs) 497
Bowling
Harris 28-5-98-2. Shreck 28-4-109-0. Cairns 18-5-63-1. Franks 19-3-102-2.
Clough 16-0-76-1. Pietersen 4-0-43-0.
Fall of Wickets 1 60, 2-197, 3-295, 4-297, 5-434, 6-474

NOTTS              First Innings              Second Innings
DJ Bicknell        c Prior b Kirtley   15     c Montgomerie b Kirtley 75
JER Gallian (capt) b Kirtley            6     lbw b Kirtley       0
GE Welton          c Yardy b Kirtley   12     c Cottey b Hutchison 8
RJ Warren          c Cottey b M-Jenkins 42    not out           114
KP Pietersen       c Adams b Kirtley  139     c and b Montgomerie 81
CL Cairns          c Prior b M-Jenkins  1     not out             7
*CMW Readc         Montgomerie b M Ahmed 0
PJ Franks          c Yardy b Hutchison 43
GD Clough          c Adams b M Ahmed   1b
AJ Harris          b Kirtley            1
CE Shreck          not out              0
Extras             b 3, lb 12, nb 6    21     b 4, lb 2           6
                   (87.5 overs)       296     (4 wkts, 73 overs) 291
Bowling
Kirtley 23-9-60-5. Hutchison 17-5-60-1. M Ahmed 28.5-2-87-2. Yardy 5-0-14-0.
M-Jenkins 14-1-60-2.
Kirtley 11-4-32-2. Hutchison 16-2-66-1. Yardy 13-2-50-0. M Ahmed 9-2-41-0.
M-Jenkins 12-2-43-0. Cottey 9-1-44-0. Montgomerie 3-0-9-1.
Fall of Wickets 1-16, 2-35, 3-46, 4-127, 5-139, 6-140, 7-254, 8-290, 9-296,
10-296
1-1, 2-34, 3-144, 4-275
```

Match drawn – Nottinghamshire (8pts),
Sussex (12pts)

```
     LANCASHIRE v. WARWICKSHIRE – at Old Trafford
LANCASHIRE         First Innings
AJ Swann           c Brown b Carter    15
IJ Sutcliffe       b Brown             86
MB Loye            lbw b Brown         14
SG Law             not out            236
MJ Chilton         c Frost b Waqar Younis 30
CL Hooper          c Brown b Carter    35
G Chapple          b Smith            132
WK Hegg            not out              7
Extras             b 8, lb 6, w 6      20
                   (6 wkts, 129 overs) 575
Bowling
Waqar Younis 24-5-79-1. Carter 24-1-133-2. Richardson 29-3-112-0.
Brown 30-7-117-2. Smith 15-0-97-1. Bell 7-0-23-0.
Fall of Wickets 1-37, 2-85, 3-134, 4-212, 5-314, 6-542

WARWICKSHIRE       First Innings              Second Innings
MJ Powell          b Martin            28     b Chapple          21
NV Knight          c Hegg b Wood       27     b Wood             56
MA Wagh            c Swann b Chapple    1     not out            76
IR Bell            c Hegg b Chapple    48     c Law b Martin     28
JO Troughton       c Hegg b Hooper     16     c Swann b Martin    4
T Frost            c Hegg b Chapple     7     not out             3
DR Brown           not out             52
NMK Smith          c Hegg b Hooper     10
NM Carter          c Law b Chapple      4
Waqar Younis       c Wood b Keedy      22
A Richardson       c Swann b Wood       1
Extras             (b 4, lb 8, w 5, nb 19) 36
                   (all out, 81 overs) 255
Bowling
Martin 17-1-55-1. Chapple 21-4-82-4. Wood 8-1-33-2. Keedy 22-12-31-1.
Hooper 13-3-42-2.
Martin 18.4-5-57-2. Wood 9-1-26-1. Keedy 24-3-74-0.
Chapple 9-1-34-1. Hooper 12-4-13-0.
Fall of Wickets 1-34, 2-35, 3-65, 4-98, 5-134, 6-137, 7-163, 8-179, 9-251, 10-255
1-76, 2-91, 3-163, 4-183
```

Match drawn – Lancashire (12pts)
Warwickshire (7.75pts)

```
      ESSEX v. LEICESTERSHIRE – at Southend
LEICESTERSHIRE     First Innings
JK Maunders        c Foster b Middlebrook 44
DI Stevens         c and b Sharif     149
DL Maddy (capt)    lbw b Sharif        41
BJ Hodge           c Flower b Sharif   74
TR Ward            lbw b McCoubrey    168
*PA Nixon          lbw b Middlebrook   30
JN Snape           not out             52
DD Masters         b Middlebrook        8
C E Dagnall
M J A Whiley
R M Amin
Extras             lb 18, w 8, nb 8    34
                   (7 wkts, 131.5 overs) 600
Bowling
Napier 22-3-115-0. McCoubrey 16-2-102-1. Middlebrook 41.5-6-150-3.
Palladino 28-8-76-0. Sharif 17-1-103-3. Bopara 7-0-36-0.
Fall of Wickets 1-108, 2-184, 3-314, 4-350, 5-471, 6-591, 7-600

ESSEX              First Innings              Second Innings
WI Jefferson       lbw b Dagnall        7     not out            54
RS Bopara          c Maunders b Amin   18
A Flower           c Nixon b Whiley   127     not out            39
A Habib            c Nixon b Maddy      7
RC Irani (capt)    b Maddy              9
*JS Foster         b Hodge             50
AP Palladino       b Dagnall            1
JD Middlebrook     not out             82     (2) c Ward b Dagnall 13
GR Napier          h Marlly            17
ZK Sharif          lbw b Maddy          0
AGAM McCoubrey     c Whiley b Masters   0
Extras             lb 6, w 4, nb 18    28     b 1, lb 1, w 1, nb 2 5
                   (113.2 overs)      351     (1 wkt, 46.1 overs) 111
Bowling
Dagnall 22-5-58-2. Whiley 19-3-62-1. Masters 18.2-4-53-1. Amin 23-3-82-1.
Maddy 17-9-42-4. Hodge 9-2-35-1. Snape 5-2-13-0.
Masters 9-5-17-0. Maddy 6-3-8-0. Amin 11.1-2-38-0. Dagnall 5-2-13-1.
Whiley 3-0-8-0. Snape 8-2-19-0. Hodge 4-1-6-0.
Fall of Wickets 1-13, 2-68, 3-87, 4-97, 5-215, 6-227, 7-291, 8-346, 9-346, 10-351
1-16
```

Match drawn – Essex (9pts),
Leicestershire (12pts)

Jason Brown's off spin brought him 6 for 42, and Ben Phillips ended up with 3 for 21 following his two strikes with the new ball on the previous evening that had initially undermined Somerset. The Northants first innings featured a crisply struck 83 from Tim Roberts, a 25-year-old former county colt making a belated championship debut for his native county following first-class appearances for Lancashire and British Universities, and an unbeaten 38 from Shantry.

Derbyshire ultimately had tail-enders Tom Lungley and Neil Gunter to thank for avoiding a record eighth successive championship defeat, after they and Durham had tried to engineer a result at Derby. The loss of the second day to rain left Durham with two ways of forcing victory following a fine opening day in which they had scored 434 for 7. Nicky Peng had fallen one run short of a century while putting on 197 for the fifth wicket with Vince Wells, who himself made it to 106, and at the start of the third day it was left to Phil Mustard to lead the charge to 501 for 8 declared by hitting a forceful 70 not out. Now Durham had the mind to try to bowl Derbyshire out twice, but Michael Di Venuto put pay to this plan by scoring 143 after adding 197 for the first wicket with Steve Selwood (62). Chris Bassano and Dominic Cork then took Derbyshire past the follow-on target, setting up a declaration at 361 for 5 midway through the final morning. In response, Durham attempted their second route to victory by declaring their second innings on 110 for 2 and leaving Derbyshire to chase 251 in 55 overs. Selwood launched the victory assault with 88 and at 176 for 4 the home side required a

Round 13: 23–28 July 2003 Division Two

NORTHAMPTONSHIRE v. SOMERSET – at Northampton

NORTHANTS	First Innings		Second Innings	
MEK Hussey (capt)	b Blackwell	20		
TW Roberts	st Turner b Blackwell	83		
PA Jaques	c Turner b Blackwell	41		
DJG Sales	b Blackwell	38		
MJ Powell	run out	18		
*TMB Bailey	lbw b Jones	0		
GP Swann	c Burns b Jones	44		
BJ Phillips	c Turner b Blackwell	12		
AJ Shantry	not out	38		
A Nel	b McLean	22		
JF Brown	c Burns b Jones	1		
Extras	lb 8	8		
	(93.1 overs)	325		

Bowling
McLean 15-2-51-1. Gilder 4-0-32-0. Jones 17.1-2-61-3. Blackwell 38-6-96-5. Dutch 16-3-62-0. Burns 3-0-15-0.
Fall of Wickets 1-62, 2-131, 3-170, 4-191, 5-192, 6-232, 7-252, 8-262, 9-322, 10-325.

SOMERSET	First Inning		Second Innings	
PD Bowler	c Bailey b Phillips	14	(8) c Jaques b Brown	8
MJ Wood	c Powell b Nel	10	(1) c Shantry b Phillips	6
JDC Bryant	b Phillips	0	c Bailey b Phillips	15
J Cox	lbw b Nel	22	c Jaques b Brown	24
M Burns (capt)	run out	15	c Phillips b Brown	55
ID Blackwell	lbw b Shantry	5	c Hussey b Nel	40
*RJ Turner	not out	10	(2) lbw b Phillips	0
KP Dutch	c Powell b Shantry	0	(7) c Powell b Brown	7
NAM McLean	c Nel b Shantry	0	c Roberts b Brown	0
PS Jones	b Brown	8	b Brown	8
GM Gilder	c Sales b Nel	12	not out	0
Extras			b 2, lb 3	5
	(36.2 overs)	96	(63.1 overs)	168

Bowling
Nel 13.2-2-51-3. Phillips 11-6-20-2. Brown 7-3-17-1. Shantry 5-3-8-3.
Nel 16-4-48-1. Phillips 11-3-21-3. Shantry 8-2-19-0. Brown 22.1-7-42-6.
Swann 6-0-33-0.
Fall of Wickets 1-15, 2-15, 3-46, 4-47, 5-66, 6-66, 7-66, 8-66, 9-81, 10-96
1-2, 2-9, 3-32, 4-59, 5-142, 6-142, 7-157, 8-157, 9-165, 10-168

*Northamptonshire beat Somerset by an innings and 61 runs –
Northamptonshire (20pts), Somerset (3pts)*

DERBYSHIRE v. DURHAM – at Derby

DURHAM	First Innings		Second Innings	
JJB Lewis (capt)	c Sutton b Cork	77	not out	41
MA Gough	c Cork b Gunter	36	c Kaif b Gunter	31
GJ Muchall	c Kaif b Wharton	9	c Di Venuto b Dean	0
GJ Pratt	c Di Venuto b Gunter	4	not out	33
N Peng	lbw b Wharton	99		
VJ Wells	c and b Lungley	106		
*P Mustard	not out	70		
GD Bridge	lbw b Lungley	4		
LE Plunkett	b Dean	29		
N Killeen	not out	13		
N G Hatch did not bat				
Extras	lb 23, w 5, nb 26	54	lb 3, w 2	5
	(8 wkts, 108.4 overs)	501	(2 wkts, 14.1 overs)	110

Bowling
Cork 20.5-3-92-1. Dean 31-5-138-1. Lungley 14.4-0-91-2. Gunter 13.1-2-48-2.
Wharton 27-4-103-2. Khan 2-1-6-0.
Dean 6-1-29-1. Gunter 6-0-57-1. Cork 1.1-0-10-0. Di Venuto 1-0-11-0.
Fall of Wickets 1-110, 2-120, 3-133, 4-162, 5-359, 6-389, 7-398, 8-475
1-52, 2-53

DERBYSHIRE	First Innings		Second Innings	
SA Selwood	c and b Bridge	62	(2) b Gough	88
MJ Di Venuto	lbw b Plunkett	143	(1) lbw b Plunkett	8
M Kaif	c Gough b Bridge	31	c Mustard b Killeen	7
RM Khan	c Gough b Killeen	7	c Muchall b Hatch	23
CWG Bassano	not out	44	c Mustard b Hatch	0
*LD Sutton	c Wells b Killeen	20	run out	36
DG Cork (capt)	not out	39	c Killeen b Gough	1
T Lungley			not out	10
NEL Gunter			not out	9
K J Dean				
L J Wharton				
Extras	b 1, lb 6, nb 8	15	b 7, lb 15	22
	(5 wkts, 93 overs)	361	(7 wkts, 55.4 overs)	204

Bowling
Plunkett 16-1-67-1. Hatch 14-1-70-0. Killeen 26-4-94-2. Wells 4-0-23-0. Bridge 33-10-100-2.
Plunkett 8-0-41-1. Killeen 12-2-28-1. Hatch 10-2-29-2. Bridge 18-3-61-0.
Gough 7.4-3-23-2.
Fall of Wickets 1-197, 2-241, 3-255, 4-255, 5-302
1-8, 2-15, 3-64, 4-72, 5-176, 6-178, 7-179

*Match drawn – Derbyshire (10pts),
Durham (10pts)*

YORKSHIRE v. HAMPSHIRE – at Scarborough

YORKSHIRE	First Innings		Second Innings	
MJ Wood (capt)	c Crawley b Tremlett	155	lbw b Mascarenhas	43
SP Fleming	c Tremlett b Bruce	16	c Francis b Bruce	53
VJ Craven	lbw b Mascarenhas	47	c Mascarenhas b Udal	38
MJ Lumb	lbw b Mascarenhas	64	c Tremlett b Udal	59
Yuvraj Singh	c Francis b Udal	26	not out	0
C White	lbw b Mascarenhas	0		
*SM Guy	c Brunnschweiler b Tremlett	13		
AKD Gray	lbw b Udal	30		
CEW Silverwood	not out	4		
RJ Sidebottom	c Tremlett b Bruce	0		
SP Kirby	c Adams b Udal	0		
Extras	lb 8, w 1, nb 20	29	b 3, lb 3, nb 12	18
	(130 overs)	384	(4 wkts, 39.5 overs)	211

Bowling
Tremlett 27-5-94-2. Mascarenhas 31-9-51-3. Hamblin 8-0-35-0. Bruce 23-4-101-2.
Udal 33-11-70-3. Katich 8-1-25-0.
Tremlett 8-2-32-0. Mascarenhas 9-2-39-1. Udal 10.5-1-42-2. Bruce 7-0-65-1.
Hamblin 5-0-27-0.
Fall of Wickets 1-55, 2-149, 3-303, 4-303, 5-303, 6-326, 7-380, 8-380, 9-383, 10-384
1-89, 2-109, 3-211, 4-211

HAMPSHIRE	First Innings		Second Innings	
DA Kenway	b Kirby	0	lbw b Kirby	5
JHK Adams	c Gray b Silverwood	0	c and b Gray	47
SM Katich	not out	143	b Craven	4
JP Crawley (capt)	c Guy b Kirby	0	c Wood b Craven	32
JD Francis	lbw b Silverwood	9	c Wood b Gray	2
JRC Hamblin	b Silverwood	4	c Wood b Gray	0
AD Mascarenhas	c Fleming b Sidebottom	4	not out	33
SD Udal	b Craven	26		
*I Brunnschweiler	lbw b Silverwood	34		
CT Tremlett	c Fleming b Sidebottom	19		
JTA Bruce	b Craven	2		
Extras	b 4, lb 5, nb 43	52	lb 9, w 1, nb 12	22
	(67 overs)	289	(6 wkts, 70.4 overs)	180

Bowling
Kirby 16-1-79-2. Silverwood 15-1-86-4. Sidebottom 11-1-28-2. Gray 16-0-49-1.
Craven 9-1-38-1.
Silverwood 16-3-40-0. Kirby 13-1-59-1. Craven 14-2-43-2. Gray 26-12-43-3.
Yuvraj Singh 4.4-1-4-0.
Fall of Wickets 1, 2-2, 3-4, 3-7, 4-96, 5-96, 6-107, 7-159, 8-232, 9-284, 10-289
1-12, 2-30, 3-83, 4-96, 5-105, 6-111

Match drawn – Yorkshire (11pts), Hampshire (9pts)

GLOUCESTERSHIRE v. WORCESTERSHIRE – at Cheltenham

GLOS	First Innings		Second Innings	
WPC Weston	c Solanki b Hall	28	(2) c Rhodes b Kabir Ali	25
CM Spearman (capt)	c Rhodes b Hayward	12	(1) b Kabir Ali	0
JN Rhodes	b Mason	19	not out	58
MGN Windows	lbw b Kabir Ali	23	lbw b Hall	12
APR Gidman	c Rhodes b Hayward	12	c Hayward b Batty	13
Shoaib Malik	c Batty b Mason	20	c Singh b Batty	0
MA Hardinges	c Rhodes b Hayward	17	not out	10
MCJ Ball	c Singh b Batty	29		
*SP Pope	not out	17		
JMM Averis	c Rhodes b Batty	26		
J Lewis	c Solanki b Mason	47		
Extras	b 2, lb 10, w 5, nb 22	39	b 4, lb 3, nb 8	15
	(73.1 overs)	271	(5 wkts, 41 overs)	133

Bowling
Kabir Ali 17-2-64-1. Hayward 17-3-77-3. Hall 14-6-29-1. Mason 16.1-7-48-3.
Batty 8-0-41-2. Solanki 1-1-0-0.
Kabir Ali 12-2-43-2. Hayward 7-2-17-0. Mason 8-4-23-0. Batty 8-1-19-2.
Hall 6-2-24-1.
Fall of Wickets 1-26, 2-69, 3-85, 4-117, 5-117, 6-157, 7-178, 8-199, 9-213, 10-271
1-0, 2-50, 3-96, 4-115, 5-115

WORCS	First Innings			
SD Peters	c Gidman b Averis	14		
A Singh	b Shoaib Malik	50		
GJ Batty	c Averis b Hardinges	24		
GA Hick	c Ball b Shoaib Malik	9		
BF Smith (capt)	c Pope b Lewis	92		
VS Solanki	lbw b Averis	35		
AJ Hall	lbw b Averis	73		
*SJ Rhodes	c Gidman b Lewis	63		
Kabir Ali	c Ball b Shoaib Malik	34		
MS Mason	not out	3		
M Hayward	c Rhodes b Lewis	0		
Extras	b 12, lb 12, nb 18	42		
	(124 overs)	439		

Bowling
Lewis 29-3-136-3. Averis 34-13-84-3. Hardinges 8-0-60-1. Shoaib Malik 35-10-76-3. Ball 14-2-43-0. Gidman 4-0-16-0.
Fall of Wickets 1-33, 2-83, 3-102, 4-103, 5-186, 6-294, 7-354, 8-434, 9-439, 10-439

*Match drawn – Gloucestershire (9pts),
Worcestershire (12pts)*

further 75 from 61 balls. Then, however, Wells ran out Luke Sutton for 36 and, with Derbyshire settling for the draw, Lungley and Gunter had held out for ten overs as the home side finished on 204 for 7.

Yorkshire captain Matthew Wood also issued Hampshire with a fourth-innings challenge at Scarborough to breathe life into another match that could have expired altogether following a third-day washout. Wood set Hampshire a target of 307 in what turned out to be 71 overs and, at 111 for 6, the visitors looked to be in distinct danger of losing the match. Shaun Udal, however, then joined James Hamblin in an unbroken seventh-wicket stand of 69. It was frustrating for Yorkshire, who would also have had Hampshire in greater trouble on day two but for an unbeaten 143, out of a first-innings total of 289, from Simon Katich. The Australian left-hander hit a six and 20 fours in a 194-ball effort which inspired some useful lower-order contributions following an initial dive to 107 for 6. The opening day had belonged to Wood, whose 155 was his 12th first-class hundred and his third score of the season above 150.

Worcestershire would most probably have defeated Gloucestershire in their Cheltenham stronghold but for the inclement weather which interrupted both the first and final days and also washed away play on the third altogether. It took a beefy 47 in 33 balls from last man Jon Lewis, featuring three sixes and four fours, to lift Gloucestershire's first innings to 271, but this was revealed in all its inadequacy by Worcestershire's subsequent march to 439. Anurag Singh, Ben Smith, Andrew Hall and Steve Rhodes all passed the

half-century mark and Gloucestershire were a shaky-looking 133 for 5 in their second innings, and indebted to an unbeaten half-century from Jonty Rhodes, when time ran out.

ROUND 14: 30 JULY–3 AUGUST 2003

Division One

The much-anticipated, top-of-the-table clash between Sussex and Surrey at Hove fizzled out

Chris Adams bounced back to form in Sussex's big match with Surrey ... but faced criticism all the same for settling for the draw.

limply on the third afternoon when Chris Adams, the home captain, decided to go off for bad light with his side 143 runs ahead at 69 for 2 in their second innings – and with 37 overs of the day still to be bowled. When Sussex finally resumed, the

next morning, Adams also chose not to declare until they had reached 302 for 5. By now, the game had ceased to exist as a contest, and Surrey merely batted out time reaching 114 for 1. In terms of points gained, Sussex came out marginally in front of their rivals at 12 to 11, but the draw – and the manner of it – was a great disappointment to all those who had looked forward to Sussex's challenge of Surrey's supremacy. Some criticized Adams harshly for what they saw as an over-cautiousness born out of a lack of confidence in his team's ability to unseat the defending champions. Adams rigorously defended his position, saying that Sussex would only earn the right to become champions over the whole season's course … and not by gambling on success in this one fixture. Whatever, the Sussex action did smack somewhat of safety-first tactics – and one was left wondering if they had not missed an opportunity to test out Surrey's own resolve on the final day. With a bat in his hand, however, Adams had illustrated beyond all doubt on the opening day that he possessed 'bottle' and the love of a scrap. Woefully out of touch for most of the summer, he responded to the importance of the occasion by returning to form in the most glorious fashion. His 107 was his first championship century in 15 months, and it also followed an opening partnership of 149 between Richard Montgomerie and Murray Goodwin. Adams added a further 82 with Montgomerie (90)

Round 14: 30 July–3 August 2003
Division One

SUSSEX v. SURREY – at Hove

SUSSEX	First Innings		Second Innings	
RR Montgomerie	b Salisbury	90	(2) lbw b Bicknell	2
MW Goodwin	b Ormond	75	(1) c Ward b Saqlain Mushtaq	29
PA Cottey	lbw b Saqlain Mushtaq	1	c Ramprakash b Azhar Mahmood	41
CJ Adams (capt)	c Batty b Ormond	107	lbw b Saqlain Mushtaq	23
*TR Ambrose	c Azhar Mahmood b Salisbury	43	not out	76
RSC M-Jenkins	b Bicknell	40	b Salisbury	45
MJ Prior	c Thorpe b Ormond	0	not out	50
MJG Davis	c Clarke b Ormond	0		
M Ahmed	c Batty b Azhar Mahmood	26		
PM Hutchison	c Ward b Bicknell	5		
RJ Kirtley	not out	1		
Extras	b 6, lb 13, nb 22	31	b 9, lb 8, nb 14	31
	(126 overs)	429	(5 wkts, 87.5 overs)	302

Bowling
Bicknell 26–5–94–2. Ormond 25–6–106–4. Hollioake 7–3–23–0. Azhar Mahmood 18–5–61–1. Saqlain Mushtaq 36–5–84–1. Salisbury 14–0–42–2.
Bicknell 16–5–54–1. Ormond 10–3–17–0. Saqlain Mushtaq 35–7–97–2. Azhar Mahmood 4–1–3–1. Salisbury 22–0–98–1. Hollioake 0.5–0–11–0.
Fall of Wickets 1–149, 2–150, 3–232, 4–330, 5–363, 6–363, 7–367, 8–415, 9–423, 10–429
1–7, 2–67, 3–89, 4–108, 5–228

SURREY	First Innings		Second Innings	
IJ Ward	lbw b Kirtley	20	lbw b Kirtley	33
*JN Batty	c Ambrose b Hutchison	12	not out	65
MR Ramprakash	c Ambrose b Kirtley	104	not out	14
GP Thorpe	c Davis b M-Jenkins	23		
R Clarke	c M Ahmed b M-Jenkins	12		
AJ Hollioake (capt)	lbw b M Ahmed	13		
Azhar Mahmood	lbw b M Ahmed	9		
MP Bicknell	lbw b M Ahmed	42		
IDK Salisbury	st Ambrose b M Ahmed	1		
Saqlain Mushtaq	b M-Jenkins	68		
J Ormond	not out	42		
Extras	b 1, lb 6, nb 2	9	lb 2	2
	(102.3 overs)	355	(1 wkt, 26 overs)	114

Bowling
Kirtley 28–4–90–2. Hutchison 16–2–58–1. M Ahmed 38–7–123–4. M-Jenkins 17.3–3–67–3. Davis 3–0–10–0.
Kirtley 6–1–23–0. Hutchison 7–1–30–0. M-Jenkins 3–0–17–0. M Ahmed 6–1–26–0. Davis 4–1–16–1.
Fall of Wickets 1–32, 2–32, 3–75, 4–89, 5–116, 6–126, 7–215, 8–217, 9–301, 10–355
1–82

Match drawn – Sussex (12pts), Surrey (11pts)

KENT v. ESSEX – at Canterbury

KENT	First Innings		Second Innings	
DP Fulton (capt)	c Flower b Grant	12	not out	94
RWT Key	lbw b Palladino	6	(4) c Foster b McCoubrey	4
ET Smith	c Flower b Palladino	108	c Flower b Grant	32
MA Carberry	c and b Grant	6	(2) c Foster b Napier	36
MJ Walker	c Jefferson b McCoubrey	5	c Flower b Napier	23
MA Ealham	c Foster b Palladino	3	c Jefferson b Grant	8
*GO Jones	b Palladino	5	c Irani b Grant	31
A Khan	c Irani b Palladino	12	c Jefferson b Middlebrook	4
MJ Saggers	c Foster b Palladino	4	lbw b Middlebrook	4
M Muralitharan	c Robinson b Middlebrook	4	lbw b Middlebrook	1
A Sheriyar	not out	1	b Middlebrook	0
Extras	b 2, w 1, nb 18	21	b 8, lb 4, nb 22	34
	(40.3 overs)	189	(81.2 overs)	284

Bowling
Grant 10–2–63–2. Palladino 15–5–41–6. Napier 5–1–23–0. McCoubrey 5–0–33–1. Middlebrook 5.3–0–27–1.
Grant 15–0–61–3. Palladino 16–2–58–0. Napier 16.5–4–68–2. Middlebrook 30.2–5–78–4. McCoubrey 3.1–1–7–1.
Fall of Wickets 1–8, 2–21, 3–33, 4–65, 5–102, 6–128, 7–164, 8–170, 9–187, 10–189
1–48, 2–103, 3–115, 4–169, 5–176, 6–237, 7–266, 8–282, 9–284, 10–284

ESSEX	First Innings		Second Innings	
DDJ Robinson	c Jones b Ealham	25	b Khan	42
WI Jefferson	c Jones b Khan	6	c Walker b Muralitharan	5
A Flower	c Jones b Ealham	39	(4) b Khan	83
A Habib	c Muralitharan b Ealham	0	(5) b Muralitharan	14
RC Irani (capt)	c Jones b Khan	52	(6) b Khan	14
*JS Foster	c Jones b Saggers	0	(7) lbw b Muralitharan	31
JD Middlebrook	b Khan	15	(8) c Walker b Muralitharan	5
GR Napier	c and b Khan	16	(9) lbw b Muralitharan	5
AP Palladino	not out	4	(3) b Saggers	8
JB Grant	lbw b Ealham	1	b Muralitharan	4
AGAM McCoubrey	c Jones b Ealham	0	not out	0
Extras	b 5, lb 2, nb 12	19	b 4, lb 7, w 1, nb 12	24
	(50.1 overs)	183	(80.1 overs)	235

Bowling
Saggers 13–5–29–1. Khan 15–0–65–4. Sheriyar 2–0–15–0. Ealham 17–8–26–5. Muralitharan 22–9–41–0.
Saggers 15–4–40–1. Khan 11–2–61–2. Ealham 12–3–32–0. Muralitharan 28.1–6–61–6. Sheriyar 14–6–30–1.
Fall of Wickets 1–14, 2–75, 3–82, 4–95, 5–107, 6–146, 7–159, 8–174, 9–175, 10–183
1–20, 2–51, 3–63, 4–118, 5–141, 6–188, 7–194, 8–221, 9–235, 10–235

Kent beat Essex by 55 runs – Kent (17pts), Essex (3pts)

LEICESTERSHIRE v. LANCASHIRE – at Leicester

LEICESTERSHIRE	First Innings		Second Innings	
JK Maunders	c Hooper b Martin	21	run out	75
DI Stevens	c Hooper b Chapple	54	c Swann b Keedy	50
DL Maddy	lbw b Wood	19	lbw b Keedy	14
BJ Hodge	c Hegg b Wood	5	c Hooper b Chapple	38
TR Ward	c Swann b Keedy	20	c Hegg b Chapple	0
*PA Nixon	c Swann b Martin	19	c Hooper b Martin	35
JN Snape	c Wood b Keedy	27	c Hegg b Wood	36
PAJ DeFreitas (capt)	c Hegg b Keedy	57	c Hegg b Wood	0
DD Masters	not out	10	c Hegg b Wood	1
RM Amin	c Loye b Wood	1	not out	6
DE Malcolm	c Hogg b Keedy	3	b Chapple	14
Extras	b 8, lb 15, w 1, nb 14	23	lb 5, w 1, nb 14	20
	(73.4 overs)	259	(93 overs)	287

Bowling
Martin 17–1–77–2. Chapple 15–4–53–1. Wood 16–3–59–3. Hogg 10–3–29–0. Hooper 6–2–15–0. Keedy 9.4–3–17–4.
Martin 26–11–51–1. Chapple 23–4–84–3. Wood 10–1–42–3. Keedy 21–4–59–2. Hooper 8–1–25–0. Hogg 5–1–21–0.
Fall of Wickets 1–32, 2–65, 3–73, 4–103, 5–146, 6–146, 7–220, 8–243, 9–244, 10–259
1–63, 2–106, 3–161, 4–161, 5–200, 6–246, 7–247, 8–257, 9–262, 10–287

LANCASHIRE	First Innings		Second Innings	
MJ Chilton	c Nixon b DeFreitas	14	b DeFreitas	9
AJ Swann	b Malcolm	7	c Nixon b DeFreitas	1
G Keedy	c Stevens b DeFreitas	6		
MB Loye	lbw b DeFreitas	45	(3) not out	21
SG Law	lbw b Maddy	186	(4) c Nixon b DeFreitas	15
CL Hooper	c Stevens b DeFreitas	117	(5) not out	20
G Chapple	c Nixon b DeFreitas	8		
*WK Hegg (capt)	c DeFreitas b Masters	27		
KW Hogg	c Maddy b DeFreitas	12		
J Wood	not out	8		
PJ Martin	c Ward b Masters	19		
Extras	b 7, lb 16, w 5, nb 2	30	lb 2	2
	(135.2 overs)	479	(3 wkts, 20.2 overs)	68

Bowling
DeFreitas 41–14–88–6. Malcolm 27–5–102–1. Maddy 15–3–56–1. Masters 31.2–4–107–2. Amin 12–1–68–0. Snape 8–1–28–0.
DeFreitas 10.2–5–24–3. Masters 9–0–36–0. Amin 1–0–6–0.
Fall of Wickets 1–20, 2–28, 3–44, 4–137, 5–384, 6–400, 7–413, 8–435, 9–459, 10–479
1–5, 2–10, 3–28

Lancashire beat Leicestershire by 7 wickets –
Lancashire (22pts), Leicestershire (4pts)

NOTTINGHAMSHIRE v. MIDDLESEX – at Trent Bridge

NOTTS	First Innings		Second Innings	
DJ Bicknell	c and b Dawes	39	lbw b Keegan	2
GE Welton	lbw b Keegan	1	c Weekes b Keegan	69
V Atri	c Nash b Noffke	5	c Nash b Dawes	2
RJ Warren	c Nash b Noffke	33	c Nash b Dawes	9
KP Pietersen	c and b Noffke	67	b Dawes	1
CL Cairns (capt)	lbw b Cook	5	c Weekes b Dawes	41
*CMW Read	c Joyce b Weekes	26	c Nash b Keegan	38
PJ Franks	c Nash b Noffke	28	c Weekes b Dawes	0
GJ Smith	b Noffke	27	not out	3
SCG MacGill	not out	5	b Keegan	2
CE Shreck	c Weekes b Keegan	1	c Nash b Keegan	0
Extras	lb 4, nb 4	8	b 2, lb 3, nb 2	7
	(81.3 overs)	254	(56.3 overs)	169

Bowling
Noffke 21–5–52–5. Keegan 19.3–4–71–2. Cook 16–4–49–1. Dawes 15–2–59–1. Joyce 2–0–8–0. Weekes 8–2–11–1.
Noffke 9.4–3–33–0. Keegan 12.3–3–39–5. Cook 13–5–38–0. Dawes 18–6–46–5. Weekes 3.2–1–8–0.
Fall of Wickets 1–2, 2–13, 3–67, 4–98, 5–119, 6–188, 7–202, 8–246, 9–249, 10–254
1–13, 2–49, 3–67, 4–73, 5–94, 6–169, 7–169, 8–169, 9–169, 10–169

MIDDLESEX	First Innings		Second Innings	
AJ Strauss (capt)	c Atri b Smith	29	c Read b Cairns	8
SG Koenig	lbw b MacGill	75	c Pietersen b Cairns	10
OA Shah	c Read b MacGill	13	c Pietersen b MacGill	41
BL Hutton	lbw b MacGill	16	lbw b Shreck	29
EC Joyce	c Read b Cairns	36	lbw b MacGill	14
PN Weekes	st Read b MacGill	6	c Welton b Smith	11
*DC Nash	c Warren b Franks	36	not out	14
AA Noffke	b Smith	20	not out	18
SJ Cook	not out	19		
CB Keegan	b Smith	4		
JH Dawes	c Read b Smith	9		
Extras	b 7, lb 8, nb 6	21	b 1, lb 1, w 1	3
	(98.4 overs)	254	(6 wkts, 50.1 overs)	146

Bowling
Smith 19.4–6–57–4. Shreck 16–7–31–0. Cairns 18–3–61–1. MacGill 30–8–78–4. Franks 15–1–36–1.
Smith 15–5–37–1. Cairns 10–1–43–2. Franks 3–2–2–0. MacGill 18.1–4–48–2. Shreck 4–1–14–1.
Fall of Wickets 1–54, 2–82, 3–120, 4–155, 5–159, 6–187, 7–246, 8–246, 9–250, 10–278
1–9, 2–26, 3–81, 4–87, 5–114, 6–116

Middlesex beat Nottinghamshire by 4 wickets –
Middlesex (19pts), Nottinghamshire (5pts)

and then 98 with Tim Ambrose, and a Sussex first-innings total of 429 put them into a strong position. It looked stronger still when Surrey slipped to 126 for 6 in reply. Were the champions cracking? If they were, they were soon made good again by an international-class century from Mark Ramprakash (104). First of all Martin Bicknell came to his aid as Ramprakash went about rebuilding the innings, although even at 217 for 8 early on the third day Surrey were in deep trouble. Ramprakash was ninth out only after an 84-run stand with Saqlain Mushtaq, and then Jimmy Ormond biffed an unbeaten 42 from 41 balls after joining the Pakistani, who hit three sixes and eight fours in his 68, in a last-wicket stand worth 54. Perhaps it was this enviable depth in batting that Adams feared. In the end, all the chatter was just that: the bottom line was that the championship battle went on with honours here just about even.

Kent hauled themselves out of the relegation zone by beating Essex – who they leapfrogged as well as Warwickshire – by 55 runs at Canterbury. Ed Smith, David Fulton, Mark Ealham and Amjad Khan were all home heroes, but the man who made the final difference between the sides was Sri Lankan off spinner Muttiah Muralitharan, marking his Kent championship debut by taking 6 for 61 in the Essex second innings. Smith, though, held the Kent first innings together single-handedly by scoring 108 – his fourth consecutive first-class hundred and making him only the third Kent batsman to do this after Wally Hardinge in 1913 and Frank Woolley in 1929. Tony Palladino, a 20-year-old seamer from Anglia University, took 6 for 41 on his championship debut – an analysis which mocked the fact that his four previous first-class victims, taken for the Cambridge UCCE team, had cost 113 runs each. Ealham, with 5 for 26 from 17 overs, and Khan (4 for 65) led a Kent fightback in the field as Essex were themselves bowled out for 183, six runs short of the home side's first-innings score. Now it was Fulton's turn to wage a lone struggle, and he was cruelly left stranded on 94 not out when James Middlebrook suddenly cut short the Kent second innings on 284 by taking a hat-trick! It was, however, the first time that Fulton had carried his bat, and his five-and-a-half hour innings had given his team a good chance of victory. Andy Flower was soon revealed as the only man who could deny Kent, and Murali wrapped things up once Alamgir Sheriyar had removed Flower for 83, via an inside edge.

The middle-order powerhouse of Stuart Law and Carl Hooper was at the heart of Lancashire's seven-wicket win over Leicestershire at Grace Road. Law hit 186 and Hooper 117 as the pair reacted to Lancashire's early decline to 44 for 3, in reply to the home side's first-innings 259, by adding 247 for the fifth wicket to inspire a drive towards 479. Phil DeFreitas, with six wickets in another determined performance, was the only bowler who demanded their respect – and DeFreitas even managed to pick up three more wickets when Lancashire, who had dismissed Leicestershire for 287 second time around, set out in pursuit of a small winning score.

The ball was always on top of the bat at Trent Bridge, where Middlesex fought their way to a four-wicket win over Nottinghamshire. Kevin Pietersen's 67 and Sven Koenig's 75 stood out as Middlesex gained a slight first-innings advantage, but Notts looked as if they were in a position to tip the balance back in their favour when they reached the end of day three at 160 for 5 in their second innings and with Chris Cairns and Chris Read having already added 66. However, the next morning, Chad Keegan and Joe Dawes engineered a collapse to 169 all out and, despite slipping to 116 for 6 themselves, Middlesex were seen home by David Nash and Ashley Noffke, whose first-day 5 for 50 were his best championship figures of the summer to date.

Division Two

Worcestershire held off a brave Glamorgan challenge at New Road to maintain their drive towards Division One status. In the end they clinched victory by just 14 runs after Robert Croft and David Harrison had fashioned a last-wicket stand of 56. Glamorgan, needing 339, were on 324 for 9 when Harrison – having just cover driven Kabir Ali for four – miscued the next ball to backward point where Gareth Batty clung on to the catch to spark scenes of jubilation. Harrison made 27 and Croft was unbeaten on 51 to add to his second-innings haul of 4 for 69. Jimmy Maher had led the run chase with 95, and Mark Wallace hit 55, but Glamorgan were let down by their first-innings batting display. Being bowled out for just 156, in reply to a Worcestershire first-innings total of 237 that was based on half-centuries from Batty and David Leatherdale, left the Welsh county with too much ground to make up once Ben Smith (87) and Stephen Peters (56) had ensured there was no Worcestershire second-innings collapse.

Hampshire captain John Crawley was either carried away by his side's first-innings bowling performance or his own return to batting form, because he miscalculated his declaration badly against Northamptonshire at Southampton. Northants, bowled out for 176 first time around after collapsing from an overnight 76 without loss following a second-day washout, romped home by five wickets – and with 13 overs in hand – after Crawley had set them 330 to win in what became 107 overs. Mike Hussey, the Northants captain, scored 100 and it was his partnership of 159 in 41 overs with David Sales, who made 75, that formed the basis of a county record sixth successive championship victory for Northants. Earlier, the match had belonged to Simon Katich, Hampshire's Australian left-hander, who hit 117 and 79 not out and in between took 4 for 21 with his left-arm chinamen. Crawley's second-innings unbeaten 81 was, in the end, his one consolation from a game his team had controlled for so long.

Only a meagre 67 balls were bowled on the first day, and Gloucestershire's centrepiece Cheltenham Festival fixture with Yorkshire remained bedevilled by poor weather as it squelched its way towards a draw. At least those being wined and dined in the many tents around the boundary had other pleasures to concentrate on as the action rather limped along in between the showers. They also had a decent sighting of fiery fast bowler Steve Kirby, who continued the upward curve on his career graph by taking six first-innings Gloucestershire wickets, and a heart-warming 68 from Gavin Hamilton in his first championship appearance since his decision to try to play county cricket as a specialist batsman following his chronic loss of confidence in his bowling. There was also some sparkling strokeplay on the final

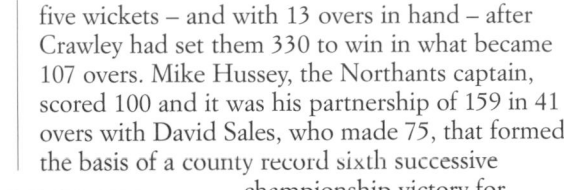

Here comes the 'Rawalpindi Express': Somerset felt the full force of Shoaib Akhtar's pace when they were derailed in spectacular fashion at Chester-le-Street.

day from Craig Spearman, Matt Windows and Shoaib Malik – and another four wickets for Kirby.

Peter Anderson, the Somerset chief executive, was a most visible visitor on the opening day of his county's fixture against Durham at faraway Chester-le-Street. Anderson had made headlines after publicly confirming that the club had, indeed, sent out letters to ten of their players warning them that their individual performances needed to improve if they were to have a future with Somerset. He responded to questions about why he made the long journey to the North East by saying: 'I want to see if our action has had any effect.' Sadly, he had his answer in three days. Somerset, replying to Durham's first-innings 345, were blown away for 139 and – after then dismissing Durham for a second-innings 168 – slid ignominiously to a hapless 56, the season's lowest total. Shoaib Akhtar may have bowled with terrifying pace – he took 4 for 39 in Somerset's first innings and then 4 for 9 in seven overs when they batted again – but this was still humiliation and more for the West Country county. Vince Wells was the first support act for Shoaib, taking 4 for 16, before Neil Killeen did the job in the second innings. The youthful quartet of Gordon Muchall, Gary Pratt, Nicky Peng and Graeme Bridge all batted well for Durham in their first innings, but the eventual win margin of 318 runs

also said much for the total lack of self-belief in a Somerset side who were 8 for 6 at one stage in their sorry second innings.

Round 14: 30 July–3 August 2003
Division Two

WORCESTERSHIRE v. GLAMORGAN – at Worcester

WORCS	First Innings		Second Innings	
SD Peters	c Wallace b Harrison	29	b Croft	56
A Singh	c Wallace b SD Thomas	30	c Maher b Wharf	10
GA Hick	c Wharf b Harrison	1	b Wharf	6
BF Smith (capt)	c Powell b Harrison	0	b Harrison	87
VS Solanki	c Maynard b Harrison	4	c IJ Thomas b Croft	8
DA Leatherdale	c IJ Thomas b Wharf	50	b Wharf	15
GJ Batty	c IJ Thomas b Wharf	60	lbw b Kasprowicz	5
*SJ Rhodes	c Powell b Croft	0	c Hughes b Croft	20
Kabir Ali	not out	38	not out	28
MS Mason	c Croft b Wharf	16	c Kasprowicz b Croft	1
M Hayward	b Wharf	4	b Kasprowicz	4
Extras	lb 9	9	b 1, lb 10, w 4, nb 2	17
	(63 overs)	237	(83.4 overs)	257

Bowling
Kasprowicz 16–3–43–0. Wharf 16–3–63–4. Croft 9–2–43–1. S. D. Thomas 6–0–22–1. Harrison 16–5–52–4.
Kasprowicz 19.4–5–46–2. Wharf 15–4–38–3. S. D. Thomas 9–0–38–0. Harrison 20–5–55–1. Croft 20–2–69–4.
Fall of Wickets 1–45, 2–46, 3–46, 4–64, 5–65, 6–166, 7–175, 8–183, 9–237, 10–237
1–28, 2–40, 3–106, 4–120, 5–147, 6–163, 7–216, 8–222, 9–228, 10–257

GLAMORGAN	First Innings		Second Innings	
JP Maher	c Rhodes b Hayward	0	c Hick b Mason	95
J Hughes	b Mason	24	c Batty b Kabir Ali	30
DS Harrison	b Hayward	0	(11) c Batty b Kabir Ali	27
IJ Thomas	c Solanki b Leatherdale	53	(3) c Hick b Mason	1
MJ Powell	b Mason	0	(4) b Kabir Ali	3
MP Maynard	c Peters b Mason	12	(5) c Peters b Hayward	19
*MA Wallace	c Solanki b Batty	29	(6) b Batty	55
RDB Croft (capt)	lbw b Leatherdale	0	(7) not out	51
SD Thomas	lbw b Kabir Ali	21	(8) lbw b Batty	10
MS Kasprowicz	b Kabir Ali	0	b Kabir Ali	0
AG Wharf	not out	0	(9) lbw b Leatherdale	13
Extras	lb 3, nb 5	8	b 8, lb 10, nb 2	20
	(51.1 overs)	156	(97 overs)	324

Bowling
Hayward 11–2–34–2. Kabir Ali 13–2–55–2. Mason 12–3–22–3. Batty 10.1–2–24–1. Leatherdale 5–2–18–2.
Kabir Ali 29–6–96–4. Hayward 11–1–75–1. Mason 23–6–58–2. Batty 23–3–66–2. Leatherdale 7–3–11–1.
Fall of Wickets 1–0, 2–0, 3–56, 4–70, 5–90, 6–106, 7–106, 8–146, 9–156, 10–156
1–51, 2–65, 3–72, 4–119, 5–210, 6–210, 7–229, 8–262, 9–268, 10–324

Worcestershire beat Glamorgan by 14 runs – Worcestershire (18pts), Glamorgan (3pts)

HAMPSHIRE v. NORTHAMPTONSHIRE – at Southampton

HAMPSHIRE	First Innings		Second Innings	
DA Kenway	c Powell b Greenidge	6	lbw b Brown	46
JHK Adams	c Hussey b Shantry	32	hit wkt b Nel	12
SM Katich	c Powell b Nel	117	not out	79
JP Crawley (capt)	c Roberts b Greenidge	8	not out	81
JD Francis	lbw b Brown	4		
JRC Hamblin	c Brophy b Brown	4		
AD Mascarenhas	c Powell b Shantry	31		
SD Udal	c Hussey b Brown	16		
*I Brunnschweiler	lbw b Nel	7		
CT Tremlett	c Brophy b Shantry	29		
JTA Bruce	not out	4		
Extras	b 1, w 2, nb 18	21	lb 1, nb 8	9
	(73.4 overs)	278	(2 wkts, 46.2 overs)	227

Bowling
Nel 21–4–79–2. Greenidge 15–1–74–2. Shantry 11.4–2–44–3. Brown 26–7–80–3.
Nel 13.2–2–47–1. Greenidge 10–2–53–0. Shantry 7–2–42–0. Brown 13–2–58–1. White 3–0–26–0.
Fall of Wickets 1–7, 2–64, 3–87, 4–97, 5–134, 6–195, 7–222, 8–225, 9–244, 10–278
1–19, 2–96

NORTHANTS	First Innings		Second Innings	
MEK Hussey (capt)	c Katich b Tremlett	13	(2) c Tremlett b Bruce	100
TW Roberts	c Adams b Tremlett	60	(1) c Brunnschweiler b Tremlett	10
PA Jaques	c Kenway b Tremlett	9	c Francis b Udal	34
DJG Sales	c Brunnschweiler b Katich	16	lbw b Bruce	75
MJ Powell	lbw b Katich	31	not out	44
RA White	lbw b Katich	12	c Brunnschweiler b Udal	27
*GL Brophy	c Francis b Katich	0	not out	2
AJ Shantry	c Francis b Udal	0		
CG Greenidge	b Udal	6		
A Nel	not out	5		
JF Brown	c Adams b Udal	0		
Extras	b 6, lb 2, w 2, nb 14	24	b 12, lb 7, nb 16	35
	(55.3 overs)	176	(5 wkts, 93.4 overs)	330

Bowling
Tremlett 13–4–49–3. Mascarenhas 14–3–49–0. Bruce 7–1–37–0. Udal 13.3–7–12–3. Katich 8–1–21–4.
Tremlett 20–4–54–1. Mascarenhas 16.4–5–28–0. Udal 34–5–114–2. Katich 10–0–56–0. Bruce 13–1–59–2.
Fall of Wickets 1–76, 2–89, 3–103, 4–150, 5–157, 6–157, 7–160, 8–162, 9–176, 10–176
1–24, 2–87, 3–246, 4–251, 5–318

Northamptonshire beat Hampshire by 5 wickets – Northamptonshire (17pts), Hampshire (5pts)

GLOUCESTERSHIRE v. YORKSHIRE – at Cheltenham

GLOS	First Innings		Second Innings	
CM Spearman (capt)	b Silverwood	0	c White b Kirby	94
WPC Weston	c Guy b Kirby	0	(7) not out	0
THC Hancock	c Guy b Silverwood	35	(2) b Kirby	0
MGN Windows	b Kirby	73	(3) c Hamilton b Kirby	57
APR Gidman	c Guy b Craven	43	(4) c Wood b Kirby	14
Shoaib Malik	c Fleming b Kirby	0	(5) st Guy b Dawson	60
*RC Russell	not out	35	(6) c Dawson b Gray	18
ID Fisher	c Fleming b Kirby	18		
MCJ Ball	c Gray b Kirby	24		
JMM Averis	c and b Kirby	0		
AM Smith	c Fleming b Dawson	0		
Extras	b 10, lb 6, w 3, nb 16	35	b 2, lb 4, nb 14	20
	(69.5 overs)	263	(6 wkts, 40 overs)	284

Bowling
Silverwood 14–3–81–2. Kirby 24–4–101–6. Craven 12–5–37–1. Gray 8–2–22–0. Dawson 3.5–1–6–1.
Silverwood 13–2–48–0. Kirby 13–2–82–4. Dawson 12–0–77–1. Craven 1–0–12–0. Gray 10–2–59–1.
Fall of Wickets 1–0, 2–4, 3–84, 4–153, 5–153, 6–184, 7–214, 8–260, 9–260, 10–263
1–38, 2–170, 3–198, 4–221, 5–260, 6–284

YORKSHIRE	First Innings		Second Innings	
C White	c Russell b Smith	4		
SP Fleming	c Russell b Smith	0	lbw b Shoaib Malik	16
VJ Craven	lbw b Averis	7	not out	20
MJ Lumb	c Russell b Ball	37	not out	4
GM Hamilton	c Gidman b Shoaib Malik	68		
*SM Guy	lbw b Ball	8		
MB Gray (capt)	c sub b Ball	23		
MJ Wood	not out	15	(1) lbw b Fisher	33
RKJ Dawson	c Ball b Averis	15		
CEW Silverwood	c Hancock b Fisher	15		
SP Kirby	lbw b Fisher	0		
Extras	b 5, lb 9, w 2, nb 18	34	b 2	2
	(79 overs)	226	(2 wkts, 40 overs)	75

Bowling
Smith 15–3–32–2. Averis 12–2–26–2. Gidman 4–1–16–0. Shoaib Malik 19–3–60–1. Fisher 8–0–31–2. Ball 21–6–47–3.
Smith 5–1–18–0. Averis 2–0–3–0. Ball 7–3–29–0. Shoaib Malik 12–6–10–1. Fisher 8–3–13–1.
Fall of Wickets 1–3, 2–16, 3–16, 4–107, 5–119, 6–175, 7–175, 8–195, 9–226, 10–226
1–43, 2–55

Match drawn – Gloucestershire (9pts), Yorkshire (8pts)

DURHAM v. SOMERSET – at Chester-le-Street

DURHAM	First Innings		Second Innings	
JJB Lewis (capt)	b McLean	2	c Durston b Jones	25
MA Gough	c Durston b Johnson	19	(8) c Bryant b McLean	0
GJ Muchall	b Jones	65	(2) c Johnson b Laraman	20
GJ Pratt	b Blackwell	51	c sub b McLean	41
N Peng	c Bryant b Johnson	58	(3) b Laraman	1
VJ Wells	b Jones	3	(5) b Jones	5
*P Mustard	c and b McLean	31	(6) c Johnson b Durston	37
GD Bridge	b McLean	42	(7) b Jones	8
Shoaib Akhtar	c Webley b Burns	26	(10) not out	5
N Killeen	c Burns b Laraman	26	(9) b Jones	11
AM Davies	not out	1	(11) b Jones	5
Extras	b 5, lb 10, w 2, nb 2	19	b 3, lb 3, nb 4	10
	(115.1 overs)	345	(44.5 overs)	168

Bowling
McLean 22–8–56–3. Johnson 28–0–109–2. Jones 22–5–76–2. Laraman 18–4–45–1. Blackwell 20–6–33–1. Durston 2–0–7–0. Burns 3.1–2–4–1.
McLean 10–2–28–2. Johnson 4–1–18–0. Laraman 8–2–26–2. Jones 9.5–2–42–5. Burns 4–0–19–0. Blackwell 3–0–13–0. Durston 6–1–16–1.
Fall of Wickets 1–2, 2–53, 3–141, 4–143, 5–146, 6–207, 7–285, 8–285, 9–339, 10–345
1–40, 2–46, 3–49, 4–56, 5–137, 6–139, 7–141, 8–157, 9–162, 10–168

SOMERSET	First Innings		Second Innings	
J Cox	lbw b Wells	29	(2) c Mustard b Shoaib Akhtar	1
JDC Bryant	c Mustard b Davies	5	(1) c Mustard b Killeen	0
M Burns (capt)	not out	35	lbw b Shoaib Akhtar	0
T Webley	lbw b Wells	0	c Peng b Shoaib Akhtar	0
ID Blackwell	c Wells b Bridge	14	c Mustard b Killeen	6
AW Laraman	c sub b Shoaib Akhtar	9	b Shoaib Akhtar	6
RJ Turner	c Mustard b Shoaib Akhtar	7	lbw b Davies	6
WJ Durston	c Bridge b Shoaib Akhtar	9	c Mustard b Killeen	6
RL Johnson	c Mustard b Shoaib Akhtar	6	run out	6
PS Jones	b Wells	25	not out	9
NAM McLean	b Wells	0	b Killeen	14
Extras	b 2, lb 1, nb 2	5	nb 2	2
	(52 overs)	139	(19.4 overs)	56

Bowling
Shoaib Akhtar 14–4–39–4. Killeen 11–2–38–2. Davies 12–4–36–1. Wells 10–4–16–4. Muchall 3–1–9–0. Bridge 2–0–8–1.
Shoaib Akhtar 7–2–9–4. Killeen 9.4–2–30–4. Davies 3–1–17–1.
Fall of Wickets 1–33, 2–35, 3–47, 4–77, 5–92, 6–100, 7–106, 8–106, 9–139, 10–139
1–1, 2–1, 3–1, 4–1, 5–2, 6–8, 7–20, 8–32, 9–39, 10–56

Durham beat Somerset by 318 runs – Durham (20pts), Somerset (3pts)

ROUND 15: 13–17 AUGUST 2003

Division One

No fewer than five Middlesex players were presented with their county caps at lunchtime on the first day of the game against Kent … but it was a Sri

Lankan visitor, who had never previously made a first-class appearance at Lord's, who ultimately stole the show. Muttiah Muralitharan's match figures of 9 for 141 may have been only his eighth best in 15 championship games for Kent and, previously, for Lancashire, but he was still far too good for much of the Middlesex batting. Initially, Murali was made to work hard for his successes as Middlesex rallied from 190 for 7 to reach a first-innings 407. Simon Cook, one of the five newly capped players alongside Ben Hutton, Joe Dawes, Chad Keegan and Ashley Noffke, celebrated by hitting 65 and joining wicketkeeper David Nash in an eighth-wicket stand of 125 in 44 overs. Nash showed a good technique against Murali and had reached his century by the close of the first day. He departed having reached 113 the following morning, but Keegan's unbeaten 36 further boosted Middlesex from their overnight 364 for 8. Kent's reply was founded on fine innings from David Fulton (86) and Andrew Symonds (71), but their surge to a 70-run first-innings lead was the result of late middle-order strokeplay from Mark Ealham, Amjad Khan and Martin Saggers. Khan hit a career-best 78 from 115 balls, before linking up with Saggers and Alamgir Sheriyar with the ball to wreck the start of the Middlesex second innings. By the close of day three, Middlesex were 141 for 6 – after slipping initially to 69 for 5 – as Saggers took 3 for 21. Khan dismissed Sven Koenig for nought and Sheriyar removed Hutton. Murali (4 for 38) then

Round 15: 13–17 August 2003 Division One

MIDDLESEX v. KENT – at Lord's

MIDDLESEX	First Innings		Second Innings	
AJ Strauss (capt)	c Jones b Khan	12	c Jones b Saggers	9
SG Koenig	c Ealham b Muralitharan	57	lbw b Khan	0
OA Shah	b Khan	0	c Jones b Saggers	12
BL Hutton	c Jones b Saggers	17	c Jones b Sheriyar	3
EC Joyce	b Muralitharan	43	lbw b Saggers	17
PN Weekes	lbw b Muralitharan	11	c Jones b Muralitharan	51
*DC Nash	run out	113	c Ealham b Muralitharan	23
JWM Dalrymple	c Walker b Muralitharan	5	c Symonds b Muralitharan	28
SJ Cook	lbw b Saggers	65	c Walker b Muralitharan	0
CB Keegan	not out	36	c and b Symonds	2
JH Dawes	b Muralitharan	18	not out	0
Extras	b 1, lb 8, w 3, nb 18	30	b 1, lb 13, w 2, nb 4	20
	(115 overs)	407	(69.2 overs)	165

Bowling
Saggers 26–3–95–2. Khan 17–1–100–2. Sheriyar 15–6–40–0. Ealham 15–3–42–0. Muralitharan 38–4–103–5. Symonds 4–1–18–0.
Saggers 17–4–31–3. Khan 7–2–38–1. Muralitharan 21.2–8–38–4. Sheriyar 4–2–6–1. Symonds 11–0–27–1. Ealham 9–7–11–0.
Fall of Wickets 1-31, 2-35, 3-58, 4-119, 5-149, 6-160, 7-190, 8-315, 9-381, 10-407
1-8, 2-25, 3-28, 4-48, 5-69, 6-108, 7-154, 8-154, 9-165, 10-165

KENT	First Innings		Second Innings	
DP Fulton (capt)	c Cook b Dalrymple	86	b Dawes	1
RWT Key	b Cook	40	not out	45
MA Carberry	lbw b Dawes	49	c Nash b Keegan	4
A Symonds	b Keegan	71	not out	41
MJ Walker	lbw b Weekes	17		
MA Ealham	lbw b Dawes	58		
*GO Jones	c Nash b Keegan	2		
A Khan	lbw b Dawes	78		
MJ Saggers	b Cook	44		
M Muralitharan	c Shah b Dalrymple	12		
A Sheriyar	not out	0		
Extras	b 1, lb 13, w 4, nb 2	20	b 4	4
	(137.2 overs)	477	(2 wkts, 24.2 overs)	96

Bowling
Dawes 32–3–119–3. Keegan 35–8–92–2. Cook 26.2–3–113–2. Weekes 19–1–64–1. Dalrymple 25–3–75–2.
Dawes 5–1–12–1. Keegan 6–1–20–1. Cook 2–0–18–0. Joyce 1–0–4–0. Weekes 5.2–1–23–0. Dalrymple 5–0–15–0.
Fall of Wickets 1-64, 2-172, 3-218, 4-272, 5-276, 6-282, 7-415, 8-422, 9-471, 10-477
1-4, 2-23

Kent beat Middlesex by 8 wickets – Kent (22pts), Middlesex (7pts)

SURREY v. NOTTINGHAMSHIRE – at Whitgift School

SURREY	First Innings	
IJ Ward	b Shreck	17
*JN Batty	c Warren b Smith	17
MR Ramprakash	not out	279
GP Thorpe	c Read b Cairns	99
R Clarke	st Read b MacGill	36
AD Brown	c Read b Franks	32
AJ Hollioake (capt)	lbw b Franks	0
Azhar Mahmood	c Pietersen b Smith	25
MP Bicknell	c and b Cairns	9
IDK Salisbury	c Smith b Franks	65
Saqlain Mushtaq	c Read b Smith	14
Extras	b 16, lb 13, w 5, nb 30	64
	(140.3 overs)	693

Bowling
Smith 27.3–7–110–3. Shreck 25.4–4–112–1. Franks 22–2–91–3. Cairns 27–3–133–2. MacGill 35–3–196–1. Pietersen 4–0–22–0.
Fall of Wickets 1-33, 2-41, 3-282, 4-345, 5-392, 6-392, 7-442, 8-457, 9-586, 10-693

NOTTS	First Innings		Second Innings	
DJ Bicknell	lbw b Bicknell	14	c sub b Azhar Mahmood	3
GE Welton	c Thorpe b Bicknell	0	c Clarke b Azhar Mahmood	0
U Afzaal	c Azhar Mahmood b Bicknell	4	lbw b Bicknell	5
RJ Warren	lbw b Salisbury	76	c Batty b Azhar Mahmood	0
KP Pietersen	c Azhar Mahmood b Bicknell	79	c Clarke b Bicknell	16
CL Cairns (capt)	b Bicknell	4	c Azhar Mahmood b Salisbury	93
*CMW Read	c Batty b Bicknell	4	c Azhar Mahmood b Salisbury	49
PJ Franks	c Thorpe b Saqlain Mushtaq	8	b Hollioake	27
GJ Smith	c Clarke b Saqlain Mushtaq	6	c Brown b Saqlain Mushtaq	42
SCG MacGill	st Batty b Salisbury	0	c Brown b Saqlain Mushtaq	7
CE Shreck	not out	0	not out	0
Extras	b 5, lb 5, nb 4	14	b 16, lb 8, w 1, nb 4	29
	(72 overs)	240	(55 overs)	242

Bowling
Bicknell 15–3–42–5. Azhar Mahmood 11–3–32–0. Saqlain Mushtaq 21–4–80–3. Clarke 7–0–32–0. Salisbury 18–6–44–2.
Bicknell 13–2–34–2. Azhar Mahmood 9–1–45–4. Clarke 4–0–22–0. Saqlain Mushtaq 15–1–49–2. Hollioake 8–0–41–1. Salisbury 11–2–42–1.
Fall of Wickets 1-1, 2-11, 3-20, 4-133, 5-186, 6-196, 7-224, 8-224, 9-237, 10-240
1-0, 2-6, 3-18, 4-19, 5-35, 6-45, 7-129, 8-233, 9-239, 10-242

Surrey beat Nottinghamshire by an innings and 211 runs – Surrey (22pts), Nottinghamshire (4pts)

SUSSEX v. LANCASHIRE – at Hove

SUSSEX	First Innings		Second Innings	
RR Montgomerie	c Law b Martin	72	(2) c Sutcliffe b Martin	70
MW Goodwin	b Hegg b Wood	9	(1) c Sutcliffe b Martin	1
PA Cottey	c Schofield b Hogg	18	c Hegg b Martin	0
CJ Adams (capt)	lbw b Schofield	140	c and b Chapple	190
*TR Ambrose	c Schofield b Wood	18	c and b Chapple	44
RSC M-Jenkins	c Law b Wood	18	lbw b Chapple	13
MJ Prior	c Hegg b Keedy	9	c Sutcliffe b Wood	35
MJG Davis	lbw b Hooper	3	not out	14
M Ahmed	lbw b Schofield	60		
PM Hutchison	lbw b Schofield	0		
BV Taylor	not out	4		
Extras	b 8, lb 6, w 1, nb 10	25	b 2, lb 8, nb 4	14
	(100.3 overs)	385	(7 wkts, 104.4 overs)	383

Bowling
Martin 15–2–64–1. Wood 17–2–64–3. Chilton 12–2–33–0. Hogg 8–2–24–1. Keedy 24–6–76–1. Hooper 12–2–48–1. Chapple 7–0–48–0. Schofield 5.3–2–14–3.
Martin 21–5–61–3. Chapple 21–3–89–3. Hooper 22–4–65–0. Wood 17.4–2–72–1. Keedy 19–3–61–0. Schofield 4–0–25–0.
Fall of Wickets 1-12, 2-60, 3-132, 4-156, 5-190, 6-252, 7-257, 8-332, 9-332, 10-385
1-2, 2-2, 3-155, 4-268, 5-313, 6-348, 7-383

LANCASHIRE	First Innings		Second Innings	
MJ Chilton	c Montgomerie b Davis	65	b Taylor	9
IJ Sutcliffe	c Prior b M Ahmed	43	c Montgomerie b Taylor	9
MB Loye	c Goodwin b Taylor	2	lbw b M Ahmed	33
SG Law	c Montgomerie b M Ahmed	96	c Adams b Taylor	1
CL Hooper	c and b M Ahmed	23	c Adams b Taylor	7
CP Schofield	b M Ahmed	3	b Davis	18
G Chapple	c Goodwin b Taylor	54	lbw b M Ahmed	7
*WK Hegg (capt)	c Montgomerie b M Ahmed	31	c Montgomerie b M Ahmed	25
PJ Martin	b Taylor	30	c Prior b M Ahmed	0
J Wood	lbw b M Ahmed	30	lbw b M Ahmed	4
G Keedy	not out	0	not out	2
Extras	b 10, lb 3, nb 8	21	b 6, lb 7, nb 12	25
	(121 overs)	377	(73.2 overs)	139

Bowling
Hutchison 14–2–50–0. Taylor 24–8–56–3. M Ahmed 48–10–124–6. M-Jenkins 9–1–48–0. Davis 26–2–86–1.
Hutchison 2–0–20–0. Taylor 26–12–42–4. M Ahmed 33.2–14–49–5. Davis 12–6–15–1.
Fall of Wickets 1-99, 2-102, 3-150, 4-189, 5-192, 6-289, 7-307, 8-321, 9-358, 10-377
1-27, 2-28, 3-56, 4-64, 5-97, 6-109, 7-128, 8-132, 9-132, 10-139

Sussex beat Lancashire by 252 runs – Sussex (21pts), Lancashire (7pts)

WARWICKSHIRE v. LEICESTERSHIRE – at Edgbaston

LEICESTERSHIRE	First Innings		Second Innings	
JK Maunders	c Knight b Bell	38	c Brown b Carter	10
DL Maddy	c Waqar Younis b Collymore	51	c Carter b Wagh	44
BJ Hodge	lbw b Waqar Younis	35	lbw b Waqar Younis	35
TR Ward	b Waqar Younis	42	(9) lbw b Waqar Younis	4
JL Sadler	not out	59	(4) lbw b Wagh	4
*PA Nixon	lbw b Waqar Younis	35	(7) not out	33
DG Brandy	b Richardson	6	(5) c Bell b Waqar Younis	0
PAJ DeFreitas (capt)	c Frost b Richardson	0	(10) b Wagh	37
VC Drakes	lbw b Wagh	17	(11) lbw b Wagh	3
DD Masters	st Frost b Wagh	2	(8) b Richardson	3
MJA Whiley	b Brown	16	(6) c Wagh b Waqar Younis	4
Extras	b 4, lb 21, w 9, nb 4	38	b 2, lb 18, w 1, nb 4	25
	(97 overs)	346	(71.4 overs)	195

Bowling
Waqar Younis 18–2–52–3. Carter 16–5–53–0. Richardson 16–3–55–3. Collymore 18–4–71–1. Bell 3–0–11–1. Brown 14–1–31–1. Wagh 15–5–48–1.
Waqar Younis 13–1–37–4. Carter 8–3–11–1. Collymore 10–2–36–0. Richardson 17–5–34–1. Brown 13–2–37–0. Wagh 10–2–20–4.
Fall of Wickets 1-103, 2-107, 3-228, 4-235, 5-235, 6-252, 7-252, 8-277, 9-301, 10-346
1-29, 2-98, 3-112, 4-112, 5-116, 6-117, 7-128, 8-129, 9-195, 10-195

WARWICKSHIRE	First Innings		Second Innings	
MJ Powell (capt)	c Maddy b Masters	28	b DeFreitas	13
NV Knight	b Drakes	0	not out	122
A Richardson	b Drakes	3	(3) lbw b Maddy	58
IR Bell	c Hodge b Masters	45	(4) retired hurt	7
MA Wagh	lbw b Masters	23	(5) not out	55
JO Troughton	c Hodge b Whiley	41		
*T Frost	c Nixon b Whiley	10		
DR Brown	not out	56		
NM Carter	c Nixon b Maddy	30		
Waqar Younis	b Maddy	61		
CD Collymore	b Maddy	0		
Extras	lb 12, w 6, nb 12	30	b 5, lb 2, w 1, nb 4	12
	(68.2 overs)	277	(2 wkts, 58.5 overs)	267

Bowling
Drakes 15–4–42–2. Whiley 16–1–77–2. Masters 10–1–40–3. DeFreitas 16–1–67–0. Maddy 9.2–3–29–3. Brandy 2–0–10–0.
Drakes 12–5–31–0. Whiley 7–0–59–0. DeFreitas 14–3–40–1. Masters 13–2–59–0. Maddy 12–1–51–1. Sadler 0.5–0–20–0.
Fall of Wickets 1-1, 2-35, 3-54, 4-58, 5-63, 6-86, 7-138, 8-180, 9-272, 10-277
1-20, 2-127

Warwickshire beat Leicestershire by 8 wickets – Warwickshire (19pts), Leicestershire (6pts)

The wizard of spin: Muttiah Muralitharan of Kent.

took over, with only Paul Weekes showing further resistance, and Middlesex's decline to 165 left Kent with a simple task as they completed an eight-wicket victory.

The first county championship fixture at Whitgift School featured a thumping innings-and-211-run win for Surrey against Nottinghamshire … and provided a showcase for the beautiful batting skills of Mark Ramprakash. Notts had reduced Surrey to 41 for 2 on the first morning, but a third-wicket stand of 241 between Ramprakash and Graham Thorpe soon had them fearing the worst. And worse it duly became, to the tune of 488 for 8 by the end of the opening day and a massive 693 overall. Ramprakash remained throughout the innings, with a chanceless, eight-and-a-half hour 279 not out. It was a career best, his ninth double-hundred and it made a mess, in particular, of Australian leg spinner Stuart MacGill's figures: 1 for 196 from 35 overs. In all, Ramprakash faced 400 balls, hitting four sixes and 40 fours, and Notts'

misery in the field was complete as Ian Salisbury and Saqlain Mushtaq scored 65 and 50 respectively from Nos. 10 and 11. Thorpe, incidentally, had made 99, despite not being 100 per cent fit with a back injury. Martin Bicknell's 5 for 42 then ensured no Notts revival with the bat, and soon they were following on and 45 for 6 as Bicknell and Azhar Mahmood wreaked havoc with the new ball. Chris Read's 111-ball 93 bravely delayed the end. 'I want to bring in three new players, and we have got to get rid to get them in,' said Mick Newell, the Notts director of cricket. 'We have to take a look at the staff and get a better top three.'

Chris Adams and Mushtaq Ahmed played like giants among men as Sussex underlined their serious championship aspirations with a significant 252-run win against fellow challengers Lancashire at Hove. Honours were even midway through the match, but then Adams and Mushtaq, having already played leading roles, hauled Sussex towards a crushing win by the skill and urgency of their cricket. Richard Montgomerie, with 72 and 70, and Billy Taylor, with a last-afternoon 4 for 42, can both claim a sizeable proportion of the credit – but it was the Sussex captain and his champion leg spinner who battered Lancashire into submission. On the opening day Adams made 140 from 191 balls, with five sixes and 16 fours, and was supported vitally by Mushtaq's late-order 60 as Sussex reached 385 all out. Lancashire's reply brought some magnificent, confrontational cricket as Mushtaq single-handedly denied them – in the end – a first-innings lead. Stuart Law hit 96 and both Mark Chilton and Glen Chapple made half-centuries, but Mushtaq ultimately snared both Law and Carl Hooper in a crucial passage of play and went on to take 6 for 124 from 48 overs. Montgomerie then helped Adams to add 153 for the third wicket as Sussex recovered from 2 for 2 at the start of their second innings. Adams' second hundred of the match was a brilliant demonstration of willpower and awareness of the wider picture: his first 50 took him 137 balls as his side fought to regain control, his second 50 occupied just 46 balls, and then there were sixes galore as he sprinted on to 190 to set up a declaration at 383 for 7. Lancashire were then overwhelmed as Taylor's honest and inspired seamers provided the ideal support for another five-wicket haul from the irrepressible Mushtaq.

Warwickshire eased their own relegation worries and almost certainly condemned Leicestershire to Division Two with an eight-wicket win at Edgbaston. The visitors began the game well enough, reaching 346 with half-centuries from Darren Maddy, Brad Hodge and John Sadler. Indeed, at 86 for 6 in reply, Warwickshire were looking distinctly in trouble before Waqar Younis emerged at No. 10 to hit 61 and provide excellent support for Dougie Brown, who remained unbeaten on 56. Waqar then made inroads with the ball, and by the close of day two Leicestershire were themselves 121 for 6 in their second innings. That became 195 all out the next morning, with both Waqar and Mark Wagh picking up four wickets. Nick Knight, with 122 not out, dashingly led the way to a victory target of 265.

Division Two

Derbyshire put an end to their unwanted run of a record seven successive defeats, plus a draw, by seeing off Hampshire in considerable style at the Rose Bowl. Victory came inside two days, by an innings and 43 runs, as Dominic Cork cast off the disappointments and frustrations of such a poor season to take his first ten-wicket match haul outside Derby. It was the former England all-rounder's fourth career match analysis of ten wickets or more, and his first-innings figures of 6 for 28 were his best return for eight summers. John Crawley, the Hampshire captain, suffered a back spasm when he was on 43, and the home side's batting effort fell away alarmingly once Crawley was prevented from taking any significant part in the rest of the match. Bowled out for 143 and 155, with Cork and Graeme Welch both picking up four wickets in the second innings, Hampshire were appalling. Only Simon Katich, with 48 not out despite feeling unwell with flu, could hold up his head at the end of the match. Cork also made a contribution with the bat for Derbyshire, rallying them from 115 for 5 with a pugnacious 40. Hampshire's spirit visibly drained away when Nathan Dumelow struck 75 off 77 balls, with a six and 13 fours, to lead the lower-order charge to 341.

Worcestershire beat Yorkshire by five wickets after an extraordinary first day at Scarborough. No fewer than 25 wickets fell, with Kabir Ali taking 8 for 53 and then Steve Kirby replying with 6 for 51, but the pitch was blameless amid the carnage. This was confirmed when John Jameson, the ECB pitch inspector, arrived before play on day two and soon passed the surface fit for first-class cricket. Whether the batting on both sides was first-class on that crazy opening day was, however, open to debate with Yorkshire only reaching 130 thanks to an unbeaten

42 from Richard Dawson before Kirby and Chris Silverwood cut down the Worcestershire reply for 91. By the close, Yorkshire were already 137 for 5 in the second innings and seemingly on top. Eventually totalling 238, they left their visitors needing 278 for victory. At 188 for 5, the game was in the balance, but Ben Smith was joined by Yorkshireman Gareth Batty in an unbroken stand of 90, the biggest of the

Still fighting after all these years: Dominic Cork was at last rewarded for his never-say-die attitude by taking ten wickets and leading Derbyshire to an innings victory at the Rose Bowl.

match, to carry the day. Smith's 87 not out contained ten fours, while Batty's unbeaten 54 took him just 59 balls. Having claimed the extra half-hour, Worcestershire had won the match inside two days.

Glamorgan's match against Durham at Cardiff seemed to be in danger of becoming a stalemate on its third afternoon. Then, Mike Kasprowicz was called up to bowl with Durham at 119 for 1 in their second innings … and suddenly the game was all but over that night! In an amazing spell, Kasprowicz reduced Durham to 174 all out in just 64 deliveries after tea, finishing with 9 for 36, the season's best analysis. Just 12 runs short of completing victory by stumps, Glamorgan's third-wicket pair were forced to return the following morning to wrap things up. Yet there had been no sign of such drama on the first two-and-a-half days. Durham had overcome an early slump against Robert Croft's off spin to reach 355, with Nicky Peng scoring his third championship hundred and both Graeme Bridge and Nicky Phillips providing late-order resistance. Glamorgan, however, still won themselves a significant first-innings lead as Mark Wallace made 117 and Adrian Dale, Matthew Maynard and Alex Wharf all hit half-centuries.

Northamptonshire were happy enough with the full 12 points available for a draw, as they consolidated their second place in the division following a high-scoring affair against Somerset at Taunton. A career-best 140 from Ian Blackwell, which included four sixes and in which he reached three figures in 113 balls, dominated the opening day. Blackwell was then joined by Aaron Laraman in a sixth-wicket partnership worth 183, and then tail-

Round 15: 13–17 August 2003
Division Two

HAMPSHIRE v. DERBYSHIRE – at Southampton

HAMPSHIRE	First Innings		Second Innings	
DA Kenway	c Di Venuto b Welch	17	lbw b Dean	11
JHK Adams	c Bassano b Dean	8	lbw b Cork	0
SM Katich	lbw b Cork	7	not out	48
JP Crawley (capt)	c Di Venuto b Cork	49	(7) b Welch	16
JD Francis	c Sutton b Cork	11	(4) c Di Venuto b Cork	3
AD Mascarenhas	c Sutton b Welch	0	(5) b Cork	6
SD Udal	lbw b Cork	0	(6) b Welch	12
W PUJC Vaas	c Bassano b Welch	1	c Kaif b Dumelow	2
*I Brunnschweiler	lbw b Cork	16	lbw b Cork	5
CT Tremlett	not out	22	c Cork b Welch	30
JTA Bruce	b Cork	0	b Welch	1
Extras	b 2, lb 2, nb 8	12	b 5, lb 6, w 2, nb 8	21
	(44.5 overs)	143	(42.3 overs)	155

Bowling
Cork 15.5-7-28-6. Dean 14-4-50-3. Gunter 5-0-30-0.
Cork 12-1-39-4. Dean 10-1-40-1. Welch 9.3-2-27-4. Gunter 3-0-18-0. Dumelow 8-2-20-1.
Fall of Wickets 1-14, 2-27, 3-36, 4-99, 5-100, 6-101, 7-104, 8-104, 9-143, 10-143
1-11, 2-11, 3-17, 4-24, 5-55, 6-79, 7-98, 8-103, 9-153, 10-155

DERBYSHIRE	First Innings	
SA Selwood	c Katich b Mascarenhas	29
MJ Di Venuto	c Brunnschweiler b Vaas	20
RM Khan	b Vaas	0
M Kaif	lbw b Vaas	36
CWG Bassano	lbw b Vaas	39
*LD Sutton	c Brunnschweiler b Udal	18
DG Cork (capt)	lbw b Udal	40
G Welch	b Mascarenhas	27
NRC Dumelow	lbw b Mascarenhas	75
NEL Gunter	not out	20
KJ Dean	lbw b Mascarenhas	12
Extras	b 2, lb 14, w 1, nb 8	26
	(95.3 overs)	341

Bowling
Vaas 26-8-82-4. Tremlett 19-1-80-0. Mascarenhas 26.3-11-45-4. Udal 17-3-63-2. Bruce 7-0-55-0.
Fall of Wickets 1-27, 2-27, 3-87, 4-91, 5-115, 6-185, 7-199, 8-290, 9-311, 10-341

*Derbyshire beat Hampshire by an innings and 43 runs –
Derbyshire (20pts), Hampshire (3pts)*

YORKSHIRE v. WORCESTERSHIRE – at Scarborough

YORKSHIRE	First Innings		Second Innings	
MJ Wood	lbw b Kabir Ali	4	c and b Hayward	16
SP Fleming	lbw b Kabir Ali	31	c Rhodes b Kemp	35
A McGrath (capt)	lbw b Kabir Ali	11	lbw b Mason	15
MJ Lumb	lbw b Kabir Ali	0	c Rhodes b Kemp	4
VJ Craven	b Kabir Ali	7	c Solanki b Kemp	17
C White	c Solanki b Kabir Ali	1	b Mason	54
*SM Guy	c Rhodes b Kabir Ali	0	(8) lbw b Mason	2
AKD Gray	b Mason	11	(9) c Hick b Hayward	27
RKJ Dawson	not out	42	(10) c Solanki b Kemp	24
CEW Silverwood	c Khalid b Kabir Ali	7	(11) not out	0
SP Kirby	b Hayward	4	(7) c Solanki b Kemp	15
Extras	lb 1	1	lb 2, w 1, nb 6	9
	(31.2 overs)	130	(70.2 overs)	238

Bowling
Kabir Ali 16-4-53-8. Hayward 7.2-2-39-1. Mason 8-1-37-1.
Kabir Ali 12-2-51-1. Hayward 8.2-0-48-2. Kemp 18-6-44-4. Mason 19-6-53-3. Batty 13-2-40-0.
Fall of Wickets 1-4, 2-26, 3-26, 4-34, 5-57, 6-57, 7-72, 8-80, 9-93, 10-130
1-21, 2-67, 3-67, 4-78, 5-124, 6-150, 7-168, 8-197, 9-238, 10-238

WORCS	First Innings		Second Innings	
SD Peters	c Fleming b Kirby	6	c McGrath b Kirby	15
A Singh	lbw b Silverwood	1	c Gray b Silverwood	41
GA Hick	c Dawson b Kirby	16	b Kirby	47
BF Smith (capt)	c Guy b Silverwood	0	not out	87
VS Solanki	lbw b Silverwood	0	st Guy b Gray	2
JM Kemp	c and b Kirby	6	b Dawson	22
*SJ Rhodes	c Gray b Kirby	10		
GJ Batty	c Guy b Kirby	6	(7) not out	54
Kabir Ali	c Guy b Kirby	0		
MS Mason	b Kirby	25		
M Hayward	not out	1		
Extras	lb 1, w 1, nb 12	14	b 1, lb 5, w 1, nb 2	9
	(28 overs)	91	(5 wkts, 76.2 overs)	278

Bowling
Silverwood 10-4-33-3. Kirby 14-5-51-6. Craven 4-2-6-1.
Silverwood 18-3-59-1. Kirby 22-6-79-2. Craven 4-1-26-0. McGrath 11-2-39-0. Gray 14.2-3-52-1. Dawson 7-0-17-1.
Fall of Wickets 1-3, 2-17, 3-22, 4-24, 5-36, 6-38, 7-53, 8-53, 9-70, 10-91
1-21, 2-96, 3-115, 4-134, 5-188

*Worcestershire beat Yorkshire by 5 wickets –
Worcestershire (17pts), Yorkshire (3pts)*

GLAMORGAN v. DURHAM – at Cardiff

DURHAM	First Innings		Second Innings	
JJB Lewis (capt)	c Wallace b Kasprowicz	13	lbw b Kasprowicz	68
MA Gough	c Hughes b Wharf	30	c and b Cosker	25
ML Love	c Wallace b Croft	38	lbw b Kasprowicz	36
GJ Pratt	b Croft	36	c Maynard b Kasprowicz	18
N Peng	b Cosker	133	lbw b Kasprowicz	0
VJ Wells	b Croft	1	lbw b Kasprowicz	3
*P Mustard	lbw b Croft	0	c Hughes b Kasprowicz	3
GD Bridge	c Maher b Croft	49	b Kasprowicz	3
NC Phillips	b Kasprowicz	39	b Kasprowicz	6
N Killeen	not out	0	b Kasprowicz	0
AM Davies	c Wallace b Croft	1	not out	1
Extras	b 1, lb 8, nb 6	15	lb 9, nb 2	11
	(117.1 overs)	355	(66.2 overs)	174

Bowling
Kasprowicz 24-10-41-2. Wharf 17-1-76-1. Harrison 15-5-55-0. Dale 4-0-26-0. Croft 35.1-12-98-6. Cosker 22-9-50-1.
Kasprowicz 20.2-6-36-9. Croft 26-10-53-0. Wharf 7-1-28-0. Harrison 4-0-15-0. Cosker 8-1-31-1. Maher 1-0-2-0.
Fall of Wickets 1-28, 2-51, 3-124, 4-133, 5-141, 6-141, 7-237, 8-353, 9-354, 10-355
1-61, 2-119, 3-136, 4-136, 5-136, 6-144, 7-160, 8-165, 9-169, 10-174

GLAMORGAN	First Innings		Second Innings	
JP Maher	c Pratt b Killeen	8	c Mustard b Phillips	35
J Hughes	b Bridge	39	lbw b Davies	11
A Dale	c Pratt b Phillips	66	not out	14
MJ Powell	c Peng b Phillips	14	not out	19
*MA Wallace	lbw b Phillips	117		
MP Maynard	lbw b Bridge	70		
RDB Croft (capt)	lbw b Bridge	25		
AG Wharf	lbw b Bridge	50		
MS Kasprowicz	b Phillips	24		
DS Harrison	c and b Phillips	6		
DA Cosker	not out	3		
Extras	b 7, lb 14, w 1	22	b 4, lb 3	7
	(132.5 overs)	444	(2 wkts, 16.1 overs)	86

Bowling
Killeen 17-4-50-1. Davies 21-4-77-0. Wells 10-3-26-0. Bridge 38-10-114-4. Phillips 44.5-8-144-5. Gough 2-0-12-0.
Killeen 2-0-17-0. Davies 6-0-29-1. Phillips 6.1-0-27-1. Pratt 1-0-5-0. Bridge 1-0-1-0.
Fall of Wickets 1-17, 2-65, 3-112, 4-161, 5-245, 6-331, 7-383, 8-421, 9-437, 10-444
1-34, 2-52

*Glamorgan beat Durham by 8 wickets –
Glamorgan (22pts), Durham (6pts)*

SOMERSET v. NORTHAMPTONSHIRE – at Taunton

SOMERSET	First Innings		Second Innings	
MJ Wood	c Hussey b Cawdron	30	b Cawdron	100
NJ Edwards	c Powell b Nel	9	b Greenidge	10
M Burns (capt)	b Greenidge	28	c Bailey b Cawdron	13
J Cox	b Nel	30	retired hurt	64
T Webley	b Brown	32	not out	41
ID Blackwell	b Nel	140	c Bailey b Greenidge	38
AW Laraman	c Bailey b Greenidge	70	not out	8
*CM Gazzard	c Bailey b Cook	41		
PS Jones	c Hussey b Brown	63		
NAM McLean	b Greenidge	16		
GM Gilder	not out	7		
Extras	b 1, lb 6, w 1, nb 2	10	lb 5, nb 13	18
	(126.2 overs)	476	(4 wkts, 96 overs)	292

Bowling
Nel 31-10-113-3. Greenidge 28.2-4-111-3. Cawdron 18-3-80-1. Cook 18-7-47-1. Brown 31-5-118-2.
Nel 18-3-53-0. Greenidge 17-2-74-2. Brown 26-6-81-0. Cawdron 11-3-76-2. Cook 10-3-38-0. Jaques 3-0-8-0. Hussey 5-1-6-0. Roberts 4-0-4-0. Sales 1-0-4-0. Bailey 1-0-3-0.
Fall of Wickets 1-23, 2-59, 3-77, 4-106, 5-160, 6-343, 7-347, 8-449, 9-457, 10-476
1-30, 2-63, 3-169, 4-267

NORTHANTS	First Innings	
MEK Hussey (capt)	not out	331
TW Roberts	b Blackwell	45
PA Jaques	c Gazzard b Burns	38
DJG Sales	b Blackwell	125
MJ Powell	c Burns b Blackwell	3
JW Cook	c Cox b Jones	15
*TMB Bailey	not out	101
CG Greenidge		
MJ Cawdron		
A Nel		
JF Brown		
Extras	b 6, lb 11, nb 6	23
	(5 wkts, 169 overs)	681

Bowling
McLean 26-3-99-0. Jones 34-3-162-1. Blackwell 53-4-206-3. Laraman 24-1-91-0. Burns 18-1-53-1. Edwards 8-0-35-0. Webley 5-1-10-0. Cox 1-0-8-0.
Fall of Wickets 1-84, 2-169, 3-390, 4-416, 5-439

*Match drawn – Somerset (10pts),
Northamptonshire (12pts)*

ender Steffan Jones blasted a championship-best 63 off 62 balls to haul Somerset up to 476. By the close of the second day, though, Northants were already 322 for 2 in reply, with Mike Hussey on 144 and David Sales on 84. The pair eventually took their third-wicket stand to 221, before Sales departed for 125, but the indefatigable Hussey motored on to 331 not out – the highest individual innings in Northants' history – with five sixes and 38 fours. Hussey's declaration finally arrived at 681 for 5, after Toby Bailey had completed a maiden hundred in an unbroken sixth-wicket stand of 242. Somerset, however, having reached 26 without loss overnight after being given an awkward 12 overs to bat on the third evening, managed to see it out for a draw at 292 for 4, with Matthew Wood scoring a fine 100.

Round 16: 19–24 August 2003

Division One

Surrey's grasp of the championship slipped at Grace Road, when two of the most inexperienced young batsmen in English cricket successfully fought one of the most pugnacious of rearguard actions. Leicestershire, already doomed to relegation, only emerged with six points in all for their efforts – but, in terms of club morale towards the end of a difficult season, it was priceless. The first two days had all been about Rikki Clarke, himself only 21 and being watched here by Rod Marsh, his former ECB National Academy boss and now an England selector. Clarke's classy 139 from 199 balls, with a six and 21 fours, helped to propel Surrey towards a first-innings score of 501. After half-centuries from Ian Ward, Jon Batty and Mark Ramprakash, who hit three sixes in his 55, Clarke and Graham Thorpe (87) added a highly entertaining 169 for the fourth wicket. Things began to go wrong for Surrey, however, even before they were bowling Leicestershire out for a first-innings 166, with Clarke picking up a career-best 4 for 21 with his seamers. Perhaps Clarke had benefited from the chance to bowl more after Azhar Mahmood had suffered a broken nose when he top-edged a sweep at Jeremy Snape's off spin into his face, but Surrey were still going to miss having the Pakistani all-rounder to lead their attack. Mahmood did manage to send down a few overs late on day three, but by then Leicestershire were prospering in their second innings after having been forced to follow on. John Maunders, a 22-year-old left-hander playing in only his tenth first-class match, was joined by Australian

Brad Hodge in a second-wicket stand that eventually realized 281. Hodge was all belligerence, scoring 116 of his 157 in boundaries, but opener Maunders was quite content to provide the anchor role as he reached the end of the third day on 126 not out. It was his maiden first-class hundred, and on the final morning he ground on to 171 as Leicestershire attacked the tiring Surrey bowlers mercilessly by accelerating from their overnight 348 for 2 to 636 for 4 declared. John Sadler, a 21-year-old signed from Yorkshire the previous winter, also made a maiden first-class hundred before taking advantage of some occasional bowling from Ward and Thorpe to go on to 145. Adam Hollioake, the Surrey captain, had turned to Ward and Thorpe as a last throw of the dice, introducing them when Leicestershire's lead had already reached 148, he hoped that quick runs might induce a cavalier declaration from the home side. Leicestershire, however, had no intention of taking the bait. Instead, they milked Ward (12 overs for 64) and Thorpe (1 for 73 from 11 overs) before allowing Surrey to bat out the final session. Besides Mahmood, Surrey also had Hollioake, Ramprakash and James Ormond all nursing minor ailments by the end of the match, and their failure to finish off Leicestershire left them five points adrift of leaders Sussex, with three games still to play. To those down at Hove, meanwhile, Maunders had emerged as one of the unlikeliest heroes of the summer for his 390-ball epic and eight-and-a-half hours of defiance.

Lancashire, the other county with championship aspirations, suffered a similar fate to Surrey as they failed to capitalize on enforcing the follow-on against Middlesex at Old Trafford. Another sound pitch aided batsmen intent on survival – although Lancashire came far closer than Surrey in their attempts to force a result on the final afternoon. Lancashire began the game by destroying the visiting bowlers and running up a monstrous 734 for 5 declared. It was, unsurprisingly, the highest first-class score ever recorded at Old Trafford and, when the declaration finally came at 3.25pm on day two, the assault had become raw plunder. Mark Chilton and Mal Loye had launched Lancashire by both scoring hundreds in a second-wicket partnership of 259 on the opening day. Then came Stuart Law and Carl Hooper, with 144 and 201 respectively as they heaped misery and humiliation on the Middlesex bowlers. Law's fifth ton of the season was only ended by a run out, while Hooper smashed no fewer than 11 sixes – three of them in four balls from Joe Dawes – to underline his total mastery. Hooper's second hundred took him just 68 balls, a magnificent way to celebrate becoming only the second batsman (after Mark Ramprakash earlier in the season) to record first-class centuries against all 18 counties. To Middlesex's credit, however, they had reached 156 for 1 by the close of the second day with Andy Strauss, their captain, leading the way with an unbeaten 99. Strauss completed his century from the third ball the following morning, and went on to make 155 in a second-wicket stand of 235 with Owais Shah. Ben Hutton, like Shah, also reached three figures, and Middlesex's own first innings did not end until they had totalled 544. They were still forced to follow on, though, and despite another half-century from Strauss they were just eight runs ahead at 198 for 7 in their second innings with 40 minutes of the match still remaining. Enter Sven Koenig, batting at No. 9 because of a split finger, and the opener was just the man to help Paul Weekes bat it out. It was the fifth time that Lancashire had made an opponent follow on in the campaign, but the fourth time it had not brought victory. Mike Watkinson, the Lancashire coach, said afterwards that the Manchester rain and not their own failings had frustrated them the most. 'I feel we would have won all three of our previous three matches here – against Notts, Essex and Warwickshire – if it had not been for the weather,' he said.

After the substandard nature of the pitch for the third Test between England and South Africa, it was a source of much embarrassment for the

Nottinghamshire club when their subsequent home championship fixture, against Kent, became the shortest match to date in the 2003 competition. Kent won by nine wickets, midway through the second day, and 16 of the 31 dismissals that

Round 16: 19–24 August 2003 Division One

LEICESTERSHIRE v. SURREY – at Leicester

SURREY	First Innings		Second Innings	
IJ Ward	lbw b Maddy	59	run out	23
*JN Batty	c Maddy b DeFreitas	50	lbw b DeFreitas	30
MR Ramprakash	c sub b Maddy	55		
GP Thorpe	c Nixon b Snape	87	(3) not out	52
R Clarke	c Nixon b Snape	139	(4) not out	3
Saqlain Mushtaq	lbw b Drakes	13		
AJ Hollioake (capt)	b Drakes	21		
Azhar Mahmood	retired hurt	30		
IDK Salisbury	not out	24		
J Ormond	c Nixon b Snape	0		
TJ Murtagh	c Maddy b Drakes	6	lb 7, nb 2	9
Extras	b 8, lb 2, w 1, nb 6	17		
	(134.1 overs)	501	(2 wkts, 28 overs)	117

Bowling
DeFreitas 29–10–87–1. Drakes 21.1–2–85–3. Dagnall 23–3–88–0. Maddy 14–1–40–2. Masters 16–0–78–0. Snape 30–6–108–3. Hodge 1–0–5–0.
DeFreitas 9–2–31–1. Drakes 8–1–41–0. Masters 6–1–19–0. Dagnall 3–0–14–0. Brandy 2–1–5–0.
Fall of Wickets 1–93, 2–145, 3–178, 4–347, 5–378, 6–420, 7–456, 8–481, 9–501 1–32, 2–89

LEICESTERSHIRE	First Innings		Second Innings	
JK Maunders	c Batty b Ormond	12	c Batty b Salisbury	171
DL Maddy	lbw b Murtagh	12	c Batty b Clarke	20
BJ Hodge	b Clarke	20	c Batty b Salisbury	157
JL Sadler	b Clarke	31	c Hollioake b Thorpe	145
JN Snape	c and b Clarke	10		
*PA Nixon	lbw b Salisbury	30	(5) not out	44
DG Brandy	b Murtagh	4	(6) not out	31
PAJ DeFreitas (capt)	b Murtagh	4		
VC Drakes	run out	10		
CE Dagnall	not out	22		
DD Masters	c Ward b Clarke	1		
Extras	b 4, lb 4, nb 2	10	b 18, lb 21, nb 29	68
	(58.1 overs)	166	(4 wkts, 158 overs)	636

Bowling
Ormond 9–1–30–1. Murtagh 12–2–68–3. Saqlain Mushtaq 8–4–18–0. Clarke 12.1–4–21–4. Salisbury 13–5–21–1.
Ormond 25–5–91–0. Murtagh 18–2–62–0. Saqlain Mushtaq 26–8–57–0. Clarke 18–3–82–1. Salisbury 25–5–92–2. Hollioake 9–0–39–0. Azhar Mahmood 14–3–37–0. Ward 12–0–64–0. Thorpe 11–1–73–1.
Fall of Wickets 1–24, 2–30, 3–58, 4–89, 5–98, 6–108, 7–112, 8–129, 9–153, 10–166 1–49, 2–330, 3–465, 4–588

Match drawn – Leicestershire (6pts), Surrey (12pts)

LANCASHIRE v. MIDDLESEX – at Old Trafford

LANCASHIRE	First Innings	
MJ Chilton	b Abdul Razzaq	125
IJ Sutcliffe	c Hutton b Dawes	4
MB Loye	c Nash b Abdul Razzaq	137
SG Law	run out	144
CL Hooper	c Joyce b Keegan	201
CP Schofield	not out	58
G Chapple	not out	21
*W K Hegg (capt)	(did not bat)	
P J Martin	(did not bat)	
J Wood	(did not bat)	
G Keedy	(did not bat)	
Extras	b 8, lb 13, w 1, nb 22	44
	(5 wkts, 162 overs)	734

Bowling
Dawes 30–5–125–1. Keegan 34–6–124–1. Abdul Razzaq 29–1–170–2. Dalrymple 24–3–96–0. Hutton 1–1–0–0. Weekes 33–5–145–0. Joyce 11–1–53–0.
Fall of Wickets 1–24, 2–283, 3–304, 4–586, 5–699

MIDDLESEX	First Innings		Second Innings	
AJ Strauss (capt)	c Keedy b Martin	155	c Schofield b Hooper	63
SG Koenig	c Sutcliffe b Schofield	13	(9) not out	16
OA Shah	b Keedy	147	lbw b Martin	15
BL Hutton	c sub b Keedy	107	(2) c Chilton b Keedy	10
EC Joyce	b Hooper	3	(4) c sub b Hooper	41
Abdul Razzaq	c Martin b Keedy	22	c Hegg b Hooper	26
PN Weekes	c Hegg b Martin	24	not out	26
*DC Nash	c Hooper b Chapple	15	(5) c and b Hooper	23
JWM Dalrymple	b Keedy	17	(8) c sub b Keedy	0
CB Keegan	b Keedy	18		
JH Dawes	not out	0		
Extras	b 4, lb 9, nb 10	23	b 7, lb 7, nb 4	18
	(164 overs)	544	(7 wkts, 78 overs)	237

Bowling
Martin 17–6–44–2. Chapple 19–0–71–1. Keedy 52–10–188–5. Schofield 34–5–120–1. Hooper 26–9–53–1. Wood 13–1–43–0. Law 3–0–12–0.
Martin 9–3–17–1. Wood 4–0–29–0. Keedy 29–8–76–2. Chapple 6–1–18–0. Hooper 18–3–51–4. Schofield 11–2–34–0. Law 1–0–6–0.
Fall of Wickets 1–59, 2–294, 3–338, 4–343, 5–374, 6–450, 7–508, 8–508, 9–543, 10–544 1–29, 2–61, 3–107, 4–157, 5–176, 6–197, 7–198

Match drawn – Lancashire (10pts), Middlesex (10pts)

NOTTINGHAMSHIRE v. KENT – at Trent Bridge

NOTTS	First Innings		Second Innings	
DJ Bicknell	c Walker b Saggers	5	st Jones b Muralitharan	46
V Atri	b Saggers	5	c Key b Saggers	3
GE Welton	lbw b Khan	7	c Jones b Ealham	43
KP Pietersen	c Carberry b Saggers	100	lbw b Symonds	13
BM Shafayat	lbw b Symonds	23	lbw b Symonds	0
CL Cairns (capt)	lbw b Symonds	0	c Ealham b Muralitharan	6
*CMW Read	c Key b Ealham	5	lbw b Muralitharan	0
PJ Franks	lbw b Symonds	17	not out	5
GJ Smith	b Saggers	0	c Walker b Muralitharan	0
SCG MacGill	not out	7	b Muralitharan	0
CE Shreck	lbw b Saggers	0	b Muralitharan	0
Extras	lb 2, nb 6	8	b 4, lb 5, w 1	10
	(40.5 overs)	177	(39.3 overs)	126

Bowling
Saggers 13.5–2–42–5. Khan 8–2–41–1. Sheriyar 2–0–24–0. Ealham 7–4–14–1.
Symonds 9–2–38–3. Muralitharan 1–0–16–0.
Saggers 7–4–20–1. Khan 4–0–31–0. Muralitharan 15.3–3–36–6. Ealham 6–1–18–1. Symonds 7–2–12–2.
Fall of Wickets 1–6, 2–17, 3–17, 4–73, 5–73, 6–92, 7–151, 8–154, 9–177, 10–177 1–13, 2–92, 3–110, 4–110, 5–119, 6–119, 7–124, 8–124, 9–124, 10–126

KENT	First Innings		Second Innings	
DP Fulton (capt)	c Franks b Smith	43	c Atri b Shreck	11
RWT Key	b Cairns	11	not out	46
MM Carberry	c Franks b Smith	5	not out	8
A Symonds	lbw b Franks	1		
MJ Walker	c Read b Shreck	11		
MA Ealham	lbw b Cairns	83		
*GO Jones	c Atri b Smith	0		
A Khan	c Welton b Shreck	46		
MJ Saggers	b MacGill	3		
M Muralitharan	c Bicknell b MacGill	15		
A Sheriyar	not out	4		
Extras	b 8, lb 9, w 1, nb 6	24		
	(60.3 overs)	242	(1 wkt, 13.3 overs)	65

Bowling
Smith 11–1–47–2. Cairns 14–2–59–3. Franks 11–2–36–1. Shreck 13–0–55–2. MacGill 11.3–1–19–2.
Smith 4–0–21–0. Cairns 4–0–14–0. Franks 3–0–20–0. Shreck 2.3–0–10–1.
Fall of Wickets 1–26, 2–31, 3–50, 4–63, 5–106, 6–164, 7–194, 8–210, 9–234, 10–242 1–51

Kent beat Nottinghamshire by 9 wickets – Kent (18pts), Nottinghamshire (3pts)

ESSEX v. SUSSEX – at Colchester

SUSSEX	First Innings	
RR Montgomerie	b Palladino	97
MW Goodwin	b Mohammad Akram	210
PA Cottey	run out	23
CJ Adams (capt)	b Mohammad Akram	0
*TR Ambrose	c Flower b Mohammad Akram	4
RSC M-Jenkins	c Foster b Middlebrook	10
MJ Prior	not out	153
MJG Davis	b Mohammad Akram	8
M Ahmed	b Mohammad Akram	0
JD Lewry	c sub b Middlebrook	70
BV Taylor	b Dakin	3
Extras	lb 9, nb 20, p 5	34
	(119 overs)	612

Bowling
Mohammad Akram 29–2–130–5. Dakin 20–1–120–1. Napier 24–5–149–0. Palladino 16–6–40–1. Middlebrook 26–1–126–2. Robinson 4–0–33–0.
Fall of Wickets 1–202, 2–270, 3–270, 4–303, 5–325, 6–438, 7–452, 8–454, 9–595, 10–612

ESSEX	First Innings		Second Innings	
DDJ Robinson	c Cottey b M Ahmed	64	run out	12
WI Jefferson	c Goodwin b M Ahmed	55	c and b M-Jenkins	59
A Flower	c Ambrose b Lewry	50	c Prior b M Ahmed	32
A Habib	lbw b M Ahmed	0	b M Ahmed	11
RC Irani (capt)	c Adams b Taylor	6	c Ambrose b Taylor	38
*JS Foster	c Montgomerie b Davis	31	lbw b M Ahmed	3
JM Dakin	lbw b Davis	6	c Goodwin b Taylor	7
JD Middlebrook	c Lewry b M-Jenkins	33	c Davis b Taylor	5
GR Napier	lbw b M Ahmed	34	not out	21
Mohammad Akram	not out	0	lbw b Taylor	10
AP Palladino	absent inj		absent inj	
Extras	lb 5, nb 2	7	b 2, lb 3, nb 6	11
	(wkts, 77.5 overs)	283	(9 wkts, 68.3 overs)	209

Bowling
Lewry 12–4–46–1. Taylor 17–3–52–1. M Ahmed 25–2–87–4. M-Jenkins 11.5–2–32–1. Davis 12–0–61–2.
Taylor 16.3–6–50–4. Lewry 8–1–28–0. M Ahmed 28–7–83–3. Davis 4–1–13–0. M-Jenkins 12–4–30–1.
Fall of Wickets 1–101, 2–144, 3–144, 4–163, 5–208, 6–214, 7–219, 8–281, 9–283 1–24, 2–109, 3–123, 4–130, 5–164, 6–164, 7–172, 8–185, 9–209

Sussex beat Essex by an innings and 120 runs – Sussex (22pts), Essex (5pts)

occurred in the 158.2 overs of play were either lbw or bowled. Low bounce and a cracked appearance did not condemn the pitch officially, however. The umpires, John Steele and John Holder, said that the bounce had not become inconsistent enough for action to be taken. Others, however, accused the ECB of not making an example of Trent Bridge because of sensitivity following the misbehaviour of the Test match surface. Whatever, Kent deserved their win because they bowled and batted far better as a team. Kevin Pietersen produced a quite brilliant innings of 100 from 97 balls in the Notts first innings of 177, even seeing off Muttiah Muralitharan after just one over that cost 16 as he swung him high and hard for two sixes and a four. But Martin Saggers, with five wickets, and Andrew Symonds, chipping in with 3 for 38 with his seamers, took overall control for Kent – and by the end of day one the visitors had won a lead of 65 as David Fulton, with a dogged 43, Mark Ealham with a skilful 83 and Amjad Khan with a hard-hit 46-ball 46 played equally important knocks. At 92 for 1 in their second innings, however, Notts still had hopes as Darren Bicknell and Guy Welton both battled their way into the 40s. It proved an illusion as Muralitharan took six wickets in 12 balls to finish off the innings for just 126.

Sussex's move to the top of the championship table, meanwhile, came at Colchester, where the feebleness of the Essex attack was fully and ruthlessly exposed. The youthful Tony Palladino was the only bowler who could be spared criticism as Sussex ran up an intimidating 521 for 8 on the opening day, and seamer Palladino was carried off on a stretcher after tea with a suspected dislocated collarbone. Murray Goodwin and Richard Montgomerie set the tone for the day by putting on 202 in just 45 overs for the first wicket. Montgomerie fell for 97, but Goodwin flew past his 1,000 runs for the season and scored 101 in the afternoon session as he completed a career-best 210 from 270 balls. Matt Prior then caught the mood, reaching an 86-ball hundred just before the close and batting with immense flair while going on to a career-best 153 not out the next day. Prior, who had strode to three figures by hitting

Graham Napier for successive sixes, was joined by Jason Lewry in a ninth-wicket stand of 141 in just 19 overs which made sure Essex had no way back into the match, especially on a pitch beginning to offer appreciable turn. Lewry posted a career best 70, from 65 balls, while Prior hit three sixes and 19 fours overall in his 134-ball exhibition. Facing such a daunting total of 612, Essex predictably fell foul of Mushtaq Ahmed. The leg spinner picked up seven wickets as they were bowled out for 283 and 209, losing by an innings and 120 runs, and seamer Billy Taylor also picked up four second-innings scalps. To set the seal on a painful few days, Essex officials also confirmed that the future of the Colchester festival week was in grave doubt, despite continued good attendances, because of the borough council's apparent unwillingness to support financially the provision of county cricket at Castle Park.

David Sales of Northamptonshire: back to his best following a long injury lay-off in 2001.

Division Two

Promotion was all but assured for Northamptonshire after they had crushed Derbyshire by an innings and 231 runs at Derby. The home side's fate was all too predictable from the moment that they succumbed for just 138 on the opening day, with only 21-year-old rookie batsman Rawait Khan showing any sort of resistance with 76, his maiden first-class 50. Khan was last out, after the seamers of Jeff Cook and Carl Greenidge had done most of the damage. Then came the powerful Northants top order, employing the sledgehammer to crack a nut. Mike Hussey and Phil Jaques both scored centuries in a second-wicket stand of 233 in 52 overs, setting the stage for David Sales to hit an unbeaten 200 from 217 deliveries. Sales' stand of 196 in 34 overs with Cook (85) enabled Northants to declare at 647 for 5, the third highest total in the county's history. 'A lead of 509 – will that be enough?' asked one wag among Derbyshire members resigned to their team's imminent demise. There was at least some initial resistance, before Steve Selwood had his wrist broken by a ball from Andre Nel and had to retire hurt, and then further grit from Michael Di Venuto (116) and Luke Sutton (56). But Jason Brown took 4 for 60 from 42 overs of patient and skilled off spin, and there was another useful three-wicket haul for Greenidge as Derbyshire were

dismissed for 278. It was the home side's eighth defeat in ten matches, and their heaviest since 1975, but Northants' seventh win in eight.

Durham moved into third place, ahead of a congested mid-table grouping, by taking maximum points from their innings-and-115-run victory against struggling Hampshire at Chester-le-Street. The win was based on a sumptuous 273 from Martin Love, the elegant Australian, who hit 36 fours – most of them stroked through the covers – and two sixes in the same Chaminda Vaas over. It took him seven-and-a-half hours, but it was the highest score by a Durham batsman and also the biggest on the ground. By the close of the second day Hampshire were already 88 for 4 in reply to Durham's 515, and that became 211 all out despite half-centuries from John Francis and Nic Pothas. Graeme Bridge and Paul Collingwood were the chief destroyers with the ball here, but the Hampshire second-innings slump to 189 was all about Neil Killeen, whose career-best 7 for 70 was also his first five-wicket haul for four years.

A valuable and determined 103 from Stephen Peters, and a season's best 5 for 46 for fast bowler Nantie Hayward, inspired Worcestershire to an eight-wicket win over Somerset at New Road which kept them at the top of the Division Two table. The visitors started well, with youngster Neil Edwards striking nine fours in a 39-ball 45 and both Matthew

Round 16: 19–24 August 2003 Division Two

DERBYSHIRE v. NORTHAMPTONSHIRE – at Derby

DERBYSHIRE	First Innings		Second Innings	
SA Selwood	c Roberts b Nel	1	(2) retired hurt	33
MJ Di Venuto	b Nel	0	(1) b Brown	116
RM Khan	b Greenidge	76	c Powell b Brown	8
M Kaif	c Sales b Cook	31	lbw b Cawdron	14
CWG Bassano	b Cook	1	c Bailey b Brown	0
LD Sutton	b Cawdron	0	b Brown	56
DG Cork (capt)	c Jaques b Cook	0	c Roberts b Greenidge	12
*G Welch	b Cook	3	c Roberts b Greenidge	8
NRC Dumelow	c Bailey b Greenidge	15	not out	6
KJ Dean	b Greenidge	0	b Greenidge	1
Mohammad Ali	not out	1	b Greenidge	0
Extras	b 1, lb 2, w 2, nb 4	9	b 7, lb 5, w 2, nb 10	24
	(49.3 overs)	138	(99.4 overs)	278

Bowling
Nel 15-5-40-2. Greenidge 10.3-2-33-3. Cawdron 9-2-27-1. Cook 15-6-35-4.
Nel 20-6-57-1. Greenidge 19.4-1-75-3. Cook 6-0-33-0. Brown 42-16-60-4.
Cawdron 14-1-41-1.
Fall of Wickets 1-1, 2-4, 3-83, 4-88, 5-95, 6-96, 7-109, 8-133, 9-133, 10-138
1-99, 2-132, 3-135, 4-220, 5-249, 6-264, 7-272, 8-278, 9-278

NORTHANTS	First Innings	
MEK Hussey (capt)	run out	115
TW Roberts	lbw b Dean	12
PA Jaques	b Dean	123
DJG Sales	not out	200
MJ Powell	c Khan b Dean	50
JW Cook	c Welch b Dean	85
*TMB Bailey	not out	22
MJ Cawdron		
A Nel		
CG Greenidge		
JF Brown		
Extras	b 15, lb 1, w 4, nb 20	40
	(5 wkts, 136.3 overs)	647

Bowling
Cork 21.1-0-83-0. Dean 30.5-3-145-4. Mohammad Ali 23.3-3-118-0. Welch
25-2-112-0. Dumelow 26.1-1-131-0. Khan 1-0-7-0. Selwood 7-0-28-0.
Di Venuto 2-0-7-0.
Fall of Wickets 1-28, 2-261, 3-274, 4-413, 5-609

*Northamptonshire beat Derbyshire by an innings and 231 runs –
Northamptonshire (22pts), Derbyshire (1pts)*

DURHAM v. HAMPSHIRE – at Chester-le-Street

DURHAM	First Innings	
JJB Lewis (capt)	c Pothas b Mullally	11
N Peng	c Pothas b Mascarenhas	30
ML Love	b Udal	273
PD Collingwood	c Smith b Tomlinson	9
GJ Pratt	lbw b Mascarenhas	66
AM Thorpe	c Adams b Udal	35
*P Mustard	c Vaas b Mullally	4
GD Bridge	lbw b Mascarenhas	23
N Killeen	c Pothas b Mullally	16
AM Davies	c Pothas b Vaas	1
NG Hatch	not out	1
Extras	b 11, lb 13, nb 12	36
	(131.5 overs)	515

Bowling
Vaas 27-2-115-1. Mullally 29-3-121-3. Mascarenhas 32-9-71-3. Tomlinson
18-0-105-1. Udal 16.5-3-50-2. Katich 9-1-29-0.
Fall of Wickets 1-25, 2-62, 3-73, 4-234, 5-315, 6-320, 7-378, 8-445, 9-489,
10-515

HAMPSHIRE	First Innings		Second Innings	
JHK Adams	c Mustard b Davies	21	c Mustard b Killeen	36
JP Crawley (capt)	c Collingwood b Davies	29	c Collingwood b Killeen	4
SM Katich	b Davies	16	b Killeen	2
RA Smith	lbw b Collingwood	1	lbw b Hatch	49
JD Francis	c Peng b Collingwood	65	c Mustard b Killeen	6
*N Pothas	c Peng b Bridge	50	b Davies	47
AD Mascarenhas	lbw b Hatch	12	h Dwier	2
SD Udal	b Bridge	10	c Love b Killeen	5
WPUJC Vaas	c Love b Bridge	0	not out	5
AD Mullally	c Mustard b Collingwood	0	lbw b Killeen	14
JA Tomlinson	not out	0	c Lewis b Killeen	10
Extras	b 1, lb 4, nb 2	7	b 4, lb 1	5
	(91.1 overs)	211	(61.2 overs)	189

Bowling
Killeen 15-8-30-0. Hatch 18-4-57-1. Collingwood 16.1-4-38-3. Davies
18-5-34-2. Bridge 24-6-47-4.
Davies 19-7-49-2. Killeen 20.2-6-70-7. Hatch 7-3-24-1. Collingwood 7-2-23-0.
Bridge 8-2-18-0.
Fall of Wickets 1-50, 2-66, 3-67, 4-80, 5-161, 6-190, 7-203, 8-211, 9-211, 10-211
1-8, 2-18, 3-63, 4-79, 5-117, 6-158, 7-159, 8-163, 9-177, 10-189

*Durham beat Hampshire by an innings and 115 runs –
Durham (22pts), Hampshire (4pts)*

WORCESTERSHIRE v. SOMERSET at Worcester

SOMERSET	First Innings		Second Innings	
MJ Wood	c Rhodes b Batty	53	run out	6
NJ Edwards	c Hick b Mason	45	b Hayward	1
M Burns (capt)	c Hick b Hayward	89	c Hick b Hayward	13
J Cox	c Rhodes b Mason	0	lbw b Mason	0
T Webley	c Rhodes b Harrity	20	c Hick b Hayward	4
ID Blackwell	lbw b Batty	21	c Hick b Hayward	9
AW Laraman	c Rhodes b Mason	29	lbw b Hayward	35
*RJ Turner	c Rhodes b Hayward	4	lbw b Batty	26
PS Jones	c Kemp b Hayward	0	lbw b Hayward	25
RL Johnson	c Hayward b Batty	24	c Batty b Harrity	0
NAM McLean	not out	4	not out	7
Extras	w 3, nb 4	7	b 6, lb 10, w 5	21
	(74.4 overs)	296	(40.5 overs)	147

Bowling
Mason 19-1-56-3. Hayward 11-2-53-3. Harrity 15-5-53-1. Kemp 5-0-23-0. Batty
24.4-3-111-3.
Hayward 13.5-4-46-5. Mason 14-4-31-1. Harrity 7-2-26-2. Batty 6-1-28-1.
Fall of Wickets 1-63, 2-154, 3-155, 4-201, 5-239, 7-263, 8-263, 9-284, 10-296
1-3, 2-18, 3-18, 4-31, 5-48, 6-49, 7-90, 8-134, 9-134, 10-147

WORCS	First Innings		Second Innings	
SD Peters	c and b Johnson	103	lbw b Batty	54
A Singh	c Turner b Laraman	14	c Laraman b Blackwell	44
GA Hick	b Laraman	23	not out	13
*SJ Rhodes	lbw b Jones	25		
BF Smith (capt)	b McLean	48	(4) not out	2
VS Solanki	lbw b Laraman	0		
JM Kemp	c Turner b Johnson	32		
GJ Batty	not out	52		
MS Mason	c Jones b Blackwell	13		
MA Harrity	lbw b Blackwell	7		
M Hayward	c Laraman b Blackwell	0		
Extras	b 5, lb 5, nb 4	14	lb 3	3
	(103.5 overs)	331	(2 wkts, 38.2 overs)	116

Bowling
McLean 21-9-60-1. Johnson 21-7-43-2. Laraman 18-5-49-3. Jones 15-4-65-1.
Blackwell 24.5-6-91-3. Burns 4-0-13-0.
McLean 8-2-29-0. Johnson 5-1-15-0. Blackwell 14-3-39-1. Laraman 3-1-10-0.
Jones 6-2-6-1. Edwards 2.2-0-14-0.
Fall of Wickets 1-38, 2-68, 3-143, 4-198, 5-223, 6-229, 7-286, 8-301, 9-331, 10-331
1-94, 2-102

*Worcestershire beat Somerset by 8 wickets –
Worcestershire (20pts), Somerset (5pts)*

Wood and Mike Burns making attractive half-centuries. But Peters' hundred, supported by Ben Smith and Gareth Batty, enabled Worcestershire to gain a slender first-innings lead, and the match turned when Somerset lost the first four wickets of their second innings in 13 overs as Day Two drew to a close. Wood was run out by a direct hit from square leg by Vikram Solanki, and Hayward claimed the first two victims of his five-wicket haul. Bowling Somerset out for 147 left Worcestershire with a straightforward-looking victory target – and Peters, with 54, and Anurag Singh made sure of no late dramas with a 94-run opening partnership.

ROUND 17: 25–29 AUGUST 2003

Division One

If Surrey had felt the championship trophy slipping from their grasp after failing to finish off Leicestershire in their previous match, then an eight-wicket defeat at the hands of Lancashire must have left them feeling as though it was now in their fingertips. Bowled out for a sorry 138 in their second innings, Surrey also left Old Trafford having suffered their first defeat in the championship for more than a year. The match began well enough for the champions, with Jon Batty and Graham Thorpe

adding 104 for the second wicket. Even after a collapse to 148 for 5, the determined Batty was joined by Azhar Mahmood in a sixth-wicket partnership of 113. Mahmood made 63, but Batty was still there at the close on 152 not out and Surrey were in sight of a fourth batting bonus point at 330 for 9. They did not get it, however, being bowled out for 337 early on day two as Batty became the first Surrey batsman for 133 years to carry his bat at Old Trafford. A sizeable first-innings lead looked probable, though, as Lancashire fell away following a third-wicket stand of 109 between 23-year-old Mark Currie (56) and the in-form Australian Stuart Law (67). Yet Carl Hooper was still there, and 268 for 9 became 341 all out as last man Gary Keedy helped the West Indian to add a precious 79 runs for the tenth wicket. Well, to be precise, Keedy scored one run! Hooper was magnificent, hitting five sixes and farming the strike so expertly that Keedy hardly had to face a ball while his partner raced from 49 to 114. Surrey were driven to distraction by Hooper's dominance, and Tim Murtagh's missed catch at square leg when the man from Guyana was on 88 did not help their spirits. On a third day shortened by rain to just 42 overs, Surrey then slumped to 137 for 9 as they found the slow left arm spin of Keedy even more difficult to deal with. Keedy's 4 for 57 was a fine piece of

Round 17: 25–29 August 2003 Division One

LANCASHIRE v. SURREY – at Old Trafford

SURREY	First Innings		Second Innings	
IJ Ward	c Hegg b Martin	10	c Chilton b Martin	3
*JN Batty	not out	154	c Law b Martin	0
GP Thorpe	lbw b Chapple	57	c Hegg b Wood	38
R Clarke	st Hegg b Keedy	11	lbw b Chapple	1
AD Brown	c Sutcliffe b Keedy	1	b Keedy	61
AJ Hollioake (capt)	b Martin	0	(7) c Law b Keedy	8
Azhar Mahmood	c Hegg b Keedy	63	(6) c Martin b Keedy	8
IDK Salisbury	c Currie b Schofield	5	c Hegg b Keedy	0
Saqlain Mushtaq	c Hegg b Wood	11	c Hegg b Martin	11
J Ormond	b Wood	0	run out	7
TJ Murtagh	b Martin	5	not out	0
Extras	b 8, lb 6, nb 6	20	b 1, nb 1	1
	(102.4 overs)	337	(43.1 overs)	138

Bowling
Martin 14.4-2-54-3. Chapple 21-4-87-1. Hooper 18-6-38-0. Wood 15-4-64-2. Keedy 24-9-62-3. Schofield 10-2-18-1.
Martin 12-5-20-3. Chapple 7-1-24-1. Keedy 14.1-1-57-4. Wood 7-0-29-1. Hooper 3-0-7-0.
Fall of Wickets 1-10, 2-114, 3-143, 4-147, 5-148, 6-261, 7-298, 8-329, 9-330, 10-337
1-1, 2-10, 3-23, 4-93, 5-108, 6-119, 7-119, 8-122, 9-137, 10-138

LANCASHIRE	First Innings		Second Innings	
MJ Chilton	b Murtagh	27	not out	33
IJ Sutcliffe	c Hollioake b Azhar Mahmood	8	c Batty b Azhar Mahmood	47
MR Currie	c Azhar Mahmood b Ormond	56	c and b Salisbury	13
SG Law	c Brown b Salisbury	67	not out	35
CL Hooper	c Salisbury b Azhar Mahmood	114		
CP Schofield	lbw b Salisbury	0		
G Chapple	c Azhar Mahmood b Ormond	1		
*WK Hegg (capt)	c Ormond b Azhar Mahmood	19		
PJ Martin	c Clarke b Azhar Mahmood	8		
J Wood	b Salisbury	6		
G Keedy	not out	1		
Extras	b 8, lb 7, w 3, nb 16	34	b 2, lb 1, nb 4	7
	(94.2 overs)	341	(2 wkts, 30.4 overs)	135

Bowling
Ormond 20-3-70-2. Azhar Mahmood 24.2-3-76-4. Murtagh 5-1-26-1. Saqlain Mushtaq 20-2-58-0. Clarke 6-0-26-0. Salisbury 19-2-70-3.
Ormond 5-1-25-0. Azhar Mahmood 7-1-28-1. Saqlain Mushtaq 13-3-49-0. Salisbury 5-0-19-1. Brown 0.4-0-11-0.
Fall of Wickets 1-18, 2-60, 3-169, 4-175, 5-178, 6-183, 7-221, 8-251, 9-262, 10-341
1-69, 2-92

Lancashire beat Surrey by 8 wickets –
Lancashire (20pts), Surrey (6pts)

WARWICKSHIRE v. MIDDLESEX – at Edgbaston

WARWICKSHIRE	First Innings		Second Innings	
MJ Powell (capt)	c Shah b Hutton	73	lbw b Keegan	1
NV Knight	b Keegan	10	b Cook	9
MA Wagh	st Nash b Weekes	62	lbw b Bloomfield	46
IR Bell	c Weekes b Keegan	27	b Keegan	0
JO Troughton	b Cook	0	c Nash b Bloomfield	64
DR Brown	c Strauss b Cook	71	b Bloomfield	9
AF Giles	b Hutton	7	c and b Weekes	9
*KJ Piper	c Dalrymple b Keegan	0	c Cook b Keegan	42
Waqar Younis	c Cook b Weekes	0	not out	13
CD Collymore	not out	11	c Cook b Bloomfield	1
A Richardson	run out	0	c Dalrymple b Keegan	4
Extras	b 1, lb 2, w 1, nb 12	21	b 4, lb 5	9
	(80.5 overs)	290	(64 overs)	198

Bowling
Keegan 23.5-5-76-3. Bloomfield 12-0-74-0. Cook 22-9-46-2. Hutton 10-0-43-2. Joyce 2-0-15-0. Weekes 11-2-28-2.
Keegan 25-4-67-4. Cook 17-5-53-1. Bloomfield 15-1-57-4. Weekes 5-2-8-1. Dalrymple 2-0-4-0.
Fall of Wickets 1-21, 2-117, 3-155, 4-156, 5-230, 6-251, 7-261, 8-264, 9-288, 10-290
1-12, 2-12, 3-20, 4-75, 5-75, 6-99, 7-180, 8-182, 9-184, 10-198

MIDDLESEX	First Innings		Second Innings	
AJ Strauss (capt)	c Piper b Collymore	0	lbw b Wagh	61
RMS Weston	c Piper b Collymore	31	b Waqar Younis	1
BL Hutton	lbw b Waqar Younis	5	lbw b Collymore	37
OA Shah	lbw b Collymore	54	c Piper b Richardson	25
EC Joyce	c and b Wagh	107	b Waqar Younis	9
PN Weekes	lbw b Brown	23	lbw b Richardson	4
*DC Nash	c Brown b Giles	4	c Piper b Waqar Younis	5
JWM Dalrymple	c Piper b Collymore	12	b Richardson	0
SJ Cook	c Troughton b Waqar Younis	9	lbw b Waqar Younis	3
CB Keegan	c Wagh b Waqar Younis	9	not out	9
TF Bloomfield	not out	9	b Waqar Younis	9
Extras	b 4, lb 8, w 5, nb 6	23	lb 1, nb 8	9
	(86 overs)	286	(64.5 overs)	171

Bowling
Waqar Younis 18-5-69-4. Collymore 14-1-42-3. Richardson 10-1-50-0. Giles 28-9-69-1. Bell 2-0-14-0. Wagh 3-0-12-1. Brown 11-2-18-1.
Waqar Younis 13.5-2-49-5. Collymore 15-5-39-1. Richardson 18-4-40-3. Brown 4-1-14-0. Wagh 8-1-30-1. Giles 6-2-7-0.
Fall of Wickets 1-0, 2-24, 3-98, 4-99, 5-151, 6-166, 7-199, 8-232, 9-242, 10-286
1-17, 2-109, 3-118, 4-141, 5-151, 6-154, 7-154, 8-158, 9-159, 10-171

Warwickshire beat Middlesex by 31 runs – Warwickshire (19pts),
Middlesex (5pts)

NOTTINGHAMSHIRE v. LEICESTERSHIRE – at Trent Bridge

NOTTS	First Innings		Second Innings	
DJ Bicknell	c Nixon b Maddy	59	c DeFreitas b Drakes	1
GE Welton	c Hodge b DeFreitas	60	lbw b DeFreitas	0
RJ Warren	lbw b DeFreitas	5	c DeFreitas b Drakes	4
KP Pietersen	lbw b DeFreitas	0	b DeFreitas	16
BM Shafayat	c Brandy b DeFreitas	68	c Sadler b Masters	13
CL Cairns (capt)	lbw b Maddy	15	lbw b DeFreitas	75
*CMW Read	c Sadler b Maddy	16	lbw b Drakes	65
PJ Franks	c Nixon b DeFreitas	36	not out	32
RJ Logan	lbw b DeFreitas	1	not out	1
SCG MacGill	c Walker b DeFreitas	0		
CE Shreck	not out	0		
Extras	b 9, lb 2, nb 18	29	b 1, lb 8, w 1, nb 12	22
	(106.4 overs)	290	(7 wkts, 57.4 overs)	241

Bowling
DeFreitas 26.4-9-51-7. Drakes 29-9-80-0. Maddy 23-3-62-3. Masters 14-6-29-0. Brandy 2-0-21-0. Walker 7-0-18-0. Snape 5-1-18-0.
DeFreitas 17-3-62-3. Drakes 15-4-58-3. Masters 11-2-52-1. Maddy 10.4-2-48-0. Walker 3-2-1-0. Brandy 1-0-11-0.
Fall of Wickets 1-132, 2-136, 3-136, 4-145, 5-164, 6-216, 7-285, 8-289, 9-289, 10-290
1-1, 2-1, 3-27, 4-29, 5-72, 6-180, 7-205

LEICESTERSHIRE	First Innings		
JK Maunders	lbw b Shreck	33	
DL Maddy	b Shreck	9	
BJ Hodge	not out	302	
JL Sadler	lbw b Shreck	2	
*PA Nixon	lbw b MacGill	65	
DG Brandy	st Read b MacGill	19	
JN Snape	c Franks b Shreck	48	
PAJ DeFreitas (capt)	c MacGill b MacGill	0	
VC Drakes	not out	4	
D D Masters			
G W Walker			
Extras	b 12, lb 11, w 2, nb 16	41	
	(7 wkts, 105 overs)	523	

Bowling
Cairns 22-1-109-0. Franks 22-2-98-0. Shreck 25-6-100-5. Logan 8-1-46-0. MacGill 27-2-135-2. Shafayat 1-0-12-0.
Fall of Wickets 1-45, 2-54, 3-60, 4-338, 5-385, 6-497, 7-498

Match drawn – Nottinghamshire (8pts),
Leicestershire (12pts)

Rolling back the years: Waqar Younis reminded spectators (and the Middlesex batsmen!) of his great days with a lethal spell at Edgbaston.

sustained attacking bowling, prompting Hooper to call him the best spinner of his type in England. Only a 70-run partnership between Thorpe and Alistair Brown (61) held up Lancashire for long, and on the final morning they were soon bowled out. Urged on by the home supporters, who sensed that this was a win that could give their own team a good chance of taking Surrey's title, Lancashire's top order then cruised to their victory target of 135.

Waqar Younis rolled back the years at Edgbaston to bring Warwickshire a victory over Middlesex which, on the third evening, had looked almost impossible. Andrew Strauss had just fallen for a fine 61, and Owais Shah had arrived at the crease and duly driven his third delivery for six to take Middlesex to 115 for 2 as they chased 203 to win.

Then, however, the umpires offered Shah and Ben Hutton – who was on 36 not out – the chance to go off for bad light. The batsmen took it, and Middlesex duly lost their momentum. The next morning Hutton fell almost immediately and Waqar, supported by the reliable Alan Richardson, smelt blood. There were still seven wickets left, and only 62 further runs were needed, but Waqar revived memories of his greatest days as Pakistan's feared spearhead as he sprinted in to take 5 for 40 with his familiar mixture of aggression and lethal swinging yorkers. He might indeed be several years older than his 'official' age of 31, as legend has it, and he is definitely not as fast as he was in his considerable pomp, but Waqar was still potent enough to propel Warwickshire to the 31-run win which almost certainly ensured their Division One status. As for Middlesex, they lost their last seven wickets for 30 runs and were left to rue their decision to take the bad light offer of the day before. Excellent seam bowling from Chad Keegan and Tim Bloomfield, who shared eight wickets as Warwickshire were dismissed for a second-innings 198, had given them the edge after the two teams were level on points at the midway stage. Ed Joyce's dedicated and skilful 107 had kept Middlescx in the game after half-centuries from Michael Powell, Mark Wagh and the in-form Dougie Brown had taken Warwickshire to 290 in their first innings. But this, in the end, will be remembered as Waqar's match – especially as he had also taken 4 for 69 in the Middlesex first innings.

A washed-out third day was typical of the wretched luck afflicting Leicestershire, as it clearly cost them the chance of beating fellow relegation candidates Nottinghamshire at Trent Bridge. In the end, Leicestershire ran out of time on the final day with Notts only eight runs in front on 241 for 7 in their second innings. Chris Cairns and Chris Read had held the visitors up with a sixth-wicket partnership of 108, after the home side had slumped to 72 for 5, but Paul Franks and Richard Logan were also in stubborn mood as the best efforts of Phil DeFreitas and Vasbert Drakes came up just short. DeFreitas had also taken a superb season's best of 7 for 51 as Notts were dismissed for a first-innings 290, but the draw was also especially tough for Brad Hodge to take after he had scored a career-best 302 not out. The Australian was in such pulsating form that Paul Nixon made only 65 in a fourth-wicket stand worth 278, and Hodge finally brought up his first triple hundred with his 49th boundary. He faced only 280 balls, and his epic innings was not only the highest championship score at Trent Bridge, but also the best by a Leicestershire player – eclipsing the 261 of Phil Simmons against Northants in 1994. Charlie Shreck, the six-foot-six-inch tall Cornishman, deserves a mention for his figures of 5 for 100 amid the carnage of Leicestershire's Hodge-driven surge to 523 for 7 declared, and Bilal Shafayat made a mature 68 in the Notts first innings, but this was a match snatched away from the visitors by the weather.

Division Two

Conservative batting and an unwillingness to give their fellow promotion rivals even a sniff of a chance of a successful last-day run chase almost certainly cost Glamorgan a priceless win over Yorkshire at Colwyn Bay. On a sluggish pitch, Michael Powell was the outstanding home batsman on show, and his innings of 146 and 85 always kept the Welsh county in the ascendancy. An eighth-wicket stand of 137 between Alex Wharf and Mike Kasprowicz helped to take Glamorgan to a first-innings 466 but, even then, the pair decided to come off for bad light nine overs from the scheduled end of day one when the total was on 380 for 7. That loss of time, and especially the defensive strategy which lay behind it, would come back to haunt Glamorgan. Yorkshire responded solidly, with Matthew Wood hitting 126

to go past 1,000 championship runs for the season and Anthony McGrath impressing with 92. Glamorgan's second innings was based initially on a second-wicket partnership worth 116 between Mark Wallace and Adrian Dale, before Powell and David Hemp came together at 158 for 4 and put the home side into an impregnable position. Incredibly, with an overnight lead of 314, Glamorgan captain Robert Croft allowed the innings to meander on for another 17 overs on the final morning before his declaration came, with Hemp still unbeaten on 85, and Yorkshire were set the task of scoring 381 from 77 overs. At 124 for 6, Glamorgan looked like winning, but McGrath, making a strong case for an England recall, found a willing accomplice in Richard Dawson in a match-saving stand of 64 for the seventh wicket. When Dawson fell for 22, time was almost up and McGrath was 127 not out when the draw was confirmed. How Croft must have wished then either for the nine overs Glamorgan had passed up on the first evening, or for the 17 overs they had used up by batting on at the start of that day. Croft himself took 4 for 80 from 42 overs, but in his defence he was also unfortunate that poor light on the final afternoon forced him to keep his quicker bowlers out of the attack for the last 60 overs.

Somerset made the highest score in their history at Taunton, but even with 705 for 9 declared they were unable to beat Hampshire due to regular weather interruptions over all four days. Neil Edwards, a 19-year-old left-hander from Cornwall in just his third championship appearance, hit 27 fours in a 186-ball 160. However, this was merely a warm-up act for Ian Blackwell, whose powerful hitting brought him two sixes and 32 fours in a 211-ball 189. Also filling their boots on a wonderful batting surface, and against some very ordinary bowling, were James Bryant, Aaron Laraman and Rob Turner, who scored 67 not out from 72 balls. It all added up to a potentially decisive 310-run first-innings lead, following Hampshire's dismissal for what proved to be a seriously below-par total of 395, but less than 47 overs were possible on the last day and the visitors escaped with

Round 17: 25–29 August 2003 Division Two

GLAMORGAN v. YORKSHIRE – at Colwyn Bay

GLAMORGAN	First Innings		Second Innings	
JP Maher	c Fleming b Silverwood	53	lbw b Gough	0
*MA Wallace	lbw b Kirby	31	c Gray b Dawson	61
A Dale	lbw b Silverwood	0	c Blakey b Yuvraj Singh	47
MJ Powell	c Silverwood b Yuvraj Singh	146	b Dawson	85
MP Maynard	c Blakey b Silverwood	32	c Gray b Dawson	3
DL Hemp	b Kirby	25	not out	85
RDB Croft (capt)	lbw b Silverwood	0	b Gough	5
AG Wharf	c Blakey b Gray	79	not out	23
MS Kasprowicz	c Dawson b McGrath	51		
DS Harrison	lbw b McGrath	1		
DA Cosker	not out	5		
Extras	b 9, lb 10, nb 24	43	b 7, lb 4, w 6, nb 10	27
	(114 overs)	466	(6 wkts, 82.5 overs)	336

Bowling
Gough 20-3-73-0. Kirby 26-1-158-2. Silverwood 19-2-56-4. Dawson 17-4-70-0. Gray 18-2-45-1. McGrath 10-2-37-2. Yuvraj Singh 4-1-8-1.
Gough 14-2-33-2. Kirby 5-0-30-0. Dawson 34-7-119-3. Silverwood 9-1-46-0. Yuvraj Singh 12.5-1-65-1. Gray 2-0-11-0. McGrath 6-0-21-0.
Fall of Wickets 1-82, 2-85, 3-102, 4-162, 5-280, 6-284, 7-323, 8-460, 9-461, 10-466
1-2, 2-118, 3-144, 4-158, 5-277, 6-292

YORKSHIRE	First Innings		Second Innings	
MJ Wood	c Dale b Croft	126	lbw b Kasprowicz	0
SP Fleming	c Dale b Croft	61	lbw b Cosker	16
A McGrath (capt)	c Powell b Cosker	92	not out	127
MJ Lumb	b Croft	5	lbw b Croft	1
Yuvraj Singh	b Cosker	2	c Cosker b Croft	6
SP Kirby	c Croft b Cosker	11		
*RJ Blakey	lbw b Kasprowicz	36	(6) lbw b Kasprowicz	0
AKD Gray	not out	48	(7) c Wallace b Croft	13
RKJ Dawson	c Powell b Harrison	7	(8) lbw b Croft	22
CEW Silverwood	b Kasprowicz	9	(9) not out	2
D Gough	b Kasprowicz	12		
Extras	b 4, lb 9	13	b 4, lb 2	6
	(128.2 overs)	422	(7 wkts, 94 overs)	193

Bowling
Kasprowicz 19.2-5-60-3. Wharf 7-0-35-0. Cosker 39-8-109-3. Croft 37-4-125-3. Harrison 16-2-67-1. Dale 10-3-13-0.
Kasprowicz 8-1-30-2. Harrison 4-0-13-0. Croft 42-14-80-4. Cosker 38-17-62-1. Maynard 2-0-2-0.
Fall of Wickets 1-104, 2-259, 3-280, 4-285, 5-295, 6-307, 7-380, 8-389, 9-406, 10-422
1-6, 2-45, 3-58, 4-78, 5-89, 6-124, 7-188

Match drawn – Glamorgan (12pts), Yorkshire (12pts)

SOMERSET v. HAMPSHIRE – at Taunton

HAMPSHIRE	First Innings		Second Innings	
DA Kenway	c Edwards b Johnson	100	c Turner b McLean	8
JHK Adams	b McLean	14	b Blackwell	50
JP Crawley (capt)	c Blackwell b McLean	60	c Blackwell b McLean	1
RA Smith	not out	56		
*N Pothas	b Jones	21		
LR Prittipaul	c Burns b Johnson	39	(4) not out	56
AD Mascarenhas	lbw b Blackwell	5		
JRC Hamblin	c Turner b Johnson	31	(5) not out	53
SD Udal	b Jones	30		
CT Tremlett	c Laraman b Jones	12		
JA Tomlinson	c Turner b Jones	0		
Extras	lb 17, nb 10	27	lb 4, w 1, nb 4	9
	(106.3 overs)	395	(3 wkts, 48 overs)	177

Bowling
McLean 21-6-68-2. Johnson 28-9-90-3. Jones 21.3-3-102-4. Laraman 23-5-71-0. Burns 4-0-27-0. Blackwell 9-5-20-1.
McLean 8.3-2-37-2. Johnson 6-0-17-0. Laraman 2-0-6-0. Blackwell 18-3-48-1. Jones 7-1-31-0. Webley 1-0-16-0. Edwards 4.3-1-10-0. Bryant 1-0-8-0.
Fall of Wickets 1-35, 2-175, 3-195, 4-219, 5-234, 6-293, 7-300, 8-364, 9-388, 10-395
1-14, 2-16, 3-96

SOMERSET	First Innings		
MJ Wood	c Kenway b Tremlett	8	
NJ Edwards	c Mascarenhas b Tomlinson	160	
JDC Bryant	c Pothas b Kenway	73	
M Burns (capt)	c Mascarenhas b Udal	10	
T Webley	b Tremlett	59	
ID Blackwell	c Tremlett b Prittipaul	189	
AW Laraman	not out	52	
*RJ Turner	not out	67	
PS Jones	c Udal b Tremlett	20	
RL Johnson	c Crawley b Tremlett	19	
N A M McLean	(did not bat)		
Extras	b 14, lb 2, w 4, nb 28	48	
	(9 wkts, 145 overs)	705	

Bowling
Tremlett 33-4-152-4. Mascarenhas 23-5-108-0. Tomlinson 28-4-142-1. Prittipaul 17-1-101-1. Udal 42-3-177-1. Kenway 2-0-9-1.
Fall of Wickets 1-26, 2-173, 3-189, 4-304, 5-448, 6-564, 7-616, 8-663, 9-705

Match drawn – Somerset (12pts), Hampshire (10pts)

Michael Powell of Glamorgan ... one of the most underrated of county batting talents.

ROUND 18:
3–8 SEPTEMBER 2003

Division One

When the end of their challenge finally came, it was not pretty. Surrey, who had been slipping slowly but surely out of the championship race for several weeks, suddenly plunged out of realistic contention when they were thrashed by an innings and 155 runs by Kent at Canterbury. For the home side, it was sweet revenge for the previous year's defeat to a Surrey side that had chased more than 400 in the fourth innings and confirmation that, on form during the second half of the season, they were more than a match for any side in the country. Injuries and England call-ups did not help Surrey in this game, but there was still an air of weariness about their performance that suggested that they had known their reign as county champions was about to end. David Fulton and Michael Carberry, the Kent openers, had put on an unbroken stand of 158 by lunch on the first day, and although they added just two more runs to their partnership before Carberry fell for 92 the die had been cast. Carberry, with 16 fours and a six from 112 balls, had also made a point against the club which had released him the previous winter, while Fulton made 71. Only Franklyn Rose, a temporary replacement for Saqlain Mushtaq, looked threatening in a tired Surrey attack, and Andrew Symonds was just the man to take full advantage as he thrashed a six and 17 fours in a quick-fire and merciless century. Mark Ealham, with 93, and Geraint Jones, building on his claims to succeed Alec Stewart as England wicketkeeper with 53, ensured that the Kent total reached commanding proportions at 535. Not even the keenest of Kent fans, though, could have expected what happened next as Surrey were tumbled out for 125 in just 28.5 overs. Martin Saggers swung the new ball to telling effect, picking up 4 for 40, while Amjad Khan provided the ideal pace foil with 3 for 50. Muttiah Muralitharan merely came on to knock over the tail with two cheap wickets. Following on, the excellent Saggers claimed two more wickets while Murali, capped at the tea interval on this dramatic second day, responded by taking three wickets in 20 overs

a draw at 177 for 3. In what proved to be his last first-class innings before retirement, Robin Smith wound up a truly top-class batting career by scoring 56 not out in the Hampshire first innings. Smith had retired hurt on seven on the opening day, because of more trouble from a chronic hamstring problem, but he then returned to the crease the following day to make sure he bowed out in better style.

before the close. Surrey, at 169 for 7 at the day's end, were doomed. The next morning brought a brief passage of aggressive defiance from Rose and James Ormond, but Muralitharan and Saggers grabbed another wicket each to finish with figures of

4 for 90 and 3 for 37 respectively. 'The dressing room is like a morgue,' confirmed Keith Medlycott, the Surrey manager, afterwards.

At Hove, where Sussex had started their fixture against Middlesex 24 hours later than at Canterbury, there was one of the biggest cheers of the match when the news of Surrey's first-innings collapse against Kent was reported to the home crowd. The Sussex faithful, however, had to endure the sight of the Middlesex third-wicket pair, Andrew Strauss and Owais Shah, adding 219 in superlative style before their side began to engineer a turnaround. Middlesex slipped from 309 for 3 to 392 all out by the close of the opening day, with the last five wickets tumbling for 18 runs in just 27 deliveries. At the heart of all this, of course, was Mushtaq Ahmed – even though the Pakistani leg spinner had to wait until his 27th over for his first success. Bowling unchanged for more than four hours, Mushtaq finished with figures of 6 for 145 to renew Sussex hopes that had seemed to be fading fast when Strauss and Shah were flowing to their respective centuries. Quite astonishing cricket, however, still lay ahead. On the second day, Sussex were soon up against it again as they slid to 107 for 6, only for Matt Prior and Mark Davis to fashion the most dramatic counter-attack of the summer. Prior went for his strokes with remarkable self-confidence for a player who is still only 21, while Davis steadily accumulated his runs. They put on 195, with Prior

Round 18: 3–8 September 2003
Division One

KENT v. SURREY – at Canterbury

KENT — **First Innings**

DP Fulton (capt)	c Batty b Rose	71
MA Carberry	c Batty b Rose	92
AGR Loudon	lbw b Murtagh	9
A Symonds	st Batty b Salisbury	121
MJ Walker	c Brown b Clarke	25
MA Ealham	lbw b Murtagh	93
*GO Jones	c Batty b Murtagh	53
RS Ferley	c Clarke b Rose	4
A Khan	c Batty b Clarke	25
MJ Saggers	not out	10
M Muralitharan	c Ramprakash b Murtagh	5
Extras	lb 11, nb 16	27
	(120.2 overs)	535

Bowling

Ormond 10–0–48–0. Rose 28–8–103–3. Murtagh 27.2–2–130–4. Clarke 21–1–95–2. Hollioake 7–1–35–0. Salisbury 27–4–115–1.

Fall of Wickets: 1-160, 2-175, 3-191, 4-262, 5-368, 6-451, 7-472, 8-506, 9-528, 10-535

SURREY — **First Innings / Second Innings**

	First Innings		Second Innings	
IJ Ward	b Saggers	3	b Muralitharan	53
*JN Batty	b Saggers	28	lbw b Ealham	17
MR Ramprakash	b Saggers	4	lbw b Saggers	15
N Shahid	lbw b Saggers	4	c Fulton b Saggers	1
AD Brown	c Fulton b Khan	2	b Muralitharan	40
R Clarke	c Jones b Khan	26	c Loudon b Muralitharan	13
AJ Hollioake (capt)	lbw b Khan	1	st Jones b Ferley	6
IDK Salisbury	c Walker b Muralitharan	16	lbw b Saggers	7
J Ormond	b Symonds	1	c Walker b Muralitharan	32
FA Rose	c Ferley b Muralitharan	4	c Saggers b Ferley	36
TJ Murtagh	not out	17	not out	12
Extras	b 5, lb 5, w 1, nb 10	21	b 8, lb 13, nb 2	23
	(28.5 overs)	125	(70 overs)	255

Bowling

Saggers 10–1–40–4. Khan 11–0–50–3. Muralitharan 4.5–2–11–2. Symonds 3–0–14–1. Saggers 14.5–5–37–3. Symonds 10–3–36–0. Ealham 6–1–17–1. Khan 4–0–11–0. Muralitharan 25–5–90–4. Ferley 11–2–43–2.

Fall of Wickets: 1-6, 2-19, 3-27, 4-30, 5-64, 6-78, 7-79, 8-99, 9-100, 10-125
1-23, 2-62, 3-68, 4-112, 5-144, 6-155, 7-159, 8-183, 9-215, 10-255

Kent beat Surrey by an innings and 155 runs – Kent (22pts), Surrey (3pts)

SUSSEX v. MIDDLESEX – at Hove

MIDDLESEX — **First Innings / Second Innings**

	First Innings		Second Innings	
AJ Strauss (capt)	c Prior b M-Jenkins	138	c Ambrose b Lewry	4
SG Koenig	b Lewry	5	lbw b M-Jenkins	16
BL Hutton	lbw b Lewry	1	c M-Jenkins b Taylor	36
OA Shah	lbw b M Ahmed	140	st Ambrose b Davis	34
EC Joyce	lbw b M Ahmed	22	b M Ahmed	31
PN Weekes	c Ambrose b M Ahmed	31	c Prior b M Ahmed	65
*DC Nash	c Adams b M Ahmed	15	(8) b Lewry	5
SJ Cook	b Davis	11	(9) b M Ahmed	11
CT Peploe	not out	0	(7) lbw b Lewry	13
CB Keegan	c Adams b M Ahmed	3	not out	3
JH Dawes	c Prior b M Ahmed	0	lbw b M Ahmed	2
Extras	b 7, lb 4, nb 6	26	b 11, lb 11, nb 8	30
	(100 overs)	392	(96.2 overs)	250

Bowling

Lewry 20–6–53–2. Taylor 15–2–66–0. M Ahmed 40–4–145–6. M-Jenkins 14–2–46–1. Davis 11–0–62–1.
Lewry 25–8–73–3. Taylor 10–1–30–1. M-Jenkins 3–3–12–1. M Ahmed 35.2–8–80–4. Davis 19–4–33–1.

Fall of Wickets: 1-17, 2-33, 3-252, 4-309, 5-334, 6-374, 7-387, 8-392, 9-390, 10-392
1-4, 2-42, 3-79, 4-124, 5-152, 6-201, 7-215, 8-241, 9-244, 10-250

SUSSEX — **First Innings / Second Innings**

	First Innings		Second Innings	
MW Goodwin	lbw b Dawes	14	(2) lbw b Dawes	4
RR Montgomerie	c Nash b Dawes	21	(1) not out	54
PA Cottey	c Hutton b Keegan	15	lbw b Dawes	7
CJ Adams (capt)	c Nash b Cook	20	c Hutton b Weekes	30
*TR Ambrose	c Hutton b Keegan	12	not out	11
RSC M-Jenkins	c Hutton b Dawes	8		
MJ Prior	c Shah b Weekes	148		
MJG Davis	c Dawes b Keegan	168		
M Ahmed	c Shah b Weekes	57		
JD Lewry	c Peploe b Keegan	21		
BV Taylor	not out	35		
Extras	b 5, lb 2, w 7, nb 4	18	b 1, lb 1	2
	(152.2 overs)	537	(3 wkts, 27.5 overs)	108

Bowling

Dawes 35–2–126–3. Keegan 32.4–4–120–4. Cook 30–7–83–1. Peploe 28–2–100–0. Weekes 27–3–101–2.
Keegan 7–2–29–0. Dawes 7–3–25–2. Cook 2–0–9–0. Peploe 6–2–20–0. Weekes 5.5–0–23–1.

Fall of Wickets: 1-26, 2-37, 3-66, 4-70, 5-82, 6-107, 7-302, 8-399, 9-431, 10-537
1-10, 2-22, 3-92

Sussex beat Middlesex by 7 wickets – Sussex (22pts), Middlesex (7pts)

WARWICKSHIRE v. LANCASHIRE – at Edgbaston

WARWICKSHIRE — **First Innings / Second Innings**

	First Innings		Second Innings	
MJ Powell (capt)	c Hegg b Chapple	0	c Law b Chapple	4
NV Knight	lbw b M-Jenkins	28	b Chapple	3
MA Wagh	b Chapple	20	c Crook b Wood	16
IJL Trott	b Hogg	126	c Loye b Keedy	43
IR Bell	c Hooper b Hogg	3	b Keedy	46
TL Penney	lbw b Wood	19	b Hogg	2
DR Brown	not out	140	b Crook	44
*KJ Piper	c Hooper b Wood	0	c Sutcliffe b Chapple	6
MM Betts	lbw b Crook	73	b Chapple	0
CD Collymore	c Hegg b Keedy	0	b Chapple	0
A Richardson	c Hooper b Keedy	2	not out	4
Extras	b 1, lb 14, w 2, nb 6	23	lb 2, w 1, nb 16	19
	(132.5 overs)	449	(57.1 overs)	187

Bowling

Chapple 28–6–92–3. Wood 23–3–101–2. Hogg 24–7–66–2. Crook 12–1–52–1. Keedy 26.5–4–84–2. Hooper 7–0–16–0. Chilton 10–4–15–0. Law 2–0–8–0.
Chapple 20–7–86–5. Wood 9–1–32–1. Hogg 7–3–24–1. Keedy 18–9–33–2. Hooper 2–0–4–0. Crook 1.1–0–6–1.

Fall of Wickets: 1-0, 2-33, 3-62, 4-68, 5-91, 6-317, 7-357, 8-446, 9-447, 10-449
1-6, 2-11, 3-39, 4-111, 5-114, 6-126, 7-143, 8-143, 9-143, 10-187

LANCASHIRE — **First Innings**

MJ Chilton	b Richardson	121
IJ Sutcliffe	c Piper b Collymore	16
MB Loye	c Richardson b Wagh	102
G Keedy	c Penney b Wagh	0
SG Law	c Wagh b Richardson	168
CL Hooper	c Collymore b Wagh	177
G Chapple	st Piper b Wagh	60
*WK Hegg (capt)	c Trott b Wagh	12
KW Hogg	c Collymore b Wagh	31
SP Crook	c sub b Wagh	27
J Wood	not out	0
Extras	b 8, lb 5, nb 48	67
	(174.5 overs)	781

Bowling

Betts 26–2–151–0. Collymore 30–5–99–1. Richardson 45–8–128–2. Bell 16–5–70–0. Wagh 39.5–2–222–7. Trott 12–0–70–0. Powell 6–0–28–0.

Fall of Wickets: 1-42, 2-264, 3-264, 4-266, 5-626, 6-669, 7-716, 8-730, 9-764, 10-781

Lancashire beat Warwickshire by an innings and 145 runs – Lancashire (21pts), Warwickshire (6pts)

ESSEX v. NOTTINGHAMSHIRE – at Chelmsford

NOTTS — **First Innings / Second Innings**

	First Innings		Second Innings	
DJ Bicknell	c Cook b Mohammad Akram	8	b Mohammad Akram	3
JER Gallian (capt)	c Irani b Clarke	65	c Clarke b Middlebrook	79
*CMW Read	b Dakin	5	c Foster b Clarke	27
RJ Warren	c Foster b Clarke	41	c Foster b Clarke	15
KP Pietersen	b Dakin	2	c Foster b Clarke	11
CL Cairns	b Dakin	70	c Pettini b Clarke	5
BM Shafayat	c Foster b Mohammad Akram	5	c Foster b Dakin	10
PJ Franks	not out	49	c Flower b Middlebrook	23
PJ McMahon	c Foster b Clarke	0	lbw b Napier	1
SCG MacGill	b Napier	9	not out	14
CE Shreck	c Foster b Dakin	19	c Pettini b Napier	14
Extras	b 5, lb 6, nb 2	13	b 4, lb 8, w 2	2
	(77.5 overs)	284	(86.4 overs)	204

Bowling

Mohammad Akram 23–7–65–2. Dakin 16.5–3–53–4. Napier 17–5–42–1. Clarke 16–3–70–3. Middlebrook 5–0–43–0.
Mohammad Akram 27–5–56–1. Dakin 18–6–30–1. Napier 19.4–5–56–2. Clarke 19–6–34–4. Middlebrook 8–3–16–2.

Fall of Wickets: 1-14, 2-19, 3-72, 4-79, 5-177, 6-190, 7-218, 8-218, 9-242, 10-284
1-5, 2-49, 3-90, 4-102, 5-108, 6-129, 7-173, 8-188, 9-192, 10-204

ESSEX — **First Innings / Second Innings**

	First Innings		Second Innings	
WI Jefferson	lbw b Cairns	1	c Gallian b McMahon	38
AN Cook	lbw b Shreck	13	not out	69
A Flower	c McMahon b Shreck	53	not out	45
ML Pettini	c Franks b Shreck	20		
RC Irani (capt)	c Gallian b MacGill	51		
*JS Foster	c Cairns b McMahon	58		
GR Napier	c Pietersen b McMahon	5		
JD Middlebrook	c Pietersen b Cairns	34		
JM Dakin	c Gallian b McMahon	47		
Mohammad Akram	c and b McMahon	0		
AJ Clarke	not out	32	nb 2	2
Extras	b 4, lb 9, w 2, nb 6	21		
	(106.5 overs)	335	(1 wkt, 34.1 overs)	154

Bowling

Cairns 22–4–89–2. Shreck 22–9–67–3. Franks 11–5–28–0. MacGill 24–3–79–1. McMahon 27.5–7–59–4.
Cairns 4–2–11–0. Shreck 6–1–21–0. MacGill 12–4–47–0. McMahon 7.1–2–54–1. Franks 5–1–21–0.

Fall of Wickets: 1-2, 2-31, 3-89, 4-118, 5-170, 6-175, 7-234, 8-268, 9-272, 10-335
1-80

Essex beat Nottinghamshire by 9 wickets – Essex (20pts), Nottinghamshire (5pts)

hitting 148 from 153 balls, with 25 boundaries. Then came Mushtaq, whose impish 57 was again the lead act in a stand of 97 with Davis. By the close – with Davis on 97 not out – Sussex were 401 for 8, but the best was still to come! As Davis ground on to a career-best 168 – a seven-and-a-half hour epic which contained two driven sixes off Paul Weekes – first Jason Lewry, and then last man Billy Taylor, kept him company. Taylor, in particular, drove the wilting Middlesex bowlers to distraction as he held firm for 40 overs, and 146 balls, to make a career-best 35 not out. His stand with Davis was worth 106, and it lifted the Sussex total to a scarcely believable total of 537. The last four wickets had raised 430 runs and even the gathering of some of the county's former players, attending their annual lunch that day, had seen nothing like it. By the close, each of Sussex's frontline bowlers had taken a wicket as Middlesex struggled to 157 for 5. The match was all but over, and so it proved on the final morning as Mushtaq (4 for 80) and Lewry (3 for 73) hastened Middlesex to 250 all out. Mushtaq's fifth ten-wicket match haul of the season took his overall tally to 99, while Richard Montgomerie's forceful unbeaten 54 soon swept Sussex to their modest victory target. With two matches still to play, Sussex now required just ten more points to become county champions for the first time in their history.

Lancashire, to their credit, were keeping up their chase with an awesome show of strength against Warwickshire at Edgbaston. They also demonstrated fine team spirit, too, after a last-day thunderstorm took away 35 overs from their attempt to bowl out Warwickshire for a second time. Every player, plus the coach and scorer, marched from the dressing room to help the ground staff remove the covers and get the field ready for play. Fittingly, their reward was to dismiss the home side for 187, with Glen Chapple taking 5 for 86. The victory, by an innings and 145 runs, was set up by irresistible batting on the second and third days, following Warwickshire's initially confident progress to a first-innings 449. Jonathan Trott, who hit 16 fours and a six in his innings of 126, was joined by Dougie Brown in a sixth-wicket stand worth 216 – just four runs short of the county record. Brown, who had to retire hurt on 112 with a calf muscle strain, then returned to the crease the next morning, accompanied by a runner, to reach an unbeaten 140. With Mel Betts thumping 12 fours and a six in a career-best 73, Warwickshire perhaps felt they were assured of a draw at least in their continuing bid to avoid the drop into Division Two. How wrong they were. Their attack was first softened

Young and gifted: Matt Prior of Sussex, who inspired a remarkable lower-order performance against Middlesex.

up by Mark Chilton and Mal Loye, who scored their sixth and fourth hundreds of the season respectively while adding 222 for the second wicket. At 278 for 4 overnight, Lancashire were then powered on to a massive 781 by Stuart Law and Carl Hooper. Law's 168, from 271 balls and containing 23 fours, was almost sedate compared to Hooper's 177. The West Indian faced 223 balls, striking eight sixes and 16 fours, and the 360 they put on was by some distance a Lancashire record for the fifth wicket. It was also only 11 runs short of the county record for any wicket, and as Law tucked in greedily and Hooper sent a stream of skimming drives away it became almost embarrassingly easy. Chapple also made 60 as Warren Hegg was prevented from declaring towards the end of the day by poor light that would have had the visiting batsmen opting to stay in the sanctuary of the pavilion. The only Warwickshire bowler to emerge from the carnage with any sort of satisfaction was Mark Wagh, whose gamely flighted off breaks brought him career-best figures (but decidedly strange ones) of 7 for 222.

Nottinghamshire, meanwhile, became the first county to be relegated when they lost by nine wickets to Essex at Chelmsford. Jason Gallian, the Notts skipper, batted with customary diligence to score 65 and 79 in his first game back since breaking a thumb five weeks previously, but only Chris Cairns (70 from 73 balls in the first innings) and Paul Franks matched his determination at the crease in another deeply flawed team performance. Perhaps the match was won and lost, though, when Jon Dakin followed up his first-innings haul of 4 for 53 by scoring 47 in a last-wicket stand worth 63 with Andy Clarke that won Essex a valuable 51-run lead at the midway point. Clarke, playing for a new contract, then picked up 4 for 34 as Notts could make only 204 second time around. Will Jefferson (38), the 18-year-old Alistair Cook (69 not out) and Andy Flower (45 not out) made no mistake as the home side eased to their victory target.

Division Two

There were 11 wickets for Jon Lewis and eight for slow left-armer Ian Fisher at Bristol as Gloucestershire squeezed past a Derbyshire side beset by nerves with the winning post in sight. The eventual margin of the home sides's victory was just 20 runs, keeping alive Gloucestershire's promotion ambitions but merely adding to the woes of their opponents. Set 290 on the final day, Derbyshire were going along well on 230 for 5 after fine innings from Michael Di Venuto (80) and Steve Stubbings (63), but Fisher, resurrecting his stop-start career, took 5 for 73 while the dependable Lewis added 4 for 66 to his heroic first-innings figures of 7 for 117 as Derbyshire subsided to 269 all out. Gloucestershire were also indebted, on day three, to an 86-ball 87 from Craig Spearman that kept them going forward in the face of a spirited Derbyshire seam attack, but Jonty Rhodes – who made a first-innings 137 – was dropped at slip off Dominic Cork at just 29. The two Derbyshire players who definitely did not deserve to be on the losing side were Di Venuto, who also hit 75 in their first innings, and 25-year-old Stubbings, who had marked his championship return with 103. Putting a long absence due to poor form behind him, Stubbings

Not good enough for Australia? Mike Hussey piles up the runs for Northamptonshire in his continued search for international honours.

reached his brave comeback hundred with a towering straight six. The only slight irritant for winners Gloucestershire, though, was that they had missed out on maximum batting bonus points by the narrowest of margins by being stranded on 399 for 8 at the end of 130 overs.

Yorkshire maintained their bid for promotion by seeing off Somerset by nine wickets at Headingley.

Matthew Hoggard, in his first championship appearance since May, confirmed his recovery from a long-standing knee injury by taking 7 for 49 as Somerset were bowled out for 228 despite a late rally from 120 for 8 led by Steffan Jones (61 not out) and Richard Johnson. A match-winning, first-innings lead was then won by the audacious hitting of Darren Gough, who included 16 fours in his 72-ball 83. Yorkshire had earlier recovered from a first-evening mini-slump from 72 for 1 to 86 for 3 as Craig White (93) was joined by his former Australian Under 19 team-mate Damien Martyn in a rousing fourth-wicket stand. Martyn, the late-season overseas replacement for Stephen Fleming, had reached 87 when he top-edged a hook at Johnson and the ball squeezed between the grille and peak of his helmet to break his nose. Neil Edwards made a spirited 90 at the start of the Somerset second innings, and there was further resistance from both Jamie Cox and Ian Blackwell, but the Yorkshire bowlers worked their way steadily through the visiting ranks, and an eventual 313 all out meant a relaxed stroll to victory on the third afternoon for Matthew Wood and Anthony McGrath, who both scored unbeaten half-centuries.

The prolific Northamptonshire pair of Mike Hussey and Phil Jaques were at it again as Durham were overwhelmed by an innings and 85 runs at Wantage Road. Jeff Cook's medium pacers undermined a Durham batting effort that showed a lack of discipline on day one, with only Paul Collingwood exuding any signs of permanence as the visitors were bowled out for 190. Cook returned

Round 18: 3–8 September 2003
Division Two

GLOUCESTERSHIRE v. DERBYSHIRE – at Bristol

GLOS	First Innings		Second Innings	
CM Spearman (capt)	lbw b Welch	21	(2) c Sutton b Havell	87
WPC Weston	c Gait b Havell	34	(1) lbw b Welch	6
THC Hancock	c Sutton b Cork	8	lbw b Havell	15
JN Rhodes	c Di Venuto b Dean	137	run out	2
MGN Windows	c Sutton b Havell	49	c Sutton b Havell	8
APR Gidman	lbw b Havell	46	b Dumelow	17
ID Fisher	c Di Venuto b Dean	24	lbw b Welch	10
MCJ Ball	c Stubbings b Welch	26	not out	22
RJ Sillence	b Cork	13	c Sutton b Welch	3
J Lewis	lbw b Welch	0		
*SP Pope	not out	0	(10) not out	14
Extras	b 1, lb 17, w 3, nb 14	35	b 9, lb 9, w 1, nb 6	25
	(131.5 overs)	401	(8 wkts, 66 overs)	209

Bowling
Dean 27–7–98–2. Welch 36–8–93–3. Cork 27.5–7–75–2. Havell 30–8–93–3. Dumelow 8–3–8–0. Hewson 3–0–12–0.
Cork 11–4–37–0. Welch 18–8–37–3. Dean 2–2–32–0. Dumelow 16–6–51–1. Havell 12–3–34–3.
Fall of Wickets 1–41, 2–58, 3–78, 4–174, 5–273, 6–346, 7–361, 8–391, 9–401, 10–401
1–34, 2–90, 3–94, 4–111, 5–132, 6–156, 7–162, 8–171

DERBYSHIRE	First Innings		Second Innings	
AI Gait	c Pope b Lewis	10	(2) c Pope b Sillence	12
MJ Di Venuto	c Windows b Fisher	75	(1) b Fisher	80
RM Khan	b Lewis	39	c Gidman b Lewis	10
SD Stubbings	c Weston b Lewis	103	c Ball b Lewis	63
DR Hewson	lbw b Lewis	0	c Hancock b Fisher	13
*LD Sutton	c Pope b Lewis	34	b Lewis	41
KJ Dean	b Fisher	0	(10) c Hancock b Lewis	2
DG Cork (capt)	c Weston b Lewis	10	(7) c Spearman b Fisher	19
G Welch	lbw b Lewis	1	(8) st Pope b Fisher	6
NRC Dumelow	c Hancock b Fisher	24	(9) lbw b Fisher	11
PM Havell	not out	0	not out	3
Extras	b 4, lb 7, w 1, nb 12	24	b 1, lb 3, w 2, nb 4	10
	(93.2 overs)	321	(89.2 overs)	269

Bowling
Lewis 27.2–3–117–7. Sillence 20–3–81–0. Gidman 3–2–1–0. Ball 20–6–45–0. Fisher 23–8–66–3.
Lewis 26.2–9–66–4. Sillence 10–2–42–1. Gidman 12–4–30–0. Ball 22–7–54–0. Fisher 19–2–73–5.
Fall of Wickets 1–38, 2–115, 3–145, 4–145, 5–217, 6–218, 7–241, 8–254, 9–299, 10–321
1–22, 2–46, 3–155, 4–182, 5–194, 6–230, 7–238, 8–253, 9–256, 10–269

Gloucestershire beat Derbyshire by 20 runs – Gloucestershire (21pts), Derbyshire (5pts)

YORKSHIRE v. SOMERSET – at Headingley

SOMERSET	First Innings		Second Innings	
MJ Wood	lbw b Hoggard	3	lbw b Gough	1
NJ Edwards	c Dawson b Hoggard	7	c and b Kirby	90
M Burns (capt)	c Lumb b Hoggard	28	c sub b Wood	34
J Cox	c Blakey b Gough	11	lbw b Kirby	59
T Webley	c Kirby b Hoggard	22	lbw b McGrath	12
ID Blackwell	b Hoggard	0	c Kirby b Dawson	48
*RJ Turner	b Hoggard	11	lbw b Gough	13
GM Andrew	c Dawson b Gough	11	c Gough b Dawson	9
PS Jones	not out	61	not out	14
RL Johnson	c Hoggard b Kirby	30	not out	14
NAM McLean	c McGrath b Hoggard	15	lbw b Hoggard	2
Extras	b 2, lb 5, w 1, nb 21	29	lb 4, w 2, nb 12	16
	(62.3 overs)	228	(98.5 overs)	313

Bowling
Gough 20–8–42–2. Hoggard 22.4–9–49–7. Kirby 14.5–1–82–1. Dawson 3–0–35–0. Craven 2–0–13–0.
Hoggard 20.5–2–57–2. Gough 19–2–58–2. Craven 12–3–28–0. McGrath 14–2–43–1. Dawson 18–2–59–2. Wood 2–0–4–1. Kirby 13–0–61–2
Fall of Wickets 1–13, 2–33, 3–45, 4–75, 5–75, 6–91, 7–108, 8–120, 9–199, 10–228
1–1, 2–94, 3–157, 4–180, 5–231, 6–266, 7–278, 8–291, 9–301, 10–313

YORKSHIRE	First Innings		Second Innings	
C White	b Jones	93	b Johnson	8
MJ Wood	c Turner b Andrews	40	not out	53
A McGrath (capt)	c Turner b Andrews	0	not out	67
MJ Lumb	c Turner b Johnson	2		
DR Martyn	retired hurt	87		
VJ Craven	c Turner b Johnson	3		
*RJ Blakey	c Turner b Jones	21		
RKJ Dawson	c and b Burns	47		
D Gough	c Cox b Johnson	83		
MJ Hoggard	not out	11		
SP Kirby	absent ill			
Extras	b 4, lb 10, w 1, nb 2	17	lb 4	4
	(9 wkts, 92.4 overs)	410	(1 wkt, 26.1 overs)	132

Bowling
McLean 19–1–90–0. Johnson 27.4–8–92–3. Jones 18–0–86–2. Andrews 11–2–48–2. Blackwell 14–1–53–0. Edwards 1–0–6–0. Burns 2–0–21–1.
McLean 6–1–21–0. Johnson 6–0–31–1. Jones 6–1–28–0. Andrews 4–0–36–0. Edwards 3–0–6–0. Wood 1.1–0–6–0.
Fall of Wickets 1–72, 2–72, 3–79, 4–225, 5–248, 6–264, 7–372, 8–410
1–29

Yorkshire beat Somerset by 9 wickets – Yorkshire (22pts), Somerset (3pts)

NORTHAMPTONSHIRE v. DURHAM – at Northampton

DURHAM	First Innings		Second Innings	
JJB Lewis (capt)	c Powell b Nel	0	b Greenidge	22
GJ Muchall	c Bailey b Hussey	23	c Powell b Cook	62
ML Love	c Powell b Cook	25	c Roberts b Brown	84
PD Collingwood	c Swann b Cook	68	c Sales b Swann	10
GJ Pratt	lbw b Nel	26	c Hussey b Brown	5
AM Thorpe	c Jaques b Cook	10	c Powell b Swann	4
*P Mustard	c Jaques b Cook	10	c Powell b Brown	35
GD Bridge	not out	33	not out	33
Shoaib Akhtar	c Nel b Brown	9	c Hussey b Brown	0
NC Phillips	b Cook	1	lbw b Brown	0
N Killeen	lbw b Cook	0	c Powell b Swann	0
Extras	b 1, lb 4	5	lb 2, lb 6	8
	(60.3 overs)	190	(88.3 overs)	263

Bowling
Nel 15–3–39–2. Greenidge 10–3–41–0. Cook 9.3–2–31–5. Hussey 3–1–5–1. Brown 11–0–44–2. Swann 4–0–23–0.
Nel 12–2–52–0. Greenidge 10–2–26–1. Brown 34–8–90–5. Swann 24.3–5–77–3. Cook 8–2–10–1.
Fall of Wickets 1–0, 2–40, 3–52, 4–125, 5–152, 6–168, 7–168, 8–181, 9–188, 10–190
1–79, 2–111, 3–123, 4–154, 5–183, 6–211, 7–262, 8–262, 9–262, 10–263

NORTHANTS	First Innings	
MEK Hussey (capt)	b Bridge	187
TW Roberts	c Pratt b Shoaib Akhtar	0
PA Jaques	b Bridge	147
DJG Sales	lbw b Phillips	79
MJ Powell	c Mustard b Shoaib Akhtar	10
JW Cook	lbw b Bridge	12
*TMB Bailey	c Muchall b Phillips	10
GP Swann	not out	50
A Nel	not out	22
CG Greenidge		
JF Brown		
Extras	b 8, lb 6	14
	(7 wkts, 129.2 overs)	538

Bowling
Shoaib Akhtar 21–3–91–2. Killeen 20–5–59–0. Bridge 42–6–180–3. Phillips 35.2–3–160–2. Collingwood 11–0–34–0.
Fall of Wickets 1–1, 2–269, 3–396, 4–427, 5–440, 6–453, 7–489

Northamptonshire beat Durham by an innings and 85 runs – Northamptonshire (22pts), Durham (2pts)

HAMPSHIRE v. WORCESTERSHIRE – at Southampton

WORCS	First Innings		Second Innings	
SD Peters	c Adams b Mascarenhas	87	c Pothas b Tomlinson	23
GA Hick	c Prittipaul b Tomlinson	8	lbw b Mascarenhas	42
Kadeer Ali	c Prittipaul b Mascarenhas	6	c Pothas b Vaas	79
BF Smith (capt)	c Pothas b Tomlinson	16	c and b Vaas	11
VS Solanki	c Pothas b Mascarenhas	8	c Pothas b Vaas	77
JM Kemp	c Kenway b Prittipaul	90	c Kenway b Udal	33
*DJ Pipe	not out	104	(8) b Udal	0
GJ Batty	c Pothas b Prittipaul	7	(7) c Mascarenhas b Udal	0
MS Mason	c Mascarenhas b Prittipaul	0	(10) not out	5
MA Harrity	c Prittipaul b Tremlett	1		
M Hayward	c Pothas b Tremlett	25		
Kabir Ali	(did not bat)		(9) c Kenway b Udal	20
Extras	b 3, lb 2, w 1	6	lb 11, w 7, nb 8	26
	(99.4 overs)	364	(9 wkts, 92.5 overs)	313

Bowling
Tremlett 21.4–5–78–2. Vaas 19–1–71–0. Tomlinson 17–1–69–3. Mascarenhas 18–7–54–7. Udal 8–1–38–0. Katich 9.1–32–0. Prittipaul 7–1–17–3.
Tremlett 7–1–32–0. Vaas 22–7–42–3. Mascarenhas 18–4–54–1. Tomlinson 15–2–61–1. Udal 21.5–2–69–4. Prittipaul 4–0–13–0. Katich 5–0–31–0.
Fall of Wickets 1–55, 2–77, 3–98, 4–106, 5–179, 6–316, 7–323, 8–323, 9–330, 10–364
1–53, 2–87, 3–107, 4–243, 5–256, 6–259, 7–264, 8–302, 9–313

HAMPSHIRE	First Innings		Second Innings	
DA Kenway	b Pipe b Mason	3	c Pipe b Mason	44
JHK Adams	c Pipe b Hayward	3	c Kemp b Hayward	6
SM Katich (capt)	c Kabir Ali b Batty	70	run out	42
JP Crawley (capt)	c Pipe b Hayward	35	b Batty	99
LR Prittipaul	c Peters b Kabir Ali	19	c Pipe b Kabir Ali	35
*N Pothas	c and b Batty	7	c Hick b Mason	2
AD Mascarenhas	c Pipe b Mason	24	b Mason	16
SD Udal	c Peters b Kabir Ali	50	c Pipe b Batty	29
W PUJC Vaas	c Mason b Batty	35	not out	0
CT Tremlett	run out	0	st Pipe b Batty	0
JA Tomlinson	not out	0	c Kemp b Batty	0
Extras	b 6, lb 8, w 3, nb 2	19	b 4, lb 8, w 7, nb 4	23
	(87 overs)	265	(88.2 overs)	311

Bowling
Hayward 18–4–50–2. Mason 19–5–47–2. Harrity 9–4–26–0. Batty 26–8–77–3. Kabir Ali 11–1–40–2. Kemp 4–0–11–0.
Kabir Ali 16–1–60–1. Hayward 17–3–52–0. Batty 34.2–10–94–4. Mason 18–3–66–3. Kemp 3–1–10–0.
Fall of Wickets 1–9, 2–9, 3–73, 4–107, 5–136, 6–167, 7–189, 8–241, 9–255, 10–265
1–12, 2–89, 3–121, 4–213, 5–225, 6–251, 7–251, 8–301, 9–305, 10–311

Worcestershire beat Hampshire by 101 runs – Worcestershire (21pts), Hampshire (5pts)

career-best figures of 5 for 31 and, by the close, Hussey and Jaques had already swept Northants to 166 for 1 in reply. Jaques had completed his fifth championship hundred of the season just before stumps, from 104 balls, and there were two sixes and 23 fours in his eventual 147 as the two Australians posted 268 for the second wicket. David Sales then scored 79 and Graeme Swann an unbeaten 50, but Northants' remorseless progress to 538 for 7 declared was mainly due to the 187 made in seven-and-a-half hours of unflagging concentration by Hussey. Gordon Muchall and Martin Love tried hard to play the similar sort of innings that Durham needed from someone if they were to save the game, but Jason Brown and Swann chipped away with their off breaks and, in the end, Durham could not even see out the third day. Brown's 5 for 90 included three wickets in four balls towards the end of the innings.

Division Two leaders Worcestershire proved too strong for lowly Hampshire over four days at Southampton's Rose Bowl, but at least the home side could reflect on a performance in which they fought every step of the way. Stephen Peters, Justin Kemp and, in particular, the reserve wicketkeeper Jamie Pipe excelled with the bat on day one, as Worcestershire totalled 364. The 25-year-old Pipe, deputizing for the injured Steve Rhodes, scored his maiden first-class hundred and finished unbeaten on 104 to show that his days as Rhodes' understudy might be drawing to a close. He added 137 for the sixth wicket with Kemp, and his innings contained a six and 18 fours. Hampshire were 99 runs adrift after the first innings, despite 70 from Simon Katich and a half-century eighth-wicket stand between Shaun Udal and Chaminda Vaas. Udal, taking 4 for 69 and moving past 600 first-class wickets in the process, did his best to slow the Worcestershire advance towards a second-innings declaration on day three, following attractive 70s from Kadeer Ali and Vikram Solanki. A brilliant pick up and throw from cover by Ben Smith then ran out Katich for 42 just before the close, and only John Crawley's 88 held up Worcestershire for longer than they wished on the final day. Gareth Batty picked up four wickets and Matt Mason three as Worcestershire completed a deserved victory by 101 runs.

ROUND 19: 10–15 SEPTEMBER 2003

Division One

Sussex suffered a horrible attack of stage fright as all eyes turned on to their visit to Lancashire – the one side who could still deny them a historic first

Mal Loye continued his prolific first season at Lancashire with 144 against Sussex.

championship title. In the end, they slunk away from Old Trafford vowing to learn the lessons of a thumping innings-and-19-run defeat. Too timid throughout, they gained only four bonus points from the game, leaving them requiring a minimum of six points from their final match against Leicestershire at Hove. Lancashire's maximum 22-point haul meanwhile – giving them a total of 63 out of a possible 66 from their last three games – kept alive their own hopes of a first outright title since 1934. Poor weather badly affected the first two days, which should have played into Sussex's hands as they sought the draw that would have clinched them their holy grail, but Lancashire, who were 225 for 2 after day one and 368 for 5 after the 43 further overs possible on the second day, declared at 450 for 6 and by the close of day three had Sussex following on and already in trouble again at 21 for 2. Tony Cottey's dismissal for 40 sparked a slump from 121 for 1 to 251 all out in the Sussex first innings, with only Murray Goodwin showing the necessary steel and skill against the slow left-arm spin of Gary Keedy. Goodwin carried his bat for 118, despite suffering a deep gash to his right eyebrow after misjudging an attempt to hook a ball from Peter Martin when he was on 87. Play was held up for ten minutes as both team physios carried out running repairs to staunch the flow of blood. At the close, Goodwin needed seven stitches to repair the cut properly, and in the Sussex second innings he batted, bandaged up, at No. 6. Even a bloodied Goodwin, though, was better than anything else Sussex could offer with the bat – the Zimbabwean again top scoring with 57 as Keedy, with another five-wicket haul, spun them to 180 all out. Earlier, Mal Loye and Stuart Law had made the 27th and 28th individual hundreds of Lancashire's own title challenge … their best tally since, yes, 1934!

Essex were confirmed as the third relegated club when they lost by nine wickets to Warwickshire at Chelmsford. The home side began the game hopelessly, plunging to 73 for 7 before Graham Napier at No. 8, John Stephenson at No. 9 and Andy Clarke at No. 10 fashioned a recovery to 256 all out. Napier scored 48, Stephenson an unbeaten 75 and Clarke a career-best 41, but by the end of day two Warwickshire were exactly 200 runs ahead at 456 for 7. Mark Wagh's 116 and half-centuries for Nick Knight, Jon Trott and Dougie Brown were followed, the next morning, by a hard-hit 45 not out from Waqar Younis which pushed Warwickshire's total up to 503. An opening stand of 122, however, between Will Jefferson and young Alistair Cook, was followed

by a defiant championship-best innings from Mark Pettini (78), and Essex reached the end of the third day still dreaming of a miracle. Enter Waqar, the dream-breaker. With a burst of 5 for 12 in 24 balls,

Round 19: 10–15 September 2003
Division One

LANCASHIRE v. SUSSEX – at Old Trafford

LANCASHIRE — First Innings
MJ Chilton	c Ambrose b Taylor	6
IJ Sutcliffe	c Davis b Lewry	38
MB Loye	c Montgomerie b M-Jenkins	144
SG Law	not out	163
CL Hooper	lbw b Lewry	33
CP Schofield	b Taylor	1
G Chapple	b Lewry	14
*WK Hegg (capt)	not out	26
P J Martin		
J Wood		
G Keedy		
Extras	b 4, lb 12, w 1, nb 8	25
	(6 wkts, 126.3 overs)	450

Bowling
Lewry 26.3-3-125-3. Taylor 35-8-114-2. M-Jenkins 23-7-73-1. M Ahmed 37-6-99-0. Davis 5-1-23-0.
Fall of Wickets 1-21, 2-66, 3-363, 4-363, 5-368, 6-414

SUSSEX — First Innings / Second Innings
	First Innings		Second Innings	
MW Goodwin	not out	118	(6) lbw b Keedy	57
RR Montgomerie	lbw b Keedy	10	(1) lbw b Martin	2
PA Cottey	c Chapple b Wood	40	(4) c sub b Wood	32
CJ Adams (capt)	c Chapple b Wood	1	(2) c Law b Wood	35
*TR Ambrose	b Wood	0	c Sutcliffe b Wood	2
RSC M-Jenkins	c Hegg b Keedy	2	(7) b Martin	6
MJ Prior	c Law b Keedy	2	(8) c Schofield b Keedy	10
MJG Davis	c Law b Keedy	2	(9) c Sutcliffe b Keedy	11
M Ahmed	c Chilton b Hooper	54	(10) c Law b Schofield	16
JD Lewry	b Hooper	0	(11) not out	7
BV Taylor	c Schofield b Keedy	0	(3) lbw b Keedy	0
Extras	b 9, lb 3, nb 8	20	lb 2	2
	(73 overs)	251	(87 overs)	180

Bowling
Martin 15-4-40-0. Chapple 15-2-54-0. Keedy 28.5-5-106-5. Wood 9-3-17-3. Hooper 5-0-17-2. Schofield 1-0-5-0.
Martin 20-7-43-2. Wood 14-4-27-2. Keedy 32 6 61-5. Hooper 17-3-33-0. Schofield 4-0-14-1.
Fall of Wickets 1-28, 2-122, 3-126, 4-126, 5-143, 6-147, 7-157, 8-238, 9-240, 10-251
1-20, 2-21, 3-61, 4-67, 5-73, 6-96, 7-125, 8-146, 9-164, 10-180

Lancashire beat Sussex by an innings and 19 runs – Lancashire (22pts), Sussex (4pts)

ESSEX v. WARWICKSHIRE – at Chelmsford

ESSEX — First Innings / Second Innings
	First Innings		Second Innings	
WI Jefferson	lbw b Brown	33	c Brown b Wagh	62
AN Cook	lbw b Collymore	0	b Wagh	55
A Flower	run out	13	c Piper b Wagh	28
ML Pettini	b Collymore	0	c Knight b Wagh	78
HC Irani (capt)	c Wagh b Waqar Younis	9	c Knight b Brown	18
*JS Foster	b Richardson	15	c Piper b Waqar Younis	23
JD Middlebrook	b Richardson	1	b Waqar Younis	0
GR Napier	c Wagh b Brown	48	not out	3
JP Stephenson	not out	75	c Knight b Waqar Younis	10
AJ Clarke	c Troughton b Richardson	41	b Waqar Younis	6
Mohammad Akram	lbw b Waqar Younis	6	b Waqar Younis	3
Extras	b 6, lb 3, nb 6	15	b 6, lb 4, nb 8	16
	(66.2 overs)	256	(108.1 overs)	302

Bowling
Waqar Younis 15.2-3-69-2. Collymore 16-3-60-2. Richardson 20-6-51-3. Brown 9-3-41-2. Wagh 6-1-26-0.
Waqar Younis 25.1-4-77-5. Collymore 11-2-57-0. Wagh 41-9-111-4. Richardson 16-7-25-0. Troughton 2-1-1-0. Brown 14-5-20-1.
Fall of Wickets 1-7, 2-11, 3-44, 4-59, 5-88, 6-139, 7-213, 8-213, 9-238, 10-256
1-122, 2-137, 3-188, 4-223, 5-279, 6-279, 7-281, 8-292, 9-298, 10-302

WARWICKSHIRE — First Innings / Second Innings
	First Innings		Second Innings	
MJ Powell (capt)	lbw b Middlebrook	30	c Middlebrook b M Akram	10
NV Knight	st Foster b Middlebrook	64	not out	24
MA Wagh	c Foster b Middlebrook	116	not out	23
IJL Trott	lbw b Middlebrook	65		
IR Bell	lbw b Stephenson	13		
JO Troughton	c Jefferson b Mohammad Akram	28		
DR Brown	lbw b Napier	77		
*KJ Piper	c Foster b Napier	24		
Waqar Younis	not out	45		
A Richardson	b Napier	0		
CD Collymore	c Foster b Middlebrook	1		
Extras	b 5, lb 6, w 1, nb 28	40	b 1, lb 1, nb 2	4
	(111.3 overs)	503	(1 wkt, 15.4 overs)	61

Bowling
Mohammad Akram 24-0-151-1. Napier 19-2-80-3. Clarke 10-1-50-0. Middlebrook 48.3-8-154-5. Stephenson 8-0-46-1. Cook 2-0-11-0.
Mohammad Akram 5-1-16-1. Middlebrook 7.4-2-29-0. Napier 3-0-14-0.
Fall of Wickets 1-65, 2-172, 3-255, 4-281, 5-335, 6-361, 7-421, 8-488, 9-488, 10-503
1-22

Warwickshire beat Essex by 9 wickets – Warwickshire (22pts), Essex (5pts)

LEICESTERSHIRE v. KENT – at Leicester

LEICESTERSHIRE — First Innings / Second Innings
	First Innings		Second Innings	
JK Maunders	c Walker b Khan	129	not out	2
DI Maddy	c Jones b Sheriyar	1	not out	1
BJ Hodge	c Walker b Ealham	31		
JL Sadler	c Ealham b Muralitharan	20		
TR Ward	c Smith b Saggers	15		
*PA Nixon	c Ealham b Muralitharan	23		
CE Dagnall	lbw b Muralitharan	0		
JN Snape	not out	45		
PAJ DeFreitas (capt)	st Jones b Muralitharan	8		
VC Drakes	c Ealham b Muralitharan	18		
DD Masters	c Fulton b Muralitharan	3		
Extras	b 3, lb 8, w 1, nb 10	22	nb 2	2
	(82.1 overs)	295	(no wkt, 1.4 overs)	5

Bowling
Saggers 15-2-63-1. Sheriyar 10-1-48-1. Khan 15-2-67-1. Symonds 7-2-23-0. Ealham 13-2-32-1. Muralitharan 22.1-4-51-6. Walker 1-0-1-0. Key 0.4-0-4-0.
Fall of Wickets 1-16, 2-71, 3-111, 4-132, 5-139, 6-139, 7-232, 8-261, 9-291, 10-295

KENT — First Innings / Second Innings
	First Innings		Second Innings	
DP Fulton (capt)	c Hodge b Drakes	13	c Hodge b Dagnall	21
RWT Key	b DeFreitas	11	b Dagnall	15
ET Smith	b Drakes	21	c Nixon b Maddy	30
A Symonds	lbw b DeFreitas	2	c Nixon b Masters	0
MJ Walker	c Nixon b Dagnall	24	c Nixon b Masters	35
MA Ealham	lbw b Dagnall	13	lbw b DeFreitas	1
*GO Jones	lbw b Dagnall	9	lbw b DeFreitas	1
A Khan	lbw b Maddy	0	b Drakes	26
MJ Saggers	c Snape b Maddy	4	not out	26
M Muralitharan	run out	12	c Sadler b Masters	0
A Sheriyar	not out	4	c Masters b Maddy	11
Extras	lb 9, nb 8	17	lb 10, nb 2	12
	(49.3 overs)	130	(45.5 overs)	169

Bowling
DeFreitas 16-5-44-2. Drakes 15-4-29-2. Masters 6-2-5-0. Dagnall 9-1-37-3. Maddy 3.3-2-6-2.
DeFreitas 11-3-16-2. Drakes 9-2-33-1. Maddy 10.5-1-43-2. Dagnall 6-1-23-2. Masters 9-0-44-3.
Fall of Wickets 1-23, 2-41, 3-58, 4-62, 5-96, 6-109, 7-110, 8-110, 9-122, 10-130
1-33, 2-58, 3-59, 4-87, 5-88, 6-104, 7-124, 8-140, 9-140, 10-169

Leicestershire beat Kent by 10 wickets – Leicestershire (19pts), Kent (3pts)

MIDDLESEX v. NOTTINGHAMSHIRE – at Lord's

NOTTS — First Innings / Second Innings
	First Innings		Second Innings	
DJ Bicknell	c Nash b Bloomfield	35	lbw b Dawes	42
JER Gallian	c Strauss b Dawes	73	c Dalrymple b Joyce	116
BM Shafayat	c Nash b Hutton	5	c sub b Weekes	6
RJ Warren	b Keegan	123	not out	113
KP Pietersen	c Joyce b Weekes	70	b Strauss	68
CL Cairns	run out	1		
*CMW Read	c Nash b Dalrymple	16	not out	3
PJ Franks	b Weekes	1		
SCG McGill	c Weekes b Dalrymple	0		
PJ McMahon	b Keegan	7	(6) c Nash b Koenig	30
CE Shreck	not out	4		
Extras	b 6, lb 11, w 5, nb 4	26	b 10, lb 10, w 1, nb 8	29
	(98 overs)	361	(5 wkts, 109 overs)	407

Bowling
Dawes 28-3-93-1. Keegan 25-2-105-2. Bloomfield 6.4-1-25-1. Hutton 5-1-26-1. Weekes 23.2-3-72-2. Joyce 3-0-18-0. Dalrymple 7-2-5-2.
Dawes 13-2-47-1. Keegan 13-2-37-0. Weekes 23-6-32-1. Dalrymple 20-2-71-0. Hutton 10-0-70-0. Joyce 7-1-23-1. Shah 8-0-36-0. Strauss 5-0-27-1. Koenig 5-0-19-1. Nash 5-0-25-0.
Fall of Wickets 1-70, 2-106, 3-146, 4-274, 5-275, 6-317, 7-320, 8-321, 9-346, 10-361
1-86, 2-115, 3-234, 4-345, 5-397

MIDDLESEX — First Innings
AJ Strauss (capt)	c and b Cairns	15
SG Koenig	lbw b Shreck	13
BL Hutton	c Pietersen b MacGill	20
OA Shah	b Warren b Franks	87
EC Joyce	c Read b Cairns	14
PN Weekes	c MacGill b Franks	38
*DC Nash	not out	53
JWM Dalrymple	c Pietersen b MacGill	26
CB Keegan	lbw b MacGill	17
JH Dawes	b Cairns	14
TF Bloomfield	lbw b MacGill	0
Extras	b 3, lb 5, w 11, nb 10	29
	(94 overs)	326

Bowling
Cairns 30-8-101-3. Shreck 14-5-36-1. Franks 12-3-54-2. MacGill 33-6-98-4. McMahon 5-0-29-0.
Fall of Wickets 1-28, 2-43, 3-85, 4-121, 5-197, 6-230, 7-274, 8-304, 9-325, 10-326

Match drawn – Middlesex (10pts), Nottinghamshire (11pts)

the former Pakistan captain recalled his most destructive years as Essex tumbled to 302 all out.

Relegated Leicestershire finally achieved their first win of the season, skittling out Kent twice on a pitch offering variable bounce at Grace Road. Matthew Walker was top scorer in both innings, with 24 and 35, as Kent folded to 130 and 169 in reply to a Leicestershire first-innings total of 295 that was built around a superb 129 from 189 balls by John Maunders. For once, Muttiah Muralitharan's six-wicket analysis counted for little as Leicestershire were faced with the task of scoring just five second-innings runs to complete victory.

One of the most pointless days of cricket ever seen at Lord's provided the sad end to Middlesex's meeting with Nottinghamshire. Rain affected the first two days, but Notts won themselves a modest first-innings lead and, on 48 without loss second time around, began the final day 83 runs to the good. A declaration, however, never came – and, by late afternoon, ten Middlesex players had been given a bowl in an attempt to relieve the boredom. Those who operate the big electric scoreboard at Lord's ran out of space in which to indicate the identity of the tenth bowler and, instead, flashed up a message to David Nash, the Middlesex wicketkeeper now about to purvey his flighted filth: 'Sorry, Nashy, there's no room for you!' Russell Warren added an unbeaten 113 to his first-innings 123, which at least made the last day memorable for him, while Jason Gallian batted well earlier in the innings to hit 116. The Notts captain had also made 73 on the opening day, but the Middlesex support was distinctly underwhelmed by his negative approach as the game drifted to a draw.

Division Two

Worcestershire took a giant step nearer the Division Two title by denting Yorkshire's own promotion prospects with a 71-run win at New Road. Their 21-point haul, clinched with 20 overs to spare as Nantie Hayward and Gareth Batty bowled out Yorkshire for 164 on the final afternoon, meant that a draw against second-placed Northants in the season's final round of matches would be sufficient to crown them champions of the second tier. Home skipper Ben Smith led from the front with a first-innings 110 – his first championship hundred since the season's opening day – and followed it up with a gritty 57 in the second innings. Kadeer Ali helped Smith to put on 182 for Worcestershire's third wicket before unluckily falling for 99 as he gloved a legside delivery. Steve Kirby did his best to check Worcestershire's

progress with his fifth five-wicket return of the championship summer, but it took an eighth-wicket partnership between Craig White (66) and Richard Dawson, who was dropped at slip off Batty on 3 and went to a 93-ball 60, to push Yorkshire's noses in front after the first innings. Chris Silverwood then took 5 for 63 on a pitch whose bounce was growing more variable, while Worcestershire were grateful not only for Smith's half-century but also for a welcome return to form for Graeme Hick, whose 57 was his first championship 50 in 12 innings.

Glamorgan last pair David Hemp and Dean Cosker failed by only 20 runs to bring off a heroic victory against Northamptonshire at Cardiff. The Welsh county, needing a stiff 382 to win, looked out of contention at 283 for 9 despite a defiant 78 from Matthew Maynard, but then Cosker joined Hemp in a last-ditch bid that garnered 78 runs. At 361, however, Cosker failed for once to get fully forward against the off breaks of Jason Brown – who, by then, was in his 63rd over – and was lbw for 42. Distraught, Cosker was later to be found slumped in the corner of the Glamorgan dressing room berating himself with the words: 'Why didn't I get forward?' Hemp finished up on 85 not out. Northants always had the upper hand in the match, however, from the moment that the prolific Mike Hussey's 147 took them to 319 all out on the first day. Hussey also made 50 in the second innings, looking for a long while that he would go on to a sixth successive championship hundred. Graeme Swann's 5 for 37 had given Northants a 116-run first-innings lead to build upon but, in the end, Andre Nel's second-innings 42 batting from No. 10 assumed vital proportions. Defeat was tough to take for Robert Croft, after the Glamorgan captain had picked up match figures of 10 for 147 with two five-wicket hauls.

The defeats suffered by Yorkshire and Glamorgan enabled Gloucestershire to move back into third place and put themselves in pole position to grab the third promotion place. Jonty Rhodes marked his last appearance at Bristol, and the penultimate first-class match of his iconic career, by scoring two hundreds in the match for the first time. He tamed a Durham attack spearheaded by the fearsome Shoaib Akhtar, although the sluggishness of the Nevil Road pitch was, no doubt, a contributory factor. Rhodes made 103 on the opening day, hitting three sixes and ten fours in the process, and Tim Hancock also impressed before falling three runs short of a first championship century at Bristol. A career-best 5 for 30 from Ian Fisher, following an incisive three-wicket burst with the new ball from Jon Lewis, then cut down Durham for 218 in reply to Gloucestershire's 374 – leaving the stage clear again for Rhodes to spark emotional farewell scenes by reaching 102. Ian Harvey and Jack Russell also hit out jauntily before a declaration came at 288 for 7, and Rhodes admitted after his innings that he had greatly benefited from Russell's presence at the crease when nerves had afflicted him during the approach of his second ton. Durham's resistance on the third evening and final morning revolved around Martin Love, their classical Australian batsman, and when he was out for 97 (to add to his first-innings 98) the game was up, bar Liam Plunkett's unbeaten 40. Again, Fisher and Lewis were the Gloucestershire bowling heroes with figures of 5 for 93 and 3 for 64 respectively.

Perhaps the greatest individual performance of the entire county summer, however, took place at Taunton where Ian Blackwell entered Somerset folklore with an amazing innings of 247 not out. Blackwell came in to bat, against his former county Derbyshire, with Dominic Cork rampant and his side in some trouble at 31 for 4 on the first morning. Soon, it was 112 for 7 and the powerful Blackwell was in danger of running out of partners. A cricketing legend, though, was about to be created. Richard Johnson and then Simon Francis hung on at the other end while Blackwell went into overdrive. Suddenly, the boundary boards – and the surrounding buildings beyond it

– were being peppered by a wondrous barrage of magnificently struck drives, pulls and cuts. Even the appearance of last man Nixon McLean did not bring an end to the entertainment – after, that is,

Round 19: 10–15 September 2003
Division Two

WORCESTERSHIRE v. YORKSHIRE – at Worcester

WORCS	First Innings		Second Innings	
SD Peters	b Dawson	44	c and b Silverwood	0
GA Hick	c Dawson b Hoggard	7	b Craven	57
Kadeer Ali	c Blakey b Silverwood	99	b Hoggard	21
BF Smith (capt)	lbw b Kirby	110	b Craven	57
A Singh	b Kirby	17	c Blakey b Silverwood	14
JM Kemp	c Dawson b Kirby	20	lbw b Kirby	33
GJ Batty	c McGrath b Hoggard	34	lbw b Silverwood	21
*DJ Pipe	c McGrath b Craven	10	b Silverwood	1
Kabir Ali	c Blakey b Silverwood	3	lbw b Silverwood	3
DH Wigley	c Blakey b Kirby	15	c Blakey b Kirby	8
M Hayward	not out	6	not out	7
Extras	b 10, lb 5, w 6, nb 6	27	b 9, lb 13, w 3, nb 4	29
	(130.3 overs)	389	(77.1 overs)	251

Bowling
Hoggard 26–6–85–2. Silverwood 28–9–56–1. Kirby 32.3–4–122–5. Dawson 29–12–61–1. McGrath 7–0–25–0. Craven 8–1–25–1.
Silverwood 21–7–63–5. Kirby 28.1–7–62–2. Hoggard 13–4–41–1. Dawson 6–0–34–0. Craven 9–1–29–2.
Fall of Wickets: 1–15, 2–82, 3–264, 4–292, 5–304, 6–323, 7–361, 8–365, 9–370, 10–389
1–2, 2–58, 3–134, 4–155, 5–185, 6–203, 7–222, 8–227, 9–229, 10–251

YORKSHIRE	First Innings		Second Innings	
CR Taylor	c Batty b Kemp	40	lbw b Hayward	14
MJ Wood	c Kadeer Ali b Kabir Ali	37	c Pipe b Hayward	14
A McGrath (capt)	c Pipe b Hayward	47	lbw b Wigley	6
MJ Lumb	c and b Kemp	61	b Batty	23
VJ Craven	b Batty	45	c Kemp b Batty	24
SP Kirby	c Pipe b Hayward	2	(10) lbw b Hayward	8
C White	lbw b Wigley	66	(6) lbw b Hayward	9
*RJ Blakey	c Pipe b Hayward	3	(7) not out	31
RKJ Dawson	c Kabir Ali	60	(8) c Hick b Hayward	18
CEW Silverwood	c Batty b Wigley	6	(9) c Hick b Batty	6
MJ Hoggard	not out	0	run out	1
Extras	b 14, lb 11, w 2, nb 16	43	lb 6, nb 4	10
	(116.1 overs)	405	(56 overs)	164

Bowling
Kabir Ali 23–2–108–2. Hayward 28–10–74–3. Wigley 19.1–5–56–2. Kemp 12–0–62–2. Batty 34–10–80–1.
Hayward 19–5–37–4. Wigley 10–4–39–1. Batty 20–4–57–4. Kemp 7–1–25–0.
Fall of Wickets: 1–69, 2–127, 3–151, 4–254, 5–258, 6–285, 7–289, 8–393, 9–405, 10–405
1–18, 2–33, 3–35, 4–73, 5–98, 6–98, 7–130, 8–137, 9–163, 10–164

Worcestershire beat Yorkshire by 71 runs –
Worcestershire (21pts), Yorkshire (8pts)

GLAMORGAN v. NORTHAMPTONSHIRE – at Cardiff

NORTHANTS	First Innings		Second Innings	
MEK Hussey (capt)	b Croft	147	(2) c Maynard b Croft	50
TW Roberts	c Wallace b Wharf	41	(1) c Wallace b Kasprowicz	6
PA Jaques	lbw b Croft	3	c and b Wharf	0
DJG Sales	lbw b Croft	17	lbw b Kasprowicz	52
MJ Powell	lbw b Cosker	3	c Wallace b Wharf	1
JW Cook	c Maher b Croft	3	b Croft	37
*TMB Bailey	lbw b Kasprowicz	11	c Maynard b Croft	7
GP Swann	lbw b Kasprowicz	0	c Wallace b Wharf	39
MJ Cawdron	lbw b Croft	5	c and b Croft	1
A Nel	b Kasprowicz	19	c Kasprowicz b Croft	42
JF Brown	not out	19	not out	9
Extras	b 6, lb 10	26	b 9, lb 2, nb 10	21
	(81.3 overs)	319	(79.1 overs)	265

Bowling
Kasprowicz 20–2–58–3. Wharf 13–2–83–1. Harrison 9–2–47–0. Cosker 11–4–32–1. Croft 28.3–6–93–5.
Kasprowicz 13–3–41–2. Wharf 16–2–83–3. Harrison 4–3–12–0. Cosker 22–5–64–0. Croft 24.1–12–54–5.
Fall of Wickets: 1–95, 2–142, 3–184, 4–219, 5–222, 6–253, 7–253, 8–260, 9–287, 10–319
1–6, 2–7, 3–80, 4–85, 5–154, 6–154, 7–181, 8–199, 9–207, 10–265

GLAMORGAN	First Innings		Second Innings	
JP Maher	c Hussey b Cawdron	29	st Bailey b Brown	35
*MA Wallace	lbw b Cawdron	10	run out	38
A Dale	c Hussey b Cook	24	c Roberts b Swann	16
MJ Powell	c Roberts b Swann	40	b Brown	11
MP Maynard	c Powell b Swann	48	c and b Swann	78
DI Hemp	lbw b Swann	20	not out	85
RDB Croft (capt)	c Powell b Brown	1	b Cook	31
AG Wharf	c Sales b Brown	4	b Cook	4
MS Kasprowicz	not out	0	c Bailey b Cook	4
DS Harrison	b Swann	0	b Cook	4
DA Cosker	lbw b Swann	1	lbw b Brown	42
Extras	b 2, lb 3, w 1	6	b 10, lb 5, nb 2	17
	(71 overs)	203	(147.2 overs)	361

Bowling
Nel 12.3–3–24–0. Cawdron 11.3–2–58–2. Brown 24–8–56–2. Cook 7–2–23–1. Swann 16–4–37–5.
Nel 1–0–7–0. Cawdron 14–3–48–0. Cook 20–5–66–4. Hussey 3–0–9–0. Brown 62.2–24–100–3. Swann 47–8–116–2.
Fall of Wickets: 1–20, 2–53, 3–86, 4–141, 5–170, 6–171, 7–187, 8–203, 9–203, 10–203
1–63, 2–88, 3–91, 4–106, 5–154, 6–154, 7–181, 8–199, 9–207, 10–265

Northamptonshire beat Glamorgan by 20 runs –
Northamptonshire (20pts), Glamorgan (4pts)

GLOUCESTERSHIRE v. DURHAM – at Bristol

GLOS	First Innings		Second Innings	
WPC Weston	c Mustard b Shoaib Akhtar	12	(2) c Bridge b Shoaib Akhtar	7
CM Spearman (capt)	lbw b Bridge	59	(1) b Shoaib Akhtar	8
THC Hancock	b Collingwood	97	c Peng b Plunkett	32
JN Rhodes	c Peng b Phillips	103	(5) st Mustard b Bridge	102
MGN Windows	c Mustard b Phillips	28	(6) c Bridge b Plunkett	12
IJ Harvey	b Bridge	29	(7) c Mustard b Shoaib Akhtar	41
*RC Russell	b Bridge	5	(8) not out	34
ID Fisher	c Mustard b Shoaib Akhtar	18	(9) not out	12
MA Hardinges	lbw b Bridge	4		
MCJ Ball	b Mustard	3	(4) b Shoaib Akhtar	8
J Lewis	not out	0		
Extras	lb 8, nb 2	10	b 7, lb 5	12
	(109 overs)	374	(7 wkts, 67 overs)	288

Bowling
Shoaib Akhtar 14–3–30–3. Plunkett 12–3–53–0. Collingwood 8–0–36–1. Phillips 43–9–139–2. Bridge 32–8–98–4.
Shoaib Akhtar 17–3–48–4. Plunkett 16–3–61–2. Phillips 2–0–51–0. Bridge 11–1–96–1. Collingwood 5–0–27–0.
Fall of Wickets: 1–14, 2–109, 3–240, 4–293, 5–322, 6–347, 7–360, 8–360, 9–373, 10–374
1–29, 2–52, 3–67, 4–100, 5–122, 6–195, 7–258

DURHAM	First Innings		Second Innings	
JJB Lewis (capt)	lbw b Lewis	16	b Hardinges	28
GJ Muchall	c Russell b Lewis	1	b Lewis	11
ML Love	st Russell b Fisher	98	c Spearman b Fisher	97
PD Collingwood	lbw b Lewis	11	c Harvey b Lewis	0
GJ Pratt	c Spearman b Hardinges	1	st Russell b Fisher	67
N Peng	lbw b Harvey	0	c Russell b Fisher	38
*P Mustard	c and b Fisher	31	c Windows b Fisher	7
GD Bridge	c Spearman b Fisher	5	absent hurt	
Shoaib Akhtar	st Russell b Fisher	34	(8) c Harvey b Fisher	14
LE Plunkett	c Ball b Fisher	0	(9) not out	40
NC Phillips	not out	11	(10) c Hardinges b Lewis	5
Extras	lb 4, nb 6	10	b 4, lb 6, w 2, nb 4	16
	(61.1 overs)	218	(94.3 overs)	318

Bowling
Lewis 19–7–52–3. Harvey 13–4–41–1. Hardinges 10–5–28–1. Ball 10–2–63–0. Fisher 9.1–1–35–5.
Lewis 20.3–5–64–3. Harvey 13–5–58–0. Hardinges 9–4–30–1. Ball 26–7–63–0. Fisher 26–9–64–3.
Fall of Wickets: 1–11, 2–32, 3–56, 4–57, 5–84, 6–159, 7–170, 8–173, 9–173, 10–218
1–42, 2–42, 3–42, 4–143, 5–220, 6–227, 7–252, 8–278, 9–318

Gloucestershire beat Durham by 126 runs –
Gloucestershire (21pts), Durham (4pts)

SOMERSET v. DERBYSHIRE at Taunton

SOMERSET	First Innings		Second Innings	
MJ Wood	lbw b Dean	14	b Mohammad Ali	72
MJ Edwards	b Cork	10	b Havell	28
M Burns (capt)	lbw b Cork	0	c Di Venuto b Mohammad Ali	58
T Webley	lbw b Cork	6	b Dumelow	12
JC Hildreth	b Cork	9	b Cork	4
ID Blackwell	not out	247	c Havell b Dumelow	4
*RJ Turner	lbw b Dean	16	not out	18
GM Andrew	b Cork	0	c Adnan b Dumelow	0
RL Johnson	lbw b Cork	25	lbw b Cork	6
SRG Francis	c Gait b Mohammad Ali	18	lbw b Cork	4
NAM McLean	b Mohammad Ali	39	c Sutton b Cork	4
Extras	b 4, lb 7, w 1, nb 6	18	b 5, lb 1, nb 6	6
	(65 overs)	409	(76.3 overs)	214

Bowling
Cork 20.3–9–92–6. Dean 22.4–118–2. Havell 7–0–66–0. Mohammad Ali 13.3–83–2. Dumelow 3–0–36–0.
Cork 20.3–7–35–4. Dean 2–0–21–0. Havell 8–0–45–1. Mohammad Ali 17.9–38–2. Dumelow 29–9–76–3.
Fall of Wickets: 1–19, 2–26, 3–26, 4–31, 5–42, 6–75, 7–112, 8–176, 9–246, 10–409
1–87, 2–124, 3–165, 4–170, 5–185, 6–186, 7–191, 8–206, 9–214, 10–214

DERBYSHIRE	First Innings		Second Innings	
AI Gait	b Francis	110	(3) b Blackwell	49
MJ Di Venuto	c Turner b Johnson	46	(1) c Turner b Francis	23
RM Khan	c Turner b Francis	24	c Webley b Blackwell	22
SD Stubbings	c Turner b Francis	93	c Andrew b Francis	9
Hassan Adnan	not out	33	c Johnson b Francis	32
*LD Sutton	c Turner b Francis	10	c Turner b Andrew	49
DG Cork (capt)	c Turner b Johnson	5	st Turner b Blackwell	6
NRC Dumelow	c Wood b Johnson	26	b Andrew	1
Mohammad Ali	c Turner b McLean	7	c Webley b Andrew	0
KJ Dean	b McLean	7	b Blackwell	1
PM Havell	not out	1	not out	0
Extras	b 8, w 2, nb 2	12	lb 2, w 1	3
	(9 wkts, 123.3 overs)	400	(64 overs)	196

Bowling
McLean 27–6–86–2. Johnson 36–9–98–2. Andrew 12–2–42–1. Francis 23.3–4–94–4. Burns 3–1–14–0. Blackwell 22–6–58–0.
McLean 9–1–25–0. Johnson 11–1–47–0. Blackwell 27–7–65–4. Francis 13–1–43–3. Andrew 4–0–14–3.
Fall of Wickets: 1–64, 2–96, 3–281, 4–282, 5–292, 6–293, 7–345, 8–352, 9–362, 10–196
1–43, 2–78, 3–97, 4–105, 5–178, 6–179, 7–188, 8–188, 9–193, 10–196

Somerset beat Derbyshire by 27 runs –
Somerset (22pts), Derbyshire (8pts)

Journey into legend: Ian Blackwell's power-hitting at Taunton has already entered Somerset folklore.

the West Indian fast bowler was dropped at slip before he had scored. Far from it. With McLean batting sensibly to reach 39, a Somerset record tenth-wicket stand of 163 was raised and, when the carnage finally subsided, Blackwell remained 247 not out and the total was 409. He had belted 11 sixes and 27 fours, and his last-wicket partnership with McLean – eclipsing the 143 of Jim Bridges and Holland Gibbs in 1919 – had taken just 15 overs. 'Towards the end of my innings I was feeling so confident that, for the first time in my career, I thought I could hit every ball for six,' said Blackwell. Derbyshire, to their credit, responded to Blackwell's great onslaught by carefully building a total of 400 for 9 declared themselves – though by more workaday means. Andrew Gait, with 110, and Steve Stubbings (93) confirmed their respective returns to form in a third-wicket stand of 185 in 29 overs, while Hasan Adnan made 59 not out on debut. Then, when Cork added 4 for 35 to his first innings 6 for 92, as Somerset were bowled out for 214, it seemed as if Derbyshire could actually have the last laugh. At 178 for 4, they seemed certain to do so, but

Blackwell – who else? – chipped away with his left-arm spin to take 4 for 65 and three wickets apiece for Francis and Gareth Andrew helped to send the visitors sliding to 196 all out, and defeat by 27 runs. Blackwell, for one, deserved no less.

ROUND 20: 17–20 SEPTEMBER 2003

Division One

At 1.43pm on a sunny Thursday down by the sea, 18 minutes after a lunch interval spent in delicious anticipation, Sussex won the first county title in their long history. A short ball from Phil DeFreitas was pulled like a pistol crack to the midwicket boundary by Murray Goodwin, signalling scenes of jubilant celebration carried off with customary grace and charm around the old Hove ground. Goodwin's stroke had brought up the Sussex 300 and, after they had bowled out Leicestershire for 179 on the opening day, their total of six bonus points was enough to take them out of reach of second-placed Lancashire. Chris Adams, the captain who had linked up so well with Peter Moores, the coach, was fittingly at the crease when the title was secured. His great jump of joy, as he danced down the pitch to embrace Goodwin, was symbolic of the moment when the hearts of thousands upon thousands of Sussex folk leapt in unison. It had been 164 years since the formation of the club, 139 years since the first unofficial recognition of an annual champion county, and a mere 113 summers since the county championship was officially endorsed. And, now, Sussex had actually won! Play was halted for almost ten minutes as the rest of the Sussex squad came out on to the field, first to greet Adams and Goodwin and then to pose for the photographs they will cherish. Finally, as the cricket began to continue, the Sussex players embarked on a modest half lap of honour around the boundary edge. Champagne corks were already popping all around the ground, from the deckchairs to the terraces, to the committee room and pavilion, and also in the press box where Christopher Martin-Jenkins, *The Times* cricket correspondent, was toasting with colleagues the achievement of both his county and his son Robin. It was a joyous occasion, indeed, in beautiful late-summer weather, and the rest of the afternoon for a near-capacity crowd was spent luxuriating in the emotion of it all. The strokeplay from the middle also formed a majestic backdrop to such celebration: Adams soon completed a century of huge personal satisfaction, containing four sixes, and Goodwin gave the impression he didn't want his own involvement in the day to end. On and on he went, until even Duleepsinhji's individual record score of 333, set in 1930, fell to him. Tim Ambrose also joined the on-field party, with 82, and Sussex even capped their most memorable day by taking two Leicestershire wickets before the close after declaring themselves on a mammoth 614 for 4.

The following day, after many hours of partying, was one of sore heads and Jason Lewry – although credit must also go to the Leicestershire pair of David Masters and John Sadler. Masters, resuming as nightwatchman of the evening before, took advantage of some less-than-waspish Sussex bowling to reach a maiden first-class hundred, while the 21-year-old Sadler hit two sixes and 22 fours in 145, his second hundred in ten first-class innings. The pair added 208 for the fifth wicket, but then Lewry raised himself for a final burst of 5 for 6 in 25 balls that gave him overall career-best figures of 8 for 106 and completed a Sussex victory by an innings and 55 runs. The Sussex total of points, 257, was a record for Division One and their ten wins in the campaign equalled Surrey's Division One record.

One more player in particular, however, needs to be mentioned in conjunction with this Sussex triumph. Mushtaq Ahmed, the rejuvenated Pakistan leg spinner, had struck the blow which initially diverted this game Sussex's way – as he had done so

often along their 2003 road to glory. Leicestershire had reached 111 for 1 on the opening morning when, on the stroke of lunch, Mushtaq produced a

Round 20: 17–20 September 2003
Division One

SUSSEX v. LEICESTERSHIRE – at Hove

LEICESTERSHIRE	First Innings			Second Innings	
JK Maunders	c Lewry b M-Jenkins	21		c M-Jenkins b Lewry	15
DL Maddy	c Cottey b Taylor	55		(7) lbw b Lewry	29
BJ Hodge	b M Ahmed	36		(5) c Ambrose b Lewry	1
JL Sadler	st Ambrose b M Ahmed	145		(6) b Lewry	145
*PA Nixon	c Ambrose b Taylor	1		(8) c Goodwin b Lewry	0
LJ Wright	c Montgomerie b M Ahmed	0		(9) not out	11
JN Snape	c Ambrose b Lewry	13		(2) c Adams b Taylor	1
PAJ DeFreitas (capt)	b M-Jenkins	23		(10) b Lewry	0
VC Drakes	c Ambrose b M-Jenkins	8		(11) c Ambrose b Lewry	0
GW Walker	not out	4		c sub b Lewry	21
DD Masters	b M Ahmed	2		(3) c M-Jenkins b Taylor	119
Extras	b 5, lb 6, w 1, nb 4	16		b 8, lb 14, nb 16	38
	(69.5 overs)	179		(88.1 overs)	380

Bowling
Lewry 15-4-37-1. Taylor 18-6-40-2. M-Jenkins 12-6-20-3. M Ahmed 24.5-3-71-4.
Lewry 24.1-3-106-8. Taylor 21.2-6-84-2. M-Jenkins 9.4-0-60-0. Davis 25-9-75-0. Cottey 4-0-15-0. Goodwin 3-0-17-0. Adams 1-0-1-0.
Fall of Wickets 1-42, 2-111, 3-117, 4-117, 5-118, 6-118, 7-142, 8-167, 9-174, 10-179
1-16, 2-20, 3-65, 4-69, 5-277, 6-353, 7-353, 8-370, 9-370, 10-380

SUSSEX	First Innings	
RR Montgomerie	c Nixon b DeFreitas	10
MW Goodwin	not out	335
PA Cottey	c Nixon b DeFreitas	56
CJ Adams (capt)	c Drakes b Walker	102
*TR Ambrose	b Sadler b Hodge	82
RSC M-Jenkins		
MJ Prior		
MJG Davis		
M Ahmed		
JD Lewry		
BV Taylor		
Extras	b 12, lb 9, nb 8	29
	(4 wkts, 126 overs)	614

Bowling
DeFreitas 28-4-94-2. Drakes 19-2-64-0. Masters 18-0-88-0. Maddy 4-0-21-0. Wright 19-0-95-0. Snape 12-0-72-0. Walker 19-1-92-1. Hodge 6-0-51-1. Maunders 1-0-16-0.
Fall of Wickets 1-24, 2-151, 3-418, 4-614

Sussex beat Leicestershire by an innings and 55 runs – Sussex (22pts), Leicestershire (1pt)

NOTTINGHAMSHIRE v. LANCASHIRE – at Trent Bridge

NOTTS	First Innings			Second Innings	
DJ Bicknell	b Wood	75		c Hooper b Chapple	53
JER Gallian (capt)	c Keedy b Hogg	83		lbw b Chapple	2
*CMW Read	c Hegg b Wood	9		lbw b Chapple	2
RJ Warren	b Wood	75		lbw b Chapple	0
KP Pietersen	c Hegg b Hooper	52		b Chapple	37
BM Shafayat	lbw b Martin	22		c Hegg b Chapple	26
SR Patel	c sub b Keedy	9		c Law b Hogg	55
PJ Franks	c Chapple	14		not out	100
GJ Smith	not out	9		c Law b Sutcliffe	9
SCG MacGill	b Chapple	4		not out	16
A J Harris	(did not bat)				
Extras	b 3, lb 6, w 3, nb 8, p 5	25		b 8, lb 6, nb 5	19
	(9 wkts, 100 overs)	376		(8 wkts, 83.5 overs)	319

Bowling
Martin 21-4-66-1. Chapple 23-2-78-2. Hogg 13-2-71-1. Wood 19-4-80-3. Keedy 15-2-51-1. Hooper 9-2-16-1.
Martin 8.5-0-55-0. Chapple 33-8-98-6. Wood 11-1-43-0. Keedy 16-4-40-0. Hogg 9-0-50-1. Sutcliffe 4-1-11-1. Loye 2-0-8-0.
Fall of Wickets 1-165, 2-175, 3-183, 4-270, 5-318, 6-342, 7-360, 8-362, 9-376
1-8, 2-116, 3 22, 4-85, 5-116, 6-186, 7-211, 8-211, 9-216, 10-219
1-54, 2-134, 3-137, 4-137, 5-168, 6-169, 7-194, 8-211, 9-239, 10-243

LANCASHIRE	First Innings			Second Innings	
MJ Chilton	b Smith	7		c Read b MacGill	27
IJ Sutcliffe	c Read b Smith	37		b Franks	65
MB Loye	lbw b Smith	9		lbw b Franks	28
SG Law	c Bicknell b Smith	51		b Franks	3
CL Hooper	b Smith	4		lbw b Franks	0
KW Hogg	c Shafayat b MacGill	46		b MacGill	53
G Chapple	c Patel b Harris	25		lbw b MacGill	0
*WK Hegg (capt)	lbw b Franks	11		c Gallian b Smith	12
PJ Martin	c Read b Franks	4		c Pietersen b Smith	16
G Keedy	not out	3		(11) not out	2
J Wood	lbw b MacGill	3		c Gallian b MacGill	20
Extras	b 2, lb 9, w 1, nb 2	14		b 1, lb 9, w 1, nb 6	17
	(66.4 overs)	219		(73.2 overs)	243

Bowling
Smith 20-7-61-5. MacGill 14.4-2-52-2. Franks 17-7-36-2. Harris 15-2-59-1.
Smith 19.2-3-61-2. Franks 18-5-62-4. MacGill 22-4-67-4. Harris 6-1-33-0. Patel 8-5-10-0.
Fall of Wickets 1-8, 2-36, 3-109, 4-124, 5-147, 6-186, 7-211, 8-211, 9-216, 10-219
1-54, 2-134, 3-137, 4-137, 5-168, 6-169, 7-194, 8-211, 9-239, 10-243

Nottinghamshire beat Lancashire by 233 runs – Nottinghamshire (21pts), Lancashire (4pts)

SURREY v. ESSEX – at The Oval

SURREY	First Innings			Second Innings	
SA Newman	c Foster b Napier	9		c Cook b Mohammad Akram	0
JN Batty	b Napier	87		c Foster b Mohammad Akram	47
N Shahid	c Pettini b Middlebrook	67		c Cook b Mohammad Akram	0
R Clarke	b Middlebrook	4		b Mohammad Akram	18
AD Brown	c Bopara b Middlebrook	17		b Mohammad Akram	0
JGE Benning	hit wkt b Mohammad Akram	18		c Foster b Mohammad Akram	5
*BJM Scott	not out	58		c Foster b Mohammad Akram	4
IDK Salisbury (capt)	c Flower b Bopara	14		lbw b Napier	29
TJ Murtagh	c Napier b Mohammad Akram	21		b Mohammad Akram	0
PJ Sampson	lbw b Middlebrook	3		not out	32
NC Saker	b Napier	1		b Napier	4
Extras	lb 7, w 4, nb 8	19		lb 7, w 1, nb 8	16
	(81.3 overs)	318		(57.3 overs)	194

Bowling
Mohammad Akram 21-5-93-2. Napier 18.3-4-58-3. Clarke 7-2-32-0. Middlebrook 28-3-93-4. Stephenson 2-0-12-0. Bopara 5-0-23-1.
Mohammad Akram 21-9-49-8. Napier 12.3-1-54-2. Clarke 7-1-19-0. Stephenson 12-2-39-0. Middlebrook 5-0-26-0.
Fall of Wickets 1-17, 2-120, 3-130, 4-164, 5-195, 6-222, 7-241, 8-300, 9-313, 10-318
1-0, 2-0, 3-24, 4-26, 5-122, 6-125, 7-134, 8-138, 9-194, 10-194

ESSEX	First Innings			Second Innings	
WI Jefferson	c Brown b Sampson	0		c Scott b Sampson	22
AN Cook	c Scott b Saker	84		c Scott b Sampson	18
A Flower (capt)	not out	201			
ML Pettini	c Newman b Benning	70		(3) not out	4
RS Bopara	c Newman b Salisbury	31		(4) not out	2
*JS Foster	lbw b Clarke	36			
JD Middlebrook	c Scott b Clarke	3			
GR Napier	b Murtagh	1			
JP Stephenson	c Scott b Murtagh	1			
AJ Clarke	c Scott b Clarke	8			
Mohammad Akram	lbw b Sampson	0			
Extras	b 1, lb 5, w 1, nb 22	29		lb 1, nb 2	3
	(106.5 overs)	464		(2 wkts, 9.1 overs)	49

Bowling
Sampson 14.5-1-85-2. Clarke 20-1-104-3. Murtagh 27-4-89-2. Saker 16-1-71-1. Salisbury 21-1-70-1. Benning 8-1-39-1.
Sampson 5-0-16-2. Saker 4.1-0-32-0.
Fall of Wickets 1-0, 2-157, 3-272, 4-343, 5-429, 6-433, 7-440, 8-442, 9-457, 10-464
1-36, 2-47

Essex beat Surrey by 8 wickets – Essex (22pts), Surrey (6pts)

KENT v. WARWICKSHIRE – at Canterbury

KENT	First Innings	
DP Fulton (capt)	c Piper b Richardson	51
RWT Key	lbw b Brown	54
ET Smith	c Wagh b Trott	213
A Symonds	c and b Wagh	88
MJ Walker	c Piper b Trott	121
*GO Jones	c Piper b Trott	0
MA Ealham	c Piper b Trott	30
JC Tredwell	lbw b Trott	4
RS Ferley	c Piper b Trott	4
K Khan	lbw b Trott	7
MJ Saggers	not out	0
Extras	b 6, lb 12, nb 4	22
	(156.1 overs)	594

Bowling
Collymore 24-2-71-0. Carter 18-1-90-0. Richardson 26-4-87-1. Brown 24-6-80-1. Wagh 30-2-122-1. Bell 16-3-53-0. Trott 11.1-2-39-7. Troughton 7-0-34-0.
Fall of Wickets 1-95, 2-123, 3-267, 4-534, 5-534, 6-553, 7-570, 8-585, 9-593, 10-594

WARWICKSHIRE	First Innings			Second Innings	
MJ Powell (capt)	c Tredwell b Ealham	6		c Key b Tredwell	110
NV Knight	c Ferley b Ealham	25		c Walker b Symonds	1
MA Wagh	c Jones b Saggers	6		b Symonds	0
IJL Trott	c Jones b Symonds	53		c Walker b Ealham	7
IR Bell	c Jones b Symonds	54		c Jones b Ealham	0
JO Troughton	lbw b Ealham	26		c Walker b Ealham	20
DR Brown	c Ferley b Symonds	8		c Key b Tredwell	21
KJ Piper	b Ealham	3		run out	39
NM Carter	c Saggers b Ealham	15		lbw b Ferley	38
A Richardson	c Walker b Ealham	44		c and b Ferley	7
CD Collymore	not out	0		not out	10
Extras	b 4, lb 8, nb 12	24		nb 4	4
	(70.5 overs)	267		(68.4 overs)	257

Bowling
Saggers 15-2-67-2. Khan 15-0-70-0. Ealham 15.5-7-35-6. Tredwell 8-2-19-0. Symonds 12-2-42-2. Ferley 5-1-22-0.
Saggers 7-0-19-0. Symonds 10-4-24-2. Ferley 14.4-2-45-3. Ealham 13-2-52-2. Khan 7-1-32-0. Tredwell 17-0-58-2.
Fall of Wickets 1-55, 2-87, 3-112, 4-203, 5-249, 6-249, 7-251, 8-256, 9-256, 10-267
1-10, 2-16, 3-45, 4-55, 5-123, 6-157, 7-180, 8-236, 9-240, 10-257

Kent beat Warwickshire by an innings and 70 runs – Kent (22pts), Warwickshire (3pts)

fizzing leg break which beat Brad Hodge's defensive bat and clipped the off stump. It was Mushtaq's 100th first-class victim of the season, and he became the first bowler since Andy Caddick in 1998 (and first spinner since Anil Kumble in 1995) to perform the feat. Soon, Leicestershire were 118 for 6 and Mushtaq had finished with 4 for 71. His 103 victims had earned him an extra £10,500 under the special incentive scheme Sussex had offered as part of a one-year contract, now about to be extended. The best bit of business done all summer? Undoubtedly, and that the return on Mushtaq's signing was at least worth ten-fold to Sussex was almost spookily underlined when Adams received the championship cheque … for £105,000.

Second-placed Lancashire may have had the consolation of the £50,000 runners-up prize, but this was their fourth second-place finish in six years and there was a distinct air of despondency about their 233-run surrender to Nottinghamshire at Trent Bridge. A short boundary on one side was found with regularity on day one when Notts, boosted by an opening partnership of 165 between Darren Bicknell and Jason Gallian, went on to score 376 for 9 declared. Russell Warren and Kevin Pietersen also added 87 for the fourth wicket, and on the second day some superb in-swing bowling from Greg Smith wrecked the prolific Lancashire top order. Smith removed the first five batsmen and soon Notts had a 157-run first-innings lead. Glen Chapple was then the only Lancashire bowler to fight against the flowing tide, taking six wickets in a spell of 29 overs that was broken only by lunch on the third day. Paul Franks, though, was joined by former England Under 19 captain Samit Patel in a stand which made sure the match would go Notts' way. Patel impressed with 55, and Franks completed an unbeaten 100 with two sixes and a four from successive Peter Martin deliveries. Iain Sutcliffe and Kyle Hogg batted well on the last day, but four wickets apiece for Franks and Stuart MacGill meant, at least, that Notts could end a largely unhappy season on a high note.

Surrey, their hopes of retaining their title long gone, fielded a youthful side for the last match of the season and were well beaten by Essex at The Oval. Jon Batty and Nadeem Shahid did put on 103 for the second wicket, and young wicketkeeper Ben Scott did end up unbeaten on 58 on his debut, but Surrey's first innings 318 was made to look horribly inadequate as Andy Flower took command of the Essex reply. The Zimbabwean was joined in a second-wicket stand of 157 by Alistair Cook,

formerly of Bedford School, who reached 50 from just 32 balls and went on to score a highly promising 84, and then a third-wicket stand of 115 by another youngster, Mark Pettini, whose 70 from 79 balls contained 13 fours. Flower completed the third double-hundred of his career shortly before Essex were all out for 464. Surrey's batting was then blown away by the pace and swing of Mohammad Akram, the former Pakistan fast bowler who took the first eight wickets to fall and looked to be on course for all ten before tiredness set in. It was left to Graham Napier to remove the last two batsmen and, with Surrey dismissed for 194, it was not long before relegated Essex were eight-wicket winners.

Despite his omission from England's overseas tours, Ed Smith finished his memorable summer in fine style with a career-best 213 at Canterbury. The rest of Kent's top five all passed 50, too, with Andrew Symonds crashing 88 and Matthew Walker staying to hit 121 and, with Smith, helped double the total from 267 for 3. At 534 for 3 there was only one team who were going to win this contest, but Warwickshire's Jon Trott then embarked on perhaps the most remarkable bowling spell of the season. Introduced as the seventh bowler, and with a combined return of 0–176 from his previous 38 first-class overs for the county, the 22-year-old proceeded to take 7 for 39 with his gentle out-swingers either side of lunch! By the close of the second day Warwickshire were 200 for 3 in reply to Kent's 594 and looking as if they would make a scrap of it. Mark Ealham, however, then produced a spell of 4.5–2–9–4 the following morning to give himself overall figures of 6 for 35, his best return since 1996. Bowled out for 267, Warwickshire were now following on, and despite 110 from their captain Mike Powell, to add to his first-innings 61, there was little other resistance. The visitors were dismissed again for 257, and Kent had confirmed themselves as worthy of fourth place with victory by an innings and 70 runs.

Division Two

How ironic it was, at the end of a gorgeous summer and with warm sunshine again being experienced by the rest of England, that Yorkshire's hopes of promotion to Division One should have been ultimately scuppered by rain. Their frustration was considerable, and understandable, when the third and fourth days of their showdown with Gloucestershire at Headingley were badly affected by the weather. Until then, indeed, a Yorkshire victory seemed certain following a majestic innings of 238 by Australian batsman Damien Martyn, their latest import. Gloucestershire, who themselves needed just a draw to clinch the third promotion place behind Worcestershire and Northamptonshire, had only managed to avoid the follow-on because of an unlikely ninth-wicket stand of 97 between Ian Fisher and Jon Lewis. Now, with a mere 7.5 overs of play being possible on day three, and then drizzle and bad light ruling out of the final session of the match, they were able to escape with the draw that they needed to earn themselves Division One championship status for the first time. Yorkshire, who had begun the last day with an overall advantage of 161 at 29 for 2 in their second innings, carved their way to a declaration at 121 for 7 after just another 13.1 overs. In theory, they now had a minimum of 81 overs in which to bowl Gloucestershire out, and by tea the visitors were tottering at 93 for 5 with at least 40 overs still remaining. During the interval, however, rain began to fall – and although the players emerged to try to resume, they were forced off without another ball being bowled. If Yorkshire supporters will not want to remember the way the match ended, though, they will certainly be recalling Martyn's strokeplay for many a long year. Joining Matthew Wood on the first morning at 51 for 3, Martyn tucked into the

Gloucestershire bowling with rare flair. His timing was superb, his range of strokes breathtaking and his technique immaculate. He first claimed the fastest

Round 20: 17–20 September 2003
Division Two

YORKSHIRE v. GLOUCESTERSHIRE – at Headingley

YORKSHIRE	First Innings		Second Innings	
C White	c Harvey b Smith	0	c sub b Lewis	2
MJ Wood	c sub b Gidman	116	c Russell b Lewis	25
A McGrath (capt)	c Hancock b Harvey	28	c Hancock b Harvey	1
MJ Lumb	lbw b Harvey	4	b Harvey	31
DR Martyn	b Gidman	238	c Dawson b Lewis	17
*RJ Blakey	b Fisher	9	c Spearman b Lewis	21
RKJ Dawson	not out	48	b Harvey	5
D Gough	c Weston b Fisher	10	not out	2
CEW Silverwood	c Russell b Lewis	4	not out	7
SP Kirby	c Rhodes b Lewis	5		
MJ Hoggard	b Harvey	2		
Extras	lb 6, nb 6	12	lb 6, nb 4	10
	(100 overs)	476	(7 wkts, 23 overs)	121

Bowling
Smith 10-1-57-1. Lewis 22-5-91-2. Harvey 20-4-91-3. Gidman 20-1-121-2. Fisher 7R-5-110-2.
Lewis 12-1-71-4. Harvey 11-1-44-3.
Fall of Wickets 1-0, 2-47, 3-51, 4-381, 5-396, 6-408, 7-436, 8-445, 9-467, 10-476
1-4, 2-7, 3-43, 4-69, 5-92, 6-100, 7-108

GLOS	First Innings		Second Innings	
WPC Weston	b Silverwood	84	(2) lbw b Hoggard	4
CM Spearman (capt)	c Martyn b Hoggard	41	(1) c Gough b Kirby	8
THC Hancock	b Dawson b Silverwood	0	c Dawson b McGrath	48
JN Rhodes	b Silverwood	5	b McGrath	16
MGN Windows	lbw b Silverwood	0	b Gough	4
APR Gidman	b Gough	8	not out	9
IJ Harvey	b McGrath	70	not out	1
*RC Russell	c Dawson b McGrath	0		
ID Fisher	b sub b McGrath	71		
J Lewis	b Silverwood	36		
AM Smith	not out	1		
Extras	b 8, lb 7, nb 8	23	b 1, nb 2	3
	(96.2 overs)	344	(5 wkts, 41 overs)	93

Bowling
Hoggard 21-3-72-1. Silverwood 25.1-7-75-5. Kirby 13.5-3-63-0. Gough 22-4-83-1. McGrath 11.2-2-26-3. Dawson 3-0-10-0.
Silverwood 9-4-19-0. Hoggard 10-5-26-1. Gough 10-5-17-1. Kirby 8-2-19-1.
McGrath 4-1-11-2.
Fall of Wickets 1-79, 2-94, 3-100, 4-108, 5-116, 6-209, 7-210, 8-247, 9-344, 10-344
1-4, 2-25, 3-63, 4-78, 5-92

Match drawn – Yorkshire (12pts),
Gloucestershire (10pts)

NORTHAMPTONSHIRE v. WORCESTERSHIRE – at Northampton

NORTHANTS	First Innings		Second Innings	
MEK Hussey (capt)	run out	4	(2) c Pipe b Batty	79
TW Roberts	c Hick b Hayward	6	(1) c Hick b Hayward	0
PA Jaques	c Pipe b Khalid	29	c Mason b Khalid	39
DJG Sales	b Khalid	32	c Peters b Khalid	29
GL Brophy	lbw b Batty	25	b Khalid	60
JW Cook	b Khalid	57	c Leatherdale b Batty	31
GP Swann	c Hayward b Batty	1	(8) c Solanki b Khalid	69
*TMB Bailey	c Pipe b Khalid	13	(7) b Hayward	22
MJ Cawdron	c and b Batty	18	b Mason	18
MS Panesar	not out	6	run out	0
JF Brown	b Hayward	0	not out	2
Extras	b 5, lb 8	13	b 12, lb 14, w 2, nb 2	30
	(75.3 overs)	196	(94.4 overs)	379

Bowling
Mason 11-3-19-0. Hayward 11.3-0-41-2. Batty 32-11-53-4. Khalid 21-1-70-3.
Hayward 10-2-37-2. Mason 11.4-3-28-1. Batty 24-4-94-2. Khalid 28-5-131-4. Hick 21-5-63-0.
Fall of Wickets 1-6, 2-10, 3-73, 4-75, 5-126, 6-130, 7-153, 8-170, 9-184, 10-196
1-0, 2-62, 3-108, 4-207, 5-248, 6-263, 7-339, 8-368, 9-369, 10-379

WORCS	First Innings		Second Innings	
SD Peters	b Swann	69	b Panesar	50
GA Hick	c Brophy b Cook	0	lbw b Cawdron	4
Kadeer Ali	b Swann	0	b Brown	30
BF Smith (capt)	b Swann	14	b Panesar	53
VS Solanki	st Bailey b Swann	0	c Wallace b Brown	0
DA Leatherdale	b Swann	20	c Swann b Brown	61
GJ Batty	c Hussey b Panesar	1	c and b Brown	20
*BJ Pipe	not out	13	c sub b Brown	35
MS Mason	b Swann	0	st Bailey b Swann	27
SA Khalid	(did not bat)		c Swann b Brown	8
M Hayward	(did not bat)		not out	4
Extras	b 1, lb 3	4	b 4, lb 11	15
	(8 wkts, 55.3 overs)	172	(76.5 overs)	311

Bowling
Cawdron 4-0-22-0. Cook 5-3-8-1. Swann 18.3-5-66-6. Brown 11-1-35-0. Panesar 17-4-37-1.
Cawdron 7-2-15-1. Cook 6-2-14-0. Brown 24-5-87-6. Swann 19-2-86-1. Panesar 24-2-92-3.
Fall of Wickets 1-4, 2-37, 3-109, 4-124, 5-133, 6-134, 7-164, 8-172
1-7, 2-80, 3-88, 4-88, 5-181, 6-223, 7-242, 8-285, 9-298, 10-311

Northamptonshire beat Worcestershire by 92 runs –
Northamptonshire (16pts), Worcestershire (3pts)

DURHAM v. GLAMORGAN – at Chester-le-Street

GLAMORGAN	First Innings		Second Innings	
JP Maher	b Davies	63	c Love b Wells	24
*MA Wallace	c Mustard b Killeen	121	hit wkt b Shoaib Akhtar	4
A Dale	c Collingwood b Wells	1	c Bridge b Killeen	0
MJ Powell	c Wells b Davies	5	b Davies	198
MP Maynard	lbw b Killeen	12	hit wkt b Shoaib Akhtar	102
DL Hemp	run out	0	c Collingwood b Shoaib Akhtar	3
RDB Croft (capt)	c and b Bridge	5	c Mustard b Shoaib Akhtar	7
AG Wharf	c Wells b Bridge	0	b Bridge	4
SD Thomas	b Bridge	7	not out	69
MS Kasprowicz	b Wells	4	not out	34
DS Harrison	not out	0		
Extras	b 7, lb 6, w 1, nb 2	16	b 12, lb 8, nb 2	22
	(70.4 overs)	270	(8 wkts, 83 overs)	464

Bowling
Shoaib Akhtar 7-1-19-0. Killeen 16-6-59-2. Davies 16.5-5-52-2. Collingwood 10-1-49-0. Wells 13-4-52-2. Bridge 9-3-26-3.
Shoaib Akhtar 17-1-84-4. Killeen 14-2-61-1. Davies 15-0-95-1. Wells 7-0-45-1. Collingwood 4-0-21-0. Bridge 26-0-138-1.
Fall of Wickets 1-127, 2-154, 3-171, 4-213, 5-222, 6-249, 7-249, 8-260, 9-266, 10-270 1-5, 2-10, 3-65, 4-296, 5-322, 6-334, 7-345, 8-371

DURHAM	First Innings		Second Innings	
JJB Lewis (capt)	c Maher b Kasprowicz	0	c Wallace b Kasprowicz	0
N Peng	c Wallace b Harrison	9	c Powell b Harrison	16
ML Love	c Wallace b Harrison	0	lbw b Kasprowicz	4
PD Collingwood	c Wallace b Harrison	50	not out	21
GJ Pratt	c Hemp b Wharf	59	c Wallace b Kasprowicz	0
VJ Wells	not out	30	lbw b Kasprowicz	0
*P Mustard	c Maher b Kasprowicz	5	b Kasprowicz	5
GD Bridge	c Hemp b Wharf	10	b Harrison	0
Shoaib Akhtar	c Wallace b Dale b Wharf	9	b Kasprowicz	37
N Killeen	b Kasprowicz	8	b Kasprowicz	0
AM Davies	c Wallace b Thomas	21	b Kasprowicz	14
Extras	b 1, lb 12, w 2, nb 12	27	lb 6, lb 8	14
	(58.3 overs)	247	(24.5 overs)	118

Bowling
Kasprowicz 22-3-65-4. Harrison 11-1-57-2. Thomas 8.3-0-37-1. Wharf 12-0-66-3. Croft 5-2-9-0.
Kasprowicz 12.5-2-45-9. Harrison 8-2-38-1. Wharf 4-0-29-0.
Fall of Wickets 1-0, 2-9, 3-11, 4-113, 5-146, 6-155, 7-184, 8-180, 9-199, 10-247 1-4, 2-20, 3-28, 4-36, 5-36, 6-42, 7-44, 8-82, 9-82, 10-118

Glamorgan beat Durham by 369 runs –
Glamorgan (19pts), Durham (4pts)

DERBYSHIRE v. HAMPSHIRE – at Derby

DERBYSHIRE	First Innings		Second Innings	
AI Gait	c Prittipaul b Hamblin	63	(2) c Pothas b Tomlinson	71
MJ Di Venuto	c Pothas b Hamblin	35	(1) c Pothas b Tomlinson	52
RM Khan	c Prittipaul b Udal	6	b Bruce	58
SD Stubbings	c Prittipaul b Udal	30	lbw b Bruce	8
Hasan Adnan	b Hamblin	84	b Udal	14
*LD Sutton	c Bruce b Hamblin	17	c Katich b Mascarenhas	30
DG Cork (capt)	c Tomlinson b Bruce	26	(9) not out	1
G Welch	lbw b Ucal	14	(7) b Tomlinson	19
NRC Dumelow	c Katich b Hamblin	1	(8) c Prittipaul b Tomlinson	19
Mohammad Ali	c Bruce b Udal	18	c and b Tomlinson	0
PM Havell	not out	0	b Tomlinson	0
Extras	b 1, lb 5, w 5, nb 15	29	b 6, lb 7, nb 6	19
	(84.3 overs)	317	(95.1 overs)	289

Bowling
Mascarenhas 14-4-38-0. Tomlinson 13-2-58-0. Bruce 13-4-54-1. Hamblin 22-3-93-6. Udal 19.3-2-52-3. Katich 3-1-3-0.
Mascarenhas 16-5-43-1. Tomlinson 19.1-6-63-6. Bruce 14-3-60-2. Hamblin 6-1-30-0. Udal 29-14-50-1. Katich 11-5-30-0.
Fall of Wickets 1-82, 2-112, 3-117, 4-180, 5-213, 6-252, 7-298, 8-298, 9-307, 10-317 1-71, 2-90, 3-108, 4-160, 5-215, 6-260, 7-288, 8-289, 9-289, 10-289

HAMPSHIRE	First Innings		Second Innings	
DA Kenway	lbw b Mohammad Ali	21	not out	16
JHK Adams	b Havell	60	not out	10
SM Katich	c Havell b Welch	122		
JP Crawley (capt)	lbw b Welch	59		
LR Prittipaul	lbw h Welch	19		
*N Pothas	c Khan b Havell	4		
JRC Hamblin	b Dumelow	96		
AD Mascarenhas	c Sutton b Welch	21		
SD Udal	c Gait b Mohammad Ali	57		
JTA Bruce	c Di Venuto b Havell	12		
JA Tomlinson	not out	0		
Extras	b 12, lb 7, w 1, nb 42	62	nb 2	2
	(127.4 overs)	580	(no wkt, 4.2 overs)	28

Bowling
Cork 4-0-28-0. Welch 41-7-163-4. Mohammad Ali 36-4-166-2. Dumelow 26-9-75-1. Havell 20.4-1-129-3.
Welch 2.2-0-18-0. Dumelow 2-0-10-0.
Fall of Wickets 1-138, 2-142, 3-295, 4-346, 5-365, 6-366, 7-478, 8-542, 9-577, 10-580

Hampshire beat Derbyshire by 10 wickets –
Hampshire (22pts), Derbyshire (6pts)

first-class hundred of the season in just 65 balls; then, from 63 balls, he added another! In all, he faced only 159 balls, hitting seven sixes and 38 fours, and his stand of 330 for the fourth wicket with Wood, who made 116, was a Yorkshire record. Martyn's great Australian predecessor, Don Bradman, once scored 309 in a day at Headingley – against England in 1930 – but Martyn's first 200 runs, made in 176 minutes, were chalked up faster than Bradman's double-hundred on that famous occasion.

The meeting of the two other promoted clubs at Northampton, meanwhile, provoked considerable bad feeling and controversy as Northants and Worcestershire battled for the honour, and added prize money, of becoming Division Two champions. The home side had prepared a pitch that spun sharply from the first morning, had included three specialist slow bowlers, and it all seemed to be going according to plan when they won the toss and batted first. Despite Mike Hussey running himself out, attempting a suicidal second run to Vikram Solanki at fine leg, Northants looked to be on target for some vital batting points. But Gareth Batty and Shaftab Khalid, the two Worcestershire off spinners, bowled with control and skill to dismiss the home side for 196 – just four runs short of a precious first point. Stephen Peters then made 69, but by the close of the opening day Worcestershire were struggling themselves at 139 for 6. When Graeme Swann then took his figures to 6 for 66 by bowling Matt Mason the following morning, leaving Worcestershire on 172 for 8, the visitors promptly declared to deny Northants the third and final bowling point which, mathematically, could have earned them the title if they had gone on to win. As it was, and despite a second-innings charge to 379, Northants were docked eight points by an ECB pitch panel, who ruled that the original surface had been 'poor' and had taken too much spin too early. Northants then went on to bowl out Worcestershire for 311, despite half-centuries from Peters, Ben Smith and Batty, with Jason Brown taking 5 for 89 and Monty Panesar picking up three wickets with his slow left-arm. But it was a hollow victory, by 92 runs. Kepler Wessels, the Northants coach, said: 'We made 379 on that pitch against an England spinner (Batty) and another who is going to the National Academy this winter (Khalid). Either there is not much wrong with the pitch or the future of England's spin bowling doesn't look too bright.' Worcestershire's decision to declare their first innings had brought predictable jeers from the Northants crowd, but their director of cricket Tom

Moody said: 'The bottom line is that we are here to win the division, and so we took the first opportunity we had to do that. We'd have liked to have played the game from the word go, but we arrived here to find what can only be described as a very ordinary pitch.'

Durham's batsmen might well be having nightmares, now, about fast bowler Mike Kasprowicz. The big Queenslander added to an already impressive record against Durham by taking 9 for 45 in the second innings to speed Glamorgan to victory by 369 runs at Chester-le-Street. It was the biggest win in Glamorgan's history, in terms of runs, and Kasprowicz was irrepressible as he cut down the Durham second innings for 118 inside 25 overs. They were 44 for 7 at one stage, before Shoaib Akhtar blazed 37. Kasprowicz's remarkable 12.5-over spell gave him match figures of 13 for 110, and also followed the 9 for 36 he took against Durham at Cardiff a month earlier. Indeed, his previous two meetings with Durham had brought him match analyses of 11 for 77 and 11 for 105. What made his latest nine-wicket burst so much more impressive, though, was that immediately before it he was at the crease with Darren Thomas knocking up an unbroken ninth-wicket stand of 93 as Glamorgan romped to a declaration at 464 for 8. Michael Powell's magnificent 198, in which he figured in a fourth-wicket partnership of 231 with Matthew Maynard (102), was another memorable feature of this Glamorgan win, at the end of a season in which they had clearly under-performed as a team in championship competition. Going into this final match, with just an outside mathematical chance of gaining the third promotion spot, Glamorgan were launched by an opening stand of 127 between Jimmy Maher and Mark Wallace, who hit a fine 121, but then fell away to 270 all out. Durham's first innings, originally rallied from 11 for 3 by Paul Collingwood and Gary Pratt, who both scored half-centuries, was then closed on 247 by Kasprowicz and Alex Wharf – despite an unbeaten 58 from Vince Wells.

The wooden spoon, meanwhile, went to Derbyshire after their failure to beat Hampshire at Derby in a basement meeting of the bottom two. Dominic Cork announced just before the start of the match that he had asked to be released from his contract, and the Derbyshire captain's request was granted. Cork hit five fours in a tempestuous 20 during the Derbyshire first innings of 317, and then bowled four overs costing 28 that evening.

Champions! Led by their captain, Chris Adams, the Sussex players get down to some serious celebrating at Hove.

A hamstring problem prevented him from bowling again in the match, and he was left on one not out when Derbyshire were bowled out for 289 in their second innings. It was a sad end to Cork's 14-year career at the county, but the announcement of Dave Houghton's installation as the new director of cricket was soon followed by the indication that Cork's six seasons as captain were to end and that a new era was about to start. Like Derbyshire, there is really only one way for Hampshire to go after a forgettable championship campaign. At least, for them, this was an emphatic way to sign off – their ten-wicket win being rounded off by a career-best 6 for 63 from left-arm seamer James Tomlinson. There was a six-wicket, career-best haul in the Derbyshire first innings, too, for all-rounder James Hamblin – who then hit 96 as Hampshire ran up 580. Simon Katich, Hampshire's one consistent top-order batsman throughout the season, scored 122 and there were also half-centuries for Jimmy Adams, Derek Kenway, John Crawley and Shaun Udal. All that Derbyshire had to cling on to was the continued return to form of Andrew Gait, who made 63 and 71, the passing of 1,500 first-class runs by Michael Di Venuto, and the promise in the middle order of Hasan Adnan, with 84 on his second appearance, and a second-innings 58 from Rawait Khan. In truth, however, it was not much for Derbyshire fans; instead, the all-pervading thought was the fact that, in 1997 when Cork had taken over as captain, a certain Chris Adams had left a club yet again suffering upheaval to seek his cricketing fortune on the south coast … the rest, as they say, is history.

DIVISION ONE FINAL POSITIONS

	P	W	L	D	Bat	Bowl	Pts
Sussex	**16**	**10**	**4**	**2**	**62**	**47**	**257.00**
Lancashire	16	6	2	8	64	43	223.00
Surrey	16	6	3	7	63	44	219.00
Kent	16	6	5	5	47	47	198.00
Warwickshire	16	4	5	6	50	37	171.50
Middlesex	16	3	3	10	46	41	169.00
Essex	16	3	5	7	34	45	156.00
Nottinghamshire	16	2	8	6	36	45	132.00
Leicestershire	16	1	6	9	36	40	125.50

Slow Over Rate Fines

Nottinghamshire	0.75	v. Warwickshire (Trent Bridge, 18 April)
Warwickshire	0.25	v. Nottinghamshire (Trent Bridge, 18 April)
Nottinghamshire	0.25	v. Surrey (Trent Bridge, 9 May)
Warwickshire	1.00	v. Leicestershire (Leicester, 2 July)
Warwickshire	0.25	v. Lancashire (Old Trafford, 27 July)
Leicestershire	0.50	v. Warwickshire (Edgbaston, 14 August)
Warwickshire	1.00	v. Middlesex (Edgbaston, 26 August)

DIVISION TWO FINAL POSITIONS

	P	W	L	D	Bat	Bowl	Pts
Worcestershire	**16**	**10**	**1**	**5**	**42**	**44**	**245.75**
Northamptonshire*	16	10	2	4	45	44	237.00
Gloucestershire	16	5	2	9	38	46	190.00
Yorkshire	16	4	5	7	54	47	183.50
Glamorgan	16	5	5	6	45	45	183.00
Durham	16	5	7	4	31	43	159.25
Somerset	16	4	8	4	41	44	157.00
Hampshire	16	2	6	8	36	44	140.00
Derbyshire	16	2	11	3	30	44	114.00

* Eight points deducted for a substandard pitch
  v. Worcestershire (Northampton) 17–20 September

Slow Over Rate Fines

Durham	0.25	v. Somerset (Taunton, 23 April)
Yorkshire	0.25	v. Glamorgan (Headingley, 21 May)
Yorkshire	0.25	v. Somerset (Taunton, 27 June)
Worcestershire	0.25	v. Derbyshire (Worcester, 15 August)
Yorkshire	1.00	v. Worcestershire (Worcester, 12 Sept)
Durham	0.50	v. Glamorgan (Chester-le-Street, 17 September)
Glamorgan	1.00	v. Durham (Chester-le-Street, 17 September)

COUNTY CHAMPIONSHIP FEATURES 2003

INDIVIDUAL SCORES OVER 200

MW Goodwin	335*	Sussex v. Leicestershire	at Hove
MEK Hussey	331*	Northants v. Somerset	at Taunton
BJ Hodge	302*	Leicestershire v. Notts	at Trent Bridge
MR Ramprakash	279*	Surrey v. Nottinghamshire	at Whitgift School
ML Love	273	Durham v. Hampshire	at Chester-le-Street
MEK Hussey	264	Northants v. Gloucs	at Gloucester
ID Blackwell	247*	Somerset v. Derbyshire	at Taunton
DR Martyn	238	Yorkshire v. Gloucs	at Headingley
SG Law	236*	Lancashire v. Warwicks	at Old Trafford
RJ Blakey	223*	Yorkshire v. Northants	at Headingley
PA Jaques	222	Northants v. Yorkshire	at Northampton
KP Pietersen	221	Notts v. Warwicks	at Edgbaston
ET Smith	213	Kent v. Warwicks	at Canterbury
MW Goodwin	210	Sussex v. Essex	at Colchester
MJ Wood	207	Yorkshire v. Somerset	at Taunton
N Hussain	206	Essex v. Kent	at Chelmsford
ET Smith	203	Kent v. Lancashire	at Blackpool
A Flower	201*	Essex v. Surrey	at The Oval
CL Hooper	201	Lancashire v. Middlesex	at Old Trafford
DJG Sales	200*	Northants v. Derbyshire	at Derby

BEST INNINGS BOWLING (7 WICKETS OR MORE)

MS Kasprowicz	9-36	Glamorgan v. Durham	at Cardiff
MS Kasprowicz	9-45	Glamorgan v. Durham	at Chester-le-Street
Mohammad Akram	8-49	Essex v. Surrey	at The Oval
Kabir Ali	8-53	Worcestershire v. Yorks	at Scarborough
Kabir Ali	8-58	Worcestershire v. Derbys	at Worcester
Mohammad Sami	8-64	Kent v. Nottinghamshire	at Maidstone
SP Kirby	8-80	Yorkshire v. Somerset	at Taunton
JD Lewry	8-106	Sussex v. Leicestershire	at Hove
GP Swann	7-33	Northants v. Derbyshire	at Northampton
IJL Trott	7-39	Warwicks v. Kent	at Canterbury
MJ Hoggard	7-49	Yorkshire v. Somerset	at Headingley
Mohammad Sami	7-50	Kent v. Nottinghamshire	at Maidstone
PAJ DeFreitas	7-51	Leics v. Nottinghamshire	at Trent Bridge
JF Brown	7-69	Northants v. Durham	at Chester-le-Street
N Killeen	7-70	Durham v. Hampshire	at Chester-le-Street
Mushtaq Ahmed	7-85	Sussex v. Warwickshire	at Hove
RJ Sidebottom	7-97	Yorkshire v. Derbyshire	at Headingley
J Lewis	7-117	Gloucs v. Derbyshire	at Bristol
MA Wagh	7-222	Warwickshire v. Lancashire	at Edgbaston

COUNTY CHAMPIONSHIP FEATURES 2003

BEST MATCH BOWLING

Mohammad Sami	15-114	Kent v. Nottinghamshire	at Maidstone
MS Kasprowicz	13-110	Glamorgan v. Durham	at Chester-le-Street
SP Kirby	13-154	Yorkshire v. Somerset	at Taunton
Mushtaq Ahmed	12-244	Sussex v. Nottinghamshire	at Horsham
MS Kasprowicz	11-77	Glamorgan v. Durham	at Cardiff
Mushtaq Ahmed	11-140	Sussex v. Warwicks	at Hove
Mushtaq Ahmed	11-173	Sussex v. Lancashire	at Hove
J Lewis	11-183	Gloucestershire v. Derbys	at Bristol
DG Cork	10-67	Derbyshire v. Hampshire	at Southampton
PAJ DeFreitas	10-113	Leics v. Nottinghamshire	at Trent Bridge
ID Fisher	10-123	Gloucestershire v. Durham	at Bristol
JD Lewry	10-124	Sussex v. Essex	at Arundel
DG Cork	10-127	Derbyshire v. Somerset	at Taunton
Mohammad Akram	10-142	Essex v. Surrey	at The Oval
RDB Croft	10-147	Glamorgan v. Northants	at Cardiff

HIGHEST TEAM TOTALS

781	Lancashire v. Warwickshire	at Edgbaston
734 for 5dec	Lancashire v. Middlesex	at Old Trafford
705 for 9dec	Somerset v. Hampshire	at Taunton
693	Surrey v. Nottinghamshire	at Whitgift School
681 for 5dec	Northamptonshire v. Somerset	at Taunton
673 for 8dec	Yorkshire v. Northamptonshire	at Headingley
647 for 5dec	Northamptonshire v. Derbyshire	at Derby
646	Nottinghamshire v. Warwickshire	at Edgbaston
636 for 4dec	Leicestershire v. Surrey	at Leicester
622 for 8dec	Northamptonshire v. Gloucestershire	at Gloucester
620 for 7dec	Middlesex v. Leicestershire	at Southgate
619 for 7dec	Sussex v. Nottinghamshire	at Horsham
614 for 4dec	Sussex v. Leicestershire	at Hove
612	Sussex v. Essex	at Colchester
611 for 9dec	Gloucestershire v. Somerset	at Taunton

LOWEST TEAM TOTALS

56	Somerset v. Durham	at Chester-le-Street
79	Nottinghamshire v. Essex	at Trent Bridge
89	Derbyshire v. Gloucestershire	at Derby
91	Worcestershire v. Yorkshire	at Scarborough
93	Yorkshire v. Durham	at Headingley
96	Derbyshire v. Worcestershire	at Worcester
96	Somerset v. Northamptonshire	at Northampton
98	Gloucestershire v. Worcestershire	at Worcester
104	Glamorgan v. Hampshire	at Southampton
106	Sussex v. Warwickshire	at Edgbaston
108	Derbyshire v. Northamptonshire	at Northampton
114	Kent v. Surrey	at The Oval
116	Middlesex v. Sussex	at Lord's
116	Derbyshire v. Glamorgan	at Swansea
118	Durham v. Glamorgan	at Chester-le-Street

COUNTY CHAMPIONSHIP FEATURES 2003

COUNTY CHAMPIONSHIP FEATURES 2003

LEADING RUN SCORERS

Player	Runs	Matches
SG Law (Lancashire)	1820	16
MEK Hussey (Northamptonshire)	1697	14
MJ Di Venuto (Derbyshire)	1520	16
MW Goodwin (Sussex)	1496	16
KP Pietersen (Nottinghamshire)	1488	15
PA Jaques (Northamptonshire)	1409	16
AJ Strauss (Middlesex)	1401	16
ET Smith (Kent)	1352	13
MJ Wood (Yorkshire)	1339	16
MP Maynard (Glamorgan)	1297	16
JN Rhodes (Gloucestershire)	1293	15
BJ Hodge (Leicestershire)	1293	15
MR Ramprakash (Surrey)	1239	14
MJ Powell (Glamorgan)	1234	16
MA Wagh (Warwickshire)	1228	16

MOST SIXES

Player	Sixes	Matches
CL Hooper (Lancashire)	41	13
KP Pietersen (Nottinghamshire)	26	15
ID Blackwell (Somerset)	21	13
A Flintoff (Lancashire)	19	5
AG Wharf (Glamorgan)	17	16
BL Hutton (Middlesex)	16	16
MJ Prior (Sussex)	16	16
JN Rhodes (Gloucestershire)	15	15
CJ Adams (Sussex)	15	16
A Nel (Northamptonshire)	14	13
MP Maynard (Glamorgan)	14	16
MR Ramprakash (Surrey)	13	14
RL Johnson (Somerset)	12	9
MEK Hussey (Northamptonshire)	12	14
AJ Hollioake (Surrey)	11	13

LEADING WICKET-TAKERS

Player	Wickets	Matches
Mushtaq Ahmed (Sussex)	103	16
MS Kasprowicz (Glamorgan)	77	15
J Lewis (Gloucestershire)	74	14
SP Kirby (Yorkshire)	67	14
M Hayward (Worcestershire)	67	16
JF Brown (Northamptonshire)	65	13
RDB Croft (Glamorgan)	62	16
NAM McLean (Somerset)	62	16
G Keedy (Lancashire)	60	12
CB Keegan (Middlesex)	60	16
PAJ DeFreitas (Leicestershire)	58	15
Kabir Ali (Worcestershire)	54	12
MJ Saggers (Kent)	54	13
G Welch (Derbyshire)	53	14
GJ Batty (Worcestershire)	53	16

LEADING CATCHES (EXCLUDING WICKETKEEPERS)

Player	Catches	Matches
MJ Powell (Northamptonshire)	29	15
MJ Di Venuto (Derbyshire)	25	16
RR Montgomerie (Sussex)	22	16
MJ Walker (Kent)	22	16
GA Hick (Worcestershire)	19	13
VS Solanki (Worcestershire)	18	13
CJ Adams (Sussex)	18	16
MA Ealham (Kent)	18	16
PN Weekes (Middlesex)	18	16
Azhar Mahmood (Surrey)	17	10
MEK Hussey (Northamptonshire)	17	14
A Flower (Essex)	17	16
SG Law (Lancashire)	17	16
KP Pietersen (Nottinghamshire)	16	15
JER Gallian (Nottinghamshire)	15	12

LEADING DISMISSALS (WICKETKEEPERS)

Player	Dismissals	Matches
RJ Turner (Somerset)	65	15
GO Jones (Kent)	55	16
MA Wallace (Glamorgan)	51	16
WK Hegg (Lancashire)	49	16
PA Nixon (Leicestershire)	48	16
JS Foster (Essex)	47	16
DC Nash (Middlesex)	43	16
P Mustard (Durham)	42	12
SJ Rhodes (Worcestershire)	40	11
N Pothas (Hampshire)	40	13
RC Russell (Gloucestershire)	37	11
TMB Bailey (Northamptonshire)	35	14
T Frost (Warwickshire)	33	12
RJ Blakey (Yorkshire)	31	10
TR Ambrose (Sussex)	30	10

MOST HUNDREDS

Player	Hundreds	Matches
ET Smith (Kent)	7	13
SG Law (Lancashire)	7	16
MEK Hussey (Northamptonshire)	6	14
MJ Chilton (Lancashire)	6	16
CL Hooper (Lancashire)	5	13
MR Ramprakash (Surrey)	5	14
MB Loye (Lancashire)	5	15
JN Rhodes (Gloucestershire)	5	15
MP Maynard (Glamorgan)	5	16
MJ Wood (Yorkshire)	5	16
MJ Di.Venuto (Derbyshire)	5	16
PA Jaques (Northamptonshire)	5	16
SM Katich (Hampshire)	4	13
KP Pietersen (Nottinghamshire)	4	15
BJ Hodge (Leicestershire)	4	15

COUNTY CHAMPIONSHIP FEATURES 2003

MOST FIFTIES (EXCLUDING CENTURIES)

Player	Fifties	Matches
KP Pietersen (Nottinghamshire)	10	15
BF Smith (Worcestershire)	10	16
JJB Lewis (Durham)	10	16
TR Ambrose (Sussex)	9	15
JP Crawley (Hampshire)	8	16
MJ Di Venuto (Derbyshire)	8	16
GP Thorpe (Surrey)	7	11
DJ Bicknell (Nottinghamshire)	7	14
PA Cottey (Sussex)	7	15
JN Rhodes (Gloucestershire)	7	15
SG Koenig (Middlesex)	7	15
CM Spearman (Gloucestershire)	7	15
DR Brown (Warwicks)	7	16
RR Montgomerie (Sussex)	7	16
M Burns (Somerset)	7	16

MOST BALLS BOWLED

Player	Balls bowled	Matches
Mushtaq Ahmed (Sussex)	5019	16
RDB Croft (Glamorgan)	4271	16
JF Brown (Northamptonshire)	3702	13
MS Kasprowicz (Glamorgan)	3435	15
CB Keegan (Middlesex)	3383	16
JD Middlebrook (Essex)	3357	15
J Lewis (Gloucestershire)	3308	14
G Keedy (Lancashire)	3191	12
PAJ DeFreitas (Leicestershire)	3171	15
NAM McLean (Somerset)	3129	16
GJ Batty (Worcestershire)	3092	16
G Chapple (Lancashire)	2966	16
Saqlain Mushtaq (Surrey)	2826	14
AD Mascarenhas (Hampshire)	2803	16
SP Kirby (Yorkshire)	2778	14

HUNDREDS IN EACH INNINGS

Name	For	Against	Venue	Date	1st	2nd
MJ Powell	Glamorgan	v. Worcs	Cardiff	27 June	125	142
ET Smith	Kent	v. Notts	Maidstone	9 July	149	113
CJ Adams	Sussex	v. Lancashire	Hove	14 August	140	190
JN Rhodes	Gloucs	v. Durham	Bristol	10 September	103	102
RJ Warren	Notts	v. Middlesex	Lord's	10 September	123	113*

FASTEST COUNTY CHAMPIONSHIP 100

DR Martyn	65 balls	Yorkshire v. Gloucs	at Headingley	17 September

DAVID FULTON'S VIEW

After suffering a horrific pre-season eye injury, Kent captain DAVID FULTON made perhaps the most courageous comeback of the 2003 English summer. He writes here about his personal trauma, and about the health of the county game.

The England captain, ex-England players, various journalists and even a chat show host have all called for changes to our domestic game.

Now, I'm not claiming to be an expert. I've never played for my country, never experienced the pressures of international cricket or the pride of wearing the three lions on my chest to do battle with the old enemy in the baggy green.

County cricket with Kent is as far as I've got and all I've ever known. I love what I do and am incredibly proud to be a county cricketer and Kent captain.

I realized just how much I loved it when earlier this year it was nearly all taken away from me. During pre-season, a ball fired at 90mph from the bowling machine went freakishly straight through the gap between the grille and peak of my batting helmet and hit me flush on the right eye.

Rushed to hospital, I had my torn eyelid and tear duct pieced back together in a three-hour operation, but still the experts weren't sure if I'd ever see out of the eye again.

I lay in hospital for a week, allowed only to go to the toilet and back. My head had to be kept still and upright at all times and every couple of hours I was wheeled off to have my eye pressure checked.

The hardest part was knowing that we were a week away from our opening game of the season against Leicestershire and I was not going to be there. I'd plotted and schemed all winter for this campaign: signed new players, worked with others on their games and in the gym on their fitness, brought in team-builders and motivational speakers for pre-season. We were also unbeaten in all our warm-up games – we had been so ready.

Having come so close to losing a career in county cricket – something I love and value – I get protective when others knock it. It upsets me when Michael Vaughan says the system isn't producing enough mentally tough cricketers. I'm gutted and angry when county cricket gets the blame for England losing a Test match, because no one gives it any credit when England wins.

We didn't hear 'well done the first-class game for giving us James Kirtley' after one of county cricket's most loyal and honest servants made good the big leap and won us a Test match at Trent Bridge in mid-August.

Any re-vamp of our domestic structure, indeed, requires cool-headed objectivity and not a reactionary call for revolution when our national side has a bad day.

I'm all for trying to narrow the gap between county and international cricket, but in recent years, despite Lord MacLaurin's attempt to raise the standard, this gap has got wider.

Duncan Fletcher's tight control of centrally contracted players might make sense for Team England, but taking the country's best players out of county cricket is in no one's long-term interests.

Forgive me for using myself by way of illustration, but in 2001 I scored nearly 1,900 first-class runs yet didn't get picked for my country. The perception must have been that despite dominating the county scene I would not have been good enough to cut it in the Ashes series against Australia that was then going on.

In other words, the England selectors thought county cricket couldn't be trusted. And they may have had a point: I scored three hundreds that season against a Somerset side shorn of the services of Andrew Caddick – a bowler who had previously got me out for a pastime.

This season, in an effort to improve the standard, whilst simultaneously raising the profile of the game, two overseas players per county have been re-introduced. It's a move that has worked.

The county performances of Ed Smith, Kirtley and Martin Bicknell have been rewarded by England selection – a clear indication in itself that some of our first-class game's credibility has been restored, at least in the eyes of the selectors.

Playing day in day out, as I have done since my comeback from the eye injury, there is no doubt in my mind that the quality of county cricket in 2003 has been better. Facing Waqar Younis and Corey Collymore at Edgbaston, or bowling to Stuart Law and Carl Hooper on a flat one at Old Trafford, means the 'average' county performer has had to lift his game quickly or be exposed as not good enough.

The British public, furthermore, whilst not exactly grabbing cricket to its bosom, has at least popped in more often to take a look. The fantastic weather, combined with the Twenty20 Cup phenomenon, will have been a factor, but also the pulling power of overseas players like Muttiah Muralitharan and Shoaib Akhtar – which the new regulations have made possible – must not be overlooked.

The main drawback of having two overseas stars per county has been the huge contrasts in quality of the foreign players. At one end of the scale you have the likes of Mushtaq Ahmed, Saqlain Mushtaq, Murali, Law and Hooper. At the other (no disrespect intended) you have players such as Collins Obuya, Imran Tahir and Yuvraj Singh.

Also, because to some extent your success as a side depends on your ability to lure the big guns, this might in the future mean some counties having to forego domestic talent in order to stockpile the finances.

Attracting the best in the world, though, is only the tip of the iceberg. The real challenge for county cricket is to replicate the intensity of the international game.

At its fiercest, cricket should be 'a war' every ball. The opening bowlers, for instance, should be pounding their rock-hard leather missile with seam bolt upright into a good length, continually asking questions of a batsman's technique and temperament. Fielders should be using every ounce of mental and physical energy to stop a batsman scoring a run.

Good teams can keep up this kind of fierce, concentrated intensity for longer – but not forever. Over the course of a long county season, however, teams struggle to maintain their intensity for a whole four-day match. Bowlers playing five days a week, week in week out, will inevitably tire. Fielders will have a 'here we go again' mentality rather than diving for every ball as if their lives depended on it.

At Kent, this season, we played a televised day-night National League match against Worcestershire which finished just 37 hours before we took the field for a championship match at Lord's against Middlesex. We played with fire and passion to give Worcestershire a good hammering, but it was like trying to raise the dead two mornings later!

If we want to move forward as a game we have to cut the amount of cricket played. If everyone was that 15 per cent fresher, for example, there would be fewer niggles, less lethargy and more full-throttle cricket.

Players aren't moaning about their lot when they say they play too much. It's not a case of spoilt, lazy sportsmen not realizing how good they've got it.

I know how lucky I am to be hitting a ball around a field with my mates, representing my county and getting paid for the privilege. Players are simply saying they want to play better. Give them a week off and they can prepare themselves properly. They can make technical adjustments, be fitter and stronger and most importantly play hard, intense cricket rather than having to pace themselves to get through a season.

Play less play better. It's a pretty simple message that gets reiterated every year, yet nothing gets done.

We don't need to scrap six counties as some commentators suggest. I agree that if we had a blank sheet of paper and were starting from scratch, 12 would be about the right number, but the fact is we have to do what's possible and not what's fantasy.

Eighteen counties are here to stay for the foreseeable future – they are set in stone within a constitution more complex than the matrix – so let's work with the system rather than bash our heads against it.

Whether it's three divisions of six, or two divisions of nine, or one division of 18, I don't really mind so long as the competition's worth fighting for and the right amount of cricket is being played. Get this right and the right kind of cricket will be played, followed by the right kind of cricketer.

Personally, I would have a top division of the best seven counties with the remaining 11 playing against each other just the once in Division Two. Counties in the top division would play each other home and away with the bottom two relegated.

Top division sides would receive better ECB handouts and would be rewarded by better prize money than the Division Two sides. This system would see a significant reduction in the numbers of games in both four-day and one-day cricket for all counties, whilst having plenty to play for.

Finally, I would like formally to congratulate Sussex on a fantastic achievement in winning the county championship. Peter Moores, Chris Adams and co. have become a real force to be reckoned with on the circuit, and Sussex produced some stunning cricket this summer.

Mushtaq Ahmed may have earned most of the plaudits but, make no mistake about it, theirs was a real team effort and symbolized everything that is good about the game in this country. County cricket is not that broke. Let's stop knocking it and start doing it better.

David Fulton still does not have full vision is his right eye. After returning to the Kent team, he played in 11 championship matches last season, scoring 674 runs at an average of 37.44. He writes a regular column for the Kent on Sunday *newspaper.*

NATIONAL CRICKET LEAGUE
By Mark Baldwin

27 April 2003: Division One
at Chelmsford
Surrey 268 for 8 (45 overs) (Azhar Mahmood 98,
AJ Hollioake 77)
Essex 253 (43 overs) (RC Irani 64)
Surrey (4pts) won by 15 runs

at Bristol
Gloucestershire 143 (43.3 overs) (MS Mason 4 for 35)
Worcestershire 98 for 2 (24.4 overs) (GA Hick 52*)
*Worcestershire (4pts) won by 35 runs – DL Method:
target 64 from 24.4 overs*

at Canterbury
Kent 254 for 4 (45 overs) (MJ Walker 82*)
Leicestershire 200 (39.2 overs) (PD Trego 4 for 39)
Kent (4pts) won by 54 runs

at Edgbaston
Warwickshire 158 for 9 (42 overs) (AF Giles 61*)
Yorkshire 160 for 4 (35 overs) (MJ Lumb 61)
Yorkshire (4pts) won by 6 wickets

A buccaneering stand of 154 in 21 overs between
Adam Hollioake and Azhar Mahmood not only
rescued Surrey from the depths of 82 for 6 against
Essex at Chelmsford, but also proved the basis for a
hard-fought 15-run victory. It was, unsurprisingly, a
county one-day league record for the seventh wicket
and Hollioake's 66-ball 77 contained four sixes.
Mahmood reacted to the sight of Hollioake finally
chopping a ball from Scott Brant onto his stumps by
simply intensifying his own assault. When he was
finally bowled by Jon Dakin, the Pakistan all-rounder
had included three sixes and nine fours in his 73-ball
98. Will Jefferson then launched the Essex reply with a
fusillade of boundaries in his quick-fire 47, but Ronnie
Irani's 64 off 60 balls ended at just the wrong time for
the home side who lost too many wickets to careless
shots. In the end, another two overs were still available
when – instead of pushing singles – Graham Napier
tried to slog Mahmood and skied to mid-on. Saqlain
Mushtaq's 3 for 27 from his nine-over allocation was
by far the most important bowling spell of the game.
Graeme Hick's unbeaten 52, made from 56 balls on
a pitch on which Gloucestershire had struggled to
143 all out, earned Worcestershire a comfortable win
on Duckworth-Lewis calculations when rain arrived
at Bristol. Earlier, the Australian-bred paceman Matt
Mason had impressed with four wickets in a strong-

Pakistan all-rounder Azhar Mahmood was in exhilarating
early-season form at Chelmsford.

looking and well-balanced Worcestershire attack.
Kent proved too strong in all departments for
Leicestershire at Canterbury, taking command from
the early overs when Mark Ealham thumped 41 from
just 26 balls. Matthew Walker's unbeaten 82 ensured
a challenging total, and Kent's satisfaction at a good
day's work was completed when Peter Trego, their
21-year-old off-season signing from Somerset, added
four wickets to his spritely, unbeaten 31 and Geraint
Jones, the wicketkeeper, again overshadowed his
predecessor, Paul Nixon, by taking a county
competition record of six catches.
Nick Knight announced his retirement from one-
day international cricket at Edgbaston, where another
left-handed opener, Yorkshire's Michael Lumb,
played the match-winning innings. Knight fell for just
seven, during a fine new-ball spell from Chris
Silverwood, and Warwickshire needed a gutsy,
unbeaten 61 from 66 balls by Ashley Giles to post any
sort of target for Yorkshire. Lumb's early assault on
the home bowling, his 61 coming off just 40 balls, left
Yorkshire able simply to jog over the finishing line.

Division Two

at Taunton
Somerset 233 for 9 (45 overs) (ME Trescothick 74,
D Pretorius 4 for 31)

Durham 215 for 3 (32.4 overs) (GJ Pratt 101*, N Peng 92)
Durham (4pts) won by 7 wickets – DL Method: target 215 from 40 overs

at Old Trafford
Northamptonshire 196 for 2 (37 overs) (MEK Hussey 84 (PA Jaques 65)
Lancashire 151 (33.4 overs)
Northamptonshire (4pts) won by 45 runs

at Lord's
Derbyshire 203 (45 overs) (MJ Di Venuto 61, CWG Bassano 52, SJ Cook 4 for 30)
Middlesex 205 for 5 (43.5 overs) (PN Weekes 76)
Middlesex (4pts) won by 5 wickets

Nicky Peng and Gary Pratt, two of Durham's legion of emerging young players, figured in a partnership of 164 in just 23 overs at Taunton. The result of their alliance was a morale-shattering, seven-wicket home defeat for Somerset, for whom even Marcus Trescothick found himself being outplayed. Trescothick had made 74 from 86 balls in Somerset's 233 for 9, a total which might have been more but for some fine pace bowling from South African Dewald Pretorius. But then came Peng's 92 off 94 balls and, even more impressive, Pratt's 101 not out. His hundred was completed off only 79 deliveries, which put him alongside Dean Jones as the holder of Durham's fastest one-day league century.

Mike Hussey defied jet lag to lead Northamptonshire to a convincing 45-run win over Lancashire at Old Trafford. Hussey, who had arrived from Australia less than 48 hours earlier, hit an unbeaten 84 and then ran out the dangerous Andrew Flintoff for seven in a match reduced to 37 overs per side. Phil Jaques, his fellow Aussie left-hander, added to his own growing reputation by contributing 65 to a second-wicket partnership of 155 in 24 overs.

Simon Cook's four wickets, and a fine all-round performance by Paul Weekes, set up Middlesex's five-wicket win against Derbyshire at Lord's. Cook's most important strike came when he dismissed Michael Di Venuto for 61. That ended the Australian's third-wicket stand of 76 with Chris Bassano, who then fell to Abdul Razzaq as Derbyshire lost four wickets for 11 runs in five overs – with Cook taking three of them. Weekes followed up his three tail-end wickets by scoring 76 from the top of the order and dominating an opening stand of 96 with his captain, Andy Strauss. Owais Shah's stylish 48 maintained the Middlesex momentum, and victory finally arrived with seven balls to spare.

4 May 2003: Division One

at The Oval
Surrey 281 for 8 (45 overs) (MR Ramprakash 63, GP Thorpe 58)
Warwickshire 256 (43.1 overs) (NV Knight 105, AJ Tudor 4 for 45)
Surrey (4pts) won by 25 runs

at Leicester
Glamorgan 249 for 5 (45 overs) (DL Hemp 83*)
Leicestershire 205 (41.3 overs) (DL Maddy 80)
Glamorgan (4pts) won by 44 runs

Surrey made it two wins out of two to take an early lead at the top of the National League table after beating Warwickshire by 25 runs in a match which they always controlled. A jaw-dropping reverse sweep for six by Graham Thorpe, off Ashley Giles, was one of the many high points of a powerful Surrey batting display – Thorpe's 58, Mark Ramprakash's 63 and a fine 47 at the head of the order by Ian Ward – which ensured a highly competitive total. In reply, only Nick Knight, with a brave hundred, looked to be in Surrey's class as he led a spirited recovery from 127 for 7. In the end, with Graham Wagg clubbing 31 not out from just 11 balls, which included three sixes off Saqlain Mushtaq, the margin of victory did not truly reflect Surrey's dominance.

Despite being boosted by the arrival from Delhi, only six hours earlier, of their second overseas player, Virender Sehwag, Leicestershire tumbled to a 44-run defeat against defending champions Glamorgan. The Welsh county were hauled up to 249 for 5 by an unbroken partnership of 59 in just 32 balls between David Hemp and Mark Wallace. The left-handed Hemp, one of the most pleasing strokemakers in the game on his day, ended the innings unbeaten on 83 from 96 deliveries. Sehwag hit four boundaries in his 23, but the Glamorgan seam attack bowled tidily and Robert Croft's off spin brought him three important wickets just when the Leicestershire late middle order was attempting to give Darren Maddy (80) the support he deserved for leading some sort of rally from 75 for 5.

Division Two

at Chester-le-Street
Durham 167 for 7 (45 overs) (RM Haq 4 for 36)
Scotland 168 for 6 (44.2 overs)
Scotland (4pts) won by 4 wickets

at Southampton
Hampshire 144 for 9 (45 overs)
Sussex 101 (36.4 overs)
Hampshire (4pts) won by 43 runs

at Northampton
Nottinghamshire 294 for 8 (45 overs) (CMW Read
119*, KP Pietersen 77)
Northamptonshire 295 for 5 (44.3 overs) (DJG Sales
133*, PA Jaques 68)
Northamptonshire (4pts) won by 5 wickets

at Derby
Derbyshire 220 for 7 (45 overs) (SA Selwood 88*,
CWG Bassano 57)
Somerset 205 (41.1 overs) (RL Johnson 53)
Derbyshire (4pts) won by 15 runs

The Scottish Saltires began their first season in the
National League by recording a famous debut victory
against Durham at Chester-le-Street. A group of their
supporters in the 2,000 crowd, sporting kilts and
sporrans, did a jig of delight in front of the pavilion
after Colin Smith cut the winning boundary in the
final over to clinch a four-wicket victory over Durham.
It was a win they fully deserved, too, against a county
team boasting a new-ball attack of two overseas
internationals, with England's Steve Harmison in
support. Durham's performance, in truth, was not a
very good one, with only Gordon Muchall and Gary
Pratt producing anything approaching quality with the
bat as they stuttered to 167 for 7 from their 45-over
allocation. The Saltires were indebted mainly to Majid
Haq, a short and slightly tubby 20-year-old off spinner
from Paisley who gained a four-wicket reward for
flighting the ball cleverly and giving it a good rip.
Douglas Lockhart and Ryan Watson launched
Scotland's reply with a solid opening stand worth 75,
and Harmison's inability to bowl tidily enough to keep
the part-time Scotland batsmen quiet perfectly
summed up Durham's overall embarrassment.

A poor pitch at the Rose Bowl produced a low-
scoring contest in which Hampshire's struggle to 144
for 9 proved 43 runs too many for Sussex. Robin
Smith battled hard in the conditions to reach 44,
while Nic Pothas' unbeaten 30 brought a late impetus
to the innings. Sussex, however, never got going in
reply, with Chris Tremlett's height exacerbating the
inconsistent bounce in the pitch and Murray
Goodwin holing out at long on to give off spinner
Shaun Udal the first of his three cheap wickets.

No sooner had Chris Read underlined his claims
for an England one-day place by taking an unbeaten

hundred off Northamptonshire than David Sales had
won the match by hitting an even better century of his
own. Sales treated his home crowd at Wantage Road
to a brilliant 133 not out from just 120 balls, hitting a
six and 14 fours as he eventually guided his side past
Nottinghamshire's challenging total of 294 for 8 with
three balls in hand. Phil Jaques scored 68 to help Sales
add a decisive 149 in 21 overs for the third wicket,
with Sales going on to make the highest league score
by a Northants player for 20 years. Read, however,
could count himself unlucky to be on the losing side
after carrying his bat for 119, from 108 balls and with
three sixes and 15 fours. Promoted to open by his
county, on account of his England hopes, Read
featured in stands of 82 for the second wicket with
Jason Gallian and then a blistering 116 with Kevin
Pietersen, whose 77 took only 63 balls and included
two sixes and nine fours. Ultimately, though, it was
not enough as Sales took the Notts attack apart.

**David Sales: his 133 not out against Nottinghamshire was the
highest one-day league score by a Northamptonshire batsman
for 20 years.**

Derbyshire withstood a late assault from Somerset's Richard Johnson to complete a 15-run victory at Derby. After being lifted to 220 for 7 by, in the main, an unbeaten 88 from Steve Selwood, Derbyshire had reduced their visitors to 108 for 7 by the time Johnson strode in at No. 9. His lusty 53 from 47 balls, and a 53-run ninth-wicket stand with Nixon McLean, threatened to ruin the home side's day, but Dominic Cork, the Derbyshire captain, brought himself back to deceive Johnson with a low full toss, which he hit straight to a fielder. McLean's own bid for victory was ended by a good ball from Graeme Welch with four overs still remaining.

5 May 2003: Division One

at Headingley
Essex 211 for 6 (45 overs) (WI Jefferson 57, A Habib 50)
Yorkshire 54 (20.2 overs) (GR Napier 4 for 18, SA Brant 4 for 25)
Essex (4pts) won by 157 runs

at Bristol
Gloucestershire 311 for 4 (45 overs) (WPC Weston 92, CM Spearman 89, THC Hancock 82)
Leicestershire 254 (43.5 overs) (PAJ DeFreitas 90, DI Stevens 65)
Gloucestershire (4pts) won by 57 runs

at Cardiff
Kent 192 for 9 (45 overs) (RWT Key 68)
Glamorgan 195 for 3 (36.2 overs) (RDB Croft 59, MJ Powell 58)
Glamorgan (4pts) won by 7 wickets

at Worcester
Worcestershire 244 for 5 (45 overs) (GA Hick 81, Kadeer Ali 52)
Surrey 247 for 9 (41.3 overs) (AD Brown 81, MR Ramprakash 67)
Surrey (4pts) won by one wicket

There was humiliation at Headingley for Yorkshire, bowled out for their lowest score in 40 years of one-day cricket by Essex. The damage was done by Scott Brant and Graham Napier, with four wickets apiece, and it took just 20.2 overs for the home side's demise to 54 all out. Essex, who had earlier seen Will Jefferson and Aftab Habib reach half-centuries in a solid batting effort, won by 157 runs. The ball swung and seamed all day, but the Yorkshire batting did not show any of the self-discipline evident in an Essex line-up missing the injured duo of Andy Flower and Ronnie Irani. A hamstring injury for Darren Gough, suffered at the start of his fourth over and which prevented him from batting later, set the seal on a day Yorkshire were left wanting to forget.

A short, and rather inadequate, boundary on one side of the ground contributed to a high-scoring affair at Bristol, which was won by 57 runs by Gloucestershire after a top-order assault by Craig Spearman, Philip Weston and Tim Hancock. Spearman and Weston struck ten sixes between them, but Hancock played perhaps the most destructive innings of all as he raced to 82 from 57 balls, including six more sixes. When Matt Windows also thumped a six and a four from the final over, Gloucestershire had totalled 331 for 4 – their highest league effort at their headquarters. In reply, Leicestershire looked towards the swashbuckling Indian, Virender Sehwag, or the destructive Trevor Ward, but both fell early on to Jon Lewis – Sehwag to a leading edge back to the bowler and Ward to a good catch at mid-on by Hancock. Darren Stevens did reach 50 from 48 balls, and Phil DeFreitas later delayed the end with an entertaining 90 off 64 balls, but Gloucestershire were always in control.

The defending champions Glamorgan, inspired by their stand-in captain, Robert Croft, crushed Kent, the 2001 winners, by seven wickets at Cardiff. Despite Rob Key's well-constructed 68, and some late-order defiance from the wicketkeeper with Welsh blood, Geraint Jones, Kent's 192 for 9 seemed totally inadequate once Croft, who had also taken three important wickets with his off breaks, bludgeoned 59 in the role of pinch-hitter. Michael Powell also scored a breezy 50, before being stumped off a wide, and Matthew Maynard remained at the crease to usher Glamorgan home with 52 balls to spare.

Surrey maintained their 100 per cent record at the top of the table, despite the alarming collapse which almost saw them toss away victory at Worcester. At 157 for 1, with Alistair Brown and Mark Ramprakash having added an exhilarating 153 for the second wicket, Surrey looked to be in a position to cruise past Worcestershire's total of 244 for 5. Sure enough, Graham Thorpe's 38 saw them comfortably to 209 for 3, but then the England left-hander was run out by a throw from the deep by Nantie Hayward. Suddenly, six wickets had gone down in seven frantic overs and, in the end, it needed a calm little innings by Martin Bicknell and a cover-driven four by last man Jimmy Ormond to deny Worcestershire. Graeme Hick and Kadeer Ali both batted well, earlier, to ensure that an 85-run opening stand between Stephen Peters and Vikram Solanki was not wasted.

Division Two

at Hove
Sussex 217 for 3 (45 overs) (CJ Adams 109*, RSC Martin-Jenkins 68*)
Northamptonshire 221 for 6 (44.4 overs) (PA Jaques 68)
Northamptonshire (4pts) won by 4 wickets

at Southampton
Hampshire 198 for 5 (45 overs) (RA Smith 92)
Middlesex 201 for 6 (45 overs) (PN Weekes 53)
Middlesex (4pts) won by 4 wickets

at Chester-le-Street
Durham 186 for 8 (44 overs) (GJ Pratt 66*)
Lancashire 188 for 5 (42.2 overs) (AJ Swann 73*)
Lancashire (4pts) won by 5 wickets

at Trent Bridge
Derbyshire 252 (45 overs) (SA Selwood 67, DR Hewson 50, S Elworthy 4 for 41)
Nottinghamshire 254 for 9 (44.2 overs) (KP Pietersen 130*)
Nottinghamshire (4pts) won by one wicket

An ongoing verbal battle between Sussex captain Chris Adams and Northamptonshire's South African fast bowler Andre Nel enlivened proceedings at genteel Hove. With Sussex on 34 for 3, Adams was on the receiving end of some of Nel's thoughts when he played and missed early in his innings on a testing surface. But, later on, when the bowler returned, Adams was well into the process of putting on an unbroken 183 in 30 overs with Robin Martin-Jenkins, who contributed his highest one-day score of 68 not out. Clubbing Nel for six, Adams could not resist marching down the pitch to confront the South African with some well-chosen words of his own. After completing his century, he then hit Nel for another six, his fourth, before the two players exchanged a brief handshake at the end of Sussex's 217 for 3. Northants, though, had the last word – a solid middle-order batting display, led by Phil Jaques, earned them victory by four wickets with two balls to spare and kept them at the top of the Division Two table.

Veterans Robin Smith and Wasim Akram both produced quality performances for Hampshire at Southampton, but could not prevent defeat by Middlesex. It was close, though, with victory coming off the final ball when, with two runs required, Ben Hutton flat-batted a ball from Chris Tremlett through the covers for four. Smith scored 92 from 132 balls in Hampshire's innings of 198 for 5, and Wasim removed the Middlesex top order to return figures of

3 for 17 from his nine overs. Paul Weekes, however, survived Wasim's new-ball spell to reach 53 and Abdul Razzaq later provided perhaps the turning point of the game when he hit three sixes off the suffering Shaun Udal. Razzaq fell to the fourth ball of the final over, for 30, but Hutton did the rest.

A 24-ball 42 from Andy Flintoff, including 38 runs in boundaries, gave Lancashire the mid-innings impetus they needed to overhaul Durham's total of 186 for 8. Gary Pratt's unbeaten 66, in low-scoring conditions at Chester-le-Street, had given the home side a chance – and with Lancashire on 78 for 4 from 22 overs, they were looking for inspiration. They found it in Flintoff, who tore into Steve Harmison, Michael Gough and Danny Law. When he was caught at the wicket off Law, it was a relatively straightforward task for Warren Hegg and Alec Swann, who finished on 73 not out, to steer the visitors home.

Derbyshire were left stunned by the power of Kevin Pietersen at Trent Bridge, losing by one wicket a match they had good reason to believe they would win after totalling 252 and then reducing Nottinghamshire first to 68 for 4 and later to 140 for 6. Pietersen, however, would not go away and eventually hit his 13th four to go to 130 not out and win the game with four deliveries to spare. What an innings it was, with five sixes besides and taking just 109 balls. Yet, at the start, Pietersen was almost circumspect as he helped Chris Cairns to launch the Notts recovery in a fifth-wicket stand of 68. When Cairns fell for 40, however, Pietersen decided all-out attack was his only option. His second 50 took only 24 balls, and off spinner Nathan Dumelow was despatched for four sixes in rapid succession. Notts began the last ten overs still requiring 103, but at times the 22-year-old Pietersen made it look as if the boundary ropes had been pulled in ten yards or so when he was facing. He dominated a seventh-wicket partnership of 79 in seven overs with Paul Franks and stayed to the finish. Pietersen, South African-born but with a British passport courtesy of an English mother, qualifies for England in 2005. On this evidence, that day cannot come around fast enough.

9 May 2003: Division Two

at The Grange
Somerset 179 for 3 (16 overs) (ME Trescothick 80*)
Scotland 181 for 4 (14.3 overs) (RR Watson 103*)
Scotland (4pts) won by 6 wickets

Remarkable hitting by Ryan Watson, Scotland's Zimbabwean opener, earned the home side a

Graham Napier, with 3 for 9 from seven overs, did much to undermine Kent's challenge at Chelmsford as Essex ran out three-wicket winners. Ronnie Irani also played his part with the ball as the visitors struggled to 176 all out, but Essex themselves were a shaky 137 for 7 – despite a fifth-wicket stand of 59 between Paul Grayson and James Foster – before being guided home by James Middlebrook and Napier. Ben Trott included the prized scalps of Nasser Hussain, for seven, and Andy Flower, for a duck, in his nine-over spell of 3 for 22, but it wasn't enough to prevent the visitors from sliding to defeat.

18 May 2003: Division One

at The Oval
Surrey 322 for 7 (45 overs) (MR Ramprakash 107*, Azhar Mahmood 70, PD Trego 4 for 66)
Kent 316 for 7 (45 overs) (ET Smith 99, MJ Walker 80*)
Surrey (4pts) won by 6 runs

A remarkable century from Ryan Watson, off only 43 balls, left Somerset shell-shocked in Scotland.

memorable six-wicket win over Somerset in Edinburgh. Rain, which arrived after just four overs of Somerset's innings, cut the match to a 16-over-per-side affair – but not even a total of 179 for 3, in which Marcus Trescothick blitzed 80 not out from 44 balls, could save the first-class county from defeat against the rampant Saltires. Watson's 103 not out was an astonishing effort, spanning just 43 balls and featuring seven sixes and ten fours. He added 84 with James Brinkley (48) for the second wicket, and, in the end, the Scots passed the Somerset score with nine balls remaining. Watson has designs on playing international cricket for Zimbabwe, and on this evidence it looks like an achievable ambition.

10 May 2003: Division One

at Chelmsford
Kent 176 (45 overs)
Essex 179 for 7 (43 overs)
Essex (4pts) won by 3 wickets

at Leicester
Leicestershire 247 for 8 (45 overs) (DI Stevens 63, V Sehwag 54, RJ Sidebottom 5 for 42)
Yorkshire 181 (44.2 overs) (CE Dagnall 4 for 41)
Leicestershire (4pts) won by 66 runs

at Cardiff
Gloucestershire 133 for 9 (26 overs) (AG Wharf 4 for 18)
Glamorgan 135 for 0 (21.2 overs)
(IJ Thomas 71*, RDB Croft 60*)
Glamorgan (4pts) won by 10 wickets

at Edgbaston
Warwickshire 143 (18.4 overs)
Essex 146 for 2 (19.1 overs) (WI Jefferson 50)
Essex (4pts) won by 8 wickets

A record run aggregate for the one-day league was posted at The Oval, where Kent got themselves into the perfect position to overhaul Surrey's massive total of 322 for 7 … and blew it. Requiring 35 more to win from the last five overs, with six wickets remaining, Kent somehow managed to lose by six runs, despite Matthew Walker finishing unbeaten on 80. Walker had put Kent thrillingly on course for victory with a

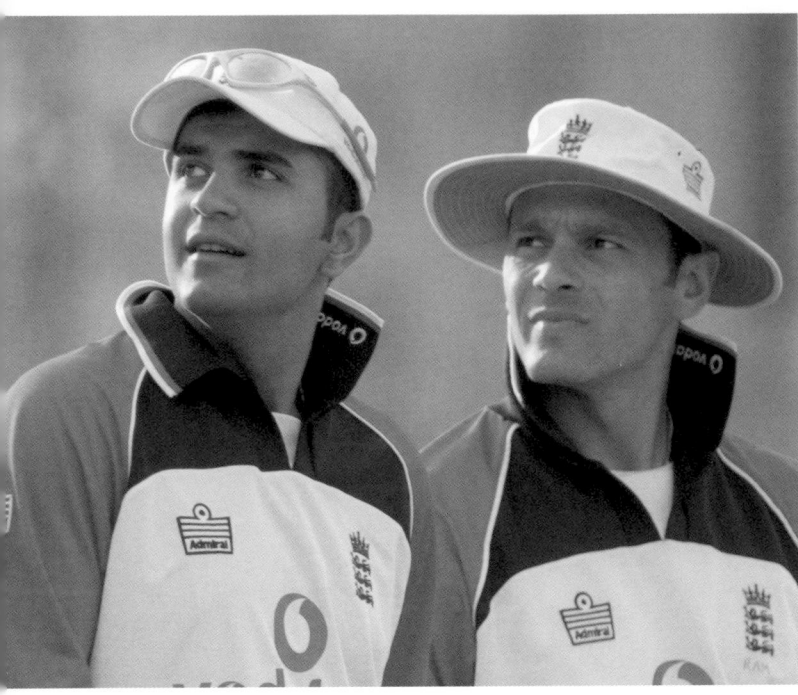

Springtime century-makers both: Usman Afzaal (left) for Nottinghamshire and Mark Ramprakash for Surrey.

stand of 162 from a mere 102 balls with Ed Smith. From 137 for 4 in the 25th over, their partnership transformed the innings, with Smith's 99 taking him just 86 balls. They plundered 23 from one Adam Hollioake over, the 34th, but when Smith fell, the Kent lower-middle order proved themselves incapable of giving Walker the strike. He faced only six of the last 21 deliveries, and Hollioake achieved a private act of revenge by bowling the final over admirably, when 11 were needed at its start. The Surrey innings had earlier been a showcase for the strokemaking talents of Mark Ramprakash (107 from 99 balls) and Azhar Mahmood, whose innings of 70 took just 41 deliveries.

Yorkshire were never in the hunt against Leicestershire at Grace Road after slumping to 28 for 5 at the start of their reply to the home side's challenging total of 247 for 8. Ryan Sidebottom's five-wicket haul could not prevent Darren Stevens and Virender Sehwag from reaching fine half-centuries and Brad Hodge from hitting 47. Charlie Dagnall excelled with the ball for Leicestershire, taking 4 for 41.

Play began two hours late at Cardiff, and Gloucestershire struggled against the Glamorgan

seamers. By contrast, Robert Croft and Ian Thomas were untroubled as they raced to a modest victory target with 28 balls to spare.

A similar story occurred at Edgbaston, after the match had got under way belatedly at 4.30pm. Warwickshire's batsmen were over-frantic in their approach to the reduced-overs match, and even managed to allow themselves to be bowled out well inside the 20-over allocation. Essex then had few alarms as Will Jefferson and Andy Flower inspired an eight-wicket win.

Division Two

at Taunton
Somerset 293 for 4 (35 overs) (J Cox 110, CM Gazzard 58, JDC Bryant 56*)
Nottinghamshire 265 (33 overs) (U Afzaal 105, JER Gallian 69)
Somerset (4pts) won by 49 runs – DL Method: target 309 from 35 overs

at Old Trafford
Lancashire 231 for 4 (30 overs) (SG Law 98, CL Hooper 51*)
Hampshire 150 (23.3 overs)
Lancashire (4pts) won by 70 runs – DL Method: target 221 from 28 overs

at Northampton
Northamptonshire 131 for 9 (33 overs)
Derbyshire 5 for 0 (3 overs)
No result. Northamptonshire (2pts) Derbyshire (2pts). Match abandoned – rain

A 201-run partnership for the third wicket between Usman Afzaal and Jason Gallian looked to be putting Nottinghamshire on course for a stiff revised Duckworth-Lewis target of 315 in 35 overs, following Somerset's own blazing progress to 293 for 4 in a weather-reduced encounter at Taunton. Afzaal (105) reached his hundred in just 68 balls, while Gallian hit 69, but Notts then lost their last eight wickets for just 64 to fall a hefty 49 runs short. Somerset's Jamie Cox had earlier stroked an 81-ball century, launching the home innings with a 131-run stand for the first wicket with promising youngster Carl Gazzard.

Stuart Law's brilliance shone out from Lancashire's 70-run win over Hampshire at Old Trafford. The Australian's 98 took him only 81 balls, and included three sixes and seven fours, and he put on 102 with Mal Loye for the third wicket and then a thrilling stand of 91 in 11 overs with Carl Hooper. The watching James Anderson was then awarded his county cap during the interval, before the home fans settled down to see Hampshire dismissed for 150 as they cracked in the face of Lancashire's intimidating 30-over score.

Derbyshire were robbed by the weather at Northampton, where the home side struggled to just 131 for 9, with Dominic Cork leading a good seam effort with 3 for 22. After the Derbyshire reply had reached just five without loss, however, the rains came.

19 May 2003: Division Two

at The Grange
Middlesex 88 for 4 (20.2 overs)
Scotland Did not bat
No result. Scotland (2pts) Middlesex (2pts)

There was no result either at Edinburgh, where Middlesex limped to 88 for 4 against the Scottish Saltires before the weather closed in.

20 May 2003: Division Two

at The Grange
Scotland 206 (44 overs) (JC Kent 85, DR Hewson 4 for 25)
Derbyshire 139 for 4 (22.2 overs)
Derbyshire (4pts) won by 6 wickets – DL Method: target 139 from 27 overs

The Scots suffered their first defeat of the season in the competition when Derbyshire successfully chased a reduced Duckworth-Lewis target. Savage early hitting from Shahid Afridi, whose 19-ball 35 included two sixes, set them on their way to a six-wicket win, despite steady bowling from Craig Wright. The Saltires' 206 was earlier based on the classy accumulation of South African Jon Kent (85), although the Scots were disappointed with a slide from 149 for 3 as Dominic Hewson picked up 4 for 25 with his medium pacers.

25 May 2003: Division One

at Worcester
Worcestershire 271 for 4 (45 overs) (GA Hick 108, BF Smith 51)
Kent 132 (31.5 overs) (DA Leatherdale 5 for 36)
Worcestershire (4pts) won by 139 runs
at Headingley

Yorkshire 153 for 7 (32 overs)
Glamorgan 165 for 6 (27.1 overs) (CEW Silverwood 4 for 45)
Glamorgan (4pts) won by 4 wickets – DL method: target 164 from 32 overs

at Bristol
Gloucestershire v. **Surrey**
Match abandoned – 2pts each

Graeme Hick scored the 153rd century of his senior career, in all forms of cricket, to make light of a pitch of uneven bounce and spearhead Worcestershire's 139-run hammering of Kent at New Road. Hick, two days past his 37th birthday, was head and shoulders above any other batsman on view and dominated a stand of 127 in 22 overs with Stephen Peters which set Worcestershire up for a big total. Andrew Hall then struck three sixes in a 27-ball, unbeaten 47 and David Leatherdale's skiddy medium pace then proved ideal in the conditions as Kent's reply disintegrated.

Yorkshire had scored 93 for 3 from 21.2 overs when an original 40-over contest at Headingley was further reduced by rain to 32 overs per side. Under the Duckworth-Lewis regulations, Glamorgan needed to score 12 runs more than the eventual Yorkshire total for victory, but despite Chris Silverwood's four wickets and a return to action for Darren Gough, they made it comfortably. Michael Powell top scored with 47.

Gloucestershire's eagerly-awaited clash with leaders Surrey at Bristol unfortunately fell foul of the weather and was abandoned without a ball being bowled.

Division Two

at Chester-le-Street
Durham v. **Derbyshire**
Match abandoned – 2pts each

at Southampton
Hampshire 248 for 3 (45 overs) (DA Kenway 115, JP Crawley 66, SM Katich 51*)
Somerset 149 (39.2 overs) (AD Mascarenhas 4 for 33)
Hampshire (4pts) won by 99 runs

at Old Trafford
Scotland 192 for 8 (45 overs) (CJO Smith 60, JG Williamson 60)
Lancashire 151 (42.1 overs)
Scotland (4pts) won by 41 runs
at Horsham

Robin Smith (left) and Derek Kenway teamed up to see off the Scottish Saltires' challenge in Edinburgh.

Nottinghamshire 258 for 6 (40 overs) (U Afzaal 83, CL Cairns 53*)
Sussex 150 (31.3 overs) (GD Clough 4 for 32)
Nottinghamshire (4pts) won by 97 runs – DL Method: target 248 from 37 overs

at Shenley
Middlesex 200 for 7 (45 overs) (EC Joyce 61, DC Nash 50)
Northamptonshire 204 for 2 (44.3 overs) (MEK Hussey 86*, DJG Sales 75*)
Northamptonshire (4pts) won by 8 wickets

Rain put pay to Durham's scheduled meeting with Derbyshire at Chester-le-Street, but there were only minimal interruptions elsewhere in the division.

Derek Kenway hit his first one-day hundred as Hampshire overpowered Somerset at the Rose Bowl. John Crawley and Simon Katich also impressed with fluent half-centuries, but the day belonged to Kenway, whose 115 from 143 balls featured 14 fours. His 138-run opening stand with Crawley provided the base for a Hampshire total of 248 for 3, and Dimitri Mascarenhas then picked up four cheap wickets as Somerset folded to a disappointing 149 all out in reply.

Scotland's players, meanwhile, were able to celebrate a third league win of the season when they were rewarded for some highly disciplined bowling with the prized scalp of Lancashire at Old Trafford. Greig Williamson struck three sixes in a middling Saltires total, but then three wickets apiece for Ryan Watson and Craig Wright contributed to a Lancashire slide to 151 all out. Wright, the Scottish

skipper, said: 'This win has to be the highlight of our campaign so far.'

Chris Cairns only arrived at Heathrow Airport at 11.55am on the flight bringing him back from New Zealand's tour of Sri Lanka, but he was still able to be driven to Horsham and then smash an unbeaten 53 from just 35 balls to set the seal on a stroke-filled Nottinghamshire total of 258 for 6. Usman Afzaal's 83 had taken him 98 balls, and his partnership with Kevin Pietersen had already raised 75 in 11 overs before Cairns arrived. A shower of rain during the interval left Sussex needing 248 from 37 overs to win, but a series of over-ambitious shots soon led to their dismissal for 150, with Gareth Clough picking up four deserved wickets.

Northamptonshire put a run of bad championship form to one side as they secured a comprehensive eight-wicket victory against Middlesex at Shenley. Mike Hussey and David Sales saw Northants home with an unbroken partnership of 142 in 32 overs, and some good new-ball bowling by the visitors had earlier prevented Middlesex from achieving a really testing total. Indeed, only three late sixes from Simon Cook enabled them to reach 200.

1 June 2003: Division One

at Leicester
Leicestershire 234 for 6 (45 overs) (BJ Hodge 63)
Gloucestershire 235 for 7 (43.4 overs) (MGN Windows 76)
Gloucestershire (4pts) won by 3 wickets

Gloucestershire completed the double over Leicestershire, beating them by three wickets and with eight balls to spare on their own turf at Grace Road. The home side's 234 for 6 was based on 63 from Brad Hodge, a determined 39 off 32 balls from Jeremy Snape against his former club ... and 46 extras. Matt Windows led the successful chase, being joined in a third-wicket stand of 100 in 18 overs by Chris Taylor and himself hitting eight fours and a straight six off Charlie Dagnall in a 91-ball 76.

Division Two

at The Grange
Scotland 201 for 8 (45 overs) (JC Kent 57)
Hampshire 202 for 4 (43 overs) (RA Smith 82*, DA Kenway 51)
Hampshire (4pts) won by 6 wickets
Rahul Dravid made 25 on his Scotland debut at

Edinburgh, although Jon Kent top scored with 57 as the Saltires totalled 201 for 8. It might have been enough if the Scots had not then dropped both Derek Kenway and Robin Smith early in their innings. Kenway made 51 and Smith stayed to score an unbeaten 82 from 84 balls and steer Hampshire home by six wickets with two overs in hand.

8 June 2003: Division One

at Swansea
Glamorgan 209 for 9 (39 overs) (A Dale 60, DL Hemp 59, Kabir Ali 4 for 38)
Worcestershire 184 (36.2 overs) (AG Wharf 4 for 24)
Glamorgan (4pts) won by 31 runs – DL Method: target 215 from 39 overs

at The Oval
Essex 220 (44.2 overs) (DDJ Robinson 78, Azhar Mahmood 6 for 37)
Surrey 221 for 7 (42.5 overs) (GP Thorpe 79*)
Surrey (4pts) won by 3 wickets

at Gloucester
Gloucestershire 307 for 8 (45 overs) (CM Spearman 153, WPC Weston 61)
Warwickshire 229 (40.2 overs) (NV Knight 70, JO Troughton 53, IR Bell 50)
Gloucestershire (4pts) won by 78 runs

at Tunbridge Wells
Kent 208 for 7 (45 overs)
Yorkshire 186 for 9 (45 overs) (MJ Lumb 77)
Kent (4pts) won by 22 runs

Glamorgan made it five wins out of five by beating Worcestershire at Swansea. Adrian Dale and David Hemp added 112 for the fifth wicket in 18 overs, and then some fine seam bowling from Alex Wharf (4 for 24) undermined the visitors. Robert Croft also picked up three good wickets with his off spin and the margin of victory in the end was 31 runs.

A burst of five wickets in 16 balls from Azhar Mahmood halted Essex in their stride at The Oval, limiting the visitors to 220 all out when a total of around 250 had looked probable. Mahmood finished with 6 for 37, and then Graham Thorpe marshalled the run chase with an unbeaten 79. Victory, which pushed Surrey's unbeaten run up to 14 matches in all competitions, eventually came with three wickets and 2.1 overs remaining.

Craig Spearman, the cavalier Kiwi, made

Gloucestershire's highest individual one-day league innings as Warwickshire were overwhelmed by 78 runs at Gloucester. Spearman's magnificent 153 took him just 123 balls, and featured five sixes and 15 fours. He dominated an opening partnership of 171 with Phil Weston, whose contribution was 61. It was certainly leading from the front – Spearman was Gloucestershire's acting captain in the absence of Mark Alleyne who missed the game with a side strain. In reply, Nick Knight threatened for Warwickshire by hitting 70 off 53 balls, with two sixes and nine fours, while Ian Bell and Jim Troughton both scored half-centuries. After Spearman's onslaught, however, the home side always had something in hand.

Kent held their nerve with both bat and ball to see off Yorkshire by 22 runs at Tunbridge Wells. Steady, rather than spectacular, batting saw Kent mount a defendable total on a sluggish pitch, and then a three-wicket new-ball burst by Ben Trott immediately put Yorkshire up against it. Trott bowled his nine-over allocation straight through, and Kent's other bowlers maintained the pressure as the visitors attempted to rebuild the innings. Michael Lumb made 77, and Richard Blakey also fought hard, but the required run rate went up and up until even frantic slogging was not enough.

Division Two

at Old Trafford
Nottinghamshire 100 for 6 (17 overs)
Lancashire 114 for 3 (15.3 overs)
Lancashire (4pts) won by 7 wickets – DL Method: target 112 from 17 overs

at Southampton
Hampshire 203 for 5 (45 overs) (JP Crawley 102)
Durham 196 for 8 (45 overs) (AD Mascarenhas 4 for 44)
Hampshire (4pts) won by 7 runs

at Lord's
Sussex 161 for 7 (39 overs) (MW Goodwin 81*)
Middlesex 133 (33.2 overs) (AJ Strauss 57, KJ Innes 5 for 41)
Sussex (4pts) won by 49 runs – DL Method: target 183 from 39 overs

at Bath
Somerset 143 (32.3 overs) (KP Dutch 50, MJ Cawdron 4 for 31)
Northamptonshire 131 for 3 (27.3 overs) (MEK Hussey 54)
Somerset (4pts) won by 12 runs
Only three overs had been bowled at Old Trafford

when a prolonged downpour forced a four-hour stoppage. The match between Lancashire and Nottinghamshire then became a 17-over-per-side contest, but at least there was still some rich entertainment for the home supporters as Andy Flintoff joined forces with Carl Hooper to sweep Lancashire to victory with nine balls to spare in an unbroken fourth-wicket stand of 88. Flintoff finished off the match in style, too, hammering a six over midwicket off Paul Franks.

John Crawley made what was only his second one-day league century in 13 seasons as Hampshire squeezed past Durham by seven runs at Southampton. Alan Mullally's nine overs cost just 15 runs, while Dimitri Mascarenhas also made a significant contribution to Hampshire's successful defence of 203 for 5 by taking four wickets.

A sudden and dramatic change in fortune for Kevin Innes, the medium pacer, inspired Sussex's first win of the season at Lord's. On a bowler-friendly surface, Murray Goodwin had fought hard to finish with 81 not out, but even his 112-run stand with Tim Ambrose had only managed to lift Sussex to a 39-over total of 161 for 7. Needing 182, under Duckworth-Lewis regulations, Middlesex

Five-wicket hero: a stunning 15-ball burst by Kevin Innes inspired Sussex to their first win of the season.

seemed to be cruising at 115 for 3 by the 28th over, but Innes, whose first four overs had cost 34 runs, then returned to take 5 for 6 in just 15 balls as the home side lost their last seven wickets for 18 runs in a total of 33 deliveries.

Northamptonshire's fifth win, stretching their unbeaten run to six matches, was a straightforward affair once Somerset had been tumbled out for 143 at Bath, with Mike Cawdron picking up 4 for 31. Another half-century from the relentless Mike Hussey then ensured there would be no slip-ups by the visitors, despite a short rain break.

15 June 2003: Division One

at Chelmsford
Warwickshire 307 for 5 (45 overs) (IR Bell 125, IJL Trott 59)
Essex 182 (27.5 overs) (GR Napier 52, IR Bell 5 for 41)
Warwickshire (4pts) won by 125 runs

at Worcester
Worcestershire 193 for 7 (45 overs) (SD Peters 50)
Leicestershire 198 for 8 (42.1 overs) (PAJ DeFreitas 68, DL Maddy 56, DA Leatherdale 4 for 41)
Leicestershire (4pts) won by 2 wickets

at Beckenham
Kent 222 for 8 (45 overs) (GO Jones 74*, A Symonds 56)
Gloucestershire 223 for 4 (41.2 overs) (MGN Windows 58*)
Gloucestershire (4pts) won by 6 wickets

An irresistible all-round performance from Ian Bell, the 21-year-old surely destined for higher honours, shone brightly out of Warwickshire's 125-run trouncing of Essex at Chelmsford. Bell hit his first one-day hundred (125), added 173 in 28 overs with Jon Trott, and then took 5 for 41 with his medium pacers as the Essex batsmen perished in a do-or-die attempt to chase Warwickshire's imposing total of 307 for 5. At least there was some entertainment for the home supporters as they saw their side fall way short: five different players hit sixes, including Graham Napier, whose 28-ball 52 featured three 'maximums'.

A late wobble left Leicestershire needing their ninth-wicket pair of Trevor Ward and David Masters to score 21 further runs from the last eight overs at Worcester. They were equal to the task, which meant that fine early batting from Phil DeFreitas (68 from 91 balls) and Darren Maddy (56 off 69) was not wasted. Worcestershire's total

All-round talent: Ian Bell of Warwickshire was in irresistible form with both bat and ball at Chelmsford.

of 193 for 7 was below par in the conditions, but credit must go to a disciplined bowling effort by the visitors.

Kent could not mark their return to the metropolitan north-west of the county by beating Gloucestershire at Beckenham, In fact, they played well below their potential on a beautiful pitch and a fast-scoring outfield, with only a solid half-century from acting captain Andrew Symonds and a chirpy unbeaten 74 from Geraint Jones lifting them above 200. The visitors were never in trouble, winning with 22 balls to spare, but at least Kent's enterprise in coming back to the redeveloped former Lloyds Bank Sports Ground – where they played one championship match in 1954 – was rewarded by a 4,000 crowd. A full festival week at Beckenham, including a championship fixture, was planned for 2004 and beyond.

Division Two

at Derby
Lancashire 251 for 6 (45 overs) (MB Loye 63)
Derbyshire 246 for 9 (45 overs) (LD Sutton 83, G Chapple 4 for 37)
Lancashire (4pts) won by 5 runs

at Northampton
Northamptonshire 148 (44.3 overs)
Sussex 135 (42.2 overs)
Northamptonshire (4pts) won by 13 runs

at Trent Bridge
Durham 183 (44.5 overs) (ML Love 55)
Nottinghamshire 176 (44.5 overs) (N Killeen 5 for 22)
Durham (4pts) won by 7 runs

at Taunton
Scotland 296 for 4 (45 overs) (R Dravid 120*, RR Watson 75)
Somerset 299 for 9 (44.1 overs) (J Cox 82, CM Gazzard 81)
Somerset (4pts) won by one wicket

There was an exciting finish at Taunton, where Somerset squeezed home by one wicket against the Scottish Saltires after successfully chasing down a score of 296 for 4. It took a last-wicket stand of nine runs, however, to do it – with No. 11 Simon Francis hitting the winning blow when he leg-glanced the first ball of the final over, from Paul Hoffman, to the boundary. Rahul Dravid made a brilliant 120 not out for the Scots, and Ryan Watson also hit 75 as he added 117 for the third wicket with the elegant Indian. Somerset's reply was always up with the required rate, following a second-wicket stand of 160 in just 19 overs between Carl Gazzard, whose 81 took him 61 balls, and Jamie Cox.

A spirited fightback by Luke Sutton and Dominic Cork narrowly failed to inspire Derbyshire to an unlikely victory over Lancashire at Derby. At 61 for 5, in reply to a Lancashire total of 251 for 6 built around 63 from Mal Loye and forthright 40s from both Stuart Law and Iain Sutcliffe, the home side looked buried. But Cork joined Sutton in a stand worth 114 in 19 overs and, although both fell before the end – Sutton for a league-best 83 off 85 balls and Cork for 49 – Derbyshire reached the final over needing ten runs to win. Peter Martin, however, then produced a magnificent over of near-yorkers to concede just four singles, and Lancashire ran out winners by five runs.

Rahul Dravid was the wicket every Scottish Saltires opponent coveted in the National League.

undermined the Notts innings, picking up five wickets with both movement off the seam and unrelenting accuracy. Durham's eventual seven-run win owed much to him, and to Martin Love's 55 in the bowler-friendly conditions.

An even lower-scoring match at Northampton saw the home team win a tense affair by 13 runs, but not before the Sussex ninth-wicket pair of Mark Davis and Paul Hutchison had edged them closer than they expected following a collapse to 98 for 8. Phil Jaques' run out of Hutchison was, in the end, a key moment.

17 June 2003: Division Two

at Richmond
Middlesex 255 for 9 (45 overs) (PN Weekes 80, EC Joyce 59*)
Scotland 143 (30.1 overs) (CB Keegan 5 for 48)
Middlesex (4pts) won by 112 runs

The Scottish Saltires received their first real battering of the league season when they lost by 112 runs to Middlesex at Richmond. Paul Weekes and Owais Shah added 98 in 93 balls for the county side, and Ed Joyce's unbeaten 59 then ensured a decent total. The Scots, though, made a terrible start and, when Rahul Dravid was out in the 12th over, they were left reeling on 36 for 5 and beyond any hope of victory. A 14-ball 33 from Paul Hoffman breathed some defiance, but Chad Keegan's 5 for 48 spearheaded an efficient Middlesex display in the field.

22 June 2003: Division One

at Edgbaston
Glamorgan 193 (44 overs) (DR Brown 4 for 37)
Warwickshire 179 for 8 (38.5 overs) (NV Knight 75)
Warwickshire (4pts) won by 2 wickets – DL Method: target 179 in 39 overs

at Headingley
Leicestershire 251 for 8 (45 overs) (BJ Hodge 104, V Sehwag 65)
Yorkshire 233 (44.4 overs) (TT Bresnan 61, Yuvraj Singh 50)
Leicestershire (4pts) won by 18 runs

Nick Knight's masterly 75, supported by a typically ebullient 49 off 53 balls by Dougie Brown, guided

Nottinghamshire had a similar near miss at Trent Bridge, after a fine effort from the lower-middle order. Notts had required 68 from the last ten overs on a slow, low pitch, but Gareth Clough struck an unbeaten 42 from 51 balls to take the home side to within seven runs of a tie. As at Derby, only four runs came from the final over – which had begun with 11 runs still needed. Neil Killeen had earlier

Warwickshire through some sticky moments en route to a two-wicket victory against previously unbeaten Glamorgan at Edgbaston. Warwickshire were initially 16 for 3, and then 44 for 4, before Brown joined Knight in a stand of 82 for the fifth wicket. The home side eventually crept over the finishing line with one ball remaining, having been set a revised target of 179 in 39 overs by the Duckworth-Lewis regulations. Earlier Robert Croft had plundered 42 of Glamorgan's first 50 runs, but Brown (with 4 for 37) checked their progress with his first significant contribution to a fine afternoon's work.

Brad Hodge, Leicestershire's Australian batsman, found his league touch after a couple of excellent Twenty20 Cup knocks to score the century at Headingley which ultimately proved too much for Yorkshire. The eventual winning margin was only 18 runs, but that was due to a defiant 45-ball 61 at the end by Tim Bresnan. Leicestershire had looked firm

favourites from the moment that Yuvraj Singh was brilliantly held one-handed by a diving Jeremy Snape after hitting a fluent 50. Hodge, whose second 50 had taken him just 37 balls, added 126 in 24 overs for the second wicket with Virender Sehwag.

Division Two

at Old Trafford
Durham 197 for 7 (45 overs) (ML Love 53)
Lancashire 198 for 7 (43.5 overs) (G Chapple 77*)
Lancashire (4pts) won by 3 wickets

at Trent Bridge
Middlesex 234 (44 overs) (OA Shah 106, RJ Logan 4 for 44)
Nottinghamshire 233 for 8 (45 overs) (KP Pietersen 82, GE Welton 50)
Middlesex (4pts) won by one run

An unbeaten 77 off 109 balls from Glen Chapple, who had earlier taken 3 for 38, swept Lancashire home by three wickets at Old Trafford. Chapple led a stirring rally after Liam Plunkett, the young Durham fast bowler, had wrecked the top order with three quick wickets. Plunkett also forced Iain Sutcliffe to retire hurt with a broken cheekbone, after he missed an attempted hook, and so Lancashire were effectively 24 for 5 in reply to Durham's 197 for 7 before Chapple arrived at the crease.

Owais Shah's 106 from 101 balls, with two sixes and ten fours, was the first one-day league century by a Middlesex batsman against Nottinghamshire in the 35 years of the competition. Shah's effort also proved enough for the visitors to come away from Trent Bridge with victory … albeit by the narrowest of margins. Kevin Pietersen's 70-ball 82 put Notts well in contention, and the last over was reached with 11 runs still required. It came down to Richard Logan facing Paul Weekes' final delivery with one run needed for the tie, but the attempt at a scrambled single failed with Logan being run out at the bowler's end.

6 July 2003: Division One

at Maidstone
Kent 291 for 4 (45 overs) (ET Smith 122, MA Ealham 50*)
Glamorgan 239 (41.4 overs) (MP Maynard 72)
Kent (4pts) won by 52 runs

at The Oval
Yorkshire 199 (41.5 overs) (SP Fleming 90)

Born strokemaker: Owais Shah, one of county cricket's most stylish batsmen.

Surrey 200 for 3 (38.1 overs) (MA Butcher 104, MR Ramprakash 60*)
Surrey (4pts) won by 7 wickets

at Worcester
Worcestershire 218 for 8 (45 overs) (A Singh 97)
Warwickshire 219 for 2 (41.1 overs) (IR Bell 97*, IJL Trott 56*)
Warwickshire (4pts) won by 8 wickets

Ed Smith's first hundred in one-day cricket, celebrated by two successive sixes off Robert Croft, was followed by a withering late assault from Mark Ealham on the Maidstone ground where, in 1995, he hit a 44-ball league century. Here, Ealham's plunder was a mere unbeaten 50 from 22 balls, but the cumulative effect of Kent's charge to 291 for 4 – in which Smith's 122 took him just 107 balls – still left the opposition shell-shocked. Glamorgan's top order then failed to negotiate the pace of Mohammad Sami, and it was left to Matthew Maynard's 72 off 76 balls to bring them some honour in an eventual 52-run defeat.

For a man who has never played in a one-day international, despite more than 50 Test appearances, Mark Butcher looked a pretty good practioner of the limited-overs game at The Oval, as Surrey cruised to a seven-wicket win over Yorkshire with almost seven overs to spare. Then again, Butcher's 104 out of 166, from 108 balls, was unbelievably his first one-day hundred in county cricket – in his 146th match. Stephen Fleming hit 90 off 107 balls for Yorkshire, but their 199 was made to look as inadequate as it had at first appeared as Butcher was joined by Mark Ramprakash in a high-class stand of 158 in 30 overs.

A closer contest than Warwickshire's eventual winning margin of eight wickets might suggest, the West Midlands derby at New Road nevertheless provided a showcase for the batting talents of Ian Bell and Jon Trott. In the end, the pair stayed on to add an unbroken 159 in 30 overs, with Bell just failing to complete his hundred before the victory was clinched, but it was tougher going early on as Worcestershire fought hard to stay in the game. Anurag Singh's determined 97 had been the feature of their own score of 218 for 8.

Division Two

at Lord's
Middlesex 255 for 6 (45 overs) (DC Nash 62, Abdul Razzaq 61*)

Lancashire 257 for 5 (43.4 overs) (CL Hooper 88*, MB Loye 78)
Lancashire (4pts) won by 5 wickets

at The Grange
Scotland 222 for 7 (45 overs) (R Dravid 129*, RJ Logan 4 for 32)
Nottinghamshire 224 for 6 (42.1 overs) (CL Cairns 65*, PJ Franks 55)
Nottinghamshire (4pts) won by 4 wickets

at Northampton
Northamptonshire 228 for 8 (45 overs) (PA Jaques 117)
Hampshire 229 for 6 (44.3 overs) (JP Crawley 77*, SM Katich 54)
Hampshire (4pts) won by 4 wickets

at Taunton
Sussex 286 for 5 (45 overs) (MW Goodwin 123, CJ Adams 69*)
Somerset 196 (38.3 overs) (KA Parsons 74)
Sussex (4pts) won by 90 runs

Cool strokeplay from Carl Hooper was the eventual difference between the two sides in a high-scoring affair between Middlesex and Lancashire at Lord's. David Nash and Ed Joyce had earlier rallied the home side from 60 for 4, with Nash scoring 62 in a stand worth 94, but it was Abdul Razzaq's 31-ball unbeaten 61 which really enabled Middlesex to set a demanding target. Mal Loye's 78 was an important contribution, but nothing could compare with Hooper's unhurried chase – with the former West Indies captain flicking three sixes and seven fours in his 68-ball masterclass.

Rahul Dravid was another dreamy strokemaker in fine fettle, with the Indian finishing on 129 not out from 128 balls as Scotland totalled 222 for 7 against Northamptonshire in Edinburgh. The Scots could not defend their score, however, as Paul Franks (55 off 43 balls) and Chris Cairns, who hit an unbeaten 65 from 56 deliveries, saw the East Midlands county home with almost three overs to spare.

A beautifully paced 77 not out by Hampshire captain John Crawley, occupying 72 balls, made sure Phil Jaques had the disappointment of finishing up on the losing side at Northampton despite having struck a fine 117 from 113 balls. Jaques' second 50 took him just 33 deliveries and he hit four sixes and 12 fours, but Hampshire eventually passed the Northants total of 228 for 8 with three balls to spare.

Powerful batting from Murray Goodwin and Chris Adams earned Sussex only their second win of the season in a bottom-of-the-table battle with Somerset at Taunton. Goodwin reached his first hundred of the season, in all cricket, while Adams contributed a muscular 69 not out from 63 balls to their stand of 115 in 17 overs. It was Sussex's highest league total for four years, with 103 runs coming from the final ten overs of the innings, and when Somerset lost four wickets in their first ten overs the contest was all over bar Keith Parsons' defiant 74. The match included a memorable moment, however, for 18-year-old Somerset debutant Mike Parsons. Taunton-born, he took the wicket of Matt Prior with the first ball of the game – and, obviously, his first ball in senior cricket.

7 July 2003: Division Two

at The Grange
Durham 267 for 7 (45 overs) (GJ Muchall 87)
Scotland 153 (36 overs) (RM Haq 55*, Shoaib Akhtar 4 for 34)
Durham (4pts) won by 114 runs

Hammer of the Scots: the pace of Pakistan's Shoaib Akhtar was too much for the Saltires in Edinburgh.

The Scots were scattered by Shoaib Akhtar in Edinburgh, with Durham avenging their earlier defeat at the hands of the Saltires on home soil. Pakistan paceman Shoaib, operating with a breeze at his back, was simply too quick for the Scottish top order – although it was Neil Killeen at the other end who accounted for Rahul Dravid. The sum of their destruction, however, was a scoreboard which soon read 6 for 5 in reply to Durham's 267 for 7. Some resistance was forthcoming from Craig Wright and young Majid Haq – once Shoaib's blitz was over, that is – but the Scots never looked remotely capable of matching a Durham total in which Gordon Muchall, aged just 20, impressed with 87.

9 July 2003: Division Two

at The Grange
Scotland 168 for 7 (39 overs) (J Wood 4 for 22)
Lancashire 170 for 0 (29 overs) (MB Loye 88*, MJ Chilton 69*)
Lancashire (4pts) won by 10 wickets – DL Method: target 169 from 39 overs

There was revenge in Edinburgh, too, for Lancashire, who had travelled north of the border keen to redress the balance after their May defeat at Old Trafford. Victory came by the emphatic margin of ten wickets, after John Wood had included the prized scalp of Rahul Dravid in his spell of 4 for 22. The Saltires' total of 168 for 7 owed much to Craig Wright's unbeaten 46, but not even a 12-over interruption for rain could help them. An adjusted target, calculated on the Duckworth-Lewis scale, was reached with no fewer than ten overs to spare by Lancashire's unbeaten openers Mal Loye and Mark Chilton.

13 July 2003: Division One

at Cardiff
Essex 267 for 6 (45 overs) (N Hussain 144*, RC Irani 63)
Glamorgan 269 for 2 (38.1 overs) (JP Maher 142, RDB Croft 64)
Glamorgan (4pts) won by 8 wickets

at Oakham School
Leicestershire 295 for 7 (45 overs) (V Sehwag 76, TR Ward 68, DL Maddy 58)
Worcestershire 219 (41.5 overs) (SD Peters 82)
Leicestershire (4pts) won by 76 runs

at Edgbaston
Surrey 242 for 9 (45 overs) (MR Ramprakash 57, Waqar Younis 4 for 35)

Warwickshire 244 for 4 (42.1 overs) (NV Knight 74, IR Bell 59*, IJL Trott 51)
Warwickshire (4pts) won by 6 wickets

Nasser Hussain scored an unbeaten 144 from 137 balls for Essex against Glamorgan at Cardiff, but then found himself upstaged by Jimmy Maher and Robert Croft. Hussain's two sixes and 17 fours, plus powerful batting from Ronnie Irani (63), enabled Essex to reach 267 for 6 from their 45 overs. Glamorgan, however, raced home with almost seven overs to spare after Maher and Croft had battered the Essex attack into submission with a club one-day league record opening stand worth 181 in 26 overs. Croft was not sluggish, but he was by far the pedestrian partner with 64 as left-hander Maher sprinted to his maiden league century. The Queenslander went to 50 in just 36 balls, and his hundred came up in 94 balls. Eventually, he was caught on the boundary for 142 from a remarkable reverse pull.

A beautiful pitch, festival atmosphere, a brass band and soaring temperatures beneath an azure sky: these were just some of the delights on offer at Oakham School as Leicestershire completed an eighth consecutive one-day victory by holding their nerve against Worcestershire in the field. Trevor Ward and Virender Sehwag had launched the home side's innings in considerable style, putting on 129 for the first wicket in just 15 overs. Ward's 44-ball 68 included 56 runs in boundaries, while Sehwag made 76 from 59 balls, including three sixes and eight fours. An eventual total of 295 for 7 also owed much to Darren Maddy's 58, but Stephen Peters was in equally bright form at the top of the Worcestershire innings with a 92-ball 82. Peters was well supported first by Anurag Singh and then by Ben Smith and, at 176 for 2 with 15 overs to go, the visitors seemed primed for a final dash to the winning line. Jeremy Snape, however, then took three wickets in 16 balls and – overall – Worcestershire's challenge died as five wickets fell for 13 in six overs.

Waqar Younis, relishing the challenge of playing against his old club, took four important wickets as Warwickshire ended Surrey's run of 11 National League games without defeat. A near full-strength Surrey side struggled somewhat to 198 for 8 before Ian Salisbury struck his fellow leg spinner, Collins Obuya, for three sixes and a four in the final over – before being caught off the last ball for 33. Obuya had earlier taken the scalps of Adam Hollioake and Azhar Mahmood in a tidy spell, but Surrey's 242 for 9 was still only about par. A 6,000 crowd then greatly enjoyed a second-wicket Warwickshire stand of 131 between Nick Knight (74) and Jon Trott, before Ian Bell hit an unbeaten 59 from 47 balls to revive an innings which had suddenly faltered at 152 for 4, following the loss of three wickets for just one run.

Division Two

at Chester-le-Street
Northamptonshire 215 for 7 (45 overs) (MEK Hussey 112*)
Durham 166 (43 overs)
Northamptonshire (4pts) won by 49 runs

at Southgate
Middlesex 337 for 5 (45 overs) (Abdul Razzaq 79, OA Shah 74, AJ Strauss 74, PN Weekes 65)
Somerset 305 for 9 (45 overs) (KP Dutch 65, ID Blackwell 64, WJ Durston 51*)
Middlesex (4pts) won by 32 runs

at Southampton
Hampshire 208 for 7 (45 overs) (SM Katich 56)
Nottinghamshire 212 for 5 (44.4 overs) (JER Gallian 60, CL Cairns 57*)
Nottinghamshire (4pts) won by 5 wickets

at Arundel
Sussex 232 for 6 (45 overs) (MW Goodwin 129*, DR Hewson 4 for 40)
Derbyshire 235 for 4 (41.4 overs) (CWG Bassano 126*)
Derbyshire (4pts) won by 6 wickets

Northamptonshire went back to the top of Division Two with a victory over Durham at Chester-le-Street built upon a determined unbeaten 112 from Mike Hussey, their captain. Hussey batted throughout the innings, finally finding solid support from Toby Bailey after a slide to 150 for 7. Their unbroken 65-run stand ultimately made all the difference, with Durham's batsmen also struggling to break free on an awkward pitch and finally subsiding to 166 all out.

Abdul Razzaq clouted 79 from 49 balls, peppering the hospitality tents at Southgate with five sixes, to set the seal on a record Middlesex limited-overs total of 337 for 5. Andrew Strauss and Paul Weekes had launched the innings with an opening stand of 150 in 24 overs, and then Razzaq's partnership with Owais Shah for the third wicket raised another 114 in 14 overs – of which Shah scored 29. When Razzaq fell, Shah went on to 74 from 57 balls to show that he was no slouch either. In all, Middlesex took 112 runs from their last eight overs. In reply Somerset lost wickets too regularly to suggest that they could overhaul the Middlesex total, but both Keith Dutch (65) and Ian Blackwell (64) blazed away profitably for a while, and 22-year-old Wes Durston finished on 51 not out from 44 balls. In the end, Somerset topped 300 too, making it a day for bowlers to forget as 642 runs were plundered from the 90 overs bowled.

Chris Read, fresh from his successes as England's new one-day wicketkeeper, struck Wasim Akram for two fours in the final over to give Nottinghamshire victory over Hampshire at the Rose Bowl with just two balls to spare. Notts had been making hard work of chasing 209 until Chris Cairns entered at No. 6 to share partnerships of 62 with Jason Gallian and then an unbroken decisive one of 55 with Read. Cairns finished on a run-a-ball 57 not out, while Read's unbeaten 33 took him 32 balls.

After making just 39 runs from his previous eight championship innings, Chris Bassano suddenly found enviable batting form as he struck an unbeaten 126 to sweep Derbyshire to a straightforward six-wicket win over Sussex at Arundel. Employing the lofted drive with great success and style, Bassano reached three figures from 114 balls and dominated a 126-run third-wicket partnership in 26 overs with Mohammad Kaif. Dominic Hewson then added a useful 34 to the four wickets he had taken earlier in a Sussex innings based on Murray Goodwin's 129 not out from 130 balls.

17 July 2003: Division One

at Chelmsford
Essex 252 for 8 (45 overs) (N Hussain 98)
Gloucestershire 255 for 3 (35 overs) (CM Spearman 101, IJ Harvey 96)
Gloucestershire (4pts) won by 7 wickets

The awesome hitting of Craig Spearman and Ian Harvey left the Essex attack in shreds at Chelmsford, as Gloucestershire overhauled a total of 252 for 8 with an almost unbelievable ten overs in hand. Nasser Hussain's 98 had underpinned the Essex innings, but when Harvey joined Spearman following the fall of Phil Weston, with the score on 78, the evening's fireworks began. Spearman's 101 took him 93 balls, with three sixes and nine fours, but it was Harvey who really laid into the inexperienced Essex bowlers. The Australian all-rounder's 96, from just 55 balls, included 74 runs in boundaries.

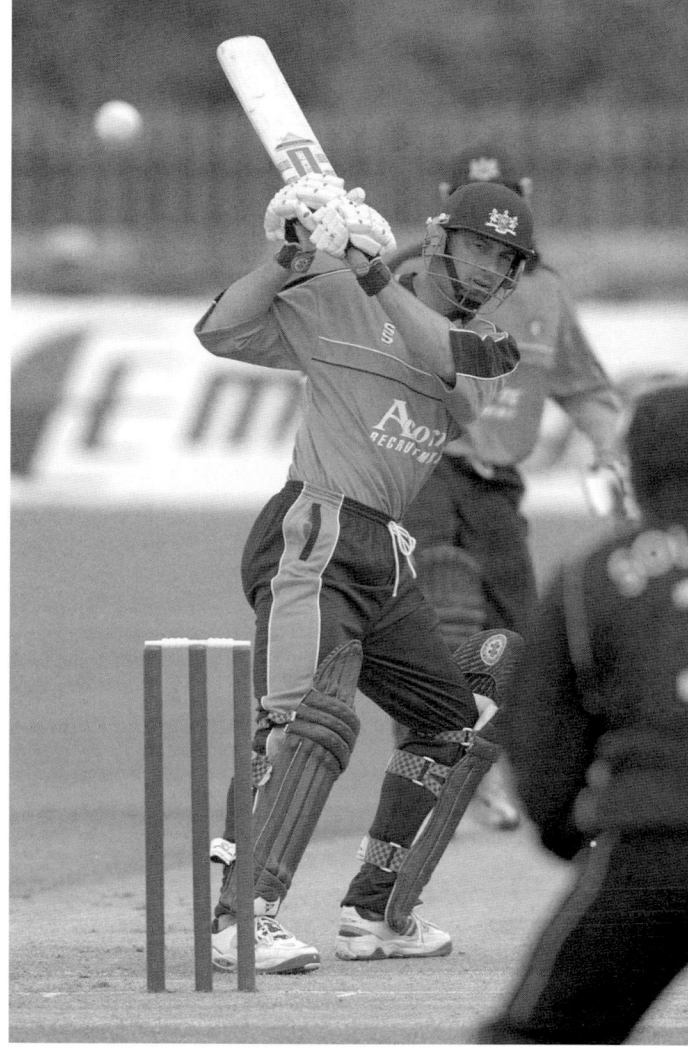

Big hitter: few batsmen in the game can match the top-order aggression of Gloucestershire opener Craig Spearman.

21 July 2003: Division Two

at Trent Bridge
Nottinghamshire 249 for 6 (45 overs) (RJ Warren 91, KP Pietersen 58)
Hampshire 250 for 4 (45 overs) (SM Katich 67, JP Crawley 58, DA Kenway 50)
Hampshire (4pts) won by 6 wickets

John Francis drove Greg Smith for two as Hampshire secured a thrilling last-ball victory at Trent Bridge to push themselves into the Division Two promotion zone. Francis and Dimitri Mascarenhas saw them home, just, after being left to score 16 from the final two overs and seven from the last. Earlier, Simon Katich had made 67 from 73 balls while both Derek Kenway and John Crawley hit assured 50s. That Hampshire faced a challenging total was largely down to Russell Warren, who scored 91 off 112 balls, and Kevin Pietersen (58), although Chris Read provided late impetus to the home side's innings with a jaunty unbeaten 38 from just 20 deliveries.

22 July 2003: Division Two

at Hove
Sussex 169 for 9 (45 overs)
Durham 161 (44 overs) (GJ Muchall 58)
Sussex (4pts) won by 8 runs

From the depths of 26 for 5, 20-year-old Gordon Muchall fashioned a Durham recovery that failed by just eight runs to match Sussex's 169 for 9 in a low-scoring affair under the Hove lights. It was rough on Muchall, who had been run out for 58 with just 15 runs needed for victory when Matthew Prior produced a direct hit from cover. A quick-fire 32 from 34 balls by Phil Mustard had also boosted the Durham cause, but eventually Neil Killeen missed a full toss from Billy Taylor and was lbw for ten with nine needed from seven deliveries. Sussex earlier had Mark Davis and Paul Hutchison to thank for rallying them from 126 for 8, although it was also unfortunate for Durham at this stage that Shoaib Akhtar, their strike bowler, had to go off with ankle trouble after injuring it in his delivery stride.

23 July 2003: Division Two

at Derby
Derbyshire 244 for 9 (42 overs) (MJ Di Venuto 76, PJ Franks 4 for 12)
Nottinghamshire 245 for 5 (41 overs) (CL Cairns 66*)
Nottinghamshire (4pts) won by 5 wickets

At 135 for 5, with 109 runs still required from the last 12 overs, Nottinghamshire were in dire need of inspiration as they tried to overhaul Derbyshire's 244 for 9 in a 42-over contest at Derby. They got it, in the shape of Chris Cairns, whose unbeaten 66 was supported by a perky 39 not out from Chris Read. Cairns' 50 took him just 28 balls, and the hail of fours and sixes was so intense that, in the end, Notts got home with a full over to spare. Derbyshire had been granted nine wides before the fourth legitimate

ball had been delivered, as Richard Logan suffered a nightmare first over, and Michael Di Venuto (76) also raced to his half-century from 36 balls. At 187 for 2, with 51 balls remaining, Derbyshire should have totalled far more. In the end, it was that failure as much as anything which cost them dear.

27 July 2003: Division One

at Guildford
Worcestershire 219 for 6 (45 overs) (BF Smith 93*)
Surrey 140 (37.1 overs) (MS Mason 4 for 34, Kabir Ali 4 for 30)
Worcestershire (4pts) won by 79 runs

at Cheltenham
Glamorgan 197 (37.2 overs)
Gloucestershire 199 for 3 (36.5 overs) (MGN Windows 54*)
Gloucestershire (4pts) won by 7 wickets

at Southend
Essex 203 for 6 (45 overs) (WI Jefferson 61)
Leicestershire 166 (42.2 overs)
Essex (4pts) won by 37 runs

at Scarborough
Yorkshire 197 for 8 (45 overs)
Kent 179 (43.5 overs) (VJ Craven 4 for 22)
Yorkshire (4pts) won by 18 runs

A below-strength Surrey batting line-up was exposed at Guildford by Kabir Ali, who took four wickets in his seven-over new-ball spell to put Worcestershire on the road to an eventual victory by 79 runs. An excellent unbeaten 93 from Ben Smith had anchored Worcestershire's 219 for 6, but any interval talk about this total not being enough on a usually fast-scoring ground was soon cut short by Kabir's burst. What is more, Matt Mason then replaced him to take the next four wickets at similarly low cost – and only some unscientific hitting by Saqlain Mushtaq then delayed the end.

Gloucestershire took advantage of Surrey's demise to go back on top of Division One with an emphatic seven-wicket win against Glamorgan before a big festival crowd at Cheltenham. In a match cut to 38 overs per side, the Gloucestershire bowling and fielding was top-class as the visitors were dismissed for a below-par 197. A cultured 49 from Alex Gidman, full of crisp drives, and a punchy unbeaten 54 from Matt Windows then capped a consistent batting performance and a thoroughly satisfying day for the home county.

Vibrant fielding was also behind Essex's 37-run win over Leicestershire at Southend. Three run outs helped them to close out the visitors as they defended a modest total of 203 for 6 with great spirit. A late, unbeaten 32 from 18-year-old Ravinder Bopara also caught the eye.

There was some curious Scarborough fare on offer in the sunshine at North Marine Road, where a 50-yard boundary on one side could not offset the difficulties of a seaming pitch. In a low-scoring affair, enlivened only when Tim Bresnan and Chris Silverwood were hitting out lustily at the end of the Yorkshire innings, Kent seemed in control of the game for long periods before losing their way against the gentle medium pace of Vic Craven, who finished with 4 for 22. Muttiah Muralitharan took 2 for 25 from nine overs on his Kent debut.

Division Two

at Northampton
Northamptonshire 234 for 8 (45 overs) (TW Roberts 64, DJG Sales 56)
Middlesex 238 for 5 (43.4 overs) (OA Shah 83*)
Middlesex (4pts) won by 5 wickets

Middlesex beat leaders Northamptonshire for the first time in ten meetings to push themselves into the Division Two promotion race. Tim Roberts hit 64 from 80 balls to give Northants a flowing start, and David Sales' 65-ball 56 was another major contribution to their eventual total of 234 for 8. But Owais Shah, dropped at long off by Ben Phillips when he was on 35, surged on to 83 not out from 86 balls to guide Middlesex to their target. Shah hit two sixes and six fours and his last 48 runs took him just 27 deliveries as he flourished in an unbroken sixth-wicket stand of 81 in nine overs with Ben Hutton.

28 July 2003: Division Two

at Old Trafford
Lancashire 129 for 8 (20 overs)
Somerset Did not bat
No result. Lancashire (2pts) Somerset (2pts)
Match abandoned as a draw – rain

Continued squalls of rain finally put pay to Lancashire's home match with Somerset at Old Trafford, although the two points the home side took from the no result enabled them to pull alongside Northants at the head of the Division Two table.

Dimitri Mascarenhas took 4 for 22 as Hampshire breezed past Northants at Southampton.

29 July 2003: Division One

at Worcester
Worcestershire 117 for 5 (18 overs)
Glamorgan 122 for 7 (18 overs)
Worcestershire (4pts) won by 3 runs – DL Method: target 126 from 18 overs

Alex Wharf failed to hit David Leatherdale for four

from the final ball, leaving Worcestershire the winners over Glamorgan by three runs in a New Road contest trimmed to 18 overs per side after rain delayed the start until 7.15pm. Glamorgan, in fact, needed just 18 runs from three overs, but Leatherdale's penultimate over allowed just three runs. Ten were then required from that last over, but again Leatherdale proved too canny for the visiting tail. Unhappily, too, for Glamorgan, who would have gone top of the division if they had won, an unpleasant injury to Adrian Dale in the penultimate over may have cost them the match. Dale had made 16 from as many balls when he top-edged a short ball from Kabir Ali into his right eye. The ball squeezed between the grille and lid of his batting helmet, and he was forced to retire hurt with a nasty gash. In such a tight affair, the six which Ben Smith lifted off Owen Parkin from the final ball of the Worcestershire innings also proved to be vital in the shake-up.

30 July 2003: Division Two

at Southampton
Hampshire 216 for 8 (45 overs) (DA Kenway 78, MJ Cawdron 4 for 52)
Northamptonshire 162 (42.5 overs) (DJG Sales 73, SD Udal 4 for 40, AD Mascarenhas 4 for 22)
Hampshire (4pts) won by 54 runs

A crowd of more than 6,000 turned up for the floodlit fixture between Hampshire and leaders Northamptonshire at the Rose Bowl, and the home fans saw Dimitri Mascarenhas produce the decisive performance of the match. Mascarenhas wrecked the Northants top order with an outstanding new-ball spell of 9–3–22–4, and at 50 for 5 the visitors were out of the running to overhaul Hampshire's 216 for 8. David Sales did hit a defiant 73, but Shaun Udal's off spin wrapped up the Northants tail.

3 August 2003: Division One

at Cheltenham
Yorkshire 183 (41.5 overs) (JMM Averis 4 for 50)
Gloucestershire 184 for 2 (32.4 overs) (CM Spearman 93*, WPC Weston 62)
Gloucestershire (4pts) won by 8 wickets

at Canterbury
Kent 254 for 9 (45 overs) (MA Ealham 73, GO Jones 58)
Essex 254 for 9 (45 overs) (A Flower 100, WI Jefferson 58, MJ Saggers 4 for 36)
Match tied – Kent (2pts), Essex (2pts)

at Leicester
Leicestershire 172 (45 overs) (PA Nixon 51, Waqar Younis 4 for 37)
Warwickshire 173 for 6 (41.5 overs) (NV Knight 50)
Warwickshire (4pts) won by 4 wickets

With a familiar brand of intimidatory out-cricket, Gloucestershire overwhelmed Yorkshire by bowling them out for 183 and then breezing to victory by eight wickets at Cheltenham. The visitors even made it as far as 62 without loss before Gloucestershire began to undermine their innings and chip away constantly at their self-confidence. Then, after an opening stand of 143, the effervescent Craig Spearman – along with Phil Weston – sped away to an unbeaten 93 to strengthen Gloucestershire's position at the top of the National League. Weston made a fine 62 off 72 balls, while Spearman's six and 15 fours helped to take his season's league aggregate to 570 runs at an average of 70.

Mohammad Akram almost pulled off a sensational win for Essex against Kent at Canterbury, where he needed to hit Muttiah Muralitharan for six from the final ball. He hit it hard and high for four instead to clinch a thrilling tie, but the ball landed just yards short of the boundary rope. It was a memorable end to a fine day's cricket, in which Kent's 254 for 9 was built around a stand of 127 in 117 balls between Geraint Jones (58) and Mark Ealham (73), and Essex's challenge was launched by Andy Flower's 86-ball 100 and a 132-run opening partnership with Will Jefferson. With 32 runs required from the last three overs, however, and with Muralitharan ready to bowl two of them, it was a time for more heroics. Aftab Habib, Graham Napier and especially last man Akram, who also reverse swept Murali for four earlier in that dramatic final over, provided them. Essex, remarkably, had also totalled 254 for 9.

Leicestershire never recovered from being reduced to 23 for 3 by Waqar Younis and Neil Carter, and Warwickshire eventually eased to a four-wicket victory at Grace Road with 19 balls in hand, despite a mid-innings wobble. Paul Nixon battled to 51 in a bid to lead a Leicestershire recovery, but a second-wicket partnership of 81 between Nick Knight and Ian Bell set the visitors up for a successful chase.

Division Two

at Derby
Derbyshire 259 for 8 (45 overs) (MJ Di Venuto 106, TF Bloomfield 4 for 25)

Middlesex 260 for 6 (44 overs) (OA Shah 66,
AJ Strauss 57, PN Weekes 54)
Middlesex (4pts) won by 4 wickets

at Chester-le-Street
Durham 187 (44.2 overs)
Somerset 189 for 6 (39 overs) (ID Blackwell 79*,
Shoaib Akhtar 5 for 35)
Somerset (4pts) won by 4 wickets

at Cleethorpes
Lancashire 210 for 9 (45 overs) (CL Hooper 71)
Nottinghamshire 185 (42.2 overs) (KP Pietersen 54,
U Afzaal 51)
Lancashire (4pts) won by 25 runs

at Hove
Sussex 270 for 4 (45 overs) (MW Goodwin 106,
CJ Adams 95*)
Scotland 272 for 4 (43.3 overs) (JC Kent 115*, R Dravid 69)
Scotland (4pts) won by 6 wickets

Michael Di Venuto scored 48 of his first 53 runs in boundaries, on his way to a maiden one-day league hundred, but he still finished up on the losing side at Derby as Middlesex produced a far more even team batting performance. A Derbyshire total of 259 for 8 was challenging, but Middlesex openers Paul Weekes and Andy Strauss both topped 50 before Owais Shah and David Nash saw the visitors to within six runs of victory with a fifth-wicket stand of 82 in 13 overs.

The rapid yorkers of Shoaib Akhtar brought him fine figures of 5 for 35 on a slow Chester-le-Street pitch, but the Pakistani paceman could not rid Durham of Ian Blackwell. In the end, with 79 not out, Blackwell proved the difference between the two sides as he guided Somerset to a four-wicket win. There were three sixes for Blackwell, whose power enabled him to pull off shots out of the range of everyone else on view.

Nottinghamshire's return to the Chichester Road ground at Cleethorpes, after a four-year absence, drew a 3,000 crowd but ended up in the disappointment of a narrow Lancashire win, by 25 runs. Notts faltered badly in pursuit of the visitors' 210 for 9, after Kevin Pietersen's 46-ball 54 had put them ahead of the clock. Pietersen was then run out by a direct hit from Chris Schofield at backward point, and Usman Afzaal then began to run out of partners as he attempted to play the anchor role. Earlier, Carl Hooper had struck three sixes in his 106-ball 71, while Stuart Law (47 from 45 balls) and

Glen Chapple, with a late 36-ball 37, had boosted the Lancashire total.

Jon Kent, a South African with aspirations to play full-time county cricket, put himself in the shop window with a brilliant unbeaten 115 from 113 balls as the Scottish Saltires shocked Sussex at Hove. Kent struck a six over the short legside boundary, plus 13 fours, and lost little in comparison to the immaculate Rahul Dravid (69) in a match-winning, fourth-wicket stand of 167 in 29 overs. The Scots, in fact, still had nine balls in hand when they sailed past the Sussex total of 270 for 4. Murray Goodwin hit his third century in four National League innings and Chris Adams pounded a six and 12 fours in an 83-ball 95 not out.

4 August 2003: Division Two

at Southampton
Scotland 225 for 5 (45 overs) (R Dravid 81, JC Kent 78*)
Hampshire 226 for 3 (44 overs) (JP Crawley 83*,
JD Francis 62*)
Hampshire (4pts) won by 7 wickets

at Old Trafford
Derbyshire 197 (43.4 overs) (M Kaif 70)
Lancashire 199 for 2 (35.3 overs) (CL Hooper 79*,
MB Loye 62*)
Lancashire (4pts) won by 8 wickets

Hampshire moved into second place in Division Two, but they were pushed all the way by a brave performance from the Scottish Saltires at the Rose Bowl. When Rahul Dravid and Jon Kent were adding 103 in 18 overs for the fourth wicket, a total of around 250 looked possible, but after the Indian's dismissal for 81 in the 36th over the scoring rate dropped and, although Kent finished on 78 not out, the Scots had to be content with 225 for 5. Three wickets for Craig Wright, in a disciplined spell of medium-pace bowling, held Hampshire back for a while, and at 100 for 3 in the 23rd over there was still much work to be done. John Crawley, however, played with great skill in a superbly paced 83 not out while John Francis produced some eye-catching drives in an unbeaten 62. Their eventual unbroken stand of 126 was enough to bring victory with an over to spare.

Mohammad Kaif and Michael Di Venuto apart, there is a frail look to the Derbyshire batting line-up, and so it proved at Old Trafford as the visitors were bowled out for 197 – with Kaif making 70 and Di Venuto 40. Derbyshire fell away alarmingly from 157 for 4, with Carl Hooper picking up three

The power of 'The Lord': Alistair Brown lives up to his dressing–room nickname once again with some serious strokeplay at The Oval.

wickets with his off spin, and the West Indian was later in commanding form with the bat as he finished on 79 not out. Entering the fray at 93 for 2, Hooper dominated an unbroken stand of 106 with Mal Loye that took Lancashire to their target and also stretched their lead at the top of the division.

5 August 2003: Division One

at Chelmsford
Essex 298 for 5 (45 overs) (N Hussain 161*, A Flower 57, DA Cosker 5 for 54)
Glamorgan 153 (26.1 overs) (MP Maynard 50, GR Napier 4 for 26)
Essex (4pts) won by 145 runs

at The Oval
Surrey 297 for 6 (45 overs) (AD Brown 84, MR Ramprakash 83)
Gloucestershire 231 (40 overs) (CM Spearman 85)
Surrey (4pts) won by 66 runs

Nasser Hussain, a last-minute addition to the Essex line-up, demolished Glamorgan at Chelmsford with a

limited-overs career-best score of 161 not out from 147 balls. His previous best was the 144 not out he scored against the Welsh county at Cardiff the previous month, and once again he treated the Glamorgan attack with contempt. Driving and cutting with a casual ease, he struck a six and 21 fours and utterly dominated a magnificent opening partnership of 176 with Andy Flower, who made 57. Only when Jon Dakin appeared at No. 7 to smash an unbeaten 40 at the death did Hussain accept the role of second fiddle. The defending National League champions then saw their reply under lights fade out as early as the 16th over when Graham Napier's third wicket in ten balls left Glamorgan reeling at 94 for 5.

Surrey struck a significant blow, in the context of the destination of the league title, when they overpowered Gloucestershire by 66 runs at The Oval. Alistair Brown, so often the man for the big occasion, fuelled Surrey's drive to an intimidating score of 297 for 6 by hammering 84 from 61 balls at the top of the innings, with three sixes and 12 fours. Mark Ramprakash accelerated on to 83 once Brown had departed, while both Graham Thorpe and Rikki

Clarke hit out profitably. Craig Spearman immediately took up the challenge for Gloucestershire, scoring 85 off 73 balls with three sixes and ten fours, but three run outs in the space of four overs undermined the chase. Clarke scored two brilliant direct hits to send back Alex Gidman and Matt Windows, while Shoaib Malik was beaten by Thorpe's accurate throw. There were two more run outs later on as well, claiming Tim Hancock and Martyn Ball, as Gloucestershire fell away to 231 all out.

Division Two

at Chester-le-Street
Durham 199 (43.1 overs)
Nottinghamshire 203 for 6 (38.3 overs) (KP Pietersen 72)
Nottinghamshire (4pts) won by 4 wickets

at Taunton
Somerset 283 for 8 (45 overs) (J Cox 130,
TF Bloomfield 4 for 58)
Middlesex 216 (39.1 overs) (EC Joyce 59)
Somerset (4pts) won by 67 runs

at Hove
Hampshire 250 for 6 (45 overs) (SM Katich 57,
JP Crawley 55, JRC Hamblin 53)
Sussex 181 (35.3 overs) (AD Mascarenhas 4 for 24)
*Hampshire (4pts) won by 62 runs – DL Method: target
244 from 41 overs*

A thrilling duel between Kevin Pietersen and Shoaib Akhtar provided the highlight of Nottinghamshire's eventual four-wicket win at Durham. Pietersen fell to Shoaib for 72, but not before he had led Notts out of the mire of 56 for 5. Durham's 199 had not left them with much to defend, but when Pietersen was joined by Chris Read the home side were in control. Not for long. Pietersen, after a cautious start, signalled his intentions by plundering 24 from the first over bowled by Graeme Bridge, the slow left-armer. A two was followed by a brace of languidly struck straight sixes. Then came a four to midwicket and, finally, a massive swung six to the same area which made Pietersen the first man to clear Chester-le-Street's lofty pavilion roof. Shoaib was now summoned back into the attack, but although he succeeded in having Pietersen well held at backward point, a platform had been established for Read, with 46 not out, and Paul Franks, with an unbeaten 31, to coast to victory with an unbroken stand of 88.

Jamie Cox scored 130 off 120 balls, with two sixes and 14 fours, to show that he at least had been inspired by the motivational talk given to the entire Somerset squad by Ian Botham, their great former all-rounder. To be fair to his team-mates, though, this was a much-improved team performance as Middlesex were defeated by 67 runs in front of an appreciative audience at Taunton. Cox received solid support all the way down the order, and every Somerset bowler contributed to Middlesex's dismissal for 216.

One of the hottest days of the year still led to the Duckworth-Lewis system being invoked at Hove. A sudden sea fret? No, this delightfully English quirk of the season was because of a sudden failure of four of the ground's eight dedicated floodlights. Play was suspended at 8.10pm and, although power was soon restored, Sussex's target in reply to Hampshire's 250 for 6 came down to 244 from 41 overs. Not that it did them one bit of good, as Sussex had by then already lost four wickets inside the first nine overs for just 19. Dimitri Mascarenhas was again in blistering form with the new ball, taking 4 for 24 as the Sussex slump became 37 for 5. A perky lower-order effort then limited the damage, but Hampshire were good value for the win that maintained their promotion push. John Crawley's 55 earlier was his fifth half-century in seven league innings, while James Hamblin and Simon Katich also passed 50 as the visitors posted 108 for the first wicket.

6 August 2003: Division One

at Headingley
Warwickshire 273 for 6 (45 overs) (NV Knight 95,
JO Troughton 77)
Yorkshire 274 for 3 (38.2 overs) (SP Fleming 139*,
MJ Wood 65)
Yorkshire (4pts) won by 7 wickets

Yorkshire's emphatic seven-wicket win over Warwickshire at Headingley, only their third of the season, included a cameo appearance from Michael Vaughan, the new England captain. Vaughan bowled five overs for 32 in Warwickshire's well-constructed 273 for 6, in which both Nick Knight (95) and Jim Troughton (77) impressed during a stand of 97, and then emerged to score a brisk 22 after watching Stephen Fleming and Matthew Wood put on a dazzling first-wicket partnership of 167 in only 21 overs. Wood pulled and cut with great power in his 63-ball 65, but it was New Zealand captain Fleming who stole the show with a

Jamie Cox, the key batsman in Somerset's line-up, was out of luck against Hampshire at Taunton.

breathtaking unbeaten 139. He reached his first hundred for Yorkshire from a mere 76 balls, and hit four sixes and 18 fours overall.

Division Two

at Northampton
Northamptonshire 319 for 7 (45 overs) (MEK Hussey 123, PA Jaques 76, DJG Sales 53)
Scotland 244 (43.4 overs) (R Dravid 114)
Northamptonshire (4pts) won by 75 runs

The Scottish Saltires were given the runaround in blistering conditions at Northampton, where Mike Hussey spearheaded a gallop to 319 for 7 – the highest total the Scots had conceded in the league. Hussey's 123 took him just 115 balls, and both Phil Jaques (76 from 77 balls) and David Sales (53) joined in the fun. Rahul Dravid did his best to make a game of it, reaching his third league century from just 90 balls and going on to 114, but he did not receive the sort of support he needed.

10 August 2003: Division One

at Cardiff
Warwickshire 196 (43.5 overs)
(TL Penney 64*)
Glamorgan 198 for 3 (40.5 overs)
(RDB Croft 70)
Glamorgan (4pts) won by 7 wickets

at Leicester
Essex 212 for 6 (43.3 overs)
(A Flower 103)
Leicestershire 90 for 4 (15.4 overs)
Leicestershire (4pts) won by 6 wickets – DL Method: target 89 from 16 overs

Glamorgan revived fast-fading hopes of retaining their title by beating Warwickshire in convincing fashion at Cardiff. Five defeats in the previous six matches had all but cost them their chance of a successful title defence, but with two meetings with Surrey still ahead of them they rightly reasoned that anything was possible. Robert Croft, the Glamorgan captain, read the riot act to his players following the defeat at Essex, and it was Croft who led the charge to overhaul Warwickshire's 196 by racing to a 46-ball 50 and finally scoring 70 from the head of the order. After Croft's innings, it was left to Matthew Maynard and David Hemp to take the home side across the winning line.

Several tropical-like thunderstorms burst over Grace Road and reduced Leicestershire's chase of Essex's 212 for 6 to an eventual Duckworth-Lewis exercise. After the first deluge had prematurely ended the Essex innings, Leicestershire were initially left needing 219 from 43 overs. At 36 without loss, from 7.2 overs, the players were forced again from the field and – after an hour's break – only two more balls were possible before yet another downpour arrived. Eventually, the storms gave way to evening sunshine, and Leicestershire re-emerged requiring another 49 runs from 50 remaining deliveries. In the end, they scrambled home by six wickets, with two balls to spare, but a key moment came when Graham Napier dropped a top-edge from Darren Maddy when 12 runs were still required off ten balls.

Division Two

at Derby
Sussex 160 for 6 (32 overs) (MJ Prior 60*)
Derbyshire 163 for 4 (30.5 overs) (M Kaif 55*)
Derbyshire (4pts) won by 6 wickets – DL Method: target 163 from 32 overs

at Lord's
Middlesex 210 for 8 (45 overs) (EC Joyce 77, SJ Cook 67*, N Killeen 5 for 33)
Durham 203 for 6 (45 overs) (GJ Pratt 63*, TF Bloomfield 4 for 36)
Middlesex (4pts) won by 7 runs

at Taunton
Hampshire 329 for 6 (45 overs) (SM Katich 106, JP Crawley 92, JD Francis 50)
Somerset 219 (36.1 overs)
Hampshire (4pts) won by 116 runs – DL Method: target 336 from 45 overs

Heavy showers also caused three interruptions at Derby, where Sussex were boosted to a 32-over score of 160 for 6 by Matthew Prior's unbeaten 60. Derbyshire, requiring a Duckworth-Lewis adjusted target of 163 from their 32 overs, rallied from 65 for 3 through a decisive partnership of 64 in ten overs between Mohammad Kaif and Dominic Hewson. Kaif was still there on 55 when victory arrived by six wickets.

Middlesex kept their cool on a sweltering day at Lord's to recover from 66 for 6 and then to hold their nerve in the field and earn themselves a seven-run win over Durham. The batting recovery came courtesy of Ed Joyce and Simon Cook, who both made their highest one-day scores in a seventh-wicket partnership of 116. Neil Killeen, taking 5 for

33 in three fine spells, did his best to bowl Durham to victory, but all his efforts proved in vain as Tim Bloomfield produced figures of 4 for 36 to inspire Middlesex. For long periods, however, it seemed that excellent innings from Nicky Peng, Gordon Muchall and Gary Pratt, who ended up unbeaten on 63, would win the day for Durham, but Bloomfield, who had taken two important wickets in his new-ball spell, then returned to claim two more at the death to put the brakes on Durham's march to victory.

Hampshire's batsmen had a wonderful time of it at Taunton, amassing the county's highest total in their one-day league history and – in so doing – setting up the victory which put them on top of Division Two. Simon Katich led the way with a powerful 106, but John Crawley's 64-ball 92 was the most elegant innings of the day and John Francis struck 50 off just 39 balls towards the end. The fall of Jamie Cox in the opening over of the Somerset reply, edging perhaps the only ball of the day that deviated markedly from a magnificent batting surface, was a blow that the home side could not overcome and only Ian Blackwell, with a 24-ball 43, threatened heroics as Hampshire closed efficiently on a 116-run win.

11 August 2003: Division One

at Canterbury
Worcestershire 225 for 8 (45 overs) (VS Solanki 70)
Kent 226 for 2 (36.2 overs) (A Symonds 93*, MA Carberry 79)
Kent (4pts) won by 8 wickets

Spectacular hitting from Michael Carberry and Andrew Symonds rushed Kent to an eight-wicket victory under the Canterbury floodlights against fellow strugglers Worcestershire. The visitors started stylishly, through Vikram Solanki's 85-ball 70, but Kent's trio of off spinners – James Tredwell, Muttiah Muralitharan and Symonds – put an effective brake on the Worcestershire innings until Matt Mason carved the last two balls, from Murali, for six. Carberry, however, took just 42 balls to reach his first league 50 and had scored 79 from 74 deliveries when he carved to point. Symonds, now joined by the industrious Matthew Walker, had already completed his half-century off a mere 38 balls, and he stayed to finish the job with 93 not out – an innings which included three huge legside sixes off Kabir Ali, Justin Kemp and Solanki.

12 August 2003: Division Two

at Northampton
Somerset 202 for 9 (45 overs)
Northamptonshire 206 for 6 (43.3 overs) (PA Jaques 73, MEK Hussey 53)
Northamptonshire (4pts) won by 4 wickets

Twelve months previously, Northamptonshire had found themselves in prime position to gain promotion from Division Two, but blew it with five defeats in six matches. Their determination not to repeat that experience was evident from the steely way they disposed of Somerset by four wickets at Northampton. At 70 for 1, Somerset were looking on course for a sizeable score, but a superb three-wicket spell of off spin from Jason Brown eventually left them scrambling to get past 200. The Northants chase was then set up by two of the other central figures in the county's 2003 successes: Mike Hussey and Phil Jaques. Hussey (53) was joined in a second-wicket stand of 104 by Jaques, who went on to make an excellent 73.

13 August 2003: Division One

at Edgbaston
Leicestershire 178 (40.4 overs) (BJ Hodge 55)
Warwickshire 182 for 2 (30.5 overs) (NM Carter 75, IR Bell 54*)
Warwickshire (4pts) won by 8 wickets

Neil Carter was a real danger to Leicestershire's health during an emphatic Warwickshire win under lights at Edgbaston. First he clean bowled Phil DeFreitas, who had opened in a bid to do some of the damage that Carter himself was later to inflict with the bat, and then struck Darren Stevens such a nasty blow on the shoulder that he caused him to retire hurt with a fractured collarbone. Only Brad Hodge (55) flourished in a disappointing Leicestershire total of 178, and then Carter came out to club a brutal 75 from just 37 balls – with six sixes and seven fours – to put the result beyond doubt.

Division Two

at Hove
Sussex 112 (32.1 overs) (KW Hogg 4 for 24)
Lancashire 113 for 3 (26.5 overs) (MB Loye 58)
Lancashire (4pts) won by 7 wickets

Championship contenders Sussex remained rock bottom of the National League after taking a severe seven-wicket beating by Lancashire at Hove. Sussex batted appallingly to be dismissed for just 112 on a blameless pitch, with Kyle Hogg the chief beneficiary with 4 for 24. Mal Loye then set about the Sussex bowlers to put the conditions into perspective with a lordly 58 and put Lancashire back on top of the division table.

17 August 2003: Division One

at Whitgift School
Surrey 298 for 5 (45 overs) (MR Ramprakash 101, GP Thorpe 77*)
Glamorgan 240 (39.4 overs) (MJ Powell 60)
Surrey (4pts) won by 58 runs

at Scarborough
Worcestershire 170 (44.5 overs) (BF Smith 56)
Yorkshire 171 for 7 (42 overs) (MJ Wood 60)
Yorkshire (4pts) won by 3 wickets

Class innings from exiled Test pair Mark Ramprakash and Graham Thorpe underpinned a Surrey victory at Whitgift School, strengthening the county's title bid and almost certainly casting off

Kyle Hogg, the young Lancashire seamer who wrecked the Sussex batting at Hove.

Glamorgan's loosening grip on the National League in the process. Ramprakash scored 101 off 93 balls, including three sixes and 11 fours, while Thorpe remained unbeaten on 77 from 72 balls, with two sixes and eight fours. Their third-wicket stand of 120 in 19 overs entranced the home crowd, while Adam Hollioake's late 16-ball 41 (four sixes, two fours) wowed them. Martin Bicknell's early dismissal of Jimmy Maher did not help the Glamorgan cause, but Michael Powell and Matthew Maynard, in particular, kept up a muscular chase until Hollioake's three wickets accelerated their decline to 240 all out, and defeat by 58 runs.

Steve Kirby snatched three early wickets at Scarborough to undermine Worcestershire's decision to bat first. From 43 for 4, they rallied to 170 through Ben Smith's 56 and an undefeated 35 from Yorkshireman Steve Rhodes. Matthew Wood, however, played Yorkshire's anchor role well with 60 and not even some over-the-top aggression from Nantie Hayward, who took three wickets and bowled with great speed, could prevent the home side from progressing steadily to a three-wicket win.

Division Two

at Southampton
Derbyshire 158 for 9 (45 overs) (CT Tremlett 4 for 26)
Hampshire 162 for 4 (35.4 overs)
Hampshire (4pts) won by 6 wickets

at Lord's
Middlesex 300 for 4 (45 overs) (OA Shah 91*, PN Weekes 72, CB Keegan 50)
Nottinghamshire 263 (43.1 overs)
Middlesex (4pts) won by 37 runs

Hampshire secured their tenth league victory in 11 games by overcoming Derbyshire by six wickets in a fine all-round display at Southampton. Dimitri Mascarenhas, perhaps the outstanding new-ball bowler of the season in this competition, stifled the Derbyshire top order by taking 2 for 11 from his nine overs and did not concede a run off the bat until the middle of his sixth over. Chris Tremlett then took four wickets at low cost, and, despite Dominic Cork's 49, a Derbyshire total of 158 for 9 provided Hampshire with a comfortable canter to victory.

Owais Shah revealed once again the high talent that once promised a successful Test career by plundering the Nottinghamshire bowling to the tune of 91 not out from 56 balls at Lord's. There were two sixes and 11 fours in an innings that, following

on from half-centuries by Paul Weekes and Chad Keegan, pushed Middlesex up to 300 for 4. Jamie Dalrymple, who had struck the final ball of the Middlesex innings for six over long off, then teamed up with fellow off spinner Weekes to strangle a Notts reply in which six batsmen were out between the scores of 29 and 38.

19 August 2003: Division Two

at Old Trafford
Middlesex 278 for 4 (45 overs) (AJ Strauss 127, EC Joyce 70)
Lancashire 281 for 3 (43.3 overs) (SG Law 78, IJ Sutcliffe 71, CL Hooper 51*)
Lancashire (4pts) won by 7 wickets

Lancashire made it a third successful floodlit chase in a row when they saw off a sturdy Middlesex challenge at Old Trafford. An animated crowd of 7,500 witnessed a thrilling chase as Iain Sutcliffe, Stuart Law, Carl Hooper and Mark Chilton hunted down a Middlesex total of 278 for 4 that had been built upon a superb 127 from Andrew Strauss – the first one-day century of his career. Ed Joyce hit 70 from 76 balls as he helped Strauss to add 157 in 25 overs for the third wicket, but Sutcliffe and Law, who hit three sixes, kicked off the Lancashire effort with a second-wicket stand of 155 in 24 overs that put the home side ahead of the asking rate. After they both fell to spin, Hooper and Chilton added a further unbroken 92 with some style.

20 August 2003: Division One

at Leicester
Leicestershire 217 for 8 (45 overs) (DL Maddy 66, AJ Hollioake 4 for 35)
Surrey 218 for 3 (28.2 overs) (AD Brown 89, IJ Ward 70*)
Surrey (4pts) won by 7 wickets

Dropping Alistair Brown on one, as Darren Maddy did at first slip early in the Surrey reply to Leicestershire's 217 for 8 at Grace Road, must rank as one of the daftest things to do in a one-day context. Sadly for Maddy, his error had predictably dire consequences as hurricane-force Brown struck two sixes and 14 fours in a 66-ball 89 that settled the match. The fact that Maddy had worked so hard earlier to bolster the Leicestershire innings, with a gutsy 66, only added to his misery. With Ian Ward anchoring the Surrey reply with an unbeaten 70, victory soon arrived with 16.4 overs to spare as

Michael Di Venuto won the battle of the Aussie left-handers at Derby, where his 130 trumped Mike Hussey's earlier 103.

Adam Hollioake added a pair of big sixes to his four wickets.

24 August 2003: Division One

at Colwyn Bay
Glamorgan 238 for 8 (45 overs) (MJ Powell 61, JP Maher 53)
Yorkshire 237 (45 overs) (MJ Lumb 92, DA Cosker 4 for 37)
Glamorgan (4pts) won by one run

at Edgbaston
Kent 212 (44.5 overs) (MJ Walker 72, Waqar Younis 4 for 20)
Warwickshire 213 for 6 (42.2 overs) (MA Wagh 66)
Warwickshire (4pts) won 4 wickets

at Worcester
Worcestershire 146 (44.2 overs) (JM Kemp 50, MW Alleyne 4 for 26)
Gloucestershire 148 for 6 (40.5 overs) (APR Gidman 67*)
Gloucestershire (4pts) won by 4 wickets

Darren Gough made a dramatic return to county cricket, following his decision to retire from Tests, but even his best efforts could not prevent Yorkshire from experiencing the frustration of a one-run defeat against Glamorgan at Colwyn Bay. Gough first impressed with the ball by taking 2 for 30 from his nine overs as the home side reached 238 for 8 on the back of excellent half-centuries from Jimmy Maher and Michael Powell. Then, coming in to bat with Yorkshire slipping out of contention at 150 for 7, he played the supporting role well as Michael Lumb took 37 from Robert Croft's last three overs and then set about Dean Cosker by sweeping the slow left-armer for a six and a four. On 92, however, Lumb top-edged a catch and left Gough in charge with 30 required from four overs, with two wickets remaining. It all boiled down to last man Matthew Hoggard needing two runs for victory, and one to tie, from the final ball. Hoggard, who had earlier bowled well in his first match since May, drove Michael Kasprowicz's delivery hard into the ground. Gough, at the non-striker's end after scoring 24 from 27 balls, had already set off, but Kasprowicz leapt into the air to grab the bouncing ball and threw down the stumps at the batsman's end.

A lacklustre performance by Kent condemned them to a four-wicket defeat to Warwickshire at Edgbaston, although the visitors were not helped by losing the toss and being forced to bat first on a pitch containing early moisture. Matthew Walker, Geraint Jones and Mark Ealham fashioned a reasonable recovery from 53 for 4, but then sloppy fielding let down Kent in the field as Mark Wagh played a match-winning innings of 66 from 87 balls. Perhaps the key partnership for Warwickshire was the 64 in 12 overs added by Wagh and Ian Bell, in which the two young Englishmen played Muttiah Muralitharan with confidence until Bell, on 30, overdid a sweep shot.

Alex Gidman struck the hardest psychological blow at Worcester, in a dress rehearsal for the following weekend's Cheltenham & Gloucester Trophy final. Gidman's assured unbeaten 67, the highest score of a low-scoring affair on a seaming surface, took Gloucestershire to a four-wicket win over a Worcestershire side missing the thrust of Andrew Hall and Kabir Ali. Mark Alleyne's 4 for 26 included a double-wicket maiden.

Division Two

at Derby
Northamptonshire 251 for 5 (45 overs) (MEK Hussey 103, MJ Powell 70)
Derbyshire 254 for 7 (43 overs) (MJ Di Venuto 130)
Derbyshire (4pts) won by 3 wickets

at Chester le Street
Hampshire 131 (39.5 overs) (GD Bridge 4 for 20)
Durham 132 for 3 (25.3 overs) (N Peng 56*)
Durham (4pts) won by 7 wickets

at Trent Bridge
Nottinghamshire 292 for 5 (45 overs) (CL Cairns 91*, CMW Read 79*, RSC Martin–Jenkins 4 for 50)

Sussex 221 (44.3 overs)
Nottinghamshire (4pts) won by 71 runs

Michael Di Venuto trumped the earlier century of his fellow left-handed Australian opener Mike Hussey with a brilliant 130 to set up a three-wicket Derbyshire win against Northamptonshire at Derby. Hussey's 103 off 130 balls, supported by Mark Powell's one-day best of 70, left Derbyshire to chase 252. That they achieved their target was almost entirely down to Tasmanian Di Venuto, who reached his hundred in only 70 balls and went on to his competition-best score before finally falling with the victory line in sight.

Hampshire endured possibly their worst performance of the league summer to plunge to a seven-wicket defeat in little more than 65 overs' worth of 'action' at Chester-le-Street. Not that Durham were complaining after halting an unwanted run of five successive defeats by dismissing Hampshire for 131. Nicky Peng, with 56 not out, and Paul Collingwood (48) then made short work of knocking off the runs, but most of the credit for Durham went to Steve Harmison and Liam Plunkett for wrecking the Hampshire top order with pace and movement. Graeme Bridge, the left-arm spinner, then weighed in with four wickets to clean up the tail.

The 35-year-old one-day league gained a new sixth-wicket partnership record at Trent Bridge, where Chris Cairns and Chris Read added an unbroken 167 from just 20 overs to take Nottinghamshire to a match-winning total of 292 for 5 against Sussex. The visitors barely raised a challenge with the bat after suffering in the field as Cairns, with five sixes and four fours in his 72-ball unbeaten 91, and Read, who struck 79 not out from 73 balls, cut loose.

26 August 2003: Division Two

at The Grange
Scotland 119 (40.2 overs)
Northamptonshire 123 for 2 (21.5 overs)
Northamptonshire (4pts) won by 8 wickets

at Chester-le-Street
Sussex 137 (38.5 overs) (SJ Harmison 4 for 43)
Durham 141 for 6 (36.2 overs)
Durham (4pts) won by 4 wickets

Northamptonshire revived their promotion challenge by thrashing the Scottish Saltires for the second time during the course of the season. The county's convincing eight-wicket win in Edinburgh, set up by a fine all-round performance in the field which left the Scots all out for just 119, pushed them four points ahead of fourth-placed Middlesex.

Paul Collingwood impressed under the Chester-le-Street lights to hit the 45 which kept Durham on course for an eventual four-wicket victory over Sussex. In a low-scoring affair on a tricky pitch, Collingwood's confident strokeplay stood out, as did a fierce four-wicket display from Steve Harmison, who confirmed his return to fitness after being sidelined from the Headingley Test.

27 August 2003: Division One

at Bristol
Kent 251 for 7 (45 overs) (MJ Walker 101, ET Smith 59, IJ Harvey 4 for 55)
Gloucestershire 215 (43 overs)
(M Muralitharan 5 for 34)
Kent (4pts) won by 36 runs

Surrey were left as clear title favourites after Gloucestershire, their only realistic challengers, were humbled by Kent at Bristol. The eventual margin of victory was 36 runs, but, in truth, Kent always looked in control under the floodlights once Gloucestershire had uncharacteristically let them get away when they were in the field. At 20 for 2, David Fulton's decision to bat first looked shaky, especially with the ball wobbling around, but Ed Smith and Matthew Walker gradually gained the upper hand in a third-wicket stand that altered the flow of the match. They added 152 in 30 overs, accelerating rapidly towards the end of their alliance, with Smith scoring 59 and Walker an impressive 101. No Gloucestershire batsman approached their level of achievement, while Kent always had Muttiah Muralitharan up their sleeves to prevent any late break-out. The Sri Lankan maestro gleefully worked his way through the middle and lower order to finish with figures of 5 for 34.

Kent's Matthew Walker kept up his impressive one-day league form with a fine 101 against Gloucestershire at Bristol.

28 August 2003: Division One

at Colchester
Worcestershire 141 for 3 (25 overs)
Essex 86 for 8 (9.5 overs)
Essex (4pts) won by 2 wickets – DL Method: target 83 from 10 overs

A bad groin injury to Darren Robinson brought into question the wisdom of restarting a floodlit match between Essex and Worcestershire that was bedevilled by rain at Colchester. Play was initially stopped after an hour, and the outfield was still extremely wet from the heavy rainfall when the match resumed at 8pm with Worcestershire's innings now due to run for a further 8.1 overs in a

contest reduced to 25 overs per side. Robinson, slipping as he threw the ball in from the deep on the run, needed medical attention for fully ten minutes before being lifted from the turf on a stretcher and carried off to hospital with his legs strapped together. Another thundery shower at 9pm then brought a further delay, after Essex had scored just six without loss from 1.2 overs as they set off in pursuit of an original 173 off 25. Again, however, the decision was made to restart the game in sopping conditions at 9.50pm, with Essex now requiring 83 from a total of ten overs. Both sides, of course, were desperate for a win as they attempted to pull away from the relegtion zone – but Worcestershire were also appearing in the Cheltenham & Gloucester Trophy final in less than 48 hours, which meant their players were taking a big risk of injury. As it was, no further fielders suffered an accident as Essex almost made a mess of the seemingly simple task of scoring 22 from the final four overs of their amended allocation with five wickets in hand. With just one ball left, and with three-quarters of an initially healthy crowd long gone for the night, Andy Clarke (effectively the last man with Robinson in hospital) cut his first ball from Gareth Batty for four. The time? 10.40pm.

Division Two

at The Grange
Scotland 191 for 9 (39 overs)
(PM Hutchison 4 for 29)
Sussex 173 for 9 (31 overs) (CD Hopkinson 67*)
Sussex (4pts) won by one wicket – DL Method: target 170 from 31 overs

Carl Hopkinson, a 21-year-old all-rounder, took 3 for 19 and then hit a nerveless unbeaten 67 to guide Sussex to the one-wicket win against Scotland in Edinburgh which raised hopes that they could avoid finishing with the league's wooden spoon. It was a real personal triumph for a youngster trying to make his way in the game, and snatching this chance to perform in the absence of many of Sussex's more established stars, who were resting up in preparation for the final push for glory in the county championship. The Saltires, at 105 for 1 with all their middle-order big guns still to come, looked set for a sizeable total, but Hopkinson removed both Ryan Watson (48) and Colin Smith (38) before trapping the dangerous Jon Kent lbw. Mark Davis, the Sussex acting captain, then caught Rahul Dravid off his own bowling, for just one, and, in the end, the Scots could only reach 191 for 9 in an innings

cut to 39 overs because of a sharp shower. Another burst of rain during the tea interval left Sussex to score 170 from 31 overs, under the Duckworth-Lewis regulations, and at 69 for 6 they were in deep trouble. Hopkinson, though, was still there and, despite losing Paul Hutchison in a final over which began with only two more runs required, he was finally given the strike by Billy Taylor (after three dot balls) and proceeded to stroke Watson's last ball of the match to the boundary.

31 August 2003: Division One

at Headingley
Surrey 202 (44.2 overs) (AD Brown 50, A McGrath 4 for 41)
Yorkshire 200 for 8 (45 overs) (MP Vaughan 90)
Surrey (4pts) won by 2 runs

Michael Vaughan was badly let down by the Yorkshire tail as Surrey took a giant stride towards the league title with a remarkable two-run victory at Headingley. This match was a rarity for the two counties in that they were both almost at full-strength – and Yorkshire should have won it after Vaughan's high-class 90 took them to the brink of victory. The England captain was run out attempting a second to midwicket from the first ball of the penultimate over, but at that stage – with just five more runs needed from 11 balls – it did not look as though Vaughan's failure to beat Ian Ward's throw would have serious consequences. But Rikki Clarke then bowled Richard Dawson and did not concede another run for the remainder of the over. In fading light, Azhar Mahmood then bowled Richard Blakey and just one single had been scored from the preceding ten deliveries when Darren Gough faced the final ball of the match suddenly needing to hit it for four. He managed only a single, and Vaughan's 120-run fifth-wicket stand with Vic Craven had all been for nothing. Earlier a 49-ball 50 from Alistair Brown and an unbeaten 46 from Clarke had held Surrey's innings together and had ensured that Surrey at least had some sort of total to defend.

Division Two

at Derby
Durham 216 for 7 (45 overs) (PD Collingwood 54)
Derbyshire 205 (44.1 overs) (MJ Di Venuto 63, CWG Bassano 51, GD Bridge 4 for 39)
Durham (4pts) won by 11 runs.
at Trent Bridge

Northamptonshire 296 for 5 (45 overs) (TW Roberts 131, MEK Hussey 59)
Nottinghamshire 84 (21 overs)
Northamptonshire (4pts) won by 212 runs

Durham won a close encounter with Derbyshire at Derby by 11 runs, with Graeme Bridge's 4 for 39 undermining the home side when they looked on course for victory. Durham's 216 for 7 was based on a solid top-order effort which included a half-century from Paul Collingwood, but Derbyshire were well placed at 113 for 1 after a 97-run second-wicket stand between Michael Di Venuto and Chris Bassano. However, then Bridge had Di Venuto stumped and also clean bowled Chris Harris, Rawait Khan and Luke Sutton. With Bassano falling to Steve Harmison, it was left to Steve Stubbings (45) and the tail to take Derbyshire close, but they came up short.

Tim Roberts hit a breathtaking 131 from 112 balls, his first limited-overs century, as Northamptonshire routed a sorry Nottinghamshire by 212 runs at Trent Bridge. At one stage, when Notts were 18 for 6 in reply to Northants' 296 for 5, it seemed as if Glamorgan's unwanted record 220-run hammering by Somerset at Neath in 1990 was in severe danger of being 'bettered'. It was not to be, however, as Samit Patel, missed at second slip when he was on ten, went on to marshal the tail with 33 not out and raised Notts' total to the comparative riches of 84 all out. It was still a sad day for Notts, however, near the end of a wretched season, with Andre Nel and Carl Greenidge

doing all the damage with the new ball by taking three wickets apiece. Roberts, 25, completely overshadowed his prolific captain Mike Hussey in an opening stand worth 172, and he reached both his 50 and his century with sixes.

1 September 2003: Division One

at Edgbaston
Gloucestershire 246 for 6 (45 overs) (APR Gidman 73)
Warwickshire 244 for 7 (45 overs) (TL Penney 88*)
Gloucestershire (4pts) won by 2 runs

Two days after being crowned as Cheltenham & Gloucester Trophy winners, Gloucestershire were given the fright of their lives by Warwickshire's Trevor Penney at Edgbaston. Resuscitating an innings which had declined to 98 for 5 soon after he had come in at No. 6, Penney hit 88 not out from 92 balls to take Warwickshire to the very brink of overhauling Gloucestershire's 246 for 6. Dougie Brown was his partner in a stand worth 99 in 17 overs for the sixth wicket, but after Keith Piper was bowled, Penney soon found himself and new partner Waqar Younis needing to score 39 more from the final two overs of the match. Amazingly, after a whirl of boundaries, Penney faced up to Mark Alleyne's last ball needing just four to win. Agonizingly for Penney, a clever paddle off his pads then went straight to short fine leg, when five yards either side would have meant a glorious winning hit. For Gloucestershire, the increasingly impressive Alex Gidman top scored with 73, while Jonty Rhodes made 45 after announcing that he was going to retire from first-class cricket at the end of the season.

Division Two

at Taunton
Lancashire 310 for 7 (45 overs) (MJ Chilton 103, CL Hooper 82, SG Law 51)
Somerset 286 (42.5 overs) (KA Parsons 90, G Chapple 4 for 60)
Lancashire (4pts) won by 24 runs

Put into bat for some strange reason, on a perfect Taunton pitch, Lancashire then gratefully piled up their biggest one-day league total before reducing Somerset to 87 for 5 in reply. Keith Parsons, with a defiant 90, rallied the lower order, however, and Somerset eventually did well to reach 286 in reply to Lancashire's massive 310 for 7. Troubled times still

Tim Roberts overpowered the Nottinghamshire attack at Trent Bridge with 131 from just 112 balls.

Trevor Ward dedicated his match-winning hundred at Cardiff to the memory of his late mother.

afflicted the West Country county, however, and Peter Anderson, the Somerset chief executive, wrote in the match programme: 'We will be trying to sign new players to try to halt the terrible downwards spiral the club now finds itself in.' For Lancashire, Mark Chilton made a responsible 103, Stuart Law a fluent 51 off 44 balls and Carl Hooper an often-breathtaking 82 from 78 balls which contained five sixes and four fours.

2 September 2003: Division One

at Cardiff
Glamorgan 226 for 7 (45 overs) (MJ Powell 91*)
Leicestershire 227 for 7 (45 overs) (TR Ward 104, PA Nixon 67*, DS Harrison 4 for 44)
Leicestershire (4pts) won by 3 wickets

Fuelled by his emotions, Trevor Ward played one of the most heart-warming innings of the summer to inspire Leicestershire to a wonderful, last-ball, three-wicket win against Glamorgan at Cardiff. Ward dedicated his magnificent, classy 104 to the memory of his late mother as he rallied his side from the depths of 52 for 5. Paul Nixon, concentrating almost exclusively on singles, gave Ward the support he deserved as he unravelled a series of majestic strokes. They had soon transformed the match with a stand of 125 and, when a clearly emotionally drained Ward was finally caught in the deep, Nixon was joined by Jeremy Snape in another spirited stand of 45 that carried Leicestershire to within five runs of their target of 227. Snape then fell for 21, but Nixon held his nerve during a tense final over and capped a thrilling chase by driving the final ball, from Adrian Davies, to the wide midwicket boundary. Earlier Michael Powell had made the most of being dropped twice, on 48 and 58, to score a one-day league best of 91 not out from 92 balls.

3 September 2003: Division One

at Canterbury
Kent 142 (31.4 overs) (A Symonds 53, AJ Hollioake 6 for 17)
Surrey 143 for 5 (37 overs)
Surrey (4pts) won by 5 wickets

Adam Hollioake recorded the extraordinary bowling analysis of 4.4–0–17–6 at Canterbury as Surrey inflicted a first floodlit defeat on Kent, and in the process all but assured themselves of the National League title. Kent, having chosen to bat on a decent enough pitch, had reached 109 for 3 with Andrew Symonds surging past a 37-ball half-century when Surrey skipper Hollioake introduced himself into the attack in the 25th over. His third ball accounted for David Fulton, caught behind as he nibbled outside off stump, and he then had Symonds lbw for 53. Hollioake continued to bowl straight and with canny little changes of pace, but Kent's middle and lower order subsided embarrassingly and 142 all out was nowhere near enough in the conditions. To their credit, Kent fought hard to make amends in the field, but Mark Ramprakash held the Surrey innings together and a 7,000 crowd went home disappointed.

Division Two

at Hove
Middlesex 248 for 6 (45 overs) (PN Weekes 91,
RSC Martin-Jenkins 4 for 46)
Sussex 249 for 2 (43.2 overs) (MW Goodwin 118*,
CJ Adams 115*)
Sussex (4pts) won by 8 wickets

Thrilling batting from Murray Goodwin and Chris
Adams took Sussex off the bottom of the table and
also severely dented Middlesex's promotion hopes
under the floodlights at Hove. Coming together with
their side on 21 for 2 in reply to Middlesex's 246 for
6, Goodwin and Adams won the game with a
competition-record third-wicket partnership of 228
in 36 overs. Goodwin was 118 not out at the end,
and Adams was on 115, and the pair had matched
each other stroke for stroke. Neither man needed to
resort to slogging at any stage, and there were only
ten fours in Adams' hundred, reached off 116 balls.
Goodwin's century, which took him just three balls
longer, included 16 boundaries. Robin Martin-
Jenkins also played a significant part in the Sussex
victory, with his 4 for 46 slowing an intended late
Middlesex charge after Paul Weekes (91) and Ed
Joyce had put on 83 for the fourth wicket.

7 September 2003: Division One

at Bristol
Gloucestershire 232 for 7 (45 overs) (MGN Windows
83*)
Essex 227 (45 overs) (A Flower 90, RC Irani 61,
IJ Harvey 5 for 38)
Gloucestershire (4pts) won by 5 runs

at Worcestershire
Worcestershire 223 for 7 (45 overs) (GA Hick 52)
Yorkshire 227 for 3 (43.4 overs) (MJ Wood 91,
MJ Lumb 62*)
Yorkshire (4pts) won by 7 wickets

The bowling skills of Ian Harvey clinched
Gloucestershire the victory they needed over Essex at
Bristol in order to keep up at least the mathematical
chance of denying Surrey the National League trophy.
With Essex requiring nine runs from the final over to
overhaul Gloucestershire's 232 for 7, of which Harvey
had already made a 23-ball 43, the Australian all-
rounder conceded just three runs, took two wickets and
also ran out Mohammad Akram. With six needed off
the last ball, James Middlebrook had his off stump

removed by yet another perfect yorker. Harvey's first
spell had cost just seven runs, and he finished with 5 for
38. It all capped another combative Gloucestershire
performance in the field after Essex had initially reached
168 for 1 with Andy Flower and Ronnie Irani putting
on 115 and looking as if they were going to win the
game on their own. Matt Windows' 95-ball unbeaten 83
had been the best Gloucestershire innings on a day in
which they did not play at their best, but still won.

Both teams were fittingly attired in black for a
basement battle at New Road in which Yorkshire
kept their own flickering survival chances alive by
condemning Worcestershire to relegation. Matthew
Hoggard's 3 for 29 and Matthew Wood's 91 were two
good reasons why Yorkshire emerged as winners by
seven wickets, but Craig White also batted well for
40, in an opening partnership of 75 with Wood, while
Michael Lumb finished on 62 not out after figuring in
a 114-run alliance with Wood. Yorkshire still required
17 from three overs when Vic Craven strode in to get
off the mark with a six, and then Lumb pummelled
Kabir Ali for successive boundaries to end the contest
with eight balls remaining.

Division Two

at Derby
Scotland 201 for 8 (45 overs) (RR Watson 70)
Derbyshire 202 for 2 (38.4 overs) (CWG Bassano 108*)
Derbyshire (4pts) won by 8 wickets

at Southampton
Lancashire 204 for 5 (45 overs) (CL Hooper 73,
G Chapple 66*)
Hampshire 159 (41.3 overs) (N Pothas 58)
Lancashire (4pts) won by 45 runs

at Northampton
Northamptonshire 241 for 6 (45 overs) (PA Jaques 67,
MEK Hussey 55)
Durham 214 (42.3 overs) (AM Thorpe 76,
GP Swann 4 for 57)
Northamptonshire (4pts) won by 27 runs

at Trent Bridge
Nottinghamshire 279 for 5 (45 overs) (KP Pietersen 141*)
Somerset 244 for 8 (45 overs) (CM Gazzard 76)
Nottinghamshire (4pts) won by 35 runs

Scotland slid to the bottom of the National League
pile when they were beaten by eight wickets by
Derbyshire at Derby. Ryan Watson's 70, and a late
39-ball assault from Ian Stanger (42 not out) enabled

them to top 200, which was a good effort after they had been reduced to what was effectively 25 for 6 by the swing of Kevin Dean and Dominic Cork. Colin Smith was taken to hospital after ducking into a Cork bouncer, but later ignored medical advice and kept wicket despite mild concussion. He caught Michael Di Venuto, too, but Chris Bassano took Derbyshire home at a canter with an unbeaten 108.

Lancashire's push for the Division Two title continued with an efficient 45-run win against Hampshire at the Rose Bowl. Carl Hooper was again central to their success, scoring 73 from 88 balls and then picking up three wickets with his deceptively gentle off breaks. Hooper rebuilt a Lancashire innings which was stuttering at 52 for 4 in the 20th over, while Glen Chapple also produced an excellent all-round display that included an unbeaten 66.

Northamptonshire remained hard on Lancashire's heels with a hard-fought 27-run victory over Durham at Northampton that also secured their promotion to the top flight of the one-day league. The home side were once more grateful to their Australian left-handers, Mike Hussey and Phil Jaques, who both hit half-centuries to put them on course for a defendable total. A third Australian-born left-hander, Ashley

Thorpe, then led the Durham chase with a powerful competition-best 76, while Paul Collingwood and Gary Pratt also batted attractively, scoring 43 and 40 respectively. However, once Thorpe was bowled, heaving at Graeme Swann, the remaining six Durham wickets fell in just seven overs.

Two days after playing down suggestions that he might be leaving Nottinghamshire, the talented Kevin Pietersen produced the sort of scintillating innings which underlined what the county would miss if he did opt for pastures new. Pietersen's 141 not out at Trent Bridge, which took him only 104 balls and featured three sixes and 17 fours, was his third hundred in four one-day meetings with Somerset. Despite Carl Gazzard's 76, Somerset were always struggling to match Notts' 279 for 5, and in the end fell 35 runs short.

9 September 2003: Division One

at Edgbaston
Warwickshire 250 for 4 (45 overs) (NV Knight 122, IJL Trott 51*)
Worcestershire 173 for 6 (35.3 overs)
Warwickshire (4pts) won by 18 runs – DL Method: target 192 from 35.3 overs

Knight on the attack: Nick Knight, one of the best one-day batsmen produced by England, is pictured in full flow.

Worcestershire donated six penalty runs to their West Midlands rivals Warwickshire for a slow over rate, and when rain arrived at 9.55pm to bring an end to the floodlit frolics they were deemed to be 18 runs short of where they needed to be on Duckworth-Lewis computations. There was no doubt, however, that Warwickshire deserved to be winners. They had run up 250 for 4 from their 45 overs (including the penalty) with Nick Knight scoring 122 from 131 balls, before limiting Worcestershire to 173 for 6 from 35.3 overs largely through some superb seam bowling from Corey Collymore and Alan Richardson.

10 September 2003: Division One

at Chelmsford
Yorkshire 174 (43.5 overs) (AJ Clarke 4 for 28)
Essex 177 for 6 (42.5 overs) (ML Pettini 59)
Essex (4pts) won by 4 wickets

Essex recovered from being 61 for 5 in reply to Yorkshire's 174 thanks to a gutsy sixth-wicket stand of 88 in 18 overs between Mark Pettini and James Middlebrook. Pettini was caught for 59, but former Yorkshire off spinner Middlebrook stayed to finish on 46 not out and completed the four-wicket win which kept Essex in Division One and condemned Yorkshire to relegation. Darren Gough, so miffed at being left out of England's winter one-day squad announced earlier in the day, top scored for Yorkshire with a 41-ball 33 from No. 9 and then had Andy Flower taken at first slip in his second over, but, in the end, there was yet more disappointment for both him and his county.

14 September 2003: Division One

at Cardiff
Surrey 198 for 9 (45 overs) (MR Ramprakash 53, AJ Hollioake 51, A Dale 4 for 35)
Glamorgan 190 (43.4 overs)
Surrey (4pts) won by 8 runs

at Leicester
Leicestershire 98 (35.1 overs) (MA Ealham 4 for 19, A Khan 4 for 26)
Kent 101 for 2 (19.2 overs)
Kent (4pts) won by 8 wickets

Surrey's consolation for having the county championship taken from their grasp was the National League trophy, a success they confirmed by defeating Glamorgan by eight runs at Cardiff –

the scene of their 1996 Sunday League triumph. The club's celebrations, after Rikki Clarke had uprooted David Harrison's middle stump with nine wanted from nine balls, were tempered however by the news that Ian Ward, the opener, had decided to leave the club in search of 'new inspiration'. Half-centuries from Mark Ramprakash and Adam Hollioake took Surrey to 198 for 9, on a pitch offering some uneven bounce and aid to the spinners, but it was the controlled medium pace of both Hollioake and Clarke which did most to restrict the Glamorgan reply.

Kent destroyed Leicestershire at Grace Road to take the final relegation issue to the final week. If Leicestershire had won, they would have sent their opponents down – but instead they were tumbled out for just 98 with both Amjad Khan and Mark Ealham picking up impressive four-wicket returns. Khan began the rout by taking four wickets in 13 deliveries with the new ball, and then Ealham took over with his nip and cut which was ideally suited to a receptive surface. Two early wickets for Phil DeFreitas failed to deflect Kent from their course, and Rob Key was joined by Andrew Symonds in an unbroken partnership of 62 as victory arrived by eight wickets.

Division Two

at Old Trafford
Lancashire 125 (41 overs) (MJG Davis 4 for 14)
Sussex 128 for 1 (18.2 overs) (RR Montgomerie 66*, MW Goodwin 59)
Sussex (4pts) won by 9 wickets

at Lord's
Hampshire 277 for 7 (45 overs) (SM Katich 106, N Pothas 78, PN Weekes 4 for 45)
Middlesex 278 for 4 (44.5 overs) (PN Weekes 104)
Middlesex (4pts) won by 6 wickets

at Trent Bridge
Scotland 183 (44.1 overs) (JE Brinkley 67)
Nottinghamshire 185 for 3 (37.4 overs) (CL Cairns 76*)
Nottinghamshire (4pts) won by 7 wickets

at Taunton
Somerset 243 for 9 (45 overs) (ID Blackwell 60, MJ Wood 58)
Derbyshire 249 for 8 (44.5 overs) (MJ Di Venuto 113)
Derbyshire (4pts) won by 2 wickets

Plans for an Old Trafford trophy celebration had to be shelved when Sussex beat Lancashire with embarrassing ease to leave the home side sweating on their last-day visit to Division Two title rivals Northamptonshire. The margin was nine wickets after Lancashire had folded to 125 all out, with Billy Taylor picking up 3 for 23 and the off spin of Mark Davis earning him career-best one-day figures of 4 for 14. Richard Montgomerie then reached his 50 in just 36 balls, and by the end had raced on to 66 not out. Murray Goodwin, with 59, joined in an exuberant opening stand of 112 from 95 balls.

Middlesex kept alive their hopes of snatching the third promotion spot by beating their jittery rivals, Hampshire, by six wickets at Lord's. Hampshire, fuelled by an opening partnership of 144 between Nic Pothas (78) and century-maker Simon Katich, totalled 277 for 7, but a crowd of around 4,000 lapped up the sunshine and the shot-making as Middlesex replied strongly. Paul Weekes all but matched Katich's effort with 104, his second league hundred, and with Chad Keegan took Middlesex to 178 for 2 from 30 overs, 19 more than Hampshire had managed at the same stage. Owais Shah and Ed Joyce then pressed the accelerator again with a superb stand of 57 in six overs. With ten still needed, however, Shah was dropped at long off from the last ball of the penultimate over. When the first ball of the final over, from Dimitri Mascarenhas, was powered over the extra-cover boundary for six by Shah, it looked all over. Shah clipped the next ball to midwicket, though, and it was three scrambled singles that ultimately took Middlesex past the winning post with a ball to spare.

Chris Cairns, in what was expected to be his final innings for Nottinghamshire, took his leave with a powerful unbeaten 76 from 73 balls as Scotland were seen off by seven wickets at Trent Bridge. Cairns shared an unbroken fourth-wicket stand of 111 in 19 overs with Jason Gallian as Notts sauntered past a Saltires total of 183 that owed much to James Brinkley's 67.

Michael Di Venuto scored 113, his third league ton of the season, to inspire Derbyshire to an eventual two-wicket victory over Somerset at Taunton. From 190 for 2, though, in pursuit of the home side's 243 for 9, Derbyshire lost six wickets in seven overs and, in the end, after requiring just three from the final over, they were indebted to Nathan Dumclow's straight six off Simon Francis from the penultimate ball to secure their victory.

21 September 2003: Division One

at Canterbury
Kent 267 for 7 (45 overs) (ET Smith 74)

Warwickshire 163 (37.2 overs)
Kent (4pts) won by 104 runs

at The Oval
Leicestershire 283 for 9 (45 overs) (DL Maddy 69, JGE Benning 4 for 43)
Surrey 115 (22 overs) (PAJ DeFreitas 5 for 40)
Leicestershire (4pts) won by 168 runs

at Worcester
Worcestershire 213 (42.4 overs) (Kabir Ali 92)
Essex 217 for 6 (42 overs) (WI Jefferson 74)
Essex (4pts) won by 4 wickets

at Headingley
Yorkshire 213 for 7 (45 overs) (JJ Sayers 62, MCJ Ball 5 for 33)
Gloucestershire 214 for 7 (44.1 overs) (MGN Windows 91*, ND Thornicroft 5 for 42)
Gloucestershire (4pts) won by 3 wickets

Kent ensured their survival in Division One with an emphatic 104-run victory over Warwickshire at Canterbury in front of 5,500 supporters relishing the warm last-day sunshine of a cricket summer to remember. Ed Smith kicked off a solid Kent batting display with 74 from 109 balls, while Andrew Symonds offered a 56-ball 49, Matthew Walker a rapid 37 and Mark Ealham two sixes and two fours in a frisky 25. Amjad Khan then lopped off the top of the Warwickshire order with three new-ball strikes and only a defiant 48 from Michael Powell, down at No. 7 in his last match as captain, delayed the end. For Kent, at the end of a frustrating season overall, there was the satisfaction that they had sent Leicestershire down in the third relegation position, thereby confirming themselves as the only county never to have experienced Division Two life in either the one-day league or the county championship.

Leicestershire thumped an under-strength Surrey by 168 runs at The Oval, but it was all in vain as news of Kent's win filtered through. Darren Maddy top scored with 69 in a consistent batting display that was rewarded with a total of 283 for 9, and then the evergreen Phil DeFreitas sealed yet another successful personal season by taking 5 for 40 as Surrey declined swiftly to 115 and their heaviest defeat in the 35-year history of the competition. Afterwards, it was a rather subdued squad that paraded the National League trophy and were presented with their medals.

Essex soared into third place by beating bottom-placed Worcestershire by four wickets at Worcester. Kabir Ali, batting at No. 3, entertained the crowd with a career-best one-day innings of 92 from 93 balls, but no other home batsman could get going. Will Jefferson then cover drove beautifully to make 74 and Mark Pettini added to his growing reputation by scoring 36.

Runners-up Gloucestershire had Matt Windows and Martyn Ball to thank for their three-wicket win against relegated Yorkshire at Headingley. Joe Sayers, the former England Under 19 captain, scored 62 on his league debut to take Yorkshire to 130 for 1 in the 31st over, but then Ball snatched one-day best figures of 5 for 33 to reduce them to 164 for 6 in the space of ten overs. It took a confident 33 off 29 balls from Tim Bresnan to boost the Yorkshire total to 213 for 7. Gloucestershire were themselves 37 for 4 before Windows – with support first from Alex Gidman and then Jack Russell – saw them home with an unbeaten 91. Nick Thornicroft, one of seven players under the age of 25 in the Yorkshire line-up, finished with figures of 5 for 42.

Division Two

at Derby
Derbyshire 172 for 7 (45 overs)
Hampshire 163 (44.3 overs) (SM Katich 56)
Derbyshire (4pts) won by 9 runs

at Chester-le-Street
Middlesex 112 for 9 (30 overs)

(Shoaib Akhtar 4 for 21)
Durham 114 for 1 (15.4 overs) (N Peng 66*)
Durham (4pts) won by 9 wickets

at Northampton
Northamptonshire 240 (44.5 overs) (PA Jaques 107)
Lancashire 243 for 1 (36.4 overs) (MB Loye 104*, SG Law 79*, IJ Sutcliffe 54)
Lancashire (4pts) won by 9 wickets

at Hove
Somerset 377 for 9 (45 overs) (ID Blackwell 111, M Burns 91)
Sussex 186 (30.2 overs) (KP Dutch 4 for 34)
Somerset (4pts) won by 191 runs

Mal Loye bit the hand that used to feed him as Lancashire overwhelmed Northamptonshire at Wantage Road in the battle to decide who were Division Two champions and who were runners-up. Loye, who left Northants the previous winter, made plain his joy when reaching a match-winning century. He finished on 104 not out and, with Stuart Law (79 not out) added an unbroken 131 for the second wicket as victory arrived by the crushing margin of nine wickets and with 8.2 overs in hand. Iain Sutcliffe's 54 had helped Loye to post 112 for the opening wicket, and for Northants only Phil Jaques, with 107 from 109 balls, matched the dominance of the Lancashire top three.

Hampshire secured the third promotion position, despite losing at Derbyshire to record an extraordinary fourth consecutive defeat. Middlesex's collapse at Durham allowed John Crawley's team to celebrate, rather shamefacedly, following a nine-run loss at Derby. Having restricted the home side to 172 for 7, Hampshire reached 123 for 2 and then 143 for 3 before contriving to lose their last seven wickets for 20 runs.

Middlesex ran into Shoaib Akhtar at his most lethal at Chester-le-Street, with the self-styled 'Rawalpindi Express' taking 4 for 21 to blow the visitors completely off the rails. They had journeyed to the North East knowing that victory would take them up to Division One, if Hampshire lost at Derby. But soon they were 27 for 7, with Neil Killeen doing almost as much damage with his medium pacers at

Emotional return: Mal Loye, back on home turf at Wantage Road, clearly relished the match-winning hundred he scored for Lancashire.

the other end to Shoaib's lightning bolts. A brave eighth-wicket stand of 80 between Ben Hutton and Chad Keegan, mostly constructed after Shoaib and Killeen had finished their permitted six-over spells, took Middlesex to 112 for 9 in a game reduced to 30 overs per side. Durham's batsmen, however, needed just 15.4 overs to knock off the runs, with Nicky Peng thrashing 66 not out.

Ian Blackwell continued his magnificent late-season form to hit 111 off a mere 56 balls as Somerset at least managed to end a deflating season with a 191-run thrashing of Sussex, the newly crowned county championship kings. The Sussex attack was pulverized in front of a Hove crowd still flushed from the championship triumph, with Robin Martin-Jenkins conceding 70 from his seven overs, Carl Hopkinson going for 80 off nine, Paul Hutchison 72 off his nine, and Mike Yardy 39 off three. The upshot was a record Somerset total of 377 for 9, with Mike Burns also plundering 91 from 81 balls. In reply, Sussex subsided to 186 all out, with Keith Dutch adding 4 for 34 to his earlier quick-fire 44.

FINAL TABLES

DIVISION ONE

	P	W	L	Tie	NR	Pts
Surrey	**16**	**12**	**3**	**0**	**1**	**50**
Gloucestershire	16	11	4	0	1	46
Essex	16	8	7	1	0	34
Warwickshire	16	8	8	0	0	32
Glamorgan	16	8	8	0	0	32
Kent	16	7	8	1	0	30
Leicestershire	16	7	9	0	0	28
Yorkshire	16	5	11	0	0	20
Worcestershire	16	4	12	0	0	16

DIVISION TWO

	P	W	L	Tie	NR	Pts
Lancashire	**18**	**14**	**3**	**0**	**1**	**58**
Northamptonshire	18	12	5	0	1	50
Hampshire	18	11	7	0	0	44
Middlesex	18	10	7	0	1	42
Nottinghamshire	18	9	9	0	0	36
Derbyshire	18	8	8	0	2	36
Durham	18	7	10	0	1	30
Sussex	18	6	12	0	0	24
Somerset	18	5	12	0	1	22
Scotland	18	4	13	0	1	18

FEATURES OF NATIONAL LEAGUE 2003

HIGHEST TOTAL

377-9 (45 overs)	Somerset v. Sussex at Hove	21 September

HIGHEST TOTAL BATTING SECOND

316-7 (45 overs)	Kent v. Surrey at The Oval	18 May

LOWEST TOTAL

54 (20.2 overs)	Yorkshire v. Essex at Headingley	5 May

HIGHEST INDIVIDUAL SCORE

161* N Hussain	Essex v. Glamorgan at Chelmsford	5 August

59 centuries were scored in the competition

SIX WICKETS IN AN INNINGS

6-17 AJ Hollioake	Surrey v. Kent at Canterbury	3 September
6-37 Azhar Mahmood	Surrey v. Essex at The Oval	8 June

There were 86 instances of four wickets in an innings

TIED MATCHES

Kent tied with Essex at Canterbury	3 August

WINNING BY ONE WICKET

Nottinghamshire beat Derbyshire at Trent Bridge	5 May
Surrey beat Worcestershire at Worcester	5 May
Somerset beat Scotland at Taunton	15 June
Sussex beat Scotland at The Grange	28 August

WINNING BY MORE THAN 150 RUNS

212	Northamptonshire beat Nottinghamshire at Trent Bridge	31 August
191	Somerset beat Sussex at Hove	21 September
168	Leicestershire beat Surrey at The Oval	21 September
157	Essex beat Yorkshire at Headingley	5 May

There were 11 instances of a side winning by more than 100 runs (including the four matches above)

WINNING BY ONE RUN

Middlesex beat Nottinghamshire at Trent Bridge	22 June
Glamorgan beat Yorkshire at Colwyn Bay	24 August

NO PLAY POSSIBLE

Gloucestershire v. Surrey at Bristol	25 May
Durham v. Derbyshire at Chester-le-Street	25 May

NATIONAL LEAGUE: DIVISION ONE FEATURES 2003

BATTING: LEADING AVERAGES

Batting	M	Inns	NO	Runs	HS	Av	SR	100	50
N Hussain (Essex)	5	5	2	431	161*	143.66	91.70	2	1
TL Penney (Warwicks)	11	8	5	273	88*	91.00	102.24	–	2
MR Ramprakash (Surrey)	13	12	3	686	107*	76.22	78.22	2	6
MGN Windows (Gloucs)	15	15	7	510	91*	63.75	77.27	–	5
A Symonds (Kent)	9	9	2	375	93*	53.57	96.89	–	3
MJ Walker (Kent)	16	15	4	573	101	52.09	81.27	1	3
CM Spearman (Gloucs)	15	15	1	717	153	51.21	104.82	2	3
SP Fleming (Yorks)	7	7	1	285	139*	47.50	104.01	1	1
IJL Trott (Warwicks)	8	8	2	284	59	47.33	74.34	–	4
GP Thorpe (Surrey)	13	12	4	378	79*	47.25	76.05	–	3
MJ Powell (Glam)	16	15	2	597	91*	45.92	83.37	–	4
NV Knight (Warwicks)	15	15	0	684	122	45.60	80.66	2	5
BF Smith (Worcs)	16	15	4	496	93*	45.09	78.48	–	3
IR Bell (Warwicks)	16	16	3	560	125	43.07	93.33	1	4
MP Maynard (Glam)	15	14	3	465	72	42.27	89.76	–	2
APR Gidman (Gloucs)	12	11	2	372	73	41.33	77.82	–	2
DL Hemp (Glam)	14	12	3	355	83*	39.44	70.15	–	2
AF Giles (Warwicks)	5	4	2	76	61*	38.00	81.72	–	1
A Flower (Essex)	15	15	1	531	103	37.92	88.50	2	2
IJ Harvey (Gloucs)	7	7	0	264	96	37.71	134.01	–	1
JM Kemp (Worcs)	7	7	2	182	50	36.40	65.70	–	1
ET Smith (Kent)	13	13	0	472	122	36.30	80.82	1	3
TR Ward (Leics)	11	11	1	338	104	33.80	83.66	1	1
WI Jefferson (Essex)	14	14	0	472	74	33.71	83.83	–	5
V Sehwag (Leics)	7	7	0	233	76	33.28	84.72	–	3
SD Peters (Worcs)	9	8	0	265	82	33.12	68.83	–	2
AD Brown (Surrey)	15	15	0	491	89	32.73	116.90	–	4
DR Brown (Warwicks)	13	10	3	223	49	31.85	96.95	–	–
DL Maddy (Leics)	16	16	1	474	80	31.60	81.58	–	5
MJ Lumb (Yorks)	15	15	1	441	92	31.50	76.82	–	4
Azhar Mahmood (Surrey)	12	11	2	277	98	30.77	128.83	–	2
A Singh (Worcs)	12	12	0	357	97	29.75	69.86	–	1
BJ Hodge (Leics)	16	16	0	475	104	29.68	74.80	1	2
RDB Croft (Glam)	16	16	1	445	70	29.66	84.28	–	4
JP Maher (Glam)	10	10	0	295	142	29.50	88.32	1	1
RWT Key (Kent)	14	14	1	381	68	29.30	67.07	–	1
TT Bresnan (Yorks)	11	8	1	204	61	29.14	85.35	–	1
GA Hick (Worcs)	13	13	1	349	108	29.08	89.25	1	3
DDJ Robinson (Essex)	7	6	0	173	78	28.83	59.86	–	1
AJ Hall (Worcs)	5	5	1	115	47*	28.75	87.12	–	–
WPC Weston (Gloucs)	14	14	0	395	92	28.21	68.81	–	3
SJ Rhodes (Worcs)	13	7	4	84	35*	28.00	62.22	–	–
RC Irani (Essex)	13	13	1	332	64	27.66	78.11	–	3
A Habib (Essex)	8	8	1	193	50	27.57	83.91	–	1
THC Hancock (Gloucs)	7	6	0	162	82	27.00	77.88	–	1
IJ Ward (Surrey)	11	11	1	257	70*	25.70	86.24	–	1
MA Wagh (Warwicks)	9	9	1	204	66	25.50	58.28	–	1
AJ Hollioake (Surrey)	15	15	0	377	77	25.13	99.47	–	2
GO Jones (Kent)	16	13	1	300	74*	25.00	79.36	–	2

Qualification: average of 25 or above (minimum of five innings)

LEADING RUN SCORERS – TOP 20

Batting	Inns	Runs
CM Spearman (Gloucs)	717	15
MR Ramprakash (Surrey)	686	13
NV Knight (Warwicks)	684	15
MJ Powell (Glam)	597	16
MJ Walker (Kent)	573	16
IR Bell (Warwicks)	560	16
A Flower (Essex)	531	15
MGN Windows (Gloucs)	510	15
BF Smith (Worcs)	496	15
AD Brown (Surrey)	491	15
BJ Hodge (Leics)	475	16
DL Maddy (Leics)	474	16
ET Smith (Kent)	472	13
WI Jefferson (Essex)	472	14
MP Maynard (Glam)	465	14
RDB Croft (Glam)	445	16
MJ Lumb (Yorks)	441	15
N Hussain (Essex)	431	5
WPC Weston (Gloucs)	395	14
MJ Wood (Yorks)	390	16

BOWLING: LEADING AVERAGES

Bowling	O	M	Runs	W	Av	Best	4i	Econ
GR Napier (Essex)	108	11	536	33	16.24	4-18	2	4.96
IJ Harvey (Gloucs)	60.2	2	311	17	18.29	5-38	2	5.15
AJ Hollioake (Surrey)	82.5	1	443	23	19.26	6-17	2	5.34
Waqar Younis (Warwicks)	83.3	4	404	20	20.20	4-20	3	4.83
M Muralitharan (Kent)	68	9	269	13	20.69	5-34	–	3.95
Kabir Ali (Worcs)	85.1	10	472	22	21.45	4-30	2	5.54
DA Leatherdale (Worcs)	80.2	3	375	17	22.05	5-36	2	4.66
RJ Sidebottom (Yorks)	69.5	4	333	15	22.20	5-42	1	4.76
SA Brant (Essex)	53.4	2	294	13	22.61	4-25	1	5.47
A Khan (Kent)	47	4	231	10	23.10	4-26	1	4.91
M Hayward (Worcs)	58	2	289	12	24.08	3-32	–	4.98
AP Davies (Glam)	59.5	3	338	14	24.14	3-31	–	5.64
AJ Clarke (Essex)	58.5	4	314	13	24.15	4-28	1	5.33
PD Trego (Kent)	39.2	1	244	10	24.40	4-39	2	6.20
MCJ Ball (Gloucs)	102	1	522	21	24.85	5-33	1	5.11
TT Bresnan (Yorks)	79.5	5	374	15	24.93	3-29	–	4.68
PAJ DeFreitas (Leics)	111	5	480	19	25.26	5-40	1	4.32
AG Wharf (Glam)	88.5	2	510	20	25.50	4-18	2	5.74
Azhar Mahmood (Surrey)	89	4	466	18	25.88	6-37	1	5.23
A Symonds (Kent)	71	4	286	11	26.00	2-33	–	4.02
CEW Silverwood (Yorks)	79	12	339	13	26.07	4-45	1	4.29
JN Snape (Leics)	92.2	1	370	14	26.42	3-14	–	4.00
AM Smith (Gloucs)	87.4	8	325	12	27.08	2-22	–	3.70
BJ Trott (Kent)	70.2	4	354	13	27.23	3-19	–	5.03
MS Mason (Worcs)	125	18	524	19	27.57	4-34	2	4.19
GJ Batty (Worcs)	87	7	336	12	28.00	3-51	–	3.86
JC Tredwell (Kent)	90.2	0	406	14	29.00	3-38	–	4.49
MS Kasprowicz (Glam)	125.5	14	584	20	29.20	3-20	–	4.64
CE Dagnall (Leics)	94.5	8	533	18	29.61	4-41	1	5.62
DA Cosker (Glam)	95	1	506	17	29.76	5-54	2	5.32
MW Alleyne (Gloucs)	79.2	4	371	12	30.91	4-26	1	4.67
J Ormond (Surrey)	86	4	410	13	31.53	3-46	–	4.76
RDB Croft (Glam)	112	0	577	18	32.05	3-33	–	5.15
DR Brown (Warwicks)	86.3	6	490	15	32.66	4-37	1	5.66
JMM Averis (Gloucs)	100	7	560	17	32.94	4-50	1	5.60
R Clarke (Surrey)	64	1	396	12	33.00	3-48	–	6.18
A Dale (Glam)	85.5	1	435	13	33.46	4-35	1	5.06
NM Carter (Warwicks)	105.3	4	512	14	36.57	2-19	–	4.85
MA Ealham (Kent)	115.3	7	505	13	38.84	4-19	1	4.37
MP Bicknell (Surrey)	91	9	436	11	39.63	2-30	–	4.79

Qualification: average of 40 or less (minimum of ten wickets)

LEADING WICKET-TAKERS – TOP 20

Batting	W	O
GR Napier (Essex)	33	108
AJ Hollioake (Surrey)	23	82.5
Kabir Ali (Worcs)	22	85.1
MCJ Ball (Gloucs)	21	102
Waqar Younis (Warwicks)	20	83.3
AG Wharf (Glam)	20	88.5
MS Kasprowicz (Glam)	20	125.5
PAJ DeFreitas (Leics)	19	111
MS Mason (Worcs)	19	125
Azhar Mahmood (Surrey)	18	89
CE Dagnall (Leics)	18	94.5
RDB Croft (Glam)	18	112
IJ Harvey (Gloucs)	17	60.2
DA Leatherdale (Worcs)	17	80.2
DA Cosker (Glam)	17	95
JMM Averis (Gloucs)	17	100
RJ Sidebottom (Yorks)	15	69.5
TT Bresnan (Yorks)	15	79.5
DR Brown (Warwicks)	15	86.3
AP Davies (Glam)	14	59.5

FIELDING: MOST DISMISSALS – TOP 20

GO Jones (Kent) – 33 (27 ct, 6 st); MA Wallace (Glam) – 24 (21 ct, 3 st); JN Batty (Surrey) – 23 (19 ct, 4 st); SJ Rhodes (Worcs) – 20 (15 ct, 5 st); RJ Blakey (Yorks) – 17 (15 ct, 2 st); PA Nixon (Leics) – 16 (12 ct, 4 st); KJ Piper (Warwicks) – 15 (15 ct); JS Foster (Essex) – 13 (11 ct, 2 st); DI Stevens (Leics) – 11 (11 ct); RC Russell (Gloucs) – 11 (6 ct, 5 st); NV Knight (Warwicks) – 10 (10); A Flower (Essex) – 10 (8 ct, 2 st); APR Gidman (Gloucs) – 9 (9 ct); GP Thorpe (Surrey) – 8 (8 ct); WI Jefferson (Essex) – 8 (8); MGN Windows (Gloucs) – 8 (8 ct); AD Brown (Surrey) – 8 (8 ct); BF Smith (Worcs) – 8 (8 ct)

NATIONAL LEAGUE: DIVISION TWO FEATURES 2003

BATTING: LEADING AVERAGES

Batting	M	Inns	NO	Runs	HS	Av	SR	100	50
TMB Bailey (Northants)	12	9	7	156	31*	78.00	91.22	-	-
CMW Read (Notts)	14	13	7	451	119*	75.16	107.12	1	1
CL Hooper (Lancs)	16	14	6	597	88*	74.62	97.07	-	7
N Pothas (Hants)	11	8	4	284	78	71.00	71.53	-	2
R Dravid (Scot)	11	11	2	600	129*	66.66	92.73	3	2
CJ Adams (Sussex)	12	11	4	450	115*	64.28	88.06	2	2
CL Cairns (Notts)	14	14	6	510	91*	63.75	113.33	-	6
Abdul Razzaq (Middx)	5	5	2	190	79	63.33	152.00	-	2
MEK Hussey (Northants)	18	18	3	820	123	54.66	77.28	3	6
RA Smith (Hants)	7	7	2	257	92	51.40	74.49	-	2
DJG Sales (Northants)	18	17	4	638	133*	49.07	84.16	1	4
MW Goodwin (Sussex)	18	18	3	731	129*	48.73	78.43	4	2
KP Pietersen (Notts)	18	18	2	776	141*	48.50	111.81	2	5
PA Jaques (Northants)	18	18	1	803	117	47.23	88.82	2	6
MJ Di Venuto (Derby)	15	14	0	655	130	46.78	95.90	3	3
CWG Bassano (Derby)	16	15	3	559	126*	46.58	74.73	2	3
JP Crawley (Hants)	18	18	3	692	102	46.13	82.77	1	6
PJ Martin (Lancs)	16	5	4	46	29*	46.00	60.52	-	-
SM Katich (Hants)	18	18	1	728	106	42.82	84.55	2	6
GJ Pratt (Durham)	17	16	4	510	101*	42.50	72.03	1	2
PN Weekes (Middx)	18	18	0	746	104	41.44	71.66	1	7
MB Loye (Lancs)	18	18	3	619	104*	41.26	74.39	1	5
OA Shah (Middx)	18	18	2	655	106	40.93	93.03	1	4
EC Joyce (Middx)	18	17	3	561	77	40.07	73.52	-	5
SG Law (Lancs)	18	17	2	586	98	39.06	102.26	-	4
ID Blackwell (Somerset)	17	16	1	566	111	37.73	129.22	1	3
WJ Durston (Somerset)	7	6	2	145	51*	36.25	98.63	-	1
GD Clough (Notts)	13	9	4	181	42*	36.20	82.64	-	-
JC Kent (Scot)	16	15	2	469	115*	36.07	86.85	1	3
N Peng (Durham)	15	15	2	466	92	35.84	82.33	-	3
J Cox (Somerset)	16	14	0	479	130	34.21	89.86	2	1
SJ Cook (Middx)	17	10	5	170	67*	34.00	107.59	-	1
RM Haq (Scot)	17	8	4	135	55*	33.75	79.88	-	1
G Chapple (Lancs)	16	10	3	236	77*	33.71	78.92	-	2
MJ Chilton (Lancs)	17	15	2	426	103	32.76	74.34	1	1
TW Roberts (Northants)	9	9	0	291	131	32.33	101.04	1	1
JD Francis (Hants)	11	11	2	290	62*	32.22	66.51	-	2
M Kaif (Derby)	8	8	1	225	70	32.14	68.80	-	2
GJ Muchall (Durham)	12	12	0	383	87	31.91	58.92	-	2
KA Parsons (Somerset)	18	15	0	478	90	31.86	81.15	-	2
AJ Strauss (Middx)	18	18	0	563	127	31.27	85.17	1	3
AM Davies (Durham)	12	5	4	31	19*	31.00	83.78	-	-
SA Selwood (Derby)	11	9	1	240	88*	30.00	66.66	-	2
RR Watson (Scot)	18	17	1	474	103*	29.62	81.58	1	2
ML Love (Durham)	10	10	0	288	55	28.80	70.76	-	2
RJ Turner (Somerset)	9	7	3	114	27*	28.50	65.89	-	-
RL Johnson (Somerset)	6	5	1	113	53	28.25	125.55	-	1
JER Gallian (Notts)	14	14	1	367	69	28.23	70.98	-	2
U Afzaal (Notts)	12	12	0	338	105	28.16	74.44	1	2

Qualification: average of 25 or above (minimum of five innings)

LEADING RUN SCORERS – TOP 20

Batting	Inns	Runs
MEK Hussey (Northants)	820	18
PA Jaques (Northants)	803	18
KP Pietersen (Notts)	776	18
PN Weekes (Middx)	746	18
MW Goodwin (Sussex)	731	18
SM Katich (Hants)	728	18
JP Crawley (Hants)	692	18
MJ Di Venuto (Derby)	655	14
OA Shah (Middx)	655	18
DJG Sales (Northants)	638	17
MB Loye (Lancs)	619	18
R Dravid (Scot)	600	11
CL Hooper (Lancs)	597	14
SG Law (Lancs)	586	17
ID Blackwell (Somerset)	566	16
AJ Strauss (Middx)	563	18
EC Joyce (Middx)	561	17
CWG Bassano (Derby)	559	15
CL Cairns (Notts)	510	14
GJ Pratt (Durham)	510	16

BOWLING: LEADING AVERAGES

Bowling	O	M	Runs	W	Av	Best	4i	Econ
Shoaib Akhtar (Durham)	56	4	224	17	13.17	5-35	3	4.00
D Mascarenhas (Hants)	138.5	19	585	34	17.20	4-22	4	4.21
GP Swann (Northants)	49.1	1	224	13	17.23	4-57	1	4.55
A Nel (Northants)	115.3	14	410	22	18.63	3-20	-	3.54
PJ Martin (Lancs)	117	12	460	24	19.16	3-18	-	3.93
CM Wright (Scot)	112	11	496	25	19.84	3-25	-	4.42
CT Tremlett (Hants)	79	8	342	17	20.11	4-26	1	4.32
GM Andrew (Somerset)	38.2	4	222	11	20.18	3-38	-	5.79
N Killeen (Durham)	130.2	11	505	25	20.20	5-22	2	3.87
GD Bridge (Durham)	71.2	6	286	14	20.42	4-20	2	4.00
SJ Harmison (Durham)	57.5	2	289	14	20.64	4-43	1	4.99
MJ Cawdron (Northants)	115	11	550	26	21.15	4-31	2	4.78
G Chapple (Lancs)	111.5	11	539	25	21.56	4-37	2	4.81
NAM McLean (Somerset)	87.3	3	468	21	22.28	3-51	-	5.34
RSC M-Jenkins (Sussex)	126.2	8	584	26	22.46	4-46	2	4.62
KJ Innes (Sussex)	41.2	1	226	10	22.60	5-41	1	5.46
KW Hogg (Lancs)	75	4	391	17	23.00	4-24	1	5.21
Wasim Akram (Hants)	63.4	9	231	10	23.10	3-17	-	3.62
DR Hewson (Derby)	63.1	1	349	15	23.26	4-25	2	5.52
DG Cork (Derby)	128	11	537	23	23.34	3-15	-	4.19
RJ Logan (Notts)	81	7	436	18	24.22	4-32	2	5.38
SCG MacGill (Notts)	84.1	6	419	17	24.64	3-26	-	4.97
PM Hutchison (Sussex)	86	7	398	16	24.87	4-29	1	4.62
SD Udal (Hants)	125.3	4	604	23	26.26	4-40	1	4.81
CL Hooper (Lancs)	90.1	2	379	14	27.07	3-18	-	4.20
CB Keegan (Middx)	135.3	13	635	23	27.60	5-48	1	4.68
JW Cook (Somerset)	81.4	7	416	15	27.73	3-69	-	5.09
TF Bloomfield (Middx)	67	4	362	13	27.84	4-25	1	5.40
GJ Smith (Notts)	96.5	6	421	15	28.06	3-16	-	4.34
G Welch (Derby)	117.1	12	567	20	28.35	3-44	-	4.83
AM Davies (Durham)	96	10	374	13	28.76	2-15	-	3.89
CG Greenidge (Northants)	53	6	322	11	29.27	3-24	-	6.07
MJG Davis (Sussex)	133.5	6	621	20	31.05	4-14	1	4.64
RJ Kirtley (Sussex)	62	9	317	10	31.70	3-33	-	5.11
GD Clough (Notts)	97	1	518	16	32.37	4-32	1	5.34
NRC Dumelow (Derby)	95.2	3	486	15	32.40	3-26	-	5.09
J Wood (Lancs)	111.5	8	520	16	32.50	4-22	1	4.64
ID Blackwell (Somerset)	108	5	594	18	33.00	3-27	-	5.50
PJ Franks (Notts)	83.1	3	468	14	33.42	4-12	1	5.62
JWM Dalrymple (Middx)	66	0	339	10	33.90	3-55	-	5.13

Qualification: average of 34 or less (minimum of ten wickets)

LEADING WICKET-TAKERS – TOP 20

Batting	W	O
AD Mascarenhas (Hants)	34	138.5
MJ Cawdron (Northants)	26	115
RSC Martin-Jenkins (Sussex)	26	126.2
G Chapple (Lancs)	25	111.5
CM Wright (Scot)	25	112
N Killeen (Durham)	25	130.2
PJ Martin (Lancs)	24	117
SD Udal (Hants)	23	125.3
DG Cork (Derby)	23	128
CB Keegan (Middx)	23	135.3
A Nel (Northants)	22	115.3
NAM McLean (Somerset)	21	87.3
G Welch (Derby)	20	117.1
MJG Davis (Sussex)	20	133.5
RJ Logan (Notts)	18	81
ID Blackwell (Somerset)	18	108
PN Weekes (Middx)	18	113.1
Shoaib Akhtar (Durham)	17	56
KW Hogg (Lancs)	17	75
CT Tremlett (Hants)	17	79

FIELDING: MOST DISMISSALS

WK Hegg (Lancs) – 29 (26 ct, 3 st); LD Sutton (Derby) – 22 (21 ct, 1 st); CJO Smith (Scot) – 19 (12 ct, 7 st); TMB Bailey (Northants) – 18 (13 ct, 5 st); CMW Read (Notts) – 18 (15 ct, 3 st); CM Gazzard (Somerset) – 17 (16 ct, 1 st); P Mustard (Durham) – 15 (14 ct, 1 st); TR Ambrose (Sussex) – 14 (14 ct); CL Hooper (Lancs) – 13 (13 ct); SM Katich (Hants) – 13 (13 ct); OA Shah (Middx) – 13 (13 ct); A Pratt (Durham) – 12 (11 ct, 1 st); GL Brophy (Northants) – 12 (9 ct, 3 st); N Pothas (Hants) – 12 (10 ct, 2 st); DA Kenway (Hants) – 12 (11 ct, 1 st); MB Loye (Lancs) – 12 (12 ct); GJ Pratt (Durham) – 11 (11 ct)

NATIONAL LEAGUE COUNTY COLOURS: DIVISION ONE

ESSEX CCC
National League nickname:
ESSEX EAGLES

GLAMORGAN CCC
National League nickname:
GLAMORGAN DRAGONS

GLOUCESTERSHIRE CCC
National League nickname:
GLOUCESTERSHIRE GLADIATORS

KENT CCC
National League nickname:
KENT SPITFIRES

LEICESTERSHIRE CCC
National League nickname:
LEICESTERSHIRE FOXES

SURREY CCC
National League nickname:
SURREY LIONS

WARWICKSHIRE CCC
National League nickname:
THE BEARS

WORCESTERSHIRE CCC
National League nickname:
WORCESTERSHIRE ROYALS

YORKSHIRE CCC
National League nickname:
YORKSHIRE PHOENIX

For full county details, please refer to the form charts at the back of the book.

NATIONAL LEAGUE COUNTY COLOURS: DIVISION TWO

DERBYSHIRE CCC
National League nickname:
DERBYSHIRE SCORPIONS

DURHAM CCC
National League nickname:
DURHAM DYNAMOS

HAMPSHIRE CCC
National League nickname:
HAMPSHIRE HAWKS

LANCASHIRE CCC
National League nickname:
LANCASHIRE LIGHTNING

MIDDLESEX CCC
National League nickname:
MIDDLESEX CRUSADERS

NORTHAMPTONSHIRE CCC
National League nickname:
STEELBACKS

NOTTINGHAMSHIRE CCC
National League nickname:
NOTTS OUTLAWS

SCOTLAND CC
National League nickname:
SCOTTISH SALTIRES

SOMERSET CCC
National League nickname:
SOMERSET SABRES

SUSSEX CCC
National League nickname:
SUSSEX SHARKS

For full county details, please refer to the form charts at the back of the book.

TWENTY20 CUP

By Mark Baldwin

Perhaps Atomic Kitten were a few disco steps too far, but otherwise those critics who had pooh-poohed the concept of Twenty20 cricket were left with nothing but their prejudices to fall back on after its unqualified success.

Surrey proved that class usually tells in any form of the game by holding their nerve in a tense semi-final against Gloucestershire, before knocking over Warwickshire in the final. Those games, plus Warwickshire's own semi-final win against Leicestershire, were held on one day, and at one venue.

Trent Bridge was volunteered by Nottinghamshire when Lord's could not get a music licence from Westminster Council for the aforementioned Atomic Kitten pop group, plus all the other assorted jingles and theme-tunes which punctuate the action with the same regularity as fours and sixes. And so it was, on Saturday 19 July, that Nottingham hosted not just a memorable finals day but also cricket's 'Longest Day'.

The first semi-final began at 11am, and Surrey were crowned inaugural champions under the lights at 9.35pm, some 40 minutes earlier than scheduled, with their captain Adam Hollioake brandishing a £42,000 winners' cheque and underlining the seriousness with which his team had treated the competition.

In between, a full house of 15,000 had witnessed three separate matches, 851 runs from 108.2 overs, and the fall of 36 wickets. Most importantly, the cricket itself held the attention of the spectators and the music and the gimmicks merely supported the action in the middle and did not swamp it.

John Bracewell, the Gloucestershire coach, is a man for whom innovation and an eye for detail have been watchwords during his highly successful stint at Bristol. The New Zealander outlined his support for the new competition following his team's defeat in what was really the true 'final' of finals day.

'Twenty20 will help improve the standard of one-day cricket,' said Bracewell. 'The intensity of one-day cricket has improved in the last few years, but this will take it a step further.'

It was interesting to the experienced cricket-watcher how often the hectic, all-action contests came down to a real piece of skill from a leading performer. Despite its short form, the best players were still the best players.

In the final itself, for instance, Surrey fast bowler Jimmy Ormond exploited a little extra bounce in the pitch with an expertise that others could not match. The result? His new ball spell of 4–0–11–4 decimated the Warwickshire top order and, effectively, decided the game.

Some bowlers did get hammered, and going for ten or more runs per over was commonplace, but bowlers, overall, were not quite the cannon fodder that critics of the concept had predicted. As Bracewell indicated, a grasp of specific one-day skills was essential to survival in such a harsh and unforgiving climate. Bowlers had to be ultra-accurate, and clever at mixing up their pace and length, while batsmen had to use their imagination as much as their power to keep the scoreboards roaring along.

Spinners, too, found a niche in this new, wham-bam world. Of the five bowlers who took five-wicket hauls in the group matches, two were spinners: Northants off spinner Jason Brown, with 5 for 27 against Somerset, and Warwickshire's Kenyan leg spinner Collins Obuya, with 5 for 24 against Glamorgan.

For the record, the seamers who earned five wickets in a match were Surrey's Ormond and Hollioake, with 5 for 26 and 5 for 21 against Middlesex and Hampshire respectively, and Nottinghamshire's Richard Logan (who took 5 for 26 against Lancashire).

The competition's first century was scored by Ian Harvey, the Gloucestershire all-rounder who took to Twenty20 like … well, like an Australian was bound to take to it! Andrew Symonds and Brad Hodge, two other big-hitting Aussies, got closest to the three-figure mark before Harvey finally scored a century against Warwickshire at Edgbaston on 23 June.

Gloucestershire, with 221 for 7 against a shell-shocked Glamorgan the next day at Bristol, became the first team to top 200, and statistics soon showed that there was no advantage to be gained from batting either first or second.

Conditions, however, were quite magnificent for the entire tournament. The sun shone, and wonderful temperatures brought out the families and helped them to have a good time. More than 250,000 people attended the matches, including a noticeably higher proportion of both young women and children. Almost every county attracted significantly large crowds to all their games.

The ECB and county club marketing departments had argued that English cricket needed to do something radical to attract a new audience to the game, adding that even if ten per cent of those new fans then decided to try out longer matches it would be helping to generate future growth of interest in cricket.

There can be no doubt, after the success of the Twenty20 Cup, that it has given county cricket – and the game in England in general – a massive shot in the arm at a critical time. Next year, wisely, the ECB have decided to keep the format of the competition virtually the same, although it will appear at a later time in the calendar to avoid a clash with soccer's European Championships.

The task for the 18 counties in 2004 will be to build solidly on the success and support that the Twenty20 Cup undoubtedly achieved this year. Food outlets at grounds, for instance, should be more slickly run and should provide better quality. Boundary-edge entertainment needs to be carefully monitored, especially as the potential danger to younger children from an almost constant hail of low-flying cricket balls does not bear thinking about.

The three-hour time span of matches, however, as much as the novelty factor, has been the key to tempting spectators through the county gates. For television viewers too, as much as the paying fans, the 'jazzy' features like microphone links to the players, new batsmen having just 90 seconds to get from a 'hot seat' in the boundary-edge dugouts to the crease, and cash prizes for great catches in the crowd, all add to the entertainment rather than detract from it.

What was most noticeable on finals day at Trent Bridge, despite the cumulative amount of cricket on view (almost nine hours), was that it was actually the cricket that the huge majority of people had come to see.

Indeed, as one writer put it: 'Ironically, the crowd watching Atomic Kitten during the interval before the final was reminiscent of a county championship game: sparse and pretty apathetic.'

During their own short innings, moreover, one of the three Kitten singers shouted out, rather cattily, as the volume of the heckles mounted: 'OK, one more and you can get back to your cricket!'

As Gloucestershire's Bracewell observed later: 'Twenty20 didn't need Atomic Kitten. The cricket is intense enough. It's been a great spectacle.' Miaow!

13 June 2003

North Division

at Chester-le-Street
Nottinghamshire 157 for 7 (20 overs)
(JER Gallian 62)
Durham 160 for 4 (19.1 overs)
Durham (2pts) won by 6 wickets

Midlands/West/Wales Division

at Worcester
Northamptonshire 150 for 9 (20 overs)
(MEK Hussey 67)
Worcestershire 151 for 9 (19.4 overs) (RSG Anderson 4 for 29)
Worcestershire (2pts) won by one wicket

at Taunton
Warwickshire 188 for 7 (20 overs)
(TL Penney 52)
Somerset 169 (20 overs) (KP Dutch 70)
Warwickshire (2pts) won by 19 runs

South Division

at Southampton
Hampshire 153 (19.4 overs)
Sussex 148 for 7 (20 overs) (TR Ambrose 54*)
Hampshire (2pts) won by 5 runs

at The Oval
Middlesex 155 (20 overs) (AJ Strauss 52, J Ormond 5 for 26)
Surrey 158 for 6 (19.2 overs)
Surrey (2pts) won by 4 wickets

14 June 2003

North Division

at Headingley
Yorkshire 186 for 5 (20 overs)
Derbyshire 141 (18.1 overs) (MJ Di Venuto 67)
Yorkshire (2pts) won by 45 runs

South Division

at Imber Court
Surrey 182 for 9 (20 overs) (GP Thorpe 50)
Essex 138 (18.5 overs)
(Azhar Mahmood 4 for 20)
Surrey (2pts) won by 44 runs

Midlands/West/Wales Division

at Bristol
Worcestershire 122 (19.5 overs)
Gloucestershire 126 for 6 (19.1 overs)
Gloucestershire (2pts) won by 4 wickets

16 June 2003

North Division

at Leicester
Leicestershire 174 for 6 (20 overs) (BJ Hodge 97)
Yorkshire 158 (20 overs)
(Yuvraj Singh 71)
Leicestershire (2pts) won by 16 runs

at Trent Bridge
Lancashire 120 (19.2 overs) (RJ Logan
5 for 26)
Nottinghamshire 124 for 3 (19.1 overs)
(KP Pietersen 58)
Nottinghamshire (2pts) won by 7 wickets

Midlands/West/Wales Division

at Cardiff
Northamptonshire 159 for 5 (20 overs)
(MEK Hussey 79*)
Glamorgan 136 (18.4 overs)
(RDB Croft 53)
Northamptonshire (2pts) won by 23 runs

South Division

at Beckenham
Hampshire 145 for 6 (20 overs)
(SM Katich 59*)
Kent 147 for 4 (12 overs)
(A Symonds 96*)
Kent (2pts) won by 6 wickets

at Imber Court
Sussex 143 for 8 (20 overs) (AJ Hollioake
4 for 31)
Surrey 145 for 6 (18.1 overs)
Surrey (2pts) won by 4 wickets

18 June 2003

North Division

at Leicester
Leicestershire 168 for 9 (20 overs)
(BJ Hodge 64)
Durham 122 for 9 (20 overs)
Leicestershire (2pts) won by 46 runs

Midlands/West/Wales Division

at Cardiff
Glamorgan 193 for 7 (20 overs)
Somerset 197 for 3 (18 overs) (J Cox 53)

Ian Harvey, the first century-maker in
Twenty20 cricket.

Somerset (2pts) won by 7 wickets
at Worcester
Warwickshire 175 (19.4 overs)
(NV Knight 89)
Worcestershire 155 for 5 (20 overs)
(Kadeer Ali 53)
Warwickshire (2pts) won by 20 runs

South Division

at Southampton
Essex 155 for 6 (20 overs)
Hampshire 151 for 3 (20 overs) (SM Katich 59*)
Essex (2pts) won by 4 runs

at Hove
Sussex 177 for 9 (20 overs)
Middlesex 136 (19.3 overs)
(RSC Martin-Jenkins 4 for 20)
Sussex (2pts) won by 41 runs
19 June 2003

North Division

at Derby
Nottinghamshire 94 (19.1 overs) (T Lungley 4 for 13)
Derbyshire 95 for 1 (11.3 overs)
Derbyshire (2pts) won by 9 wickets

at Old Trafford
Yorkshire 102 for 8 (20 overs)
Lancashire 104 for 3 (13.1 overs)
Lancashire (2pts) won by 7 wickets

Midlands/West/Wales Division

at Bristol
Northamptonshire 128 for 5 (20 overs)
Gloucestershire 129 for 5 (19.3 overs)
Gloucestershire (2pts) won by 5 wickets

South Division

at Richmond
Kent 161 for 8 (20 overs)
Middlesex 165 for 3 (17.2 overs) (AJ Strauss 60)
Middlesex (2pts) won by 7 wickets

20 June 2003

North Division

at Leicester

Leicestershire 178 for 7 (20 overs)
Lancashire 156 for 8 (20 overs) (G Chapple 55*)
Leicestershire (2pts) won by 22 runs

at Headingley
Yorkshire 198 for 4 (20 overs) (SP Fleming 58,
MJ Lumb 50)
Durham 143 for 8 (20 overs) (ML Love 51)
Yorkshire (2pts) won by 55 runs

Midlands/West/Wales Division

at Northampton
Northamptonshire 166 for 6 (20 overs)
(MEK Hussey 88)
Somerset 151 (20 overs) (JF Brown 5 for 27)
Northamptonshire (2pts) won by 15 runs

at Edgbaston
Warwickshire 181 for 9 (20 overs)
(NV Knight 54)
Glamorgan 113 (16.2 overs) (MP Maynard 50,
CO Obuya 5 for 24)
Warwickshire (2pts) won by 68 runs

South Division
at Chelmsford
Essex 116 (18.4 overs) (MJ Dennington 4 for 28)
Kent 120 for 7 (16.1 overs)
Kent (2pts) won by 3 wickets

21 June 2003

North Division

at Old Trafford
Lancashire 91 (17.4 overs) (DR Hewson 4 for 18)
Derbyshire 95 for 3 (15.5 overs)
(MJ Di Venuto 52*)
Derbyshire (2pts) won by 7 wickets

at Trent Bridge
Nottinghamshire 158 for 5 (20 overs)
Leicestershire 159 for 9 (20 overs)
(DL Maddy 53)
Leicestershire (2pts) won by 1 wicket

Midlands/West/Wales Division

at Taunton
Somerset 119 for 9 (20 overs)
Gloucestershire 120 for 0 (10.2 overs)
(IJ Harvey 75*)

Gloucestershire (2pts) won by 10 wickets

South Division

at Hove
Sussex 180 for 6 (20 overs)
(RSC Martin-Jenkins 56*)
Essex 173 for 4 (20 overs) (A Flower 71)
Sussex (2pts) won by 7 runs

23 June 2003

North Division

at Derby
Derbyshire 157 (19.5 overs) (N Killeen 4 for 32)
Durham 151 for 5 (20 overs) (GJ Pratt 62*)
Derbyshire (2pts) won by 6 runs

Midlands/West/Wales Division

at Cardiff
Glamorgan 170 for 4 (20 overs) (MP Maynard 72,
MJ Powell 66*)
Worcestershire 114 (19 overs)
Glamorgan (2pts) won by 56 runs

at Edgbaston
Warwickshire 134 for 7 (20 overs) (IJL Trott 65*)
Gloucestershire 135 for 2 (13.1 overs)
(IJ Harvey 100*)
Gloucestershire (2pts) won by 8 wickets

South Division

at Canterbury
Surrey 186 for 8 (20 overs)
(Azhar Mahmood 57*, MR Ramprakash 53)
Kent 168 for 9 (20 overs) (ET Smith 56)
Surrey (2pts) won by 18 runs

at Uxbridge
Hampshire 134 for 7 (20 overs)
Middlesex 136 for 2 (14.5 overs) (PN Weekes 56)
Middlesex (2pts) won by 8 wickets

24 June 2003

North Division

at Old Trafford
Lancashire 144 for 8 (20 overs)
(AJ Swann 56)
Durham 140 for 9 (20 overs) (P Mustard 61,

CL Hooper 4 for 18)
Lancashire (2pts) won by 4 runs
at Leicester
Leicestershire 171 for 8 (20 overs)
Derbyshire 170 for 9 (20 overs)
(M Kaif 53)
Leicestershire (2pts) won by 1 run

at Headingley
Yorkshire 196 for 5 (20 overs) (MJ Wood 57,
MJ Lumb 55)
Nottinghamshire 178 (18.1 overs)
Yorkshire (2pts) won by 18 runs

Midlands/West/Wales Division

at Bristol
Gloucestershire 221 for 7 (20 overs)
(CM Spearman 88)
Glamorgan 168 for 7 (20 overs)
(MP Maynard 69)
Gloucestershire (2pts) won by 53 runs

at Northampton
Warwickshire 202 for 5 (20 overs) (NV Knight 69*)
Northamptonshire 148 for 7 (20 overs)
Warwickshire (2pts) won by 54 runs

at Worcester
Worcestershire 161 for 5 (20 overs) (GJ Batty 87)
Somerset 124 (18.2 overs)
Worcestershire (2pts) won by 37 runs

South Division

at Chelmsford
Essex 175 for 5 (20 overs) (A Flower 83)
Middlesex 173 for 7 (20 overs)
Essex (2pts) won by 2 runs

at Southampton
Surrey 140 for 9 (20 overs) (SA Newman 59)
Hampshire 121 (20 overs) (AJ Hollioake 5 for 21)
Hampshire (2pts) won by 19 runs

at Hove
Kent 114 (18.5 overs)
Sussex 115 for 5 (15.5 overs)
Sussex (2pts) won by 5 wickets

FINAL GROUP TABLES

GROUP MIDLANDS/WALES/WEST

	P	W	L	NR	T	Pts	R/R
Gloucestershire	5	5	-	-	-	10	+2.187
Warwickshire	5	4	1	-	-	8	+1.072
Worcestershire	5	2	3	-	-	4	-0.459
Northamptonshire	5	2	3	-	-	4	-0.245
Somerset	5	1	4	-	-	2	-1.411
Glamorgan	5	1	4	-	-	2	-1.098

GROUP NORTH

	P	W	L	NR	T	Pts	R/R
Leicestershire	5	5	-	-	-	10	+0.860
Yorkshire	5	3	2	-	-	6	+0.457
Derbyshire	5	3	2	-	-	6	+0.604
Lancashire	5	2	3	-	-	4	-0.125
Durham	5	1	4	-	-	2	-1.020
Nottinghamshire	5	1	4	-	-	2	-0.882

GROUP SOUTH

	P	W	L	NR	T	Pts	R/R
Surrey	5	5	-	-	-	10	+1.068
Sussex	5	3	2	-	-	6	+0.617
Kent	5	2	3	-	-	4	+0.250
Middlesex	5	2	3	-	-	4	+0.196
Essex	5	2	3	-	-	4	-0.811
Hampshire	5	1	4	-	-	2	-1.321

SEMI-FINAL – LEICESTERSHIRE v. WARWICKSHIRE
19 July 2003 at Trent Bridge

LEICESTERSHIRE

TR Ward	run out	5
V Sehwag	c Knight b Waqar Younis	5
BJ Hodge	c Brown b Waqar Younis	66
DI Stevens	b Wagg	14
DL Maddy	c Carter b Obuya	26
*PA Nixon	c Obuya b Brown	7
PAJ DeFreitas (capt)	c Obuya b Waqar Younis	11
JN Snape	not out	9
JL Sadler	not out	2
DD Masters		
JO Grove		
Extras	lb 5, w 8, nb 4	17
	(20 overs) (7 wkts)	**162**

	O	M	R	W
Carter	4	0	27	0
Waqar Younis	4	0	21	3
Wagg	2	0	24	1
Brown	3	0	30	1
Obuya	4	0	35	1
Smith	3	0	20	0

Fall of Wickets 1-12, 2-12, 3-38, 4-97, 5-125, 6-137, 7-160

WARWICKSHIRE

NM Carter	c Grove b Sehwag	35
NV Knight (capt)	run out	32
IR Bell	lbw b Hodge	4
*TL Penney	not out	43
JO Troughton	not out	33
IJL Trott		
DR Brown		
GG Wagg		
CO Obuya		
NMK Smith		
Waqar Younis		
Extras	lb 2, w 9, nb 8	19
	(19.2 overs) (3 wkts)	**166**

	O	M	R	W
Maddy	3.2	0	28	0
DeFreitas	1	0	13	0
Grove	1	0	20	0
Masters	4	0	35	0
Sehwag	4	0	17	1
Hodge	4	0	27	1
Snape	2	0	24	0

Fall of Wickets 1-67, 2-83, 3-99

Umpires: JW Holder & G Sharp
Toss: Leicestershire

Warwickshire won by 7 wickets

SEMI-FINAL – SURREY v. GLOUCESTERSHIRE
19 July 2003 at Trent Bridge

SURREY

IJ Ward	b Harvey	49
AD Brown	c Windows b Lewis	18
R Clarke	st Pope b Hardinges	15
AJ Hollioake (capt)	c Gidman b Hardinges	15
Azhar Mahmood	c Rhodes b Hardinges	13
GP Thorpe	b Harvey	4
MR Ramprakash	c & b Ball	8
*JN Batty	not out	10
IDK Salisbury	b Ball	0
Saqlain Mushtaq	run out	5
J Ormond		
Extras	b 2, lb 2, w 2, nb 4	10
	(20 overs) (9 wkts)	**147**

	O	M	R	W
Smith	4	0	11	0
Lewis	4	0	37	1
Hardinges	4	0	37	3
Ball	4	0	26	2
Harvey	4	0	32	2

Fall of Wickets 1-26, 2-55, 3-91, 4-112, 5-116, 6-129, 7-137, 8-137, 9-147

GLOUCESTERSHIRE

CM Spearman (capt)	b Ormond	1
IJ Harvey	c Saqlain b Mahmood	7
JN Rhodes	c Batty b Mahmood	0
APR Gidman	b Mahmood	61
MGN Windows	b Saqlain	3
MA Hardinges	b Hollioake	24
CG Taylor	not out	21
MCJ Ball	not out	11
*SP Pope		
J Lewis		
A M Smith		
Extras	lb 5, w 3, nb 6	14
	(20 overs) (6 wkts)	**142**

	O	M	R	W
Ormond	4	0	21	1
Mahmood	4	0	28	3
Saqlain	4	0	24	1
Salisbury	4	0	34	0
Hollioake	4	0	30	1

Fall of Wickets 1-4, 2-5, 3-17, 4-35, 5-87, 6-120

Umpires: B Dudleston & G Sharp
Toss: Surrey

Surrey won by 5 runs

FINAL – SURREY v. WARWICKSHIRE
19 July 2003 at Trent Bridge

WARWICKSHIRE

Batting

NM Carter	b Ormond	8
NV Knight (capt)	b Ormond	8
IR Bell	c Clarke b Azhar Mahmood	5
JO Troughton	c Brown b Ormond	1
TL Penney	b Hollioake	33
DR Brown	c Batty b Ormond	0
*T Frost	c Ormond b Saqlain Mushtaq	31
GG Wagg	b Hollioake	5
CO Obuya	c Ward b Saqlain Mushtaq	17
NMK Smith	run out	1
Waqar Younis	not out	0
Extras	w 2, nb 4	6
	(18.1 overs)	**115**

Bowling

	O	M	R	W
Ormond	4	0	11	4
Azhar Mahmood	3	0	22	1
Saqlain Mushtaq	4	0	35	2
Clarke	4	0	20	0
Hollioake	3.1	0	27	2

Fall of Wickets
1-16, 2-20, 3-22, 4-32, 5-33, 6-63, 7-83, 8-112, 9-115, 10-115

SURREY

Batting

IJ Ward	c Waqar Younis b Wagg	50
AD Brown	not out	55
MR Ramprakash	not out	4
R Clarke		
AJ Hollioake (capt)		
Azhar Mahmood		
GP Thorpe		
*JN Batty		
IDK Salisbury		
Saqlain Mushtaq		
*J Ormond		
Extras	lb 4, w 2, nb 4	10
	(10.5 overs) (1 wicket)	**119**

Bowling

	O	M	R	W
Carter	2	0	20	0
Waqar Younis	4	0	29	0
Brown	2	0	24	0
Obuya	1	0	18	0
Wagg	1	0	20	1
Knight	0.5	0	4	0

Fall of Wickets
1-100

Umpires: B Dudleston & JW Holder
Toss: Warwickshire

Surrey won by 9 wickets

Adam Hollioake, captain of inaugural winners Surrey, stressed how seriously his team had approached the Twenty20 Cup.

CHELTENHAM & GLOUCESTER TROPHY

By Mark Baldwin

First Round: 28 August 2002

at Banbury
Lancashire Cricket Board 229 for 8 (50 overs)
(SE Dearden 67*, P Green 63)
Oxfordshire 198 (48.2 overs) (AJ Mercer 4 for 26)
Lancashire Cricket Board won by 31 runs

at Finchampstead
Ireland 113 (35 overs)
Berkshire 114 for 6 (27 overs) (PJ Prichard 51*)
Berkshire won by 4 wickets

at Kidderminster
Dorset 227 (49.4 overs) (GR Treagus 76, SWD Rintoul
55, I Jamshed 5 for 36)
Worcestershire Cricket Board 228 for 5 (46 overs)
(D Manning 80, GS Kandola 53)
Worcestershire Cricket Board won by 5 wickets

at Ratcliffe College
Denmark 249 for 6 (50 overs) (Aftab Ahmed 77,
BE McGain 51, NJ Pullen 4 for 36)
Leicestershire Cricket Board 253 for 6 (46.1 overs)
(MDR Sutliff 97, NJ Pullen 65*)
Leicestershire Cricket Board won by 4 wickets

at Camborne
Cornwall 301 for 8 (50 overs) (JP Kent 80, TG Sharp
60, BP Price 50)
Somerset Cricket Board 299 (50 overs) (AV Suppiah
70, WJ Durston 50)
Cornwall won by 2 runs

at Southgate
Middlesex Cricket Board 239 for 9 (50 overs)
(PE Wellings 59)
Derbyshire Cricket Board 201 (47.5 overs) (JP Rodham
4 for 23)
Middlesex Cricket Board won by 38 runs

at Coventry & N Warwicks
Herefordshire 276 for 6 (50 overs) (PS Lazenbury 71,
I Dawood 60)
Warwickshire Cricket Board 203 (47.5 overs) (Naved-ul-
Hasan 4 for 49)
Herefordshire won by 73 runs

at Bristol
Surrey Cricket Board 290 for 4 (50 overs)
(SV Bahutule 105, JJ Porter 96)

Gloucestershire Cricket Board 273 for 8 (50 overs)
(MA Coombes 97, BRF Staunton 56, JJ Porter 4 for 51)
Surrey Cricket Board won by 17 runs

at Dinton
Buckinghamshire 424 for 5 (50 overs) (DK Taylor 140,
PD Atkins 110, PR Sawyer 50)
Suffolk 194 (40 overs) (AD Mawson 65, RJ Catley 65,
AR Clarke 5 for 36)
Buckinghamshire won by 230 runs

at Hursley Park
Hampshire Cricket Board 280 for 6 (50 overs)
(DC Shirazi 101, L Ronchi 78, J Hibberd 4 for 48)
Wiltshire 196 (41.4 overs)
Hampshire Cricket Board won by 84 runs

at Luton
Hertfordshire 167 (45.4 overs) (SG Cordingley 58)
Bedfordshire 169 for 2 (26.1 overs) (DR Clarke 73*,
S Young 50*)
Bedfordshire won by 8 wickets

at Keswick
Cumberland 280 for 5 (50 overs) (ST Knox 108*,
AA Metcalfe 71, SA Twigs 63)
Nottinghamshire Cricket Board 194 (50 overs)
(Z Iqbal 56*, ID Austin 4 for 25)
Cumberland won by 86 runs

at Toft
Cheshire 230 for 5 (50 overs)
(KEA Upashantha 59*)
Huntingdonshire Cricket Board 218 (49 overs)
Cheshire won by 12 runs

at Northampton
Yorkshire Cricket Board 233 for 8 (50 overs)
(S Widdup 90, S Clark 52)
Northamptonshire Cricket Board 176 (43.2 overs)
(TM Baker 63)
Yorkshire Cricket Board won by 57 runs

Second Round: 12 September 2002

at Aberdeenshire
Lancashire Cricket Board 175 for 7 (50 overs)
Scotland 177 for 6 (42.4 overs)
Scotland won by 4 wickets

at Reading
Norfolk 119 (40.5 overs) (SD Myles 4 for 8)
Berkshire 123 for 4 (27.1 overs)
Berkshire won by 6 wickets

at Kidderminster
Sussex Cricket Board 225 (48.5 overs) (CM Mole 66)
Worcestershire Cricket Board 227 for 4 (43.5 overs)
(Kadeer Ali 66, GR Hill 56*, RK Illingworth 53*)
Worcestershire Cricket Board won by 6 wickets

at Maidstone
Leicestershire Cricket Board 175 (47.4 overs)
Kent Cricket Board 176 for 3 (40.4 overs)
Kent Cricket Board won by 7 wickets

at Sully
Cornwall 248 for 7 (50 overs) (JM Hands 61)
Wales 224 (48.2 overs) (PV Simmons 59)
Cornwall won by 24 runs

at Southgate
Middlesex Cricket Board 194 (44 overs)
(SK Ranasinghe 75)
Cambridgeshire 200 for 3 (44.3 overs) (SA Kellett 79)
Cambridgeshire won by 7 wickets

at Darlington
Durham Cricket Board 274 for 8 (50 overs) (GM Scott
100, A Worthy 53, OJ Hughes 51, NM Davies 4 for 72)
Herefordshire 224 (47.2 overs) (CW Boroughs 72)
Durham Cricket Board won by 50 runs

at Chelmsford
Essex Cricket Board 302 for 8 (50 overs) (Saad Janjua
91, Tauseef Ali 65, GD James 51*)
Surrey Cricket Board 253 (45.5 overs) (JAW Fry 69,
Tauseef Ali 4 for 66)
Essex Cricket Board won by 49 runs

at Beaconsfield
Buckinghamshire 160 (49.5 overs)
Shropshire 149 (48.5 overs) (AR Clarke 4 for 28)
Buckinghamshire won by 11 runs

at Southampton
Staffordshire 249 for 6 (50 overs) (GD Franklin 63,
GF Archer 58)
Hampshire Cricket Board 144 (36.4 overs)
(MJR Rindel 4 for 21)
Staffordshire won by 105 runs

at Luton
Holland 96 (34.4 overs) (S Rashid 4 for 30)
Bedfordshire 97 for 0 (15.3 overs)
(NA Stanley 56*)
Bedfordshire won by 10 wickets

at Exmouth
Devon 285 for 6 (50 overs) (RI Dawson 138, MP Hunt 70)
Cumberland 158 (43.5 overs) (MAE Richards 4 for 22)
Devon won by 127 runs

at Neston
Lincolnshire 281 for 7 (50 overs) (MC Dobson 90,
J Trower 67)
Cheshire 277 for 8 (50 overs) (MR Currie 94,
RG Hignett 84, PRJ Bryson 59, MA Fell 4 for 20)
Lincolnshire won by 4 runs

at Jesmond
Northumberland 352 (49.4 overs) (B Parker 108,
CJ Hewison 69)
Yorkshire Cricket Board 226 (47.1 overs)
Northumberland won by 126 runs

Third Round: May 2003

at Luton
Warwickshire 233 for 8 (50 overs) (WE Sneath 4 for 38)
Bedfordshire 218 for 9 (50 overs)
Warwickshire won by 15 runs

at Reading
Berkshire 110 (44.2 overs) (VJ Wells 6 for 20)
Durham 111 for 2 (23 overs) (VJ Wells 63*)
Durham won by 8 wickets

at Ascott Park
Gloucestershire 401 for 7 (50 overs) (THC Hancock 135,
JN Rhodes 87, CM Spearman 76)
Buckinghamshire 77 (25.1 overs) (JMM Averis 6 for 23)
Gloucestershire won by 324 runs

at March
Yorkshire 299 for 5 (50 overs) (MJ Wood 118*,
MJ Lumb 82, A McGrath 56)
Cambridgeshire 214 for 8 (50 overs) (NT Gadsby 53)
Yorkshire won by 85 runs

at Truro
Cornwall 140 (46.1 overs)
Kent 141 for 5 (38.4 overs)
Kent won by 5 wickets

at Exmouth
Devon 180 (49.1 overs) (ND Hancock 73*, J Wood 4 for 33)
Lancashire 182 for 1 (40.4 overs) (IJ Sutcliffe 89*,
MJ Chilton 51)
Lancashire won by 9 wickets

at Darlington
Glamorgan 312 for 9 (50 overs) (MP Maynard 115,
IJ Thomas 93)
Durham Cricket Board 226 (47.4 overs) (A Worthy 59)
Glamorgan won by 86 runs

at Chelmsford
Essex 315 for 6 (50 overs) (WI Jefferson 132,
DDJ Robinson 70)
Essex Cricket Board 273 (49.3 overs) (M Akhtar 71,
Adnan Akram 61)
Essex won by 42 runs

at Southampton
Hampshire 213 for 7 (50 overs) (SM Katich 82*)
Sussex 214 for 6 (49.3 overs) (CJ Adams 80*)
Sussex won by 4 wickets

at Canterbury
Derbyshire 299 for 5 (50 overs) (CWG Bassano 101,
DR Hewson 69, DG Cork 59)
Kent Cricket Board 128 (45.2 overs)
Derbyshire won by 171 runs

at Lincoln Lindum
Lincolnshire 279 for 7 (50 overs) MA Fell 77,
RJ Chapman 53*, J Clarke 53)
Nottinghamshire 280 for 6 (48.1 overs) (PJ Franks 84*,
U Afzaal 71)
Nottinghamshire won by 4 wickets

at Northampton
Middlesex 214 for 7 (50 overs) (EC Joyce 72,
AJ Strauss 53, GP Swann 4 for 40)
Northamptonshire 188 (48.4 overs) (JW Cook 57,
CB Keegan 4 for 35)
Middlesex won by 26 runs

at Jesmond
Leicestershire 182 for 9 (50 overs) (PA Nixon 57)
Northumberland 92 (25.4 overs) (DD Masters 4 for 15)
Leicestershire won by 90 runs

at The Grange
Scotland 138 for 9 (50 overs) (DR Lockhart 51)
Somerset 142 for 0 (19.2 overs) (ME Trescothick 103*)
Somerset won by 10 wickets

at Stone
Surrey 273 (49.3 overs) (IJ Ward 108)
Staffordshire 264 for 4 (50 overs) (GF Archer 65,
PF Shaw 55*)
Surrey won by 9 runs

at Worcester
Worcestershire 311 for 4 (50 overs)
(VS Solanki 164*)
Worcestershire Cricket Board 141 for 9 (50 overs)
Worcestershire won by 170 runs

Staffordshire, Bedfordshire, Lincolnshire and the
Essex Cricket Board were the minnows who emerged
with the greatest credit from a third round which
contained no shocks. In the two ties contested by
first-class counties, Sussex squeezed past Hampshire
and Middlesex proved too strong for
Northamptonshire.

It was at Stone where perhaps the gutsiest and
best performance of the day occurred, with
Staffordshire falling short of Surrey's 273 by just
nine runs. What is more, the minor county side lost
only four wickets in the chase – although they were
never really in with a realistic chance of beating the
competition favourites. Their tenacity, however,
almost paid off when – with 25 runs still required
from the final over – skipper Richard Harvey swung
Adam Hollioake for successive sixes. Suddenly, just
ten runs were needed from the last two balls ... but
Hollioake kept his head and a moment of near panic
for the star-studded Surrey team had passed. The
highlight of the day for Surrey – besides winning –
was Ian Ward's feat of moving from 82 to his first
one-day century with three successive sixes, off
Richard Cooper's medium pace.

Warwickshire also had a fright before seeing off
Bedfordshire at Luton's Wardown Park by 15 runs.
The close nature of the contest, on a sluggish pitch
that made strokeplay difficult, was summed up by
the fact that Warwickshire's 233 for 8 included 17
ultimately crucial runs plundered off the final over
of their innings. Will Sneath, the 26-year-old
Bedford-born fast bowler, won the Man of the
Match award for his 4 for 38, while Tim Roberts' 48
from 54 balls, which contained seven fours, was the
top score on both sides and launched a Bedfordshire
reply which, at 137 for 5 with 15 overs remaining,
precisely matched that of their first-class opponents
at the same stage.

Lincolnshire's players could not hide their
disappointment after letting Nottinghamshire off the
hook in the derby encounter at the lovely Lincoln
Lindum ground which nestles beneath the city's
cathedral. Mark Fell, their 42-year-old captain, hit 77
from 90 balls before Bobby Chapman and James
Clarke struck half-centuries from 44 and 56 deliveries
respectively to lift the minor county side to 279 for 6
– their highest total in the competition. At 125 for 5
in reply, with just under 25 overs left,
Nottinghamshire were staring defeat in the face. Paul
Franks, however, then hit a match-winning 84 not
out, from just 70 balls and including three sixes and
seven fours, to lead a Notts lower-middle-order rally.
Usman Afzaal supported Franks in an 85-run sixth-

Vikram Solanki found the Worcestershire Cricket Board bowlers to his liking at Worcester as he plundered a career-best one-day score of 164 not out.

wicket partnership, and then Gareth Clough arrived to figure in an unbroken partnership of 70. Victory for Notts finally came with 11 balls to spare.

An incestuous affair at Chelmsford ended with Essex overcoming their own Cricket Board opponents by 42 runs in a high-scoring match dominated by Will Jefferson's 141-ball 132. The Essex Board team, containing five Essex academy players, were unfazed by the prospect of chasing the county's 315 for 6 – indeed, at 218 for 3 with 13 overs remaining, they had half a chance of causing an upset. Mohammed Akhtar, however, then chipped to midwicket after hitting three sixes and four fours in a 62-ball 71, but despite the excellent groundwork provided by him, Adnan Akram (61) and Saad Janjua (37 from 18 balls) the Board XI still came up some way short of their target.

Cornwall made Kent struggle at Truro, with the county side 83 for 5 at one stage before Matthew Walker and Geraint Jones saw them to their target of 141 with no further alarms.

It was a day to forget for the Buckinghamshire bowlers at Wing as Gloucestershire amassed 401 for 7 and went on to win by 324 runs – the second highest margin of victory in all domestic one-day competitions.

Elsewhere, Vikram Solanki hammered a career-best one-day score of 164 not out as Worcestershire trounced their own Cricket Board XI at New Road, while Matthew Maynard hammered the Durham Cricket Board team for a 86-ball 115 at Darlington to spearhead a comfortable Glamorgan win.

Marcus Trescothick swept Somerset to a ten-wicket victory over Scotland in Edinburgh by smashing five sixes and 13 fours in an unbeaten 103 from 70 balls, and Vince Wells took 6 for 20 and then scored 63 not out as Durham – or, rather, Wells – trounced Berkshire by eight wickets at Reading.

Yorkshire's Matthew Wood and Derbyshire's Chris Bassano were the third round's other century makers, while Ed Joyce (72) and Chris Adams (80 not out) both played the vital innings for Middlesex and Sussex respectively in the round's two all-first-class ties.

Fourth Round: 28 May 2003

at Lord's
Middlesex 258 for 8 (50 overs) (AJ Strauss 75, PN Weekes 73, RJ Kirtley 5 for 41)
Sussex 241 for 8 (50 overs)
Middlesex won by 17 runs

at Taunton
Surrey 281 for 6 (50 overs) (GP Thorpe 102*, JN Batty 55*)
Somerset 275 for 9 (50 overs) (KA Parsons 83)
Surrey won by 6 runs

at Canterbury
Kent 194 (47.4 overs) (GS Blewett 50, AM Smith 4 for 35)
Gloucestershire 195 for 5 (45.4 overs) (CM Spearman 71)
Gloucestershire won by 5 wickets

at Edgbaston
Essex 256 for 5 (50 overs) (ML Pettini 92*, A Flower 82)
Warwickshire 257 for 7 (49.1 overs) (DR Brown 108, AF Giles 71*)
Warwickshire won by 3 wickets

at Leicester
Leicestershire 258 for 9 (50 overs) (V Sehwag 56)
Nottinghamshire 159 (40.2 overs) (CL Cairns 67)
Leicestershire won by 99 runs

at Cardiff
Glamorgan 248 for 9 (50 overs) (J Hughes 51)
Derbyshire 251 for 3 (41.1 overs) (CWG Bassano 121, AI Gait 87*)
Derbyshire won by 7 wickets

at Worcester
Worcestershire 244 for 8 (50 overs) (DA Leatherdale 80, VS Solanki 60)
Yorkshire 177 (41.1 overs) (M Hayward 5 for 49)
Worcestershire won by 67 runs

at Chester-le-Street
Lancashire 229 for 9 (50 overs) (CL Hooper 61, SG Law 59)
Durham 86 (26.3 overs)
Lancashire won by 143 runs

Yorkshire's defence of the trophy did not survive their trip to Worcester, where South African fast bowler Nantie Hayward made a nonsense of his pre-match injury alarms to rip through the holder's batting. The Worcestershire spearhead took 5 for 49 as Yorkshire, despite 47 from England's Michael Vaughan, were dismissed for 177 in reply to the home side's 244 for 8. That total was built upon two fine knocks: the first of 80 from David Leatherdale and the second by Vikram Solanki who scored 60.

The closest game of the round came at Taunton, where an unbeaten 102 from 103 balls by Graham Thorpe proved just enough for Surrey to pip Somerset

Graham Thorpe's unbeaten century at Taunton helped Surrey to squeeze past Somerset.

by six runs. Thorpe struck 13 fours, and, with Jon Batty, plundered 99 from the last ten overs of the innings. It was a good job they did, for it gave Adam Hollioake just enough runs to play with as he fought to hold off a Somerset chase which, with just 65 needed from the final ten overs and with six wickets still standing, perhaps should have succeeded. However, despite Keith Parsons' 83 and two successive slogged sixes by Ian Blackwell off Saqlain Mushtaq, wickets kept tumbling as Surrey proved the team that kept its nerve.

There were just five balls to spare at Edgbaston as Warwickshire, on the back of Dougie Brown's maiden one-day hundred and a fine unbeaten 71 from Ashley Giles, overhauled Essex's challenging total of 256 for 5. The visitors had recovered magnificently themselves following the loss of both openers for nought – Nasser Hussain run out first ball – with youngster Mark Pettini and the ever-dependable Andy Flower providing the major contributions.

Predictably, perhaps, the only batsmen to make much of a seamers' pitch at the Riverside were the classy Lancashire pair of Carl Hooper (61) and Stuart Law (59). Their efforts took the visitors to a defendable total of 229 for 9, and then Durham folded to just 86 all out in 26.3 overs with James Anderson and Peter Martin both picking up three cheap wickets.

Totals of 258 were good enough for both Leicestershire and Middlesex, at Grace Road and Lord's respectively. Virender Sehwag's half-century was the highlight of a consistent Leicestershire batting performance, and only Chris Cairns (67) could make any inroads into a home attack in which Phil DeFreitas, Charlie Dagnall and Jamie Grove all took three scalps in a comfortable 99-run win. At Lord's it was the batting of Andy Strauss and Paul Weekes, who put on 139 for the first wicket, which ultimately decided Middlesex's tie with Sussex. Defeat for the visitors, by 17 runs, was particularly hard to take for James Kirtley, who followed up a five-wicket haul by finishing with a defiant unbeaten 30.

A superb 121 from just 100 balls by Chris Bassano, plus an unbeaten 87 by Andrew Gait, enabled Derbyshire to waltz past Glamorgan's 248 for 9 with an emphatic seven wickets and almost nine overs in hand at Cardiff.

Gloucestershire, meanwhile, moved menacingly into the quarter-finals by clearing a tricky looking Kent hurdle with considerable aplomb at Canterbury. Mike Smith and James Averis were the bowling stars as Kent were dismissed for just 194,

Chris Bassano, the Derbyshire batsman, tangles with Jonty Rhodes ... and survives! But Gloucestershire, and Rhodes, were the eventual winners of a thrilling semi-final tie at Bristol.

and then Craig Spearman led the chase with an entertaining 71 as victory was achieved by five wickets and with 26 deliveries unused.

Quarter-Finals: 10–11 June 2003

at Leicester
Worcestershire 216 for 8 (50 overs) (A Singh 74, DA Leatherdale 62)
Leicestershire 141 (43.5 overs)
Worcestershire won by 75 runs

at Old Trafford
Lancashire 252 for 7 (50 overs) (MB Loye 74)
Middlesex 195 (49.1 overs) (PJ Martin 4 for 34)
Lancashire won by 57 runs

at Derby
Derbyshire 271 (50 overs) (M Kaif 81, MJ Di Venuto 51, Azhar Mahmood 4 for 49)

Surrey 134 (33.4 overs) (G Welch 4 for 26)
Derbyshire won by 137 runs

at Edgbaston
Warwickshire 204 (47.4 overs) (NV Knight 88, JO Troughton 52, IJ Harvey 5 for 23)
Gloucestershire 206 for 5 (40.5 overs) (WPC Weston 88*)
Gloucestershire won by 5 wickets

There may not have been any giant-killing in the earlier rounds, but this year's competition still produced one major cup upset when unheralded and unfancied Derbyshire routed star-studded Surrey by the glorious margin of 137 runs at Derby. Badly missing the injured Martin Bicknell, Surrey's attack was exposed by a fourth-wicket stand of 88 in 15 overs between Mohammad Kaif and Dominic Hewson. Until then, and despite 51 from opener Michael Di Venuto, the home side had rather struggled to 99 for 3 in the 25th over. Hewson's 34

Back from Oz with a vengeance ... Ian Harvey returns to help Gloucestershire move smoothly into the last four.

from 38 balls gave Kaif the initial support he craved, before the 22-year-old Indian moved smoothly on to 81 from 85 balls himself. Kaif played with classical poise on a pitch hardly ideal for fast scoring, and the Derbyshire total was boosted to an intimidating 271 by the lower-order hitting of Nathan Dumelow and Graeme Welch, who pulled Rikki Clarke for six. In reply, Surrey never looked up to the challenge. Dominic Cork sent back Alistair Brown and Clarke, first ball, and Welch snuffed out the hint of a rally from Graham Thorpe and Adam Hollioake before finishing with figures of 4 for 26.

Ian Harvey, in only his second game of the summer for Gloucestershire since returning from Australian duty in the West Indies, took 5 for 23 and also ran out Ian Bell with a brilliant throw from short midwicket as Warwickshire were trounced by five wickets at Edgbaston. Nick Knight did hit 88 and Jim Troughton 52, but the home side's total of 204 was still woefully inadequate as Phil Weston, with an unbeaten 88, guided the visitors over the finishing line with almost ten overs to spare.

In his first bowl for a month, Andrew Flintoff took a couple of late Middlesex wickets to clinch Lancashire's 57-run win at Old Trafford and prove his recovery from shoulder trouble. Flintoff, however, had failed with the bat in an unexpected middle-order stutter, leaving Mal Loye, with 74, and Glen Chapple, with a hard-hit 45 from 25 balls, to anchor the Lancashire innings and boost it to 252 for 7. The last ten overs of the Lancashire innings had produced 81 runs, and Middlesex were immediately up against it as the new-ball attack of James Anderson and Peter Martin reduced them to 22 for 3.

Poor weather at Grace Road meant that it took Worcestershire two days to see off Leicestershire by 75 runs. Half-centuries from Anurag Singh and David Leatherdale propped up the visitors on a difficult surface, before their international seam attack made light work of the Leicestershire batting after the home side had begun the reserve day on 5 for 0, but then lost Virender Sehwag to the first ball bowled.

Semi-Finals: 7 and 9 August 2003

at Bristol
Derbyshire 219 (49.3 overs) (M Kaif 72)
Gloucestershire 221 for 9 (45.5 overs) (Shoaib Malik 74)
Gloucestershire won by one wicket

at Worcester
Worcestershire 254 for 5 (50 overs)
(GA Hick 97, A Singh 63)
Lancashire 248 for 9 (50 overs)
(MB Loye 116*, AJ Hall 4 for 36)
Worcestershire won by 6 runs

The first of two thrilling semi-finals was played out in a literally red-hot atmosphere at Bristol. On one of the hottest days of a steamy summer, and in front of a noisy and involved crowd, the Gloucestershire players were uncharacteristically nervous before squeezing past Derbyshire by one wicket. Victory came when James Averis gratefully swung a low full toss from Graeme Welch away to the square leg boundary, with the bowler unwisely straining to deliver a yorker when Dominic Cork was himself straining at the leash to be given the chance of a bowl at last man Mike Smith. If Welch could have completed a maiden at Averis, which looked on the cards when the tail-ender had either left or missed the previous four deliveries, a pumped-up Cork would have had the opportunity of adding Smith, who had yet to face a ball, to his victims of a highly dramatic 45th over – Shoaib Malik and Martyn Ball. But Cork, his new David Beckham-like hairdo and alice band appearing as a mark of his 32nd birthday, was ultimately denied his shot at glory by Averis' blow. 'We set a competitive total on a wicket getting slower and lower, but I personally didn't bowl as well as I would have liked to at the start of the Gloucestershire innings,' said skipper Cork afterwards. 'No one likes losing a semi-final, but we're proud that we gave Gloucestershire such a good game.' Mark Alleyne, the Gloucestershire captain, admitted: 'That was too close for comfort, and we owe a lot to Shoaib.' Indeed they did, with the young off-spinning Pakistani all-rounder, who was substituting for Ian Harvey, taking the Man of the Match award for his calm, 83-ball 74. It seemed hardly fair that Shoaib, as a Muslim, was unable to share in his own bottle of champagne and that he was informed of Harvey's intended return for the Lord's final. Despite mishooking Cork to long leg in the frantic finish, Shoaib had rallied Gloucestershire to 193 for 5 in a 59-run, sixth-wicket stand with Alleyne and had then stayed on long enough with Ball, following the fall of Jack Russell for a duck, to take his team to the very edge of victory. Shoaib's innings had also matched that of Mohammad Kaif, who had earlier made 72 and, along with former Gloucestershire player Dominic Hewson (37), had put on 75 in 14 overs for Derbyshire's fourth wicket.

Lancashire, once the undisputed one-day kings of county cricket, lost the second semi-final at New Road when they somehow managed not to score a run off the first five balls of their last over. Worcestershire, inspired by Andrew Hall in the scarcely

Vintage Hick: the semi-final at Worcester provided Graeme Hick with the stage to remind cricket followers of his enduring quality.

believable climax to a fine match, thus won by six runs. For Lancashire, it was a fifth cup semi-final defeat in four years. At the end of a day of draining temperatures and cut-and-thrust cricket, you had to feel sorry for Mal Loye, the Lancashire opener who remained unbeaten on 116 after being out on the field for the entire match. Loye, crucially as it turned out, failed to score from the final ball of the penultimate over, bowled by Kabir Ali. If only he had pushed a single, rather than swishing to leg in the hope of something more! This, though, would be harsh criticism of Loye, who hit four sixes and nine fours in a heroic, 154-ball innings that, towards its end, seemed to be leaving him on the brink of collapse through dehydration and exhaustion. Seven runs only were required from that fateful last over, although Loye had just lost Glen

Chapple in the previous over for a spirited, 43-ball 44. He and Chris Schofield, with 32, had helped Loye to pull the match back Lancashire's way after their powerful middle-order had fallen to Hall and Matt Mason. Chapple's final scoring shot had been a carved boundary through extra-cover off Kabir, leaving a victory equation that had been 147 from 20 overs, then 82 from 12, and then 15 from two, sitting apparently prettily at eight runs from nine balls. Chapple, though, then heaved again at Kabir and was bowled, bringing in Lancashire captain Warren Hegg to join Loye.

A single had given Hegg the strike against Hall, but the first ball of the final over bowled him and Peter Martin swished at the next delivery before he, too, was castled by a near-perfect yorker. In came John Wood and he, too, swung wildly and

Bristol cream: Ian Harvey sets the seal on an emphatic Gloucestershire victory in the Cheltenham & Gloucester Trophy final by hammering 61 from just 36 balls.

missed the fourth ball of the over. Wood, in fact, looked so overwhelmed by the pressure of the situation that he didn't even attempt to run for a bye when he failed to connect with Hall's next ball. Loye had sprinted to the striker's end, by this stage knowing that Lancashire's only hope was for him to hit the very last ball of the match for six, but Wood for some reason merely wandered up the pitch in a daze as Steve Rhodes, the Worcestershire wicketkeeper, gathered the ball and lobbed it carefully to the bowler's stumps for the run out to be effected. Now Loye, joined by last man James Anderson, was faced with an impossible task and he didn't even bother to run what would have been a final single to long leg. Hall, amazingly, had delivered a double-wicket maiden and Worcestershire, their own total based on a careful 63 from Anurag Singh and a vintage 97 from 112 balls by Graeme Hick, could celebrate one of the more remarkable triumphs in domestic one-day history.

Jon Lewis celebrates his dismissal of Gareth Batty as Worcestershire's cup final blues continue at Lord's.

Final: 30 August 2003 at Lord's

If this was a last hurrah for an ageing, but still fiercely competitive, Gloucestershire side, and one soon to lose its inspirational coach John Bracewell, then it was certainly a performance to remember. Cheekily, Mark Alleyne's side sang along to the theme music from television's classic *Dad's Army* comedy series in their dressing room afterwards, while the captain and Bracewell – who is off at the end of the season to coach New Zealand – spoke proudly about the six one-day trophies in five years that their alliance has produced. None of those victories, however, was achieved in quite the same crushing manner as this latest triumph.

Worcestershire, a line-up powerfully stacked with all-rounders and highly rated pacemen and with Graeme Hick still leading the top-order batting,

were simply humbled. As a Lord's cup final beating, this was on a par with the one handed out by Australia to Pakistan in the 1999 World Cup final. After seeing Hick lift a drive, fourth ball, to be caught at extra-cover in the 17th over, it was as if all the fight went out of Worcestershire. They had begun, in fact, with a promising opening stand of 64 between Vikram Solanki and Anurag Singh, but the running out of Solanki for 40 by Jonty Rhodes and the almost immediate failure of Hick undermined their collective effort to an alarming degree.

Gloucestershire, sniffing hesitancy and a lack of self-belief in the Worcestershire ranks, mercilessly strangled the life out of their opponents. It was a team performance of stunning quality, demonstrating once again how a determined, well-led and well-drilled team can make the very best

Cheltenham & Gloucester Trophy winners Gloucestershire are the modern masters of one-day domestic cricket, with six limited-overs titles in five years.

use of its individual abilities and achieve something far in excess of their sum. Even a recurring back injury to Mike Smith, forcing their leading bowler to leave the field, failed to knock Gloucestershire out of their stride. Alex Gidman, one of the up-and-coming all-rounders in English cricket, stepped up to take two important mid-innings wickets with some disciplined medium pace bowling, and the rest of the Gloucestershire attack all played their familiar roles to perfection. Behind the stumps, the irrepressible Jack Russell celebrated both the passing of his 40th birthday in

mid-August and a late fitness test by yapping out encouragement and commands, and his quick reaction to an aborted sharp single attempt in the 24th over also ran out the Worcestershire captain, Ben Smith.

The underrated Jon Lewis cut short a lower-order mini-recovery by removing both Gareth Batty and Steve Rhodes, and veteran off spinner Martyn Ball followed up three fine catches in the slip area by dealing efficiently with No. 10 and jack. Phil Weston then relished every minute of the excellent 50-ball 46 he took off his former county,

Mark Alleyne, the Gloucestershire captain, leads the cheers at Lord's.

FINAL – GLOUCESTERSHIRE v. WORCESTERSHIRE
30 August 2003 at Lord's

WORCESTERSHIRE

	First Innings	
VS Solanki	run out	40
A Singh	c Ball b Harvey	28
GA Hick	c Windows b Harvey	0
BF Smith (capt)	run out	12
AJ Hall	lbw b Gidman	11
DA Leatherdale	c Ball b Gidman	2
GJ Batty	lbw b Lewis	20
*SJ Rhodes	c Ball b Lewis	15
Kabir Ali	not out	5
MS Mason	st Russell b Ball	0
M Hayward	c sub b Ball	4
Extras	lb 6, w 4, nb 2	12
	(46.3 overs)	149

	First Innings			
	O	M	R	W
Smith	5	0	24	0
Lewis	10	2	28	2
Harvey	10	1	37	2
Alleyne	7	0	21	0
Gidman	7	1	12	2
Ball	7.3	0	21	2

Fall of Wickets
1-64, 2-65, 3-72, 4-92, 5-96, 6-99, 7-133, 8-134, 9-136

GLOUCESTERSHIRE

	First Innings	
CM Spearman	c Smith b Kabir Ali	10
WPC Weston	c Hall b Mason	46
IJ Harvey	st sub b Batty	61
APR Gidman	not out	12
JN Rhodes	not out	7
MGN Windows		
MW Alleyne (capt)		
*RC Russell		
MCJ Ball		
J Lewis		
AM Smith		
Extras	b 4, lb 3, w 3, nb 4	14
	(3 wkts, 20.3 overs)	150

	First Innings			
	O	M	R	W
Kabir Ali	4	0	25	1
Hayward	3	0	20	0
Mason	7	0	38	1
Hall	3	0	33	0
Batty	3.3	0	27	1

Fall of Wickets
1-30, 2-108, 3-132

Umpires: MR Benson & JH Hampshire
Toss: Gloucestershire

Gloucestershire won by 7 wickets

while Harvey merrily set about the Worcestershire bowling to smash 12 boundaries in a brilliant 36-ball 61. To Worcestershire's players and followers, the reason for the early (4.10pm) finish was hard to take. To the neutral, the one-sided nature of the event was a major disappointment – although Harvey's assault was entertaining enough. For Gloucestershire's exuberant supporters, however, for whom Lord's has become something of a home-from-home in recent years, the sight of Weston's imperious driving and Harvey's explosive hitting set the seal on a perfect day out.

CRICKET WORLD CUP 2007

By SCYLD BERRY

OK, it's quiz time! Answer, please, the following question: Which two of the following countries have the strongest cricket team: A. Australia; B. Pakistan; C. Upper Volta; D. Lower Volta?

Tricky one, eh? All right, try this question which is hardly more difficult: Which two out of these four have the strongest cricket team: A. England; B. West Indies; C. Scotland; D. Bermuda?

Well, we all know that Australia and Pakistan are the two strongest teams in the first group, and – barring the odd mishap – England and the West Indies in the second. Yet even though we all know that, the ICC are devising qualifying groups for the next World Cup exactly on the lines of the one involving England, West Indies, Scotland and Bermuda. In each group four countries will play each other once to discover – well, what do you know, that the two strongest teams in the group are the two Test-playing countries.

There will be four qualifying groups in all. That means the eight main Test-playing countries – excluding Zimbabwe and Bangladesh in other words – will probably be split between the four groups. Then two minnows will be added to each group to make a total of 16 countries in all: if not Upper and Lower Volta, then two out of Bangladesh, Zimbabwe, Kenya and five Associate Member countries like Scotland, Bermuda and Namibia.

Now I know England were struggling at one stage of their qualifying match against Namibia in the last World Cup. I was in Port Elizabeth and can see it now: the exemplary pick-up by Marcus Trescothick on the cover boundary and the laser-guided throw to Alec Stewart to bring off the run out that prompted Namibia's gallant run chase to collapse.

Namibia were ahead of England's run rate at one stage, but I still think England – without any interruption from rain – would have won, even without Trescothick's throw. The amateurs had gusto and physiques like oxen and their coach Dougie Brown of Warwickshire had drilled them well, but the Namibians would not have had the savvy in a tight finish.

So I don't see the point of having four qualifying groups which are hopelessly one-sided or, to be precise, two-sided.

In all the World Cups dating back to 1975 there have really only been three serious upsets: Zimbabwe beating Australia in 1983, Kenya beating the West Indies in 1996, and Bangladesh beating Pakistan in 1999, and the circumstances surrounding the last two were – how can we say this without annoying the lawyers? – dubious and controversial.

Most of these whale v. minnow matches have been routs, mismatches, boring to watch, and of no benefit to the players of either side, let alone to the spectators. The essence of sport is competition: I will watch Australia v. Pakistan, and with considerable interest even though I'm a neutral, because the sides are roughly equally matched and therefore will spark some dramatic tension. I will even watch Upper Volta v. Lower Volta as long as the teams are playing competitively, and never mind the quality. But Australia v. Lower Volta? Uh ah.

Or, rather, I do see the point behind these World Cup mismatches and profoundly disagree with it. The 1999 tournament had 12 teams, the 2003 tournament had 14, and the next will have 16. Why? Because the ICC wants to popularize – or 'globalize' – the game so that it is played in more countries around the world: that is a part of the answer, but I'm afraid it is only the minor part.

The major part is to increase – or 'globalize' – both TV audiences and revenues. Canada played in the last World Cup, and weren't disgraced thanks to the efforts of their Australian all-rounder John Davison; and the USA will play in the next one, and probably stage a few of the games as well.

The North American market is cricket's future. Television research supplied to the ICC has shown that the big money is to be made out of expatriates – primarily, though not exclusively, Indian – living in the States and Canada, with their high incomes and their televisions which can be programmed to take channels dedicated to cricket. And thus to pay good money to watch the game on TV.

So the ICC's big idea is to make the next World Cup as global as possible, not as interesting as possible. Naturally enough, the ICC want to make all they can out of it, but I think they are going to spread the butter dangerously thinly. Boring World Cups – like the last one was if you weren't an Australian or Indian fan – do the game damage in the long run.

A World Cup should have tens of millions glued to their television screens each evening to see a big game between the best countries. Instead, the qualifying rounds of 2007 will have millions switching off to avoid another mismatch.

No less a judge than Mike Atherton, albeit a very young elder statesman, thought that only 'a handful' of games in the last World Cup were interesting: five, that is, out of 52.

That is far too few to show for taking seven weeks out of everybody's life. Let the best play the best, as it was in the 1992 tournament, when the top nine countries played each other on a league basis and the top four went through to the semi-finals. Not the best v. the worst.

As you might have guessed, I won't be breaking a leg to get on a plane to attend the qualifying rounds in 2007, when the eight countries to get through to the Super-Eights might just be Australia, England, India, New Zealand, Pakistan, South Africa, Sri Lanka and the West Indies.

At that stage the World Cup should become interesting: it should be terrific fun in fact. The Prime Ministers of each of the West Indian territories have been overseeing their territory's bid to stage fixtures: so much does cricket still mean in the Caribbean. Chris Dehring, the chief organizer, seems a fine choice too; it is a nice touch that he has a sporting background, having played both cricket and football for Jamaica.

New grounds in Grenada and St Lucia; new stands in Barbados and elsewhere to seat the capacity crowds; cruise ships to be brought in to provide extra accommodation; while nothing need be done to stoke the enthusiasm of the locals. If the West Indies reach a semi-final in Kingston, Port-of-Spain or Bridgetown, it would be one of the most dramatic occasions in sport. I can't stand the thought of the 2007 qualifying rounds; I can't wait for the knock-out stage to begin.

And why should we all have to wait so long between World Cups? Talk about sheep following sheep! World Cups in every sport, and the Olympic Games, are held every four years simply because that was the timetable which suited a few people in Greece two-and-a-half thousand years ago. Going to Olympia in the wild west of the country every four years suited

them fine: in between they had crops to cut, inter-city wars to fight, and it took a while to send out the invitations without e-mail. So why have major sporting events followed a quadrennial cycle ever since the original Olympic Games, to no obvious purpose?

I propose that Cricket World Cups should be held every three years. Then the major countries could stage a tournament every 20 years or less, not 30. Then there would be no need for the Champions Trophy, either, which is just a money-spinner to fill in the vacuum between World Cups.

Roll on the knock-out stage of the next cricket World Cup in 2007. Better still, in 2006.

Scyld Berry is cricket correspondent of the Sunday Telegraph.

Martin Suji, the Kenya fast bowler, celebrates a successful appeal for lbw against Sachin Tendulkar of India during the 2003 World Cup semi-final. David v. Goliath battles on the cricket field, however, are usually hopelessly one-sided ... in favour of Goliath.

CRICKET WORLD CUP

By Jonathan Agnew

INTRODUCTION

The eighth Cricket World Cup, which ran during February and March 2003, was the biggest and most elaborate competition cricket has ever experienced. By the time it had limped to its dull and thoroughly predictable outcome (not Australia's fault, incidentally), even the most senior ICC executives who had been flushed out to beat the drum for the tournament before the semi-finals began, must have conceded, in moments of honesty, that size is not everything.

It is true that the World Cup raised lots of money for the ICC and, therefore, for international cricket, which is a good thing. However, for evidence that raking in the cash was the driving force above all else, one needs to look no further than the mission statement of the tournament: 'Our aim is to create the right environment for the players to best display their skills and in turn further enhance the game of cricket as an outstanding spectator and television sport.'

Apart from the ghastly split infinitive, what is wrong with that? Nothing, except that it was the 13th and last declared priority of the World Cup organizing committee, when it should have been the first. It is hardly surprising, then, that cricket's greatest showpiece was ruined by politics, dogged by petty restrictions that even dictated what brand of bottled water spectators could or could not bring to the grounds and produced a string of

Ali Bacher ... the man in charge of cricket's eighth World Cup.

stultifying, utterly forgettable matches. Indeed, the only highlight was the colourful opening ceremony, but even that went on too long. We should have taken that as a clue of what was to follow.

The smooth running of the event was crucial to the South African government, which is desperate to host the football World Cup in 2010. This would encompass Southern Africa as a whole, including Zimbabwe, and there is no doubt whatsoever that the technical committee, chaired by Ali Bacher, was pressurized into refusing to allow the murderous regime of President Robert Mugabe in Zimbabwe to be used in any way to reflect badly on the region, or its safety and suitability as a World Cup venue. This was the reason for the ICC's perceived intransigence so far as England's repeated and entirely reasonable requests to reschedule their match in Harare was concerned. 'We are not a political organization,' was the ICC's mantra, yet politics controlled its decision-making throughout and ruined the tournament.

Further doubt on the ICC's ability to gather accurate security information was cast in May when the British government advised against all unnecessary travel to Kenya. British Airways stopped flying to Nairobi because of the risk of terrorist activity there barely three months after New Zealand's cricketers had refused to play their match against Kenya in Nairobi for the same reason. Again, the ICC did not budge and the match was duly forfeited. The four points that Kenya and Zimbabwe both gained from the two boycotted games helped to propel them into the Super Sixes, and, as a spectacle, the World Cup was finished.

The first fortnight was remarkably newsworthy. Apart from the political shenanigans involving England, New Zealand, Zimbabwe and Kenya, there were problems with the Indian team and 'ambush marketing'. This was a largely unknown phrase to cricket correspondents before this World Cup, but so desperate was the ICC not to compromise its $500 million deal with the Global Cricket Corporation that all sorts of measures were put in place to protect it. This did not prevent alleged infringements and, like a host of issues arising from this unhappy tournament, the matter will have to be settled in court at a later date. On a lighter note – although it caused enormous embarrassment to the South Africans – the president of the United Cricket Board, Percy Sonn, was reported to be so drunk in a hospitality box in Paarl that he 'was falling out of his trousers'. Mr Sonn survived the inevitable calls for his resignation, but was spotted only rarely in public again.

Given that World Cups are all about pitting the best players in the world against each other, and that politics had already played such a strong and unwelcome hand, the final straw was the shock announcement that Shane Warne had given a positive drugs sample in Australia shortly before the tournament, and was to fly home before Australia had bowled a ball in anger. There was still the chance that he could return to South Africa if he won his appeal, but the Australian anti-doping committee, which considered the leg spinner's plea that he had, mistakenly, taken a

diuretic, soon scotched this. The tablet, he claimed, was given to him by his mother to assist him with fluid loss. 'Much of Warne's evidence was unsatisfactory,' the verdict read, 'and the committee does not accept that he was entirely truthful…' Warne was banned from all cricket for a year, and the World Cup was deprived of one its most glittering attractions.

Given that start to Australia's defence, the domination of Ricky Ponting's team was all the more laudable. They had a hiccup or two along the way – most significantly against England and New Zealand – but they won both games when the chips were down and are, truly, a great team. They were worthy champions of a World Cup unworthy of the name. The ICC has four years to get it right by restoring the need to promote cricket as an exciting and vibrant game at the top of the agenda, rather than at the bottom. Do that, and the tournament – and, indeed, the game – has a future.

GROUP STAGES

Pool A

10 February 2003 at Harare
Zimbabwe 340 for 2 (50 overs) (CB Wishart 172*, GW Flower 78*)
Namibia 104 for 5 (25.1 overs)
Zimbabwe (4pts) won by 86 runs – DL Method: target 191 from 25.1 overs

11 February 2003 at Johannesburg
Australia 310 for 8 (50 overs) (A Symonds 143*, RT Ponting 53)
Pakistan 228 (45 overs) (IJ Harvey 4 for 58)
Australia (4pts) won by 82 runs

12 February 2003 at Paarl
India 204 (48.5 overs) (SR Tendulkar 52, TBM de Leede 4 for 35)
Holland 136 (48.1 overs) (DLS van Bunge 62, A Kumble 4 for 32, J Srinath 4 for 30)
India (4pts) won by 68 runs

13 February 2003 at Harare
Zimbabwe v. **England** – match cancelled
Zimbabwe (4pts)

15 February 2003 at Centurion Park
India 125 (41.4 overs)
Australia 128 for 1 (22.2 overs)
Australia (4pts) won by 9 wickets

Tarnished gold: Shane Warne, the world's best leg spinner and a beach-blond icon of the game, missed the World Cup because of a drugs ban.

16 February 2003 at East London
Holland 142 for 9 (50 overs) (TBM de Leede 58*,
JM Anderson 4 for 25)
England 144 for 4 (23.2 overs) (MP Vaughan 51,
NV Knight 51)
England (4pts) won by 6 wickets

16 February 2003 at Kimberley
Pakistan 255 for 9 (50 overs) (Saleem Elahi 63)
Namibia 84 (17.4 overs) (Wasim Akram 5 for 28,
Shoaib Akhtar 4 for 46)
Pakistan (4pts) won by 171 runs

19 February 2003 at Port Elizabeth
England 272 (50 overs) (AJ Stewart 60, ME Trescothick
58, RJ van Vuuren 5 for 43)
Namibia 217 for 9 (50 overs) (AJ Burger 85)
England (4pts) won by 55 runs

19 February 2003 at Harare
India 255 for 7 (50 overs) (SR Tendulkar 81)
Zimbabwe 172 (44.4 overs)
India (4pts) won by 83 runs

20 February 2003 at Potchefstroom
Australia 170 for 2 (36 overs) (DR Martyn 67*)
Holland 122 (30.2 overs)
*Australia (4pts) won by 75 runs – DL Method: target 198
from 36 overs*

22 February 2003 at Cape Town
England 246 for 8 (50 overs) (PD Collingwood 66*,
MP Vaughan 52)
Pakistan 134 (31 overs) (JM Anderson 4 for 29)
England (4pts) won by 112 runs

23 February 2003 at Pietermaritzburg
India 311 for 2 (50 overs) (SR Tendulkar 152,
SC Ganguly 112*)
Namibia 130 (42.3 overs) (Yuvraj Singh 4 for 6)
India (4pts) won by 181 runs

24 February 2003 at Bulawayo
Zimbabwe 246 for 9 (50 overs) (A Flower 62,
AM Blignaut 54)
Australia 248 for 3 (47.3 overs) (AC Gilchrist 61,
DS Lehmann 56*, DR Martyn 50*)
Australia (4pts) won by 7 wickets

25 February 2003 at Paarl
Pakistan 253 for 9 (50 overs) (Yousuf Youhana 58)
Holland 156 (39.3 overs)
Pakistan (4pts) won by 97 runs

26 February 2003 at Durban
India 250 for 9 (50 overs) (R Dravid 62,
SR Tendulkar 50)
England 168 (45.3 overs) (A Flintoff 64,
A Nehra 6 for 23)
India (4pts) won by 82 runs

27 February 2003 at Potchefstroom
Australia 301 for 6 (50 overs) (ML Hayden 88,
A Symonds 59, DS Lehmann 50*)
Namibia 45 (14 overs) (GD McGrath 7 for 15)
Australia (4pts) won by 256 runs

28 February 2003 at Bulawayo
Zimbabwe 301 for 8 (50 overs) (A Flower 71,
AM Blignaut 58)
Holland 202 for 9 (50 overs)
Zimbabwe (4pts) won by 99 runs

1 March 2003 at Centurion Park
Pakistan 273 for 7 (50 overs) (Saeed Anwar 101)
India 276 for 4 (45.4 overs) (SR Tendulkar 98, Yuvraj
Singh 50*)
India (4pts) won by 6 wickets

2 March 2003 at Port Elizabeth
England 204 for 8 (50 overs) (AJ Bichel 7 for 20)
Australia 208 for 8 (49.4 overs) (MG Bevan 74*,
AR Caddick 4 for 35)
Australia (4pts) won by 2 wickets

3 March 2003 at Bloemfontein
Holland 314 for 4 (50 overs) (KJ van Noortwijk 134*,
JF Kloppenburg 121)
Namibia 250 (46.5 overs) (BG Murgatroyd 52,
D Keulder 52, Adeel Raja 4 for 42,
JF Kloppenburg 4 for 42)
Holland (4pts) won by 64 runs

4 March 2003 at Bulawayo
Pakistan 73 for 3 (14 overs)
Zimbabwe
Match abandoned – rain
Zimbabwe (2pts) Pakistan (2pts)

Pool B

9 February 2003 at Cape Town
West Indies 278 for 5 (50 overs) (BC Lara 116)
South Africa 275 for 9 (49 overs) (G Kirsten 69,
L Klusener 57)
West Indies (4pts) won by 3 runs

10 February 2003 at Bloemfontein
Sri Lanka 272 for 7 (50 overs) (ST Jayasuriya 120,
HP Tillekeratne 81*)
New Zealand 225 (45.3 overs) (SB Styris 141)
Sri Lanka (4pts) won by 47 runs

11 February 2003 at Durban
Canada 180 (49.1 overs)
Bangladesh 120 (28 overs) (A Codrington 5 for 27)
Canada (4pts) won by 60 runs

12 February 2003 at Potchefstroom
Kenya 140 (38 overs) (RD Shah 60,
L Klusener 4 for 16)
South Africa 142 for 0 (21.2 overs) (HH Gibbs 87*,
G Kirsten 52*)
South Africa (4pts) won by 10 wickets

13 February 2003 at Port Elizabeth
New Zealand 241 for 7 (50 overs)
West Indies 221 (49.4 overs) (RR Sarwan 75,
RD Jacobs 50, AR Adams 4 for 44)
New Zealand (4pts) won by 20 runs

14 February 2003 at Pietermaritzburg
Bangladesh 124 (31.1 overs) (WPUJC Vaas 6 for 25)
Sri Lanka 126 for 0 (21.1 overs) (MS Atapattu 69*,
ST Jayasuriya 55*)
Sri Lanka (4pts) won by 10 wickets

15 February 2003 at Cape Town
Canada 197 (49 overs) (IS Billcliff 71, TM Odoyo
4 for 28)
Kenya 198 for 6 (48.3 overs) (RD Shah 61)
Kenya (4pts) won by 4 wickets

16 February 2003 at Johannesburg
South Africa 306 for 6 (50 overs) (HH Gibbs 143)
New Zealand 229 for 1 (36.5 overs)
(SP Fleming 134*, NJ Astle 54*)
*New Zealand (4pts) won by 9 wickets - DL Method:
target 226 from 39 overs*

18 February 2003 at Benoni
West Indies 244 for 9 (50 overs) (RL Powell 50)
Bangladesh 32 for 2 (8.1 overs)
Match abandoned – rain
West Indies (2pts) Bangladesh (2pts)

19 February 2003 at Paarl
Canada 36 (18.4 overs) (RAP Nissanka 4 for 12)
Sri Lanka 37 for 1 (4.4 overs)
Sri Lanka (4pts) won by 9 wickets

21 February 2003 at Nairobi
Kenya v. **New Zealand** – match cancelled
Kenya (4pts)

22 February 2003 at Bloemfontein
Bangladesh 108 (35.1 overs) (M Ntini 4 for 24)
South Africa 109 for 0 (12 overs)
(G Kirsten 52*)
South Africa (4pts) won by 10 wickets

23 February 2003 at Centurion Park
Canada 202 (42.5 overs) (JM Davison 111,
VC Drakes 5 for 44)
West Indies 206 for 3 (20.3 overs) (BC Lara 73,
WW Hinds 64)
West Indies (4pts) won by 7 wickets

24 February 2003 at Nairobi
Kenya 210 for 9 (50 overs) (KO Otieno 60,
M Muralitharan 4 for 28)
Sri Lanka 157 (44.5 overs) (CO Obuya 5 for 24)
Kenya (4pts) won by 53 runs

26 February 2003 at Kimberley
Bangladesh 198 for 7 (50 overs) (Mohammad
Ashraful 56)
New Zealand 199 for 3 (33.3 overs)
(CD McMillan 75)
New Zealand (4pts) won by 7 wickets

27 February 2003 at East London
South Africa 254 for 8 (50 overs) (HH Dippenaar 80,
GC Smith 63)
Canada 136 for 5 (50 overs) (I Maraj 53*)
South Africa (4pts) won by 118 runs

28 February 2003 at Cape Town
Sri Lanka 228 for 6 (50 overs) (ST Jayasuriya 66)
West Indies 222 for 9 (50 overs) (S Chanderpaul 65,
CH Gayle 55, WPUJC Vaas 4 for 22)
Sri Lanka (4pts) won by 6 runs

1 March 2003 at Johannesburg
Kenya 217 for 7 (50 overs) (MO Odumbe 52*)
Bangladesh 185 (47.2 overs)
(MO Odumbe 4 for 38)
Kenya (4pts) won by 32 runs

3 March 2003 at Benoni
Canada 196 (47 overs) (JM Davison 75,
JDP Oram 4 for 52)
New Zealand 197 for 5 (23 overs) (SB Styris 54*)
New Zealand (4pts) won by 5 wickets

3 March 2003 at Durban
Sri Lanka 268 for 9 (50 overs) (MS Atapattu 124,
PA de Silva 73)
South Africa 229 for 6 (45 overs) (HH Gibbs 73)
Match tied
South Africa (2pts), Sri Lanka (2pts) – DL Method: target
230 from 45 overs

4 March 2003 at Kimberley
West Indies 246 for 7 (50 overs) (CH Gayle 119,
S Chanderpaul 66)
Kenya 104 (35.5 overs) (VC Drakes 5 for 33)
West Indies (4pts) won by 142 runs

Serious political wrangling at the start of the
tournament was to have major consequences in both
groups that began the 2003 Cricket World Cup. In
Group B, New Zealand made it clear from the
outset that they were not willing to play their match
in Nairobi. New Zealand claimed to have credible
evidence of a terrorist cell working in the city and
given that the Kiwis had only recently witnessed a
bomb blast in Karachi, it was clear that the position
taken by the team was more than simply posturing.
The refusal of the ICC to move the match resulted
in Kenya picking up the four points on offer and
this, in turn, had a major bearing in Kenya reaching
the semi-finals of the tournament.

In Group A, England had serious misgivings
about travelling to Harare. Pressure was growing at
home for the team to boycott the game and the
team, although mindful of the consequences of
surrendering four points, was inclined to agree.
However, because the ICC regulations required
teams to supply proof of fears about safety and
security to themselves, rather than of the starvation,
rape and murder of the host country's citizens, in
order for the games to be played elsewhere, England
had little option but to make the most of an alleged
death threat to the players and their families from an
unknown group called the Sons and Daughters of
Zimbabwe. With little credible evidence – save the
letter itself – this failed and England's bid to reach
the Super Sixes was seriously damaged before the
tournament had begun. To embarrass the ICC still
further, Henry Olonga and Andy Flower then wore
black armbands and issued a fiercely critical
statement about the regime of President Robert
Mugabe in Zimbabwe's first home game.

Group A contained Australia, Pakistan, India,
England, Zimbabwe and the 'minnows' Namibia
and Holland. Neither of the part-timers provided
anything bordering on a shock, but in the match

Andrew Symonds played perhaps the most important innings
of his career at the Wanderers to kick-start Australia's World
Cup defence.

played between the two of them, Holland won by 64
runs having run up an impressive total of 314 for 4.

The first game of interest in Group A featured
Australia and Pakistan in Johannesburg. With Shane
Warne packing his bags for home and at 148 for 5 in
the 30th over, Australia – the defending champions
– were struggling and it seemed that the tournament
might get under way with a major upset. However,
Andrew Symonds hit a blistering 143 from 125 balls.
Waqar bowled two beamers at the Queenslander as
Pakistan's frustration mounted. Gillespie struck in
his first over, Lee softened up the middle order and
it was Hogg and Harvey who picked up the wickets
as Pakistan fell 83 runs short.

Australia had ruthlessly dealt with India at
Centurion before England had even played a game.
Finally, England started, disposing of Holland in East
London where James Anderson claimed 4 for 25 and
Knight and Vaughan both made 51. England then
moved along the coast to face Namibia and although
their margin of victory – 55 runs – was fairly
comfortable, the fact is that Jan-Berry Burger, with a
hard-hitting 85, almost caused an embarrassment.

With other results going as expected, England flew into Cape Town to meet Pakistan knowing, realistically, they had to beat them as well as India to go into the Super Sixes. Collingwood's 66 not out followed 52 from Vaughan and a target of 247 under lights was a stiff proposition. Pakistan were blown away by some superb swing bowling from 20-year-old Anderson, who dismissed Inzamam and Yousuf Youhana both first ball and, with White and Flintoff chipping away at the lower order, Pakistan were dismissed for 134. As a result, England still had a sniff of qualifying.

Australia defied the wishes of Prime Minister John Howard and travelled to Bulawayo where they beat Zimbabwe by seven wickets, and after Pakistan had dealt with Holland in Paarl, it was time for England to meet India in a match that would decide England's destiny. If they lost, England would have to beat Australia to have any chance to moving through to the Super Sixes, and it was a cruel blow when Hussain lost the toss and condemned his team to bat under the Durban floodlights. India's 250 for 9 was manageable, but England were soon undone by some superb swing bowling from Ashish Nehra. Using the conditions perfectly – although there is also a chance that England were psyched out – he took 6 for 23 as England were skittled out for 168.

Two titanic clashes still remained in this group. First, India lined up against Pakistan at Centurion with Pakistan's campaign in deep trouble. Saeed Anwar got his team away to an excellent start with 101 and Younis Khan pushed the innings along with 32 to set India 274 to win. In an electric atmosphere, Tendulkar chose the moment to bat at his very best. He raced to 98 from only 75 balls as India galloped towards victory, and after he had fallen to Shoaib, Yuvraj and Dravid saw the Indians home with six wickets and four overs in hand.

This left England and Zimbabwe chasing one place in the Super Sixes. At St George's Park, England almost managed to achieve the unthinkable and defeat Australia. Having scored 204 for 8, England seemed quietly confident on a pitch that was becoming wretchedly slow and difficult to bat on. After 15 overs of their reply, Australia were 60 for 4, and this became 112 for 6. Bevan was still there, though, and this gave Andy Bichel his first opportunity to prove his worth. They took Australia to within 14 runs of victory in two overs when, inexplicably, Hussain chose to bowl young Anderson rather than the experienced Caddick. Bichel struck

ten runs from the first two balls and this effectively ended the contest with Bevan on 74 not out.

England's hopes of qualification then rested on Pakistan taking four points from their game in Zimbabwe to deny the hosts and allow England through but, ironically, it poured with rain in Bulawayo and the two points Zimbabwe earned from the washout prompted Hussain to resign as England's one-day captain, and condemned his players to an early flight home.

Naturally enough, the main interest in Group B focussed on the home team, South Africa. There was

Taking centre stage: Brian Lara launches his World Cup with a brilliant hundred against South Africa.

an expectation, bordering on an arrogant assumption, that South Africa would at least reach the final, and, quite possibly, topple Australia. Indeed, there was a feeling amongst the locals that there was only one team capable of doing that: South Africa. Their dream was to end, literally, in tears.

Also in the group were West Indies, New Zealand, Sri Lanka, Bangladesh, Canada and Kenya. It was widely assumed that Bangladesh, Canada and Kenya would fail to make the Super Six, but thanks to home wins over Sri Lanka and Bangladesh – which put its Test status firmly in its true perspective – and New Zealand's boycott, Kenya went through at the expense of the West Indies.

Yet it was the West Indies that showed the early form by defeating South Africa in the tournament's opening match at Newlands, Cape Town. This went against the script as far as the locals – and the tournament's organizers – were concerned, but the latter, at least, could point to an exciting and unpredictable start to the World Cup.

Brian Lara took centre stage there, with an exquisite 116 that set South Africa 279 to win. Kirsten replied with 69, but wickets fell steadily until Klusener revived memories of 1999 with a rousing innings from No. 8. With eight needed from three balls, however, the left-hander perished on the boundary having made 57 from 48 balls, and the West Indies won by three runs.

That was possibly the best match of the tournament. Sri Lanka caused a surprise in Bloemfontein, where they beat New Zealand by 47 runs. New Zealand were already up against it by forfeiting their game in Kenya, and they were undone by Jayasuriya, who scored 120 to set New Zealand 273 to win. Fleming's men fell 47 runs short.

Canada thoroughly embarrassed Bangladesh by beating them by 60 runs in Durban. Austin Codrington claimed 5 for 27 as Bangladesh were skittled for only 120.

South Africa earned their first points by thrashing Kenya by ten wickets and the spotlight then focussed on New Zealand's vital match with the West Indies in Port Elizabeth. The Kiwis had to win and, thanks to Andre Adams' rather fortuitous bowling, they managed to do just that. The West Indies, chasing 242, were reduced to 46 for 5 and although Jacobs scored 50 and Sarwan 75, they fell 21 runs short of victory. New Zealand could breathe again.

Chaminda Vaas claimed a hat-trick with the first three balls of the match at Paarl as Sri Lanka humbled Bangladesh, and Kenya were made to work hard for their win over Canada before the next

As easy as 1–2–3: Sri Lanka's Chaminda Vaas plucks out the Bangladesh top order with a hat-trick from the first three balls of the game in Paarl.

important game in the group between South Africa and New Zealand at Johannesburg. This provided another clue that this was not to be South Africa's tournament. After Gibbs had rattled up a breathtaking 143 from 141 balls, including 19 fours and three sixes, Klusener bludgeoned 33 from 21 balls and New Zealand were set an unlikely 307 to stay in the World Cup. The enormous, utterly partisan crowd were soon silenced by an innings of genuine brilliance by Stephen Fleming. Never can the left-hander's placement have been more precise and he was particularly severe on Allan Donald, who was increasingly looking well past his sell-by date. There was a power failure and two breaks for rain, the second of which transformed New Zealand's target. From needing 125 to win from 20 overs, the revised Duckworth-Lewis target was 45 runs from nine. The crowd hated it, and New Zealand cruised home by nine wickets with Fleming undefeated on 134.

Sri Lanka bowled Canada out for 36 in Paarl, but John Davison then scored the fastest-ever World Cup century for Canada in their next game against the West Indies. It was the result in Nairobi, however, where Kenya beat Sri Lanka, that was to have the greatest impact on the tournament.

Kenya scored 210 for 9, which did not seem likely to challenge Sri Lanka's strokeplayers but, one by one, they came unstuck against Collins Obuya's flighted leg spin. Obuya took 5 for 24 as Sri Lanka caved in for 157, and this was the moment Kenya found themselves hurtling towards the Super Sixes.

The contest between Sri Lanka and the West Indies at Newlands had always promised to be a Group B decider, and so it was to prove. Sri Lanka made 228 for 6, with Jayasuriya scoring a sedate 66 from 99 balls as the West Indies bowled tidily. However, Vaas was soon amongst the wickets – including Lara for one – and Sarwan was then forced to retire to hospital after being hit on the head by Fernando. Chanderpaul scored 65, but with hopes fading, Sarwan reappeared with his team needing 60 from seven overs with three wickets in hand. Playing some outrageous strokes, Sarwan took the West Indies to within seven of victory before running out of partners. Although they had produced some good cricket, the West Indies knew this result signalled the end of the road.

All that remained was the fate of South Africa – and what a finale this was to be. Sri Lanka were their opponents under floodlights in Durban and South Africa's exit must rank as cricket's greatest blunder. Chasing 269 – a large total under lights – South Africa had made a decent start with Gibbs and Smith putting on 65 in good time. Gibbs fell for 73 and the middle order faltered as Jayasuriya turned the screw with his typically frugal left-arm spin. Pollock made 25 before being run out by a hair's breadth, and the promised rain then arrived. Nothing heavy, mind you, just steady rain. Duckworth-Lewis was now a real possibility and South Africa had to be ahead of the rate in case the umpires called the players from the field. The rain became more persistent and when Boucher swung the penultimate ball of the 45th over for six, he punched the air. The score was now exactly that shown on the Duckworth-Lewis sheet. Boucher blocked the final ball to midwicket, the umpires uprooted the stumps and the truth then dawned on everyone: Boucher had presumed that the score on the read-out was enough to win. In fact, it was to tie, which was not enough to propel South Africa into the Super Sixes. A photograph showing a tearful Pollock graphically summed up the mood of the nation as, once again, the locals pointed to sheer bad luck accounting for South Africa's exit. Bad luck? Try unprofessionalism and crass stupidity, and it cost both Pollock the captaincy and the tournament the vital ingredient of the involvement of the home team.

Final Table – Pool A

	P	W	L	T	NR	R/R	Pts
Australia	6	6	0	0	0	2.04	24
India	6	5	1	0	0	1.11	20
Zimbabwe*	6	3	2	0	1	0.50	14
England*	6	3	3	0	0	0.82	12
Pakistan	6	2	3	0	1	0.23	10
Netherlands	6	1	5	0	0	-1.45	4
Namibia	6	0	6	0	0	-2.95	0

*Zimbabwe awarded four points after England refused to play in Harare.

Final Table – Pool B

	P	W	L	T	NR	R/R	Pts
Sri Lanka	6	4	1	1	0	1.20	18
Kenya*	6	4	2	0	0	-0.69	16
New Zealand*	6	4	2	0	0	0.99	16
South Africa	6	3	2	1	0	1.73	14
West Indies	6	3	2	0	1	1.10	14
Canada	6	1	5	0	0	-1.99	4
Bangladesh	6	0	5	0	1	-2.05	2

*Kenya awarded four points after New Zealand refused to play in Nairobi.

SUPER SIXES

7 March 2003 at Centurion Park
Australia 319 for 5 (50 overs) (RT Ponting 114, AC Gilchrist 99, DR Martyn 52)
Sri Lanka 223 (47.4 overs) (PA de Silva 92)
Australia (4pts) won by 96 runs

7 March 2003 at Cape Town
Kenya 225 for 6 (50 overs) (KO Otieno 79*)
India 226 for 4 (47.5 overs) (SC Ganguly 107*, Yuvraj Singh 58*)
India (4pts) won by 6 wickets

8 March 2003 at Bloemfontein
Zimbabwe 252 for 7 (50 overs) (HH Streak 72*, T Taibu 53)
New Zealand 253 for 4 (47.2 overs) (NJ Astle 102*, CL Cairns 54)
New Zealand (4pts) won by 6 wickets

10 March 2003 at Johannesburg
India 292 for 6 (50 overs) (SR Tendulkar 97, V Sehwag 66)
Sri Lanka 109 (23 overs) (A Nehra 4 for 35, J Srinath 4 for 35)
India (4pts) won by 183 runs

11 March 2003 at Port Elizabeth
Australia 208 for 9 (50 overs) (AJ Bichel 64,
MG Bevan 56, SE Bond 6 for 23)
New Zealand 112 (30.1 overs) (B Lee 5 for 42)
Australia (4pts) won by 96 runs

12 March 2003 at Bloemfontein
Zimbabwe 133 (44.1 overs) (A Flower 63)
Kenya 135 for 3 (26 overs)
Kenya (4pts) won by 7 wickets

14 March 2003 at Centurion Park
New Zealand 146 (45.1 overs) (Z Khan 4 for 42)
India 150 for 3 (40.4 overs) (M Kaif 68*, R Dravid 53*)
India (4pts) won by 7 wickets

15 March 2003 at East London
Sri Lanka 256 for 5 (50 overs) (MS Atapattu 103*)
Zimbabwe 182 (41.5 overs)
Sri Lanka (4pts) won by 74 runs

15 March 2003 at Durban
Kenya 174 for 8 (50 overs) (SO Tikolo 51)
Australia 178 for 5 (31.2 overs) (AC Gilchrist 67)
Australia (4pts) won by 5 wickets

Had the ICC been taken to court at this stage of the
tournament, they might very well have been
successfully sued under the Trades Description Act.
'Super' Six this was not: 'Insipid' Six would have
been far more appropriate since, before a single
delivery of this supposed cut-and-thrust section of
the World Cup was bowled, we all knew which four
teams would progress to the semi-finals. Even Kenya
could afford to lose every match and qualify if the
other games all went according to form and logic.
What a farce!

What was needed was an upset or two, and the
only likely way that Kenya's passage to the semi-
finals could be blocked was for New Zealand to beat
India. This contest did not take place until the death
throes and, as it happened, India completely
annihilated the Kiwis. Besides, by then, Kenya had
already progressed by virtue of their victory over
crisis-stricken Zimbabwe.

Australia confirmed their place in the semi-finals
in their opening match of the Super Six in which
they thrashed Sri Lanka – the last team to beat them
in a one-day international – at Centurion Park.
Ponting scored a masterful 114 from 109 balls, but

**Shane Bond took 6 for 23 against Australia at Port Elizabeth,
but New Zealand still could not win.**

this was put in the shade by Gilchrist's whirlwind 99
from just 88 deliveries. Sri Lanka's reply was
derailed when Lee hit Jayasuriya on the hand with
only six runs on the board. The fast bowler then
removed Atapattu, Jayawardene and Arnold and Sri
Lanka fell to a 96-run defeat.

A more experienced team than Kenya might have
beaten India under the lights at Newlands. Chasing
226, India were 24 for 3 and, when Dravid was caught
and bowled by Obuya, 108 for 4. But they were
steered to victory by Ganguly, who made 107 not out.

Next day at Bloemfontein, Zimbabwe crashed to
106 for 6 against New Zealand, but were rescued by
some astonishing lower-order hitting by Heath
Streak. The captain scored an unbeaten 72 from 82
balls and was ably assisted by young Taibu (53) and
Ervine, whose 31 not out came from only 14
deliveries. Suddenly New Zealand were faced with a

target of 253, which was only negotiated with 16 balls to spare thanks to Astle's unbeaten 102.

Badly needing a close contest, the bandwagon trundled north to Johannesburg where India mauled Sri Lanka by the massive margin of 183 runs. Tendulkar and Sehwag posted an opening stand of 153 in 27 overs, despite a curious phase in which they did not attempt to score from 19 successive deliveries between overs 13 and 15. Tendulkar was dropped on 61, but failed by three runs to reach his century when he edged De Silva to Sangakkara. Ganguly – in tremendous form – raced to 48 leaving Sri Lanka to score 293. In the 15th over they were 59 for 6 thanks to Srinath's four wickets and, mercifully, the tail surrendered meekly as Sri Lanka were dismissed in 23 overs.

The fifth Super Six match might have produced the game of the tournament. Fuelled by decades of sporting rivalry, New Zealand and Australia met at Port Elizabeth with the Kiwis needing to win the match to have any chance of progressing to the semi-finals. At 84 for 7, Australia seemed down and out thanks to a brilliant spell of genuine pace bowling from Shane Bond. He blasted out the first four batsmen, including Ponting for six but, not for the first time, Australia were rescued by Bevan who, with Bichel – fast becoming Australia's man of the World Cup – added 97 for the seventh wicket. Bichel played so fluently that the more experienced Bevan scored only 38 of them and by the time that Lee arrived to smash two sixes, the force was with Australia, despite Bond finishing with figures of 6 for 23. After 15 overs, New Zealand were 67 for 4 and floundering in their chase for 209. Cairns began aggressively, but was dismissed by Bichel and a rampant Lee ran through the tail to finish with 5 for 42. St George's Park was, indeed, beginning to look like Australia's lucky ground.

By beating Zimbabwe at Bloemfontein, in front of a minuscule crowd, Kenya sealed their position in the semi-finals. It was another ghastly game in which Zimbabwe succumbed to Kenya's medium pacers and the leg spinner, Obuya, to be dismissed for 133. The only question that remained was whether or not Kenya could hold their nerve, and although they faltered slightly at 33 for 2, the experienced pair of Odoyo and Odumbe steered them to their target with 24 overs still remaining.

And so to the one game in the Super Sixes that might have had some bearing on the make-up of one position in the semi-finals. Sri Lanka's position would have been threatened had New Zealand been able to defeat India at Centurion but, typically in this competition, the big occasion produced a total

The pace of Brett Lee was a major factor in Australia's success.

anti-climax. This is to take nothing away from Zaheer Khan and Ashish Nehra, whose opening spells wrecked New Zealand's innings. The Kiwis were 98 for 7 in the 30th over and they hobbled on to score 146 before being bowled out in the 46th over. There was a flicker of excitement when Sehwag, Tendulkar and Ganguly fell to Tuffey and Bond with only 21 on the board, but Kaif and Dravid played with great common sense and patience to score half-centuries and overhaul the target in the 41st over.

The only memorable aspect of the eighth Super Six match at East London between Sri Lanka and Zimbabwe was the retirements of Andy Flower and Henry Olonga, the men who had so bravely worn black armbands in Harare to 'mourn the death of democracy' in Zimbabwe. Flower's departure for Essex had been widely known; Olonga's decision not to return to Zimbabwe because he feared for his safety was not. Flower's career ended with the worst lbw decision of the tournament just as he was threatening Sri Lanka's total of 256 for 5. 'You must be joking,' Flower said to umpire Jerling as the finger was raised, and Zimbabwe's lower order fell in a heap as they crashed to a 74-run defeat.

The final match of the round between Australia and Kenya was as meaningless as it was one-sided. Kenya's total of 174 for 8 was overhauled with 18 overs to spare to leave Australia, Kenya, Sri Lanka and India in the semi-finals. But then we had known that already!

1ST SEMI-FINAL
18 March 2003 at Port Elizabeth
Australia 212 for 7 (50 overs) (A Symonds 91*)
Sri Lanka 123 for 7 (38.1 overs)
Australia won by 48 runs – DL Method: target 172 from 38.1 overs

Australia's path to the semi-final had not been entirely straightforward, but it shows the true strength of a team when it can repeatedly drag itself out of trouble. At 144 for 5, Australia were in a predicament bordering on desperate. True, Port Elizabeth had shown itself to be a chasing team's nightmare, with the pitch quickly adopting all the qualities of a blancmange but, at that moment, Sri Lanka knew they had the champions on the ropes. Even Michael Bevan, one-day cricket's mastermind, had been disposed of for a duck.

Although Andrew Symonds began some careful restoration of the innings, he was badly missed on 33 by wicketkeeper Sangakkara, and Sri Lanka's fleeting chance had gone. The burly Queenslander quickly changed gear to score an unbeaten 91 from 118 balls as he and Bichel added 37 in the last seven overs and Australia were able to set Sri Lanka 213 to win a place in the final.

Brett Lee worked up a ferocious pace from the Duck Pond End, and spectacularly splattered Atapattu's stumps in the fourth over. This started a procession, and when Arivinda de Silva – in his final innings for his country – was brilliantly run out by Bichel in his follow through for 11, Sri Lanka were 51 for 5 and the game was effectively over.

2ND SEMI-FINAL
20 March 2003 at Durban
India 270 for 4 (50 overs) (SC Ganguly 111, SR Tendulkar 83)
Kenya 179 (46.2 overs) (SO Tikolo 56)
India won by 91 runs

Kenya's heroic, but unrealistic, run finally came to an end under the lights in Durban in a one-sided game that failed to attract a full house. Hopefully

Kenya's success in the World Cup will have done a great deal for the game of cricket there, but however hard the delegation from the ICC tried to sell the success of the World Cup to the English media before this semi-final began, the fact that any team can progress to this stage having beaten Canada, Bangladesh and Sri Lanka in the first round and then only Zimbabwe in the Super Sixes exposes serious flaws in the tournament which must be eradicated.

Steve Tikolo's team all played with smiles on their faces, but one sensed that they felt utterly out of place by the time the semi-finals came around.

For India, this match represented an enormous banana skin, but their captain, Saurav Ganguly, made absolutely sure that there would not be a slip-up by scoring an excellent century which, after Tendulkar's 83, gave Kenya far too many to chase.

At 63 for 5, another hopelessly one-sided and utterly boring game was doing nothing for the image of cricket and although Tikolo scored a brave half-century, it was clear that the Indians had the final on their mind and the match ended anti-climactically.

Saurav Ganguly, the India captain, leads from the front against the gallant Kenyans.

WORLD CUP FINAL
23 March 2003 at the Wanderers, Johannesburg

There was little doubt that the best two teams in the tournament were brought together for the World Cup final and that probably the finest one-day team of all time – Australia – retained their crown. The strength of Ricky Ponting's squad is best illustrated by the manner in which the absence of both Shane Warne and Jason Gillespie – which would surely have scuppered any other team – was shrugged off almost nonchalantly. It merely gave an opportunity to others, and Andy Bichel in particular, and they all more than rose to the occasion.

India's decision to put Australia in to bat caused more than just a murmur of interest, bordering on disbelief, in the media centre, but India had won key matches chasing runs and, importantly, had been trounced by Australia earlier in the tournament when they had chosen to bat first. To be fair, the moment Saurav Ganguly realized that the decision was his to make, he would have known he was on a hiding to nothing.

It was not long before the ball was flying around the Wanderers, and this was to be the pattern of Australia's innings. When Adam Gilchrist was dismissed in the 15th over for 57 from 48 balls, Australia had already rattled up 105. India's nerves

FINAL – AUSTRALIA v. INDIA
23 March 2003 at Johannesburg

AUSTRALIA

*AC Gilchrist	c Sehwag b Harbhajan Singh	57
ML Hayden	c Dravid b Harbhajan Singh	37
RT Ponting (capt)	not out	140
DR Martyn	not out	88
D S Lehmann		
A Symonds		
M G Bevan		
G B Hogg		
A J Bichel		
B Lee		
G D McGrath		
Extras	b 2, lb 12, w 16, nb 7	37
	(50 overs) (2 wkts)	359

	O	M	R	W
Khan	7	0	67	0
Srinath	10	0	87	0
Nehra	10	0	57	0
Harbhajan Singh	8	0	49	2
Sehwag	3	0	14	0
Tendulkar	3	0	20	0
Mongia	7	0	39	0
Yuvraj Singh	2	0	12	0

Fall of Wickets
1-105, 2-125

INDIA

SR Tendulkar	c & b McGrath	4
V Sehwag	run out	82
SC Ganguly (capt)	c Lehmann b Lee	24
M Kaif	c Gilchrist b McGrath	0
*R Dravid	b Bichel	47
Yuvraj Singh	c Lee b Hogg	24
D Mongia	c Martyn b Symonds	12
Harbhajan Singh	c McGrath b Symonds	7
Z Khan	c Lehmann b McGrath	4
J Srinath	b Lee	1
A Nehra	not out	8
Extras	b 4, lb 4, w 9, nb 4	21
	(39.2 overs)	234

	O	M	R	W
McGrath	8.2	0	52	3
Lee	7	1	31	2
Hogg	10	0	61	1
Lehmann	2	0	18	0
Bichel	10	0	57	1
Symonds	2	0	7	2

Fall of Wickets
1-4, 2-58, 3-59, 4-147, 5-187, 6-208, 7-209, 8-223, 9-226

Umpires: SA Bucknor & DR Shepherd
Toss: India

Australia won by 125 runs

The Man of the Final: Ricky Ponting marches off to the world's acclaim.

were tangible – Zaheer Khan's first over was a ten-baller – and, ruthlessly, the Aussies seized upon this.

Matthew Hayden was the second to go – caught behind off Harbhajan for a comparatively subdued 37 from 54 balls, and this enabled Ponting and Damien Martyn to compile one of the most bruising partnerships ever seen in one-day cricket. The pair put together 234 in 30 overs – about eight runs per over – and such was Ganguly's hopeless predicament that he turned to eight bowlers in an attempt to halt the carnage. Ponting raced to 140 not out from only 121 balls – his last 90 runs came from just 47 balls in which he hit a staggering eight sixes – while Martyn finished unbeaten on 88. As is usually the case, Martyn's innings was the more understated, but it was no less impressive than his captain's. No fewer than

109 runs came from the last ten overs as Australia closed on 359 for 2 – the highest total in a World Cup final and the highest score ever made by Australia in a one-day international.

Unfortunately, the match was ruined as a contest as a result of this onslaught. An interruption for rain produced a flurry of Duckworth-Lewis sheets and, for a while, improved India's hopeless position, but when Tendulkar was dismissed in the very first over of their reply, caught and bowled as he pulled McGrath, India's supporters knew that the writing was on the wall. Sehwag scored 82 at a run-a-ball and Dravid's 47 came in a stand of 40 with Yuvraj, but once the rain clouds blew away and Australia squeezed in their mandatory 25 overs, it was only a matter of time before Ponting's hands were on the cup.

Ricky Ponting, Australia's victorious captain, lifts the World Cup trophy.

Above: Cricketing genius – Sir Garfield Sobers presents Sachin Tendulkar, of India, with the award for the best batsman of the tournament.

Opposite: Tight-knit – Australia's players show their togetherness again as they celebrate a successful defence of the World Cup trophy.

CRICKET WORLD CUP 2003 RECORDS

MOST RUNS (Top 10) – *No. of innings in brackets*

SR Tendulkar (Ind)	673 (11)
SC Ganguly (Ind)	465 (11)
RT Ponting (Aus)	415 (11)
AC Gilchrist (Aus)	408 (11)
HH Gibbs (SA)	384 (6)
MS Atapattu (SL)	382 (10)
A Flower (Zim)	332 (8)
ML Hayden (Aus)	328 (11)
A Symonds (Aus)	326 (9)
DR Martyn (Aus)	323 (10)

HIGHEST INDIVIDUAL SCORES (Top 10)

172*	CB Wishart	Zimbabwe v. Namibia at Harare, 10/02/2003
152	SR Tendulkar	India v. Namibia at Pietermaritzburg, 23/02/2003
143*	A Symonds	Australia v. Pakistan at Johannesburg, 11/02/2003
143	HH Gibbs	South Africa v. New Zealand at Johannesburg, 16/02/2003
141	SB Styris	New Zealand v. Sri Lanka at Bloemfontein, 10/02/2003
140*	RT Ponting	Australia v. India at Johannesburg, 23/03/2003
134*	SP Fleming	New Zealand v. South Africa at Johannesburg, 16/02/2003
134*	KJJ van Noortwijk	Netherlands v. Namibia at Bloemfontein, 03/03/2003
124	MS Atapattu	Sri Lanka v. South Africa at Durban, 03/03/2003
121	JF Kloppenburg	Netherlands v. Namibia at Bloemfontein, 03/03/2003
120	ST Jayasuriya	Sri Lanka v. New Zealand at Bloemfontein, 10/02/2003

HIGHEST BATTING STRIKE RATE (Top 10) – *Runs per 100 balls faced*

AJ Hall (SA)	200.00	GD McGrath (Aus)	150.00
A Nehra (Ind)	200.00	Shoaib Akhtar (Pak)	141.17
M Ntini (SA)	175.00	AM Blignaut (Zim)	138.20
RL Powell (WI)	156.94	RC Irani (Eng)	133.33
JN Gillespie (Aus)	150.00	SM Ervine (Zim)	130.30

MOST WICKETS (Top 10) – *No. of matches played in brackets*

WPUJC Vaas (SL)	23 (10)
B Lee (Aus)	22 (10)
GD McGrath (Aus)	18 (11)
Z Khan (Ind)	18 (11)
SE Bond (NZ)	17 (8)
M Muralitharan (SL)	17 (10)
VC Drakes (WI)	16 (6)
AJ Bichel (Aus)	16 (8)
J Srinath (Ind)	16 (11)
A Nehra (Ind)	15 (9)

BEST INNINGS BOWLING (Top 10)

7/15	GD McGrath	Australia v. Namibia at Potchefstroom, 27/02/2003
7/20	AJ Bichel	Australia v. England at Port Elizabeth, 02/03/2003
6/23	A Nehra	India v. England at Durban, 26/02/2003
6/23	SE Bond	New Zealand v. Australia at Port Elizabeth, 11/03/2003
6/25	WPUJC Vaas	Sri Lanka v. Bangladesh at Pietermaritzburg, 14/02/2003
5/24	CO Obuya	Kenya v. Sri Lanka at Nairobi (Gymk), 24/02/2003
5/27	A Codrington	Canada v. Bangladesh at Durban, 11/02/2003
5/28	Wasim Akram	Pakistan v. Namibia at Kimberley, 16/02/2003
5/33	VC Drakes	West Indies v. Kenya at Kimberley, 04/03/2003
5/42	B Lee	Australia v. New Zealand at Port Elizabeth, 11/03/2003

BEST BOWLING ECONOMY RATE (Top 10) – *Runs conceded per over*

JJC Lawson (WI)	2.00	JN Gillespie (Aus)	3.26
CD McMillan (NZ)	2.00	M Ntini (SA)	3.37
A Flintoff (Eng)	2.87	Ehsanul Haque (Bang)	3.40
AY Karim (Ken)	2.95	AJ Bichel (Aus)	3.45
S Chanderpaul (WI)	3.00	RJ Peterson (SA)	3.50

AUSTRALIA

ENGLAND IN AUSTRALIA
VB TRIANGULAR SERIES
AUSTRALIA REPORT

ENGLAND IN AUSTRALIA
By Jonathan Agnew

FIRST TEST
7–10 November 2002 at the Gabba, Brisbane

After seven consecutive successful Ashes series, Australia's grip on the urn seemed to be as solid as ever when the two teams lined up shortly before the start of play at the Gabba to remember those who had fallen in the Great Wars. The last post sounded, and already it seemed to have a prophetic ring to it, for Nasser Hussain had just won the toss and asked Australia to bat first. Everyone thought he was quite mad.

The only faintly credible excuse for Hussain's decision – which he admitted during the match via his exclusive newspaper column rather than through the proper channels to have been a terrible mistake – was that England's preparations for the match had been shambolic. Injuries not merely blighted the start of the tour, but key players such as Andrew Flintoff and Darren Gough had clearly not recovered from their various ailments of the summer. Steve Harmison had shin splits, Michael Vaughan's knee was touch and go and Simon Jones revealed the day before the Test that he was still troubled with the side strain that had ruled him out of the second half of the English season. Taking all of this into account, Hussain recognized that his players were unusually nervous on that hot, dry Brisbane morning and he decided that his team needed to take the field together.

Vaughan fumbled the second ball of the day in the covers and Australia were off the mark. Again, Vaughan's blemish was to set the tone for the one-sided contest that unfolded before our eyes.

At lunch on that first day, Australia were 125 for 1 from only 25 overs and Hussain already knew he had blown it. Langer had fallen to Jones for 32, and had Jones remained in control of the ball's 'further

dispersal' when he attempted to cling on to a catch from Hayden at long leg, it might have looked a little better for England. As it was, Ponting and Hayden were just setting out on their marathon partnership of 272 for the second wicket which ended shortly before the close of play on the first day. Hayden, standing tall and driving powerfully straight down the ground, was at his intimidating best, and this might account for the no fewer than

The merciless strokeplay of Matthew Hayden quickly set the tone for the Ashes series.

The long walk back: Nasser Hussain falls as England slide to defeat.

FIRST TEST – AUSTRALIA v. ENGLAND
7–10 November 2002 at Brisbane

AUSTRALIA

	First Innings		Second Innings	
JL Langer	c Stewart b Jones	32	c Stewart b Caddick	22
ML Hayden	c Stewart b Caddick	197	c & b Giles	103
RT Ponting	b Giles	123	c Trescothick b Caddick	3
DR Martyn	c Trescothick b White	26	c Hussain b Giles	64
SR Waugh (capt)	c Crawley b Caddick	7	(6) c Trescothick b Caddick	12
DS Lehmann	c Butcher b Giles	30	(7) not out	20
*AC Gilchrist	c Giles b White	0	(5) not out	60
SK Warne	c Butcher b Caddick	57		
AJ Bichel	lbw b Giles	0		
JN Gillespie	not out	0		
GD McGrath	lbw b Giles	0		
Extras	b 1, lb 11, w 1, nb 7	20	b 3, lb 5, nb 4	12
		492	(5 wkts dec.)	**296**

	First Innings				Second Innings			
	O	M	R	W	O	M	R	W
Caddick	35	9	108	3	23	2	95	3
Hoggard	30	4	122	0	13	2	42	0
Jones	7	0	32	1				
White	27	4	105	2	11	0	61	0
Giles	29.2	3	101	4	24	2	90	2
Butcher	2	0	12	0				

Fall of Wickets
1-67, 2-339, 3-378, 4-399, 5-408, 6-415, 7-478, 8-478, 9-492
1-30, 2-39, 3-192, 4-213, 5-242

ENGLAND

	First Innings		Second Innings	
ME Trescothick	c Ponting b McGrath	72	c Gilchrist b Gillespie	1
MP Vaughan	c Gilchrist b McGrath	33	lbw b McGrath	0
MA Butcher	c Hayden b McGrath	54	c Ponting b Warne	40
N Hussain (capt)	c Gilchrist b Gillespie	51	c Ponting b McGrath	11
JP Crawley	not out	69	run out	0
*AJ Stewart	b Gillespie	0	c Hayden b Warne	0
C White	b McGrath	12	c Hayden b McGrath	13
AF Giles	c Gilchrist b Bichel	13	c Gilchrist b McGrath	4
AR Caddick	c Ponting b Bichel	0	c Lehmann b Warne	4
MJ Hoggard	c Hayden b Warne	4	not out	1
SP Jones	absent injured	0	absent injured	0
Extras	b 2, lb 8, nb 7	17	lb 1, nb 4	5
	(9 wkts)	**325**	(9 wkts)	**79**

	First Innings				Second Innings			
	O	M	R	W	O	M	R	W
McGrath	30	9	87	4	12	3	36	4
Gillespie	18	4	51	2	6	1	13	1
Bichel	23	4	74	2	-	-	-	-
Warne	26.5	4	87	1	10.2	3	29	3
Waugh	4	2	5	0	-	-	-	-
Lehmann	5	0	11	0	-	-	-	-

Fall of Wickets
1-49, 2-170, 3-171, 4-268, 5-270, 6-283, 7-308, 8-308, 9-325
1-1, 2-3, 3-33, 4-34, 5-35, 6-66, 7-74, 8-74, 9-79

Umpires: SA Bucknor & RE Koertzen
Toss: England

Australia won by 384 runs

three chances that were dropped that afternoon. One – Vaughan's – was no more difficult than an underarm lob you might toss your little old granny in the back garden. Hoggard also put down a sitter and, rapidly, England's out-cricket was falling apart. This feeling of hopelessness was compounded even further when Jones, sliding to stop the ball going for four, ruptured the cruciate ligament in his right knee and was stretchered, in agony, from the field. The sad, career-threatening injury to a very likeable young man, cast a pall over the ground.

Next morning, England fought back inexplicably as Australia collapsed from 364 for 2 to 492 all out. It was still a commanding total, and it is possible that over-confidence was their downfall rather than any particular heroics by Caddick, Giles and White. After Hayden had perished for 197 to a legside catch by Stewart, Steve Waugh played a desperately scratchy innings of seven from 37 balls. He appeared tentative and utterly out of sorts. Warne biffed 57 from 65 balls, but by the end of the second day, England were well placed on 158 for 1 and the Australian media seemed genuinely relieved at the prospect of a real contest.

As pleasant as it was, our new-found optimism in English cricket could not last for long and, sure enough, the inevitable collapse was only a few overs into the third day away. England lost six wickets for 57 and since four of the top five batsmen had passed 50, their total of 325 was bitterly disappointing. Trescothick top scored with 72 – it was to be his only half-century of the series – and Crawley suggested that the Australians might take him rather more seriously this time by finishing unbeaten on 69, but the lower order was blown away, and Waugh's men were soon building on their lead of 167.

Hayden completed his second century of the match on his home ground, featuring in a stand of 153 with Martyn, and as Australia moved inexorably towards their declaration, the only item of real interest was another horrible innings by Waugh. This time he scored 12 from 42 balls and it really began to seem that he was genuinely concerned about his place in the team. Caddick got him for the second time in the match, and the manner in which Waugh was roughed up by short, fast bowling at the ribs was sure to be noted.

Certainly, in the short term, it did not matter a jot as the focus was very quickly switched to a quite dismal collapse by England in their second innings. Set an unlikely 464 to win from 137 overs, they were routed in less than 30 for a feeble 79 all out. McGrath took 4 for 36, including the unlucky Vaughan who received a dodgy lbw to the third ball of the innings, and only three Englishmen could muster double figures. Crawley was crazily run out and, in the mayhem, Stewart recorded his first pair in a long and distinguished Test career. In the match, England's lower order – Stewart included – managed to score only 51 runs between them.

SECOND TEST
21–24 November 2002 at Adelaide

Another four-day, equally emphatic victory for Australia left England needing to win the three remaining Tests to regain the Ashes. On the evidence of the first two Tests, the tourists would do well even to manage a single draw at Perth, Melbourne or Sydney. Rather than play in the first-class match at Hobart that was sandwiched between

Michael Vaughan did not deserve to be an Adelaide loser.

the first two Tests, Hussain travelled to Perth for the birth of his second child, Joel. When he returned, it was to find that the injury curse had not deserted his team, and England, for various reasons, were now without six of the original members of the squad: Thorpe, Gough, Flintoff, Giles, Jones and Crawley. Giles was, arguably, the least unfortunate of the group. He was struck on the wrist in the nets by Harmison – a short ball delivered from 18 yards, despite the bowling coach's attention having been drawn to the fact that all of his fast bowlers were running through the crease. This unprofessionalism simply would not be tolerated in the Australian team.

Giles' loss meant Dawson's gain and, under the circumstances, the young off spinner toiled away pluckily. However, had it not been for Vaughan's contributions with the bat, the large band of England supporters might not have seen much cricket on the scheduled third day, let alone the fourth. The Yorkshire opener scored 43.5 per cent of England's runs, including a brilliant 177 in

England's first-innings total of 342. Hussain supported him, making 47, but England's lower order was blown away again on the second morning, losing six wickets for 47 runs in 26 overs.

While Vaughan drove and pulled brilliantly, we were again treated to another quite unnecessary controversy involving the third umpire and a low catch which was claimed, on this occasion, by Langer. As always, the umpire ruled in the batsman's favour – it is impossible to do anything else because of the fuzzy, incoherent replay the umpire receives – and Langer's holier-than-thou attitude was remarkable for a man who had been one of the first to benefit from the system when he himself refused to walk against the West Indies two years previously. Until the decision-making power is returned to the men with the best view – the umpires in the middle – technology will continue to destroy sportsmanship and make a mockery of the game. (I will continue to labour this point until someone finally listens!)

The second day took a predictable course, and ended with Australia only 95 runs behind with eight wickets still in hand. Ponting was in ruthless form and closed the day on 83, a score he extended to 154 from 269 balls. His dismissal might have arisen from the bemusement caused by Hussain's field

More flamboyance from Ricky Ponting, Australia's century-maker in the second Test victory.

SECOND TEST – AUSTRALIA v. ENGLAND
21–24 November 2002 at Adelaide

ENGLAND

	First Innings		Second Innings	
ME Trescothick	b McGrath	35	lbw b Gillespie	0
MP Vaughan	c Warne b Bichel	177	c McGrath b Warne	41
RWT Key	c Ponting b Warne	1	(5) c Lehmann b Bichel	1
N Hussain (capt)	c Gilchrist b Warne	47	b Bichel	10
MA Butcher	c Gilchrist b Gillespie	22	(3) lbw b McGrath	4
*AJ Stewart	lbw b Gillespie	29	lbw b Warne	57
C White	c Bichel b Gillespie	1	c sub b McGrath	5
RKJ Dawson	lbw b Warne	6	c Gilchrist b McGrath	19
AR Caddick	b Warne	0	(11) not out	6
MJ Hoggard	c Gilchrist b Gillespie	6	(9) b McGrath	1
SJ Harmison	not out	3	(10) lbw b Warne	0
Extras	lb 7, nb 8	15	b 3, lb 4, nb 8	15
		342		**159**

	First Innings				Second Innings			
	O	M	R	W	O	M	R	W
McGrath	30	11	77	1	17.2	6	41	4
Gillespie	26.5	8	78	4	12	1	44	1
Bichel	20	2	78	1	5	0	31	2
Warne	34	10	93	4	25	7	36	3
Waugh	5	1	9	0	-	-	-	-

Fall of Wickets
1-88, 2-106, 3-246, 4-295, 5-295, 6-308, 7-325, 8-325, 9-337
1-5, 2-17, 3-36, 4-40, 5-114, 6-130, 7-130, 8-132, 9-134

AUSTRALIA

	First Innings	
JL Langer	c Stewart b Dawson	48
ML Hayden	c Caddick b White	46
RT Ponting	c Dawson b White	154
DR Martyn	c Hussain b Harmison	95
SR Waugh (capt)	c Butcher b White	34
DS Lehmann	c sub b White	5
*AC Gilchrist	c Stewart b Harmison	54
SK Warne	c & b Dawson	25
AJ Bichel	b Hoggard	48
JN Gillespie	not out	0
GD McGrath		
Extras	b 1, lb 17, w 7, nb 18	43
	(9 wkts dec.)	**552**

	First Innings			
	O	M	R	W
Caddick	20	2	95	0
Hoggard	26	4	84	1
Harmison	28.2	8	106	2
White	28	2	106	4
Dawson	37	2	143	2

Fall of Wickets
1-101, 2-114, 3-356, 4-397, 5-414, 6-424, 7-471, 8-548, 9-552

Umpires: SA Bucknor & RE Koertzen
Toss: England

Australia won by an innings and 51 runs

placings when Waugh joined Ponting at the crease. Setting the fielders deep for Ponting and allowing an easy single anywhere, Hussain treated Waugh as if he were a No. 11 and the Australian captain was not best pleased.

It was, in truth, rather amusing, although Waugh managed to score 34 from only 40 balls and looked more confident and secure than had been the case in Brisbane. Still the runs flowed, with a belligerent partnership of 77 between Bichel and Gilchrist, who hit four fours and two sixes in his 54, being the highlight before the declaration came with Australia's lead standing at 210. This left England's batsmen with 13 overs to face on the third day and, utterly predictably, they slumped to 36 for 3. Hussain was bowled by the last ball of the day and it was, effectively, the death knell. Again the tail was skittled with the last five wickets falling for only 29 runs. As had been the case in Brisbane, only four English batsmen reached double figures in the second innings and had more grit and determination been shown, the match might have been saved: rain meant the fifth day would have been a complete washout.

THIRD TEST
29 November–1 December 2002
at the WACA, Perth

Spectators were allowed into the WACA free of charge as early as the third afternoon in order to observe the last rites of an Ashes series that was effectively over within only 11 days. The gulf between the two teams seemed to be as wide now as it was back in 1989 when Allan Border's young team first announced its intention in England with a 4–0

series drubbing. That performance represented a remarkable turnaround by the Australians following a sequence of six series in which they had won the Ashes only once. This emphatic victory in Perth gave them their eighth successive series, equalling the record sequence of England's success between 1882 and 1891: the first eight Ashes contests in history.

This match was a bruising, bloody encounter in which England were bullied mercilessly to defeat. Brett Lee, one of the fastest bowlers in the world, was recalled for the notoriously fiery Perth pitch and he responded precisely as the selectors had expected for a man who had been dropped for the first two matches. He picked up only five wickets in the game, but he terrorized the tail-enders and despatched Alex Tudor to hospital with a sickening blow to the head. One might question whether the umpires might have done something to prevent the barrage but, in truth, this was raw, aggressive, Test-match fast bowling and, rather like watching a bloodthirsty horror movie, it had a certain fascination.

The match followed the pattern of its predecessor in Adelaide, only England scored even fewer runs in their first innings. A promising opening partnership of 47 between Vaughan and Trescothick was broken in the 13th over by a Lee thunderbolt and when Stewart aimed a horrible pull at McGrath and was caught behind, England were 111 for 5 with four batsmen having got themselves out. Butcher was run out by a direct hit from cover by Waugh after a dreadful mix-up with Vaughan, Hussain tried to hook Lee and gloved a catch to Gilchrist, and Vaughan's pull at McGrath was equally limp and ill-advised. At tea on the first day England were 156 for 8, and everyone knew the match was already set on an all-too-familiar course.

Robert Key was the only batsman to stand his ground and show some grit. He scored a plucky 47, and clearly earned a measure of respect from the Australians despite, allegedly, having been asked from the gully region what on earth he thought he was doing on the same pitch as them when he first walked out to bat. Dawson was left on 19 not out when Harmison's demise brought the tally of England's wickets to eight for only 102 runs.

Then, of course, it was a matter of sitting back and waiting to see how many the Australians would score and, at the same time, organize some alternative entertainment for the scheduled fifth day. The total of 456 gave them a lead of 271 and, as is

Flat out: Alex Tudor is struck a nasty blow by Brett Lee, and even the Australians look concerned.

Damien Martyn plays another classical stroke on his way to 71 in Perth.

THIRD TEST – AUSTRALIA v. ENGLAND
29 November–1 December 2002 at Perth

ENGLAND

	First Innings		Second Innings	
ME Trescothick	c Gilchrist b Lee	34	c Gilchrist b Lee	4
MP Vaughan	c Gilchrist b McGrath	34	run out	9
MA Butcher	run out	9	(4) lbw b McGrath	0
N Hussain (capt)	c Gilchrist b Lee	8	(5) c Gilchrist b Warne	61
RWT Key	b Martyn	47	(6) lbw b McGrath	23
*AJ Stewart	c Gilchrist b McGrath	7	(7) not out	66
C White	c Martyn b Lee	7	(8) st Gilchrist b Warne	15
AJ Tudor	c Martyn b Warne	0	(9) retired hurt	3
RKJ Dawson	not out	19	(3) c Waugh b Gillespie	8
CEW Silverwood	c Hayden b Gillespie	10	(11) absent injured	0
SJ Harmison	b Gillespie	6	(10) b Lee	5
Extras	lb 2, nb 7	9	b 8, lb 5, w 1, nb 15	29
		185	(8 wkts)	**223**

	First Innings				Second Innings			
	O	M	R	W	O	M	R	W
McGrath	17	5	30	2	21	9	24	2
Gillespie	17.2	8	43	2	15	4	35	1
Lee	20	1	78	3	18.1	3	72	2
Warne	9	0	32	1	26	5	70	2
Martyn	1	1	0	1	2	0	9	0

Fall of Wickets
1-47, 2-69, 3-83, 4-101, 5-111, 6-121, 7-135, 8-156, 9-173
1-13, 2-33, 3-34, 4-34, 5-102, 6-169, 7-208, 8-222

AUSTRALIA

	First Innings	
JL Langer	run out	19
ML Hayden	c Tudor b Harmison	30
RT Ponting	b White	68
DR Martyn	c Stewart b Tudor	71
DS Lehmann	c Harmison b White	42
SR Waugh (capt)	b Tudor	53
*AC Gilchrist	c Tudor b White	38
SK Warne	run out	35
B Lee	c Key b White	41
JN Gillespie	b White	27
GD McGrath	not out	8
Extras	b 4, lb 5, nb 15	24
		456

	First Innings			
	O	M	R	W
Silverwood	4	0	29	0
Tudor	29	2	144	2
Harmison	28	7	86	1
White	23.1	3	127	5
Butcher	10	1	40	0
Dawson	5	0	21	0

Fall of Wickets
1-31, 2-85, 3-159, 4-226, 5-264, 6-316, 7-348, 8-416, 9-423

Umpires: SA Bucknor & RE Koertzen
Toss: England

Australia won by an innings and 48 runs

the Australian way, their innings consisted of solid contributions all the way down. Ponting played well for 68 and Martyn, who scored 71, is always a pleasure to watch. The most important contribution came from Waugh, who reached 53 before being bowled by Tudor, but this was enough at least to postpone the decision about his future as captain for another month. To add to England's unbelievable run of injuries, Silverwood – who had been called up as a replacement for Gough – managed to bowl just four overs before breaking down with an ankle injury. This gave Hussain another unenviable challenge in the field and, curiously, England's most economical bowler – largely because a high percentage of his deliveries were unreachable – was Harmison. Unwisely, this 'economy' played a part in his selection for the one-day series that followed and, ultimately, the World Cup, in which he did not bowl a single ball. There can never have been many more absurd choices for a one-day tournament.

With 18 overs of the third day still remaining, the Test was over. England subsided to 34 for 4, and the end might have come even sooner had Hussain not been dropped first ball, and then battled away for four hours for 61. His dismissal by Warne was disputable and as the England captain returned to the sanctuary of the dressing room, a prying television camera caught him explode in rage. Kicking wildly at an innocent kit bag, the picture of Hussain's utterly uncontainable frustration was made complete by Silverwood's crutches, which were leaning up against the wall. This sorry, yet mildly amusing, scene perfectly summed up the tour.

The medics were required again soon enough when Tudor was stretchered off, and although Stewart made 66, he did little to protect the tail from a rampant Lee. Harmison's wicket sealed the series – a forlorn swipe from so far down the legside that he was barely standing on the pitch – to complete the sixth of the last 11 Tests at the WACA to finish within three days.

FOURTH TEST
26–30 December 2002 at MCG, Melbourne

England have become adept at producing something verging on serious competition when Ashes series have already been lost, and one might be forgiven if a glance at the scorecard suggests they fought with greater tenacity at the MCG than elsewhere on this tour. The fact, though, is that an unsettled forecast and a ruthless pursuit of a 5–0 whitewash prompted Steve Waugh to declare his first innings closed some 100 runs prematurely. This enabled England to get back into the game and produce some excitement on the final morning as Australia chased a small target to win the match, but Vaughan, Key and White apart, there were no heroes to speak of in the England camp.

Australia's imposing score might have been considerably smaller had Hayden been caught from the first ball he received from Caddick. Harmison, at long leg, had been quite deliberately brought closer than he should have been by Hussain, so the top-edge pull lobbed over the fielder's head and landed well inside the boundary. And so it was that England were again rocked back onto their heels from the word 'go' and Australia's openers put on the small matter of 195!

Caddick finally got his man, but only after he had scored 102 from only 150 balls, including ten fours and three sixes. Ponting and Martyn both missed out for once, but it was Langer who held centre stage.

The left-hander might not be the most glamorous member of this team, but he is a meticulous batsman who rarely misses out on a good pitch. He raised the tempo by reaching his 13th Test century with a straight-driven six off Dawson and by the close of the first day had reached 146 out of Australia's 356 for 3.

England's attack looked threadbare, with White as first change, and Butcher was called up to bowl 13 overs as Waugh dominated proceedings on the second morning. He put on 129 for the fourth wicket with Langer and it was a major surprise when he edged a nondescript delivery from White to Foster – keeping wicket in place of the injured Stewart – for 77. Langer, though, remained undeterred as he guided the debutant Martin Love through his first nervous moments of Test cricket. Love was already well known to England's bowlers having scored two double centuries against them earlier in the tour. Now, in the company of Langer, who was showing no sign of tiring, he added 151 in a quiet, unassuming and largely legside manner which suggested he was perfectly comfortable at this level.

Finally Langer succumbed when, after ten hours, he sliced a cut at a short ball from Dawson to Caddick at point. He faced 407 balls, hitting 30 fours and a six and, in scoring 250, made the fourth

Michael Vaughan's defiance is not enough as England go 4–0 down at Melbourne.

highest score by an Australian at the MCG. Six runs and the wicket of Gilchrist later – he aimed a mighty slog at Dawson – and Waugh declared. In the session that followed, England lost Vaughan, Trescothick and Butcher and were still 255 runs away from saving the follow-on at the close. Hussain was lucky still to be there after another ruling by the third umpire that an apparently perfectly good catch taken by Gillespie (a good sport) had possibly not carried. More piety from Langer followed: 'In an ideal world there should be more onus on the players.' If Mr Langer ever sets an example of this, we will be delighted to report it.

Hussain did not last long on the third morning, however, adding just seven to his overnight 17, but he was the third wicket to fall. Dawson, the nightwatchman, and Key fell in successive overs to MacGill and Lee, and when the leg spinner removed Hussain, England were 118 for 8, still 234 runs short of avoiding the follow-on. It might as well have been a million. At least White rose to the occasion. He is not a man who has necessarily excelled against Australia, and there was widespread bewilderment in the country when he was called up for the tour with a bowling average of 189 and a batting average of 7. 'Jeez! Surely those figures are the wrong way round, mate?' Under the circumstances, therefore, it was desperate to see him get so close to a superb century, only to be cruelly let down by a cowardly slog at Gillespie by Caddick. White's 85 not out came from only 135 balls, which was brisk under the circumstances, and when Harmison was last out on the stroke of tea on the third day, England were 270 all out, and soon following on, 281 runs behind.

The pattern up to now had been that England would collapse in their second innings and be beaten on the fourth day, but Vaughan took the opportunity to show, once again, what an extremely fine player he is. His 145 was his sixth Test century of the calendar year and when he passed 45, he passed Dennis Amiss' English record of 1,381 runs in a year. Key supported him well for 52, but when he fell to the first ball after a drinks break, England had a lead of six, but with only five lower-order wickets in hand. Crawley and White added a precious 55 and Dawson made 15 as the tail added exactly 100, and when Harmison was cleaned up by Gillespie, it left Australia needing 107 to win. By the close of play, they had knocked off eight, leaving 99 to secure their fourth victory on the final day.

What drama we savoured on that last day! Hayden fell to the very first ball to an excellent catch at deep square leg as he pulled Caddick.

FOURTH TEST – AUSTRALIA v. ENGLAND
26–30 December 2002 at Melbourne Cricket Ground

AUSTRALIA

	First Innings				Second Innings			
JL Langer	c Caddick b Dawson	250			lbw b Caddick			24
ML Hayden	c Crawley b Caddick	102			c sub b Caddick			1
RT Ponting	b White	21			c Foster b Harmison			30
DR Martyn	c Trescothick b White	17			c Foster b Harmison			0
SR Waugh (capt)	c Foster b White	77			c Butcher b Caddick			14
ML Love	not out	62			not out			6
*AC Gilchrist	b Dawson	1			not out			10
SCG MacGill								
B Lee								
JN Gillespie								
GD McGrath								
Extras	lb 11, w 5, nb 5	21			b 8, lb 5, nb 9			22
	(6 wkts dec.)	551			(5 wkts)			107

	First Innings				Second Innings			
	O	M	R	W	O	M	R	W
Caddick	36	6	126	1	12	1	51	3
Harmison	36	7	108	0	11.1	1	43	2
White	33	5	133	3	-	-	-	-
Dawson	28	1	121	2	-	-	-	-
Butcher	13	2	52	0	-	-	-	-

Fall of Wickets
1-195, 2-235, 3-265, 4-394, 5-545, 6-551
1-8, 2-58, 3-58, 4-83, 5-90

ENGLAND

	First Innings				Second Innings			
ME Trescothick	c Gilchrist b Lee	37			lbw b MacGill			37
MP Vaughan	b McGrath	11			c Love b MacGill			145
MA Butcher	lbw b Gillespie	25			c Love b Gillespie			6
N Hussain (capt)	c Hayden b MacGill	24			c & b McGrath			23
RKJ Dawson	c Love b MacGill	6			(9) not out			15
RWT Key	lbw b Lee	0			(5) c Ponting b Gillespie			52
JP Crawley	c Langer b Gillespie	17			(6) b Lee			33
C White	not out	85			(7) c Gilchrist b MacGill			21
*JS Foster	lbw b Waugh	19			(8) c Love b MacGill			6
AR Caddick	b Gillespie	17			c Waugh b MacGill			10
SJ Harmison	c Gilchrist b Gillespie	2			b Gillespie			7
Extras	b 3, lb 10, nb 14	27			b 3, lb 21, w 2, nb 6			32
		270						387

	First Innings				Second Innings			
	O	M	R	W	O	M	R	W
McGrath	16	5	41	1	19	5	44	1
Gillespie	16.3	7	25	4	24.4	6	71	3
MacGill	36	10	108	2	48	10	152	5
Lee	17	4	70	2	27	4	87	1
Waugh	4	0	13	1	2	0	9	0

Fall of Wickets
1-13, 2-73, 3-94, 4-111, 5-113, 6-118, 7-172, 8-227, 9-264
1-67, 2-89, 3-169, 4-236, 5-287, 6-342, 7-342, 8-356, 9-378

Umpires: DL Orchard & RB Tiffin
Toss: Australia

Australia won by 5 wickets

Langer and Ponting added exactly 50 at a cracking rate before Ponting was trapped down the legside for 30. Three balls later, Martyn was caught behind for a duck and Waugh strode to the crease with his team needing a further 49 to win with seven wickets in hand. When he was on four, Waugh clearly edged Harmison to Foster, but such was the noise generated by the Barmy Army that, initially, no one appealed. It was several seconds later that a quizzical Foster raised the question with umpire Orchard who, understandably, turned it down. Next ball, Waugh thrashed a catch straight to Hussain to mid-off who threw the ball in the air in celebration. Waugh walked off, unaware for some considerable time that Mr Orchard had called no-ball.

Finally Waugh's unusual innings came to an end on 14, and when Langer was lbw to Caddick for 24, Australia were 90 for 5, still needing 17 to win. Any hopes of an unlikely victory, though, were ruthlessly and calmly extinguished by Love and Gilchrist with the final run being knocked off ten minutes before lunch.

FIFTH TEST
2–6 January 2003 at the SCG, Sydney

This was a match in which, without Warne and McGrath, Australia were able to take a glance into the future. They may not have liked what they saw. Deprive any team of bowlers of that quality and, of course, the difference will be seen. It is just that everyone has become so accustomed to Australia seeming able to cope with every eventuality that this particular exercise was so interesting. Lee, the persevering Bichel and, until he was injured, Gillespie all worked hard, but Gillespie was able to bowl only 18 overs in England's second innings of 452 for 9, and not even Australia could stem the flow of runs.

There were many highlights, not least England's first victory at the SCG since 1978–79, in front of several thousand English supporters – some more vociferous than others. Vaughan, again, batted supremely well to record his third century of the series, Butcher scored a fine 124 and Caddick took seven wickets in Australia's second innings. But all of these worthy achievements were put well and truly in the shade by one of the most remarkable moments of theatre it has ever been my pleasure to see.

It is true that, probably, one had to have been in Australia for the couple of months that preceded this match in order to appreciate fully the magnitude of Steve Waugh's century on the second day. His

Steve Waugh handed the Australian selectors a sharp reminder that his Test career is far from over with a knock of 102.

place in the team had become the major talking point the length and breadth of the vast continent, and it seemed as if the selectors had made up their minds that this was to be his swansong. If there is anything an Australian likes, it is for an underdog to stand up and make his mark.

And so it was shortly before tea on the second afternoon that Waugh stepped onto his home ground in bright sunshine and before a vast crowd which was 100 per cent behind him – including the Brits. Australia were 56 for 3 in reply to England's 362 and the innings needed a steadying hand. In fact, during a breathtaking final session, 170 runs were scored: 93 of them by Waugh.

I remember settling into the commentator's seat for the final 20 minutes of play without even considering that Waugh might get his hundred that day. He was in the mid-80s at the time and it seemed inconceivable that England would allow him to get the runs he needed, but make him endure a sleepless night instead.

When Dawson trotted up to bowl the last over of the day, Waugh was 95 not out – five runs away from equalling Don Bradman's tally of 29 Test centuries. That fact meant nothing: here was a man who was ramming home his point to the selectors. How dare they consider finishing his career? The atmosphere in the famous old ground was a mixture of unrestrained joy and disbelief. This really did surpass all expectation, and now there was the real chance that Waugh could finish it that evening. He blocked the first three balls, and some of us thought that was it. However, he drove the fourth through the covers and ran three: 98 not out with two balls to go, but at the wrong end! Gilchrist masterfully engineered a single, to everyone's delight, and after what seemed an age as Hussain time and again minutely adjusted the field, Waugh smashed the final ball of the day through the covers for four. It was one of those moments that one could never forget, and I feel hugely privileged to have been the man on air at the time, charged with describing the drama, tension and excitement of one of cricket's greatest moments.

Typically, Waugh failed to add to his overnight 102, but the entertainment continued in the form of a terrific innings by Gilchrist. He raced to 133 from only 121 balls with 18 fours and, with some doughty support from Gillespie, he took Australia to the most slender advantage of just a single run.

Now it was Vaughan's turn to step into the limelight. For me, this was his best innings of the series and it was cruel that, for the third time, he came within a whisker of a double century without being able to pass the landmark. This time he was on 183 when he was despatched by an lbw decision that might well have been too high. With Hussain, who scored 72, he had added 189 and Stewart chipped in with a useful 38 to enable England to declare and set Australia 452 to win in 110 overs. It was hardly a generous target, but Australia had made a whitewash their ambition, and Hussain was hardly going to make it easy for them.

Tempers in the Australian dressing room clearly became fraught as the finest team in the world found themselves under pressure for once. Hayden fell to a debatable lbw decision, but his behaviour, which resulted in a broken window in the pavilion door, was utterly unacceptable. Gilchrist was also cited for an incident in the middle and, all in all, it was most unsavoury for a team which constantly reminds us of the importance of sportsmanship. Even the locals referred to them as 'The Unlovables'.

There was no stopping Caddick on the final day as a wearing pitch produced awkward bounce, and there are few better bowlers when his tail is up. Gilchrist and Lee added 42 and suggested that Australia could save the game before Gilchrist received a brute from Caddick that flew, hit the glove and resulted in a catch for Butcher at slip. The game was up and, on the old hill, the Barmy Army celebrated as if England had just won the Ashes themselves. One day they will, but it is difficult to see it happening for a while yet.

Steve Waugh displays the Ashes vase after a Test match of great personal satisfaction at Sydney.

FIFTH TEST – AUSTRALIA v. ENGLAND
2–6 January 2003 at Sydney Cricket Ground

ENGLAND

	First Innings		Second Innings	
ME Trescothick	c Gilchrist b Bichel	19	b Lee	22
MP Vaughan	c Gilchrist b Lee	0	lbw b Bichel	183
MA Butcher	b Lee	124	c Hayden b MacGill	34
N Hussain (capt)	c Gilchrist b Gillespie	75	c Gilchrist b Lee	72
RWT Key	lbw b Waugh	3	c Hayden b Lee	14
JP Crawley	not out	35	c Hayden b Lee	8
*AJ Stewart	b Bichel	71	not out	38
RKJ Dawson	c Gilchrist b Bichel	2	c & b Bichel	12
AR Caddick	b MacGill	7	c Langer b MacGill	8
MJ Hoggard	st Gilchrist b MacGill	0	b MacGill	0
SJ Harmison	run out	4	not out	20
Extras	b 6, lb 3, nb 13	22	b 9, lb 20, w 2, nb 10	41
		362	(9 wkts. dec.)	**452**

	First Innings				Second Innings			
	O	M	R	W	O	M	R	W
Gillespie	27	10	62	1	18.3	4	70	1
Lee	31	9	97	2	31.3	5	132	3
Bichel	21	5	86	3	25.3	3	82	2
MacGill	44	8	106	2	41	8	120	3
Waugh	4	3	2	1	6	2	5	0
Martyn	-	-	-	-	3	1	14	0

Fall of Wickets
1-4, 2-32, 3-198, 4-210, 5-240, 6-332, 7-337, 8-348, 9-350
1-37, 2-124, 3-313, 4-344, 5-345, 6-356, 7-378, 8-407, 9-409

AUSTRALIA

	First Innings		Second Innings	
JL Langer	c Hoggard b Caddick	25	lbw b Caddick	3
ML Hayden	lbw b Caddick	15	lbw b Hoggard	2
RT Ponting	c Stewart b Caddick	7	(4) lbw b Caddick	11
DR Martyn	c Caddick b Harmison	26	(5) c Stewart b Dawson	21
SR Waugh (capt)	c Butcher b Hoggard	102	(6) b Caddick	6
ML Love	c Trescothick b Harmison	0	(7) b Harmison	27
*AC Gilchrist	c Stewart b Harmison	133	(8) c Butcher b Caddick	37
AJ Bichel	c Crawley b Hoggard	4	(3) lbw b Caddick	49
B Lee	c Stewart b Hoggard	0	c Stewart b Caddick	46
JN Gillespie	not out	31	not out	3
SCG MacGill	c Hussain b Hoggard	1	b Caddick	1
Extras	b 2, lb 6, w 2, nb 9	19	b 6, lb 8, w 3, nb 3	20
		363		**226**

	First Innings				Second Innings			
	O	M	R	W	O	M	R	W
Hoggard	21.3	4	92	4	13	3	35	1
Caddick	23	3	121	3	22	5	94	7
Harmison	20	4	70	3	9	1	42	1
Dawson	16	0	72	0	10	2	41	1

Fall of Wickets
1-36, 2-45, 3-56, 4-146, 5-150, 6-241, 7-267, 8-267, 9-349
1-5, 2-5, 3-25, 4-93, 5-99, 6-109, 7-139, 8-181, 9-224

Umpires: DL Orchard & RB Tiffin
Toss: England

England won by 225 runs

SERIES AVERAGES
Australia v. England

AUSTRALIA

Batting	M	Inns	NO	Runs	HS	Av	100	50	c/st
ML Hayden	5	8	0	496	197	62.00	3	-	8/-
JN Gillespie	5	5	4	61	31*	61.00	-	-	-/-
AC Gilchrist	5	8	2	333	133	55.50	1	2	23/2
JL Langer	5	8	0	423	250	52.87	1	-	2/-
RT Ponting	5	8	0	417	154	52.12	2	1	6/-
ML Love	2	4	2	95	62*	47.50	-	1	4/-
DR Martyn	5	8	0	320	95	40.00	-	3	2/-
SK Warne	3	3	0	117	57	39.00	-	1	1/-
SR Waugh	5	8	0	305	102	38.12	1	2	2/-
DS Lehmann	3	4	1	97	42	32.33	-	-	2/-
B Lee	3	3	0	87	46	29.00	-	-	2/-
AJ Bichel	3	4	0	101	49	25.25	-	-	2/-
GD McGrath	4	2	1	8	8*	8.00	-	-	2/-
SCG MacGill	2	2	0	2	1	1.00	-	-	-/-

Bowling	Overs	Mds	Runs	Wkts	Av	Best	5/inn	10m
GD McGrath	162.2	53	380	19	20.00	4-36	-	-
SR Waugh	25	8	43	2	21.50	1-2	-	-
DR Martyn	6	2	23	1	23.00	1-0	-	-
JN Gillespie	181.5	53	492	20	24.60	4-25	-	-
SK Warne	131.1	29	347	14	24.78	4-93	-	-
AJ Bichel	94.3	14	351	10	35.10	3-86	-	-
SCG MacGill	169	36	486	12	40.50	5-152	1	-
B Lee	144.4	26	536	13	41.23	3-78	-	-

Also bowled: DS Lehmann 5-0-11-0

ENGLAND

Batting	M	Inns	NO	Runs	HS	Av	100	50	c/st
MP Vaughan	5	10	0	633	183	63.30	3	-	-/-
AJ Stewart	4	8	2	268	71	44.66	-	3	11/-
JP Crawley	3	6	2	162	69*	40.50	-	1	3/-
N Hussain	5	10	0	382	75	38.20	-	4	3/-
MA Butcher	5	10	0	318	124	31.80	1	1	6/-
ME Trescothick	5	10	0	261	72	26.10	-	1	5/-
C White	4	8	1	154	85*	22.00	-	1	1/-
RWT Key	4	8	0	141	52	17.62	-	1	1/-
RKJ Dawson	4	8	2	87	19*	14.50	-	-	2/-
JS Foster	1	2	0	25	19	12.50	-	-	3/-
CEW Silverwood	1	1	0	10	10	10.00	-	-	-/-
AF Giles	1	2	0	17	13	8.50	-	-	3/-
SJ Harmison	4	8	2	47	20*	7.83	-	-	1/-
AR Caddick	4	8	1	52	17	7.42	-	-	3/-
AJ Tudor	1	2	1	3	3*	3.00	-	-	2/-
MJ Hoggard	3	6	1	12	6	2.40	-	-	1/-

Also batted: SP Jones played in one Test but did not bat

Bowling	Overs	Mds	Runs	Wkts	Av	Best	5/inn	10m
AF Giles	53.2	5	191	6	31.83	4-101	-	-
SP Jones	7	0	32	1	32.00	1-32	-	-
AR Caddick	171	28	690	20	34.50	7-94	1	1
C White	122.1	14	532	14	38.00	5-127	1	-
SJ Harmison	132.3	28	455	9	50.55	3-70	-	-
MJ Hoggard	103.3	17	375	6	62.50	4-92	-	-
AJ Tudor	29	2	144	2	72.00	2-144	-	-
RKJ Dawson	96	5	398	5	79.60	2-121	-	-

Also bowled: CEW Silverwood 4-0-29-0; MA Butcher 25-3-104-0

VB TRIANGULAR SERIES
By Jonathan Agnew

For the three teams involved – Australia, England and Sri Lanka – this rather disjointed series was the last chance to play one-day cricket before the World Cup. It was clear that Australia, as the tournament favourites, had no more than the minutest tinkering to perform in order to put out the strongest limited-overs team in the world. Sri Lanka had just been hammered in South Africa, while England's selection policy over the past two years had been so chaotic that virtually anyone could secure a place in the World Cup on the back of a decent showing in the nets.

Injuries had, again, not helped England's preparations in the least. Darren Gough was back in Milton Keynes and Andrew Flintoff still was not fit. Jeremy Snape and Ashley Giles both had broken bones while, crucially, Michael Vaughan was rested from the early round of games which took place before Christmas.

In the opening match of the series at Sydney, England posted a creditable 251 for 8 from 50 overs, with Knight scoring an unbeaten 111 and Trescothick 60. Australia reminded us of their superiority by breezing past their target with five overs to spare. Two days later, in Melbourne, Australia ran up 318 for 6. Although Knight scored another 70, England were never in the game, which fizzled out at 92 for 5.

Then followed two of the direst matches imaginable as a curiously disinterested Sri Lanka failed on both occasions even to attempt victory. Perhaps they were distracted by the absurd bonus point ruling which actually rewards teams for failing to win? Whatever it was, this was no way to play one-day cricket and at Brisbane they meandered to 249 for 6 chasing England's 292 and in Perth it was even worse: 163 all out in reply to 258 for 9. Australia thrashed Sri Lanka two days later and at the half-way stage, five matches had produced four games of pure tedium.

Post England's Sydney Test celebrations, the VB Series limped into action again but, happily, with a resounding Sri Lankan win over Australia who conceded 343 for 5 – centuries for Jayasuriya and Atapattu – and then replied with only 264. A narrow encounter followed in Hobart where Australia beat England by only seven runs and Sri Lanka's victory in Sydney gave them a chance of reaching the finals at England's expense. However, Knight's 88 and four wickets by Caddick in Adelaide gained England's revenge and enabled them to line up against Australia in the best-of-three final.

Brett Lee's burst denied England one-day victory at the MCG.

The first, in Sydney, was an utter embarrassment. England were skittled for 117 and Australia raced to their target without losing a wicket in only 74 balls. With talk of going home for a few days in the air, many expected England to roll over again in Melbourne. In fact they lost a game they should have won where England, chasing Australia's 229, needed 14 to win from the last three overs with four wickets in hand. But, revved up by the excitable crowd, Brett Lee charged in to remove Flintoff, Blackwell and Caddick to finish with 5 for 30 and prove yet again that Australia appear to have the answer for every situation.

Match One
13 December 2002 at Sydney Cricket Ground
England 251 for 8 (50 overs) (NV Knight 111*,
ME Trescothick 60, N Hussain 52, B Lee 4 for 47)
Australia 252 for 3 (45 overs) (ML Hayden 98,
AC Gilchrist 53)
Australia (5pts) won by 7 wickets – England (1pt)

Match Two
15 December 2002 at Melbourne Cricket Ground
Australia 318 for 6 (50 overs) (AC Gilchrist 124,
RT Ponting 119)
England 229 (48 overs) (NV Knight 70, C White 57*)
Australia (6pts) won by 89 runs

Match Three
17 December 2002 Woolloongabba, Brisbane
England 292 (50 overs) (N Hussain 79,
AJ Stewart 64)
Sri Lanka 249 for 6 (50 overs) (DPMD Jayawardene 71,
RP Arnold 60*)
England (5pts) won by 43 runs – Sri Lanka (1pt)

Match Four
20 December 2002 at WACA Ground, Perth
England 258 for 9 (50 overs) (PD Collingwood 100,
CRD Fernando 4 for 48)
Sri Lanka 163 (43.4 overs)
England (6pts) won by 95 runs

Match Five
22 December 2002 at
WACA Ground, Perth
Australia 305 for 5
(50 overs)
(DS Lehmann 119,
ML Hayden 64)
Sri Lanka 163 (43 overs)
*Australia (6pts) won by
142 runs*

Match Six
9 January 2003 at
Sydney Cricket Ground
Sri Lanka 343 for 5
(50 overs)
(ST Jayasuriya 122,
MS Atapattu 101)
Australia 264 (49.3 overs)
(ST Jayasuriya 4 for 39)
*Sri Lanka (6pts) won by
79 runs*

Nick Knight: consistently
England's best one-day
batsman for a decade.

Match Seven

10 January 2003 at Bellerive Oval, Hobart
Australia 271 for 4 (50 overs) (DR Martyn 101*,
MG Bevan 52)
England 264 for 7 (50 overs) (NV Knight 85,
ME Trescothick 82)
Australia (5pts) won by 7 runs – England (1pt)

Match Eight

13 January 2003 at Sydney Cricket Ground
Sri Lanka 284 for 7 (50 overs) (ST Jayasuriya 106,
PA de Silva 51)
England 253 (49.2 overs) (ME Trescothick 85,
PA de Silva 4 for 30)
Sri Lanka (5pts) won by 31 runs – England (1pt)

Match Nine

15 January 2003 at Woolloongabba, Brisbane
Sri Lanka 211 for 9 (50 overs) (MS Atapattu 70,
DPMD Jayawardene 56)
Australia 214 for 6 (48.5 overs) (M Muralitharan
4 for 27)
Australia (5pts) won by 4 wickets – Sri Lanka (1pt)

Match Ten

17 January 2003 at Adelaide Oval
England 279 for 7 (50 overs) (NV Knight 88,
AJ Stewart 51)
Sri Lanka 260 (49.2 overs) (ST Jayasuriya 99,
KC Sangakkara 56, AR Caddick 4 for 35)
England (5pts) won by 19 runs – Sri Lanka (1pt)

Match Eleven

19 January 2003 at Adelaide Oval
England 152 (48.3 overs) (PD Collingwood 63*)
Australia 153 for 6 (47.3 overs) (DR Martyn 59)
Australia (5pts) won by 4 wickets – England (1pt)

Match Twelve

21 January 2003 at Melbourne Cricket Ground
Sri Lanka 214 for 8 (50 overs)
Australia 215 for 1 (34.3 overs) (RT Ponting 106*,
ML Hayden 80*)
Australia (6pts) won by 9 wickets

FIRST FINAL – AUSTRALIA v. ENGLAND
23 January 2003 at Sydney Cricket Ground

ENGLAND

ME Trescothick	c Gilchrist b Lee	0
NV Knight	c Gilchrist b Lee	5
MP Vaughan	lbw b Bichel	21
N Hussain (capt)	b Williams	1
*AJ Stewart	c Gilchrist b Williams	12
PD Collingwood	st Gilchrist b Warne	43
ID Blackwell	c Ponting b Bichel	0
RC Irani	c Bichel b Lee	10
AR Caddick	not out	12
JM Anderson	c Gilchrist b Bichel	0
MJ Hoggard	c Gilchrist b Bichel	0
Extras	lb 7, w 5, nb 1	13
	(41 overs)	**117**

	O	M	R	W
Williams	10	2	22	2
Lee	10	1	29	3
Bichel	7	2	18	4
Warne	10	0	28	1
Hogg	4	0	13	0

Fall of Wickets
1-1, 2-11, 3-19, 4-33, 5-45, 6-45, 7-79, 8-115, 9-117

AUSTRALIA

*AC Gilchrist	not out	69
ML Hayden	not out	45
RT Ponting (capt)		
DR Martyn		
MG Bevan		
A Symonds		
B Lee		
GB Hogg		
AJ Bichel		
BA Williams		
SK Warne		
Extras	lb 2, w 2	4
	(14.2 overs) (0 wkt)	**118**

	O	M	R	W
Caddick	3	0	31	0
Anderson	4	0	35	0
Hoggard	3.2	0	36	0
Irani	2	0	14	0

Umpires: DL Orchard & SJA Taufel
Toss: England

<u>**Australia won by 10 wickets**</u>

SECOND FINAL – AUSTRALIA v. ENGLAND
25 January 2003 at Melbourne Cricket Ground

AUSTRALIA

*AC Gilchrist	c Anderson b Flintoff	26
ML Hayden	c sub b Irani	69
RT Ponting (capt)	c Flintoff b Caddick	1
DR Martyn	c Stewart b Caddick	11
MG Bevan	retired hurt	10
A Symonds	b Irani	8
GB Hogg	not out	71
SK Warne	c & b Irani	0
B Lee	c Blackwell b Anderson	18
AJ Bichel	not out	11
BA Williams		
Extras	b 2, lb 1, w 1	4
	(50 overs) (7 wkts)	**229**

	O	M	R	W
Caddick	10	2	23	2
Anderson	9	0	57	1
Flintoff	10	0	56	1
Blackwell	10	0	32	0
Irani	10	1	46	3
Vaughan	1	0	12	0

Fall of Wickets
1-39, 2-40, 3-56, 4-98, 5-147, 6-148, 7-196

ENGLAND

ME Trescothick	c Bichel b Lee	0
NV Knight	c Symonds b Lee	5
RC Irani	c Symonds b Williams	7
MP Vaughan	c Ponting b Warne	60
N Hussain (capt)	b Hogg	28
*AJ Stewart	c Lee b Warne	60
PD Collingwood	not out	25
A Flintoff	b Lee	16
ID Blackwell	c Martyn b Lee	1
AR Caddick	b Lee	4
JM Anderson	run out	0
Extras	lb 7, w 4, nb 7	18
	(49.3 overs)	**224**

	O	M	R	W
Lee	9.3	0	30	5
Williams	10	1	46	1
Bichel	10	0	42	0
Hogg	10	1	41	1
Warne	10	0	58	2

Fall of Wickets
1-8, 2-18, 3-20, 4-88, 5-151, 6-182, 7-216, 8-218, 9-224

Umpires: DB Hair & RB Tiffin
Toss: Australia

Australia won by 5 runs

AUSTRALIA REPORT
By Jim Maxwell

Between a semi-final loss in the Champions Trophy in Sri Lanka in August 2002 and an unsurprising win over Bangladesh in Darwin in August 2003, Australia continued to dominate all opposition, maintaining the high standards expected of the most entertaining Australian team in memory.

Twelve Tests and three series were won comfortably, with losses at the end of the Ashes and Caribbean campaigns making no difference to the outcome of the series. The loss in Antigua was an amazingly inspiring result for the West Indies, who chased down a record 418 in the last innings. It revealed how easily momentum can swing when one side has nothing to lose and the other is mentally and physically drained.

England grabbed a win in Sydney in similar circumstances at the end of the Ashes series, buoyed by some exceptional batting from Michael Vaughan, and a deteriorating fourth-innings pitch.

In limited-overs internationals, Australia were irrepressible, completing a staggering 33 wins, including a record-breaking streak of 21 consecutive victories, against five losses.

Australia's World Cup performance was resounding, producing an unblemished record that showed the gap between Australia and the rest. The team's potency reverberated through Ricky Ponting's spectacular batting in the final against India at the Wanderers. It was an awesome display, and it left India gasping.

Australian cricket has hit many peaks of excellence in the last decade, playing ruthlessly yet entertainingly under the laconic Steve Waugh and, more recently, his impressive limited-overs successor, Ricky Ponting.

There are several factors behind Australia's consistently high standard of play. A synopsis would jump on these key words: organization, skill, commitment, leadership, belief, structure and, most importantly, culture.

This particular type of intellectual development, or culture, embraces the gamut of Australian cricket – from playing in the backyard, imitating the heroes of the day, to the full-blown experience of wearing the country's most powerful sporting icon, the baggy green cap.

Added in is a clearly defined path which identifies adolescent talent and nurtures it through rigorous graduation levels, with the process being supported by quality personnel and proper corporate governance. The focus is firmly aimed at producing the best national team, and parochial interests have been diffused by a redefined brief for the variously elected directors from each state, including former players like Allan Border.

The rewards for the players flow through state-based contracts to Cricket Australia's contracted list of 24. The deal struck by the Players' Association under the leadership of former Test off spinner Tim May is generous, with bonuses locked in if the game's revenues continue to grow.

Like a mining or tech boom, Cricket Australia has struck gold in recent seasons, but losses from Bangladesh's winter visit, a plateau in earnings from television rights and sponsorship, and the growing costs in running a cricket bureaucracy, will force pay-packet renegotiations.

For the elite team a successful culture has grown through the captaincy tenures of Border, Mark Taylor and Steve Waugh, Bob Simpson's disciplined coaching, the fine tuning of John Buchanan's mentoring regimens, and the preventative care of physiotherapist Errol Alcott, supported by fitness co-ordinator Jock Campbell.

The flesh around those bones is a group of experienced, highly motivated players, including the most accomplished strike bowlers of their generation in Glenn McGrath and Shane Warne, now joined by Jason Gillespie and Brett Lee, plus the best batsman-wicketkeeper the game has ever seen, Adam Gilchrist.

The depth of that experience showed up in the World Cup when Andy Bichel seamlessly substituted for the injured Gillespie, and became a match-winning contributor.

Bichel and Michael Bevan destroyed England's vestigial hopes at Port Elizabeth with their unbroken eighth-wicket partnership of 73, after Bichel had taken seven of the eight English wickets to fall for just 20 runs. Bichel's significant contribution throughout the World Cup was one of several positive outcomes for players who were given little chance of appearing regularly from the outset.

Warne's last-minute withdrawal also gave Andrew Symonds an opportunity, which he grabbed devastatingly against Pakistan with his maturest performance, a Man of the Match-winning 143 from 125 deliveries.

Symonds said he was angry about Warne's dramatic revelation regarding a positive drug sample, and felt motivated to show that he and the rest of his disappointed team-mates could perform and win without their champion wrist-spinner.

While Ponting's team was gallumphing across the veldt, Steve Waugh, the forgotten hero of previous World Cup successes and spurned one-day leader, had agreed to lead the team to the Caribbean after a period of deliberation about his future.

Speculation about the timing of Waugh's retirement, or the selectors' decision to push him, had been rife throughout the summer. Following the retention of the Ashes, and a memorable century in front of a rapturous SCG home crowd in the fifth Test, Waugh was certainly in control of his destiny.

A string of impressive innings in domestic cricket had convinced Waugh that he had the form and the desire to play on. Another Test hundred in Barbados, during a 3–1 series win, followed by two not out centuries against Bangladesh, fortified the record-breaking leader, who was now looking ahead to the next major event: to win a series in India in

End of one Waugh: for stylish Mark, being left out of the 2002–03 Ashes series signalled the finish of a great international career.

September 2004, when he'd be 39, and with Border's run-scoring record probably eclipsed.

Waugh has outlasted his twin brother Mark, who was dropped at the start of the Ashes series. The graceful Waugh 'junior' immediately announced his retirement from international cricket. He continued to play domestic cricket, where he coveted the NSW captaincy, but finished the season playing under Steve when the Blues claimed trophies in both the one-day and first-class competitions.

When Mark was replaced by Darren Lehmann in the Test XI, pundits were still asking the question that had lingered for months: name an Australian team without M.Waugh and tell me it's stronger?

Mark's catching skills were exceptional, and although his footwork had deteriorated, he could bat from memory better than most. And at 32, with his best years behind him, picking Lehmann ahead of a 21-year-old talent like Michael Clarke, was contrary to the time-honoured investment in youth that had flung the likes of Neil Harvey, Doug Walters and Steve Waugh himself into the cauldron.

Conservative selectors, feeling that Lehmann deserved a chance to play a series, were caught up in the so-called 'professionalism' of contemporary cricket, where players are expected to earn their place over several seasons of accomplishment, not one or two. And with so many earning a living from cricket into their 30s, the chances for young players, particularly batsmen, now seem limited.

The selectors appear bulletproof at present because their selections are producing a consistently high standard. Judging when to make changes in the longer-term interests of the side is their dilemma, because the combined blight of injuries and faltering form can happen suddenly, damaging confidence and performance.

In 2002–03 there were no signs of deterioration, however, and here's a snapshot of the personalities and combinations that sustained Australia at the top of the ratings.

Ponting flourished, carrying his World Cup final form through to the Caribbean where he scored 523 runs in three Tests, before missing the epic fourth Test with a debilitating virus. On his own admission, Ponting's batting reached a peak against the West Indies. Three centuries in five innings, including his highest score of 206 in Trinidad, were masterpieces of controlled aggression.

Daring cross-batted shots and straight driving featured powerfully, and like all the best players he could not be contained. When Ian Healy appointed him as the chorus leader of the team's triumphal song, 'Beneath the Southern Cross I stand, a sprig of wattle in my hand,' Ponting became a respected elder in the dressing room.

He supplanted Gilchrist as the Test vice-captain, too, and must be wondering when he will get the chance to succeed Steve Waugh. Like Waugh before Taylor stood down, or Bradman behind Woodfull, the moment is ripe.

Gilchrist's durability is remarkable. He has not missed a Test since replacing Healy in 1999, doing knee squats behind the stumps at a strike rate comparable to his astonishing rate of scoring.

Consistently ranked in the top five batsmen in both forms of the game, Gilchrist bats at No. 7 in Test matches with a free spirit that is rarely tempered by apparent scoreboard anxiety. Wyatt Earp couldn't have had faster hands than Gilchrist, and few batsmen are capable of changing the course of a match as he does. Although more accomplished standing back than he is over the stumps, the quality of his keeping is often underrated. Hopefully his knees will last long enough for

Ricky Ponting was at the peak of his considerable powers when he took his World Cup final form to the Caribbean.

another Ashes series in 2005.

Opening batsmen are best in pairs. Matthew Hayden and Justin Langer, like their brilliant predecessors Taylor and Slater, or Simpson and Lawry or Woodfull and Ponsford, or the best of all Hobbs and Sutcliffe, play for each other as much as themselves.

Averaging over 70 since the association began at The Oval in 2001, the two left-handers are experts at destroying bowlers, and they have enjoyed particular prosperity facing some inexperienced, inadequate attacks. Hayden has developed his game more roundly than Langer, encouraging Steve Waugh to say 'he's as good as anyone around' after a seven-hour 119 that single-handedly outscored Pakistan's paltry 59 and 53 in the 50-degree Sharjah heat.

Langer often looks more vulnerable than his statuesque partner, but his record shows how determinedly he grasps opportunities, as he did so convincingly at the MCG when making 250 against England, and again in the Caribbean with two centuries and a series average of 69. Langer's self-discipline is impressive, remembering that he is the only established Test batsman who has never been regarded as a one-day player.

Gillespie was described by his captain as the best fast bowler in the game at the end of the West Indies series. On unsympathetic pitches he took 17 wickets at 20.76. In the Ashes rubber, he led the attack with 20 wickets at 24.60. Significantly he played through both series, allowing for the elbow injury that curtailed his fifth Test appearance in Sydney.

Gillespie's Test career was spasmodic before improved recuperative and preventative care was initiated by physio Alcott. Gillespie's commitment to fitness is as routined as yoga or morning prayers observance. A spate of exercises in the pool, and the wearing of the revolutionary therapeutic bodysuit skin, have ensured Gillespie's survival. Like McGrath, he nowadays bowls unwaveringly at the off stump, and if the conditions attract swing he's lethal.

McGrath himself, however, may be reaching the end of an illustrious career. After taking 19 wickets in four Ashes Tests, fatigue forced him out of the final Test. Following a refreshed World Cup campaign he understandably opted out of two Tests in the West Indies after his wife Jane had again been diagnosed with cancer.

He returned in Barbados and was short of match condition and down on pace, a factor that became more obvious when he played against Bangladesh. An ankle injury has been annoying him for a long time, and the signs of battle fatigue are omnipresent, but hopefully not overwhelming.

Warne's skill produced 27 wickets in three Tests against Pakistan, and another 14 in the Ashes series before a shoulder injury forced him out of the last two Tests. Bluff and experience now count more than huge leg breaks and flippers, though, and the 12-month ban for drug abuse has cast doubts over his return. His careless behaviour has also put the authorities into damage control, and as long as Stuart MacGill continues to take wickets, as he did so effectively in the Caribbean and against the Bangladeshis, Warne cannot expect automatic selection.

Lee's improvement was stark in the World Cup, and he maintained excellent rhythm in the West Indies with 17 wickets at 28.82. His attacking method relies on bounce and movement. Lee's fitness is the key to his success, and this was underlined watching him bowl a nine-over spell in Trinidad's dripping humidity.

Bichel, Lehmann and Damien Martyn, until he was injured, all made excellent contributions, and Bevan continued his unique role as a one-day specialist. For the future, Michael Clarke's forthright brilliance stands out.

Indeed, this golden era in Australian cricket should continue as long as other countries struggle to match the aggression and organization of these confident sportsmen.

A study in speed: Jason Gillespie was hailed as the world's best fast bowler by his captain at the end of the West Indies series.

FIRST TEST – AUSTRALIA v. BANGLADESH
18–21 July 2003 at Darwin

BANGLADESH

	First Innings		Second Innings	
Hannan Sarkar	lbw b McGrath	0	c Gilchrist b Gillespie	35
Javed Omar	c Gilchrist b Gillespie	5	lbw b McGrath	5
Habibul Bashar	b Lee	16	b MacGill	54
Mohammad Ashraful	c Gillespie b McGrath	23	c Gilchrist b Lee	7
Al Sahariar	b Lee	0	c & b MacGill	36
Alok Kapali	lbw b MacGill	0	lbw b MacGill	0
*Khaled Mashud	lbw b McGrath	11	c Gilchrist b MacGill	6
Khaled Mahmud (capt)	c Gilchrist b MacGill	21	b Gillespie	5
Mashrafe Mortaza	c Gilchrist b Gillespie	3	(10) run out	15
Tapash Baisya	not out	2	(9) lbw b MacGill	4
Manjural Islam	c Langer b Lee	1	not out	0
Extras	b 1, lb 5, w 6, nb 3	15	lb 6, w 2, nb 3	11
		97		**178**

	First Innings				Second Innings			
	O	M	R	W	O	M	R	W
McGrath	13	6	20	3	10	0	25	1
Gillespie	8	1	27	2	16	3	48	2
Lee	8.2	2	23	3	12	5	34	1
MacGill	13	4	21	2	13.1	1	65	5

Fall of Wickets
1-4, 2-26, 3-36, 4-39, 5-40, 6-60, 7-87, 8-91, 9-94
1-8, 2-89, 3-112, 4-112, 5-112, 6-122, 7-143, 8-152, 9-171

AUSTRALIA

	First Innings	
JL Langer	lbw b Kapali	71
ML Hayden	b Mortaza	11
RT Ponting	c Omar b Baisya	10
DS Lehmann	c Omar b Mortaza	110
SR Waugh (capt)	not out	100
ML Love	b Mortaza	0
*AC Gilchrist	b Islam	43
B Lee	run out	23
JN Gillespie	not out	16
GD McGrath		
SCG MacGill		
Extras	b 5, lb 8, w 7, nb 3	23
	(7 wkts dec.)	**407**

	First Innings			
	O	M	R	W
Islam	24	4	78	1
Mortaza	23	7	74	3
Baisya	21.5	4	69	1
Mahmud	28	2	98	0
Kapali	18	2	65	1
Ashraful	2	0	9	0
Bashar	1	0	1	0

Fall of Wickets
1-13, 2-43, 3-184, 4-243, 5-244, 6-313, 7-377

Umpires: RE Koertzen & DR Shepherd
Toss: Australia

Australia won by an innings and 132 runs

SECOND TEST – AUSTRALIA v. BANGLADESH
25–29 July 2003 at Cairns

BANGLADESH

	First Innings		Second Innings	
Hannan Sarkar	lbw b MacGill	76	c Hayden b MacGill	55
Javed Omar	c Gilchrist b Lee	26	lbw b Gillespie	8
Habibul Bashar	c & b MacGill	46	c Langer b Lee	25
Mohammad Ashraful	c Gilchrist b Gillespie	0	c Ponting b MacGill	0
Sanwar Hossain	b MacGill	46	c Ponting b MacGill	16
Alok Kapali	c Love b MacGill	5	c Langer b MacGill	17
*Khaled Mashud	c Love b Gillespie	44	lbw b Gillespie	14
Khaled Mahmud (capt)	lbw b MacGill	0	b MacGill	17
Tapash Baisya	c Gilchrist b McGrath	25	lbw b Gillespie	0
Mashrafe Mortaza	c Lee b Gillespie	8	not out	3
Anwar Hossain Monir	not out	0	b Gillespie	4
Extras	lb 8, nb 11	19	lb 2, nb 2	4
		295		**163**

	First Innings				Second Innings			
	O	M	R	W	O	M	R	W
McGrath	17.1	2	57	1	15	9	22	0
Gillespie	25	7	57	3	12.4	3	38	4
Lee	18	1	88	1	11	2	45	1
MacGill	24	9	77	5	20	3	56	5
Waugh	5	3	4	0	-	-	-	-
Lehmann	3	1	4	0	-	-	-	-

Fall of Wickets
1-47, 2-155, 3-156, 4-156, 5-170, 6-230, 7-230, 8-281, 9-295
1-12, 2-87, 3-90, 4-90, 5-123, 6-136, 7-156, 8-156, 9-156

AUSTRALIA

	First Innings	
JL Langer	c Omar b Mortaza	1
ML Hayden	b Hossain	50
RT Ponting	c Ashraful b Hossain	59
DS Lehmann	c Ashraful b Baisya	177
SR Waugh (capt)	not out	156
ML Love	not out	100
*AC Gilchrist		
B Lee		
JN Gillespie		
GD McGrath		
SCG MacGill		
Extras	lb 11, w 1, nb 1	13
	(4 wkts dec.)	**556**

	First Innings			
	O	M	R	W
Mortaza	25	7	60	1
Baisya	26	5	96	1
Hossain Monir	21	4	95	0
Mahmud	19	3	75	0
Hossain	30	2	128	2
Kapali	14.2	0	69	0
Ashraful	4	0	22	0

Fall of Wickets
1-14, 2-105, 3-132, 4-382

Umpires: RE Koertzen & DR Shepherd
Toss: Australia

Australia won by an innings and 98 runs

SERIES AVERAGES
Australia v. Bangladesh

AUSTRALIA

Batting	M	Inns	NO	Runs	HS	Av	100	50	c/st
DS Lehmann	2	2	0	287	177	143.50	2	-	-/-
ML Love	2	2	1	100	100*	100.00	1	-	2/-
AC Gilchrist	2	1	0	43	43	43.00	-	-	9/-
JL Langer	2	2	0	72	71	36.00	-	1	3/-
RT Ponting	2	2	0	69	59	34.50	-	1	2/-
ML Hayden	2	2	0	61	50	30.50	-	1	1/-
B Lee	2	1	0	23	23	23.00	-	-	2/-
SR Waugh	2	2	2	256	156*	-	2	-	-/-
JN Gillespie	2	1	1	16	16*	-	-	-	1/-
GD McGrath	2	0	0	0	0	-	-	-	-/-
SCG MacGill	2	0	0	0	0	-	-	-	2/-

Bowling	Overs	Mds	Runs	Wkts	Av	Best	5/inn	10m
SCG MacGill	70.1	17	219	17	12.88	5-56	3	1
JN Gillespie	61.4	14	170	11	15.45	4-38	-	-
GD McGrath	55.1	17	124	5	24.80	3-20	-	-
B Lee	49.2	10	190	6	31.66	3-23	-	-

Also bowled: SR Waugh 5-3-4-0; DS Lehmann 3-1-4-0

BANGLADESH

Batting	M	Inns	NO	Runs	HS	Av	100	50	c/st
Hannan Sarkar	2	4	0	166	76	41.50	-	2	-/-
Habibul Bashar	2	4	0	141	54	35.25	-	1	-/-
Sanwar Hossain	1	2	0	62	46	31.00	-	-	-/-
Khaled Mashud	2	4	0	75	44	18.75	-	-	-/-
Al Sahariar	1	2	0	36	36	18.00	-	-	-/-
Javed Omar	2	4	0	44	26	11.00	-	-	3/-
Khaled Mahmud	2	4	0	43	21	10.75	-	-	-/-
Tapash Baisya	2	4	1	31	25	10.33	-	-	-/-
Mashrafe Mortaza	2	4	1	29	15	9.66	-	-	-/-
Mohammad Ashraful	2	4	0	30	23	7.50	-	-	2/-
Alok Kapali	2	4	0	22	17	5.50	-	-	-/-
Anwar Hossain Monir	1	2	1	4	4	4.00	-	-	-/-
Manjural Islam	1	2	1	1	1	1.00	-	-	-/-

Bowling	Overs	Mds	Runs	Wkts	Av	Best	5/inn	10m
Mashrafe Mortaza	48	14	134	4	33.50	3-74	-	-
Sanwar Hossain	30	2	128	2	64.00	2-128	-	-
Manjural Islam	24	4	78	1	78.00	1-78	-	-
Tapash Baisya	47.5	9	165	2	82.50	1-69	-	-
Alok Kapali	32.2	2	134	1	134.00	1-65	-	-

Also bowled: Habibul Bashar 1-0-1-0; Mohammad Ashraful 6-0-31-0; Anwar Hossain Monir 21-4-95-0; Khaled Mahmud 47-5-173-0

ONE-DAY INTERNATIONALS v. BANGLADESH

Match One
2 August 2003 at Cairns
Bangladesh 105 (34 overs) (B Lee 4 for 25)
Australia 107 for 2 (22.3 overs)
Australia won by 8 wickets

Match Two
3 August 2003 at Cairns
Bangladesh 147 (45.1 overs)
Australia 148 for 1 (20.2 overs) (DR Martyn 92*)
Australia won by 9 wickets

Match Three
6 August 2003 at Darwin
Australia 254 for 7 (50 overs) (RT Ponting 101, MG Bevan 57)
Bangladesh 142 (47.3 overs) (IJ Harvey 4 for 16)
Australia won by 112 runs

STOP PRESS:

Matthew Hayden, the Australia opener, made cricket history on 10 October 2003, just as this book was going to press. Hayden scored 380 against Zimbabwe in Perth, in the First Test of their short series, to replace Brian Lara as the owner of Test cricket's highest individual innings. Lara himself had taken the record away from Sir Garry Sobers when he scored 375 for the West Indies against England in Antigua in 1994. Full details of Hayden's feat, plus comprehensive reports and records of the 2003-04 'Cricket Year', will be contained in next year's book.

INDIA

By Qamar Ahmed

The ever-changing pattern of India's performances on the international circuit, and at times the inconsistency of their star performers, worried many as the season progressed.

The quality of their cricket in England during the summer of 2002 boded well for the season ahead, and they managed to share the Champions Trophy with Sri Lanka after the final was twice washed out at Colombo because of rain. Then came a heart-warming 2–0 win in a three-match Test series at home against the West Indies – their first series win against the West Indians since Sunil Gavaskar's team triumphed 1–0 in the six-match home series of 1979 – which was followed by a 4–3 triumph in the one-day series.

Soon, however, their graph started to nosedive during their tour of New Zealand, where they lost the first Test at Wellington by ten wickets inside three days and the second Test by four wickets. A 2–0 defeat in the Tests and then a loss in the one-day series was not the ideal preparation for the World Cup in South Africa, which was due to start a few weeks later.

That India went on to contest the World Cup final is evidence in itself of the unpredictability of cricket, but it also revealed the high quality of many of the Indian players. Sachin Tendulkar, Saurav Ganguly, Virender Sehwag, Rahul Dravid, the youngsters Yuvraj Singh and Mohammad Kaif, and the bowlers Zaheer Khan, Ashish Nehra and Harbhajan Singh all featured prominently, redeeming both themselves and their country's cricket in the process.

Their World Cup successes also helped Indian cricket to redefine itself and, since the tournament, a lot of thinking has gone into reshaping the domestic game to help keep a pipeline of talented players going. However, controversy over the World Cup payments seems to have dragged on. The ICC is seen in India to be hanging on to the money owed to the BCCI. This leads to the belief that, as far as the ICC is concerned, there has always been one rule for India and Asia and another for the rest.

Then came the controversy of marketing during the World Cup and the fear of some of the Cup's sponsors who imagined that their sales would be hit by ambush marketing of products endorsed by Indian cricketers. The ICC, it seemed, was prepared to pander so much to its commercial interests that it appeared to place the Global Cricket Corporation above the India team in its list of priorities. Lest one forgets, the tournament would hardly have been worth the 'World' in its title had India not been allowed to participate.

That everyone was only too willing to stay on a confrontational course with the Indian Board's

World cricket's most powerful man? Jagmohan Dalmiya, the president of the Indian Cricket Board.

The banned Mohammad Azharuddin failed in his attempt to follow Ajay Jadeja back into Indian domestic cricket.

firebrand president, Jagmohan Dalmiya, showed up the cricket world for what it is – a house divided.

The controversies that raged both before and during the event – and the poor tour of New Zealand that preceded it – should have meant that India were in no shape to perform in the World Cup tournament itself. As it was, the only disappointment came with their collapse in the final against Australia – especially as Indian fans around the world had by then begun to believe that a second World Cup triumph was possible.

What sparked the great optimism over the final was India's win against arch rivals Pakistan at Centurion

Park. A fourth successive triumph in World Cups over Pakistan flew mainly off the blade of Sachin Tendulkar, whose punishing and entertaining 98 off Pakistan's quick bowlers settled the issue.

Back in India, meanwhile, former captain Mohammad Azharuddin's attempt to clear his name from the allegations of match fixing and to have his life ban lifted, failed to come to fruition. Ajay Jadeja's ban, however, was quashed by the High Court in India as he was allowed to participate in domestic cricket. It seemed a case of one law for one and one law for another.

India's success in the World Cup did generate

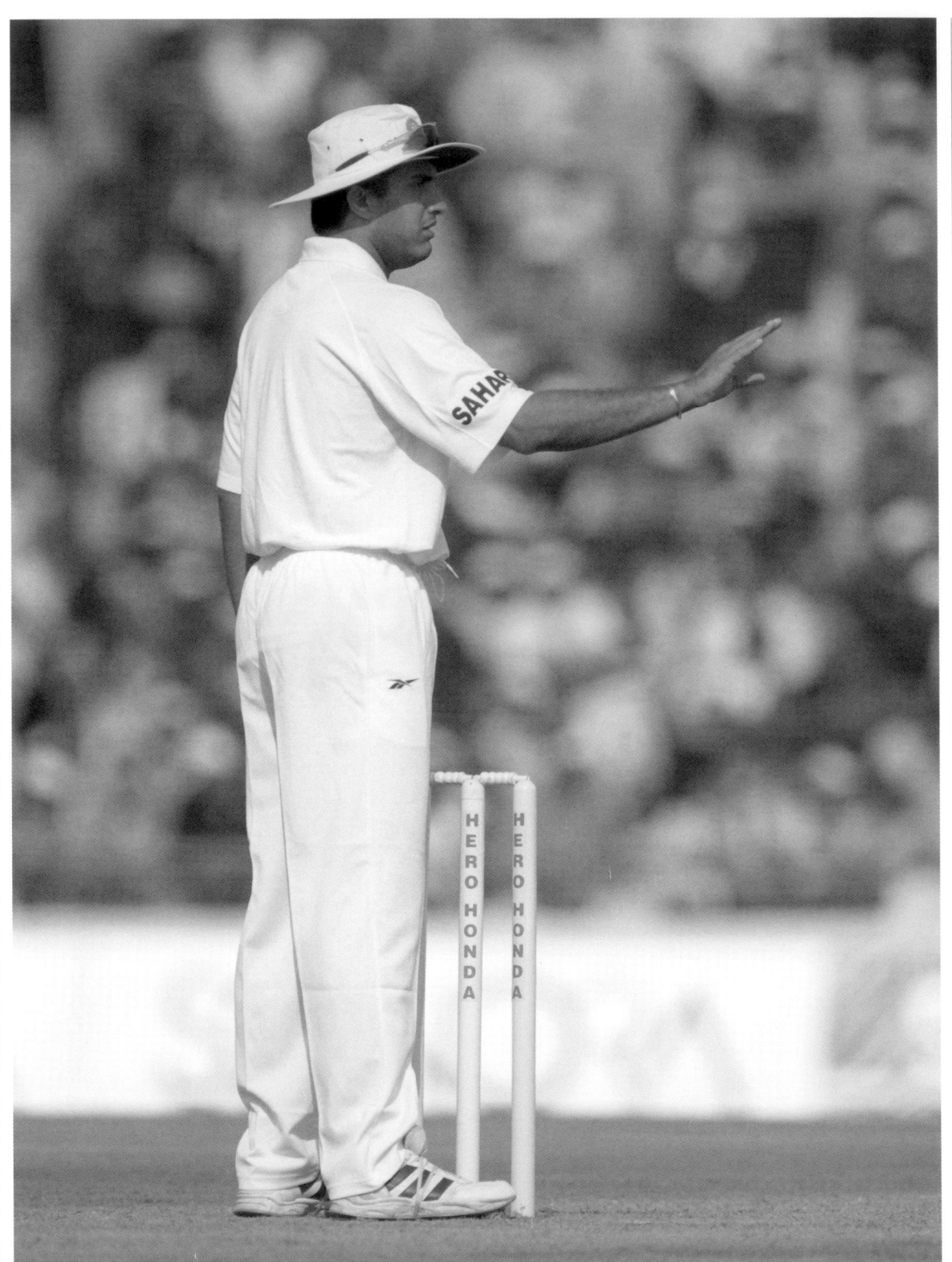

greater interest in Indian cricket. A number of reforms to the domestic game have been undertaken and new sponsors have been lining up to become involved, which in turn means that greater financial incentives are now in place for both players and umpires.

Saurav Ganguly and his players are preparing to flex their muscles on the field and Dalmiya still rules supreme off it. Indian cricket and its players remain a potent force – a force which the ICC has failed to recognize in the past. The Indian Cricket Board can afford to write off the withheld World Cup money and still be rolling in millions. The Indian market remains a bubbling base that can fund Indian cricket.

World cricket would not be the same without India's active role and co-operation. Imagine, for instance, a World Cup without India or the India-Pakistan showdown that is always the World Cup's greatest sideshow.

The saddest aspect of the past 12 months, however, has been the fact that India and Pakistan have still not been able to play each other at international level in their respective home territories because of the mindless political wrangling surrounding Kashmir. The last Test series between the two countries was held in India two years ago, despite threats by political extremists opposed to Pakistan's visit, and it was a huge success. That the crowds flocked to Chennai, Delhi and Calcutta confirmed cricket lovers' approval of matches between the two countries.

That recent attempts to bring India into Pakistan for a Test series have failed to materialize makes the game itself much poorer. One can only hope that behind-the-scenes attempts to resurrect international cricketing relations between these two great cricket nations continue and that during the next year players of these neighbouring countries will grace each other's grounds once again.

On the domestic front, Mumbai lifted the coveted Ranji Trophy after beating Tamil Nadu by 141 runs in the final to record their 35th success in the competition. Tamil Nadu, chasing 377 to win in the fourth innings, were all out for 255. Hemang Badani's 109 in the final was in vain. In the Deodhar Trophy, North Zone beat the South Zone in the final, while the Duleep Trophy was taken by Elite B.

Opposite: Saurav Ganguly has strengthened his position as captain of India in 2002–03, and has grown in authority both on and off the field of play.

FIRST TEST – INDIA v. WEST INDIES
9–13 October 2002 at Mumbai

INDIA

	First Innings	
SB Bangar	c Sarwan b Dillon	55
V Sehwag	c Jacobs b Dillon	147
R Dravid	retired hurt	100
SR Tendulkar	c Jacobs b Dillon	35
SC Ganguly (capt)	lbw b Cuffy	4
VVS Laxman	st Jacobs b Nagamootoo	45
*PA Patel	not out	21
Harbhajan Singh	c Jacobs b Cuffy	0
A Kumble	c Hooper b Nagamootoo	0
Z Khan	lbw b Nagamootoo	0
J Srinath	c Jacobs b Hooper	31
Extras	lb 7, w 3, nb 9	19
	(9 wkts)	457

	First Innings			
	O	M	R	W
Dillon	31.2	9	54	3
Collins	28	7	76	0
Cuffy	28.4	7	88	2
Nagamootoo	47	12	132	3
Hooper	11.5	3	40	1
WW Hinds	4	0	11	0
RO Hinds	10	0	40	0
Gayle	2	1	3	0
Sarwan	1	0	6	0

Fall of Wickets
1-201, 2-213, 3-280, 4-296, 5-401, 6-407, 7-408, 8-408, 9-457

WEST INDIES

	First Innings		Second Innings	
CH Gayle	lbw b Khan	7	c Ganguly b Singh	42
WW Hinds	c sub b Singh	1	b Singh	40
RR Sarwan	lbw b Kumble	22	c Tendulkar b Kumble	17
M Dillon	b Srinath	21	(9) c Dravid b Singh	0
S Chanderpaul	c & b Kumble	54	(4) not out	36
CL Hooper (capt)	c Bangar b Khan	23	(5) c & b Singh	1
RO Hinds	lbw b Khan	9	(6) c Sehwag b Kumble	2
*RD Jacobs	c Ganguly b Khan	0	(7) c Ganguly b Kumble	0
MV Nagamootoo	c Singh b Kumble	9	(8) c Ganguly b Singh	18
PT Collins	lbw b Kumble	0	c Dravid b Singh	8
CE Cuffy	not out	4	c & b Singh	0
Extras	lb 5, nb 2	7	b 8, lb 15, nb 1	24
		157		188

	First Innings				Second Innings			
	O	M	R	W	O	M	R	W
Srinath	11	5	16	1	4	2	19	0
Khan	16	3	41	4	4	0	26	0
Singh	21	8	37	1	28.3	11	48	7
Kumble	24.4	5	51	4	25	8	50	3
Sehwag	2	0	7	0	–	–	–	–
Bangar	–	–	–	–	6	1	20	0
Tendulkar	–	–	–	–	1	0	2	0

Fall of Wickets
1-7, 2-27, 3-43, 4-59, 5-103, 6-119, 7-123, 8-145, 9-146
1-60, 2-105, 3-107, 4-110, 5-117, 6-117, 7-158, 8-158, 9-184

Umpires: EAR de Silva & DR Shepherd
Toss: India

India won by an innings and 112 runs

SECOND TEST – INDIA v. WEST INDIES
17–21 October 2002 at Chennai

WEST INDIES

	First Innings		Second Innings	
CH Gayle	c Tendulkar b Singh	23	c Kumble b Srinath	0
WW Hinds	lbw b Kumble	18	c Ganguly b Singh	61
RR Sarwan	b Srinath	19	lbw b Khan	78
S Chanderpaul	c Patel b Kumble	27	c Singh b Srinath	3
CL Hooper (capt)	c Ganguly b Khan	35	c Patel b Kumble	46
RO Hinds	lbw b Kumble	16	c Kumble b Singh	7
*RD Jacobs	c Sehwag b Singh	9	c Patel b Khan	3
GR Breese	c Sehwag b Singh	5	c Ganguly b Singh	0
M Dillon	b Kumble	4	lbw b Singh	4
PT Collins	not out	1	not out	6
JJC Lawson	c Ganguly b Kumble	0	b Khan	2
Extras	b 8, lb 1, nb 1	10	b 12, lb 3, w 1, nb 3	19
		167		**229**

	First Innings				Second Innings			
	O	M	R	W	O	M	R	W
Srinath	10	5	14	1	9	4	16	2
Khan	10	3	21	1	12.4	5	23	3
Bangar	6	3	29	0	–	–	–	–
Singh	29	13	56	3	30	6	79	4
Kumble	23.3	10	30	5	26	3	87	1
Sehwag	1	0	8	0	2	0	9	0

Fall of Wickets
1-40, 2-46, 3-62, 4-117, 5-135, 6-142, 7-161, 8-166, 9-166
1-0, 2-96, 3-107, 4-179, 5-208, 6-210, 7-210, 8-214, 9-222

INDIA

	First Innings		Second Innings	
SB Bangar	c Hooper b Dillon	40	c Gayle b Hooper	20
V Sehwag	b Collins	61	st Jacobs b Hooper	33
R Dravid	b Lawson	11	not out	6
SR Tendulkar	b Lawson	43	not out	16
SC Ganguly (capt)	lbw b Dillon	0		
VVS Laxman	c & b Breese	24		
*PA Patel	st Jacobs b Breese	23		
Harbhajan Singh	b Dillon	37		
J Srinath	run out	39		
A Kumble	not out	12		
Z Khan	run out	4		
Extras	b 4, lb 10, w 1, nb 7	22	lb 3, nb 3	6
		316	(2 wkts)	**81**

	First Innings				Second Innings			
	O	M	R	W	O	M	R	W
Dillon	26	11	44	3	5	1	10	0
Collins	23	5	59	1	2	0	7	0
Lawson	20	4	63	2	2	0	2	0
Breese	26.1	3	108	2	5.1	0	27	0
Hooper	6	2	19	0	7	1	32	2
R O Hinds	5	1	9	0	–	–	–	–

Fall of Wickets
1-93, 2-109, 3-155, 4-155, 5-180, 6-204, 7-255, 8-281, 9-305
1-50, 2-61

Umpires: EAR de Silva & DR Shepherd
Toss: West Indies

India won by 8 wickets

THIRD TEST – INDIA v. WEST INDIES
30 October – 4 November 2002 at Kolkata

INDIA

	First Innings		Second Innings	
SB Bangar	c Hinds b Cuffy	77	c Chanderpaul b Dillon	0
V Sehwag	lbw b Dillon	35	c Chanderpaul b Dillon	10
R Dravid	lbw b Powell	14	lbw b Powell	17
SR Tendulkar	c Gayle b Lawson	36	c Gayle b Cuffy	176
SC Ganguly (capt)	c Jacobs b Hooper	29	lbw b Cuffy	16
VVS Laxman	c Gayle b Dillon	48	not out	154
*PA Patel	c Chanderpaul b Lawson	47	run out	27
Harbhajan Singh	b Cuffy	6	c Hooper b Samuels	26
J Srinath	c Hooper b Dillon	46	c Hooper b Chanderpaul	21
A Kumble	lbw b Powell	4	not out	8
A Nehra	not out	0		
Extras	lb 7, w 1, nb 8	16	b 8, lb 7, w 1	16
		358	(8 wkts)	**471**

	First Innings				Second Innings			
	O	M	R	W	O	M	R	W
Dillon	22	3	82	3	25	6	85	2
Cuffy	25	4	84	2	17	3	52	2
Lawson	20	3	76	2	22	3	65	0
Powell	16.2	4	62	2	25	4	53	1
Hooper	15	5	36	1	20	1	63	0
Gayle	2	0	6	0	23	5	70	0
Sarwan	1	0	5	0	8	1	38	0
Samuels	–	–	–	–	16	3	21	1
Chanderpaul	–	–	–	–	3	0	9	1

Fall of Wickets
1-49, 2-72, 3-116, 4-165, 5-242, 6-271, 7-280, 8-353, 9-358
1-0, 2-11, 3-49, 4-87, 5-301, 6-373, 7-407, 8-458

WEST INDIES

	First Innings	
CH Gayle	c Sehwag b Kumble	88
WW Hinds	c Ganguly b Singh	100
RR Sarwan	st Patel b Singh	2
M Dillon	b Singh	0
S Chanderpaul	c Singh b Sehwag	140
CL Hooper (capt)	c Patel b Nehra	19
MN Samuels	c Sehwag b Singh	104
*RD Jacobs	not out	22
DB Powell	lbw b Kumble	0
JJC Lawson	lbw b Kumble	5
CE Cuffy	c Laxman b Singh	0
Extras	b 4, lb 7, nb 6	17
		497

	First Innings			
	O	M	R	W
Srinath	19	3	62	0
Nehra	23	9	66	1
Singh	57.3	15	115	5
Kumble	54	9	169	3
Bangar	6	3	14	0
Tendulkar	7	0	33	0
Sehwag	5	0	27	1

Fall of Wickets
1-172, 2-186, 3-186, 4-213, 5-255, 6-450, 7-469, 8-470, 9-496

Umpires: EAR de Silva & DR Shepherd
Toss: India

Match Drawn

SERIES AVERAGES
India v. West Indies

INDIA

Batting	M	Inns	NO	Runs	HS	Av	100	50	c/st
VVS Laxman	3	4	1	271	154*	90.33	1	-	1/-
SR Tendulkar	3	5	1	306	176	76.50	1	-	2/-
V Sehwag	3	5	0	286	147	57.20	1	1	5/-
R Dravid	3	5	2	148	100*	49.33	1	-	2/-
PA Patel	3	4	1	118	47	39.33	-	-	4/1
SB Bangar	3	5	0	192	77	38.40	-	2	1/-
J Srinath	3	4	0	137	46	34.25	-	-	-/-
Harbhajan Singh	3	4	0	69	37	17.25	-	-	5/-
SC Ganguly	3	4	0	49	29	12.25	-	-	9/-
A Kumble	3	4	2	24	12*	12.00	-	-	3/-
Z Khan	2	2	0	4	4	2.00	-	-	-/-
A Nehra	1	1	1	0	0*	-	-	-	-/-

Bowling	Overs	Mds	Runs	Wkts	Av	Best	5/inn	10m
Z Khan	42.4	12	111	8	13.87	4-41	-	-
Harbhajan Singh	166	54	335	20	16.75	7-48	2	-
A Kumble	153.2	35	387	16	24.18	5-30	1	-
J Srinath	53	19	127	4	31.75	2-16	-	-
V Sehwag	10	0	51	1	51.00	1-27	-	-
A Nehra	23	9	66	1	66.00	1-66	-	-

Also bowled: SR Tendulkar 8-0-35-0; SB Bangar 18-7-63-0

WEST INDIES

Batting	M	Inns	NO	Runs	HS	Av	100	50	c/st
MN Samuels	1	1	0	104	104	104.00	1	-	-/-
S Chanderpaul	3	5	1	260	140	65.00	1	1	3/-
WW Hinds	3	5	0	220	100	44.00	1	-	1/-
CH Gayle	3	5	0	160	88	32.00	-	1	4/-
RR Sarwan	3	5	0	138	78	27.60	-	1	1/-
CL Hooper	3	5	0	124	46	24.80	-	-	5/-
MV Nagamootoo	1	2	0	27	18	13.50	-	-	-/-
RD Jacobs	3	5	1	34	22*	8.50	-	-	5/3
RO Hinds	2	4	0	34	16	8.50	-	-	-/-
PT Collins	2	4	2	15	8	7.50	-	-	-/-
M Dillon	3	5	0	29	21	5.80	-	-	-/-
GR Breese	1	2	0	5	5	2.50	-	-	1/-
JJC Lawson	2	3	0	7	5	2.33	-	-	-/-
CE Cuffy	2	3	1	4	4*	2.00	-	-	-/-
DB Powell	1	1	0	0	0	0.00	-	-	-/-

Bowling	Overs	Mds	Runs	Wkts	Av	Best	5/inn	10m
S Chanderpaul	3	0	9	1	9.00	1-9	-	-
MN Samuels	16	3	21	1	21.00	1-21	-	-
M Dillon	109.2	30	275	11	25.00	3-44	-	-
CE Cuffy	70.4	13	224	6	37.33	2-52	-	-
DB Powell	41.2	8	115	3	38.33	2-62	-	-
MV Nagamootoo	47	12	132	3	44.00	3-132	-	-
CL Hooper	59.5	12	190	4	47.50	2-32	-	-
JJC Lawson	64	10	206	4	51.50	2-63	-	-
GR Breese	31.2	3	135	2	67.50	2-108	-	-
PT Collins	53	12	142	1	142.00	1-59	-	-

Also bowled: WW Hinds 4-0-11-0; RR Sarwan 10-1-49-0; RO Hinds 15-1-49-0; CH Gayle 27-6-79-0

ONE-DAY INTERNATIONALS
v. WEST INDIES
Match One
6 November 2002 at Jamshedpur
India 283 for 6 (50 overs) (AB Agarkar 95)
West Indies 285 for 6 (50 overs) (WW Hinds 93, RR Sarwan 83*, MN Samuels 51)
West Indies won by 4 wickets

Match Two
9 November 2002 at Nagpur
India 279 for 9 (47 overs) (VVS Laxman 99, SC Ganguly 78, R Dravid 51)
West Indies 280 for 3 (46.2 overs) (CH Gayle 103, MN Samuels 52)
West Indies won by 7 wickets

Match Three
12 November 2002 at Rajkot
West Indies 300 for 5 (50 overs) (RR Sarwan 84, S Chanderpaul 74, CH Gayle 72)
India 200 for 1 (27.1 overs) (V Sehwag 114*, SC Ganguly 72)
India won by 81 runs – DL Method: target 120 from 27.1 overs

Match Four
15 November 2002 at Ahmedabad
West Indies 324 for 4 (50 overs) (CH Gayle 140, RR Sarwan 99*)
India 325 for 5 (47.4 overs) (R Dravid 109*, VVS Laxman 66, SB Bangar 57*)
India won by 5 wickets

Match Five
18 November 2002 at Vadodara
India 290 for 8 (48 overs) (VVS Laxman 71, SC Ganguly 53, V Sehwag 52)
West Indies 291 for 5 (46.5 overs) (CH Gayle 101, WW Hinds 80)
West Indies won by 5 wickets

Match Six
21 November 2002 at Jodhpur
West Indies 201 (46.3 overs) (S Chanderpaul 58)
India 202 for 7 (46.2 overs) (R Dravid 58, Yuvraj Singh 54)
India won by 3 wickets

Match Seven
24 November 2002 at Vijayawada
West Indies 315 for 6 (50 overs) (MN Samuels 108*, RR Sarwan 83, WW Hinds 58)
India 180 (30.5 overs) (Yuvraj Singh 68, JJC Lawson 4 for 57)
West Indies won by 135 runs

NEW ZEALAND

By Bryan Waddle

New Zealand's third place in the official ICC Test match championship has never been a major focus for the national team, but privately they regard it with a measure of pride.

As motivation, it remains New Zealand's greatest challenge to beat near-neighbours Australia in a series and, in South Africa, they see a team by which they can measure the consistency of their own international performance.

In World Cup year there was little opportunity to improve their Test ranking, but with Test series against India and then away to Sri Lanka the Kiwi position was in jeopardy.

New Zealand normally have a more extensive fixture list than was the case with the two home Tests with India and a two-Test away series against Sri Lanka, so in essence it was a quiet year compared to the previous 12 months.

India's inability to perform consistently abroad is a tag they have found hard to erase, and they departed from their series in New Zealand with that reputation still very much intact. Despite boasting two batsmen, Sachin Tendulkar and Rahul Dravid, in the world's top ten, along with exciting, skilful players in Virender Sehwag, Saurav Ganguly and VVS Laxman, India's performance never lifted above mediocre on some questionable pitches.

Whether they were disinterested or preoccupied with World Cup contract negotiations, India rarely showed glimpses of the talent that makes them so formidable on the subcontinent.

Ganguly was quick to dismiss the two New Zealand pitches in Hamilton and Wellington as 'the worst in the world', but that was a lame excuse for batsmen who were unwilling, or unable, to adapt to the conditions. The Indian captain might also have conveniently forgotten pitches used in some recent clashes between the two sides in India.

New Zealand have long held the view, and justifiably, that the classy strokeplayers from the subcontinent can be negated on pitches with pace and bounce – but in striving to achieve that, produced two Test strips that were decidedly slippery.

The sight of green seamers has never gladdened the heart of batsmen, but New Zealand's inexperienced, seam-based attack probably considered Christmas had come early in this mid-December series.

Only Dravid displayed the appropriate technique on the first day in Wellington as his team-mates laboured through 58 overs in their first innings.

The pace of Shane Bond and the consistency of Daryl Tuffey combined to unsettle the Indians, while Jacob Oram made an impact early on as an all-rounder.

Mark Richardson is a player who cherishes his time at the crease. Unwanted in the New Zealand one-day side, the late-blooming left-hander says he

Another success for the spearhead of the New Zealand attack, Shane Bond.

The most underrated batsman in Test cricket? What is certain is that few match Mark Richardson for dependability and consistency.

has to make up for that by not wasting his Test match opportunities. He did that superbly in one important innings in the Wellington Test. Batting with stout concentration and application, something that has become a trademark of his play, he spent over six-and-a-half hours for 89, with his 70-run, fourth-wicket partnership with Nathan Astle giving New Zealand the advantage they needed.

The expected threat of Tendulkar, Dravid and company seldom surfaced. Dravid's 76 in Wellington and Tendulkar's 51 at the same venue were innings of exceptional class, but proved the only half-centuries the Indians could produce in the series. For New Zealand, Richardson was the only player to pass 50, underlining the fact that the series offered some woeful batting.

New Zealand's ten-wicket victory in Wellington, their 52nd win in 300 Tests, was over in just two-and-a-half days. This added to India's miserable record at the Basin Reserve – it was their fourth successive defeat on the ground.

If India were dismayed by the conditions in Wellington, they moved to Hamilton with even

greater trepidation. After a week of excessive rain in the city, which washed out the first day, they again lost a vital toss.

New Zealand's seam attack of Bond, Tuffey and Oram would not have looked out of place packing down in an All Black scrum.

Oram stands 6ft 5in tall, Tuffey is not called 'Tower' for nothing, being only marginally shorter than Oram, while former policeman Bond, at 6ft 2in, is the midget of the three. Their height gave all three a distinct advantage in helpful conditions.

The emergence of a new breed of fast bowlers was an encouraging sign for the 'Black Caps' in 2002–03, but in developing conditions for pace New Zealand were guilty of neglecting their most successful attacking weapon, the spin of Daniel Vettori.

Vettori was not needed in either Test against India, who only lasted for a total of 179 overs in their four innings.

With rain washing out the first day in Hamilton, the Test was pushed into a fourth day, but only occupied 176.5 overs, 20 less than the first Test.

It is always easy to use pitch preparation as an initial excuse for failure, but some serious self-examination by the game's elite players of their attitude and motivation would also be a useful exercise. Poor pitch preparation is not solely the domain of New Zealand, either. Indeed, it has been a long-held attitude generally within the world game that the home country has the right to prepare pitches to suit its playing resources.

Perhaps the game and the paying public deserve a better deal, however. In the push for higher payments and a share of the profits generated by international cricket, should the players ask themselves if they are often any more professional in their approach than the administrators?

After underachieving at the World Cup, New Zealand ended the year with their most commanding performance.

While a drawn series might not produce exciting cricket, most players will tell you that coming away from the arduous conditions of Sri Lanka having levelled a series with the home team feels as good as a win.

Stephen Fleming, widely regarded as one of the game's best captains, reinforced that belief not only with his astute leadership but also with some of the best batting of his career. His highest Test score, 274 not out, is also the only double hundred in his distinguished 75-Test career.

While the tall, elegant left-hander has played

some delightful innings, Fleming has earned one dubious honour – as a batsman he has struggled to convert half-centuries into hundreds. That is why his great innings in the torrid heat and humidity of the Sara Stadium in Colombo certainly erased a few personal demons.

Fleming's shortcomings in that aspect of his game also highlight a weakness New Zealand have failed to address – inconsistent top-order batting. Richardson has bedded in comfortably as an opener of class, but does not have a settled partner. Fleming, meanwhile, has had to adjust his place in the order to compensate the fluctuating form of the other batsmen. Without Nathan Astle in Sri Lanka, and with Craig McMillan struggling for form as his average slipped under 40, the top order had an unsettled look.

As John Bracewell approaches a new era as coach, after a distinguished playing career in New Zealand colours and a highly successful stint as coach of Gloucestershire in England, he will be conscious that much needs to be done in the bowling department.

There has been no obvious back-up for spinner Vettori, in particular. Paul Wiseman is the current support act, but he does not appeal as the long-term option.

New Zealand have achieved their No. 3 world ranking by virtue of a disciplined approach and a never-say-die attitude produced from a limited resource base. To push their achievements further will take both a higher level of achievement and a greater level of consistency. If that is not found, surpassing South Africa and Australia will remain an unattainable dream.

Stephen Fleming, the New Zealand captain: an innings for him to savour in the heat of Colombo.

FIRST TEST – NEW ZEALAND v. INDIA
12–16 December 2002 at Wellington

INDIA

	First Innings		Second Innings	
SB Bangar	c Styris b Tuffey	1	lbw b Oram	12
V Sehwag	b Tuffey	2	lbw b Bond	12
R Dravid	b Styris	76	b Bond	7
SR Tendulkar	lbw b Oram	8	b Bond	51
SC Ganguly (capt)	c Vincent b Bond	17	c Hart b Bond	2
VVS Laxman	c Hart b Bond	0	c Fleming b Oram	0
*PA Patel	c Vincent b Oram	8	c Fleming b Tuffey	10
AB Agarkar	c Astle b Styris	12	c McMillan b Tuffey	9
Harbhajan Singh	c McMillan b Styris	0	c Styris b Tuffey	1
Z Khan	c Oram b Bond	19	c Nehra b Oram	9
A Nehra	not out	10	not out	0
Extras	lb 1, w 1, nb 6	8	lb 1, nb 7	8
		161		**121**

	First Innings				Second Innings			
	O	M	R	W	O	M	R	W
Bond	18.4	4	66	3	13.1	5	33	4
Tuffey	16	7	25	2	9	3	35	3
Oram	15	4	31	2	12	3	36	3
Styris	6	0	28	3	4	0	16	0
Astle	3	1	10	0	–	–	–	–

Fall of Wickets
1-2, 2-9, 3-29, 4-51, 5-55, 6-92, 7-118, 8-118, 9-147
1-23, 2-31, 3-31, 4-33, 5-36, 6-67, 7-88, 8-96, 9-121

NEW ZEALAND

	First Innings		Second Innings	
MH Richardson	lbw b Khan	89	not out	14
L Vincent	c Patel b Bangar	12	not out	21
SP Fleming (capt)	b Khan	25		
CD McMillan	lbw b Bangar	9		
NJ Astle	c Singh b Khan	41		
SB Styris	st Patel b Singh	0		
JDP Oram	lbw b Singh	0		
*RG Hart	lbw b Khan	6		
DL Vettori	c Patel b Khan	21		
DR Tuffey	not out	9		
SE Bond	b Agarkar	2		
Extras	b 6, lb 12, w 2, nb 8, pen 5	33	w 1	1
		247	(0 wkt)	**36**

	First Innings				Second Innings			
	O	M	R	W	O	M	R	W
Khan	25	8	53	5	3	0	13	0
Nehra	19	4	50	0	4.3	0	21	0
Agarkar	13.1	1	54	1	–	–	–	–
Bangar	15	4	23	2	–	–	–	–
Singh	17	4	33	2	2	1	2	0
Ganguly	2	1	11	0	–	–	–	–

Fall of Wickets
1-30, 2-96, 3-111, 4-181, 5-182, 6-185, 7-201, 8-228, 9-237

Umpires: EAR de Silva & DJ Harper
Toss: New Zealand

New Zealand won by 10 wickets

SECOND TEST – NEW ZEALAND v. INDIA
19–23 December 2002 at Hamilton

INDIA

	First Innings		Second Innings	
SB Bangar	c Oram b Tuffey	1	c & b Tuffey	7
V Sehwag	c Richardson b Bond	1	(7) c Tuffey b Bond	25
R Dravid	c Hart b Tuffey	9	c sub b Oram	39
SR Tendulkar	c Styris b Tuffey	9	b Tuffey	32
SC Ganguly (capt)	c Fleming b Tuffey	5	c Hart b Oram	5
VVS Laxman	b Bond	23	b Astle	4
*PA Patel	c Hart b Oram	8	(2) b Tuffey	0
Harbhajan Singh	b Bond	20	c Hart b Tuffey	18
Z Khan	b Oram	0	c Astle b Oram	0
A Nehra	c Fleming b Bond	7	c Hart b Oram	10
T Yohannan	not out	0	not out	8
Extras	lb 12, nb 4	16	lb 1, w 2, nb 3	6
		99		**154**

	First Innings				Second Innings			
	O	M	R	W	O	M	R	W
Bond	14.2	7	39	4	10	0	58	1
Tuffey	9	6	12	4	16	3	41	4
Oram	10	1	22	2	12.5	2	41	4
Styris	2	0	10	0	–	–	–	–
Astle	3	2	4	0	5	1	13	1

Fall of Wickets
1-1, 2-11, 3-26, 4-34, 5-40, 6-70, 7-91, 8-92, 9-93
1-2, 2-8, 3-57, 4-64, 5-85, 6-110, 7-130, 8-131, 9-137

NEW ZEALAND

	First Innings		Second Innings	
MH Richardson	lbw b Khan	13	c Patel b Nehra	28
L Vincent	c Dravid b Khan	3	c Patel b Yohannan	9
SP Fleming (capt)	c & b Khan	21	c Khan b Nehra	32
CD McMillan	c Dravid b Nehra	4	lbw b Nehra	18
NJ Astle	c Singh b Nehra	0	c Patel b Khan	14
SB Styris	lbw b Singh	13	c Patel b Singh	17
JDP Oram	c Tendulkar b Singh	3	not out	26
*RG Hart	lbw b Khan	3	not out	11
DL Vettori	c Laxman b Khan	6		
DR Tuffey	run out	13		
SE Bond	not out	0		
Extras	b 1, lb 4, nb 10	15	lb 4, nb 1	5
		94	(6 wkts)	**160**

	First Innings				Second Innings			
	O	M	R	W	O	M	R	W
Khan	13.2	4	29	5	13	0	56	1
Yohannan	9	4	16	0	16	5	27	1
Nehra	8	3	20	2	16.2	4	34	3
Bangar	2	1	4	0	–	–	–	–
Singh	6	0	20	2	11	0	39	1

Fall of Wickets
1-7, 2-34, 3-47, 4-48, 5-60, 6-64, 7-69, 8-79, 9-93
1-30, 2-52, 3-89, 4-90, 5-105, 6-136

Umpires: EAR de Silva & DJ Harper
Toss: New Zealand

New Zealand won by 4 wickets

SERIES AVERAGES
New Zealand v. India

NEW ZEALAND

Batting	M	Inns	NO	Runs	HS	Av	100	50	c/st
MH Richardson	2	4	1	144	89	48.00	-	1	1/-
SP Fleming	2	3	0	78	32	26.00	-	-	4/-
DR Tuffey	2	2	1	22	13	22.00	-	-	2/-
NJ Astle	2	3	0	55	41	18.33	-	-	2/-
L Vincent	2	4	1	45	21*	15.00	-	-	2/-
JDP Oram	2	3	1	29	26*	14.50	-	-	2/-
DL Vettori	2	2	0	27	21	13.50	-	-	-/-
CD McMillan	2	3	0	31	18	10.33	-	-	2/-
RG Hart	2	3	1	20	11*	10.00	-	-	7/-
SB Styris	2	3	0	30	17	10.00	-	-	4/-
SE Bond	2	2	1	2	2	2.00	-	-	-/-

Bowling	Overs	Mds	Runs	Wkts	Av	Best	5/inn	10m
DR Tuffey	50	19	113	13	8.69	4-12	-	-
JDP Oram	48.5	10	122	11	11.09	4-41	-	-
SE Bond	56.1	16	196	12	16.33	4-33	-	-
SB Styris	13	0	62	3	20.66	3-28	-	-
NJ Astle	11	4	27	1	27.00	1-13	-	-

INDIA

Batting	M	Inns	NO	Runs	HS	Av	100	50	c/st
R Dravid	2	4	0	131	76	32.75	-	1	2/-
SR Tendulkar	2	4	0	100	51	25.00	-	1	1/-
A Nehra	2	4	2	27	10*	13.50	-	-	-/-
AB Agarkar	1	2	0	21	12	10.50	-	-	-/-
V Sehwag	2	4	0	40	25	10.00	-	-	-/-
Harbhajan Singh	2	4	0	39	20	9.75	-	-	2/-
SC Ganguly	2	4	0	29	17	7.25	-	-	-/-
Z Khan	2	4	0	28	19	7.00	-	-	2/-
VVS Laxman	2	4	0	27	23	6.75	-	-	1/-
PA Patel	2	4	0	26	10	6.50	-	-	6/1
SB Bangar	2	4	0	21	12	5.25	-	-	-/-
T Yohannan	1	2	2	8	8*	-	-	-	-/-

Bowling	Overs	Mds	Runs	Wkts	Av	Best	5/inn	10m
SB Bangar	17	5	27	2	13.50	2-23	-	-
Z Khan	54.2	12	151	11	13.72	5-29	2	-
Harbhajan Singh	36	5	94	5	18.80	2-20	-	-
A Nehra	47.5	11	125	5	25.00	3-34	-	-
T Yohannan	25	9	43	1	43.00	1-27	-	-
AB Agarkar	13.1	1	54	1	54.00	1-54	-	-

Also bowled: SC Ganguly 2-0-11-0

ONE–DAY INTERNATIONALS v. INDIA

Match One
26 December 2002 at Auckland
India 108 (32.5 overs) (JDP Oram 5 for 26)
New Zealand 109 for 7 (37.4 overs) (J Srinath 4 for 23)
New Zealand won by 3 wickets

Match Two
28 December 2002 at Napier
New Zealand 254 for 9 (50 overs) (MS Sinclair 78, NJ Astle 76)
India 219 (43.4 overs) (V Sehwag 108)
New Zealand won by 35 runs

Match Three
1 January 2003 at Christchurch
India 108 (41.1 overs)
New Zealand 109 for 5 (26.5 overs)
New Zealand won by 5 wickets

Match Four
4 January 2003 at Queenstown
India 122 (43.4 overs) (AR Adams 5 for 22)
New Zealand 123 for 3 (25.4 overs)
New Zealand won by 7 wickets

Match Five
8 January 2003 at Wellington
New Zealand 168 (42.4 overs)
India 169 for 8 (43.2 overs) (Yuvraj Singh 54)
India won by 2 wickets

Match Six
11 January 2003 at Auckland
New Zealand 199 for 9 (50 overs) (L Vincent 53*)
India 200 for 9 (48.5 overs) (V Sehwag 112)
India won by 1 wicket

Match Seven
14 January 2003 at Hamilton
India 122 (44.5 overs) (AR Adams 4 for 21)
New Zealand 125 for 4 (28.4 overs) (SP Fleming 60*)
New Zealand won by 6 wickets

PAKISTAN

By Qamar Ahmed

In the aftermath of the 11 September incident in America and the bomb blast in the front of the New Zealand touring team's hotel at Karachi last year, the game has not been the same for either Pakistan or its team's cricket.

Cancellation of the Australian team's visit to the country last October, due to security fears, and playing a 'home' series against them in Sri Lanka and Sharjah certainly marred what would have been a wonderful way to have marked the golden jubilee of Pakistan's entry into Test cricket.

Understandably, therefore, the supporters of the game in a country denied a home series for reasons other than cricket were in no mood to compromise when the performances of their country's team plummeted.

Losses in the series against Australia and South Africa, and then their failure to make it to the Super Six stages of the World Cup, were enough for the disappointed fans to burn the effigies of star players like Wasim Akram and Waqar Younis in the streets of Lahore and Karachi.

Inconsistency in both selection procedures and in the choice of captain, the frequent chopping and changing of players and infighting within the team, have all contributed to Pakistan's poor showing on the international circuit during the past year. It has been a season which none of the team members will remember fondly.

Having recorded a 2–1 victory in the one-day series against Australia in their own backyard in August last year, Pakistan seemed well on their way to achieving loftier things, but, only a few days later, they were unable to deliver what they promised as they failed to reach the final of the Morocco Cup in Tangiers. Both South Africa and Sri Lanka got the better of them to reach the final, while in a triangular tournament in Kenya they shared the trophy with Australia only after a rain-marred final. In the ICC knock-out competition in

Sri Lanka, meanwhile, they only recorded one victory – against Holland.

Worse was to come for Pakistan when they were whitewashed by the Australians in the three-match 'home' Test series that was shifted to Sri Lanka and Sharjah.

In the opening Test, having bowled out Australia for only 127 in their second innings, Pakistan failed to capitalize. Chasing 316 to win, they lost the match by 41 runs. Thus, Shoaib Akhtar's 5 for 21 and Saqlain Mushtaq's 4 for 46 were in vain.

But it was in the second Test in Sharjah that Pakistan's cricket hit a real low. They were dismissed for 59 and 53, their smallest totals in Tests, in reply to Australia's first-innings 310 and lost the match

Star of Sharjah ... Steve Waugh scored one of four Australian hundreds as Pakistan were beaten 3–0 in a 'home' series played on foreign fields.

within two days. The final Test followed a similar script as Australia won by an innings and 20 runs.

For the team, and for their fans at home, it was humiliating to see Ricky Ponting and Steve Waugh hammer the Pakistan attack to pulp as they notched up Test centuries, while the Aussie bowlers Glenn McGrath, Shane Warne and Andy Bichel made a mockery of Pakistan's dilapidated line-up. The only mitigating circumstances for Pakistan were that they were playing without Inzamam-ul-Haq, Yousuf Youhana and Wasim Akram.

'Sons of the soil betraying the nation's faith in them,' cried the *Dawn* newspaper's correspondent. 'Spineless batting,' said *The Nation*.

Waqar, retained as captain for the tour to Zimbabwe and South Africa, and for the World Cup, had by now begun to feel the pressure of being constantly let down by those who had opposed his appointment. Allegedly, senior members of the team were amongst them.

Defeat in the five match one-day series by a margin of 4–1, and then embarrassing losses in both Tests, the first at Durban by ten wickets and the second in Cape Town by an innings and 142 runs, were plainly the performances of a troubled team.

Wasim Akram, who had agreed to play in the two Tests, then changed his mind and went home and Shoaib Akhtar allegedly feigned injury to abandon the team to prepare for the World Cup. Amid the disarray, Waqar reached the landmark of 400 victims in one-day cricket during the tour, becoming only the second bowler – after Wasim – to have done so.

Herschelle Gibbs hit 228 and Graeme Smith 151 to establish a new record stand for any wicket for South Africa as they put on 368 runs for the first wicket in the second Test at Cape Town, beating the previous best of 341 between Eddie Barlow and Graeme Pollock against Australia in 1963–64. For Pakistan, Taufeeq Umar's 135 and 50 in the second innings of the match was the best for Pakistan.

Later, during the World Cup, Pakistan failed to lift its sinking morale and retain the status of a top-notch cricket-playing nation when they had to bow out of the tournament without reaching the Super Six stages of the competition. Their only consolation came with victories against the minnows Namibia and Holland, and the sight of Wasim becoming the first bowler in history to take 500 one-day international wickets.

Their manager Shaharyar Khan's remark, on arrival for the World Cup, that 'we are the first to arrive in South Africa and will be the last to leave', sounded like a big joke as Pakistan flew home a lot earlier than he had visualized.

Even given the volatility of Pakistan cricket, it was hardly a surprise when the new selection panel, chaired by Aamir Sohail, immediately dropped eight of the senior members of the World Cup squad. Omitted from the squad for the Sharjah Cup were captain Waqar Younis, Wasim Akram, Shoaib Akhtar, Saeed Anwar, Inzamam-ul-Haq, Saqlain Mushtaq, Azhar Mahmood and Shahid Afridi. They were replaced by newcomers like Mohammad Hafeez, Umar Gul and Faisal Iqbal, while coach Richard Pybus – a man with no experience of playing first-class cricket – went too and was replaced, once again, by Javed Miandad. To cap it all, Rashid Latif, who had previously announced his retirement from Test cricket, was brought back and appointed captain.

However, criticism of the drastic changes in the

Shoaib Akhtar's 5 for 21 in the first Test in Colombo saw the Aussies plunge from 61 without loss to 127 all out ... but Pakistan still lost.

team was so fierce that the selectors were forced to water down their talk of rebuilding for the future and bring back at least some of those senior players.

A disenchanted Wasim Akram, though, when ignored for Pakistan's visit to England for the NatWest Challenge series, announced his retirement from international cricket having played in 104 Tests and 356 one-day games. Also announcing his retirement, a few months later, was opening batsman Saeed Anwar, a veteran of 55 Tests and 247 one-day internationals.

Shoaib Akhtar, reprimanded for ball tampering during the series in Zimbabwe by referee Clive Lloyd, was then banned for two one-day games for allegedly scuffing up the ball illegally during the one-day series in Sri Lanka. Up to his usual tricks of leaving and joining the team during the course of the year, Shoaib failed to catch the imagination of many in the country for his wayward performances with the ball. His jibe at Wasim and Waqar, saying 'they are in decline, they were great but they are not match-winning bowlers any more. So I have to make it all happen on my own', was met with a furious reaction from Waqar. He said: 'Shoaib performs to his ability once a year and then he has the nerve to compare himself to Glenn McGrath.'

Pakistan's 2–0 win in the two-match Test series in Zimbabwe, a clean sweep in the five-match one-day series against them before the World Cup, and a 3–0 whitewash in a three-match Test series against Bangladesh at home, did, however, promise the suggestion of a little light at the end of the tunnel.

Yasir Hameed's century in each innings of his debut Test at Karachi against Bangladesh, Javed Omar and Habibul Bashar's hundreds in the series and Alok Kapali's hat-trick in the second Test at Peshawar, the first by a Bangladesh bowler, were the features of the home series.

Inzamam-ul-Haq, by now back in the fold, proved the selectors' decision to drop him was wrong as his masterly unbeaten 138 in the final Test at Multan denied Bangladesh what had looked to be their long-awaited first Test match victory.

On the domestic front, Pakistan International Airlines (PIA), under former Pakistan captain Moin Khan, were the winners of the Quaid-e-Azam Trophy first-class tournament and also the Patron's Cup one-day tournament. Yasir Hameed of PIA, with 207 in the Quaid-e-Azam Trophy final and 102 in the one-day final, was one of the top batsmen during the season.

FIRST TEST – PAKISTAN v. AUSTRALIA
3–8 October 2002 at Colombo

AUSTRALIA

	First Innings		Second Innings	
JL Langer	c Latif b Razzaq	72	c Umar b Saqlain Mushtaq	25
ML Hayden	c Nazir b Waqar Younis	4	c Umar b Saqlain Mushtaq	34
RT Ponting	c Khan b Waqar Younis	141	b Shoaib Akhtar	7
ME Waugh	c & b Saqlain Mushtaq	55	b Shoaib Akhtar	0
SR Waugh (capt)	c Khan b Saqlain Mushtaq	31	lbw b Shoaib Akhtar	0
DR Martyn	c Khan b Saqlain Mushtaq	67	c Nazir b Saqlain Mushtaq	20
*AC Gilchrist	not out	66	b Shoaib Akhtar	5
SK Warne	c Iqbal b Shoaib Akhtar	0	lbw b Shoaib Akhtar	0
B Lee	b Shoaib Akhtar	2	c Misbah-ul-Haq b Saqlain Mushtaq	12
JN Gillespie	lbw b Shoaib Akhtar	0	lbw b Sami	1
GD McGrath	b Saqlain Mushtaq	4	not out	5
Extras	b 4, lb 16, nb 5	25	b 4, lb 12, nb 2	18
		467		127

	First Innings				Second Innings			
	O	M	R	W	O	M	R	W
Waqar Younis	16	2	86	2	8	1	23	0
Shoaib Akhtar	21	5	51	3	8	2	21	5
Sami	20	3	93	0	6	0	13	1
Razzaq	17	0	78	1	-	-	-	-
Saqlain Mushtaq	40.5	6	136	4	15.5	0	46	4
Umar	2	1	3	0	2	0	8	0

Fall of Wickets
1-5, 2-188, 3-272, 4-302, 5-329, 6-457, 7-458, 8-462, 9-462
1-61, 2-74, 3-74, 4-74, 5-74, 6-85, 7-89, 8-107, 9-112

PAKISTAN

	First Innings		Second Innings	
Imran Nazir	lbw b McGrath	0	c McGrath b Warne	40
Taufeeq Umar	c Ponting b Gillespie	0	c ME Waugh b Lee	88
Abdul Razzaq	c Gilchrist b Warne	11	lbw b Warne	4
Younis Khan	c Langer b Lee	58	lbw b Warne	51
Misbah-ul-Haq	c ME Waugh b Warne	17	c SR Waugh b Warne	10
Faisal Iqbal	c ME Waugh b Warne	83	c Ponting b McGrath	39
*Rashid Latif	c Martyn b Warne	66	c Gilchrist b Gillespie	11
Saqlain Mushtaq	lbw b Warne	1	c SR Waugh b McGrath	1
Waqar Younis (capt)	lbw b Warne	14	c Gilchrist b Gillespie	1
Shoaib Akhtar	c McGrath b Warne	5	lbw b McGrath	6
Mohammad Sami	not out	0	not out	6
Extras	b 15, lb 6, nb 3	24	b 3, lb 6, nb 8	17
		279		274

	First Innings				Second Innings			
	O	M	R	W	O	M	R	W
McGrath	15	3	40	1	24.2	12	38	3
Gillespie	12	2	55	1	23.3	6	62	2
Lee	11	3	49	1	14	1	63	1
Warne	24.3	7	94	7	30.3	3	94	4
ME Waugh	3	0	20	0	2	1	8	0

Fall of Wickets
1-2, 2-4, 3-45, 4-75, 5-116, 6-219, 7-239, 8-267, 9-274
1-91, 2-117, 3-173, 4-187, 5-230, 6-248, 7-251, 8-252, 9-259

Umpires: SA Bucknor & S Venkataraghavan
Toss: Australia

Australia won by 41 runs

SECOND TEST – PAKISTAN v. AUSTRALIA
11–13 October 2002 at Sharjah

PAKISTAN

	First Innings		Second Innings	
Imran Nazir	c Warne b McGrath	0	c Gilchrist b Warne	16
Taufeeq Umar	b Lee	0	run out	0
Abdul Razzaq	c Martyn b Warne	21	retired hurt	4
Younis Khan	c Bichel b McGrath	5	lbw b McGrath	0
Misbah-ul-Haq	c ME Waugh b Bichel	2	c SR Waugh b Bichel	12
Faisal Iqbal	lbw b Warne	4	c ME Waugh b Warne	7
*Rashid Latif	not out	4	c ME Waugh b Bichel	0
Saqlain Mushtaq	lbw b Warne	0	c Warne b Lee	9
Shoaib Akhtar	c Gilchrist b Bichel	1	c SR Waugh b Warne	2
Waqar Younis (capt)	lbw b Warne	0	lbw b Warne	0
Danish Kaneria	b Lee	8	not out	1
Extras	b 8, lb 2, nb 4	14	nb 2	2
		59	(9 wkts)	**53**

	First Innings				Second Innings			
	O	M	R	W	O	M	R	W
McGrath	7	4	10	2	6	2	5	1
Lee	7.5	1	15	2	5	2	16	1
Bichel	6	2	13	2	7	1	19	2
Warne	11	4	11	4	6.5	2	13	4

Fall of Wickets
1-0, 2-1, 3-8, 4-23, 5-41, 6-46, 7-46, 8-49, 9-50
1-0, 2-13, 3-32, 4-34, 5-36, 6-50, 7-52, 8-52, 9-53

AUSTRALIA

	First Innings	
JL Langer	run out	37
ML Hayden	c Nazir b Saqlain Mushtaq	119
RT Ponting	lbw b Kaneria	44
ME Waugh	lbw b Saqlain Mushtaq	2
SR Waugh (capt)	c Sub b Saqlain Mushtaq	0
DR Martyn	c Umar b Razzaq	34
*AC Gilchrist	c Umar b Shoaib Akhtar	17
SK Warne	c Khan b Saqlain Mushtaq	19
B Lee	lbw b Razzaq	12
AJ Bichel	not out	2
GD McGrath	lbw b Razzaq	0
Extras	b 15, lb 7, nb 2	24
		310

	First Innings			
	O	M	R	W
Waqar Younis	8	2	25	0
Shoaib Akhtar	14	3	42	1
Kaneria	26	2	116	1
Razzaq	10.1	3	22	3
Saqlain Mushtaq	34	2	83	4

Fall of Wickets
1-55, 2-145, 3-148, 4-148, 5-224, 6-252, 7-285, 8-304, 9-310

Umpires: SA Bucknor & S Venkataraghavan
Toss: Pakistan

Australia won by an innings and 198 runs

THIRD TEST – PAKISTAN v. AUSTRALIA
19–23 October 2002 at Sharjah

AUSTRALIA

	First Innings	
JL Langer	b Waqar Younis	4
ML Hayden	c Iqbal b Saqlain Mushtaq	89
RT Ponting	b Waqar Younis	150
ME Waugh	c Latif b Saqlain Mushtaq	23
SR Waugh (capt)	not out	103
DR Martyn	lbw b Waqar Younis	0
*AC Gilchrist	c Latif b Kaneria	34
SK Warne	lbw b Kaneria	11
B Lee	run out	1
AJ Bichel	c Umar b Kaneria	9
GD McGrath	c Latif b Waqar Younis	3
Extras	b 4, lb 10, nb 3	17
		444

	First Innings			
	O	M	R	W
Waqar Younis	17.3	5	55	4
Sami	28	6	81	0
Saqlain Mushtaq	45	5	159	2
Kaneria	36	8	128	3
Umar	2	0	7	0

Fall of Wickets
1-4, 2-188, 3-233, 4-308, 5-308, 6-363, 7-403, 8-404, 9-418

PAKISTAN

	First Innings		Second Innings	
Taufeeq Umar	lbw b McGrath	5	c Gilchrist b McGrath	1
Imran Farhat	lbw b Warne	29	c Gilchrist b Bichel	18
Younis Khan	c Gilchrist b McGrath	5	lbw b McGrath	4
Faisal Iqbal	c Gilchrist b Warne	9	run out	2
Misbah-ul-Haq	lbw b Bichel	11	lbw b Warne	17
Hasan Raza	not out	54	c Gilchrist b Bichel	68
*Rashid Latif	c ME Waugh b Warne	17	lbw b Warne	17
Saqlain Mushtaq	b McGrath	44	lbw b Warne	10
Waqar Younis (capt)	lbw b McGrath	6	c ME Waugh b McGrath	24
Mohammad Sami	lbw b Warne	0	c Martyn b Bichel	22
Danish Kaneria	st Gilchrist b Warne	15	not out	2
Extras	b 3, lb 10, w 2, nb 11	26	lb 9, nb 9	18
		221		**203**

	First Innings				Second Innings			
	O	M	R	W	O	M	R	W
McGrath	16	4	41	4	7	2	18	3
Lee	11	1	47	0	18	5	44	0
Warne	30.1	10	74	5	21	3	56	3
Bichel	9	0	31	1	11.2	1	43	3
ME Waugh	4	0	10	0	10	3	33	0
Ponting	1	0	5	0	–	–	–	–

Fall of Wickets
1-22, 2-50, 3-50, 4-70, 5-76, 6-100, 7-191, 8-198, 9-199
1-6, 2-12, 3-18, 4-30, 5-58, 6-86, 7-102, 8-153, 9-197

Umpires: SA Bucknor & S Venkataraghavan
Toss: Australia

Australia won by an innings and 20 runs

SERIES AVERAGES
Pakistan v. Australia

PAKISTAN

Batting	M	Inns	NO	Runs	HS	Av	100	50	c/st
Hasan Raza	1	2	1	122	68	122.00	-	2	-/-
Faisal Iqbal	3	6	0	144	83	24.00	-	1	2/-
Imran Farhat	1	2	0	47	29	23.50	-	-	-/-
Rashid Latif	3	6	1	115	66	23.00	-	1	4/-
Younis Khan	3	6	0	123	58	20.50	-	2	4/-
Taufeeq Umar	3	6	0	94	88	15.66	-	1	5/-
Imran Nazir	2	4	0	56	40	14.00	-	-	3/-
Mohammad Sami	2	4	2	28	22	14.00	-	-	-/-
Abdul Razzaq	2	4	1	40	21	13.33	-	-	-/-
Danish Kaneria	2	4	2	26	15	13.00	-	-	-/-
Misbah-ul-Haq	3	6	0	69	17	11.50	-	-	1/-
Saqlain Mushtaq	3	6	0	65	44	10.83	-	-	1/-
Waqar Younis	3	6	0	45	24	7.50	-	-	-/-
Shoaib Akhtar	2	4	0	14	6	3.50	-	-	-/-

Bowling	Overs	Mds	Runs	Wkts	Av	Best	5/inn	10m
Shoaib Akhtar	43	10	114	9	12.66	5-21	1	-
Abdul Razzaq	27.1	3	100	4	25.00	3-22	-	-
Saqlain Mushtaq	135.4	13	424	14	30.28	4-46	-	-
Waqar Younis	49.3	10	189	6	31.50	4-55	-	-
Danish Kaneria	62	10	244	4	61.00	3-128	-	-
Mohammad Sami	54	9	187	1	187.00	1-13	-	-

Also bowled: Taufeeq Umar-6-1-18-0

AUSTRALIA

Batting	M	Inns	NO	Runs	HS	Av	100	50	c/st
RT Ponting	3	4	0	342	150	85.50	2	-	2/-
ML Hayden	3	4	0	246	119	61.50	1	1	-/-
SR Waugh	3	4	1	134	103*	44.66	1	-	4/-
AC Gilchrist	3	4	1	122	66*	40.66	-	1	10/1
JL Langer	3	4	0	138	72	34.50	-	1	1/-
DR Martyn	3	4	0	121	67	30.25	-	1	3/-
ME Waugh	3	4	0	80	55	20.00	-	1	8/-
AJ Bichel	2	2	1	11	9	11.00	-	-	1/-
SK Warne	3	4	0	30	19	7.50	-	-	2/-
B Lee	3	4	0	27	12	6.75	-	-	-/-
GD McGrath	3	4	1	12	5*	4.00	-	-	2/-
JN Gillespie	1	2	0	1	1	0.50	-	-	-/-

Bowling	Overs	Mds	Runs	Wkts	Av	Best	5/inn	10m
GD McGrath	75.2	27	152	14	10.85	4-41	-	-
SK Warne	124	29	342	27	12.66	7-94	2	1
AJ Bichel	33.2	4	106	8	13.25	3-43	-	-
JN Gillespie	35.3	10	117	3	39.00	2-62	-	-
B Lee	66.5	13	234	5	46.80	2-15	-	-

Also bowled: RT Ponting 1-0-5-0; ME Waugh 19-4-71-0

FIRST TEST – PAKISTAN v. BANGLADESH
20–24 August 2003 at Karachi

BANGLADESH

	First Innings		Second Innings	
Hannan Sarkar	c Latif b Shabbir	41	lbw b Hafeez	30
Javed Omar	b Gul	1	lbw b Shoaib Akhtar	13
Habibul Bashar	c Hafeez b Shoaib Akhtar	71	c Shabbir b Kaneria	108
Sanwar Hossain	lbw b Shoaib Akhtar	15	lbw b Shabbir	3
Rajin Saleh	c Gul b Kaneria	26	c Latif b Shabbir	60
Alok Kapali	c Shabbir b Kaneria	46	b Kaneria	1
*Khaled Mashud	lbw b Gul	19	st Latif b Kaneria	22
Khaled Mahmud (capt)	c Hameed b Kaneria	14	lbw b Shabbir	0
Tapash Baisya	c Umar b Shabbir	10	c Latif b Shabbir	5
Mohammad Rafique	c Latif b Shabbir	14	lbw b Shabbir	6
Mashrafe Mortaza	not out	9	not out	10
Extras	b 3, lb 5, nb 14	22	lb 11, w 1, nb 4	16
		288		**274**

	First Innings			Second Innings		
	O	M	R	W	O	M	R	W
Shoaib Akhtar	18	4	56	2	25	8	59	1
Gul	20	5	91	2	19	3	57	0
Shabbir	20.3	3	61	3	18.1	2	48	5
Kaneria	21	6	58	3	38	12	85	3
Hafeez	7	2	14	0	14	8	14	1

Fall of Wickets
1-9, 2-123, 3-123, 4-146, 5-176, 6-231, 7-251, 8-252, 9-273
1-19, 2-73, 3-83, 4-194, 5-195, 6-251, 7-251, 8-254, 9-262

PAKISTAN

	First Innings		Second Innings	
Mohammad Hafeez	c Omar b Mortaza	2	b Rafique	50
Taufeeq Umar	c Omar b Rafique	38	c Saleh b Baisya	4
Yasir Hameed	c Rafique b Mortaza	170	b Rafique	105
Inzamam-ul-Haq	c Saleh b Baisya	0	not out	35
Yousuf Youhana	c & b Saleh	46	not out	15
Misbah-ul-Haq	lbw b Mortaza	13		
*Rashid Latif (capt)	not out	54		
Shoaib Akhtar	b Rafique	1		
Shabbir Ahmed	c Saleh b Rafique	6		
Danish Kaneria	c & b Mahmud	8		
Umar Gul	run out	0		
Extras	lb 4, nb 4	8	lb 7, w 1	8
		346	(3 wkts)	**217**

	First Innings			Second Innings		
	O	M	R	W	O	M	R	W
Mortaza	19	3	68	3	18	4	62	0
Baisya	17	6	42	1	11	1	34	1
Mahmud	17	2	74	1	6	3	8	0
Rafique	32	9	76	3	26	5	61	2
Hossain	9	0	23	0	5	1	23	0
Kapali	18	3	50	0	2	0	10	0
Saleh	5	0	9	1	2	0	12	0

Fall of Wickets
1-5, 2-102, 3-103, 4-234, 5-270, 6-304, 7-307, 8-323, 9-338
1-10, 2-144, 3-170

Umpires: SA Bucknor & TH Wijewardene
Toss: Pakistan

Pakistan won by 7 wickets

SECOND TEST – PAKISTAN v. BANGLADESH
27–31 August 2003 at Peshawar

BANGLADESH

	First Innings		Second Innings	
Hannan Sarkar	c Latif b Gul	6	c Umar b Shoaib Akhtar	7
Javed Omar	b Shoaib Akhtar	119	c Latif b Shoaib Akhtar	0
Habibul Bashar	lbw b Shabbir	97	lbw b Gul	28
Mohammad Ashraful	c Latif b Shoaib Akhtar	77	c Umar b Kaneria	7
Rajin Saleh	c Latif b Kaneria	3	lbw b Shoaib Akhtar	6
Alok Kapali	c Latif b Shoaib Akhtar	4	c Latif b Shabbir	16
Khaled Mashud (capt)	lbw b Shoaib Akhtar	0	lbw b Shoaib Akhtar	0
*Khaled Mahmud	c Shabbir b Shoaib Akhtar	25	lbw b Kaneria	1
Mohammad Rafique	b Shoaib Akhtar	0	not out	9
Mashrafe Mortaza	b Gul	10	b Gul	14
Alamgir Kabir	not out	1	b Gul	4
Extras	b 4, lb 5, w 1, nb 9	19	lb 2, nb 2	4
		361		96

	First Innings				Second Innings			
	O	M	R	W	O	M	R	W
Shoaib Akhtar	22.5	4	49	6	12	2	30	4
Gul	27	3	67	2	4.5	1	16	3
Shabbir	25	7	73	1	7	2	21	1
Kaneria	41	11	110	1	10	3	27	2
Malik	12	4	27	0	-	-	-	-
Hafeez	10	4	26	0	-	-	-	-

Fall of Wickets
1-13, 2-180, 3-310, 4-315, 5-315, 6-315, 7-320, 8-320, 9-341
1-7, 2-20, 3-43, 4-43, 5-64, 6-64, 7-65, 8-75, 9-90

PAKISTAN

	First Innings		Second Innings	
Mohammad Hafeez	c Mashud b Mahmud	21	not out	102
Taufeeq Umar	c Mashud b Rafique	75	c Mortaza b Mahmud	43
Yasir Hameed	b Rafique	23	not out	18
Inzamam-ul-Haq	b Rafique	43		
Yousuf Youhana	not out	64		
*Rashid Latif (capt)	st Mashud b Rafique	40		
Shoaib Malik	lbw b Rafique	0		
Shoaib Akhtar	b Mahmud	15		
Shabbir Ahmed	c Mortaza b Kapali	8		
Danish Kaneria	lbw b Kapali	0		
Umar Gul	lbw b Kapali	0		
Extras	lb 1, nb 5	6	lb 1, w 1	2
		295	(1 wkt)	165

	First Innings				Second Innings			
	O	M	R	W	O	M	R	W
Mortaza	18	6	48	0	7	1	26	0
Kabir	13	3	61	0	7.3	1	39	0
Mahmud	21	6	42	2	14	5	28	1
Rafique	45	13	118	5	12	2	34	0
Saleh	7	2	13	0	-	-	-	-
Ashraful	2	0	9	0	1	0	7	0
Kapali	2.1	1	3	3	6	0	30	0

Fall of Wickets
1-51, 2-84, 3-159, 4-178, 5-242, 6-250, 7-265, 8-289, 9-289
1-140

Umpires: SA Bucknor & RB Tiffin
Toss: Bangladesh

Pakistan won by 9 wickets

THIRD TEST – PAKISTAN v. BANGLADESH
3–7 September 2003 at Multan

BANGLADESH

	First Innings		Second Innings	
Hannan Sarkar	c Latif b Gul	13	c Latif b Gul	3
Javed Omar	c Khan b Gul	38	c Inzamam-ul-Haq b Shabbir	16
Habibul Bashar	c Latif b Ali	72	c Latif b Gul	3
Mohammad Ashraful	lbw b Saqlain Mushtaq	12	c Butt b Shabbir	3
Rajin Saleh	run out	49	c Latif b Gul	42
Alok Kapali	b Gul	11	c Latif b Ali	22
*Khaled Mashud	c Latif b Gul	29	(8) lbw b Shabbir	28
Khaled Mahmud (capt)	lbw b Shabbir	19	(7) lbw b Shabbir	2
Mohammad Rafique	b Shabbir	11	lbw b Gul	4
Tapash Baisya	lbw b Shabbir	0	not out	14
Manjural Islam	not out	0	c Khan b Saqlain Mushtaq	5
Extras	b 4, lb 10, nb 13	27	b 5, lb 2, w 2, nb 3	12
		281		154

	First Innings				Second Innings			
	O	M	R	W	O	M	R	W
Shabbir	25.2	3	70	3	23	6	68	4
Gul	32	7	86	4	15	2	58	4
Ali	14	4	43	1	6	1	12	1
Saqlain Mushtaq	25	5	61	1	2.3	0	9	1
Hafeez	3	1	7	0	-	-	-	-

Fall of Wickets
1-28, 2-102, 3-136, 4-166, 5-179, 6-241, 7-248, 8-278, 9-278
1-4, 2-9, 3-23, 4-41, 5-77, 6-91, 7-111, 8-127, 9-137

PAKISTAN

	First Innings		Second Innings	
Mohammad Hafeez	lbw b Mahmud	21	(2) c sub b Islam	18
Salman Butt	c Mashud b Mahmud	12	(1) c sub b Islam	37
Yasir Hameed	b Rafique	39	c sub b Mahmud	18
Inzamam-ul-Haq	c Sarkar b Mahmud	10	not out	138
Younis Khan	c Mashud b Mahmud	34	run out	0
Farhan Adil	lbw b Rafique	25	c Bashar b Rafique	8
*Rashid Latif (capt)	c Kapali b Baisya	5	lbw b Mahmud	5
Saqlain Mushtaq	b Rafique	9	c Mashud b Mahmud	11
Shabbir Ahmed	lbw b Rafique	4	lbw b Rafique	13
Umar Gul	b Rafique	5	run out	5
Yasir Ali	not out	0	not out	1
Extras	b 1, lb 5, nb 5	11	lb 4, w 4	8
		175	(9 wkts)	262

	First Innings				Second Innings			
	O	M	R	W	O	M	R	W
Islam	13	3	42	0	21	2	64	2
Baisya	11	2	54	1	12	0	46	0
Mahmud	13	1	37	4	28	9	68	3
Rafique	17.4	7	36	5	30	6	80	2

Fall of Wickets
1-27, 2-36, 3-50, 4-121, 5-135, 6-152, 7-154, 8-166, 9-170
1-37, 2-62, 3-78, 4-81, 5-99, 6-132, 7-164, 8-205, 9-257

Umpires: EAR de Silva & RB Tiffin
Toss: Bangladesh

Pakistan won by 1 wicket

SERIES AVERAGES
Pakistan v. Bangladesh

PAKISTAN

Batting	M	Inns	NO	Runs	HS	Av	100	50	c/st
Yousuf Youhana	2	3	2	125	64*	125.00	-	1	-/-
Inzamam-ul-Haq	3	5	2	226	138*	75.33	1	-	1/-
Yasir Hameed	3	6	1	373	170	74.60	2	-	1/-
Mohammad Hafeez	3	6	1	214	102*	42.80	1	1	1/-
Taufeeq Umar	2	4	0	160	75	40.00	-	1	3/-
Rashid Latif	3	4	1	104	54*	34.66	-	1	17/1
Salman Butt	1	2	0	49	37	24.50	-	-	1/-
Younis Khan	1	2	0	34	34	17.00	-	-	2/-
Farhan Adil	1	2	0	33	25	16.50	-	-	-/-
Misbah-ul-Haq	1	1	0	13	13	13.00	-	-	-/-
Saqlain Mushtaq	1	2	0	20	11	10.00	-	-	-/-
Shoaib Akhtar	2	2	0	16	15	8.00	-	-	-/-
Shabbir Ahmed	3	4	0	31	13	7.75	-	-	3/-
Danish Kaneria	2	2	0	8	8	4.00	-	-	-/-
Umar Gul	3	4	0	10	5	2.50	-	-	1/-
Shoaib Malik	1	1	0	0	0	0.00	-	-	-/-
Yasir Ali	1	2	2	1	1*	-	-	-	-/-

Bowling	Overs	Mds	Runs	Wkts	Av	Best	5/inn	10m
Shoaib Akhtar	77.5	18	195	13	15.00	6-50	1	1
Shabbir Ahmed	119	23	341	17	20.05	5-48	1	-
Umar Gul	117.5	21	375	15	25.00	4-58	-	-
Yasir Ali	20	5	55	2	27.50	1-12	-	-
Danish Kaneria	110	32	280	9	31.11	3-58	-	-
Saqlain Mushtaq	27.3	5	70	2	35.00	1-9	-	-
Mohammad Hafeez	34	15	61	1	61.00	1-14	-	-

Also bowled: Shoaib Malik 12-4-27-0

BANGLADESH

Batting	M	Inns	NO	Runs	HS	Av	100	50	c/st
Habibul Bashar	3	6	0	379	108	63.16	1	3	1/-
Javed Omar	3	6	0	187	119	31.16	1	-	2/-
Rajin Saleh	3	6	0	186	60	31.00	-	1	4/-
Mohammad Ashraful	2	4	0	99	77	24.75	-	1	-/-
Mashrafe Mortaza	2	4	2	43	14	21.50	-	-	2/-
Hannan Sarkar	3	6	0	100	41	16.66	-	-	1/-
Alok Kapali	3	6	0	100	46	16.66	-	-	1/-
Khaled Mashud	3	6	0	98	29	16.33	-	-	5/1
Khaled Mahmud	3	6	0	61	25	10.16	-	-	1/-
Tapash Baisya	2	4	1	29	14*	9.66	-	-	-/-
Sanwar Hossain	1	2	0	18	15	9.00	-	-	-/-
Mohammad Rafique	3	6	1	44	14	8.80	-	-	1/-
Manjural Islam	1	2	1	5	5	5.00	-	-	-/-
Alamgir Kabir	1	2	1	5	4	5.00	-	-	-/-

Bowling	Overs	Mds	Runs	Wkts	Av	Best	5/inn	10m
Khaled Mahmud	99	26	257	11	23.36	4-37	-	-
Mohammad Rafique	162.4	43	405	17	23.82	5-36	2	-
Alok Kapali	28.1	4	93	3	31.00	3-3	-	-
Rajin Saleh	14	2	34	1	34.00	1-9	-	-
Manjural Islam	34	5	106	2	53.00	2-64	-	-
Tapash Baisya	51	9	176	3	58.66	1-34	-	-
Mashrafe Mortaza	62	14	204	3	68.00	3-68	-	-

Also bowled: Mohammad Ashraful 3-0-16-0; Sanwar Hossain 14-1-46-0; Alamgir Kabir 20.3-4-100-0

ONE-DAY INTERATIONALS v. BANGLADESH

Match One
9 September 2003 at Multan
Pakistan 323 for 3 (50 overs) (Yasir Hameed 116, Younis Khan 59*, Inzamam-ul-Haq 56*)
Bangladesh 186 (43.2 overs)
Pakistan won by 137 runs

Match Two
12 September 2003 at Faisalabad
Pakistan 243 for 8 (50 overs) (Yousuf Youhana 106)
Bangladesh 169 (42.1 overs) (Rajin Saleh 64)
Pakistan won by 74 runs

Match Three
15 September 2003 at Lahore
Pakistan 257 for 9 (50 overs) (Yousuf Youhana 65, Inzamam-ul-Haq 64*, Tapash Baisya 4 for 56)
Bangladesh 201 for 9 (44 overs) (Alok Kapali 61, Hannan Sarkar 61, Umar Gul 5 for 17)
Pakistan won by 42 runs – DL Method: target 244 from 44 overs

Match Four
18 September 2003 at Rawalpindi
Bangladesh 222 for 8 (50 overs)
Pakistan 226 for 5 (49.5 overs) (Yousuf Youhana 94*)
Pakistan won by 5 wickets

Match Five
21 September 2003 at Karachi
Pakistan 302 for 5 (50 overs) (Yasir Hameed 82, Inzamam-ul-Haq 59*, Yousuf Youhana 52)
Bangladesh 244 for 7 (50 overs) (Rajin Saleh 71, Alok Kapali 69, Hannan Sarkar 50)
Pakistan won by 58 runs

SOUTH AFRICA

By Telford Vice

Shaun Pollock is not everybody's idea of a great cricketer: not serious enough, talented but boring, disciplined but not explosive.

The list of the former South African captain's perceived weaknesses grew last season to include the claim that he was unable to comprehend a table of figures prepared according to the Duckworth-Lewis formula.

Pollock's abject desolation as he slumped, head in hands, at a window in the Kingsmead dressing room to confront the horror of his team's first-round elimination from the World Cup, is the enduring image of the tournament for every South African. Just as four years previously millions of memories had photographed that daft bit of running between the wickets by Lance Klusener and Allan Donald against Australia at Edgbaston.

On that fateful, wet night at Kingsmead, Mark Boucher blocked a ball he could have used to score what would have been the winning run. It wasn't Boucher's fault, as he was under the impression that the revised target had been reached and that South Africa had beaten Sri Lanka. They hadn't, the match was tied and the hosts were evicted from their own party. At least Klusener and Donald tried before

failing; the South Africans of 2003 appeared to fail without trying.

Thus was completed South African cricket's tragic trilogy – Hansie Cronje's corruption, the 5–1 thrashing in Test matches by Australia in 2001–02, and now this: the successful World Cup that never was.

Cronje himself paid the price for the first calamity – though being banned for life dented neither his celebrity status in South Africa, nor his earning potential – and sacked coach Graham Ford for the second.

Who would pay for the third? Eric Simons was as culpable as anyone, but he was in the midst of his honeymoon period as coach and was, therefore, untouchable. Goolam Rajah, the team manager, should have walked the plank. Except that he had been in the job for too long and had become the most powerful figure in the dressing room.

Percy Sonn, the president of the United Cricket Board (UCB), spent much of the World Cup enveloped in a cloud of alcoholic fumes. A spectator at a match at Paarl said he had seen Sonn 'falling out of his trousers'. Nobody wanted to ask what that meant. Just as nobody had the courage to pin the World Cup rap on Sonn. So he survived.

Instead, the UCB told Pollock to resign. To his eternal credit, he refused. In that instant Pollock achieved the seemingly impossible – he became bigger than the game, and he deserved to be.

'Since the Hansie issue there has been an effort to ensure the captain isn't given too much power,' Pollock said a day after the axe finally fell. 'Shared responsibility was the approach they wanted. That hasn't worked out from my perspective. As captain you want the full support to be able to do what you want.'

The UCB's response to the Cronje episode was to strip future captains of authority.

'Whatever Hansie wanted he got in terms of teams, the way forward and how to approach things,' Pollock said. 'The UCB was very worried about what had happened.

Shaun Pollock (far left) already wears a haunted look ... and the World Cup has only just begun.

'They didn't want to give that same power, and maybe that same backing and support. I'm not saying I didn't get backing and support, but it was probably not as strong as is ideal for a captain leading his country.'

With that, Pollock rejoined the team he was always more comfortable being a part of than leading.

'Despite not being captain, I'm still 100 per cent committed to South African cricket and would like to remain a positive influence in the side.' He did not resign, he said, 'as I felt that would be the soft option.'

Unusually for a member, albeit a former member, of a club that invariably inflates egos, Pollock offered Graeme Smith his sincere support.

'I've spoken to my successor and wished him well. He could be a great captain, and I would like us to get behind the new captain, focus on the positives and give him a fair chance in the interests of South African cricket.'

This was more support than Pollock had been afforded by Jonty Rhodes and Allan Donald, who both dedicated the World Cup to Cronje's memory. Herschelle Gibbs, meanwhile, said Pollock had 'a lot to learn' as captain.

'I think I had the players' respect,' Pollock said. 'I had a good relationship with each and every one of them. But guys are open to opinion and Hansie was a topic of hot debate. There were no rifts in the side, but it was probably not an ideal situation going into a World Cup.'

Pollock suggested he did not feel secure in the captaincy. 'In a way I was a makeshift captain to start off with. People were happy with the way it went, and I was retained. But it's not ideal when your captaincy is up for debate in the papers a lot of the time, and before Omar Henry was made the convenor of selectors he said he wasn't sure I was the best captain.'

History does not always get it right, but it is to be hoped that the maturity Pollock showed, when most of those around him seemed intent on shirking the responsibility for the disaster as readily as they dished out the blame, is reflected in the annals of South African cricket.

Graeme Smith: 'He could be a great captain,' says his predecessor Shaun Pollock.

That may prove a vain hope, because history is written by the survivors. The truth is that South Africa's World Cup campaign foundered months before the players had even stepped on to the field. By that stage a dearth of strong leadership from Ford and, yes, Pollock had allowed the squad to shatter into a loosely bound collection of cliques in which discipline was a fading ideal.

The UCB could also have used several pairs of bulletproof shoes. It emerged that the Board had underpaid the players by the combined sum of US$173,000 over the course of six months leading up to the World Cup. It seemed an honest error and

it was rectified after being spotted by the South African Cricketers' Association. There was little honour, however, in the UCB not sticking to its verbal agreement to a contract worth $885,000 for the players' image rights. All of which took its toll. 'This lot aren't going to win a thing – I've never seen such a divided squad,' a source close to the team said in the weeks before the tournament.

Knuckles turned white in a tight opening match against the West Indies. A nation that had been hyped into a frenzy waited for the kind of victory they had seen snatched in so many close games. It never came, and the loss shoved Pollock's team down a slope that saw them lurch from a hand injury that ended Rhodes' World Cup after two matches to that inept loss against New Zealand.

Many South Africans would like to be able to claim that they clamoured for Smith to lead them out of this wilderness. Instead, his appointment was met with scorn in the pubs as well as in the press. Who did this untested 22-year-old think he was? Who did the UCB think he was?

A tour of Bangladesh provided no meaningful answers, but Smith's consecutive double centuries against England silenced all the questioners. More importantly, Smith put the passion back into the South African team. Cronje, when he was an honest man, inspired his players with an unshakeable commitment and Pollock was a conduit for collective thinking more than a demonstrative leader, but, in Smith, South Africa have a captain who demands the hearts of his men and the blood of their opponents. He is vocal and expressive and there is fire in his eyes.

To draw a series they were set to win was a crushing disappointment for South Africa in England, but that blow was significantly softened by the feeling that the team had finally found a positive momentum to move on from the problems that have shackled their spirit in recent years.

Klusener, meanwhile, has become a metaphor for much of what was wrong with the old order. Having been rested for the Bangladesh tour after his ineffective performances in the World Cup, he was left out of the squad for England. New brooms Smith and Simons, it seemed, were less enamoured with the match-winner's surly, anti-team attitude than their predecessors. Besides, Klusener was no longer a match-winner.

Zulu dusk: the international career of Lance Klusener, the legendary hitter, looked over when he was jettisoned after the World Cup.

The player's response was to declare a labour dispute with the UCB on the grounds that he was verbally assured he would be part of the England tour party. This matter remains unresolved at the time of writing, but its ending is unlikely to be a happy one.

South Africa's home season began gently enough with a tour by Bangladesh. The visitors did little to shrug off their unwanted billing as the minnows of international cricket, and crashed to comprehensive defeats in both Test matches and in all three one-day internationals.

If the one-day series is remembered, it will be for a delivery in the second match in Benoni that beat both batsman and wicketkeeper and crossed the boundary to register five wides. Gibbs faced the ball. He was 96 not out in search of the century that would have made him the first player to score four consecutive limited-overs hundreds. The pugnacious opener had made 116 against Kenya and 116 retired against India in the Champions Trophy in Sri Lanka, and 153 in the first match of the Bangladesh series in Potchefstroom.

In Benoni, South Africa had reached 149 without loss in reply to Bangladesh's total of 154 for 9 when leg spinner Alok Kapali pushed a delivery wide down the legside. The five wides tied the scores, and Gibbs drove the next ball down the ground for a single to end the match. The Bangladeshis, however, denied that the ball had been bowled deliberately to deny Gibbs a century.

'I asked Alok to bowl down the leg,' captain Khaled Mashud said. 'Herschelle was coming down the wicket, and we felt there was a chance of a stumping. He bowled it a bit too quick and a bit too wide, but it was not intentional.'

The team manager, the magnificently named Abu Sharis Mahmood Faruque, also twitched his thin moustache in indignation at the very thought. 'I spoke to the captain regarding that, and it was unintentional,' he said. 'The captain had no motive about that. It was clear, absolutely clear.'

The Bangledeshis had the first taste of a flavour England would come to know rather too well for their liking when Smith scored a double century in East London's inaugural Test match, which South Africa won by an innings on the fourth morning.

Makhaya Ntini's pace had the visitors all but scurrying for the dressing room in the first innings, and David Terbrugge's diligent seam bowling found them out in the second.

Another Test venue was inaugurated in Potchefstroom, and South Africa wrapped the game up in three days with Gibbs, Gary Kirsten and Jacques Kallis, who also took five wickets, scoring centuries in the innings victory.

Sri Lanka arrived next and were swept aside in the limited-overs series. South Africa cantered to their third consecutive innings victory in the first Test in Johannesburg – another unfulfilling three-day affair – but Sri Lanka did well to narrow the margin to three wickets at Centurion, with Hashan Tillekeratne toughing out an admirable unbeaten century. Pollock, meanwhile, became only the fourth Test batsman to be stranded on 99 not out.

The Pakistanis promised much but delivered little. They batted magnificently to win the second one-day international, but that was their only success against the hosts.

Pakistan's performance in the Tests was lamentable. They put in a token appearance in Durban, and gave up records with impunity in Cape Town. Their troubles were compounded when a photograph of some of Bollywood's biggest names swanning about Durban with Shoaib Akhtar, who was supposedly having an injury treated in Pakistan, appeared in a local newspaper.

In Cape Town, the visitors were fined their entire match fee for a positively ponderous over rate. This series win, by the way, also earned South Africa top billing in the ICC Test championship, a fact that went down like a lumpy beer in Australia.

ONE-DAY INTERNATIONALS v. BANGLADESH

Match One
3 October 2002 at Potchefstroom
South Africa 301 for 8 (50 overs) (HH Gibbs 153, Talha Jubair 4 for 65)
Bangladesh 133 (41.5 overs) (JH Kallis 4 for 33)
South Africa won by 168 runs

Match Two
6 October 2002 at Benoni
Bangladesh 154 for 9 (50 overs)
South Africa 155 for 0 (20.2 overs) (HH Gibbs 97*)
South Africa won by 10 wickets

Match Three
9 October 2002 at Kimberley
Bangladesh 151 (43.1 overs) (Habibul Bashar 51, SM Pollock 4 for 24)
South Africa 152 for 3 (25.4 overs)
South Africa won by 7 wickets

FIRST TEST – SOUTH AFRICA v. BANGLADESH
18–22 October 2002 at East London

SOUTH AFRICA

	First Innings		
GC Smith	c Islam b Hossain	200	
HH Gibbs	c Imran b Baisya	41	
G Kirsten	c Kapali b Jubair	150	
JH Kallis	not out	75	
AG Prince	c Kapali b Jubair	2	
M van Jaarsveld	not out	39	
*MV Boucher (capt)			
CW Henderson			
DJ Terbrugge			
M Hayward			
M Ntini			
Extras	b 2, lb 1, w 4, nb 15	22	
	(4 wkts dec.)	529	

	First Innings			
	O	M	R	W
Islam	29	3	104	0
Baisya	30	3	148	1
Jubair	26	5	108	2
Rafique	23	2	85	0
Kapali	18	0	72	0
Hossain	3	0	9	1

Fall of Wickets
1-87, 2-359, 3-440, 4-448

BANGLADESH

	First Innings		Second Innings	
Javed Omar	lbw b Terbrugge	7	c Gibbs b Hayward	10
Al Sahariar	b Hayward	18	b Ntini	71
Habibul Bashar	c Boucher b Ntini	38	c Terbrugge b Hayward	21
Sanwar Hossain	c Boucher b Ntini	31	lbw b Terbrugge	49
Tushar Imran	b Ntini	0	(6) c van Jaarsveld b Henderson	8
Alok Kapali	c Kallis b Henderson	35	(7) lbw b Terbrugge	10
*Khaled Mashud (capt)	c van Jaarsveld b Hayward	4	(5) lbw b Terbrugge	33
Mohammad Rafique	not out	17	b Terbrugge	19
Tapash Baisya	c Boucher b Ntini	2	c Kirsten b Terbrugge	10
Manjural Islam	b Ntini	4	c sub b Ntini	8
Talha Jubair	c Boucher b Terbrugge	3	not out	4
Extras	lb 9, w 1, nb 1	11	b 3, lb 3, nb 3	9
		170		252

	First Innings				Second Innings			
	O	M	R	W	O	M	R	W
Hayward	15	3	50	2	16	2	65	2
Terbrugge	11.4	3	43	2	15	1	46	5
Henderson	9	2	23	1	28	8	58	1
Ntini	15	9	19	5	18.5	6	55	2
Kallis	8	2	26	0	10	3	22	0

Fall of Wickets
1-21, 2-25, 3-91, 4-97, 5-100, 6-130, 7-149, 8-155, 9-161
1-22, 2-78, 3-121, 4-158, 5-176, 6-211, 7-212, 8-231, 9-244

Umpires: DJ Harper & RB Tiffin
Toss: Bangladesh

South Africa won by an innings and 107 runs

SECOND TEST – SOUTH AFRICA v. BANGLADESH
25–29 October 2002 at Potchestroom

BANGLADESH

	First Innings		Second Innings	
Hannan Sarkar	c Kallis b Ntini	65	b Ntini	17
Al Sahariar	c Smith b Hayward	30	c Kallis b Hayward	27
Habibul Bashar	c Boucher b Pollock	40	c Boucher b Ntini	7
Sanwar Hossain	lbw b Ntini	0	c Kallis b Ntini	6
*Khaled Mashud (capt)	c van Jaarsveld b Kallis	20	(6) c Boucher b Kallis	9
Rafiqul Islam	c Gibbs b Kallis	6	(8) c Kirsten b Kallis	1
Tushar Imran	c Boucher b Pollock	8	(5) c Prince b Hayward	0
Alok Kapali	not out	38	(7) c Boucher b Kallis	23
Tapash Baisya	c van Jaarsveld b Hayward	2	c Gibbs b Kallis	0
Manjural Islam	c Smith b Henderson	0	c Gibbs b Kallis	5
Talha Jubair	run out	0	not out	1
Extras	b 4, nb 2	6	lb 8, nb 3	11
		215		**107**

	First Innings				Second Innings			
	O	M	R	W	O	M	R	W
Pollock	16	6	38	2	6	0	25	0
Ntini	21	4	69	2	12	1	37	3
Hayward	14	3	64	2	8	3	16	2
Kallis	13	4	26	2	4.3	1	21	5
Henderson	5.5	2	14	1	–	–	–	–

Fall of Wickets
1-52, 2-136, 3-136, 4-140, 5-162, 6-169, 7-184, 8-197, 9-202
1-33, 2-43, 3-52, 4-60, 5-61, 6-95, 7-101, 8-101, 9-104

SOUTH AFRICA

	First Innings	
GC Smith	c Mashud b Hossain	24
HH Gibbs	run out	114
G Kirsten	c Mashud b Jubair	160
JH Kallis	not out	139
AG Prince	c Mashud b Jubair	0
M van Jaarsveld	lbw b Baisya	11
*MV Boucher	not out	14
SM Pollock (capt)		
CW Henderson		
M Ntini		
M Hayward		
Extras	b 13, lb 2, nb 5	20
	(5 wkts dec.)	**482**

	First Innings			
	O	M	R	W
Manjural Islam	26	7	80	0
Baisya	28	3	103	1
Jubair	26	3	109	2
Kapali	20	2	75	0
Hossain	20	1	98	1
Bashar	1	0	2	0

Fall of Wickets
1-61, 2-202, 3-436, 4-436, 5-452

Umpires: DJ Harper & RB Tiffin
Toss: Bangladesh

South Africa won by an innings and 160 runs

SERIES AVERAGES
South Africa v. Bangladesh

SOUTH AFRICA

Batting	M	Inns	NO	Runs	HS	Av	100	50	c/st
G Kirsten	2	2	0	310	160	155.00	2	–	2/-
GC Smith	2	2	0	224	200	112.00	1	–	2/-
HH Gibbs	2	2	0	155	114	77.50	1	–	4/-
M van Jaarsveld	2	2	1	50	39*	50.00	–	–	4/-
AG Prince	2	2	0	2	2	1.00	–	–	1/-
JH Kallis	2	2	2	214	139*	–	1	1	4/-
MV Boucher	2	1	1	14	14*	–	–	–	9/-

Also batted: CW Henderson, M Hayward, M Ntini played in two Tests but did not bat
SM Pollock, DJ Terbrugge (1ct) played in one Test but did not bat

Bowling	Overs	Mds	Runs	Wkts	Av	Best	5/inn	10m
DJ Terbrugge	26.4	5	89	7	12.71	5-46	1	–
JH Kallis	35.3	10	95	7	13.57	5-21	1	–
M Ntini	66.5	20	180	12	15.00	5-19	1	–
M Hayward	53	11	195	8	24.37	2-16	–	–
SM Pollock	22	6	63	2	31.50	2-38	–	–
CW Henderson	42.5	12	95	3	31.66	1-14	–	–

BANGLADESH

Batting	M	Inns	NO	Runs	HS	Av	100	50	c/st
Hannan Sarkar	1	2	0	82	65	41.00	–	1	-/-
Al Sahariar	2	4	0	146	71	36.50	–	1	-/-
Mohammad Rafique	1	2	1	36	19	36.00	–	–	-/-
Alok Kapali	2	4	1	106	38*	35.33	–	–	2/-
Habibul Bashar	2	4	0	106	40	26.50	–	–	-/-
Sanwar Hossain	2	4	0	86	49	21.50	–	–	-/-
Khaled Mashud	2	4	0	66	33	16.50	–	–	3/-
Javed Omar	1	2	0	17	10	8.50	–	–	-/-
Manjural Islam	2	4	0	17	8	4.25	–	–	1/-
Talha Jubair	2	4	2	8	4*	4.00	–	–	-/-
Tushar Imran	2	4	0	16	8	4.00	–	–	1/-
Tapash Baisya	2	4	0	14	10	3.50	–	–	-/-
Rafiqul Islam	1	2	0	7	6	3.50	–	–	-/-

Bowling	Overs	Mds	Runs	Wkts	Av	Best	5/inn	10m
Sanwar Hossain	23	1	107	2	53.50	1-9	–	–
Talha Jubair	52	8	217	4	54.25	2-108	–	–
Tapash Baisya	58	6	251	2	125.50	1-103	–	–

Also bowled: Habibul Bashar 1-0-2-0; Mohammad Rafique 23-2-85-0; Alok Kapali 38-2-147-0;
Manjural Islam 55 -10-184-0

FIRST TEST – SOUTH AFRICA v. SRI LANKA
8–12 November 2002 at Johannesburg

SRI LANKA

	First Innings		Second Innings	
MS Atapattu	b Pollock	34	c Smith b Elworthy	43
RP Arnold	c Smith b Ntini	0	c Kallis b Ntini	0
*KC Sangakkara	c Smith b Elworthy	26	c Boucher b Ntini	7
DPMD Jayawardene	c Boucher b Kallis	39	c Kirsten b Pollock	1
ST Jayasuriya (capt)	c Smith b Kallis	32	b Pollock	0
HP Tillekeratne	run out	24	c Elworthy b Hall	27
KHRK Fernando	c Kirsten b Kallis	0	lbw b Elworthy	0
WPUJC Vaas	c Kallis b Hall	1	c Kirsten b Ntini	32
CRD Fernando	b Pollock	7	not out	4
M Muralitharan	c Ntini b Hall	10	b Hall	0
PDRL Perera	not out	11	b Hall	4
Extras	b 4, lb 2, w 1, nb 1	8	b 4, lb 7, w 1	12
		192		130

	First Innings				Second Innings			
	O	M	R	W	O	M	R	W
Pollock	18	8	45	2	8	3	17	2
Ntini	14	5	45	1	10	4	22	3
Elworthy	15.3	3	42	1	10	3	39	2
Kallis	17	8	35	3	11	3	40	0
Hall	11	6	19	2	2	1	1	3

Fall of Wickets
1-2, 2-46, 3-86, 4-137, 5-140, 6-140, 7-141, 8-152, 9-165
1-2, 2-16, 3-21, 4-25, 5-77, 6-81, 7-122, 8-122, 9-122

SOUTH AFRICA

	First Innings	
GC Smith	c Tillekeratne b KHRK Fernando	73
G Kirsten	c Muralitharan b KHRK Fernando	55
M van Jaarsveld	b KHRK Fernando	3
JH Kallis	c Sangakkara b Vaas	75
AG Prince	c Perera b Vaas	3
ND McKenzie	lbw b Vaas	0
*MV Boucher	c Sangakkara b Muralitharan	38
SM Pollock (capt)	c Sangakkara b CRD Fernando	38
AJ Hall	lbw b Muralitharan	31
S Elworthy	lbw b Muralitharan	6
M Ntini	not out	2
Extras	b 16, lb 10, w 5, nb 31	62
		386

	First Innings			
	O	M	R	W
Vaas	22	2	79	3
Perera	10.2	2	40	0
CRD Fernando	20	2	95	1
Muralitharan	31.2	8	83	3
KHRK Fernando	21	2	63	3

Fall of Wickets
1-133, 2-148, 3-175, 4-179, 5-180, 6-249, 7-329, 8-378, 9-378

Umpires: DJ Harper & RB Tiffin
Toss: Sri Lanka

South Africa won by an innings and 64 runs

SECOND TEST – SOUTH AFRICA v. SRI LANKA
15–19 November 2002 at Centurion

SRI LANKA

	First Innings		Second Innings	
MS Atapattu (capt)	c Kirsten b Kallis	17	c Boucher b Kallis	22
J Mubarak	c Smith b Pollock	48	c Boucher b Ntini	15
*KC Sangakkara	c Pollock b Hall	35	c Boucher b Ntini	89
DPMD Jayawardene	b Pollock	44	lbw b Ntini	40
HP Tillekeratne	not out	104	c Boucher b Kallis	6
RP Arnold	c Boucher b Kallis	2	lbw b Pollock	4
KHRK Fernando	c Kallis b Ntini	24	c Hall b Ntini	14
WPUJC Vaas	c Boucher b Ntini	7	lbw b Kallis	17
MKGCP Lakshitha	c Kirsten b Ntini	2	c Pollock b Kallis	0
CRD Fernando	c Boucher b Ntini	0	c Boucher b Elworthy	14
M Muralitharan	b Kallis	27	not out	0
Extras	lb 10, w 1, nb 2	13	b 13, lb 1, w 7, nb 3	24
		323		245

	First Innings				Second Innings			
	O	M	R	W	O	M	R	W
Pollock	29	11	51	2	17	7	45	1
Ntini	29	6	86	4	22	5	52	4
Elworthy	21	4	71	0	12	1	54	1
Kallis	15.5	2	71	3	14.2	5	39	4
Hall	14	3	34	1	8	0	29	0
Smith	–	–	–	–	4	2	12	0

Fall of Wickets
1-34, 2-90, 3-108, 4-189, 5-207, 6-263, 7-277, 8-281, 9-281
1-23, 2-60, 3-179, 4-180, 5-185, 6-205, 7-209, 8-209, 9-245

SOUTH AFRICA

	First Innings		Second Innings	
GC Smith	lbw b CRD Fernando	15	lbw b Vaas	0
HH Gibbs	run out	92	c Sangakkara b CRD Fernando	7
G Kirsten	c KHRK Fernando b CRD Fernando	11	c Mubarak b CRD Fernando	11
JH Kallis	b KHRK Fernando	84	b CRD Fernando	6
AG Prince	c Sangakkara b Vaas	20	c Sangakkara b CRD Fernando	5
ND McKenzie	lbw b Lakshitha	28	(7) b Muralitharan	39
*MV Boucher	c & b Lakshitha	63	(8) not out	22
SM Pollock (capt)	not out	99	(9) not out	6
AJ Hall	lbw b Muralitharan	0	(6) c Arnold b Muralitharan	16
S Elworthy	c Tillekeratne b Muralitharan	5		
M Ntini	c Arnold b Vaas	23	b 5, lb 1, nb 6	12
Extras	b 4, lb 10, w 4, nb 5	23		
		448	(7 wkts)	124

	First Innings				Second Innings			
	O	M	R	W	O	M	R	W
Vaas	33.3	7	81	2	8	2	28	1
Lakshitha	22	2	71	2	2	1	6	0
CRD Fernando	27	0	91	2	12	0	49	4
Muralitharan	57	10	133	2	13.3	1	35	2
KHRK Fernando	18	5	45	1	–	–	–	–
Mubarak	2	0	6	0	–	–	–	–
Jayawardene	2	1	2	0	–	–	–	–
Arnold	5	2	5	0	–	–	–	–

Fall of Wickets
1-45, 2-71, 3-211, 4-219, 5-258, 6-264, 7-396, 8-400, 9-408
1-0, 2-13, 3-23, 4-31, 5-44, 6-73, 7-112

Umpires: DJ Harper & RB Tiffin
Toss: South Africa

South Africa won by 3 wickets

SERIES AVERAGES
South Africa v. Sri Lanka

SOUTH AFRICA

Batting	M	Inns	NO	Runs	HS	Av	100	50	c/st
SM Pollock	2	3	2	143	99*	143.00	-	1	2/-
MV Boucher	2	3	1	123	63	61.50	-	1	10/-
JH Kallis	2	3	0	165	84	55.00	-	2	3/-
HH Gibbs	1	2	0	99	92	49.50	-	1	-/-
GC Smith	2	3	0	88	73	29.33	-	1	5/-
G Kirsten	2	3	0	77	55	25.66	-	1	5/-
ND McKenzie	2	3	0	67	39	22.33	-	-	-/-
AJ Hall	2	3	0	47	31	15.66	-	-	1/-
M Ntini	2	2	1	10	8	10.00	-	-	1/-
AG Prince	2	3	0	28	20	9.33	-	-	-/-
S Elworthy	2	2	0	11	6	5.50	-	-	1/-
M van Jaarsveld	1	1	0	3	3	3.00	-	-	-/-

Bowling	Overs	Mds	Runs	Wkts	Av	Best	5/inn	10m
AJ Hall	35	10	83	6	13.83	3-1	-	-
M Ntini	75	20	205	12	17.08	4-52	-	-
JH Kallis	58.1	18	185	10	18.50	4-39	-	-
SM Pollock	72	29	158	7	22.57	2-17	-	-
S Elworthy	58.3	11	206	4	51.50	2-39	-	-

Also bowled: GC Smith 4-2-12-0

SRI LANKA

Batting	M	Inns	NO	Runs	HS	Av	100	50	c/st
HP Tillekeratne	2	4	1	161	104*	53.66	1	-	2/-
KC Sangakkara	2	4	0	157	89	39.25	-	1	6/-
J Mubarak	1	2	0	63	48	31.50	-	-	1/-
DPMD Jayawardene	2	4	0	124	44	31.00	-	-	-/-
MS Atapattu	2	4	0	116	43	29.00	-	-	-/-
ST Jayasuriya	1	2	0	32	32	16.00	-	-	-/-
PDRL Perera	1	2	1	15	11*	15.00	-	-	1/-
WPUJC Vaas	2	4	0	57	32	14.25	-	-	1/-
M Muralitharan	2	4	1	37	27	12.33	-	-	1/-
KHRK Fernando	2	4	0	38	24	9.50	-	-	1/-
CRD Fernando	2	4	1	25	14	8.33	-	-	-/-
RP Arnold	2	4	0	6	4	1.50	-	-	2/-
MKGCP Lakshitha	1	2	0	2	2	1.00	-	-	1/-

Bowling	Overs	Mds	Runs	Wkts	Av	Best	5/inn	10m
KHRK Fernando	39	7	108	4	27.00	3-63	-	-
WPUJC Vaas	63.3	11	188	6	31.33	3-79	-	-
CRD Fernando	59	2	235	7	33.57	4-49	-	-
M Muralitharan	101.5	19	251	7	35.85	3-83	-	-
MKGCP Lakshitha	24	3	77	2	38.50	2-71	-	-

Also bowled: DPMD Jayawardene 2-1-2-0; RP Arnold 5-2-5-0; J Mubarak 2-0-6-0; PDRL Perera 10.2-2-40-0

ONE-DAY INTERNATIONALS
v. SRI LANKA

Match One
27 November 2002 at Johannesburg
Sri Lanka 128 (46.4 overs) (SM Pollock 4 for 18)
South Africa 129 for 4 (29.3 overs)
South Africa won by 6 wickets

Match Two
29 November 2002 at Centurion Park
South Africa 317 for 6 (50 overs) (GC Smith 99, HH Dippenaar 89, JH Kallis 53)
Sri Lanka 140 (33.2 overs)
South Africa won by 177 runs

Match Three
1 December 2002 at Benoni
South Africa 253 for 7 (50 overs) (JH Kallis 87, L Klusener 60*)
Sri Lanka 258 for 3 (41.4 overs) (MS Atapattu 123*, PA de Silva 71)
Sri Lanka won by 7 wickets

Match Four
4 December 2002 at Kimberley
Sri Lanka 184 (47.3 overs) (RP Arnold 50)
South Africa 190 for 2 (30.5 overs) (HH Gibbs 108*, JH Kallis 64*)
South Africa won by 8 wickets

Match Five
6 December 2002 at Bloemfontein
Sri Lanka 228 for 8 (50 overs) (KC Sangakkara 77*, MS Atapattu 53)
South Africa 229 for 4 (45.1 overs) (ND McKenzie 70*)
South Africa won by 6 wickets

FIRST TEST – SOUTH AFRICA v. PAKISTAN
26–29 December 2002 at Durban

SOUTH AFRICA

	First Innings		Second Innings	
GC Smith	c Kamran Akmal b Sami	16	not out	13
HH Gibbs	c Faisal Iqbal b Waqar Younis	11	not out	25
G Kirsten	c Younis Khan b Saqlain Mushtaq	56		
JH Kallis	b Sami	105		
HH Dippenaar	c Kamran Akmal b Saqlain Mushtaq	1		
ND McKenzie	b Waqar Younis	24		
*MV Boucher	c Faisal Iqbal b Saqlain Mushtaq	55		
SM Pollock (capt)	c Kamran Akmal b Waqar Younis	21		
N Boje	not out	37		
M Ntini	c Taufeeq Umar b Saqlain Mushtaq	0		
M Hayward	b Sami	10		
Extras	b 4, lb 5, nb 23	32	lb 1, nb 6	7
		368	(0 wkts)	45

	First Innings				Second Innings			
	O	M	R	W	O	M	R	W
Waqar Younis	25	3	91	3	-	-	-	-
Mohammad Sami	26	5	92	3	5	0	36	0
Abdul Razzaq	19	3	57	0	-	-	-	-
Saqlain Mushtaq	37	4	119	4	4	2	8	0

Fall of Wickets
1-27, 2-33, 3-155, 4-159, 5-214, 6-252, 7-286, 8-344, 9-344

PAKISTAN

	First Innings		Second Innings	
Taufeeq Umar	c Smith b Hayward	39	lbw b Boje	39
Saleem Elahi	c McKenzie b Ntini	39	c Smith b Ntini	18
Younis Khan	lbw b Pollock	1	c Boucher b Kallis	30
Inzamam-ul-Haq	c & b Ntini	18	c Gibbs b Boje	13
Yousuf Youhana	c Smith b Ntini	12	c McKenzie b Hayward	42
Faisal Iqbal	run out	6	b Kallis	17
Abdul Razzaq	c McKenzie b Hayward	1	c Boucher b Hayward	22
*Kamran Akmal	c Pollock b Hayward	12	c Boucher b Ntini	29
Saqlain Mushtaq	b Hayward	0	c Boucher b Pollock	4
Waqar Younis (capt)	b Hayward	28	c Kirsten b Pollock	15
Mohammad Sami	not out	0	not out	11
Extras	lb 1, w 1, nb 3	5	lb 2, w 1, nb 7	10
		161		250

	First Innings				Second Innings			
	O	M	R	W	O	M	R	W
Pollock	14	5	23	1	17.3	4	29	2
Ntini	18	4	59	3	21	2	73	2
Hayward	10.4	1	56	5	13	1	63	2
Kallis	6	0	22	0	17	5	30	2
Boje	-	-	-	-	19	2	53	2

Fall of Wickets
1-77, 2-83, 3-83, 4-107, 5-119, 6-120, 7-120, 8-120, 9-145
1-50, 2-64, 3-88, 4-132, 5-156, 6-184, 7-199, 8-216, 9-226

Umpires: SA Bucknor & S Venkataraghavan
Toss: Pakistan

South Africa won by 10 wickets

SECOND TEST – SOUTH AFRICA v. PAKISTAN
2–5 January 2003 at Cape Town

SOUTH AFRICA

	First Innings	
GC Smith	b Zahid	151
HH Gibbs	c Younis Khan b Saqlain Mushtaq	228
G Kirsten	c Younis Khan b Waqar Younis	19
JH Kallis	lbw b Mohammad Sami	31
HH Dippenaar	c Kamran Akmal b Saqlain Mushtaq	62
ND McKenzie	c Kamran Akmal b Zahid	51
*MV Boucher	b Saqlain Mushtaq	7
SM Pollock (capt)	not out	36
N Boje	not out	7
M Ntini		
M Hayward		
Extras	b 1, lb 5, w 1, nb 21	28
	(7 wkts dec)	620

	First Innings			
	O	M	R	W
Waqar Younis	28	4	121	1
Mohammad Sami	28	2	124	1
Mohammad Zahid	25	3	108	2
Saqlain Mushtaq	50	3	237	3
Younis Khan	4	0	24	0

Fall of Wickets
1-368, 2-413, 3-414, 4-463, 5-548, 6-557, 7-594

PAKISTAN

	First Innings		Second Innings	
Taufeeq Umar	c Kallis b Ntini	135	c Boucher b Pollock	67
Saleem Elahi	c Smith b Pollock	10	c Dippenaar b Ntini	0
Younis Khan	lbw b Pollock	46	c McKenzie b Kallis	2
Inzamam-ul-Haq	c Dippenaar b Hayward	32	st Boucher b Boje	60
Yousuf Youhana	c Boucher b Hayward	0	c Kallis b Boje	50
Faisal Iqbal	b Ntini	24	c Pollock b Ntini	11
*Kamran Akmal	lbw b Pollock	0	lbw b Ntini	4
Saqlain Mushtaq	c Boucher b Ntini	1	run out	9
Waqar Younis (capt)	c Kallis b Pollock	0	lbw b Hayward	9
Mohammad Sami	not out	0	not out	9
Mohammad Zahid	c Smith b Ntini	0	c Pollock b Ntini	0
Extras	lb 1, nb 3	4	lb 1, w 1, nb 3	5
		252		226

	First Innings				Second Innings			
	O	M	R	W	O	M	R	W
Pollock	23	6	45	4	12	5	32	1
Ntini	20.4	7	62	4	15.1	2	33	4
Kallis	12	2	35	0	6	1	34	1
Hayward	15	2	56	2	11	3	44	1
Boje	17	2	53	0	15	0	82	2

Fall of Wickets
1-36, 2-152, 3-208, 4-208, 5-240, 6-247, 7-251, 8-252, 9-252
1-0, 2-9, 3-130, 4-130, 5-184, 6-190, 7-203, 8-216, 9-221

Umpires: SA Bucknor & S Venkataraghavan
Toss: South Africa

South Africa won by an innings and 142 runs

SERIES AVERAGES
South Africa v. Pakistan

SOUTH AFRICA

Batting	M	Inns	NO	Runs	HS	Av	100	50	c/st
HH Gibbs	2	3	1	264	228	132.00	1	-	1/-
GC Smith	2	3	1	180	151	90.00	1	-	5/-
JH Kallis	2	2	0	136	105	68.00	1	-	3/-
SM Pollock	2	2	1	57	36*	57.00	-	-	3/-
G Kirsten	2	2	0	75	56	37.50	-	1	1/-
ND McKenzie	2	2	0	75	51	37.50	-	1	4/-
HH Dippenaar	2	2	0	63	62	31.50	-	1	2/-
MV Boucher	2	2	0	62	55	31.00	-	1	7/1
M Hayward	2	1	0	10	10	10.00	-	-	-/-
M Ntini	2	1	0	0	0	0.00	-	-	1/-
N Boje	2	2	2	44	37*	-	-	-	-/-

Bowling	Overs	Mds	Runs	Wkts	Av	Best	5/inn	10m
SM Pollock	66.3	20	129	8	16.12	4-45	-	-
M Ntini	74.5	15	227	13	17.46	4-33	-	-
M Hayward	49.4	7	219	10	21.90	5-56	1	-
JH Kallis	41	8	121	3	40.33	2-30	-	-
N Boje	51	4	188	4	47.00	2-53	-	-

PAKISTAN

Batting	M	Inns	NO	Runs	HS	Av	100	50	c/st
Taufeeq Umar	2	4	0	280	135	70.00	1	1	1/-
Inzamam-ul-Haq	2	4	0	123	60	30.75	-	1	-/-
Yousuf Youhana	2	4	0	104	50	26.00	-	1	-/-
Younis Khan	2	4	0	79	46	19.75	-	-	3/-
Saleem Elahi	2	4	0	67	39	16.75	-	-	-/-
Faisal Iqbal	2	4	0	58	24	14.50	-	-	2/-
Waqar Younis	2	4	0	52	28	13.00	-	-	-/-
Abdur Razzaq	1	2	0	23	22	11.50	-	-	-/-
Kamran Akmal	2	4	0	45	29	11.25	-	-	5/-
Saqlain Mushtaq	2	4	0	14	9	3.50	-	-	-/-
Mohammad Zahid	1	2	0	0	0	0.00	-	-	-/-
Mohammad Sami	2	4	4	20	11*	-	-	-	-/-

Bowling	Overs	Mds	Runs	Wkts	Av	Best	5/inn	10m
Saqlain Mushtaq	91	9	364	7	52.00	4-119	-	-
Waqar Younis	53	7	212	4	53.00	3-91	-	-
Muhammad Zahid	25	3	108	2	54.00	2-108	-	-
Mohammad Sami	59	7	252	4	63.00	3-92	-	-

Also bowled: Younis Khan 4-0-24-0; Abdur Razzaq 19-3-57-0

ONE-DAY INTERNATIONALS
v. PAKISTAN

Match One
8 December 2002 at Durban
South Africa 272 for 7 (50 overs) (JN Rhodes 98, GC Smith 56)
Pakistan 140 (42.5 overs)
South Africa won by 132 runs

Match Two
11 December 2002 at Port Elizabeth
Pakistan 335 for 6 (50 overs) (Saleem Elahi 135, Abdul Razzaq 112)
South Africa 153 (29 overs)
Pakistan won by 182 runs

Match Three
13 December 2002 at East London
South Africa 182 (47.5 overs)
Pakistan 120 (36.2 overs)
South Africa won by 62 runs

Match Four
16 December 2002 at Paarl
Pakistan 213 (48.4 overs) (Yousuf Youhana 61)
South Africa 214 for 1 (42 overs) (G Kirsten 102*, HH Gibbs 52)
South Africa won by 9 wickets

Match Five
18 December 2002 at Cape Town
South Africa 265 for 8 (50 overs) (HH Dippenaar 93, JN Rhodes 81, Waqar Younis 4 for 41, Saqlain Mushtaq 4 for 68)
Pakistan 231 (47.4 overs) (Younis Khan 72, Inzamam-ul-Haq 63, JH Kallis 5 for 41)
South Africa won by 34 runs

SRI LANKA

By Charlie Austin

World Cup years are always eagerly anticipated in Sri Lanka. This time though, despite a flattering place in the semi-finals, expectations were not satisfied. Sri Lanka glided through some matches with the swagger of real contenders, but stumbled through others like nervous pretenders.

It was a common theme throughout an inconsistent year. Ultimately, it was a losing year – not a single Test was won in three two-match series and only 13 wins were claimed from 33 one-day internationals.

The year had its moments, however. No one who witnessed the ICC Champions Trophy semi-final in Colombo will forget the wild, Coliseum-like atmosphere. It had all started so quietly, crowd-wise, as Adam Gilchrist and Matthew Hayden violently dispatched the new ball to all parts of the ground, but moments after Aravinda de Silva started rolling out his gentle off breaks, the game swung emphatically towards the home side. Wickets tumbled and soon 30,000 frenzied supporters were screaming 'Sri-Lan-Ka … Sri-Lan-Ka … Sri-Lan-Ka' in hair-raising unity.

This victory – achieved as it was against the bitterest foe – revived memories of Sri Lanka's 1996 World Cup triumph in Lahore. It also fuelled optimism for the upcoming tournament in South Africa. Unlike the 1996 team, however, which was blessed with rich batting resources, Sanath Jayasuriya's class of 2003 were handicapped by a brittle middle order.

Occasionally Jayasuriya, or his deputy Marvan Atapattu, papered over the cracks with match-winning solo performances, especially in the World Cup, where the pair scored heavily in all four of Sri Lanka's main triumphs: Jayasuriya against New Zealand and the West Indies in the group stages, and Atapattu when the hosts South Africa were knocked out of the tournament and again in the Super Sixes against Zimbabwe.

Before the World Cup, Sri Lanka embarked upon tough tours to South Africa and Australia. For coach Dav Whatmore it was the perfect preparation for the main event, providing time to adjust to foreign conditions, but there was also the danger that their confidence would be shattered. The opening Test against South Africa at Wanderers in October only heightened such fears.

Sri Lanka had fared well in the warm-up games, compiling decent totals on flat pitches, but the Wanderers strip for the opening Test was green and menacing. South Africa packed their side with five seamers and Sri Lanka's defiant decision to bat first backfired.

The top order battled hard for short periods, but the lower order succumbed tamely. In the first innings, the last seven wickets mustered 55 runs; in the second the last six fell for 53. Batting techniques and temperaments (on 17 occasions during the series a batsmen passed 20, but only two of those went on to pass 50) were exposed. The bowling was woefully ill-disciplined, with 62 extras being gifted in a single innings – the second highest tally in the history of Test cricket. South Africa waltzed to a three-day victory.

During the second Test at Centurion, and despite the absence of Jayasuriya, the team showed greater character, pushing the match late into the final day. Hashan Tillekeratne became the first Sri Lankan to score a Test century in South Africa; Kumar Sangakkara achieved the impossible by ruffling the normally implacable Jaques Kallis with his sharp tongue behind the stumps; and the frustratingly injury-prone Dilhara Fernando lit up the final day with raw hostility and pace. In the end, however,

Sanath Jayasuriya … some heroic performances in the final months of his four-year stint as captain.

South Africa's deep batting order was the difference between the two sides. Sri Lanka lost by three wickets.

The five match one-day series that followed was a disaster. Without the services of their best bowler, Muttiah Muralitharan, who was rushed off to Australia for hernia surgery, confidence plummeted. They lost 4–1. It would not have mattered so much if some selection issues had been eased, but the selectors were no closer to their final World Cup squad as the players jetted off to Australia.

After chucking controversies on their two previous visits to Australia in 1995–96 and 1998–99 – both of which also immediately preceded World Cup tournaments – the team was prepared for the worst as it touched down in Brisbane. But although some Australian tabloids couldn't resist trying to re-spark a debate over the legality of Muralitharan's action, the tour passed – with the exception of one racial dressing-room outburst from Darren Lehmann – relatively peaceably. Problems, though, were boiling up at home.

The World Cup contracts row was dominated by India's megastars, but Sri Lanka's players also had grievances. Despite selling the players' image rights without prior consultation, the Sri Lanka Cricket Board was reluctant to offer compensation. The players, through the recently formed Sri Lanka Cricketers' Association, took a stand demanding 20 per cent of all World Cup revenue – a five per cent portion of which was to be redistributed to underpaid club cricketers.

An acrimonious dispute ensued and the Board threatened to field a second-string side at the tournament. Finally, after the ICC-appointed deadline had passed, an agreement was reached for a 12 per cent share plus a three per cent incentive bonus.

Top bowler: Chaminda Vaas finished the 2003 World Cup as the tournament's highest wicket-taker.

Meanwhile, Sri Lanka were being thrashed on the field. They failed to win a single game in the first pre-Christmas section of the VB Series and when they were skittled for a pathetic 65 by Australia A, just days before the second round, it looked as though the wheels had fallen off.

But the return of Muralitharan coincided with Jayasuriya throwing off the shackles of poor form. Sri Lanka stunned Australia at Sydney, running up a mammoth 343 for 5 – the highest ever score against Australia. Another Jayasuriya century followed in the next match against England, and Sri Lanka's self-belief flooded back. It was all too late to reach the VB Series finals, although that at least allowed the players a few precious days at home before the World Cup.

The tournament couldn't have started better with an emphatic win against a hesitant New Zealand side. Moreover, it became clear that Sri Lanka's spin-loaded bowling attack might not be the handicap that had been feared. The South African summer had been hot and dry and the pitches offered encouragement for the likes of Muralitharan, Jayasuriya and de Silva. With Chaminda Vaas – the tournament's highest wicket-taker and a hat-trick-taker against Bangladesh – providing a constant threat with his swing, Sri Lanka soared through their first three games.

The electric Kenyans then served up a reality check with the shock defeat of the tournament. Sri Lanka still scrambled through to the Super Sixes, thanks to a heart-pounding win against the West Indies at Newlands and a farcical tie at Durban – where Shaun Pollock scribbled away the captaincy with the wrong Duckworth-Lewis target – but the embarrassment against Kenya left deep mental scars.

A chapter closed for Sri Lankan cricket when Aravinda de Silva, the country's highest run scorer in both Tests and one-day internationals, announced his retirement.

Early tournament confidence had been shattered and Sri Lanka were soundly thrashed in their first two Super Six games against India and Australia. A workmanlike victory against Zimbabwe ensured their passage to the semi-finals, but their over-reliance on a handful of key players was then

brutally exposed (the five players from the 1996 team scored 64 per cent of the runs and took 75 per cent of the wickets in the 2003 tournament).

Australia were kept to a reasonable score on a tricky Port Elizabeth pitch, but the top order crumbled against Australia's predatory bowling and intense fielding.

The disappointment of the World Cup exit was followed by the confirmation that de Silva was to retire. The departure of Sri Lanka's highest run scorer in Tests and one-day internationals and the middle-order batting rock for the best part of two decades was expected, but it was still nonetheless mourned. He was not lost from the game for long, however, as by the end of the year he was a selector and a vice-president of the Board.

Jayasuriya decided, too, that the time had come to hand over the captaincy. After four years in charge he was exhausted by the heavy burden of expectation. His consensual and honest approach had helped forge a powerful team spirit during the early years of his leadership, but that unity had long since started to diminish and the time had come for a new man.

The Sports Minister – who eventually forced the resignation of an exasperated Guy de Alwis, the chairman of selectors, with his persistent meddling in selection – tried to persuade Jayasuriya to stay on, but Sri Lanka's lacklustre performances in Sharjah, where they were defeated by Pakistan and Zimbabwe (for the first time in three years) confirmed his departure.

Atapattu, who had been widely tipped to take over, was appointed one-day captain and Tillekeratne Test captain. The selectors' justification for this shock decision was that Tillekeratne – a steady old hand – would be a perfect caretaker leader until Atapattu found his feet. However, the decision increased rather than reduced the pressure on Atapattu's shoulders – he was on trial, and the reunification of the captaincy was at stake.

Two captains also left Sri Lanka with an identity crisis. The leadership style of the two men was different: Atapattu wanted the team to be more positive, adventurous and aggressive; Tillekeratne, on the other hand, was cautious and defensive, concerned first and foremost about not losing. The

A safe pair of hands? Hashan Tillekeratne was named as Jayasuriya's successor as Test captain.

team was standing at the crossroads, unsure over its future direction.

The departure of long-term physiotherapist Alex Kontouri and coach Whatmore, who left for Bangladesh after the BCCSL decided not to renew his contract, plus the failure to secure a proper replacement, only made matters worse. With Bob Woolmer, Steve Rixon, John Bracewell, Greg Chappell and Graham Ford all making themselves unavailable, Duleep Mendis was appointed as an interim coach. It was a strange, stagnant period.

The result was directionless cricket. A two-match Test series against New Zealand was dominated by the plodding, attritional approach of both teams. New Zealand, led from the front by Stephen Fleming, who scored a massive double century in the first Test at the P. Saravanamuttu Stadium, and it was no surprise that the tourists were allowed to square the series 0–0. Despite the huge advantage of home conditions, Sri Lanka refused to force the pace or grab the initiative. Plan A was Muralitharan. Plan B was non-existent.

Then came the Bank Alfalah Cup, a tri-series also involving Pakistan that was played entirely at Dambulla because of heavy monsoon rains in the south.

The tournament was plagued by the poor quality of the pitches. It was a bowler's paradise. During the morning it retained moisture, allowing the seamers to dart the ball around dangerously, and by the afternoon the spinners became unplayable as the surface cracked and crumbled. All seven matches were low-scoring dogfights and Sri Lanka fared miserably, failing to qualify for a home series final for the first time in history.

Clearly the time had come for a break. The players were exhausted and poor results had long since bred apathy amongst fans. For years Sri Lanka had struggled to fill its fixture list, but now it was too full.

There was, though, one more tour scheduled to the West Indies. Sri Lanka performed creditably in the one-day series, stealing a dramatic last-over win at the Kensington Oval to clinch the series. Upul Chandana, a bystander throughout so much of the year, was the hero with a whirlwind 89 from 71 balls.

However, that success was followed by a 1–0 defeat in the Test series. The first match at the Beausejour Stadium in St Lucia was weather-affected and drawn. The second game was closely fought until the third and final day. Chasing 212 for victory on a difficult pitch, the West Indies rushed home thanks to the glorious dominance of Brian Lara and Ramnaresh Sarwan.

Back home, meanwhile, the beginning of the rebuilding phase – and indeed a new era in Sri Lankan cricket – drew closer as the first Cricket Board elections were held for nearly three years.

Thilanga Sumathipala, a career administrator and a powerful businessman, won a landslide victory as Board president, humiliating former captain Arjuna Ranatunga who could muster only a handful of votes. Within hours, the Australian John Dyson was announced as the new coach, and a search for a new physiotherapist and physical trainer was started.

After a period of inertia, both on and off the field, the task of rebuilding the team for another year had begun.

FIRST TEST – SRI LANKA v. NEW ZEALAND
25–29 April 2003 at Colombo

NEW ZEALAND

	First Innings		Second Innings	
MH Richardson	b Vaas	85	(7) not out	6
MJ Horne	c Dharmasena b Nissanka	4	(1) lbw b Lokuarachchi	42
SP Fleming (capt)	not out	274	(2) not out	69
MS Sinclair	c Sangakkara b Dharmasena	17	(3) c sub b Muralitharan	1
SB Styris	c Vaas b Dharmasena	63	(4) lbw b Lokuarachchi	16
JDP Oram	c Lokuarachchi b Muralitharan	33	(5) c Kaluwitharana b Muralitharan	19
*RG Hart	c Jayawardene b Muralitharan	9	(6) c Sangakkara b Muralitharan	0
DL Vettori	lbw b Dharmasena	7		
PJ Wiseman	not out	16		
DR Tuffey				
SE Bond				
Extras	b 2, lb 3, w 1, nb 1	7	b 2, lb 5, nb 1	8
	(7 wkts dec.)	515	(5 wkts dec.)	161

	First Innings				Second Innings			
	O	M	R	W	O	M	R	W
Vaas	29	8	73	1	7	2	27	0
Nissanka	23	9	53	1	6	1	18	0
Dharmasena	40	7	132	3	16	7	21	0
Muralitharan	58.5	16	140	2	30	15	41	3
Lokuarachchi	18	2	83	0	19	2	47	2
Jayasuriya	6	0	29	0	-	-	-	-

Fall of Wickets
1-20, 2-192, 3-235, 4-392, 5-471, 6-486, 7-499
1-71, 2-76, 3-108, 4-133, 5-133

SRI LANKA

	First Innings	
MS Atapattu	lbw b Tuffey	0
ST Jayasuriya	b Bond	50
WPUJC Vaas	c Fleming b Bond	4
KC Sangakkara	c Oram b Wiseman	67
DPMD Jayawardene	c Hart b Oram	58
HP Tillekeratne (capt)	b Bond	144
*RS Kaluwitharana	c Sinclair b Wiseman	76
HDPK Dharmasena	lbw b Vettori	31
KS Lokuarachchi	not out	28
RAP Nissanka	lbw b Vettori	0
M Muralitharan	lbw b Vettori	0
Extras	lb 21, w 1, nb 3	25
		483

	First Innings			
	O	M	R	W
Tuffey	17	5	54	1
Bond	28	6	97	3
Oram	30	13	62	1
Vettori	33	8	94	3
Wiseman	41	13	127	2
Styris	3	0	28	0

Fall of Wickets
1-0, 2-11, 3-114, 4-134, 5-267, 6-374, 7-444, 8-483, 9-483

Umpires: DJ Harper & SJA Taufel
Toss: New Zealand

Match Drawn

SECOND TEST – SRI LANKA v. NEW ZEALAND
3–7 May 2003 at Kandy

NEW ZEALAND

	First Innings		Second Innings	
MH Richardson	c Sangakkara b Lokuarachchi	55	c Kaluwitharana b Nissanka	55
MJ Horne	c Kaluwitharana b Vaas	1	c Tillekeratne b Muralitharan	27
SP Fleming (capt)	lbw b Nissanka	0	c Kaluwitharana b Dharmasena	33
MS Sinclair	lbw b Vaas	3	st Kaluwitharana b Muralitharan	0
SB Styris	c Tillekeratne b Muralitharan	32	c Muralitharan b Vaas	1
JDP Oram	c Kaluwitharana b Lokuarachchi	74	lbw b Muralitharan	16
*RG Hart	lbw b Muralitharan	31	c Kaluwitharana b Vaas	12
DL Vettori	run out	55	b Muralitharan	0
PJ Wiseman	b Muralitharan	7	c Tillekeratne b Vaas	29
DR Tuffey	c Jayawardene b Nissanka	15	c Jayasuriya b Muralitharan	1
SE Bond	not out	10	not out	1
Extras	b 3, lb 7, w 5, nb 7	22	b 1, lb 6, nb 1	8
		305		**183**

	First Innings				Second Innings			
	O	M	R	W	O	M	R	W
Vaas	22	8	48	2	15.3	6	31	3
Nissanka	16.5	5	41	2	10	4	18	1
Muralitharan	34	10	90	3	39	18	49	5
Jayasuriya	8	0	24	0	7	0	20	0
Dharmasena	15	5	40	0	12	2	32	1
Lokuarachchi	16	5	52	2	14	3	26	0

Fall of Wickets
1-6, 2-7, 3-11, 4-71, 5-109, 6-189, 7-222, 8-237, 9-271
1-65, 2-109, 3-110, 4-115, 5-136, 6-139, 7-139, 8-179, 9-182

SRI LANKA

	First Innings		Second Innings	
KC Sangakkara	c Hart b Tuffey	10	not out	27
ST Jayasuriya	c Fleming b Wiseman	82	c Richardson b Bond	9
DPMD Jayawardene	c Hart b Oram	15	not out	32
HP Tillekeratne (capt)	b Wiseman	93		
*RS Kaluwitharana	c Tuffey b Bond	20		
HDPK Dharmasena	c Fleming b Wiseman	5		
KS Lokuarachchi	c Tuffey b Oram	20		
WPUJC Vaas	b Oram	22		
MS Atapattu	retired hurt	2		
RAP Nissanka	b Wiseman	6		
M Muralitharan	not out	2		
Extras	b 6, lb 11, nb 4	21	lb 4	4
	(9 wkts)	**298**	(1 wkt)	**72**

	First Innings				Second Innings			
	O	M	R	W	O	M	R	W
Tuffey	20	6	45	1	9	3	18	0
Bond	25	6	78	1	6	1	19	1
Oram	20	2	54	3	-	-	-	-
Wiseman	32.3	4	104	4	9	4	20	0
Vettori	-	-	-	-	6	1	11	0

Fall of Wickets
1-30, 2-69, 3-126, 4-169, 5-189, 6-234, 7-264, 8-285, 9-298
1-14

Umpires: DJ Harper & SJA Taufel
Toss: New Zealand

Match Drawn

SERIES AVERAGES
Sri Lanka v. New Zealand

SRI LANKA

Batting	M	Inns	NO	Runs	HS	Av	100	50	c/st
HP Tillekeratne	2	2	0	237	144	118.50	1	1	3/-
DPMD Jayawardene	2	3	1	105	58	52.50	-	1	2/-
KC Sangakkara	2	3	1	104	67	52.00	-	1	3/-
RS Kaluwitharana	2	2	0	96	76	48.00	-	1	6/1
KS Lokuarachchi	2	2	1	48	28*	48.00	-	-	1/-
ST Jayasuriya	2	3	0	141	82	47.00	-	2	1/-
HDPK Dharmasena	2	2	0	36	31	18.00	-	-	1/-
WPUJC Vaas	2	2	0	26	22	13.00	-	-	1/-
RAP Nissanka	2	2	0	6	6	3.00	-	-	-/-
MS Atapattu	2	2	1	2	2*	2.00	-	-	-/-
M Muralitharan	2	2	1	2	2*	2.00	-	-	1/-

Bowling	Overs	Mds	Runs	Wkts	Av	Best	5/inn	10m
M Muralitharan	161.5	59	320	13	24.61	5-49	1	-
WPUJC Vaas	73.3	24	179	6	29.83	3-31	-	-
RAP Nissanka	55.5	19	130	4	32.50	2-41	-	-
KS Lokuarachchi	67	12	208	4	52.00	2-47	-	-
HDPK Dharmasena	83	21	225	4	56.25	3-132	-	-

Also bowled: ST Jayasuriya 21-0-73-0

NEW ZEALAND

Batting	M	Inns	NO	Runs	HS	Av	100	50	c/st
SP Fleming	2	4	2	376	274*	188.00	1	1	3/-
MH Richardson	2	4	1	201	85	67.00	-	3	1/-
JDP Oram	2	4	0	142	74	35.50	-	1	1/-
SB Styris	2	4	0	112	63	28.00	-	1	-/-
PJ Wiseman	2	3	1	52	29	26.00	-	-	-/-
DL Vettori	2	3	0	62	55	20.66	-	1	-/-
MJ Horne	2	4	0	74	42	18.50	-	-	-/-
RG Hart	2	4	0	52	31	13.00	-	-	3/-
DR Tuffey	2	2	0	16	15	8.00	-	-	2/-
MS Sinclair	2	4	0	21	17	5.25	-	-	1/-
SE Bond	2	2	2	11	10*	-	-	-	-/-

Bowling	Overs	Mds	Runs	Wkts	Av	Best	5/inn	10m
JDP Oram	50	15	116	4	29.00	3-54	-	-
DL Vettori	39	9	105	3	35.00	3-94	-	-
SE Bond	59	13	194	5	38.80	3-97	-	-
PJ Wiseman	82.3	21	251	6	41.83	4-104	-	-
DR Tuffey	46	14	117	2	58.50	1-45	-	-

Also bowled: SB Styris 3-0-28-0

WEST INDIES

By Tony Cozier

A season initially shrouded in familiar controversy, confusion and defeat ended for the West Indies in rare and significant triumph and optimism.

Their first-round elimination from the World Cup was followed, back home, by a players' strike that delayed the semi-finals of the Carib Beer Series, the annual first-class tournament in its first year under new sponsorship, a change of captain, from Carl

Hooper to Brian Lara, and also a change of coach, from Roger Harper to Gus Logie.

It was hardly ideal preparation for two difficult, successive assignments – four Tests and seven one-day internationals against Australia, fresh from their Ashes and World Cup successes, and two Tests and three one-day internationals against Sri Lanka.

The immediate consequences were predictable, as the ruthless and superior Australians handed out sound thrashings in the first three Tests. The reversal that followed, however, was extraordinary. Not only did the West Indies prevent Australia from repeating the clean sweep which occurred the last time the teams had met in Australia two years earlier, they did so with a flourish, amassing a winning total of 418 for 7 at the Antigua Recreation Ground, a feat never previously achieved in Test cricket's long history.

It might have rekindled debate over Australia's 'Dead Rubber Syndrome' affliction, that struck them for the seventh time in seven years, but, for West Indians starved of success for so long, it simply endorsed the Bard's observation that 'all's well that ends well'. Subsequent victory by seven wickets over Sri Lanka, in the second of two Tests that secured the mini-series, gave the maxim even further credence. What is more, the happy climax to the season mirrored the transformation of the new captain.

Reinstated in place of the steady, but uninspiring, Hooper, Lara kept insisting that his team was getting better with every match. With an average age of under 25, it was the youngest ever put out by the West Indies, but Lara was adamant that he and his fellow selectors had sought out and assembled players with 'the right attitude and character traits'.

He promised that he himself would be 'a different Brian Lara' after answering West Indies Cricket Board (WICB) president Wes Hall's plea to once more accept the leadership three years after he had given it up in the wake of what he termed 'modest success and devastating failure'.

He was true to his word. He led with a maturity and understanding that had been blatantly absent in

Second innings: Brian Lara made a conspicuous success of his return to the West Indies captaincy.

his first, turbulent stint, and he also batted with telling consistency. He scored hundreds in each of the first two Tests against the Australians and then 209 in the drawn first Test against Sri Lanka and a match-winning, unbeaten 80 in the second. His average for the six Tests was 83.2.

Equally crucial was the faith he and his fellow selectors placed in youth. Seven players, all under the age of 22, were introduced to the Test team for the first time. One was Omari Banks, a lanky 20-year-old who became the first Test cricketer from tiny Anguilla. Another was Fidel Edwards, a 21-year-old fast bowler from Barbados whose only first-class experience was a solitary match, and a solitary wicket, a year earlier.

Banks conceded 204 runs in his first bowl in Test cricket, but he was not broken, for, as he noted, he had three wickets to show. He was clearly made of the right stuff and, by the next Test, his unbeaten, three-and-a-half hour 47 saw the West Indies across the finishing line in the remarkable finale in Antigua.

The only evidence Lara had on Edwards was a session in the nets. Generating pace around 90 mph with out-swing produced with a slinging, round-arm action – a sort of cross between Jeff Thomson and Waqar Younis – his first day in Test cricket in the last match of the season brought him five Sri Lankan wickets that helped set up the eventual win.

Not everything Lara touched turned to gold, however. A couple of the newcomers were clearly not yet ready for such tough opposition and his decision to bowl on winning the toss in the third Test against Australia (who amassed 605 for 9) was as perverse as they come, but he was always interested in a different option.

In truth, the West Indies did not have the resources to contain Australia's confident batting on lifeless pitches. Steve Waugh, keen to reassert himself after Ricky Ponting's accomplished leadership in the World Cup, returned to oversee such commanding victories in the first three Tests that Australia's hundreds of travelling supporters turned up in Antigua carrying brooms in expectation of the first whitewash of the West Indies in the Caribbean.

Even if their brooms had to be consigned to the dustbins after the stunning outcome, their initial confidence was not misplaced. Until then, the West Indies had been simply submerged under a deluge of runs.

Australia's totals in the first three Tests were 489 at Bourda, 576 for 4 declared and 238 for 3 declared at the Queen's Park Oval and 605 for 9 declared at Kensington Oval. Six of their batsmen averaged over 50.

Ricky Ponting acknowledges the applause from the Port-of-Spain crowd for his first double-hundred in Test cricket.

Ponting's double-century in Port-of-Spain, his first in Tests, was sandwiched between single hundreds in Georgetown and Bridgetown before influenza prevented him adding to his 523 runs and 130.75 average in Antigua.

The rapacious left-handed openers, Matthew Hayden and Justin Langer, helped themselves to two hundreds each and there was one each for Darren Lehmann (his first, at the age of 33), Adam Gilchrist and Steve Waugh, taking the captain past Don Bradman's Australian record of 29.

It needed the strapping, 21-year-old Jermaine Lawson, with 7 for 78 on the first day in Antigua, to halt the trend and prove that, for all their power, these Australians are as vulnerable to genuine, hostile pace bowling as anyone else. They were tumbled for 240 in the face of the kind of West Indian blitz that had become a fading trademark.

The trouble was that the first spicy surface of the series so excited Lawson that his already dubious delivery action became even more pronounced, prompting a negative report from umpires David Shepherd and Srinivas Venkataraghavan and the mandatory remedial work ordered by the ICC.

Jermaine Lawson: from the ecstasy of a seven-wicket haul to the agony of being reported for a suspect bowling action.

The West Indies second innings also revealed the rare phenomenon of Australia under pressure in the field. It was a disturbing sight.

When Lara was fourth out at 165, the West Indies' target was so distant that the anticipated result seemed certain. Instead, Shivnarine Chanderpaul and Ramnaresh Sarwan met the crisis with belligerent hundreds that so unsettled the Australians that McGrath initiated a nasty verbal spat with Sarwan. This, in turn, drew strong condemnation from the Australian Board, and Waugh became engaged with a mid-pitch, eyeball-to-eyeball confrontation with Lara that drew Shepherd's intervention.

The match was on a knife's edge entering the last day, with the West Indies 47 short of their goal and Australia requiring four wickets. Chanderpaul's immediate removal shifted the balance markedly towards Australia, but Banks and Vasbert Drakes, the fledgling and the veteran, remained calm amidst the tension to complete the fairytale with an unbroken stand of 47.

The celebrations around the Antigua Recreation Ground were typically bacchanalian, for a sequence of nine consecutive losses to the Australians had been broken by an extraordinary performance. Yet there were signs all along that, without the banned Shane Warne and with Glenn McGrath below par after remaining in Australia for the first two Tests to tend his ailing wife, Australia's bowling lacked much of its bite on slow surfaces.

Chanderpaul's shot-filled 100, from just 72 balls, on the first day of the series had provided early evidence of that. The West Indies raised totals of 398 in a brave attempt to save that Test and 408 to avoid the follow-on in the next, with hundreds in each from Lara and Daren Ganga, the solid Trinidadian right-hander appearing at home for the first time after 17 overseas Tests.

In one of the highlights of the season, Lara had to come through a spell of searing speed and aggression from Brett Lee before lunch on the last day to pass three figures for the first time in a home Test in Port-of-Spain after ten years of trying.

But the West Indies were well beaten both times as they were in Barbados, setting up Antigua for its memorable climax.

Lara described the victory there as 'the greatest experience I've ever had' – quite a statement given that he has already had enough to fill a lifetime.

His team's inconsistency in the one-day internationals that followed would have tempered his euphoria, though. The series against both Australia (4–3) and Sri Lanka (2–1) were both lost, the West Indies' victories coming only when they had little meaning except to end Australia's record winning streak of 16 matches.

It meant that the two Tests against Sri Lanka would determine what the final appraisal of the season would be.

The first marked the inauguration of the West Indies' eighth, most modern and best-appointed Test venue, the Beausejour Stadium in St Lucia. It also happened to coincide with the start of the annual rainy season in the southern Caribbean and the loss of a day and a half to the weather committed it to a draw. But there was still time for Lara's double-century, single hundreds from Marvan Atapattu and the left-handed Wavell Hinds and a customary five-wicket haul for Muttiah Muralitharan.

The second, at Sabina Park, once more revealed Sri Lanka's aversion to foreign pitches with pace and bounce. The debutant, Edwards, rocked them on the opening day and, after Prabath Nissanka responded in kind to gain Sri Lanka a narrow first-innings lead, Corey Collymore's lively swing all but settled the issue with seven wickets. Following his five in St Lucia, it was an emphatic return to Test cricket after four years pigeonholed as a one-day specialist.

The 212 that stood between the West Indies and a happy ending was the highest total of the match, but Lara and Sarwan dismissed it out of hand with a stroke-filled partnership of 161 off 27.3 overs that ended with the scores level.

The climax was a fitting farewell for Hall. At various times feared fast bowler, team manager and selector, he had been an active and popular Board president in his two years in office before ill health forced him to resign two weeks later.

It was also compensation for the turmoil of his confrontation with the Players' Association that, he said, took him 'long time to get over'.

The Association had been taken over by a new group, headed by the Test leg spinner Dinanath Ramnarine, a year earlier and had gone to the brink of strike action over sponsorship prior to the 2002 Champions Trophy and the 2003 World Cup. It now advised its members not to take to the field on the scheduled first day of the Carib Beer Series semis.

The matter was soon resolved, but Hall called it 'the darkest day in West Indies cricket' and said that, while he could forgive those who organized it, he could not forget.

Barbados, historically the most dominant team in West Indies cricket, went on to defeat Jamaica in the final to add the Carib Beer International Challenge title to the Carib Beer Cup

they had clinched earlier. Since they also won the limited-overs Red Stripe Bowl the previous October, it was Barbados who concluded the only clean sweep of the season.

New pace ace? Fidel Edwards, of Barbados, made an exciting entry into Test cricket with 5 for 36 against a startled Sri Lanka.

FIRST TEST – WEST INDIES v. AUSTRALIA
10–14 April 2003 at Georgetown, Guyana

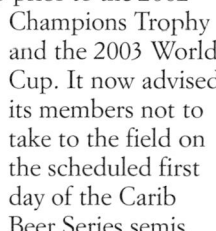

WEST INDIES

	First Innings		Second Innings	
WW Hinds	c Langer b Hogg	10	lbw b MacGill	7
DS Smith	lbw b Lee	3	c Gilchrist b Gillespie	62
D Ganga	b Gillespie	0	c Lee b Lehmann	113
BC Lara (capt)	lbw b Bichel	26	hit wicket b Hogg	110
MN Samuels	c Hayden b Hogg	0	c Ponting b MacGill	7
S Chanderpaul	lbw b Bichel	100	c Gilchrist b Gillespie	31
*RD Jacobs	not out	54	(9) c Lehmann b MacGill	11
VC Drakes	c Gilchrist b Bichel	0	(7) lbw b Gillespie	14
M Dillon	lbw b MacGill	20	(8) lbw b Gillespie	0
PT Collins	st Gilchrist b MacGill	3	not out	1
JJC Lawson	b Lee	0	lbw b Gillespie	0
Extras	b 10, lb 2, w 3, nb 6	21	b 6, lb 13, w 1, nb 22	42
		237		**398**

	First Innings				Second Innings			
	O	M	R	W	O	M	R	W
Lee	10.3	1	41	2	14	4	57	0
Gillespie	12	3	40	1	20.2	5	39	5
Bichel	8	1	55	3	13	4	40	0
Hogg	8	1	40	2	15	0	68	1
MacGill	12	4	49	2	31	5	140	3
Waugh	-	-	-	-	8	1	29	0
Lehmann	-	-	-	-	4	0	6	1

Fall of Wickets
1-9, 2-10, 3-47, 4-47, 5-53, 6-184, 7-184, 8-222, 9-236
1-52, 2-110, 3-295, 4-303, 5-354, 6-382, 7-384, 8-391, 9-397

AUSTRALIA

	First Innings		Second Innings	
JL Langer	c Hinds b Drakes	146	not out	78
ML Hayden	run out	10	c sub b Lawson	19
RT Ponting	c Samuels b Drakes	117	not out	42
DS Lehmann	c sub b Drakes	6		
SR Waugh (capt)	lbw b Dillon	25		
*AC Gilchrist	c & b Lawson	77		
GB Hogg	lbw b Collins	3		
AJ Bichel	c Hinds b Drakes	39		
B Lee	c Dillon b Drakes	20		
JN Gillespie	b Lawson	7		
SCG MacGill	not out	4		
Extras	b 18, lb 5, w 2, nb 10	35	b 1, lb 2, w 2, nb 3	8
		489	(1 wkt)	**147**

	First Innings				Second Innings			
	O	M	R	W	O	M	R	W
Dillon	23	1	116	1	6	0	21	0
Collins	23	1	96	1	6	2	14	0
Lawson	21	0	111	2	9	2	31	1
Drakes	26.1	5	93	5	8	0	28	0
Samuels	21	6	49	0	9.1	1	41	0
Ganga	1	0	1	0	4	0	9	0

Fall of Wickets
1-37, 2-285, 3-300, 4-319, 5-349, 6-362, 7-447, 8-473, 9-485
1-77

Umpires: EAR de Silva & RE Koertzen
Toss: West Indies

Australia won by 9 wickets

SECOND TEST – WEST INDIES v. AUSTRALIA
19–23 April 2003 at Port-of-Spain, Trinidad

AUSTRALIA

	First Innings		Second Innings	
JL Langer	lbw b Dillon	25	lbw b Drakes	3
ML Hayden	lbw b Dillon	30	not out	100
RT Ponting	st Baugh b Samuels	206	c Baugh b Dillon	45
DS Lehmann	c Baugh b Drakes	160	b Dillon	66
*AC Gilchrist	not out	101		
GB Hogg	not out	17		
SR Waugh				
AJ Bichel				
JN Gillespie				
B Lee				
SCG MacGill				
Extras	b 11, lb 7, w 7, nb 12	37	b 12, lb 6, w 1, nb 5	24
	(4 wkts dec.)	576	(3 wkts dec.)	238

	First Innings				Second Innings			
	O	M	R	W	O	M	R	W
Dillon	28.5	1	124	2	18.2	0	64	2
Collins	25	2	123	0	7	1	30	0
Drakes	33	3	112	1	20	4	61	1
Samuels	26	2	111	1	21	1	65	0
Bernard	11	1	61	0	-	-	-	-
Sarwan	2	0	7	0	-	-	-	-
Hinds	7	0	20	0	-	-	-	-

Fall of Wickets
1-49, 2-56, 3-371, 4-542
1-12, 2-118, 3-238

WEST INDIES

	First Innings		Second Innings	
WW Hinds	c Hayden b Lee	20	b MacGill	35
DS Smith	c Gilchrist b Gillespie	0	lbw b Gillespie	0
D Ganga	c Hayden b Lee	117	c Hayden b Gillespie	2
BC Lara (capt)	b Hogg	91	c Hayden b MacGill	122
RR Sarwan	b Lee	26	c Lehmann b Bichel	34
MN Samuels	c Bichel b MacGill	68	lbw b Bichel	1
DE Bernard	b Gillespie	7	c Hayden b Bichel	4
*CS Baugh	hit wicket b MacGill	19	c Langer b Hogg	1
VC Drakes	lbw b Lee	24	not out	26
M Dillon	lbw b Gillespie	0	c Bichel b Lee	13
PT Collins	not out	7	lbw b Gillespie	5
Extras	b 4, lb 15, w 2, nb 8	29	b 25, lb 7, w 3, nb 10	45
		408		288

	First Innings				Second Innings			
	O	M	R	W	O	M	R	W
Lee	23	4	69	4	19	4	68	1
Gillespie	28	9	50	3	17.2	3	36	3
Bichel	12	1	58	0	13	3	21	3
MacGill	27	4	98	2	20	6	53	2
Hogg	22	3	98	1	13	1	58	1
Waugh	7	2	16	0	-	-	-	-
Lehmann	-	-	-	-	7	0	20	0

Fall of Wickets
1-4, 2-25, 3-183, 4-258, 5-279, 6-300, 7-367, 8-376, 9-384
1-2, 2-12, 3-107, 4-213, 5-222, 6-228, 7-238, 8-238, 9-270

Umpires: EAR de Silva & RE Koertzen
Toss: Australia

Australia won by 118 runs

THIRD TEST – WEST INDIES v. AUSTRALIA
1–5 May 2003 at Bridgetown, Barbados

AUSTRALIA

	First Innings		Second Innings	
JL Langer	c Chanderpaul b Banks	78	lbw b Lawson	0
ML Hayden	c Gayle b Drakes	27	not out	2
RT Ponting	run out	113		
DS Lehmann	lbw b Drakes	96	(3) not out	4
SR Waugh (capt)	b Lawson	115		
*AC Gilchrist	c Smith b Banks	65		
AJ Bichel	c Lara b Banks	71		
B Lee	b Lawson	11		
JN Gillespie	not out	18		
SCG MacGill	b Lawson	0		
GD McGrath				
Extras	b 3, lb 3, w 3, nb 2	11	b 2	2
	(9 wkts dec.)	605	(1 wkt)	8

	First Innings				Second Innings			
	O	M	R	W	O	M	R	W
Lawson	32.3	2	131	3	1	0	2	1
Best	20	1	99	0	-	-	-	-
Drakes	30	2	85	2	-	-	-	-
Banks	40	2	204	3	1	0	2	0
Gayle	31	5	79	0	0.3	0	2	0
Sarwan	1	0	1	0	-	-	-	-

Fall of Wickets
1-43, 2-151, 3-292, 4-331, 5-444, 6-568, 7-580, 8-605, 9-605
1-0

WEST INDIES

	First Innings		Second Innings	
CH Gayle	b Gillespie	71	st Gilchrist b MacGill	56
DS Smith	c Gilchrist b Gillespie	59	lbw b Lee	5
D Ganga	c Bichel b Lehmann	26	lbw b Lee	6
RR Sarwan	c Gilchrist b Lee	40	lbw b MacGill	58
S Chanderpaul	c Lee b MacGill	0	(6) c Gilchrist b Gillespie	21
OAC Banks	c Ponting b Gillespie	24	(7) c Hayden b MacGill	32
*CS Baugh	c Ponting b MacGill	24	(8) run out	18
BC Lara (capt)	lbw b Bichel	14	(5) lbw b Bichel	42
VC Drakes	c Lee b MacGill	11	b MacGill	0
TL Best	not out	20	c Bichel b MacGill	0
JJC Lawson	st Gilchrist b MacGill	1	not out	5
Extras	b 11, lb 16, nb 11	38	b 13, lb 25, w 1, nb 2	41
		328		284

	First Innings				Second Innings			
	O	M	R	W	O	M	R	W
McGrath	18	7	25	0	18	4	39	0
Gillespie	21	9	31	3	28	11	37	1
Lee	25	8	77	1	15	6	44	2
MacGill	39.5	8	107	4	36	11	75	5
Lehmann	9	2	26	1	1	0	4	0
Bichel	16	3	35	1	12	2	35	1
Ponting	-	-	-	-	2	0	6	0
Waugh	-	-	-	-	4	1	6	0

Fall of Wickets
1-139, 2-142, 3-205, 4-206, 5-245, 6-245, 7-281, 8-291, 9-324
1-15, 2-31, 3-94, 4-187, 5-195, 6-256, 7-256, 8-261, 9-265

Umpires: DR Shepherd & S Venkataraghavan
Toss: West Indies

Australia won by 9 wickets

FOURTH TEST – WEST INDIES v. AUSTRALIA
9–13 May 2003 at St John's, Antigua

AUSTRALIA

	First Innings		Second Innings	
JL Langer	c Banks b Lawson	42	c Lara b Gayle	111
ML Hayden	c Drakes b Lawson	14	run out	177
ML Love	b Banks	36	(4) c sub b Banks	2
DS Lehmann	c Jacobs b Lawson	7	(5) b Dillon	14
SR Waugh (capt)	c Jacobs b Dillon	41	(6) not out	45
*AC Gilchrist	c Chanderpaul b Dillon	33	(3) c sub b Banks	6
AJ Bichel	c sub b Lawson	34	c Smith b Dillon	0
B Lee	c Jacobs b Lawson	9	c sub b Dillon	18
JN Gillespie	c Jacobs b Lawson	6	c Lara b Drakes	5
SCG MacGill	c Sarwan b Lawson	2	c Lara b Dillon	0
GD McGrath	not out	5	c Ganga b Drakes	14
Extras	b 2, lb 3, w 2, nb 4	11	b 4, lb 9, nb 12	25
		240		**417**

	First Innings				Second Innings			
	O	M	R	W	O	M	R	W
Dillon	18	2	53	2	29	3	112	4
Lawson	19.1	3	78	7	6	1	17	0
Drakes	15	2	42	0	19	1	92	2
Banks	20	2	62	1	37	5	153	2
Gayle	-	-	-	-	13	1	30	1

Fall of Wickets

1-27, 2-80, 3-93, 4-128, 5-181, 6-194, 7-224, 8-231, 9-233
1-242, 2-273, 3-285, 4-330, 5-338, 6-343, 7-373, 8-385, 9-388

WEST INDIES

	First Innings		Second Innings	
CH Gayle	b McGrath	0	c Waugh b Lee	19
DS Smith	c Gilchrist b Lee	37	c Gilchrist b Gillespie	23
D Ganga	c Gilchrist b Bichel	6	lbw b McGrath	8
VC Drakes	lbw b Lee	21	(9) not out	27
BC Lara (capt)	c Langer b Bichel	68	(4) b MacGill	60
RR Sarwan	c & b Bichel	24	(5) c & b Lee	105
S Chanderpaul	b McGrath	1	(6) c Gilchrist b Lee	104
*RD Jacobs	run out	26	(7) c Gilchrist b Lee	0
OAC Banks	not out	16	(8) not out	47
M Dillon	b Lee	9		
JJC Lawson	c Love b MacGill	14		
Extras	lb 8, w 3, nb 7	18	b 9, lb 9, w 1, nb 6	25
		240	(7 wkts)	**418**

	First Innings				Second Innings			
	O	M	R	W	O	M	R	W
McGrath	17	6	44	2	25	10	50	1
Gillespie	17	3	56	0	25	10	64	1
Bichel	14	4	53	3	15	3	49	0
Lee	15	2	71	3	23	4	63	4
MacGill	2.3	0	8	1	35.5	8	149	1
Waugh	-	-	-	-	5	0	25	0

Fall of Wickets

1-1, 2-30, 3-73, 4-80, 5-137, 6-140, 7-185, 8-197, 9-224
1-48, 2-50, 3-74, 4-165, 5-288, 6-288, 7-372

Umpires: DR Shepherd & S Venkataraghavan
Toss: Australia

West Indies won by 3 wickets

SERIES AVERAGES
West Indies v. Australia

WEST INDIES

Batting	M	Inns	NO	Runs	HS	Av	100	50	c/st
BC Lara	4	8	0	533	122	66.62	2	3	4/-
OAC Banks	2	4	2	119	47*	59.50	-	-	1/-
RR Sarwan	3	6	0	287	105	47.83	1	1	1/-
S Chanderpaul	3	6	0	257	104	42.83	2	-	2/-
CH Gayle	2	4	0	146	71	36.50	-	2	1/-
D Ganga	4	8	0	278	117	34.75	2	-	1/-
RD Jacobs	2	4	1	91	54*	30.33	-	1	4/-
DS Smith	4	8	0	189	62	23.62	-	2	2/-
VC Drakes	4	8	2	123	27*	20.50	-	-	1/-
TL Best	1	2	1	20	20*	20.00	-	-	-/-
MN Samuels	2	4	0	76	68	19.00	-	1	1/-
WW Hinds	2	4	0	72	35	18.00	-	-	2/-
CS Baugh	2	4	0	62	24	15.50	-	-	2/1
M Dillon	3	5	0	42	20	8.40	-	-	1/-
PT Collins	2	4	2	16	7*	8.00	-	-	-/-
DE Bernard	1	2	0	11	7	5.50	-	-	-/-
JJC Lawson	3	5	1	20	14	5.00	-	-	1/-

Bowling	Overs	Mds	Runs	Wkts	Av	Best	5/inn	10m
JJC Lawson	88.4	8	370	14	26.42	7-78	1	-
M Dillon	123.1	7	490	11	44.54	4-112	-	-
VC Drakes	151.1	17	513	11	46.63	5-93	1	-
OAC Banks	98	9	421	6	70.16	3-204	-	-
CH Gayle	44.3	6	111	1	111.00	1-30	-	-
PT Collins	61	6	263	1	263.00	1-96	-	-
MN Samuels	77.1	10	266	1	266.00	1-111	-	-

Also bowled: RR Sarwan 3-0-8-0; D Ganga 5-0-10-0 ; WW Hinds 7-0-20-0;
DE Bernard 11-1-61-0; TL Best 20-1-99-0

AUSTRALIA

Batting	M	Inns	NO	Runs	HS	Av	100	50	c/st
RT Ponting	3	5	1	523	206	130.75	3	-	3/-
SR Waugh	4	4	1	226	115	75.33	1	-	1/-
AC Gilchrist	4	5	1	282	101*	70.50	1	2	12/3
JL Langer	4	8	1	483	146	69.00	2	2	3/-
ML Hayden	4	8	2	379	177	63.16	2	-	7/-
DS Lehmann	4	7	1	353	160	58.83	1	2	2/-
AJ Bichel	4	4	0	144	71	36.00	-	1	5/-
GB Hogg	2	2	1	20	17*	20.00	-	-	-/-
GD McGrath	2	2	1	19	14	19.00	-	-	-/-
ML Love	1	2	0	38	36	19.00	-	-	1/-
B Lee	4	4	0	58	20	14.50	-	-	4/-
JN Gillespie	4	4	1	36	18*	12.00	-	-	-/-
SCG MacGill	4	4	1	6	4*	2.00	-	-	-/-

Bowling	Overs	Mds	Runs	Wkts	Av	Best	5/inn	10m
JN Gillespie	168.4	53	353	17	20.76	5-39	1	-
DS Lehmann	21	6	56	2	28.00	1-6	-	-
B Lee	144.3	33	490	17	28.82	4-63	-	-
AJ Bichel	103	21	346	11	31.45	3-21	-	-
SCG MacGill	204.1	46	679	20	33.95	5-75	1	-
GD McGrath	78	27	158	3	52.66	2-44	-	-
GB Hogg	58	5	264	5	52.80	2-40	-	-

Also bowled: RT Ponting 2-0-6-0; SR Waugh 24-4-76-0

FIRST TEST – WEST INDIES v. SRI LANKA
20–24 June 2003 at St Lucia

SRI LANKA

	First Innings				Second Innings			
MS Atapattu	c Lara b Hinds			118	not out			50
ST Jayasuriya	c Banks b Collymore			8	not out			72
KC Sangakkara	lbw b Gayle			56				
DPMD Jayawardene	c Lara b Banks			45				
HP Tillekrratne (capt)	b Collymore			13				
TT Samaraweera	c Jacobs b Collymore			11				
*RS Kaluwitharana	lbw b Collymore			2				
KS Lokuarachchi	c Lara b Collymore			15				
WPUJC Vaas	c Jacobs b Gayle			38				
M Muralitharan	lbw b Hinds			14				
RAP Nissanka	not out			13				
Extras	b 4, lb 4, w 5, nb 8			21	b 1, lb 2, nb 1			4
				354	(0 wkt)			**126**

	First Innings				Second Innings			
	O	M	R	W	O	M	R	W
Dillon	29	7	48	0	5	1	24	0
Collymore	29	4	67	5	3	0	8	0
Taylor	27	3	97	0	6	1	19	0
Hinds	11	4	28	2	4	0	25	0
Banks	33	8	74	1	10	0	28	0
Gayle	9.2	1	22	2	–	–	–	–
Samuels	3	0	9	0	3	1	15	0
Sarwan	2	1	1	0	3	1	4	0

Fall of Wickets
1-19, 2-127, 3-195, 4-228, 5-266, 6-269, 7-285, 8-288, 9-326

WEST INDIES

	First Innings			
CH Gayle	lbw b Muralitharan			27
D Ganga	lbw b Vaas			12
WW Hinds	run out			113
BC Lara (capt)	c Kaluwitharana b Nissanka			209
RR Sarwan	c Atapattu b Muralitharan			7
MN Samuels	st Kaluwitharana b Muralitharan			8
*RD Jacobs	lbw b Muralitharan			13
OAC Banks	not out			50
M Dillon	c Atapattu b Lokuarachchi			2
CD Collymore	c & b Muralitharan			0
JE Taylor	not out			9
Extras	b 4, lb 4, w 2, nb 17			27
	(9 wkts dec.)			**477**

	First Innings			
	O	M	R	W
Vaas	39	5	117	1
Nissanka	21.3	1	108	1
Samaraweera	8	0	53	0
Muralitharan	50	11	137	5
Lokuarachchi	20	6	54	1

Fall of Wickets
1-18, 2-66, 3-240, 4-262, 5-279, 6-305, 7-441, 8-447, 9-448

Umpires: BF Bowden & DJ Harper
Toss: Sri Lanka

Match Drawn

SECOND TEST – WEST INDIES v. SRI LANKA
27 June – 1 July 2003 at Kingston, Jamaica

SRI LANKA

	First Innings				Second Innings			
MS Atapattu	c Gayle b Drakes			15	c Jacobs b Taylor			28
ST Jayasuriya	c Jacobs b Collymore			26	lbw b Collymore			13
KC Sangakkara	lbw b Edwards			75	c Jacobs b Collymore			12
DPMD Jayawardene	c Gayle b Edwards			10	c Jacobs b Edwards			32
HP Tillekeratne (capt)	c Lara b Banks			13	(6) b Collymore			7
*RS Kaluwitharana	c Samuels b Banks			10	(5) b Taylor			23
HDPK Dharmasena	c Samuels b Collymore			6	c Lara b Collymore			20
WPUJC Vaas	not out			12	c Lara b Collymore			21
MTT Mirando	c Lara b Edwards			11	c Lara b Collymore			13
M Muralitharan	b Edwards			0	c Sarwan b Collymore			6
RAP Nissanka	c Gayle b Edwards			0	not out			0
Extras	b 1, lb 17, w 2, nb 10			30	b 4, lb 6, w 2, nb 7			19
				208				**194**

	First Innings				Second Innings			
	O	M	R	W	O	M	R	W
Collymore	15	6	28	2	16	2	57	7
Taylor	11	1	40	0	10	1	38	2
Drakes	18	3	54	1	11	3	29	0
Edwards	15.4	1	36	5	15	2	54	1
Banks	22	6	31	2	2	0	6	0
Gayle	4	3	1	0	–	–	–	–

Fall of Wickets
1-38, 2-48, 3-77, 4-109, 5-129, 6-140, 7-192, 8-204, 9-208
1-25, 2-43, 3-80, 4-118, 5-118, 6-138, 7-173, 8-176, 9-184

WEST INDIES

	First Innings				Second Innings			
CH Gayle	c Sangakkara b Nissanka			31	lbw b Vaas			0
WW Hinds	c Kaluwitharana b Nissanka			19	b Muralitharan			29
RR Sarwan	b Vaas			31	c Jayasuriya b Vaas			82
BC Lara (capt)	lbw b Muralitharan			10	not out			80
MN Samuels	c Tillekeratne b Nissanka			14	not out			0
OAC Banks	c Tillekeratne b Nissanka			2				
*RD Jacobs	lbw b Muralitharan			16				
VC Drakes	b Muralitharan			30				
JE Taylor	c Muralitharan b Dharmasena			1				
CD Collymore	c Sangakkara b Nissanka			13				
FH Edwards	not out			5				
Extras	b 5, lb 3, w 5, nb 6			19	b 7, lb 4, w 4, nb 6			21
				191	(3 wkts)			**212**

	First Innings				Second Innings			
	O	M	R	W	O	M	R	W
Vaas	15	4	33	1	12	2	54	2
Mirando	10	1	36	0	5	0	23	0
Nissanka	12.3	0	64	5	8	1	64	0
Muralitharan	11	3	23	3	15.4	1	48	1
Dharmasena	5	0	27	1	2	0	12	0

Fall of Wickets
1-54, 2-59, 3-85, 4-107, 5-110, 6-123, 7-161, 8-162, 9-174
1-1, 2-50, 3-211

Umpires: DB Hair & RB Tiffin
Toss: West Indies

West Indies won by 7 wickets

SERIES AVERAGES
West Indies v. Sri Lanka

WEST INDIES

Batting	M	Inns	NO	Runs	HS	Av	100	50	c/st
BC Lara	2	3	1	299	209	149.50	1	1	8/-
WW Hinds	2	3	0	161	113	53.66	1	-	-/-
OAC Banks	2	2	1	52	50*	52.00	-	1	1/-
RR Sarwan	2	3	0	120	82	40.00	-	1	1/-
VC Drakes	1	1	0	30	30	30.00	-	-	-/-
CH Gayle	2	3	0	58	31	19.33	-	-	3/-
RD Jacobs	2	2	0	29	16	14.50	-	-	6/-
D Ganga	1	1	0	12	12	12.00	-	-	-/-
MN Samuels	2	3	1	22	14	11.00	-	-	2/-
JE Taylor	2	2	1	10	9*	10.00	-	-	-/-
CD Collymore	2	2	0	13	13	6.50	-	-	-/-
M Dillon	1	1	0	2	2	2.00	-	-	-/-
FH Edwards	1	1	1	5	5*	-	-	-	-/-

Bowling	Overs	Mds	Runs	Wkts	Av	Best	5/inn	10m
CD Collymore	63	13	159	14	11.42	7-57	2	-
CH Gayle	13.2	4	23	2	11.50	2-22	-	-
FH Edwards	30.4	3	90	6	15.00	5-36	1	-
WW Hinds	15	4	53	2	26.50	2-28	-	-
OAC Banks	67	14	139	3	46.33	2-31	-	-
VC Drakes	29	6	83	1	83.00	1-54	-	-
JE Taylor	54	6	194	2	97.00	2-38	-	-

Also bowled: RR Sarwan 5-2-5-0; MN Samuels 6-1-24-0; M Dillon 34-8-72-0

SRI LANKA

Batting	M	Inns	NO	Runs	HS	Av	100	50	c/st
MS Atapattu	2	4	1	211	118	70.33	1	-	2/-
KC Sangakkara	2	3	0	143	75	47.66	-	2	2/-
ST Jayasuriya	2	4	1	119	72*	39.66	-	1	1/-
WPUJC Vaas	2	3	1	71	38	35.50	-	-	-/-
DPMD Jayawardene	2	3	0	87	45	29.00	-	-	-/-
KS Lokuarachchi	1	1	0	15	15	15.00	-	-	-/-
HDPK Dharmasena	1	2	0	26	20	13.00	-	-	-/-
RAP Nissanka	2	3	2	12	12*	13.00	-	-	-/-
MTT Mirando	1	2	0	24	13	12.00	-	-	-/-
RS Kaluwitharana	2	3	0	35	23	11.66	-	-	2/1
HP Tillekeratne	2	3	0	33	13	11.00	-	-	2/-
TT Samaraweera	1	1	0	11	11	11.00	-	-	-/-
M Muralitharan	2	3	0	20	14	6.66	-	-	2/-

Bowling	Overs	Mds	Runs	Wkts	Av	Best	5/inn	10m
M Muralitharan	76.4	14	209	9	23.11	5-137	1	-
HDPK Dharmasena	7	0	39	1	39.00	1-27	-	-
RAP Nissanka	42	2	236	6	39.33	5-64	1	-
WPUJC Vaas	66	11	203	4	51.00	2-54	-	-
KS Lokuarachchi	20	6	54	1	54.00	1-54	-	-

Also bowled: TT Samaraweera 8-0-53-0; MTT Mirando 15-1-59-0

ONE-DAY INTERNATIONALS v. AUSTRALIA
Match One
17 May 2003 at Kingston, Jamaica
Australia 270 for 5 (50 overs) (RT Ponting 59, DS Lehmann 55)
West Indies 205 for 8 (37 overs)
Australia won by 2 runs – DL method: target 208 from 37 overs

Match Two
18 May 2003 at Kingston, Jamaica
West Indies 163 (49 overs) (GD McGrath 4 for 31)
Australia 166 for 2 (35.1 overs) (RT Ponting 57*, ML Hayden 51)
Australia won by 8 wickets

Match Three
21 May 2003 at St Lucia
Australia 258 for 4 (50 overs) (MJ Clarke 75*, A Symonds 75)
West Indies 233 for 9 (50 overs)
Australia won by 25 runs

Match Four
24 May 2003 at Port-of-Spain, Trinidad
Australia 286 for 5 (50 overs) (AC Gilchrist 84, MJ Clarke 55*)
West Indies 219 (45.3 overs) (CH Gayle 84)
Australia won by 67 runs

Match Five
25 May 2003 at Port-of-Spain, Trinidad
West Indies 290 for 5 (50 overs) (BC Lara 80, WW Hinds 79)
Australia 251 for 9 (50 overs) (A Symonds 77)
West Indies won by 39 runs

Match Six
30 May 2003 at Grenada
Australia 252 (50 overs) (AC Gilchrist 64)
West Indies 254 for 7 (48.4 overs) (WW Hinds 125*, RR Sarwan 50)
West Indies won by 3 wickets

Match Seven
1 June 2003 at Grenada
Australia 247 for 8 (50 overs) (DS Lehmann 107, GB Hogg 53, CH Gayle 5 for 46)
West Indies 249 for 1 (43.3 overs) (WW Hinds 103*, BC Lara 75*, CH Gayle 60)
West Indies won by 9 wickets

ONE-DAY INTERNATIONALS v. SRI LANKA
Match One
7 June 2003 at Bridgetown, Barbados
Sri Lanka 201 (48.4 overs) (RS Kaluwitharana 54)
West Indies 146 (41 overs) (BC Lara 64*)
Sri Lanka won by 55 runs

Match Two
8 June 2003 at Bridgetown, Barbados
West Indies 312 for 4 (50 overs) (BC Lara 116, CH Gayle 94, MN Samuels 56*)
Sri Lanka 313 for 6 (49.3 overs) (UDU Chandana 89)
Sri Lanka won by 4 wickets

Match Three
11 June 2003 at St Vincent
Sri Lanka 191 (50 overs) (DPMD Jayawardene 51)
West Indies 160 for 4 (36.5 overs)
West Indies won by 6 wickets – DL Method: target 160 from 42 overs

CRICKET IN AFRICA

DEREK PRINGLE, the former England all-rounder, was born and raised in Nairobi and was a 16-year-old schoolboy when he saw his father Don represent East Africa at the 1975 World Cup. Here, he looks at the future for cricket in Zimbabwe and his beloved Kenya.

Andy Flower and Henry Olonga's standing in the pantheon of Zimbabwe's sportsmen and women has not yet been finalized, but the black armbands worn by the pair during the 2003 Cricket World Cup, to signify the death of democracy under the country's president, Robert Mugabe, have already assured them of a place in cricket's rich history.

Few professional sportsmen take a stance likely to cost them their jobs, let alone their lives, so this was an act of bravery worthy of the word – especially as Mugabe is also the patron of the Zimbabwe Cricket Union (ZCU).

Their actions also brought into sharp focus a country whose regime has become so abhorrent as to cause England's World Cup side, under Nasser Hussain, to make moral judgements over whether or not to play their cricket there.

After protracted discussions and a death threat, England did not play in Harare, a decision that arguably cost them a place in the second stage of the World Cup after their no-show handed Zimbabwe four crucial points.

Yet, if that was not a heavy enough price to pay, the fall-out went further as Hussain became increasingly isolated. Within months he had resigned both the Test and one-day captaincy.

For a fairly insignificant cricket power, Zimbabwe has managed to wreak havoc out of all proportion to its clout. Contrary to what many think, sport and politics make an explosive mix and the problem, at least from England's point of view, does not look like going away.

In September 2003, Vodafone, one of English cricket's principle sponsors, revealed they had deep reservations about being associated with England's proposed tour of the country in the autumn of 2004, should Mugabe and his ZANU-PF party henchmen still remain in power.

It is a difficult situation, especially after Zimbabwe's cricketers honoured their commitment to play in England during 2003. For one thing, the ECB risks financial penalty under ICC rules for cancelling tours for anything other than reasons of 'safety and security'. Yet, neither can they afford to lose Vodafone's sponsorship, worth around £4 million annually.

Whenever politics are involved, solutions are rarely simple. Mugabe may be Africa's No. 1 pariah (these days even Libya's Gaddafi has a better profile), but Zimbabwe's cricketers appear to be welcomed everywhere, though small, but vocal, protests did accompany their two Test matches in England last May.

If the interminable talking shop that presaged the World Cup fiasco is to be avoided again, a solution is needed ... and soon. For those banking on Mugabe's removal from power, however, not much will change unless his party goes too.

For meaningful progress, a coalition involving the opposition party, the Movement for Democratic Change (MDC), is the very least that is required. Only then will much-needed overseas aid start flowing again and help to quell the widespread anarchy that has taken hold as a result of food and fuel shortages.

It has left Zimbabwe cricket, granted Test status back in 1992 and with just small pools of the population to pick from, under enormous pressure. For one thing, the dire economic situation with its hyperinflation, has forced many of the better-off to flee in search of financial freedom.

Until recently, Zimbabwe's cricketers came mainly from old white families and the wealthier African ones, the very people who are now leaving the country. Cricket has begun to filter down to the less well-off, but when AIDS, violence and starvation are rife, cricket and its expensive equipment are probably the last things on your mind.

The exodus has eroded Zimbabwe's playing base, though with development projects still well funded (the ZCU is largely financially independent, with offshore accounts), playing numbers – if not quality – have been sustained.

There is still a bias towards the two main cities, Harare and Bulawayo, though projects in Masvingo, Kwekwe and Mutare have also been introduced. While expertise is in short supply, enthusiasm is not, though the ICC could help more by supplying trained coaches and ensuring that the money is spent appropriately.

Maintaining standards is vital and although no country has ever lost its Test status, and although their one-day international form is holding up, Zimbabwe's recent five-day performances have noticeably been worsening.

Although competitive in the past, one former player feels that the Zimbabwe team are now no better than an average English county side. If the decline is not arrested, therefore, the ICC will have to make a judgement over their suitability to continue playing Test cricket – especially if Bangladesh improve as quickly as many are predicting.

Remuneration for the leading players must improve, too, for the ZCU are not cash-strapped. After an acrimonious pay dispute in 1999, Zimbabwe cricket has lost Andy Flower,

Murray Goodwin and Neil Johnson – three of their best players. Their departures weren't all to do with poor pay, of course, but it played its part.

Fast-tracking black Africans into the Test team, as South Africa have tried with mixed results, has mainly brought discord within the team. When you are struggling to compete on the world stage with your best players, merit and not colour can be the only criterion for picking the side.

South Africa have the capacity to absorb the odd political selection, but not Zimbabwe. Happily, players like Tatenda Taibu and Hamilton Masakadza are worthy of their places and should serve Zimbabwe cricket well, both as players and role models for the next decade.

As with every Test-playing nation, television rights have brought untold wealth to the ZCU. Although politically corrupted, financial impropriety is not yet suspected as it is within the Kenya Cricket Association (KCA), a country hoping to follow Zimbabwe's path to Test status.

Kenyan cricket has long been bedevilled by squabbles, though television money from triangular one-day tournaments held in Nairobi over the last ten years has made the stakes far greater.

Accusations that some of it is being filtered off are rife, and sources reveal there has never been a properly audited account of the first televsion deal in 1996, thought to be worth around $US 4 million.

The Kenyan government, under new president Mwai Kibaki, has been looking into the matter, though the KCA still knows enough people in powerful places to prevent close scrutiny. Injunctions are apparently served whenever anyone gets too close.

A few years ago, a paper documenting the 'misappropriation of funds' was read out in parliament, but little came of it. As a result the new Minister for Sport (Kenya has had three in the last three years), Nagib Balala, has set up a sports trust in an effort to bypass corrupters, but it will take years to become effective.

As the international game's governing body, the ICC must act. They have been handed a dossier naming the guilty parties and containing evidence of wrongdoing, but if the ICC's anti-corruption unit have been investigating, it has been kept quiet, and as yet no official action has been taken.

Kenya's route to Test cricket is by no means assured, but before they set out on that journey the KCA must first be made to clean up its act. The ICC should put in their own professional administrators if necessary.

If that is the first prerequisite, a competitive domestic structure must follow. Kenya's progress to the World Cup semi-finals was the fairytale of the tournament and it has given them a taste for even bigger events. Before that can happen, however, a sustainable player base has to be created.

At present, only Nairobi and Mombasa have competitive leagues – enough perhaps to enable the national side to remain competitive in one-day internationals, but not in Tests.

Over the last decade, most of Kenya's first team has come from just two extended African families. African involvement needs to be nourished, though judging from the make-up of Kenya's squad for the Under 19 World Cup, which included just one black African player, politics appear to have set in. What else can explain the non-selection of a wunderkind like 15-year-old Alex Obanda, who is already scoring centuries in Nairobi's senior league?

If the ICC cannot interfere with selection, they might like to explain why a good man like Tom Tikolo, elder brother of Steve, the Kenya captain, has been made redundant in his role as an ICC development officer?

By most accounts, Tikolo senior has done a marvellous job in Uganda and Tanzania and would have done the same in Kenya were it not for the control-freaks at the KCA.

It has long been the ICC's mission to spread cricket's appeal as widely as possible, but having dispensed with the means for expansion to countries like Zimbabwe and Kenya, they need to police the methods.

Until that happens, indeed, Pliny's claim that 'There is always something new out of Africa', is unlikely to include its cricketers.

Derek Pringle is cricket correspondent of the Daily Telegraph.

One of Zimbabwe cricket's lost boys: the talented Murray Goodwin now plies his trade with Sussex.

ZIMBABWE

By Telford Vice

Moustaches abounded in a heaving Bulawayo pub on the night of 3 March 2003. Alas, Salvador Dali's was not among them. Which was a pity, because it needed the Bradman of surrealism to make sense – or even exquisite nonsense – of the scene. Particularly to this watching South African.

And sense was needed on this night above all others, as the startling truth that South Africa were about to become first-round casualties in the World Cup beamed down relentlessly from television screens that hovered above the smoke and sweaty noise.

The Bulawayo boys seemed happier about that impending fact than they would be when their own Zimbabwe side qualified for the Super Six stage of the competition, and they celebrated 'big brother's' untimely demise with gusto. Such is life in Robert Mugabe's fiefdom. Unvarnished reality is simply too daunting to face, so it is glossed luridly in fantasy.

If that entails a bunch of farmers as beefy as their herds becoming one with lithe Sri Lankans for an evening, so be it – all the better then to protest obliquely at the immoral inaction of the South African government on the horrors confronting their northern neighbours.

Cricket is usually the safest corner of this fantasy realm – win, lose or draw – because it is a place where, despite rigged elections, brutally wielded power, or rampant disease, the bars are always happily raucous. So much so that the uninformed would never guess that the mansion that hulks across the road from the ever-merry Harare Sports Club is Mugabe's own lair.

But sometimes Zimbabwe's reality invades its fantasy world – 10 February 2003 in Harare was one such time.

It began like any other match day in the Zimbabwean capital. Spectators trickled steadily towards the ground, trying to keep their minds on the pungency of a succulent summer morning and off the bayonets glinting from the muzzles of the AK47s gripped by Mugabe's soldiers nearby.

In the press box, journalists were trying to find a reason to become enthusiastic about reporting on the barely consequential matter of Zimbabwe versus Namibia. That reason was handed to each of us minutes before the first ball was bowled – every copy was signed by the authors, Andy Flower and Henry Olonga.

'We cannot in good conscience take to the field and ignore the fact that millions of our compatriots are starving, unemployed and oppressed… In all the circumstances we have decided that we will each wear a black armband for the duration of the World Cup… In doing so we are mourning the death of democracy in our beloved Zimbabwe.'

Thus the chain of events was set in motion that would lead to Flower opting for exile in England and Australia, and to Olonga having to flee from Zimbabwean secret police.

Another sad consequence of this saga was the seemingly irrevocable souring of the years of close friendship shared by Flower and his captain, Heath Streak, whose public support for World Cup matches to be played in Zimbabwe was as mealy-mouthed as it was controversial.

Brothers in arms – and armbands: Henry Olonga and Andy Flower, cricket's bravest men.

Another Harare match day dawned three days later. This time there was no statement, no crowd, no teams. No match, in fact.

It was to have been the highlight of the season, the World Cup game against England. A visit by an International Cricket Council delegation to assess player safety, the considered pronouncements of far-flung governments on whether the tournament should visit Zimbabwe at all, and umpteen meetings between the England players and officials of their Board, had kept the focus on the match mercilessly tight.

It was eventually decided that Zimbabwe was not safe for Nasser Hussain and his team, and the casting vote was a death threat issued by the so-called Sons and Daughters of Zimbabwe. That no one in Zimbabwean politics had ever heard of the organization was beside the point.

The Australians duly turned up for their Bulawayo match. They jetted in from Johannesburg cocooned in security, and scampered back 31-and-a-half hours later.

That was less time than some of the 20 spectators who were arrested at the match for wearing T-shirts emblazoned with political messages spent in jail. Two of them were 15-year-olds. One of the children, a girl, was released unharmed the next day. The other, a boy, was not as fortunate. He could not recognize his parents when the police were done with him. Either – doctors said – due to sheer trauma, being injected with an unknown substance or as a result of electrocution.

The police had another busy afternoon at the match against Holland, arresting 42 spectators. Two of them had paraded a sign that read: 'Zimbabwe needs justice.' Another two had hoisted a banner proclaiming: 'Mugabe = Hitler.' The rest had merely voiced their agreement.

The washed-out game against Pakistan ushered Zimbabwe into the second round, where they fell victim to the irresistible Kenyans in Bloemfontein. It was difficult to avoid the observation that Kenya surged to the semi-finals on a wave of optimism generated by their country's renewed commitment to democracy.

Zimbabwe's season, meanwhile, also featured a home series against Pakistan, and a tour to England after the World Cup.

Both were failures on the field and soaked in desperation off it. There were reports of Zimbabwe's teams being vetted by politicians, and it was said that Streak toed the line in return for his family's farm being left untouched by government-supported land invaders.

Hardly an eyebrow was raised when a summer of tumult ended with Alistair Campbell, Guy Whittall and Gavin Rennie having followed Flower and Olonga into the international sunset.

Zimbabwe now needs all the good men it can find, and they were a few of its best.

Heath Streak, the Zimbabwe captain, offered controversial public support for the World Cup matches.

ONE DAY INTERNATIONALS v. PAKISTAN
Match One
23 November 2002 at Bulawayo
Pakistan 302 for 4 (50 overs) (Yousuf Youhana 141*,
Inzamam-ul-Haq 55, Saleem Elahi 53)
Zimbabwe 295 for 9 (50 overs) (A Flower 77,
CN Evans 68, AM Blignaut 55)
Pakistan won by 7 runs

Match Two
24 November 2002 at Bulawayo
Pakistan 344 for 5 (50 overs) (Saleem Elahi 107,
Yousuf Youhana 76*, Taufeeq Umar 76)
Zimbabwe 140 for 6 (33 overs) (SM Ervine 61*,
Wasim Akram 4 for 22)
Pakistan won by 204 runs

Match Three
27 November 2002 at Harare
Pakistan 323 for 3 (50 overs) (Saleem Elahi 108,
Yousuf Youhana 100*, Taufeeq Umar 68)
Zimbabwe 275 for 7 (50 overs) (MA Vermeulen 79,
A Flower 63, GW Flower 54)
Pakistan won by 48 runs

Match Four
30 November 2002 at Harare
Zimbabwe 210 (49.5 overs) (GW Flower 105*,
Mohammad Sami 4 for 41)
Pakistan 211 for 2 (35.4 overs) (Faisal Iqbal 100*,
Younis Khan 56)
Pakistan won by 8 wickets

Match Five
1 December 2002 at Harare
Pakistan 300 for 7 (50 overs) (Younis Khan 90,
Yousuf Youhana 88)
Zimbabwe 230 (45.3 overs) (A Flower 72)
Pakistan won by 70 runs

ONE DAY INTERNATIONALS v. KENYA
Match One
8 December 2002 at Harare
Kenya 211 (50 overs) (HS Modi 55)
Zimbabwe 17 for 1 (5.1 overs)
No result

Match Two
11 December 2002 at Kwekwe
Zimbabwe 273 for 4 (50 overs) (TJ Friend 91,
ADR Campbell 71, A Flower 58*)
Kenya 181 for 6 (44 overs) (KO Otieno 54)
Zimbabwe won by 47 runs – DL Method: target 229 in 4 overs.

Match Three
15 December 2002 at Bulawayo
Kenya 133 (29 overs) (HK Olonga 6 for 28)
Zimbabwe 136 for 1 (16 overs) (AM Blignaut 63*,
MA Vermeulen 62*)
Zimbabwe won by 9 wickets

FIRST TEST – ZIMBABWE v. PAKISTAN
9–13 November 2002 at Harare

PAKISTAN

	First Innings		Second Innings	
Taufeeq Umar	c A Flower b Blignaut	75	c Taibu b Blignaut	111
Saleem Elahi	c Campbell b Blignaut	2	c Campbell b Olonga	0
Younis Khan	c Ebrahim b Blignaut	40	c Campbell b Olonga	8
Inzamam-ul-Haq	c sub b Olonga	39	c GW Flower b Olonga	112
Yousuf Youhana	lbw b Price	63	c Taibu b Blignaut	0
Hasan Raza	c Campbell b Mahwire	46	c Blignaut b Price	11
*Kamran Akmal	b Price	0	b Price	38
Saqlain Mushtaq	c A Flower b Whittall	2	not out	29
Waqar Younis (capt)	lbw b Blignaut	2	b Blignaut	0
Shoaib Akhtar	c GW Flower b Blignaut	1	c Taibu b Olonga	16
Mohammad Sami	not out	0	c GW Flower b Olonga	17
Extras	lb 2, w 4, nb 9	15	b 4, lb 3, w 11, nb 9	27
		285		**369**

	First Innings				Second Innings			
	O	M	R	W	O	M	R	W
Blignaut	21	4	79	5	20	1	81	3
Olonga	16	2	46	1	17.5	1	93	5
Mahwire	14.5	2	58	1	14	4	60	0
Price	16	4	56	2	24	5	66	2
Whittall	22	10	44	1	14	5	62	0

Fall of Wickets
1-7, 2-122, 3-125, 4-217, 5-246, 6-254, 7-262, 8-271, 9-274
1-10, 2-25, 3-205, 4-207, 5-238, 6-292, 7-318, 8-318, 9-339

ZIMBABWE

	First Innings		Second Innings	
DD Ebrahim	c Inzamam-ul-Haq b Sami	31	b Shoaib Akhtar	69
H Masakadza	c Akmal b Sami	9	c Elahi b Shoaib Akhtar	0
ADR Campbell (capt)	b Shoaib Akhtar	2	c Akmal b Sami	30
GW Flower	lbw b Waqar Younis	31	c Akmal b Saqlain Mushtaq	69
A Flower	c Akmal b Sami	29	c & b Shoaib Akhtar	67
GJ Whittall	b Shoaib Akhtar	7	c Khan b Saqlain Mushtaq	2
*T Taibu	not out	51	lbw b Waqar Younis	28
AM Blignaut	c Raza b Sami	50	c Khan b Saqlain Mushtaq	12
NB Mahwire	c Khan b Saqlain Mushtaq	4	lbw b Waqar Younis	3
RW Price	c Khan b Saqlain Mushtaq	2	not out	5
HK Olonga	b Shoaib Akhtar	3	b Shoaib Akhtar	5
Extras	lb 1, w 2, nb 3	6	b 8, lb 6, w 1, nb 5	20
		225		**310**

	First Innings				Second Innings			
	O	M	R	W	O	M	R	W
Waqar Younis	14	3	58	1	16	1	73	2
Shoaib Akhtar	14.5	1	43	3	18.3	4	75	4
Sami	19	3	53	4	15	3	50	1
Saqlain Mushtaq	19	5	70	2	31	5	98	3
Taufeeq Umar	–	–	–	–	1	1	0	0

Fall of Wickets
1-36, 2-41, 3-43, 4-76, 5-93, 6-136, 7-199, 8-203, 9-209
1-4, 2-51, 3-162, 4-201, 5-203, 6-251, 7-280, 8-291, 9-301

Umpires: DL Orchard & S Venkataraghavan
Toss: Zimbabwe

Pakistan won by 119 runs

SECOND TEST – ZIMBABWE v. PAKISTAN
16–20 November 2002 at Bulawayo

ZIMBABWE

	First Innings		Second Innings	
DD Ebrahim	lbw b Waqar Younis	5	lbw b Waqar Younis	7
MA Vermeulen	lbw b Shoaib Akhtar	2	lbw b Waqar Younis	26
ADR Campbell (capt)	c Akmal b Saqlain Mushtaq	46	b Sami	62
GW Flower	lbw b Saqlain Mushtaq	54	b Shoaib Akhtar	43
A Flower	c Inzamam b Shoaib Akhtar	30	lbw b Waqar Younis	13
H Masakadza	c Akmal b Saqlain Mushtaq	0	c Youhana b Saqlain Mushtaq	16
*T Taibu	c Akmal b Saqlain Mushtaq	15	c Youhana b Younis	37
AM Blignaut	c Umar b Saqlain Mushtaq	0	st Akmal b Saqlain Mushtaq	41
ML Nkala	not out	10	c Akmal b Saqlain Mushtaq	14
RW Price	b Saqlain Mushtaq	1	b Sami	12
HK Olonga	b Saqlain Mushtaq	8	not out	3
Extras	lb 3, w 1, nb 3	7	lb 5, nb 2	7
		178		**281**

	First Innings				Second Innings			
	O	M	R	W	O	M	R	W
Waqar Younis	13	6	20	1	21.2	4	78	4
Shoaib Akhtar	16	3	39	2	12	4	61	1
Mohammad Sami	15	3	38	0	19	6	47	2
Saqlain Mushtaq	25.5	2	66	7	38	9	89	3
Taufeeq Umar	2	0	12	0	-	-	-	-
Hasan Raza	-	-	-	-	1	0	1	0

Fall of Wickets
1-4, 2-8, 3-94, 4-119, 5-119, 6-155, 7-159, 8-161, 9-170
1-28, 2-37, 3-125, 4-146, 5-171, 6-171, 7-226, 8-248, 9-265

PAKISTAN

	First Innings		Second Innings	
Taufeeq Umar	c Taibu b Olonga	34	not out	21
Saleem Elahi	b Olonga	27	not out	30
Younis Khan	lbw b Blignaut	52		
Inzamam-ul-Haq	b Price	11		
Yousuf Youhana	b Price	159		
Hasan Raza	b Olonga	4		
*Kamran Akmal	lbw b Nkala	56		
Saqlain Mushtaq	c sub b Price	14		
Mohammad Sami	c Campbell b Blignaut	1		
Waqar Younis (capt)	c Ebrahim b Price	6		
Shoaib Akhtar	not out	9		
Extras	b 10, lb 5, w 2, nb 8, pen 5	30	b 1, w 1, nb 4	6
		403	(0 wkt)	**57**

	First Innings				Second Innings			
	O	M	R	W	O	M	R	W
Blignaut	22.4	5	75	2	-	-	-	-
Olonga	20	4	69	3	4.3	0	35	0
Price	51.3	14	116	4	4	1	21	0
Nkala	25	4	93	1	-	-	-	-
GW Flower	12	4	26	0	-	-	-	-
A Flower	0.2	0	4	0	-	-	-	-

Fall of Wickets
1-63, 2-64, 3-82, 4-209, 5-225, 6-346, 7-374, 8-387, 9-387

Umpires: DL Orchard & S Venkataraghavan
Toss: Zimbabwe

Pakistan won by 10 wickets

SERIES AVERAGES
Zimbabwe v. Pakistan

ZIMBABWE

Batting	M	Inns	NO	Runs	HS	Av	100	50	c/st
GW Flower	2	4	0	197	69	49.25	-	2	3/-
T Taibu	2	4	1	131	51*	43.66	-	1	4/-
ADR Campbell	2	4	0	140	62	35.00	-	1	5/-
A Flower	2	4	0	139	67	34.75	-	1	2/-
DD Ebrahim	2	4	0	112	69	28.00	-	1	2/-
AM Blignaut	2	4	0	103	50	25.75	-	1	1/-
ML Nkala	1	2	1	24	14	24.00	-	-	-/-
MA Vermeulen	1	2	0	28	26	14.00	-	-	-/-
RW Price	2	4	1	20	12	6.66	-	-	-/-
HK Olonga	2	4	1	19	8	6.33	-	-	-/-
H Masakadza	2	4	0	25	16	6.25	-	-	-/-
GJ Whittall	1	2	0	9	7	4.50	-	-	-/-
NB Mahwire	1	2	0	7	4	3.50	-	-	-/-

Bowling	Overs	Mds	Runs	Wkts	Av	Best	5/inn	10m
AM Blignaut	63.4	9	235	10	23.50	5-79	1	-
HK Olonga	58.2	7	243	9	27.00	5-93	1	-
RW Price	95.3	24	259	8	32.37	4-116	-	-
ML Nkala	25	5	93	1	93.00	1-93	-	-
GJ Whittall	36	15	106	1	106.00	1-44	-	-
NB Mahwire	28.5	6	118	1	118.00	1-58	-	-

Also bowled: A Flower 0.2-0-4-0; GW Flower 12-4-26-0

PAKISTAN

Batting	M	Inns	NO	Runs	HS	Av	100	50	c/st
Taufeeq Umar	2	4	1	241	111	80.33	1	1	1/-
Yousuf Youhana	2	3	0	222	159	74.00	1	1	2/-
Inzamam-ul-Haq	2	3	0	162	112	54.00	1	-	2/-
Younis Khan	2	3	0	100	52	33.33	-	1	4/-
Kamran Akmal	2	3	0	94	56	31.33	-	1	8/1
Saqlain Mushtaq	2	3	1	45	29*	22.50	-	-	-/-
Hasan Raza	2	3	0	61	46	20.33	-	-	1/-
Saleem Elahi	2	4	1	59	30*	19.66	-	-	1/-
Shoaib Akhtar	2	3	1	26	16	13.00	-	-	1/-
Mohammad Sami	2	3	1	18	17	9.00	-	-	-/-
Waqar Younis	2	3	0	8	6	2.66	-	-	-/-

Bowling	Overs	Mds	Runs	Wkts	Av	Best	5/inn	10m
Saqlain Mushtaq	113.5	21	323	15	21.53	7-66	1	1
Shoaib Akhtar	61.2	12	218	10	21.80	4-75	-	-
Mohammad Sami	68	15	188	7	26.85	4-53	-	-
Waqar Younis	64.2	14	229	8	28.62	4-78	-	-

Also bowled: Hasan Raza 1-0-1- 0; Taufeeq Umar 3-1-12-0

BANGLADESH

By Qamar Ahmed

At home and away, Bangladesh remained the whipping boys of the world game. Failing to win a Test or a one-day international during the year, they were faced with scathing criticism both at home and abroad.

Their enraged fans even set on fire an effigy of their Cricket Board president, Asghar Ali, in front of the board's office at Dhaka after Bangladesh failed to win a single match in the World Cup and after their defeat by one of the minnows, Canada.

Since entering the Test arena in November 2000, they have endured much misery. Their only victory in an international match remains the dubious win over Pakistan in the 1999 World Cup in England.

The past year ended with whitewashes by Pakistan in both the three-match Test series and also in the five-match one-day series. That meant they had lost 23 of their 24 Tests. Their only Test draw, against Zimbabwe in Dhaka, occurred because of rain.

It goes to their credit, however, that they were able to keep Australia in the field in the second Test at Cairns until the fourth day before losing by an innings and 98 runs – which completed a 2–0 series loss.

And had Inzamam-ul-Haq not scored that masterly unbeaten 138 when Pakistan had tottered on 148 for 6 as they chased 261 in the final Test at Multan, Bangladesh may have had their first taste of victory at Test level. Pakistan, though, took that series 3–0 and also won the one-day contest 5–0.

Darren Lehmann's 110 and 177 in the Tests at Darwin and Cairns and his captain Steve Waugh's unbeaten 100 and 156 took a heavy toll on the Bangladesh bowlers, although Waugh himself did have comforting and encouraging words for their effort in Australia. That is more than can be said for former Aussie fast bowler Dennis Lillee, who launched into a rather harsh attack on Bangladesh's status as a Test-playing nation.

New man in charge: Dav Whatmore, the former Sri Lankan coach, was appointed as the new national coach of Bangladesh.

In an article in an Australian newspaper, Lillee wrote: 'Low-ranked countries like Bangladesh and Zimbabwe should be stripped of Test status. Playing against them is nothing more than a golden opportunity to get easy wickets, easy runs and easy money.'

Perhaps Lillee failed to realize that it took New Zealand 26 years and 45 Tests to win their first match, when they beat the West Indies at Auckland in 1955–56, India 19 years and 25 Tests before they won against England in 1951–52 and South Africa 17 years and 12 Tests before they triumphed against England in 1905–06.

At least the above-mentioned countries had a long tradition of the game fully entrenched in their culture before they became Test countries. Bangladesh, however, is lacking in that, and therefore has much more ground to catch up.

Even when the region was part of Pakistan, it could produce only one Test cricketer in Niaz Ahmed, and he was not of Bengali stock. Football has always been the passion of the people of this region. They were lucky, therefore, to have been

Habibul Bashar ... one of Bangladesh's emerging stars, who topped the batting averages in the series against South Africa.

granted full membership of the ICC without cricket being played widely at school, club or university level. This, however, was not their fault.

The good news, nevertheless, is that the development of the game in the country is now accelerating quickly, with the help of good coaches and better playing facilities. Their new national coach, Dav Whatmore, is an experienced campaigner at international level and there are certainly signs of promise in Bangladesh's recent displays.

Following the chastening 2–0 home Test series defeats against both West Indies and South Africa, there were at least some eye-catching individual performances in the 3–0 Test defeat in Pakistan.

Javed Omar and Habibul Bashar scored hundreds at Karachi and Peshawar, while Alok Kapali had the honour of taking a hat-trick at Peshawar, the first Bangladesh bowler to do so.

On the domestic front, Khulana beat Dhaka by three wickets to win the final of the Ispahani Tea national league first-class tournament. Dhaka avenged that defeat, however, by beating Khulana in the final of the Ispahani one-day league by 181 runs.

Sajjadul Hasan, with 447 runs, and Hasanuzzman (444) were the most successful batsmen during the domestic season.

FIRST TEST – BANGLADESH v. WEST INDIES
8–10 December 2002 at Dhaka

BANGLADESH

	First Innings		Second Innings	
Hannan Sarkar	b Collins	0	c Ganga b Drakes	25
Anwar Hossain	c Jacobs b Drakes	2	b Drakes	12
Mohammad Ashraful	c Jacobs b Collins	6	b Drakes	0
Habibul Bashar	c Ganga b Collins	24	lbw b Collins	22
Aminul Islam	lbw b Lawson	5	lbw b Lawson	17
Alok Kapali	lbw b Drakes	52	lbw b Lawson	0
*Khaled Mashud (capt)	b Drakes	22	lbw b Lawson	0
Naimur Rahman	c Gayle b Collins	1	not out	5
Enamul Haque	b Collins	6	c Jacobs b Lawson	0
Tapash Baisya	c Jacobs b Drakes	7	b Lawson	0
Talha Jubair	not out	4	b Lawson	0
Extras	lb 6, w 1, nb 3	10	b 4, lb 3, nb 4	11
		139		87

	First Innings				Second Innings			
	O	M	R	W	O	M	R	W
Collins	17.1	7	26	5	9	2	30	1
Drakes	18	2	61	4	9	3	19	3
Lawson	9	2	24	1	6.5	4	3	6
Powell	10	2	22	0	7	1	28	0

Fall of Wickets
1-0, 2-4, 3-25, 4-40, 5-44, 6-117, 7-118, 8-124, 9-135
1-30, 2-30, 3-44, 4-80, 5-80, 6-80, 7-81, 8-83, 9-87

WEST INDIES

	First Innings	
CH Gayle	c Mashud b Baisya	51
WW Hinds	c Rahman b Baisya	75
RR Sarwan	c Rahman b Jubair	119
S Chanderpaul	c Mashud b Haque	4
MN Samuels	lbw b Jubair	91
D Ganga	run out	40
*RD Jacobs (capt)	not out	91
VC Drakes	c sub b Rahman	15
DB Powell	st Mashud b Ashraful	16
PT Collins	c Bashar b Ashraful	13
JJC Lawson	lbw b Jubair	1
Extras	lb 8, w 3, nb 9	20
		536

	First Innings			
	O	M	R	W
Baisya	34	3	117	2
Jubair	31	3	135	3
Rahman	36	5	118	1
Haque	46	13	101	1
Ashraful	13	0	57	2

Fall of Wickets
1-131, 2-132, 3-150, 4-326, 5-377, 6-417, 7-453, 8-493, 9-527

Umpires: DL Orchard & DR Shepherd
Toss: West Indies

West Indies won by an innings and 310 runs

SECOND TEST – BANGLADESH v. WEST INDIES
16–18 December 2002 at Chittagong

BANGLADESH

	First Innings		Second Innings	
Hannan Sarkar	c Gayle b Powell	15	b Drakes	13
Al Sahariar	lbw b Drakes	25	lbw b Powell	34
Habibul Bashar	c Jacobs b Powell	3	c Jacobs b Collins	0
Sanwar Hossain	c Jacobs b Lawson	36	c Gayle b Lawson	24
Mohammad Ashraful	c Powell b Collins	28	c Sarwan b Lawson	15
Alok Kapali	c Gayle b Collins	2	c Jacobs b Powell	85
*Khaled Mashud (capt)	c Sarwan b Drakes	32	lbw b Drakes	5
Enamul Haque	c Samuels b Lawson	8	not out	11
Tapash Baisya	hit wicket b Powell	5	c Chanderpaul b Powell	0
Manjural Islam	b Collins	21	b Collins	0
Talha Jubair	not out	4	b Collins	0
Extras	lb 5, nb 10	15	b 1, lb 12, w 3, nb 9	25
		194		**212**

	First Innings				Second Innings			
	O	M	R	W	O	M	R	W
Collins	16.1	3	60	3	23	8	58	3
Drakes	9	3	23	2	18	6	52	2
Powell	16	4	51	3	13	2	36	3
Lawson	22	9	55	2	18	5	53	2

Fall of Wickets
1-43, 2-43, 3-48, 4-112, 5-116, 6-125, 7-144, 8-153, 9-189
1-44, 2-45, 3-76, 4-100, 5-126, 6-137, 7-210, 8-210, 9-210

WEST INDIES

	First Innings		Second Innings	
CH Gayle	b Jubair	38	b Baisya	37
WW Hinds	c Mashud b Baisya	14	lbw b Baisya	26
RR Sarwan	c Mashud b Islam	17	c Haque b Islam	13
S Chanderpaul	c Mashud b Haque	16	not out	19
MN Samuels	c Sahariar b Jubair	31	not out	15
D Ganga	c Baisya b Hossain	63		
*RD Jacobs (capt)	c Mashud b Baisya	59		
VC Drakes	run out	26		
DB Powell	b Baisya	1		
PT Collins	not out	12		
JJC Lawson	c Bashar b Baisya	6		
Extras	b 8, lb 4, nb 1	13	lb 1	1
		296	(3 wkts)	**111**

	First Innings				Second Innings			
	O	M	R	W	O	M	R	W
Islam	21	11	34	1	8	2	38	1
Baisya	21.3	2	72	4	9	0	45	2
Jubair	20	5	58	2	3	0	20	0
Haque	19	3	62	1	-	-	-	-
Ashraful	5	0	29	0	1	0	3	0
Hossain	7	1	29	1	-	-	-	-
Kapali	-	-	-	-	0.3	0	4	0

Fall of Wickets
1-16, 2-53, 3-74, 4-99, 5-127, 6-226, 7-264, 8-278, 9-279
1-52, 2-77, 3-81

Umpires: DL Orchard & DR Shepherd
Toss: Bangladesh

West Indies won by 7 wickets

SERIES AVERAGES
Bangladesh v. West Indies

BANGLADESH

Batting	M	Inns	NO	Runs	HS	Av	100	50	c/st
Alok Kapali	2	4	0	139	85	34.75	-	2	-/-
Sanwar Hossain	1	2	0	60	36	30.00	-	-	-/-
Al Sahariar	1	2	0	59	34	29.50	-	-	1/-
Khaled Mashud	2	4	0	59	32	14.75	-	-	6/1
Hannan Sarkar	2	4	0	53	25	13.25	-	-	-/-
Habibul Bashar	2	4	0	49	24	12.25	-	-	2/-
Mohammad Ashraful	2	4	0	49	28	12.25	-	-	-/-
Manjural Islam	1	2	0	21	21	10.50	-	-	-/-
Aminul Islam	1	2	0	17	12	8.50	-	-	-/-
Enamul Haque	2	4	1	25	11*	8.33	-	-	1/-
Anwar Hossain	1	2	0	14	12	7.00	-	-	-/-
Naimur Rahman	1	2	1	6	5*	6.00	-	-	2/-
Talha Jubair	2	4	2	8	4*	4.00	-	-	-/-
Tapash Baisya	2	4	0	12	7	3.00	-	-	1/-

Bowling	Overs	Mds	Runs	Wkts	Av	Best	5/inn	10m
Sanwar Hossain	7	1	29	1	29.00	1-29	-	-
Tapash Baisya	64.3	5	234	8	29.25	4-72	-	-
Manjural Islam	29	13	72	2	36.00	1-34	-	-
Talha Jubair	54	8	213	5	42.60	3-135	-	-
Mohammad Ashraful	19	0	89	2	44.50	2-57	-	-
Enamul Haque	65	16	163	2	81.50	1-62	-	-
Naimur Rahman	36	5	118	1	118.00	1-118	-	-

Also bowled: Alok Kapali 0.3-0-4-0

WEST INDIES

Batting	M	Inns	NO	Runs	HS	Av	100	50	c/st
RD Jacobs	2	2	1	150	91*	150.00	-	2	9/-
MN Samuels	2	3	1	137	91	68.50	-	1	1/-
D Ganga	2	2	0	103	63	51.50	-	1	2/-
RR Sarwan	2	3	0	149	119	49.66	1	-	2/-
CH Gayle	2	3	0	126	51	42.00	-	1	4/-
WW Hinds	2	3	0	115	75	38.33	-	1	-/-
PT Collins	2	2	1	25	13	25.00	-	-	-/-
VC Drakes	2	2	0	41	26	20.50	-	-	-/-
S Chanderpaul	2	3	1	39	19*	19.50	-	-	1/-
DB Powell	2	2	0	17	16	8.50	-	-	1/-
JJC Lawson	2	2	0	7	6	3.50	-	-	-/-

Bowling	Overs	Mds	Runs	Wkts	Av	Best	5/inn	10m
JJC Lawson	55.5	20	135	11	12.27	6-3	1	-
VC Drakes	54	14	155	11	14.09	4-61	-	-
PT Collins	65.2	20	174	12	14.50	5-26	1	-
DB Powell	46	9	137	6	22.83	3-36	-	-

ONE DAY INTERNATIONALS
v. WEST INDIES

Match One
29 November 2002 at Chittagong
West Indies 275 for 7 (50 overs) (RL Powell 88)
Bangladesh 90 for 4 (17 overs)
No result

Match Two
2 December 2002 at Dhaka
West Indies 266 for 4 (50 overs) (RR Sarwan 102*,
MN Samuels 82)
Bangladesh 182 (48 overs) (VC Drakes 4 for 18)
West Indies won by 84 runs

Match Three
3 December 2002 at Dhaka
West Indies 281 for 5 (50 overs) (MN Samuels 77,
CH Gayle 73)
Bangladesh 195 (50 overs) Alok Kapali 89*,
VC Drakes 4 for 33)
West Indies won by 86 runs

FIRST TEST – BANGLADESH v. SOUTH AFRICA
24–28 April 2003 at Chittagong

BANGLADESH

	First Innings		Second Innings	
Javed Omar	lbw b Dawson	28	c Boucher b Ntini	71
Mehrab Hossain	c Boucher b Pollock	6	lbw b Pollock	5
Habibul Bashar	c Gibbs b Dawson	60	c Boucher b Pollock	75
Mohammad Ashraful	c Dippenaar b Adams	12	c Smith b Willoughby	28
Akram Khan	c Rudolph b Adams	13	(7) c Dippenaar b Adams	16
Alok Kapali	c Boucher b Adams	0	(5) c Boucher b Adams	7
Khaled Mahmud (capt)	b Ntini	6	(8) st Boucher b Smith	1
*Mohammad Salim	not out	16	(6) lbw b Adams	0
Tapash Baisya	c Dippenaar b Ntini	4	(10) not out	0
Enamul Haque	b Adams	1	(11) c & b Adams	11
Mashrafe Mortaza	st Boucher b Adams	20	(9) c Pollock b Adams	0
Extras	w 1, nb 6	7	b 5, lb 10, w 6, nb 2	23
		173		**237**

	First Innings				Second Innings			
	O	M	R	W	O	M	R	W
Pollock	11	2	22	1	13	9	12	2
Ntini	17	4	45	2	16	4	37	1
Dawson	13	3	37	2	12	4	48	0
Willoughby	12	5	32	0	18	6	47	1
Adams	12.3	3	37	5	18.4	5	69	5
Smith					5	2	9	1

Fall of Wickets
1-14, 2-87, 3-100, 4-124, 5-124, 6-126, 7-136, 8-144, 9-147
1-7, 2-138, 3-173, 4-183, 5-185, 6-213, 7-224, 8-224, 9-224

SOUTH AFRICA

	First Innings	
GC Smith (capt)	c Salim b Baisya	16
HH Gibbs	c Salim b Mortaza	17
JA Rudolph	not out	222
HH Dippenaar	not out	177
*M V Boucher		
N D McKenzie		
S M Pollock		
P R Adams		
A C Dawson		
M Ntini		
C M Willoughby		
Extras	b 9, lb 6, w 2, nb 21	38
	(2 wkts dec.)	**470**

	First Innings			
	O	M	R	W
Mortaza	24	3	108	1
Mahmud	17	5	56	0
Baisya	23	8	70	1
Haque	33	10	81	0
Kapali	18.5	2	71	0
Ashraful	8	0	31	0
Bashar	7	0	38	0

Fall of Wickets
1-38, 2-41

Umpires: BF Bowden & SA Bucknor
Toss: Bangladesh

South Africa won by an innings and 60 runs

SECOND TEST – BANGLADESH v. SOUTH AFRICA
1–5 May 2003 at Dhaka

SOUTH AFRICA

	First Innings	
GC Smith (capt)	c Ashraful b Baisya	15
HH Gibbs	c Baisya b Rafique	21
JA Rudolph	st Salim b Ashraful	71
HH Dippenaar	c Hossain b Rafique	1
ND McKenzie	lbw b Rafique	7
*MV Boucher	b Rafique	71
SM Pollock	lbw b Mortaza	41
RJ Peterson	c Khan b Ashraful	61
AC Dawson	c Salim b Rafique	10
PR Adams	b Rafique	9
M Ntini	not out	0
Extras	b 6, lb 6, w 1, nb 5, pen 5	23
		330

First Innings	O	M	R	W
Baisya	19	5	67	1
Mortaza	20	3	53	1
Mahmud	14	6	36	0
Rafique	37.2	7	77	6
Kapali	11	2	33	0
Ashraful	10	0	42	2
Hossain	2	0	5	0

Fall of Wickets
1-30, 2-49, 3-51, 4-63, 5-170, 6-219, 7-264, 8-294, 9-330

BANGLADESH

	First Innings		Second Innings	
Javed Omar	c sub b Ntini	11	c Pollock b Adams	27
Mehrab Hossain	c Smith b Pollock	8	run out	14
Habibul Bashar	lbw b Pollock	14	c Boucher b Peterson	33
Mohammad Ashraful	c Pollock b Ntini	15	c Pollock b Peterson	23
Akram Khan	c Boucher b Ntini	13	c Rudolph b Ntini	23
Alok Kapali	run out	1	c Ntini b Dawson	23
Khaled Mahmud (capt)	not out	20	c sub b Peterson	0
*Mohammad Salim	c Boucher b Peterson	7	c Smith b Pollock	26
Mohammad Rafique	c Pollock b Dawson	0	c Boucher b Adams	18
Tapash Baisya	b Dawson	4	not out	8
Mashrafe Mortaza	c Dippenaar b Peterson	1	b Pollock	4
Extras	lb 4, w 1, nb 3	8	b 5, w 1, nb 5	11
		102		**210**

	First Innings				Second Innings			
	O	M	R	W	O	M	R	W
Pollock	8	3	21	2	8	1	21	2
Ntini	11	4	32	3	12	2	37	1
Dawson	7	2	20	2	10	5	12	1
Peterson	8.5	1	22	2	27	13	46	3
Adams	1	0	3	0	19	3	70	2
Smith					7	0	19	0

Fall of Wickets
1-22, 2-22, 3-37, 4-53, 5-60, 6-66, 7-73, 8-77, 9-85
1-46, 2-46, 3-93, 4-119, 5-131, 6-139, 7-163, 8-190, 9-206

Umpires: BF Bowden & SA Bucknor
Toss: South Africa

South Africa won by an innings and 18 runs

SERIES AVERAGES
Bangladesh v. South Africa

BANGLADESH

Batting	M	Inns	NO	Runs	HS	Av	100	50	c/st
Habibul Bashar	2	4	0	182	75	45.50	-	2	-
Javed Omar	2	4	0	137	71	34.25	-	1	-
Mohammad Ashraful	2	4	0	78	28	19.50	-	-	1/-
Mohammad Salim	2	4	1	49	26	16.33	-	-	3/1
Akram Khan	2	4	0	65	23	16.25	-	-	1/-
Mohammad Rafique	1	2	0	18	18	9.00	-	-	-
Khaled Mahmud	2	4	1	27	20*	9.00	-	-	-
Mehrab Hossain	2	4	0	33	14	8.25	-	-	1/-
Tapash Baisya	2	4	2	16	8*	8.00	-	-	1/-
Alok Kapali	2	4	0	31	23	7.75	-	-	-
Mashrafe Mortaza	2	4	0	25	20	6.25	-	-	-
Enamul Haque	1	2	0	12	11	6.00	-	-	-

Bowling	Overs	Mds	Runs	Wkts	Av	Best	5/inn	10m
Mohammad Rafique	37.2	7	77	6	12.83	6-77	1	-
Mohammad Ashraful	18	0	73	2	36.50	2-42	-	-
Tapash Baisya	42	13	137	2	68.50	1-67	-	-
Mashrafe Mortaza	44	6	161	2	80.50	1-53	-	-

Also bowled: Mehrab Hossain 2-0-5-0; Habibul Bashar 7-0-38-0; Enamul Haque 33-10-81-0; Khaled Mahmud 31-11-92-0; Alok Kapali 29.5-4-104-0

SOUTH AFRICA

Batting	M	Inns	NO	Runs	HS	Av	100	50	c/st
JA Rudolph	2	2	1	293	222*	293.00	1	1	2/-
HH Dippenaar	2	2	1	178	177*	178.00	1	-	4/-
MV Boucher	2	1	0	71	71	71.00	-	1	9/2
RJ Peterson	1	1	0	61	61	61.00	-	1	-/-
SM Pollock	2	1	0	41	41	41.00	-	-	5/-
HH Gibbs	2	2	0	38	21	19.00	-	-	1/-
GC Smith	2	2	0	31	16	15.50	-	-	3/-
AC Dawson	2	1	0	10	10	10.00	-	-	-/-
PR Adams	2	1	0	9	9	9.00	-	-	1/-
ND McKenzie	2	1	0	7	7	7.00	-	-	-/-
M Ntini	2	1	1	0	0	*-	-	-	1/-
CM Willoughby	1	0	0	0	0	-	-	-	-/-

Bowling	Overs	Mds	Runs	Wkts	Av	Best	5/inn	10m
SM Pollock	40	15	76	7	10.85	2-12	-	-
RJ Peterson	35.5	14	68	5	13.60	3-46	-	-
PR Adams	51.1	11	179	12	14.91	5-37	2	1
M Ntini	56	14	151	7	21.57	3-32	-	-
AC Dawson	42	14	117	5	23.40	2-20	-	-
GC Smith	12	2	28	1	28.00	1-9	-	-
CM Willoughby	30	11	79	1	79.00	1-47	-	-

OTHER ONE-DAY INTERNATIONAL TOURNAMENTS

PSO TRIANGULAR TOURNAMENT 2002 IN KENYA (Pakistan, Australia and Kenya)

Match One
29 August 2002 at Nairobi
Kenya 133 (30.3 overs) (Abdul Razzaq 4 for 35)
Pakistan 134 for 6 (33.3 overs)
Pakistan won by 4 wickets

Match Two
30 August 2002 at Nairobi
Australia 332 for 5 (50 overs) (ML Hayden 146,
RT Ponting 65)
Pakistan 108 (36 overs) (JN Gillespie 5 for 22)
Australia won by 224 runs

Match Three
1 September at Nairobi
Kenya 179 (42.3 overs) (KO Otieno 59)
Pakistan 181 for 3 (38.4 overs) (Younis Khan 87*,
Misbah-ul-Haq 50*)
Pakistan won by 7 wickets

Match Four
2 September 2002 at Nairobi
Kenya 84 (35.3 overs)
Australia 85 for 2 (17 overs)
Australia won by 8 wickets

Match Five
4 September 2002 at Nairobi
Pakistan 117 (32.3 overs) (B Lee 4 for 32)
Australia 121 for 1 (19.1 overs) (ML Hayden 59*)
Australia won by 9 wickets

Match Six
5 Setember 2002 at Nairobi
Kenya 204 for 9 (50 overs) (MO Odumbe 55,
NM Hauritz 4 for 39)
Australia 205 for 5 (49.1 overs)
(SR Watson 77*)
Australia won by 5 wickets

Final
7 September 2002 at Nairobi
Pakistan 227 (50 overs) (Abdul Razzaq 59,
Misbah-ul-Haq 50, JN Gillespie 5 for 70)
Australia 67 for 1 (9.3 overs)

No result. Match abandoned – rain
*PSO Triangular Tournament shared between
Australia and Pakistan*

ICC CHAMPIONS TROPHY IN SRI LANKA

Pool One
15 September 2002 at Colombo
Australia 296 for 7 (50 overs) (DR Martyn 73)
New Zealand 132 (26.2 overs) (GD McGrath 5 for 37)
Australia won by 164 runs

19 September 2002 at Colombo
Bangladesh 129 (45.2 overs)
Australia 133 for 1 (20.4 overs) (ML Hayden 67*,
AC Gilchrist 54)
Australia won by 9 wickets

23 September 2002 at Colombo
New Zealand 244 for 9 (50 overs) (MS Sinclair 70)
Bangladesh 77 (19.3 overs) (SE Bond 4 for 21)
New Zealand won by 167 runs

Pool Two
14 September 2002 at Colombo
India 288 for 6 (50 overs) (M Kaif 111*, R Dravid 71,
DT Hondo 4 for 62)
Zimbabwe 274 for 8 (50 overs) (A Flower 145,
Z Khan 4 for 45)
India won by 14 runs

18 September 2002 at Colombo
England 298 for 8 (50 overs)
(ME Trescothick 119, N Hussain 75,
DT Hondo 4 for 45)
Zimbabwe 190 for 9 (48 overs) (HH Streak 50*,
RC Irani 4 for 37)
England won by 108 runs

22 September 2002 at Colombo
England 269 for 7 (50 overs)
(ID Blackwell 82, NV Knight 50)
India 271 for 2 (39.3 overs) (V Sehwag 126, SC Ganguly 117*)
India won by 8 wickets

Pool Three
13 September 2002 at Colombo
West Indies 238 for 8 (50 overs)

South Africa 242 for 8 (49 overs)
(JN Rhodes 61, HH Dippenaar 53, M Dillon 4 for 60)
South Africa won by 2 wickets

17 September 2002 at Colombo
West Indies 261 for 6 (50 overs) (BC Lara 111)
Kenya 232 (49.1 overs) (SO Tikolo 93)
West Indies won by 29 runs

20 September 2002 at Colombo
South Africa 316 for 5 (50 overs)
(HH Gibbs 116, GC Smith 69, JH Kallis 60)
Kenya 140 (46.5 overs) (SO Tikolo 69)
South Africa won by 176 runs

Pool Four
12 September 2002 at Colombo
Pakistan 195 (49.4 overs) (Saeed Anwar 52)
Sri Lanka 201 for 2 (36.1 overs)
(ST Jayasuriya 102*, PA de Silva 66*)
Sri Lanka won by 8 wickets

16 September 2002 at Colombo
Sri Lanka 292 for 6 (50 overs) (MS Atapattu 101)
Holland 86 (29.3 overs) (M Muralitharan 4 for 15)
Sri Lanka won by 206 runs

21 September 2002 at Colombo
Holland 136 (50 overs)
Pakistan 142 for 1 (16.2 overs)
(Imran Nazir 59, Shahid Afridi 55*)
Pakistan won by 9 wickets

Semi-finals
25 September 2002 at Colombo
India 261 for 9 (50 overs) (Yuvraj Singh 62, V Sehwag 59)
South Africa 251 for 6 (50 overs) (HH Gibbs 116, JH Kallis 97)
India won by 10 runs

27 September 2002 at Colombo
Australia 162 (48.4 overs)
Sri Lanka 163 for 3 (40 overs) (MS Atapattu 51)
Sri Lanka won by 7 wickets

Final – 29 September 2002 at Colombo
Sri Lanka 244 for 5 (50 overs) (ST Jayasuriya 74, KC Sangakkara 54)
India 14 for 0 (2 overs)
Final rained off.

Final (replay) – 30 September 2002 at Colombo
Sri Lanka 222 for 7 (50 overs) (DPMD Jayawardene 77,

RP Arnold 56)
India 38 for 1 (8.4 overs)
No result. Rained off. Trophy shared.

CHERRY BLOSSOM SHARJAH CUP 2003 (Pakistan, Zimbabwe, Sri Lanka and Kenya)

Match One
3 April 2003 at Sharjah
Pakistan 278 for 7 (50 overs) (Abdul Razzaq 76*, Younis Khan 67)
Zimbabwe 210 (44.1 overs) (DA Marillier 59)
Pakistan (6pts) won by 68 runs

Match Two
4 April 2003 at Sharjah
Sri Lanka 223 for 6 (50 overs) (KC Sangakkara 100*)
Pakistan 225 for 3 (47.2 overs) (Yousuf Youhana 64*, Younis Khan 57*, Mohammad Hafeez 50)
Pakistan (5pts) won by 7 wickets – Sri Lanka (1pt)

Match Three
5 April 2003 at Sharjah
Kenya 225 for 6 (50 overs) (DO Obuya 57)
Zimbabwe 230 for 5 (49 overs) (DA Marillier 100, GW Flower 59)
Zimbabwe (5pts) won by 5 wickets – Kenya (1pt)

Match Four
6 April 2003 at Sharjah
Sri Lanka 256 for 5 (50 overs) (KC Sangakkara 103*)
Kenya 127 (37.5 overs)
Sri Lanka (6pts) won by 129 runs

Match Five
7 April 2003 at Sharjah
Sri Lanka 193 (49.1 overs)
Zimbabwe 194 for 6 (48.4 overs) (GW Flower 61*)
Zimbabwe (5pts) won by 4 wickets – Sri Lanka (1pt)

Match Six
8 April 2003 at Sharjah
Pakistan 286 for 8 (50 overs) (Shoaib Malik 76)
Kenya 143 (31.4 overs) (MO Odumbe 54, Mohammad Sami 4 for 25)
Pakistan (6pts) won by 143 runs

Final
10 April 2003 at Sharjah
Zimbabwe 168 (49.1 overs) (T Taibu 74*)
Pakistan 172 for 2 (35.2 overs) (Taufeeq Umar 81*, Yousuf Youhana 61*)
Pakistan won by 8 wickets

ENGLAND: FIRST-CLASS COUNTIES FORM CHARTS

DERBYSHIRE

DURHAM

ESSEX

GLAMORGAN

GLOUCESTERSHIRE

HAMPSHIRE

KENT

LANCASHIRE

LEICESTERSHIRE

MIDDLESEX

NORTHAMPTONSHIRE

NOTTINGHAMSHIRE

SOMERSET

SURREY

SUSSEX

WARWICKSHIRE

WORCESTERSHIRE

YORKSHIRE

DERBYSHIRE CCC

FIRST–CLASS MATCHES
BATTING

Match	DG Cork	MJ Di Venuto	LD Sutton	G Welch	KJ Dean	AI Gait	CWG Bassano	Mohammad Ali	RM Khan	NRC Dumelow	SA Selwood	M Kaif	DR Hewson	T Lungley	LJ Wharton	SD Stubbings	PMR Havell	Shahid Afridi	Hasan Adnan	NEL Gunter	KM Krikken	Extras	Total	Wickets	Result
v. Glamorgan (Derby) 18-21 April	37	121	120	37	20	0	0	31			20			8*				14				12	420	10	
	31	61	37*	25*		6	52				10							1				22	245	6	D
v. Somerset (Derby) 30 April-3 May	25	17	38	14	1*	41	0	0			0		37					4				13	190	10	
	6	36	23*	9*		63	0				18		13					6				23	197	6	D
v. Yorkshire (Headingley) 9-12 May	92	50	127	0	0*	32	23	5			2		57	7								27	422	10	
		77	22*			25	53*				14		3									20	214	4	W
v. Durham (Chester-le-Street) 21-24 May	0	150	9	20	15	5		1			20		9		0*			0				15	244	10	
	52	4	10	23*	1	10		4			8		10		1			67				2	192	10	L
v. Worcestershire (Derby) 30 May-1 June	24	54	3	9	0	50	3*	2	5	17			0									12	179	10	
	52	4	25	51*	21	18	5	32	6	11			4									16	245	10	L
v. Glamorgan (Swansea) 4-7 June	18	29	28	16	15	23	8				13	18	20		0*							21	209	10	
		0	29	31	5	0	0				6	3	29		0*							13	116	9	L
v. Northamptonshire (Northampton) 27-29 June	16	10	25	0	3	7	1		52*		28		7		1							10	160	10	
	2	29	3	7	2	29	17*		11		0		0		1							5	106	10	L
v. Yorkshire (Derby) 2-5 July	1	27	5	0	0	17	0		60*		0		0		6							12	128	10	
	35	74	35	54	30*	6	7		25			87	8		1							21	383	10	L
v. Gloucestershire (Derby) 9-11 July	0	17	5	3	6	12	3	14*	0		12	8										9	89	10	
	39	148	81*	0	1	3	3	2	5		6	39										29	356	10	L
v. Worcestershire (Worcester) 15-18 July	12	12		28	4		16	11	15		0	31				5*				14		15	163	10	
	7	2		11*	0		4	0	0		0					30				1		11	96	10	L
v. Durham (Derby) 24-27 July	39*	143	20				44*		7		62	31										15	361	5	
	1	8	36				0		23		88	7			10*					9*		22	204	7	D
v. Hampshire (Southampton) 13-14 August	40	20	18	27	12	39			0	75	29	36								20*		25	341	10	
	–	–	–																			–	–	–	W
v. Northamptonshire (Derby) 20-22 August	1	0	0	3	0		1	1*	76	15	1	31										9	138	10	
	12	116	56	8	1		0	0	8	6*	33	14										24	278	9	L
v. South Africa (Derby) 28-30 August			46*	15*		2	6		14							44						9	136	4	
	–	–	–																			–	–	–	D
v. Gloucestershire (Bristol) 3-6 September	10	75	34	1		10			39		24		0			103	0*					24	321	10	
	19	80	41	6	2	12			10		11		13			63	2*					10	269	10	L
v. Somerset (Taunton) 10-13 September	0	46	10	7		110	6		24	26						93	7*		59*			12	400	9	
	1	23	49			49	0		22	6						9	1*		32			3	196	10	L
v. Hampshire (Derby) 17-20 September	20	35	17	14		63			18	6	1					30	0*		84			29	317	10	
	1*	52	30	17		71			0	58	19					8	0		14			19	289	10	L
Matches	16	16	16	15	14	13	12	10	9	9	9	8	8	5	5	4	3	3	2	2	1				
Innings	29	31	30	27	24	25	22	17	16	17	17	15	16	8	9	7	6	6	4	2	2				
Not Out	2	0	5	6	3	0	3	3	0	3	0	0	0	1	5	0	5	0	1	2	0				
Highest Score	92	150	127	54	30*	110	53*	31	76	75	88	87	57	29	30	103	7*	67	84	20*	14				
Runs	593	1520	982	429	148	664	277	101	336	347	333	332	222	80	46	350	10	92	189	29	15				
Average	21.96	49.03	39.28	20.43	7.05	26.56	14.58	7.21	21.00	24.79	19.59	22.13	13.88	11.43	11.50	50.00	10.00	15.33	63.00	29.00	7.50				
100s	0	5	2	0	0	1	0	0	0	0	0	0	0	0	0	1	0	0	0	0	0				
50s	3	8	2	2	0	4	2	0	2	3	2	1	1	0	0	2	0	1	2	0	0				
Catches/Stumpings	11/0	25/0	26/2	3/0	4/0	10/0	7/0	1/0	3/0	2/0	3/0	5/0	4/0	2/0	4/0	1/0	2/0	0/0	1/0	0/0	1/0				

Home Ground: Derby
Address: County Ground, Nottingham Road, Derby DE21 6DA
Tel: 01332 383211
Fax: 01332 290521
Email: derby@ecb.co.uk
Directions: By road: From the south, exit M1 at junction 25, follow A52 into Derby, take the fourth exit off Pentagon Island. From the north, exit M1 at junction 28, join A38 into Derby and then follow directional signs.
Capacity: 4,000

Other grounds used: Chesterfield
Year formed: 1870

Chief Executive: John Smedley
Other posts: *Commercial Manager:* Keith Stevenson; *County Development Officer:* Howard Dytham; *Head Groundsman:* Neil Godrich
First XI Coach: David Houghton
Captain: Michael Di Venuto
County colours: Blue, brown and gold

Honours

County Championship
1936
Sunday League/NCL
1990
Benson & Hedges Cup
1993
Gillette Cup/NatWest/C&G Trophy
1981

Website:
www.dccc.org.uk

DERBYSHIRE CCC

FIRST-CLASS MATCHES — BOWLING

First-Class Matches	KJ Dean	DG Cork	G Welch	Mohammad Ali	NRC Dumelow	T Lungley	LJ Wharton	PMR Havell	Shahid Afridi	NEL Gunter	MJ Di Venuto	DR Hewson	RM Khan	M Kaif	SA Selwood	Overs	Total	Byes/Leg-byes	Wickets	Run outs
Glamorgan (Derby) 18-21 April	17-3-65-2 / 6-2-22-0	24.2-5-83-1 / 14-1-61-3	16-3-66-0 / 8-4-10-1	17-3-79-4 / 8-0-56-0			6-0-25-1 / 10-3-23-1		10-2-29-2 / 22.4-6-69-2							90.2 / 68.4	352 / 253	5 / 12	10 / 7	
Somerset (Derby) 30 April-3 May	21-6-90-1	37-11-74-5	24.1-7-64-2	18-1-118-2					12-5-22-0							112.1	397	29	10	
Yorkshire (Headingley) 9-12 May	12.3-1-39-4 / 23-8-63-2	21-5-69-2 / 16-3-44-0	16-4-39-4 / 20-3-74-4	8-0-48-0 / 7.4-0-26-3	8-2-33-0 / 5-0-26-0											65.3 / 71.4	230 / 240	2 / 7	10 / 10	/ 1
Durham (Chester-le-Street) 21-24 May	20.4-11-41-4 / 10-5-19-1	19-2-65-0 / 23-8-49-2	21-10-53-3 / 26.4-5-60-5	14-2-49-2 / 4-3-2-2			16-3-48-1 / 3-1-5-0		10-2-27-0		3-0-5-0					103.4 / 66.4	317 / 149	29 / 14	10 / 10	
Worcestershire (Derby) 30 May-1 June	21-7-41-3 / 2-0-16-0		24.1-9-70-2 / 3-0-22-0	26-6-81-1	12-0-124-4 / 1.5-0-10-1	9-1-41-0 / 1-0-3-0										92.1 / 7.5	374 / 51	17 / -	10 / 1	
Glamorgan (Swansea) 4-7 June	22.5-4-84-3	21-5-71-2	25-7-78-1			20-3-101-4	9-2-40-0									97.5	395	21	10	
Northamptonshire (Northampton) 27-29 June	8-2-18-1 / 5-2-9-0		7-3-28-0 / 17-3-55-3		23.4-4-82-5 / 23.2-2-78-5	2-0-15-0	24-7-50-4 / 20-4-70-0							4-1-21-1		64.4 / 69	203 / 243	10 / 10	10 / 10	/ 1
Yorkshire (Derby) 2-5 July	36-7-113-2 / 7-3-12-0	15.5-3-41-1 / 7-0-20-0	41-13-102-6 / 33-0-20-0		21-3-90-0 / 3-0-13-0	16.4-1-84-1						1-0-2-0				130.4 / 20.3	444 / 68	19 / 3	10 / -	
Gloucestershire (Derby) 9-11 July	22-4-85-2 / 8.4-2-42-2	27-3-75-4 / 13-3-47-1	19.2-6-45-2 / 11-1-36-2	16-2-60-2 / 7-0-32-0	2-1-1-0											86.2 / 39.4	277 / 171	11 / 10	10 / 10	
Worcestershire (Worcester) 15-18 July	30-8-95-2	26.2-8-60-4	28-7-81-2	18-6-51-2												102.1	301	14	10	
Durham (Derby) 24-27 July	31-5-138-1 / 6-1-29-1	20.5-3-92-1 / 1.1-0-10-0			14.4-0-91-2		27-4-103-2			13.1-2-48-2 / 6-0-57-1	1-0-11-0		2-1-6-0			108.4 / 14.1	501 / 110	23 / 3	8 / 2	
Hampshire (Southampton) 13-14 August	10-2-31-1 / 10-1-40-1	15.5-7-28-6 / 12-1-39-4	14-4-50-3 / 9.3-2-27-4	8-2-20-1						5-0-30-0 / 3-0-18-0						44.5 / 42.3	143 / 155	4 / 11	10 / 10	
Northamptonshire (Derby) 20-22 August	30.5-3-145-4	21.1-0-83-0	25-2-112-0	23.3-3-118-0				26-1-131-0			2-0-7-0		1-0-7-0		7-0-28-0	136.3	647	16	5	1
South Africa (Derby) 28-30 August	24-7-87-0		28-8-82-0		14.1-4-65-2			29-6-129-4		10-3-81-1						113.1	460	16	7	
Gloucestershire (Bristol) 3-6 September	27-7-98-2 / 9-2-32-0	27.5-7-75-2 / 11-4-37-0	36-8-95-3 / 18-8-37-3	8-3-8-0 / 16-6-51-1				30-8-95-3 / 12-3-34-3				3-0-12-0				131.5 / 66	401 / 209	18 / 18	10 / 8	/ 1
Somerset (Taunton) 10-13 September	22-4-118-2 / 2-0-21-0	20-3-92-6 / 20.3-7-35-4	36-8-95-3 / 18-8-37-3	13-3-83-2 / 17-9-38-2	3-0-39-0 / 29-7-69-3			7-0-66-0 / 8-0-45-1								65 / 76.3	409 / 214	11 / 6	10 / 10	
Hampshire (Derby) 17-20 September		4-0-28-0	41-7-163-4 / 22-0-18-0	36-4-166-2 / 2-0-10-0	26-9-75-1			20.4-1-129-3								127.4 / 4.2	580 / 28	19 / -	10 / -	
Overs	444.3	445.1	483.3	221	214.5	66.2	115	106.4	54.4	45.1	6	4	3	4	7					
Maidens	107	100	121	36	43	6	24	18	15	5	0	0	1	1	0					
Runs	1593	1363	1476	1060	776	350	364	498	147	234	23	14	13	21	28					
Wickets	41	50	53	28	18	7	9	14	4	4	0	0	0	1	0					
Average	38.9	27.3	27.8	37.9	43.1	50.0	40.4	35.6	36.8	58.5	-	-	-	21.0	-					

FIELDING

LD Sutton (26 ct, 2st)
MJ Di Venuto
DG Cork
AI Gait
CWG Bassano
M Kaif
DR Hewson
KJ Dean
LJ Wharton
SA Selwood
RM Khan
G Welch
NRC Dumelow
PMR Havell
T Lungley
Hasan Adnan
SD Stubbings
KM Krikken
Mohammad Ali

DURHAM CCC

FIRST–CLASS MATCHES

BATTING

	GJ Pratt	JJB Lewis	N Peng	P Mustard	MA Gough	GJ Muchall	NC Phillips	VJ Wells	N Killeen	GD Bridge	LE Plunkett	ML Love	Shoaib Akhtar	DR Law	AM Davies	A Pratt	D Pretorius	PD Collingwood	NG Hatch	SJ Harmison	J Srinath	AM Thorpe	ID Hunter	I Pattison	JA Lowe	Extras	Total	Wickets	Result
v. Somerset	8	78	15		14	6	7	20						4		23			0	0*						10	185	10	
(Taunton) 23-26 April	21	50	4		4	4	9	0						35		27			2	13*						11	180	10	L
v. Gloucestershire	0	54	37	2		27	0							2		13	16			7*	10					15	183	10	
(Chester-le-Street) 30 April-3 May	0	55	10	73			1							2		8*					0*					10	159	6	D
v. Durham UCCE	96	6	158	5	19	9*					25*			74		1							47			10	450	8	
(Racecourse) 9-11 May		58	0	101*										13*												8	180	1	D
v. Worcestershire	38	66*	0		22	0	1*							0*		0*					1					19	146	3	
(Stockton) 14-17 May	4	43	0		1	74								0*		0*					1					28	151	7	D
v. Derbyshire	62	52		12	0	15	61	0*				54		3	5	0										53	317	10	
(Chester-le-Street) 21-24 May	2	32		17	9	4	15	0				41		7	3	1*										18	149	10	W
v. Yorkshire	4	124	2	23	10	10	19	0						4		1*								62		21	280	10	
(Headingley) 30 May-1 June	0	66	29	20	43	4	2*	0								2										25	200	10	W
v. Hampshire	43	44	0	15	0	10		10*	0					12											80	21	235	10	
(Southampton) 4-7 June	30	8	7	30	16	31*	10	0						0	0*										0	5	137	9	D
v. India A	10	20	5	2	56	121	19	1					9*				3*						44			43	333	–	
(Chester-le-Street) 27-30 June																										–	–	–	D
v. Worcestershire	23	0	7	4	3	0	36			3	28	5								5*						6	120	10	
(Worcester) 2-4 July	85	53	20	26	11	8	18			15*	0	2								10						17	265	10	L
v. Northamptonshire	150	7	18	16	9	22	6	30			38*	18								5						8	327	10	
(Chester-le-Street) 9-11 July	5	21	36	49	53	1	9*	10			0	8								3						4	199	10	L
v. Yorkshire	51	7	8	32	54	8		42		50		25							4	14*						32	327	10	
(Chester-le-Street) 15-18 July	14	41	30	34	38	30		17		1*		14*														32	251	7	W
v. Derbyshire	4	77	99	70*	36	9		106	13*	4	29															54	501	8	
(Derby) 24-27 July	33*	41*	31	0																						5	110	2	D
v. Somerset	51	2	58	31	19	65	3	26		42		26				3*										19	345	10	
(Chester-le-Street) 30 July-1 August	41	25	1	37	0	20	5	11		8		5*				5										10	168	10	W
v. Glamorgan	36	13	133	30	39	1	0*	49		38	1															15	355	10	
(Cardiff) 13-16 August	18	68	0	3	25	6	0	4	3	36							0*									11	174	10	L
v. Hampshire	66	11	30	4	16	23						273		11						9	1*	35				36	515	10	
(Chester-le-Street) 20-23 August																										–	–	–	W
v. Northamptonshire	26	0	10	23	1		0	12*	25	9								68		11						5	190	10	
(Northampton) 3-5 September	5	22	35	62	0	0	33*	84	0									10		4						8	263	10	L
v. Gloucestershire	1	16	0	31	1	11*	5	0				98	34							11						10	218	10	
(Bristol) 10-13 September	62	28	38	7	11	5					40*	97	14							0						16	318	9	L
v. Glamorgan	59	0	9	5		58*	8	10	0	0	21	50														27	247	10	
(Chester-le-Street) 17-19 September	7	0	16	5		0	0	0	4	37	14	21*														14	118	10	L
Matches	18	18	15	13	13	13	13	12	10	8	7	7	7	6	5	5	4	4	4	4	3	2	2	1	1				
Innings	33	34	25	23	25	25	22	21	18	13	12	13	14	10	8	9	7	7	5	6	5	3	2	1	2				
Not Out	1	2	0	1	0	1	5	1	4	3	5	0	2	1	3	3	3	1	2	3	3	0	0	0	0				
Highest Score	150	124	158	70*	73	121	39	106	26	50	40*	273	37	74	21	27	16	68	5	14*	13*	35	47	62	80				
Runs	1055	1188	743	486	584	620	239	420	110	240	164	778	197	127	64	93	32	169	16	38	24	50	91	62	80				
Average	32.97	37.12	29.72	22.09	23.36	25.83	14.06	21.00	7.86	24.00	23.43	59.85	16.42	14.11	12.80	15.50	8.00	28.17	5.33	12.67	12.00	16.67	45.50	62.00	40.00				
100s	1	1	2	0	0	2	0	1	0	0	0	1	0	0	0	0	0	0	0	0	0	0	0	0	0				
50s	8	11	1	1	4	3	0	2	0	1	0	4	0	1	0	0	0	2	0	0	0	0	0	1	1				
Catches/Stumpings	11/0	5/0	12/0	42/3	8/0	5/0	9/0	11/0	2/0	7/0	2/0	8/0	0/0	1/0	0/0	15/0	3/0	4/0	1/0	2/0	1/0	0/0	0/0	0/0	0/0				

Home Ground: Chester-le-Street
Address: County Ground, Riverside, Chester-le-Street, Co. Durham DH3 3QR
Tel: 0191 387 1717
Fax: 0191 387 1616
Email: marketing@durham-ccc.org.uk
Directions: *By rail:* Chester-le-Street (approx. 5 minutes by taxi or a 10-minute walk). *By road:* Easily accessible from junction 63 of the A1(M). Nearby car parking is available on match days. Disabled access: Viewing points for spectators in wheelchairs; Members' Lounge has induction loop system for members who are hard of hearing; guide dogs allowed into ground.

Capacity: 10,000
Other grounds used: Darlington CC (Feethams); Hartlepool CC; Stockton CC 01642 672835.
Year formed: 1882

Chief Executive: David Harker
Director of Cricket: Geoff Cook
Director of Operations: Lesley Williamson
First Team Coach: Martyn Moxon
Captain: Jonathan Lewis
Second XI Coach: Alan Walker
County colours: Yellow, blue, burgundy

Honours
None yet

Website:
www.durham-ccc.org.uk

DURHAM CCC

FIRST-CLASS MATCHES

BOWLING

	NC Phillips	VJ Wells	N Killeen	GD Bridge	Shoaib Akhtar	LE Plunkett	GJ Muchall	AM Davies	DR Law	NG Hatch	SJ Harmison	PD Collingwood	D Pretorius	MA Gough	J Srinath	ID Hunter	GJ Pratt	I Pattison	Overs	Total	Byes/Leg-byes	Wickets	Run outs
Somerset (Taunton) 23–26 April		11-0-35-3	12-4-31-1							20.4-7-49-3					17-4-46-2				60.4	171	10	10	1
	5.4-1-43-1	5-1-19-0	14-2-57-2							15-8-25-1					16-4-46-0				55.4	197	7	4	
Gloucestershire (Chester-le-Street) 30 April–3 May	14-4-50-2	13-3-28-1							18.2-5-30-4		30-11-58-1	20-5-94-1		24-6-64-1					119.2	341	17	10	
																			–	–	–	–	
Durham UCCE (Racecourse) 9–11 May	29-8-86-2		12-4-35-1				14-7-36-1				13-1-43-0		11-1-33-0		23-3-90-1				102	332	9	5	
	15-1-85-2		11-3-63-2					3-0-23-1			14-4-54-1		5 0 29 0		4-0-25-0				52	285	6	7	1
Worcestershire (Stockton) 14–17 May	15-0-80-0	14-2-58-2					22-2-100-1			29-14-69-3				27-10-70-3					107	395	18	10	1
																			–	–	–	–	
Derbyshire (Chester-le-Street) 21–24 May	31-8-60-3		20-5-49-1						9.3-1-35-1				17-2-96-4						77.3	244	4	10	1
	13-0-49-2		6-1-13-3	9-1-60-0					4-0-20-1				12.2-1-49-4						44.2	192	1	10	
Yorkshire (Headingley) 30 May–1 June	7.4-0-42-1		15-2-46-0			12-1-53-5	4.2-0-13-0						16-2-54-3				5.4-3-7-1		60.4	220	5	10	
			6-1-22-1			7-1-21-2	8-2-26-3						9.4-1-15-4						30.4	93	9	10	
Hampshire (Southampton) 4–7 June	36-7-129-4		28-7-57-0				28-7-109-1	18-3-70-0	22.4-2-71-4					4-2-9-0					136.4	456	11	10	1
																			–	–	–	–	
India A (Chester-le-Street) 27–30 June	34.4-126-4	16-3-41-0					12-1-49-0	31-6-104-0		33-5-77-2				3-1-12-1	18-2-55-2				147	482	18	9	
	4.0-16-0	3-0-18-0						8-3-16-1		12-2-23-2					6-1-21-0				33	95	1	3	
Worcestershire (Worcester) 2–4 July	11-1-40-3	6-1-35-0		13-5-28-1	13-4-55-2						13-3-50-4								56	218	10	10	
	11.5-2-40-2			13-2-33-2	13-0-61-3						14-3-53-2								51.5	198	11	10	1
Northamptonshire (Chester-le-Street) 9–11 July	33.5-9-92-2	14-2-31-1		19-7-49-3	19-5-78-1					21.4-6-66-3									106.4	322	6	10	
	11.1-0-54-0	4-0-14-0		6-1-25-0	6-2-44-0	4-1-26-1				7-1-39-1									38.1	206	4	2	
Yorkshire (Chester-le-Street) 15–18 July		20-10-41-2		34-9-109-2	25-6-87-3					21-3-79-1	29-7-92-2		103-2-45-3						129	448	40	10	
		9-3-20-3		1-1-0-0	10-2-38-4					6-1-20-0									36.3	129	6	10	
Derbyshire (Derby) 24–27 July		4-0-23-0	26-4-94-2	33-10-100-2			16-1-67-1			14-1-70-0				7.4-3-23-2					93	361	7	5	
			12-2-28-1	18-3-61-0			8-0-41-1			10-2-29-2									55.4	204	22	7	1
Somerset (Chester-le-Street) 30 July–1 August			10-4-16-4	11-2-28-0	2-0-8-1		14-4-39-4	3-1-9-0	12-4-36-1										52	139	3	10	
				9.4-2-30-4			7-2-9-4		3-1-17-1										19.4	56	–	10	1
Glamorgan (Cardiff) 13–16 August	44.5-8-144-5	10-3-26-0	17-4-50-1	38-10-114-4					71-4-77-0					2-0-12-0					132.5	444	21	10	
	6.1-0-27-1	2-0-17-0		1-0-1-0					6-0-29-1							1-0-5-0			16.1	86	7	2	
Hampshire (Chester-le-Street) 20–23 August			15-8-30-0	24-6-47-4			18-5-34-2			18-4-57-1	16.1-4-38-3								91.1	211	5	10	
			20.2-6-70-7	8-2-18-0			19-7-49-2			7-3-24-1	7-2-23-0								61.2	189	5	10	
Northamptonshire (Northampton) 3–5 September	35.2-3-160-2		20-5-59-0	42-6-180-3	21-3-91-2						11-0-34-0								129.2	538	14	7	
																			–	–	–	–	
Gloucestershire (Bristol) 10–13 September	43-9-139-2			32-8-98-4			14-3-30-3	12-3-53-0			8-0-36-1								109	374	18	10	
	8-2-51-0			21-1-96-1			17-3-48-4	16-3-54-2			5-0-27-0								67	288	12	7	
Glamorgan (Chester-le-Street) 17–19 September		12.4-3-52-2	16-6-59-2	9-3-26-3	7-1-19-0				16-5-52-2		10-1-49-0								70.4	270	13	10	1
		7-0-45-1	14-2-61-1	26-0-138-1	17-1-84-4				15-0-95-1		4-0-21-0								83	464	20	8	
Overs	400.4	164.4	290	289	183	164	52.2	149	103.3	149.4	161.1	61.1	79	28.4	84	51	1	5.4					
Maidens	63	36	70	59	40	34	8	35	15	28	55	7	13	5	24	6	0	3					
Runs	1513	515	946	996	580	672	216	509	353	484	441	228	317	109	226	191	5	7					
Wickets	38	22	26	25	34	19	5	11	12	13	19	4	16	3	6	3	0	1					
Average	39.8	23.4	36.4	39.8	17.1	35.4	43.2	46.3	29.4	37.2	23.2	57.0	19.8	36.3	37.7	63.7	–	7.0					

FIELDING

P Mustard (42 ct, 3st)
A Pratt
N Peng
VJ Wells
GJ Pratt
NC Phillips
ML Love
MA Gough
GD Bridge
GJ Muchall
JJB Lewis
PD Collingwood
D Pretorius
N Killeen
LE Plunkett
SJ Harmison
DR Law
J Srinath
NG Hatch

ESSEX CCC

FIRST–CLASS MATCHES
BATTING

	JS Foster	A Flower	JD Middlebrook	GR Napier	WI Jefferson	A Habib	RC Irani	DDJ Robinson	JM Dakin	AP Grayson	SA Brant	N Hussain	RS Bopara	Mohammad Akram	JB Grant	AN Cook	ML Pettini	AJ Clarke	JP Stephenson	AP Palladino	RN ten Doeschate	AC McGarry	AGA M McCoubrey	ZK Sharif	JE Bishop	Extras	Total	Wickets	Result
v. Cambridge UCCE	41	91		125	37	45	89	8*	11																	50	497	6	
(Fenner's) 12-14 April			16		102	102		13	90											2*						27	352	3	D
v. Middlesex	32	7	36	56	34	69	83	52	7	0										4*						22	402	10	
(Chelmsford) 18-21 April				18*			23*																			-	41	-	D
v. Warwickshire					20*		42*																			4	66		
(Edgbaston) 23-26 April	24	55	25	9	49	0	87	56	23	28	1*															23	380	10	D
v. Leicestershire	0	14	0*		32	35	4	33	0	0		6				50										14	188	10	
(Leicester) 30 April-3 May	23	20	19		43	15	7	15	14*			26				1										8	191	9	D
v. Lancashire	57	25	12	40	19		0	11	13	23		0	2*													13	215	10	
(Old Trafford) 14-17 May		16		3				8	1*			13*														1	42	3	D
v. Surrey	38	51	29	5	11	0	42	5	59	1		0*														11	252	10	
(Chelmsford) 21-24 May	42	6	13	15*	3	61	9	41	15	19		0														23	247	10	L
v. Nottinghamshire	12	4	0	57	0	31	9	44*	27	0				9												10	203	10	
(Trent Bridge) 30 May-1 June	85	32	3	15	10	151	4	4	20	0				15*												20	359	10	W
v. Middlesex	11	11	1	44	22	15	7	5	0	0*				48												2	166	10	
(Lord's) 4-7 June	15	3	52	3*	30	2		13	24	69				40*												18	269	8	D
v. Kent	44	13	39	19		77	0	47		6*		206		4										21		38	514	10	
(Chelmsford) 27-30 June																										-	-	-	D
v. Lancashire	0	46	9	5		19	19	18	0	1*		54						6								31	208	10	
(Chelmsford) 2-5 July	5	49	21	0*		69	9	3	17	1*		31						5								26	236	9	D
v. Sussex	12	37	14	89*		0	15	35	0	3		95						31								9	340	10	
(Arundel) 9-12 July	1	54	23	10*		53	6	0	71	2		22						6								26	274	10	L
v. Leicestershire	50	127	82*	17	7	7	9					18							5			1		0		28	351	10	
(Southend) 23-26 July		39*	13		54*																					5	111	1	D
v. Kent	0	39	15	16	4	5	52	25					1						7*				0			19	183	10	
(Canterbury) 30 July-1 August	31	83	5	5	5	14	14	42					4						8				0*			24	235	10	L
v. Sussex	31	50	33	34	55	0	3	64	6						0*											7	283	9	
(Colchester) 20-22 August	3	32	5	21*	59	11	38	12	7						10											11	209	9	L
v. Nottinghamshire	58	53	34	5	1		51		47						0	13	20	32*								21	335	10	
(Chelmsford) 3-5 September		45*				38									69*											2	154	1	W
v. Warwickshire	15	13	1	48	33	9								6		0	0	41	75*							15	256	10	
(Chelmsford) 11-14 September	23	28	0	3*	62	18								3		55	78	6	10							16	302	10	L
v. Surrey	36	201*	3	1	0									31		84	70	8	1							29	464	10	
(The Oval) 17-19 September					22									2*		18	4*									3	49	2	W

	JS Foster	A Flower	JD Middlebrook	GR Napier	WI Jefferson	A Habib	RC Irani	DDJ Robinson	JM Dakin	AP Grayson	SA Brant	N Hussain	RS Bopara	Mohammad Akram	JB Grant	AN Cook	ML Pettini	AJ Clarke	JP Stephenson	AP Palladino	RN ten Doeschate	AC McGarry	AGA M McCoubrey	ZK Sharif	JE Bishop
Matches	17	17	16	15	14	13	13	11	11	10	10	5	4	4	3	3	3	3	3	2	2	2	2	1	1
Innings	26	29	25	24	27	22	20	20	19	18	14	9	7	6	4	6	5	4	5	3	4	2	3	1	1
Not Out	0	3	1	8	3	0	0	2	2	2	6	1	3	1	1	1	1	1	1	1	0	2	1	0	0
Highest Score	85	201*	82*	89*	125	151	102	89	59	90	23	206	48	10	4	84	78	41	75*	8	31	4*	1	0	21
Runs	689	1244	484	480	781	738	597	592	411	388	37	453	163	19	11	239	172	87	137	20	48	6	1	0	21
Average	26.50	47.85	20.17	30.00	32.54	33.55	29.85	32.89	24.18	24.25	4.62	56.62	40.75	3.80	3.67	47.80	43.00	29.00	34.25	10.00	12.00	6.00	0.50	0.00	21.00
100s	0	2	0	0	1	1	1	0	0	0	0	1	0	0	0	0	0	0	0	0	0	0	0	0	0
50s	4	7	2	2	5	4	4	4	2	3	0	2	0	0	0	3	2	0	2	0	0	0	0	0	0
Catches/Stumpings	49/2	17/0	7/0	3/0	12/0	9/0	4/0	7/0	2/0	5/0	3/0	2/0	3/0	0/0	1/0	3/0	3/0	1/0	0/0	0/0	1/0	0/0	0/0	1/0	0/0

Home Ground: The County Ground, Chelmsford
Address: County Cricket Ground, New Writtle Street, Chelmsford, Essex CM2 0PD
Tel: 01245 252420   **Fax:** 01245 491607
Prospects of play: 01245 287921
Email: administration.essex@ecb.co.uk
Directions: *By rail:* Chelmsford Station (8 minutes' walk away). *By road:* M25 then A12 to Chelmsford. Exit Chelmsford and follow AA signs to 'Essex Cricket Club'.
Capacity: 6,000
Other grounds used: Castle Park, Colchester; Valentine's Park, Ilford; Southchurch Park, Southend-on-Sea.
Year formed: 1876

Chief Executive: DE East
Other posts: *Cricket Operations Manager:* Alan Lilley; *Head Groundsman:* SG Kerrison
Club Coach: Graham Gooch
Club Captain: Nasser Hussain
Team Captain: Ronnie Irani
County colours: Blue, gold and red

Honours
County Championship
1979, 1983, 1984, 1986, 1991, 1992
Sunday League/NCL
1981, 1984, 1985
Refuge Assurance Cup
1989
Benson & Hedges Cup
1979, 1998
Gillette Cup/NatWest/C&G Trophy
1985, 1997

Website:
www.essexcricket.org.uk

ESSEX CCC

FIRST-CLASS MATCHES

BOWLING

Match (date)	JD Middlebrook	GR Napier	JM Dakin	SA Brant	AP Grayson	RC Irani	Mohammad Akram	RS Bopara	JP Stephenson	AP Palladino	A Flower	DDJ Robinson	AJ Clarke	JB Grant	RN ten Doeschate	A C McGarry	AGAM McCoubrey	A Habib	JE Bishop	ZK Sharif	AN Cook	Overs	Total	Byes/Leg-byes	Wickets	Run outs
Cambridge UCCE (Fenner's) 12-14 April	12.3-4-29-2	17-5-38-1	19-7-57-1	3-1-3-0	8-4-12-1						2-0-5-1	3-0-22-0				16-7-27-5						75.3	173	7	10	
	21-4-61-2	5-0-12-0	11-6-18-1	5-1-10-0												12-4-29-0						59	163	6	4	
Middlesex (Chelmsford) 18-21 April	5-0-12-2	18-3-57-4	13-2-50-1		13-4-43-0						1.3-0-3-0	1.5-0-7-1			9-1-48-0							59	214	4	10	1
	57-11-172-5	26-11-56-1	23-6-60-1	34-5-107-2	13-4-39-0										16.3-2-41-0							172.5	495	10	10	
Warwickshire (Edgbaston) 23-26 April	19-4-62-0	13-1-62-1	23-5-79-1	30.1-5-133-3	10-1-48-0	19-5-51-2																114.1	446	11	7	
Leicestershire (Leicester) 30 April-3 May		3-0-15-0	24-6-64-4	22.1-7-54-4	2-0-15-1				19-6-55-2													68.1	201	13	10	
		6-0-30-0	6.1-1-6-2	10-2-24-2					1-0-10-0													25.1	104	9	5	
Lancashire (Old Trafford) 14-17 May	40.1-11-86-3	16-1-73-0		11-3-36-0	24-6-68-1	32-13-59-4							10-0-44-2									133.1	375	9	10	
Surrey (Chelmsford) 21-24 May	9-0-38-0	24-4-82-4	20.3-5-96-2	29-4-94-3	8-1-31-0	9-2-31-0																99.3	376	4	10	1
	26-0-117-2	21-0-124-4	17-2-55-1	19-5-62-0	4-0-16-0																	87	381	7	7	
Nottinghamshire (Trent Bridge) 30 May-1 June	16-2-64-3	18-5-66-5	8-2-22-4	8.5-3-45-6				3-2-2-0														16.5	79	12	10	
			19-8-42-1	16-7-30-1																		72	215	11	10	
Middlesex (Lord's) 4-7 June	16.1-1-63-1	24-5-74-1	35-10-86-5	31-10-67-2			15-1-61-1															121.1	363	12	10	
Kent (Chelmsford) 27-30 June	34-8-123-6	21-3-79-0		24.4-2-107-3									4.2-1-13-0						9-1-53-0			93	381	6	10	1
	47-7-138-2	27-4-90-3		20-0-75-0					7-0-21-1				13-3-48-1					2.4-0-10-1	20-3-48-1			123.4	416	34	8	
Lancashire (Chelmsford) 2-5 July	15.2-2-47-3	12-3-40-0	16-2-55-3	18-7-39-4	1-0-4-0									5-1-27-0								67.2	218	6	10	
	28-3-83-2	14-2-43-1	22-2-97-1	18-3-67-3	9-0-33-0									9-1-42-0								100	383	8	7	
Sussex (Arundel) 9-12 July	17.5-1-54-1	16-2-46-1	25-5-67-1	25-4-80-3	17-2-47-4										10-1-53-0							110.5	359	3	10	
	23.1-1-78-1	7-0-24-0	26-2-54-3	7-0-27-0	24-7-63-0																	77.1	257	11	4	
Leicestershire (Southend) 23-26 July	41.5-6-150-3	22-3-115-0						7-0-36-0							28-8-76-0	16-2-102-1				17-1-103-3		131.5	600	18	7	
Kent (Canterbury) 30 July-1 August	5.3-0-27-1	5-1-23-0							15-5-41-6				10-2-63-2			5-0-33-1						40.3	189	2	10	
	30.2-5-78-4	16.5-4-68-2							16-2-58-0				15-0-61-3			3.1-1-7-1						81.2	284	12	10	
Sussex (Colchester) 20-22 August	26-1-126-2	24-5-149-0	20-1-120-1				29-2-130-5		16-6-40-1	4-0-33-0												119	612	9	10	1
Nottinghamshire (Chelmsford) 3-5 September	5-0-43-0	17-5-42-1	16.5-3-53-4				23-7-65-2			16-3-70-3												77.5	284	11	10	
	8-3-16-2	19.4-5-56-2	18-6-30-1				22-7-56-1			19-6-34-4												86.4	204	12	10	
Warwickshire (Chelmsford) 11-14 September	48.3-8-154-5	19-2-80-3					24-0-151-1		8-0-46-1	10-1-50-0											2-0-11-0	111.3	503	11	10	
	7.4-2-29-0	3-0-14-0					5-1-16-1															15.4	61	2	1	
Surrey (The Oval) 17-19 September	28-3-93-4	18.3-4-58-3					21-5-93-4		5-0-23-1	2-0-12-0					7-2-32-0							81.3	318	7	10	
	5-0-26-0	12.3-1-54-2					21-9-49-8		2-0-12-0	12-2-39-0					7-1-19-0							57.3	194	7	10	
Overs	593	379.3	352.3	344.5	147	100	145	30	42	75	10.3	8.5	59	39.2	24	53.3	24.1	2.4	29	17	2					
Maidens	87	60	79	77	29	33	31	3	8	21	0	0	13	3	3	14	3	0	4	1	0					
Runs	1979	1506	1099	1117	453	245	560	122	162	215	29	62	205	181	122	145	142	10	101	103	11					
Wickets	56	33	40	37	9	9	20	2	3	7	2	1	7	7	0	5	3	1	1	3	0					
Average	35.3	45.6	27.5	30.2	50.3	27.2	28.0	61.0	54.0	30.7	14.5	62.0	29.3	25.9	-	29.0	47.3	10.0	101.0	34.3	-					

FIELDING

JS Foster (19 ct, 2st)
A Flower
WI Jefferson
A Habib
DDJ Robinson
JD Middlebrook
AP Grayson
RC Irani
AN Cook
ML Pettini
GR Napier
RS Bopara
SA Brant
N Hussain
JM Dakin
RN ten Doeschate
ZK Sharif
AJ Clarke
JB Grant

GLAMORGAN CCC

FIRST–CLASS MATCHES

BATTING

	RDB Croft	MA Wallace	MJ Powell	DS Harrison	MP Maynard	A Dale	AG Wharf	MS Kasprowicz	DL Hemp	J Hughes	DA Cosker	J P Maher	IJ Thomas	SD Thomas	AP Davies	AD Shaw	SP James	DD Cherry	OT Parkin	Extras	Total	Wickets	Result
v. Derbyshire	79	6	12		142	13	16	41	7					9*	9		1			17	352	10	
(Derby) 18–21 April	6	16	37		9	92	19*	13*	7								14			40	253	7	D 1
v. Hampshire	15*	37	85	6*	112	16			57					41						43	412	6	
(Cardiff) 23–26 April																				–	–	–	D 1
v. Gloucestershire	4	0	4	16	31	8	25	22	1				1		19*					8	139	10	
(Cardiff) 9–12 May	14	31	19	66	43	17	0*	78	34				13		4					36	355	10	L 2
v. Somerset	46	26	7	0	34	40	8*	13	2	2	0									22	200	10	
(Taunton) 14–17 May	0	4	16	6	30	15	2	11*	36	5	1									7	133	10	L 2
v. Yorkshire	9	94	11	1	51	0	29*	36	0	10			25							49	315	10	
(Headingley) 21–24 May																				–	–	–	D 1
v. Northamptonshire	34	32	29	33	26	37	5	21	4	24	1*									23	269	10	
(Northampton) 30 May–1 June	50*	3	8	1	11	2	17	23	9	73	0									23	220	10	W 1
v. Derbyshire	84	35	23	4	35	43	15	19	9	69	12*									47	395	10	
(Swansea) 4–7 June																				–	–	–	W
v. Worcestershire	36	9	125	11	9	0	17	19	15	1	2*									26	270	10	
(Cardiff) 27–30 June	17	3	142	4	0	1	32*	35	63	41	1*									27	366	9	D
v. Somerset	122	20	14	18*	37	13	45	24	1			21		25						9	349	10	
(Cardiff) 9–12 July	17	26	1	12*	101	7	39	0	16			62		4						22	307	10	W 2
v. Hampshire	28	0	44	0	129	123	16*	24	4	7		30								32	437	10	
(Southampton) 15–18 July	12	11	4	9	3	3	10*	14	7	6		9								16	104	10	L
v. India A	12*	29	0	7						15	1		10	0		33		9	2	22	140	10	
(Swansea) 24–26 July																				–	–	–	D
v. Worcestershire	0	29	0	0	12		0*	9		24		53	21							8	156	10	
(Worcester) 31 July–3 August	51*	55	3	27	19		13	0		30		95	1	10						20	324	10	L 3
v. Durham	25	117	14	6	70	66	50	24	39	3*	8									22	444	10	
(Cardiff) 13–16 August		19*					14*			11	35									7	86	2	W 2
v. Gloucestershire	21	8	42	0	85	32	0	4	69*			16	24							30	331	10	
(Bristol) 19–22 August	11	0	90	39*	33	27	3	25	31			11	13							8	291	10	D 3
v. Yorkshire	0	31	146	1	32	0	79	51	25	5*			53							43	466	10	
(Colwyn Bay) 25–28 August	5	61	85	3	47	23*			85*	0										27	336	6	D 1
v. Northamptonshire	1	10	40	0	48	24	4	12*	29			0	29							6	203	10	
(Cardiff) 10–13 September	31	38	11	4	78	16	4	0	85*			42	35							17	361	10	L 3
v. Durham	5	121	5	0*	12	1	0	4	36			63		7						16	270	10	
(Chester-le-Street) 17–19 September	4	4	198		102	0	34*	3				24		69*						22	464	8	W 1
Matches	17	17	17	16	16	15	15	15	12	10	8	8	7	5	2	1	1	1	1				
Innings	29	29	30	25	28	27	27	26	21	17	12	16	11	8	3	1	2	1	1				
Not Out	4	0	1	5	0	1	9	1	3	0	6	0	2	1	0	0	0	0	0				
Highest Score	122	121	198	66	142	123	79	78	85*	73	42	95	53	69*	19*	33	14	9	2				
Runs	739	856	1234	271	1297	657	475	556	607	372	80	491	182	145	32	33	15	9	2				
Average	29.56	29.52	42.55	13.55	46.32	25.27	26.39	25.27	33.72	21.88	13.33	30.69	16.55	24.17	16.00	33.00	7.50	9.00	2.00				
100s	1	2	4	0	5	1	0	0	0	0	0	0	0	0	0	0	0	0	0				
50s	4	3	3	1	4	2	2	2	5	2	0	4	1	1	0	0	0	0	0				
Catches/Stumpings	9/0	49/2	14/0	3/0	11/0	12/0	7/0	7/0	5/0	10/0	7/0	7/0	8/0	1/0	1/0	0/0	1/0	0/0	1/0				

Home Ground: Cardiff
Address: Sophia Gardens, Cardiff CF11 9XR
Tel: 029 2040 9380
Fax: 029 2040 9390
Email: glam@ecb.co.uk
Directions: *By rail:* Cardiff Central Train Station.
By road: From north, A470 and follow signs to Cardiff until junction with Cardiff bypass then A48 Port Talbot and City Centre. Cathedral Road is situated off A48 for Sophia Gardens. From east, M4 Junction 29 then A48.

Capacity: 4,000
Other grounds used: Pontypridd, Mid Glamorgan; St Helens, Swansea; Rhos-on-Sea, Colwyn Bay; Pen-y-Pound Ground, Abergavenny.
Year formed: 1888

Chief Executive: Mike Fatkin
Head Groundsman: Len Smith
Captain: Robert Croft
County colours: Navy blue and yellow/gold

Honours
County Championship
1948, 1969, 1997
Sunday League/NCL
1993, 2002

Website:
www.glamorgancricket.com

GLAMORGAN CCC

FIRST-CLASS MATCHES

BOWLING

	RDB Croft	AG Wharf	DS Harrison	MS Kasprowicz	DA Cosker	A Dale	SD Thomas	A P Davies	OT Parkin	MP Maynard	JP Maher	Overs	Total	Byes/Leg-byes	Wickets	Run outs
v. Derbyshire (Derby) 18-21 April	52.4-11-128-3	23-2-83-3		32.2-13-94-0		4-1-11-0	19.4-4-69-4	4-2-23-0				135.4	420	12	10	
	31-10-61-4	26-4-87-2		11-1-39-0				10-0-47-0				78	245	11	6	
v. Hampshire (Cardiff) 23-26 April	30.5-5-119-0	28-4-134-3	20-4-87-3		21-1-63-0		5-3-14-0	17-3-96-1				121.5	531	18	7	
												-	-	-	-	
v. Gloucestershire (Cardiff) 9-12 May	19-5-40-0	28-4-93-1	24.4-4-80-5	29-3-111-2		3-0-11-0		12-3-37-0				115.4	400	28	8	
		5-0-28-3	4-0-19-0	3-0-24-0				3-0-22-1				15	95	2	4	
v. Somerset (Taunton) 14-17 May	23-5-92-0	22-3-113-2	27-3-116-1	30-9-103-0		12-2-29-3						114	476	23	6	
												-	-	-	-	
v. Yorkshire (Headingley) 21-24 May	9-3-21-0	15.4-4-63-3	22-8-58-3	21-7-51-4		2-0-6-0						69.4	209	10	10	
	15-2-50-0	6-0-39-0	12-5-32-1	6-0-23-0		2-0-12-0						41	159	3	1	
v. Northamptonshire (Northampton) 30 May-1 June	18-4-32-1	16-4-44-1	24.3-8-64-4	24-4-77-3	10-4-17-1	3-0-16-0						95.3	262	12	10	
	15-5-34-1	8-2-41-0	6.1-0-19-2	23-3-72-6	1-0-2-0							53.1	172	4	10	1
v. Derbyshire (Swansea) 4-7 June	30.3-9-71-6	7-2-21-0	4-0-12-0	15-4-43-1	19-3-49-3							75.3	209	13	10	
	18-5-39-2	7-3-12-3	4-1-5-0	7-2-14-2	14.5-5-38-2							50.5	116	8	9	
v. Worcestershire (Cardiff) 27-30 June	28-4-99-1	16.5-1-76-3	10-3-23-1	21-5-38-3	19-1-56-2	3-0-21-0						97.5	328	10	10	
	23.4-9-54-1	10-4-13-0	11-2-32-0	16-4-35-3	19-7-34-2							79.4	175	7	6	
v. Somerset (Cardiff) 9-12 July	3-0-24-0	15-3-55-2	10.4-1-52-2	19-6-53-4			12-0-41-2					59.4	233	8	10	
	28.5-5-74-2	26-5-90-4	7-1-15-0	35-11-91-2			13-3-36-1					109.5	313	7	10	1
v. Hampshire (Southampton) 15-18 July	26-8-51-2	10-1-31-1	15-3-51-2	22.5-10-48-5		14-1-65-0						73.5	185	4	10	
	38.3-9-117-5	17-4-68-1	10-0-81-1	28-8-103-3								107.3	449	15	10	
v. India A (Swansea) 24-26 July	20-3-55-3		13-5-27-2		5-1-12-0		13-1-47-4		9-3-19-1			60	165	5	10	
			4-2-9-1		2-0-11-0		1-0-3-0		3-2-3-0			10	27	1	1	
v. Worcestershire (Worcester) 31 July-3 August	9-2-43-1	16-3-63-4	16-5-52-4	16-3-48-0			6-0-22-1					63	237	9	10	
	20-2-69-4	15-4-38-3	20-5-55-1	19.4-5-46-2			9-0-38-0					83.4	257	11	10	
v. Durham (Cardiff) 13-16 August	35.1-12-98-6	17-1-76-1	15-5-55-0	24-10-41-2	22-9-50-1	4-0-26-0						117.1	355	9	10	
	26-10-53-0	7-1-28-0	4-0-15-0	20.2-6-36-9	8-1-31-1						1-0-2-0	66.2	174	9	10	
v. Gloucestershire (Bristol) 19-22 August	43-16-82-2	21-7-53-4	13-4-45-1	27.1-5-75-3								104.1	263	8	10	
	32-10-61-4	18-2-89-1	17-5-46-2	27-5-65-0								94	280	19	7	
v. Yorkshire (Colwyn Bay) 25-28 August	37-4-125-3	7-0-35-0	16-2-67-1	19.2-5-60-3	39-8-109-3	10-3-13-0						128.2	422	13	10	
	42-14-80-4		4-0-13-0	38-17-62-1							2-0-2-0	94	193	6	7	
v. Northamptonshire (Cardiff) 10-13 September	28.3-6-93-5	13-2-83-1	9-2-47-0	20-2-58-3	11-4-32-1							81.3	319	6	10	
	24.1-12-54-5	16-2-83-3	4-3-12-0	13-3-41-2	22-5-64-0							79.1	265	11	10	
v. Durham (Chester-le-Street) 17-19 September	5-2-9-0	12-0-66-3	11-1-57-2	22-3-65-4			8.3-0-37-1					58.3	247	13	10	
		4-0-29-0	8-2-38-1	12.5-2-45-9								24.5	118	6	10	
Overs	731.5	432.3	366	572.3	264.5	48	82.1	46	12	2	1					
Maidens	192	72	84	140	67	9	0	0	6	0	0					
Runs	1928	1734	1284	1629	695	159	293	225	22	2	2					
Wickets	65	52	40	77	17	3	13	2	1	0	0					
Average	29.7	33.3	32.1	21.2	40.9	53.0	22.5	112.5	22.0	-	-					

FIELDING

51 MA Wallace (49 ct, 2st)
4 MJ Powell
2 A Dale
1 MP Maynard
0 J Hughes
RDB Croft
IJ Thomas
JP Maher
DA Cosker
MS Kasprowicz
AG Wharf
DL Hemp
DS Harrison
SP James
SD Thomas
OT Parkin
AP Davies

GLOUCESTERSHIRE CCC

FIRST-CLASS MATCHES
BATTING

Match	MGN Windows	CM Spearman	JN Rhodes	WPC Weston	J Lewis	THC Hancock	RC Russell	MCJ Ball	AM Smith	MW Alleyne	ID Fisher	APR Gidman	IJ Harvey	SP Pope	CG Taylor	RJ Sillence	IG Butler	JMM Averis	Shoaib Malik	MA Hardinges	Extras	Total	Wickets	Result	Points
v. Somerset (Bristol) 18-21 April	10	8	42	12	1*	33	11		0	19	15				42						10	203	10		
	78	8	55	12	8	44	78*		1	0	18				40						26	368	10	W	18
v. Northamptonshire (Northampton) 23-26 April	35	69	128	13		59	31*		32*												36	403	5		
																					-	-	-	D	12
v. Durham (Chester-le-Street) 30 April-3 May	44	4	60	40	10	59	65		17*	21	0				0						21	341	10		
																					-	-	-	D	10
v. Glamorgan (Cardiff) 9-12 May	63	75	47	49	37*	24	16			20	7*						13				49	400	8		
	0	39	14*	17		13			6*												6	95	4	W	22
v. Hampshire (Bristol) 14-17 May	21	103	57*	61		47				18*											9	316	4		
																					-	-	-	D	10
v. Worcestershire (Worcester) 21-24 May	14	19	14	42	0	0	38		0*	19	15					0					17	178	10		
	3	24	13	6	5	0	0		2	11	11*					0					23	98	10	L	3
v. Northamptonshire (Gloucester) 4-7 June	0		24		5	44	22	53	0*			20		45		0					17	230	10		
	150		4	11*	18	63	1	4	8			8		31		7					33	338	10	L	2
v. Hampshire (Southampton) 27-30 June	3	4	11	39	14		4	7*				16	20	14	24						29	185	10		
	40	20	151*	100	26		7	4				17	10	4	31						17	427	10	D	7
v. Somerset (Taunton) 2-5 July	19	54	50	19	5		0	0*	10			28	8	23							12	228	10		
	89	3	49	179	14		75	8*	29			128*	7	0							30	611	9	D	9
v. Derbyshire (Derby) 9-11 July	20	85	6	28	13		34*	15				25	27	1	1						22	277	10		
	0	0	62*	6								41	21*		16						25	171	5	W	19
v. Worcestershire (Cheltenham) 23-26 July	23	12	19	28	47		29					12		17*			8	20	17		39	271	10		
	12		58*	25								13							0	10*	15	133	5	D	9
v. Yorkshire (Cheltenham) 30 July-2 August	73	0	0		35	35*	24	0		18		43					0	0			35	263	10		
	57	94	0*		21	18				14									60		20	284	6	D	9
v. Glamorgan (Bristol) 19-22 August	26	1	7	42	8	64	12	8				68	13					4*			10	263	10		
	9	37	57	12		53	8	10*				50*	16								28	280	7	D	9
v. Derbyshire (Bristol) 3-6 September	49	21	137	34	8	8		26		24		46		0*		13					35	401	10		
	8	87	2	6		15		22*		10		17		14*		3					25	209	8	W	21
v. Durham (Bristol) 10-13 September	28	59	103	12	0*	97	5	3		18		29						0			20	374	10		
	12	28	102	7		32	34*	8		12*		41									12	288	7	W	21
v. Yorkshire (Headingley) 17-20 September	0	41	5	84	36	6	0		0*			71	8	70							23	344	10		
	4	8	16	4		48						9*	1*								3	93	5	D	10
Matches	16	15	15	15	13	12	10	9	8	8	8	8	6	5	4	3	3	3	2	2					
Innings	29	27	27	27	18	21	16	15	14	13	12	16	12	8	8	5	5	3	4	3					
Not Out	0	0	5	1	4	0	4	3	7	3	3	2	3	3	0	0	0	1	0	1					
Highest Score	150	103	151*	179	47	97	78*	75	17*	32*	71	68	128*	17*	45	42	13	8	60	17					
Runs	890	903	1293	877	248	720	436	304	58	193	219	407	404	65	171	98	20	12	80	27					
Average	30.69	33.44	58.77	33.73	17.71	34.29	36.33	25.33	8.29	19.30	24.33	29.07	44.89	13.00	21.38	19.60	4.00	6.00	20.00	13.50					
100s	1	1	5	2	0	0	0	0	0	0	0	1	1	0	0	0	0	0	0	0					
50s	5	7	7	2	0	5	3	2	0	0	1	2	1	0	0	0	0	0	1	0					
Catches/Stumpings	11/0	15/0	7/0	10/0	3/0	13/0	33/4	12/0	1/0	9/0	4/0	7/0	4/0	10/1	3/0	1/0	0/0	1/0	0/0	1/0					

Home Ground: Bristol
Address: The Sun Alliance Ground, Nevil Road, Bristol BS7 9EJ
Tel: 0117 910 8000 **Fax:** 0117 924 1193
Directions: By road: M5, M4, M32 into Bristol: exit at second exit (Fishponds/Horfield), then third exit – Muller Road. Almost at end of Muller Road (bus station on right), turn left at Ralph Road. Go to the top, turn left and then right almost immediately into Kennington Avenue. Follow the signs for County Cricket.
Capacity: 8,000
Other grounds used: College Ground, Cheltenham, King's School, Gloucester
Year formed: 1870

Chairman: Alan Haines
Director of Cricket: Andy Stovold
Other posts: Chief Executive: Tom Richardson; Youth Development Officer: Richard Holdsworth
Captain: Mark Alleyne
Coaching contact: Andy Stovold, Director of Coaching 0117 910 8004
County colours: Blue, brown, gold, green and red, sky blue

Honours
Sunday League/NCL
2000
Benson & Hedges Cup
1977, 1999, 2000
Gillette Cup/NatWest/C&G Trophy
1973, 1999, 2000, 2003

Website:
www.gloscricket.co.uk

GLOUCESTERSHIRE CCC

FIRST-CLASS MATCHES

BOWLING

	J Lewis	AM Smith	MCJ Ball	ID Fisher	APR Gidman	MW Alleyne	IJ Harvey	RJ Sillence	JMM Averis	IG Butler	CG Taylor	THC Hancock	MA Hardinges	Shoaib Malik	WPC Weston	Overs	Total	Byes/Leg-byes	Wickets	Run outs
Somerset (Bristol) 18-21 April	21-4-58-6	16-1-64-2	16-6-71-1		6-3-37-0		62-0-54-1									65.2	289	5	10	
	23-8-40-1	28-8-69-3			27-4-77-3		18-2-55-3									102	274	10	10	
Northamptonshire (Northampton) 23-26 April			40-9-104-5	36-6-121-3		8-3-12-1	9-1-60-0	192-5-46-1				1-0-2-0				112.2	352	9	10	
			8-6-4-2	5-0-19-0			5-1-18-0	5-1-22-1								24	69	4	3	
Durham (Chester-le-Street) 30 April-3 May	17-4-32-3	24-5-64-3		12-8-11-0		8-1-30-2		153-2-52-2								64.3	183	5	10	
	17.5-6-48-1	12-7-14-3				7-1-38-0		17-4-46-2								65.5	159	2	6	
Glamorgan (Cardiff) 9-12 May	19.2-4-61-5	9-4-24-2				2-1-7-0			12-1-45-2							42.2	139	2	10	1
	29-11-88-4	19.5-2-91-2		7-2-29-0		9-0-44-1			25-7-90-3							89.5	355	13	10	
Hampshire (Bristol) 14-17 May	29.5-12-80-4	19-4-50-1		22-2-87-1		19-5-58-0			23-7-80-3							112.5	369	14	9	
Worcestershire (Worcester) 21-24 May	18.3-8-37-3	22-4-70-5					13-6-23-1		16-4-59-2							56.3	175	9	10	
	23-7-64-1	18-5-41-4							20-3-74-4							74	212	10	10	
Northamptonshire (Gloucester) 4-7 June	35.5-6-145-1	25-5-63-1	44-6-149-3	17-1-76-0					28-2-130-3	9-0-40-0						158.5	622	19	8	
Hampshire (Southampton) 27-30 June	25-7-86-2	21-12-44-1	17-2-65-1			15-5-46-2	18.2-2-73-4									96.2	330	16	10	
	12-1-49-0	8-3-25-0	18-9-24-3			1-0-12-0	16-8-43-4									55	161	8	7	
Somerset (Taunton) 2-5 July	28-6-107-3	31-10-67-4	19-2-70-1			28-6-116-0	27-6-103-2				2-0-8-0					133	477	14	10	
	9-2-37-0	11-5-19-2	13-5-20-0			6-2-18-1									2-0-10-0	43	115	3	3	
Derbyshire (Derby) 9-11 July	11-0-48-6	11-6-14-0				1-1-0-1	13-6-18-3									36	89	9	10	
	29-7-91-0	25-5-72-2	34-11-65-4			10-1-44-0	24-7-58-3									122	356	26	10	1
Worcestershire (Cheltenham) 23-26 July	29-3-136-3		14-2-43-0		4-0-16-0				34-13-84-3				8-0-60-1	35-10-76-3		124	439	24	10	
Yorkshire (Cheltenham) 30 July-2 August		15-3-32-2	21-6-47-3	8-0-31-2	4-1-16-0						12-2-26-2			19-3-60-1		79	226	14	10	
		5-1-18-0	13-2-29-0	8-3-13-1							2-0-3-0			12-6-10-1		40	75	2	2	
Glamorgan (Bristol) 19-22 August	26.5-10-66-5		22-10-63-3		13-4-52-0	21-6-42-1			26-8-75-1		4-0-20-0					112.5	331	13	10	
	20-6-66-3		37.3-7-100-3		4-0-27-0	19-5-54-3			9-1-42-1							89.3	291	2	10	
Derbyshire (Bristol) 3-6 September	27.2-3-117-7		20-6-45-0	23-8-66-3	3-2-1-0				20-3-81-0							93.2	321	11	10	
	26.2-9-66-4		22-7-54-0	19-2-73-5	12-4-30-0				10-2-42-1							89.2	269	4	10	
Durham (Bristol) 10-13 September	19-7-52-3		10-2-63-0			13-4-41-1							10-5-28-1			61.1	218	4	10	
	20.3-5-64-3		26-7-63-0			13-5-58-0							9-4-30-1			94.3	318	10	9	
Yorkshire (Headingley) 17-20 September	22-5-91-2	10-1-57-1		28-5-110-2	20-1-121-2	20-4-91-3										100	476	6	10	
	12-1-71-4					11-1-44-3										23	121	6	7	
Overs	551.2	329.5	378.3	225.1	104	133	195.2	100.5	107.2	124	11	5	27	66	2					
Maidens	142	91	99	50	20	32	54	15	30	24	0	0	9	19	0					
Runs	1800	898	1008	767	441	460	625	408	298	478	48	22	118	146	10					
Wickets	74	38	28	28	5	9	27	9	9	17	0	0	3	5	0					
Average	24.3	23.6	36.0	27.4	88.2	51.1	23.1	45.3	33.1	28.1	-	-	39.3	29.2	-					

FIELDING

RC Russell (33 ct, 4st)
CM Spearman
THC Hancock
MCJ Ball
SP Pope (10 ct, 1st)
MGN Windows
WPC Weston
MW Alleyne
APR Gidman
JN Rhodes
ID Fisher
IJ Harvey
CG Taylor
J Lewis
MA Hardinges
JMM Averis
RJ Sillence
AM Smith

HAMPSHIRE CCC

FIRST-CLASS MATCHES
BATTING

	AD Mascarenhas	JP Crawley	DA Kenway	SD Udal	SM Katich	N Pothas	RA Smith	WS Kendall	CT Tremlett	JHK Adams	JA Tomlinson	JTA Bruce	AD Mullally	JD Francis	JRC Hamblin	Wasim Akram	LR Prittipaul	WPUJC Vaas	I Brunschweiler	AC Morris	ESH Giddins	DA Clapp	RJE Hindley	—	Extras	Total	Wickets	Result
v. Worcestershire	20	93	5		146*	22	16		11													10			11	347	10	
(Worcester) 18–21 April	38	67	1		48	77	13		9													0*			9	276	9	D
v. Glamorgan	100*	65	19	32*		87	92	32							23					46					35	531	7	
(Cardiff) 23–26 April	–																								–	–	–	D
v. Yorkshire	1	1	10	31	17	44*	30	1	2			8			18										12	175	10	
(Southampton) 30 April–3 May	–																								–	–	–	D
v. Oxford UCCE			35					114						20		69*	1								23	262	4	
(The Parks) 9–11 May	16*	68	0*											34				20	4						8	150	4	D
v. Gloucestershire	14	69	8	6	96	63	0	69	10*	6	0														28	369	9	
(Bristol) 14–17 May	–																								–	–	–	D
v. Somerset	0	0	3	5	24	34	0	49	4				0	4*											6	129	10	
(Southampton) 21–24 May	10	2	94	34	4	13	55	33	43				5*	0											13	306	10	L
v. Durham	92	29	8	60*	135	79	5	33					0	0					0						15	456	10	
(Southampton) 4–7 June	–																								–	–	–	D
v. Gloucestershire	21	15	115	5	61	21	50	22					0*		0				0						20	330	10	
(Southampton) 27–30 June	29	5	12	16*	52	14	16	2							4*										11	161	7	D
v. Northamptonshire	11	21	5	12	11	0	41	4		0*	4	8													8	125	10	
(Northampton) 2–4 July	28	16	3	14	36	5	28	3		1*	6	36													3	179	10	L
v. Glamorgan	16	24	26	4	2		22	21	0	21*	27													8	14	185	10	
(Southampton) 15–18 July	75	9	24	53	121		6	21	1	10	40													68*	21	449	10	W
v. Yorkshire	4	0	0	26	143*		19	0			2	9	0				34								52	289	10	
(Scarborough) 23–26 July	0	32	5	33*	4		47				2	35*													22	180	6	D
v. Northamptonshire	31	8	6	16	117		29	32		7*	4	4					3								21	278	10	
(Southampton) 31 July–3 August		81*	46		79*			12																	9	227	2	L
v. Derbyshire	0	49	17	0	7		22*	8	0	11								1	16						12	143	10	
(Southampton) 13–14 August	6	16	11	12	48*		30	0	1	3								2	5						21	155	10	L
v. Durham	12	29		10	16	50	1		21	0*			0	65					0						7	211	10	
(Chester-le-Street) 20–23 August	10	4		5	2	47	49		36	10			14	6					1*						5	189	10	L
v. Somerset	5	60	100	30		21	56*	12	14	0				31	39										27	395	10	
(Taunton) 26–29 August		1	8						50					53*	56*										9	177	3	D
v. Worcestershire	24	35	3	50	70	7	0	3	0*						19	35									19	265	10	
(Southampton) 3–6 September	16	88	44	29	42	3	0	6	0						35	25*									23	311	10	L
v. Derbyshire	21	59	68	57	122	4			60	1*		12			96	18									62	580	10	
(Derby) 17–20 September			16*						10*																2	28	–	W
Matches	17	16	16	15	13	13	10	9	9	9	7	7	6	6	5	4	4	3	3	2	2	1	1	1				
Innings	26	27	28	22	22	20	15	13	13	18	11	11	8	11	8	5	6	6	4	3	2	1	2	2				
Not Out	2	1	1	5	3	2	1	0	2	1	3	2	0	2	1	2	2	0	0	0	0	0	1					
Highest Score	100*	93	115	60*	143*	146*	92	114	43	60	10	21*	14	65	96	23	69*	35	34	46	0	4	10	68*				
Runs	600	878	760	483	1143	809	522	391	199	361	19	68	26	211	273	45	236	64	58	67	0	4	37	76				
Average	25.00	33.77	28.15	28.41	60.16	44.94	37.29	30.08	18.09	21.24	3.17	8.50	4.33	19.18	45.50	11.25	59.00	16.00	14.50	22.33	0.00	4.00	6.17	76.00				
100s	1	0	2	0	4	2	0	1	0	0	0	0	0	0	0	0	0	0	0	0	0	0	0	0				
50s	2	8	3	3	6	4	5	1	0	2	0	0	0	1	2	0	2	0	0	0	0	0	1	0				
Catches/Stumpings	7/0	5/0	14/0	4/0	15/0	38/2	9/0	6/0	5/0	6/0	2/0	3/0	0/0	6/0	1/0	0/0	7/0	2/0	11/0	2/0	0/0	0/0	7/0	0/0				

Home Ground: Southampton
Address: The Hampshire Rose Bowl, Botley Road, West End, Southampton SO30 3XH
Tel: 02380 472002
Fax: 02380 472122
Indoor school: 02380 472468
Email: enquiries@rosebowlplc.com
Directions: *By rail:* Southampton Parkway – 4 miles.
By road: From M27, exit junction 7 and take the A334 then the B3035 (Botley Road, West End).
Capacity: 9,950
Year formed: 1863

Chief Executive: Graham Walker
Marketing: Katie Hall
Director of Cricket: Tim Tremlett
Other posts: *Head Groundsman:* Nigel Gray
Youth Development Officer: Alan Rowe
Cricket Development Coach: Raj Maru
Women's Cricket Development Officer: Clair Slaney
Captain: Shane Warne
County colours: Navy blue, old gold

Honours

County Championship
1961, 1973
Sunday League/NCL
1975, 1978, 1986
Benson & Hedges Cup
1988, 1992
Gillette Cup/NatWest/C&G Trophy
1991

Website:
www.hampshire.cricket.org

HAMPSHIRE CCC

FIRST-CLASS MATCHES

BOWLING

	AD Mascarenhas	SD Udal	SM Katich	CT Tremlett	JTA Bruce	JA Tomlinson	AD Mullally	Wasim Akram	LR Prittipaul	WS Kendall	JRC Hamblin	WPUJC Vaas	ESH Giddins	AC Morris	DA Kenway	RJE Hindley	M Thorburn	Overs	Total	Byes/Leg-byes	Wickets	Run outs
Worcestershire (Worcester) 18-21 April	22-11-40-0	20.3-2-80-1					3-1-14-0											119	386	11	10	
	17-4-47-1	11-1-48-2																78.5	264	7	9	
Glamorgan (Cardiff) 23-26 April	19.3-9-45-1	27-5-93-0		22-7-101-3			22-5-81-1	20-4-82-1										110.3	412	10	6	
																		-	-	-	-	
Yorkshire (Southampton) 30 April-3 May	13-3-41-0	13-2-47-2	9-2-23-1	16-2-71-1			22-5-31-3	19.1-6-64-3										92.1	293	16	10	
							4-1-15-0	4-2-7-0										8	23	1	-	
Oxford UCCE (the Parks) 9-11 May	11-3-28-1	10.2-0-50-4		19-9-42-1					13-3-47-1	16-4-53-1							17-5-53-2	86.2	281	8	10	
	11-3-37-0	18-5-58-4		14-1-61-1					1-1-0-0	1.3-0-19-0	11-5-24-0						14-1-67-1	70.3	271	5	7	
Gloucestershire (Bristol) 14-17 May	20-5-74-1		20-2-73-2	12-3-35-0		9-0-62-0	22-5-67-0											83	316	5	4	1
																		-	-	-	-	
Somerset (Southampton) 21-24 May	32-11-75-2	15-3-36-1	12.5-1-48-3	12-2-28-2	15-3-39-0		30-11-67-1											116.5	308	15	10	1
	11-3-37-2	7-2-17-0	3.5-0-27-0		11-3-32-2		7-2-13-0											39.5	128	2	4	
Durham (Southampton) 4-7 June	4-1-9-0	19-3-40-1	2-0-12-0				21-4-57-3	25-7-53-3				17-4-51-3						88	235	13	10	
	6-1-13-1	4-2-4-1	16-9-39-3				2-0-3-0	14-2-44-3				10-2-29-1						52	137	5	9	
Gloucestershire (Southampton) 27-30 June	19-7-48-3	25-6-84-2		16-4-44-1			17-6-45-2	16.5-8-31-3				14-2-41-2						66.5	185	20	10	
	29-12-79-3						9.1-1-34-0	24.3-5-75-1	5-1-20-0			21-5-79-2						129.4	427	12	10	1
Northamptonshire (Northampton) 2-4 July	25-6-55-6	16.4-4-49-1	1-0-1-0		21-6-72-3	6-1-35-0												69.4	218	6	10	
	6-1-18-0	4.4-0-7-0			5-0-24-0	5-0-37-3												20.4	87	1	3	
Glamorgan (Southampton) 15-18 July	20.1-4-50-3		17-2-87-3		22-5-72-3	17-3-86-0	20-2-89-1									9-0-46-0		105.1	437	7	10	
	5.2-2-11-1				16-3-51-6	10-1-42-3												31.2	104	1	10	
Yorkshire (Scarborough) 23-26 July	31-9-51-3	33-11-70-3	8-1-25-0	27-5-94-2	23-4-101-2					8-0-35-0								130	384	8	10	
	9-2-39-1	10.5-1-42-2		8-2-32-0	7-0-65-1					5-0-27-0								39.5	211	6	4	
Northamptonshire (Southampton) 31 July-3 August	14-3-49-0	13.3-7-12-3	8-1-21-4	13-4-49-3	7-1-37-0													55.3	176	8	10	
	16.4-5-28-0	34.5-11-114-2	10-0-56-0	20-4-54-1	13-1-59-2													93.4	330	19	5	
Derbyshire (Southampton) 13-14 August	26.3-11-45-4	17-3-63-2		19-1-80-0	7-0-55-0						26-8-82-4							95.3	341	16	10	
																		-	-	-	-	
Durham (Chester-le-Street) 20-23 August	32-9-71-3	16.5-3-50-2	9-1-29-0				18-0-105-1	29-3-121-3				27-2-115-1						131.5	515	24	10	
																		-	-	-	-	
Somerset (Taunton) 26-29 August	23-5-108-0	42-3-177-1		33-4-152-4	28-4-142-1				17-1-101-1						2-0-9-1			145	705	16	9	1
																		-	-	-	-	
Worcestershire (Southampton) 3-6 September	18-7-54-2	8-1-38-0	9-1-32-0	21.4-5-78-2	17-1-69-3				7-1-17-3			19-1-71-0						99.4	364	5	10	
	18-4-54-1	21.5-2-69-4	5-0-31-0	7-1-32-0					4-0-13-0			22-7-42-3						92.5	313	11	9	
Derbyshire (Derby) 17-20 September	14-4-38-0	19.3-2-52-3	3-0-13-0		13-4-54-1	13-2-58-0					22-3-93-6							84.3	317	9	10	
	16-5-43-1	29-14-50-1	11-5-30-0		14-3-60-2	19.1-6-63-6					6-1-30-0							95.1	289	13	10	
Overs	489.1	405.1	160.4	248.4	196	150.1	185.1	123.3	42	9.3	68	94	62	155.5	2	9	31					
Maidens	150	84	29	48	39	18	43	34	6	2	13	18	13	30	0	0	6					
Runs	1287	1222	591	929	829	721	534	356	178	53	262	310	200	553	9	46	120					
Wickets	40	39	17	27	19	16	13	14	5	0	7	8	8	18	1	0	3					
Average	32.2	31.3	34.8	34.4	43.6	45.1	41.1	25.4	35.6	-	37.4	38.8	25.0	30.7	9.0	-	40.0					

FIELDING

N Pothas (38 ct, 2st)
SM Katich
DA Kenway
I Brunnschweiler
RA Smith
AD Mascarenhas
LR Prittipaul
JD Francis
JHK Adams
WS Kendall
JP Crawley
CT Tremlett
SD Udal
JTA Bruce
AC Morris
JA Tomlinson
WPUJC Vaas
JRC Hamblin

KENT CCC

FIRST-CLASS MATCHES
BATTING

Match	GO Jones	MA Ealham	MJ Walker	ET Smith	MA Carberry	JC Tredwell	MJ Saggers	A Sheriyar	RWT Key	DP Fulton	A Symonds	A Khan	GS Blewett	BJ Trott	RS Ferley	M Muralitharan	Mohammad Sami	AGR Loudon	PD Trego	MJ Banes	Extras	Total	Wickets	Result
v. Cambridge UCCE			32*	61*	137				129				11								38	408	3	
(Fenner's) 18-20 April	43*	64	92			0*					47										10	256	3	D
v. Leicestershire	38	17	1	3	55	9	9	0*	25		23		57								8	245	10	
(Canterbury) 23-26 April	104	82	38	8	36	31	47	8*	18		11		0								28	411	10	D
v. Sussex	2	24	40	23	3	32*	9	2	0				41	0							9	185	10	
(Hove) 30 April-2 May	0	15	11	33	3	10	1	7*	28				37	0							14	159	10	L
v. Middlesex	52	32	32	103	53	36	16	12*	36				60	2							38	472	10	
(Canterbury) 14-17 May																					-	-	-	D
v. Warwickshire	12	9	106	43	58	10	24*	2					71	0					13		28	376	10	
(Edgbaston) 21-24 May																					-	-	-	D
v. Lancashire	92	43	11	26	38	16	12	4	11				0	0*							14	267	10	
(Canterbury) 30 May-2 June	31	79	52	56	0	16	14	5	37				7	12*							30	339	10	L
v. Sussex	46*	9	30	13	23	16	2	7			54		46			8					21	275	10	
(Tunbridge Wells) 4-7 June	22	3	7	40	40	11	0*	4			1		0			0					3	131	10	L
v. Essex	84	34	20	0	50	16		18*	93	37	12					2					15	381	10	
(Chelmsford) 27-30 June	108*	101	65	0	8	20			33	39						1					41	416	8	D
v. Surrey	38*	5	82*	135	16				14	53				9*	2						9	352	5	
(The Oval) 2-5 July	8	5	7	0	24	17			11	30				9*	2	0					1	114	10	
v. Nottinghamshire	82	5	0			16		0	31	6	8				14*		16				35	362	10	
(Maidstone) 9-11 July			11*	113					140	18	103*										33	418	3	W
v. Lancashire	66*	95	150	203		3*			1	47	10										27	602	6	
(Blackpool) 15-18 July																					-	-	-	D
v. Essex	5	3	8	108	6		4	0*	6	12	12					4					21	189	10	
(Canterbury) 30 July-1 August	31	8	23	32	36		4	0	4	94*	17					1					34	284	10	W
v. South Africa	50		7	5	0	10	8	47					2*	10				63		15	18	235	10	
(Canterbury) 7-9 August	6		27	75	4	1	1	49					0	4				30*		24	11	232	10	L
v. Middlesex	2	58	17	49			44	0*	40	86	71	78				12					20	477	10	
(Lord's) 13-16 August				4						45*	41*										4	96	2	W
v. Nottinghamshire	0	83	11	5			3	4*	7	43	1	46				15					24	242	10	
(Trent Bridge) 20-21 August				8*						46*	11										-	65	1	W
v. Surrey	53	93	25		92	10*			71		121	25			4	5		9			27	535	10	W
(Canterbury) 4-6 September																					-	-	-	
v. Leicestershire	9	13	24	21		4	4*	11	13	2	0							12			17	130	10	
(Leicester) 10-12 September	1	1	35	30			26*	11	15	21	0	17						0			12	169	10	L
v. Warwickshire	0	30	121	213		4	0*		54	51	88	7				4					22	594	10	W
(Canterbury) 17-19 September																					-	-	-	
Matches	18	17	17	15	14	13	13	13	12	11	10	7	7	7	5	5	3	3	1	1				
Innings	27	25	27	25	24	19	20	20	20	19	16	10	12	10	6	7	4	5	1	2				
Not Out	5	0	3	1	1	3	5	9	2	1	2	0	0	4	1	0	0	1	0	0				
Highest Score	108*	101	150	213	137	36	47	18*	140	94*	121	78	71	12*	14*	15	16	63	13	24				
Runs	985	911	1051	1447	824	267	240	97	732	674	659	236	377	37	38	49	19	110	13	39				
Average	44.77	36.44	43.79	60.29	35.83	16.69	16.00	8.82	40.67	37.44	47.07	23.60	31.42	6.17	7.60	7.00	4.75	27.50	13.00	19.50				
100s	2	1	3	7	1	0	0	0	2	0	2	0	0	0	0	0	0	0	0	0				
50s	7	7	4	2	6	0	0	0	1	5	4	1	3	0	0	0	0	1	0	0				
Catches/Stumpings	54/5	18/0	22/0	10/0	2/0	15/0	3/0	3/0	10/0	4/0	6/0	1/0	7/0	2/0	4/0	1/0	0/0	3/0	1/0	1/0				

Home Ground: Canterbury
Address: St Lawrence Ground, Old Dover Road, Canterbury, Kent CT1 3NZ
Tel: 01227 456886
Fax: 01227 762168
Indoor school: 01227 473605
Email: kent@ecb.co.uk
Directions: *By rail:* Canterbury East/West
By road: AA roadsigns
Capacity: 10,000
Other grounds used: The Mote, Maidstone; The Nevill, Tunbridge Wells

Year formed: 1870

Chief Executive: Paul Millman
First Team Coach: Ian Brayshaw
Other posts: *Head Groundsman:* Mike Grantham;
Second Team Coach: Chris Stone;
Marketing Manager: Jon Fordham
Captain: David Fulton
County colours: Blue and white

Website:
www.kentcountycricket.co.uk

Honours
County Championship
1906, 1909, 1910, 1913, 1970, 1978
Joint Champions
1977
Sunday League/NCL
1972, 1973, 1976, 1995, 2001
Benson & Hedges Cup
1973, 1978
Gillette Cup/NatWest/C&G Trophy
1967, 1974

KENT CCC

FIRST-CLASS MATCHES
BOWLING

Match	MA Ealham	A Sheriyar	MJ Saggers	JC Tredwell	A Symonds	A Khan	BJ Trott	GS Blewett	RS Ferley	MA Carberry	M Muralitharan	MJ Walker	Mohammad Sami	PD Trego	AGR Loudon	RWT Key	ET Smith	Overs	Total	Byes/Leg-byes	Wickets	Run outs
v. Cambridge UCCE (Fenner's) 18-20 April	7-3-15-0	22-3-101-3	28-7-70-2	26-13-38-2	20-1-93-0		9-3-29-0				8-2-24-1							120	395	25	8	
																		-	-	-	-	
v. Leicestershire (Canterbury) 23-26 April	20-9-36-2	20-4-72-1	24-4-75-4	4-2-3-1		17-4-61-1		8-5-6-1										93	270	17	10	
	8-1-28-0	14-3-44-2	17-3-60-2	12-7-21-0		14-1-77-2		5-2-16-0										70	255	9	6	
v. Sussex (Hove) 30 April-2 May	14-4-45-2	20.2-5-66-5	20-3-77-3	9-2-38-0			9-0-53-0											72.2	279	1	10	
	10-3-34-3	14-3-34-2	13-4-49-1	19.1-4-48-4			8-2-29-0											64.1	198	4	10	
v. Middlesex (Canterbury) 14-17 May	11-4-21-2	14-0-69-0	23-9-48-4	2.4-0-2-1			20-4-68-2	1-0-1-0										71.4	221	12	10	1
	4-0-18-0	11-0-31-0	12-2-42-0	24-6-70-2			16.3-3-52-2			4-1-22-0								71.3	249	14	4	
v. Warwickshire (Edgbaston) 21-24 May	12-2-39-0	17-2-66-2	23-5-62-5	1-0-7-0			17-2-90-1							8-0-43-1				78	311	4	10	1
	9-3-35-1							6-0-27-0	6-1-11-0		4-0-25-0			5-0-26-1				30	124	-	2	
v. Lancashire (Canterbury) 30 May-2 June	23-8-54-5	20.2-6-70-2	22-3-100-1	16-3-48-1			9-3-35-0	7-0-33-0										97.2	347	7	10	1
	15-3-44-0	19-3-58-1	13-2-36-2	26.5-4-112-4					2-0-4-0									91.5	334	13	10	1
v. Sussex (Tunbridge Wells) 4-7 June	20-8-63-1	24-6-49-4	24.1-6-76-2	12-0-65-0	10-2-30-1			5-0-21-1										95.1	311	7	10	1
	10-2-37-0	23.5-1-93-4	20-4-62-1	10-2-37-2	10-1-25-2			2-0-17-0										75.5	286	15	10	1
v. Essex (Chelmsford) 27-30 June	16-2-65-2	30-5-73-4		34-4-119-2	6-0-31-0		14-3-60-0		3-0-12-0				28.4-3-150-2					131.4	514	4	10	
v. Surrey (The Oval) 2-5 July	21-3-67-1		8-1-32-0		10-0-55-0		18-5-73-4	16.2-0-76-4		11.2-2-53-1	8-0-45-1	22-3-83-1						95.2	401	15	10	
			6-2-35-0		5-0-28-0		7-0-37-1				4-0-25-0	3-0-10-0					3-1-14-0	47.2	251	4	3	
v. Nottinghamshire (Maidstone) 9-11 July	5-1-17-0	6-3-17-0	5-2-9-0				19-6-39-2						14.1-3-64-8					49.1	156	10	10	
	13-4-39-1	13-2-40-0	21-5-84-1	10-2-42-1			21-6-70-0						21.2-8-50-7					101.2	337	12	10	
v. Lancashire (Blackpool) 15-18 July	14-4-46-0	19-6-63-3	20-1-93-3	25-8-64-2	13-3-30-0		14-4-51-2											105	365	18	10	
	12-4-31-1	12-2-35-0	12-3-31-3	18-4-64-1	13-4-42-1		16-7-30-0											84	244	11	6	
v. Essex (Canterbury) 30 July-1 August	17-8-26-5		13-5-29-1		15-0-65-4						22-9-41-0							69	183	7	10	
	12-3-32-0	14-6-30-1	15-4-40-1		11-2-61-2						28.1-6-61-6							80.1	235	11	10	
v. South Africa (Canterbury) 7-9 August		15-5-44-2	16-4-63-0	8-1-50-0			12-4-62-1	11-0-68-0							10.3-1-52-1			70.3	325	6	4	
		12-7-70-0	12-3-34-2	17-0-75-3			4-0-23-0	10-0-35-2										55	243	6	7	
v. Middlesex (Lord's) 13-16 August	15-3-42-0	15-6-40-0	26-3-95-2		4-1-18-0	17-1-100-2					38-4-103-5							115	407	9	10	1
	9-7-11-0	4-2-6-1	17-4-31-3		11-0-27-1	7-2-38-1					21.2-8-38-4							69.2	165	14	10	
v. Nottinghamshire (Trent Bridge) 20-21 August	7-4-14-1		13.5-2-42-5		9-2-38-3	8-2-41-1					1-0-16-0							40.5	177	2	10	
	6-1-18-1	2-0-24-0	7-4-20-1		7-2-12-2	4-0-31-0					15.3-3-36-6							39.3	126	9	10	
v. Surrey (Canterbury) 4-6 September			10-1-40-4		3-0-14-1		11-0-50-3			4.5-2-11-2								28.5	125	10	10	
	6-1-17-1		14-5-37-3		10-3-36-0					11-2-43-2	25-5-90-4							70	255	10	10	
v. Leicestershire (Leicester) 10-12 September	13-2-32-1	10-1-48-1	15-2-63-1		7-2-23-0	15-2-67-1					22.1-4-51-6							82.1	295	11	10	
														1-0-1-0	0.4-0-4-0			1.4	5	-	-	
v. Warwickshire (Canterbury) 17-19 September	15.5-7-35-6		15-2-67-2		12-2-42-2				5-1-22-0									70.5	267	12	10	
	13-2-52-2	7-0-19-0	8-2-19-0	17-1-85-2	10-4-24-2				14.4-2-45-3									68.4	257	-	10	1
Overs	357.5	374.3	450	329.4	152	165	150.3	43	149.2	23	178	17	89.1	13	10.3	0.4	3					
Maidens	106	76	97	73	26	16	27	10	30	2	41	2	17	0	1	0	1					
Runs	1013	1257	1441	1125	517	797	649	150	532	94	447	75	357	69	52	4	14					
Wickets	38	38	58	28	16	17	13	2	16	1	33	1	18	2	1	0	0					
Average	26.7	33.1	24.8	40.2	32.3	46.9	49.9	75.0	33.2	94.0	13.5	75.0	19.8	34.5	52.0	-	-					

FIELDING

- 9 GO Jones (54 ct, 5st)
- 2 MJ Walker
- 8 MA Ealham
- 6 JC Tredwell
- 0 ET Smith
- 0 RWT Key
- GS Blewett
- A Symonds
- RS Ferley
- DP Fulton
- MJ Saggers
- AGR Loudon
- A Sheriyar
- BJ Trott
- MA Carberry
- PD Trego
- M Muralitharan
- A Khan
- MJ Banes

LANCASHIRE CCC

FIRST-CLASS MATCHES
BATTING

Match	MJ Chilton	G Chapple	SG Law	MB Love	WK Hegg	CL Hooper	IJ Sutcliffe	AJ Swann	PJ Martin	CP Schofield	G Keedy	J Wood	A Flintoff	SI Mahmood	KW Hogg	JM Anderson	MR Currie	JJ Haynes	SP Crook	PJ Horton	Extras	Total	Wickets	Result	Pos
v. Surrey	28	32	169	126	14		70	57		1			43	16	3*						40	599	10		
(The Oval) 18-21 April																								D	12
v. Nottinghamshire	14	28	6	113	0		42	15	1	3			97		0*						35	354	10		
(Old Trafford) 23-26 April			8*	7			17*	7													2	41	2	D	11
v. Middlesex	119	7*	198	30	9		27	45					111								19	565	7		
(Lord's) 9-12 May																								D	11
v. Essex	106	1	6	33	23	8	109	33	23	0						9*					24	375	10		
(Old Trafford) 14-17 May																								D	11
v. Durham UCCE	89					101		137		47				5*			97	13		2*	11	502	6		
(Racecourse) 21-23 May																								D	
v. Kent	10	66	0	27	37*	0		8	2	0			154	34							9	347	10		
(Canterbury) 30 May-2 June	5	3	67	86	35	48		4	8	4*			43	16							15	334	10	W	20
v. Leicestershire	108	15	82	54	23*	74	55						71*								21	503	6		
(Liverpool) 4-7 June	16*						5*														3	24	-	W	22
v. Essex	0	31	80	5	6	18		7	12	35*				5				12			7	218	10		
(Chelmsford) 2-5 July	70	132*	4	0	61*	50		16		38								0			12	383	7	D	8
v. Kent	114	33	29	13	10*	60		2	18	66	0				2						18	365	10		
(Blackpool) 15-18 July	2	9	0	16*		128*		1		40											15	244	6	D	12
v. Warwickshire	30	132	236*	14	7*	35	86	15													20	575	6		
(Old Trafford) 23-26 July																								D	12
v. Leicestershire	14	8	186	45	27	117		7	19	6	8*				12						30	479	10		
(Leicester) 30 July-2 August	9		15	21*	20*			1													2	68	3	W	22
v. Sussex	65	54	96	2	31	23	43	9	3	0*		30									21	377	10		
(Hove) 14-17 August	9	7	7	33	25	1	12	0	18	2*		0									25	139	10	L	7
v. Middlesex	125	21*	144	137		201	4	58*													44	734	5		
(Old Trafford) 21-24 August																								D	10
v. Surrey	27	1	67	19		114	8	8		0	1*	6					56				34	341	10		
(Old Trafford) 26-29 August	33*	35*						47									13				7	135	2	W	20
v. Warwickshire	121	60	168	102	12	177	16			0	0*				31				27		67	781	10		
(Edgbaston) 3-6 September																								W	21
v. Sussex	6	14	163*	144	26*	33	38		1												25	450	6		
(Old Trafford) 10-13 September																								W	22
v. Nottinghamshire	7	25	51	9	11	11	37		4		1*	3			46						14	219	10		
(Trent Bridge) 17-20 September	27	0	3	28	12	0	65		16		2*	20			53						17	243	10	L	4
Matches	17	16	16	15	15	14	12	10	9	9	7	6	5	4	4	3	2	2	1	1					
Innings	25	21	24	22	20	20	17	15	12	12	10	8	6	5	5	3	3	3	1	1					
Not Out	2	3	4	1	7	2	2	0	0	2	6	2	1	1	0	3	0	0	0	1					
Highest Score	125	132*	236*	144	61*	201	109	137	23	66	0	30	154	34	53	9*	97	13	27	2*					
Runs	1154	679	1820	1062	404	1219	681	355	120	310	16	67	519	62	158	12	166	25	27	2					
Average	50.17	37.72	91.00	50.57	31.08	67.72	45.40	23.67	10.00	31.00	4.00	11.17	103.80	15.50	31.60	12.00	55.33	8.33	27.00	2.00					
100s	6	2	7	5	0	6	1	1	0	0	0	0	2	0	0	0	0	0	0	0					
50s	3	3	6	2	1	3	4	1	0	2	0	0	2	0	1	0	2	0	0	0					
Catches/Stumpings	14/0	7/0	14/0	3/0	44/2	14/0	11/0	14/0	7/0	9/0	4/0	2/0	6/0	1/0	1/0	3/0	3/0	3/0	1/0	1/0					

Home Ground: Old Trafford
Address: Old Trafford, Manchester M16 0PX
Tel: 0161 282 4000 (switchboard)
0161 282 4040 (ticket/membership office)
Fax: 0161 873 8353 (ticket office)
Indoor cricket centre: 0161 282 4039
Email: enquiries@lccc.co.uk
Directions: By rail: Manchester Piccadilly or Victoria then Metro link to Old Trafford (station alongside ground). By road: M63, Stretford slip road (junction 7) on to A56; follow signs.
Capacity: 21,500
Other grounds used: Blackpool (Stanley Park); Liverpool (Aigburth); Southport (Trafalgar Road); Lytham (Church Road).
Year formed: 1864

Chairman: Jack Simmons MBE
Chief Executive: Jim Cumbes
Other posts: Head Groundsman: Peter Marron;
Sales & Marketing Manager: Geoff Durbin
Cricket Manager: Mike Watkinson
Second XI Coach: Gary Yates
Captain: Warren Hegg
County colours: Red, blue, green

Website:
www.lccc.co.uk

Honours
County Championship
1897, 1904, 1926, 1927, 1928, 1930, 193
Joint Champions
1950
Sunday League/NCL
1970, 1989, 1998, 1999
Benson & Hedges Cup
1984, 1990, 1995, 1996
Gillette Cup/NatWest/C&G Trophy
1970, 1971, 1972, 1975, 1990, 1996, 199

LANCASHIRE CCC

FIRST-CLASS MATCHES
BOWLING

Match	G Chapple	PJ Martin	CL Hooper	G Keedy	J Wood	CP Schofield	MJ Chilton	KW Hogg	JM Anderson	SI Mahmood	A Flintoff	SG Law	SP Crook	MB Loye	AJ Swann	IJ Sutcliffe	OJ Newby	Overs	Total	Byes/Leg-byes	Wickets	Run outs
v. Surrey (The Oval) 18-21 April	15-2-52-1 / 20-1-103-1					17.4-4-77-3 / 25-8-86-0	9-1-39-0 / 12-3-46-1	13-2-61-5 / 22-7-72-1		13-2-42-1 / 19-5-47-2				2-0-11-0				67.4 / 100	280 / 379	9 / 17	10 / 6	/ 1
v. Nottinghamshire (Old Trafford) 23-26 April	18.3-3-51-2	19-3-54-5		13-0-52-0				20-2-76-2			11-4-23-1	1-0-3-0						82.3 / -	275 / -	16 / -	10 / -	
v. Middlesex (Lord's) 9-12 May	17-2-63-1 / 10-4-24-0	16-3-52-0 / 12-3-25-0		22.2-5-68-6 / 23-2-82-0				19-3-90-2 / 11-1-34-0		3-0-17-1 / 4-2-6-0								77.2 / 60	304 / 176	14 / 5	10 / -	
v. Essex (Old Trafford) 14-17 May	13-3-40-0 / 43-0-18-1	12-3-32-3 / 7-2-12-1	8.5-3-34-2 / 1-1-0-0	5-0-24-1		4-0-10-0		15-1-67-4 / 7-3-11-1										57.5 / 19.3	215 / 42	8 / 1	10 / 3	
v. Durham UCCE (Racecourse) 21-23 May			6-0-11-0 / 12-3-31-0	20-1-50-0 / 4-0-11-0		31-10-64-4 / 5-1-10-0	2-0-13-0 / 2-1-2-1		24-3-76-4 / 14-4-37-5			16-3-62-0 / 8-0-35-0			18-4-41-1 / 11-3-41-0			117 / 56	327 / 175	10 / 8	9 / 6	
v. Kent (Canterbury) 30 May-2 June	15-4-43-1 / 21.2-5-66-4	20-8-52-2 / 28-3-95-1	7-1-24-0 / 19-2-55-0	23.1-4-39-5 / 29-5-79-4					12-1-40-2 / 6-0-20-1									77.1 / 103.2	267 / 339	9 / 24	10 / 10	
v. Leicestershire (Liverpool) 4-7 June	21-4-66-3 / 12-1-57-0	20-2-71-2 / 1-0-6-0	9-1-34-0 / 26.4-7-52-5	24.4-12-40-3 / 29-7-61-4					19-3-91-2 / 4-1-21-0									93.4 / 72.4	314 / 212	9 / 15	10 / 10	1
v. Essex (Chelmsford) 2-5 July	13-3-44-2 / 19-3-58-1	21-8-60-4 / 18-4-50-0	16.5-7-30-3 / 32-13-51-6			1-0-1-1 / 10-2-30-1			10-1-67-0 / 9-2-39-1									61.5 / 88	208 / 236	6 / 8	10 / 9	
v. Kent (Blackpool) 15-18 July	27-8-64-1	26-4-82-1		51-10-147-3		21-1-101-0	15-1-86-0	13-2-36-0	11-1-53-0			2-0-8-1	3-0-11-0					169 / -	602 / -	14 / -	6 / -	
v. Warwickshire (Old Trafford) 23-26 July	21-4-82-4 / 9-1-34-1	17-1-55-1 / 18.4-5-57-2	13-3-42-2 / 12-4-13-0	22-12-31-1 / 24-3-74-0	8-1-33-2 / 9-1-36-1													81 / 72.4	255 / 211	12 / 7	10 / 4	
v. Leicestershire (Leicester) 30 July-2 August	15-4-53-1 / 23-4-84-3	17-1-77-2 / 26-11-51-1	6-2-15-0 / 8-1-25-0	9.4-3-17-4 / 21-4-59-2	16-3-59-3 / 10-1-42-3			10-3-29-0 / 5-1-21-0										73.4 / 93	259 / 287	9 / 5	10 / 10	1
v. Sussex (Hove) 14-17 August	7-0-48-0 / 21-3-89-3	15-2-64-1 / 21-5-61-3	12-2-48-1 / 22-4-65-0	24-6-76-1 / 19-3-61-0	17-2-64-3 / 17.4-2-72-1	5.3-2-14-3 / 4-0-25-0	12-2-33-0	8-2-24-1										100.3 / 104.4	385 / 383	10 / 10	10 / 7	
v. Middlesex (Old Trafford) 21-24 August	19-0-71-1 / 6-1-18-0	17-6-44-2 / 9-3-17-1	26-9-53-1 / 18-3-51-4	52-10-188-5 / 29-8-76-2	13-1-43-0 / 4-0-21-0	34-5-120-1 / 11-2-34-0				3-0-12-0 / 1-0-6-0								164 / 78	544 / 237	13 / 14	10 / 7	
v. Surrey (Old Trafford) 26-29 August	21-4-87-1 / 7-1-24-1	14.4-2-54-3 / 12-5-20-3	18-6-38-0 / 3-0-7-0	24-9-62-3 / 14.1-1-57-4	15-4-64-2 / 7-0-29-1		10-2-18-1											102.4 / 43.1	337 / 138	14 / 1	10 / 10	1
v. Warwickshire (Edgbaston) 3-6 September	28-6-92-3 / 20-7-86-5		7-0-16-0 / 2-0-4-0	26.5-4-84-2 / 18-9-33-2	23-3-101-2 / 9-1-32-1		10-4-15-0	24-7-66-2 / 7-3-24-1		2-0-8-0	12-1-52-1 / 1.1-0-6-1							132.5 / 57.1	449 / 187	15 / 2	10 / 10	
v. Sussex (Old Trafford) 10-13 September	15-2-54-0	15-4-40-0 / 20-7-43-2	5-0-17-2 / 17-3-33-0	28-5-106-5 / 32-6-61-5	9-3-17-3 / 14-4-27-2	1-0-5-0 / 4-0-14-1												73 / 87	251 / 180	12 / 2	10 / 10	
v. Nottinghamshire (Trent Bridge) 17-20 September	23-2-78-2 / 33-8-98-6	21-4-66-1 / 8.5-0-55-0	9-2-16-1	15-2-51-1 / 16-4-40-0	19-4-80-3 / 11-1-43-0			13-2-71-1 / 9-0-50-1				2-0-8-0			4-1-11-1			100 / 83.5	376 / 319	9 / 14	9 / 8	
Overs	494.2	432.1	366.2	502.1	222.4	187.1	43	97	107	109	50	7	37.1	4	5	4	29					
Maidens	90	99	86	136	32	37	9	22	19	18	13	0	4	0	0	1	7					
Runs	1744	1295	912	1593	854	636	109	370	411	444	135	29	155	16	22	11	82					
Wickets	49	41	30	60	27	15	1	7	15	15	5	0	2	1	0	1	1					
Average	35.2	31.5	30.4	26.5	31.6	42.4	109.0	52.9	27.4	29.6	27.0	-	77.5	16.0	-	11.0	82.0					

FIELDING

46	WK Hegg (44 ct, 2st)
4	AJ Swann
4	SG Law
4	CL Hooper
4	MJ Chilton
1	IJ Sutcliffe
	CP Schofield
	G Chapple
	PJ Martin
	A Flintoff
	G Keedy
	MB Loye
	MA Currie
	JM Anderson
	JJ Haynes
	J Wood
	KW Hogg
	PJ Horton
	SI Mahmood
	SP Crook

LEICESTERSHIRE CCC

FIRST-CLASS MATCHES

BATTING

Match	DL Maddy	PA Nixon	BJ Hodge	DD Masters	JN Snape	PAJ DeFreitas	JK Maunders	DI Stevens	CE Dagnall	TR Ward	JL Sadler	V Sehwag	VC Drakes	DG Brandy	RM Amin	MJA Whiley	DE Malcolm	DS Brignull	RJ Cunliffe	LJ Wright	GW Walker	Extras	Total	Wickets	Result	Pts
v. Kent	63	113*		15	0	5		4	0	29	4			9			1					27	270	10		9
(Canterbury) 23-26 April	4	53		26*	34*	45				22	0			52								19	255	6	D	9
v. Essex	16	10	5	8*	2	8		65	0	44				21			7					15	201	10		8
(Leicester) 30 April-3 May	39*	17	19		5	8		1						6*								9	104	5	D	8
v. Loughborough UCCE	229*		202*							34	24											8	497	2		
(Leicester) 9-11 May																						-	-	-	W	
v. Surrey	1	22	14	33	10	65	0		23*	14	2					3						13	200	10		7
(The Oval) 14-17 May	40	1	47	0	5*	0	0		0			81										11	185	8	D	7
v. Middlesex	0	17	22	0	54	9	29				10					0*		46	0			11	198	10		7
(Leicester) 21-24 May																						-	-	-	D	7
v. Lancashire	85	0	26	0	31	16	16	65	5*		30					5						35	314	10		5
(Liverpool) 4-7 June	48	32	14	0	26	9	39	6	0*		5					6						27	212	10	L	5
v. Nottinghamshire	23	5	13	25*	0	5	3	4	0			137			1							27	243	10		8
(Leicester) 27-30 June				5			0*															-	5	1	D	8
v. Warwickshire	98	11	7	0	4	45	64	7	23		30					0*						39	328	10		10
(Leicester) 2-5 July	0	36	128		5*	6*	2	3			40											21	241	6	D	10
v. Middlesex	4	52*	52	23	3	46	55	25				130			5	6						46	447	10		7
(Southgate) 9-12 July	94	34	112	4	40*	0	0	0				13			11	3						24	335	10	L	7
v. Sussex	30	4	47	0	36	103	51	15*	4							0						30	320	10		5
(Leicester) 15-18 July	40	11	18	0	20	8	27	50	15	50						6*						13	258	10	L	5
v. Essex	41	30	74	8	52*	44	149	1		168												34	600	7		12
(Southend) 23-26 July																						-	-	-	D	12
v. Lancashire	19	19	5	10*	27	57	21	54	20							1	3					23	259	10		4
(Leicester) 30 July-2 August	14	33	38	1	36	0	75	50	0							6*	14					20	287	10	L	4
v. Warwickshire	51	0	70	9	0	38				42	59*	17	6			16						38	346	10		2
(Edgbaston) 14-16 August	44	33*	35	3	37	10				0	4	0	4									25	195	10	L	2
v. Surrey	12	30	20	1	10	4	12		22*		31		10	4								10	166	10		6
(Leicester) 21-24 August	20	44*	157				171				145			31*								68	636	4	D	6
v. Nottinghamshire	9	65	302*	48	0	33						2	4*	19								41	523	7		12
(Trent Bridge) 26-29 August																						-	-	-	D	12
v. Kent	1	3	31	3	45*	8	129	0	15	20	18											22	295	10		19
(Leicester) 10-12 September	1*						2*															2	5	-	W	19
v. Sussex	55	1	36	2	13	23	21				0	8								0	4*	16	179	10		
(Hove) 17-19 September	29	0	1	119	1	0	15				145	0								11*	21	38	380	10	L	
Matches	17	16	16	15	15	15	12	11	9	9	7	6	5	5	4	4	3	3	1	1	1					
Innings	29	27	26	23	23	25	22	19	11	15	11	10	7	9	7	6	4	4	1	2	2					
Not Out	3	4	2	3	6	2	2	0	5	0	1	0	1	2	2	2	0	0	0	1	1					
Highest Score	229*	113*	302*	119	54	103	171	149	23*	168	145	137	18	52	11	16	14	46	0	11*	21					
Runs	1110	676	1495	269	494	493	777	615	103	443	434	478	57	148	30	29	27	58	0	11	25					
Average	42.69	29.39	62.29	13.45	29.06	21.43	38.85	32.37	17.17	29.53	43.40	47.80	9.50	21.14	6.00	7.25	6.75	14.50	0.00	11.00	25.00					
100s	1	1	5	1	0	1	2	1	0	1	2	2	0	0	0	0	0	0	0	0	0					
50s	6	3	3	0	2	2	3	6	0	1	1	1	0	1	0	0	0	0	0	0	0					
Catches/Stumpings	15/0	50/2	12/0	4/0	8/0	6/0	3/0	12/0	0/0	7/0	5/0	4/0	1/0	2/0	0/0	1/0	0/0	0/0	0/0	0/0	1/0					

Home Ground: Grace Road, Leicester
Address: County Ground, Grace Road, Leicester LE2 8AD
Tel: 0116 283 2128
Fax: 0116 244 0363
Email: leicestershirecc@ukonline.co.uk
Directions: *By road:* Follow signs from city centre, or from southern ring road from M1 or A6.
Capacity: 5,500
Other grounds used: None
Year formed: 1879

Chief Executive: Kevin Hill
First XI Coach: Phil Whiticase
Other posts: *County coaches:* Russell Cobb, John Smith, Lloyd Tennant
Captain: Phil DeFreitas
County colours: Dark green and scarlet

Honours
County Championship
1975, 1996, 1998
Sunday League/NCL
1974, 1977
Benson & Hedges Cup
1972, 1975, 1985

Website:
www.leicestershireccc.com

LEICESTERSHIRE CCC

FIRST-CLASS MATCHES

BOWLING

	DD Masters	DL Maddy	PAJ DeFreitas	JN Snape	BJ Hodge	CE Dagnall	DI Stevens	MJA Whiley	VC Drakes	RM Amin	V Sehwag	DE Malcolm	DG Brandy	DS Brignull	JK Maunders	JL Sadler	GW Walker	JO Grove	LJ Wright	Overs	Total	Byes/Leg-byes	Wickets	Run outs
v. Kent (Canterbury) 23-26 April	17-5-47-1	13.2-2-59-2	13-1-60-0		14-4-43-3									11-4-30-2						68.2	245	6	10	2
	16-4-83-0	20-4-63-0	28-7-69-4	9.2-2-26-2		27-4-95-2	4-0-9-0							17-3-42-2						121.2	411	24	10	
v. Essex (Leicester) 30 April-3 May	8-3-31-3	9.3-4-19-2	18-8-34-3		16-4-49-1	1-0-4-0						10-3-39-1								62.3	188	12	10	
	7-1-31-1		11-1-43-0	3-1-13-0	16.5-3-66-5							9-3-31-3								46.5	191	7	9	
v. Loughborough UCCE (Leicester) 9-11 May	10.4-3-49-2		12-3-42-2									16-6-40-5				7-1-20-0		8-2-21-1		46.4	154	2	10	
	15-4-56-1				20-4-47-1	19-7-35-3						16-1-88-3	1.3-0-11-2		12-1-43-0					90.3	308	8	10	
v. Surrey (The Oval) 14-17 May	20-4-93-0	9-2-23-0	36-9-101-4	20.2-2-92-2	7-0-50-0	28-8-95-1	5-3-11-0		4-1-26-0	16-4-58-1										145.2	560	11	8	
v. Middlesex (Leicester) 21-24 May	10-2-33-3	13.1-1-49-5	14-4-37-1					6-0-54-1					11-3-22-0							54.1	201	6	10	
	6-1-12-1	10-2-29-1	16-7-35-1				3-1-5-1	6.5-2-27-0					8-1-28-1							49.5	142	6	5	
v. Lancashire (Liverpool) 4-7 June	17-3-68-1	15-1-84-2	31-9-73-0	11-1-48-0	2-0-10-0	28-8-81-1	1-0-15-0		1-0-1-0					21.4-3-113-2						127.4	503	10	6	
				4-0-11-0					4.2-0-10-0											8.2	24	3	–	
v. Nottinghamshire (Leicester) 27-30 June	20-7-58-2	17.5-7-52-2	30-9-68-4	4-0-11-0	4-0-12-1		19-5-69-0	1-0-1-0	14-3-40-1											109.5	326	15	10	
	12-2-62-1	7-2-15-1	10-3-23-0	6-2-22-0			16-4-61-4		13-1-90-0	3-1-30-0										67	318	15	6	
v. Warwickshire (Leicester) 2-5 July	17-4-53-5	12-3-36-1	13-9-22-1	3-0-5-1		12-3-46-0		17-3-76-2				1-0-1-0			3-1-10-0					75	253	14	10	
	14.5-3-60-2	9-1-32-0	31-10-78-6	4-1-20-0	3-0-16-0	19-5-60-1	3-0-15-0					1-0-1-0			3-1-10-0					99.5	361	12	10	1
v. Middlesex (Southgate) 9-12 July	26-6-81-3	11-1-32-0	24-5-75-1	17-0-83-1	5-2-18-1				27.4-4-118-0	34-8-137-1	16-1-66-0									160.4	620	10	7	
	3-0-17-0	1-0-10-0	3-0-19-0	2-0-17-0					5-0-32-1	8-0-49-1	2-0-10-0									24	166	12	2	
v. Sussex (Leicester) 15-18 July	27-5-89-0	17-1-70-1	29.5-10-55-5	4-0-10-0	1-0-1-0	30-10-87-2	5-1-11-0			19-5-50-2				5-0-12-0						137.5	416	31	10	
	8.2-1-31-1	7-0-23-1	2.4-0-50-1	1.5-0-6-1	6-0-28-0	2-0-20-0				11-1-41-2										38.5	166	12	5	
v. Essex (Southend) 23-26 July	18.2-4-53-1	17-9-42-4		5-2-13-0	9-2-35-1	22-5-58-2			19-3-62-1			23-3-82-1								113.2	351	6	10	
	9-5-17-0	6-3-8-0	8-2-19-0	4-1-6-0			5-2-13-1		3-0-8-0			11.1-2-38-0								46.1	111	2	1	
v. Lancashire (Leicester) 30 July-2 August	31.2-4-107-2	15-3-56-1	41-14-88-6	8-1-28-0	1-0-7-0				12-1-68-0			27-5-102-1								135.2	479	23	10	
	9-0-36-0	10.2-5-24-3							1-0-6-0											20.2	68	2	3	
v. Warwickshire (Edgbaston) 14-16 August	10-1-40-3	9.2-3-29-3	16-1-67-0					16-1-77-2	15-4-42-2			2-0-10-0								68.2	277	12	10	
	13-2-50-0	12-1-51-1	16-3-40-1					7-0-59-0	12-5-31-0							0.5-0-20-0				58.5	267	7	2	
v. Surrey (Leicester) 21-24 August	16-0-78-0	14-1-40-2	29-10-87-1	30-6-108-3	1-0-5-0	23-3-88-0			21.1-2-85-3			2-1-5-0								134.1	501	10	9	
	6-1-19-0		9-2-31-1			3-0-14-0			8-1-41-0											28	117	7	2	1
v. Nottinghamshire (Trent Bridge) 26-29 August	14-6-29-0	23-3-62-3	10.4-2-48-0	17-3-62-3	5-1-18-0				29-9-80-0			2-0-21-0						7-0-18-0		106.4	290	11	10	
	11-2-52-1	10.4-2-48-0	17-3-62-0						15-4-58-3			1-0-11-0						3-2-1-0		57.4	241	9	7	
v. Kent (Leicester) 10-12 September	6-2-5-0	3.3-2-6-2	16-5-44-2		9-1-37-3				15-4-29-2											49.3	130	9	10	1
	9-0-44-3	10.5-1-43-2	11-3-16-2		6-1-23-2				9-2-33-1											45.5	169	10	10	
v. Sussex (Hove) 17-19 September	18-0-88-0	4-0-21-0	28-4-94-2	12-0-72-0	6-0-51-1				19-2-64-0					1-0-16-0			19-1-92-1		19-0-95-0	126	614	21	4	
																				–	–	–	–	
Overs	425.3	297.1	540.3	177.3	68	295.5	23	117.3	143.1	146.1	34.2	94	8.3	68.4	9	7.5	29	20	19					
Maidens	85	59	154	25	12	70	5	14	33	24	4	22	1	14	1	1	3	3	0					
Runs	1581	1002	1443	669	274	1005	71	562	463	601	153	358	58	235	38	40	111	64	95					
Wickets	37	36	60	11	7	28	1	7	11	8	0	14	2	7	0	0	1	1	0					
Average	42.7	27.8	24.1	60.8	39.1	35.9	71.0	80.3	42.1	75.1	–	25.6	29.0	33.6	–	–	111.0	64.0	–					

FIELDING

2	PA Nixon (50 ct, 2st)
5	DL Maddy
2	BJ Hodge
2	DI Stevens
	JN Snape
	TR Ward
	PAJ DeFreitas
	JL Sadler
	V Sehwag
	DD Masters
	JK Maunders
	DG Brandy
	VC Drakes
	MJA Whiley
	GW Walker

MIDDLESEX CCC

FIRST–CLASS MATCHES
BATTING

Match	AJ Strauss	OA Shah	PN Weekes	EC Joyce	BL Hutton	DC Nash	SG Koenig	CB Keegan	SJ Cook	JH Dawes	Abdul Razzaq	JWM Dalrymple	AA Noffke	TF Bloomfield	Imran Tahir	RMS Weston	BW Gannon	CT Peploe	MJ Brown	Extras	Total	Wickets	Result	Pts
v. Oxford UCCE (The Parks) 12-14 April	76	73	8*	12		12	166													17	364	4		
	3*		17	50*	27	27		26	12											9	171	5	D	
v. Essex (Chelmsford) 18-21 April	1	13	31	28	45*	0	42	24	22	2	0									6	214	10		
	40	46	0	117	23	42	94	0	0	32*	81									20	495	10	D	8
v. Sussex (Lord's) 23-26 April	10	1	0	8	2	17	43	8	5	3*	3									16	116	10		
	83	61	33	49	11*	29	7		22*		11									24	330	7	W	17
v. Lancashire (Lord's) 9-12 May	6	81	39	53	33	13	34	21		1*		1	0							22	304	10		
	100*						71*													5	176	–	D	8
v. Kent (Canterbury) 14-17 May	3	5	3	0	74	12	42	19		16					29		1*			17	221	10		
	93	21	1*	15*	5		96					18								18	249	4	D	8
v. Leicestershire (Leicester) 21-24 May	28	28	29	0	3	3	18	32	2				40	1*						17	201	10		
	25	9	6	23	41*	11*	18													9	142	5	D	8
v. Zimbabwe (Shenley) 30 May-2 June	0	68	102*	80	2		9*									129			98	28	516	6		
	49	101*		19*												41				12	222	2	D	
v. Essex (Lord's) 4-7 June	11	4	51*	69	107	1	0	21	20		54	8								17	363	10		
																				–	–	–	D	11
v. Surrey (Lord's) 27-30 June	47	31	39	0	101	36*	22	20	0		29	23								22	370	10		
	95	7*		5*			89													22	218	2	D	10
v. Leicestershire (Southgate) 9-12 July	147	16	75	102	40	103*	20				25	33*								59	620	7		
	73*	20	29	29*																15	166	2	W	22
v. Warwickshire (Southgate) 15-18 July	37	31	10	29	38	44*	35	0			0	0	7							29	260	10		
	23			22*	102*		96					0								38	281	3	D	8
v. Surrey (Guildford) 23-26 July	87	22	0	0	2	96*	42	4	4		78	18								32	385	10		
																				–	–	–	D	11
v. Nottinghamshire (Trent Bridge) 30 July-2 August	29	13	0	36	16	36	75	4	19*	9		20								21	278	10		
	6	41	11	14	29	14*	10					18*								3	146	6	W	19
v. Kent (Lord's) 13-16 August	12	0	11	43	17	113	57	36*	65	18	5									30	407	10		
	9	12	51	17	3	23	0	2	0*		28									20	165	10	L	7
v. Lancashire (Old Trafford) 21-24 August	155	147	24	3	107	15	13	18		0*	22		17							23	544	10		
	63	15	26*	41	10	23	16*				25	0								18	237	7	D	10
v. Warwickshire (Edgbaston) 26-29 August	0	54	23	107	5		9	9			12			9*		31				23	286	10		
	61	25	7	9	37	5		3*	0			0				6				9	171	10	L	5
v. Sussex (Hove) 5-8 September	138	140	31	22	1	15	5	3	11	0								0*		26	392	10		
	4	34	65	31	36	5	16	3*	11	2								13		30	250	10	L	7
v. Nottinghamshire (Lord's) 10-13 September	15	87	38	14	20	53*	13	17		14		26	0							29	326	10		
																				–	–	–	D	10
Matches	18	18	18	18	18	17	16	16	12	9	8	6	6	3	3	2	1	1	1					
Innings	33	30	29	30	30	26	27	20	17	12	11	10	7	4	3	4	1	2	1					
Not Out	3	2	5	4	6	7	2	3	3	5	0	1	1	1	1	0	1	1	0					
Highest Score	155	147	102*	117	107	113	166	36*	65	32*	81	33*	40	9*	29	129	1*	13	98					
Runs	1529	1206	760	1023	961	752	1140	270	211	97	328	121	134	19	30	207	1	13	98					
Average	50.97	43.07	31.67	39.35	40.04	39.58	45.60	15.88	15.07	13.86	29.82	13.44	22.33	6.33	15.00	51.75	1.00	13.00	98.00					
100s	4	3	1	3	4	2	1	0	0	0	0	0	0	0	0	1	0	0	0					
50s	8	6	4	4	1	2	7	0	1	0	3	0	0	0	0	0	0	0	1					
Catches/Stumpings	6/0	11/0	20/0	7/0	17/0	42/3	3/0	5/0	5/0	3/0	2/0	3/0	2/0	2/0	0/0	0/0	0/0	2/0	2/0					

Home Ground: Lord's Cricket Ground
Address: Lord's Cricket Ground,
St John's Wood, London NW8 8QN
Tel: 020 7289 1300
Fax: 020 7289 5831
Email: enquiries.middx@ecb.co.uk
Directions: *By underground:* St John's Wood on Jubilee Line
(five minutes' walk). *By bus:* 13, 82, 113 stop along east side
of ground; 139 at south-west corner; 274 at top
of Regent's Park
Capacity: 28,000

Other grounds used: Southgate; Richmond
Year formed: 1864

Chairman: Phil Edmonds
Secretary: Vinny Codrington
Head Coach: John Emburey
Assistant Coach: Jason Pooley
Captain: Andrew Strauss
County colours: Navy

Website:
www.middlesexccc.co.uk

Honours
County Championship
1903, 1920, 1921, 1947, 1976, 1980, 1982
1985, 1990, 1993
Joint Champions
1949, 1977
Sunday League/NCL
1992
Benson & Hedges Cup
1983, 1986
Gillette Cup/NatWest/C&G Trophy
1977, 1980, 1984, 1988, 1989

MIDDLESEX CCC

FIRST-CLASS MATCHES
BOWLING

Match	CB Keegan	PN Weekes	EC Joyce	SJ Cook	BL Hutton	JH Dawes	Abdul Razzaq	AA Noffke	JWM Dalrymple	TF Bloomfield	OA Shah	AJ Strauss	Imran Tahir	CT Peploe	TA Hunt	BW Gannon	SG Koenig	DC Nash	Overs	Total	Byes/Leg-byes	Wickets	Run outs
v. Oxford UCCE (The Parks) 12–14 April	21.5-8-27-3	23-12-55-4		18-4-46-0		27-11-63-2			14-3-49-0										103.5	261	21	10	1
		13-5-26-0	2-1-1-0	9-5-7-0					8-3-9-1										32	48	5	1	
v. Essex (Chelmsford) 18–21 April	23-3-106-3	16-3-39-1	1-0-4-0	22-3-105-2		22-6-69-1	23.3-5-68-3												107.3	402	10	10	
	4-1-16-0					4-0-10-0					1-0-15-0								9	41		–	
v. Sussex (Lord's) 23–26 April	19-4-49-2	10-1-36-3			13-2-42-1	22-4-58-3	9.1-0-43-1												73.1	239	11	10	
	21-8-36-4	3-1-7-1			10-0-45-1	15.1-3-47-3	11-0-55-1												62.1	204	4	10	
v. Lancashire (Lord's) 9–12 May	27-4-120-1	27-0-91-1		2-0-14-0		6-0-13-0	30.3-5-82-3		21-2-101-1			39-8-128-1							152.3	565	16	7	
v. Kent (Canterbury) 14–17 May	28-8-72-2	28-6-70-4			7-1-45-0	28-2-90-4						20-5-68-0				23-4-102-0			134	472	25	10	
v. Leicestershire (Leicester) 21–24 May	18-4-61-5			18-4-42-4				24-4-89-1											60	198	6	10	
v. Zimbabwe (Shenley) 30 May–2 June		23-4-79-1	3-1-11-0	18-6-49-0	11-4-34-0				24-4-82-1					14-2-61-1	15-3-68-1				108	401	17	4	
		19-5-38-2	2-0-9-0	6-1-17-0	5-2-22-0				7-0-31-0	2-0-14-0				17-3-58-1	7-1-28-2				65	221	4	5	
v. Essex (Lord's) 4–7 June	16.1-3-56-2	2-1-2-0		16-7-33-3			13-0-34-1	18-6-39-3											65.1	166	2	10	1
	20-4-52-1	6-2-14-0		3-0-13-0	18-4-54-4	3-2-1-0	20-3-40-2	25-5-81-1											95	269	14	8	
v. Surrey (Lord's) 27–30 June	31-6-102-0	32.2-7-88-3	11-3-25-1	28-4-101-2				29-4-95-3	37-5-134-1										168.2	568	23	10	
v. Leicestershire (Southgate) 9–12 July	29-4-114-6	18-1-65-1	1-0-1-0				27-6-113-1	29-7-74-1	14-1-73-1										118	447	7	10	
	23-10-66-3	25-2-98-2		2-0-8-0			15-2-54-1	20-5-48-3	15-3-45-1										100	335	16	10	
v. Warwickshire (Southgate) 15–18 July	34.4-9-125-3	23-6-60-1		4-0-17-0	13-3-53-2		21-6-71-1	32-8-92-3	16-2-53-0		1-0-5-0								144.4	496	20	10	
v. Surrey (Guildford) 23–26 July	28.5-3-114-4	19-3-72-0			22-4-77-3	3-0-18-0		5-1-17-0	24-3-91-3										101.5	411	22	10	
	8-1-29-0			1-0-3-0	6-1-21-0	5-0-20-0			6-1-21-0										26	94		–	
v. Nottinghamshire (Trent Bridge) 30 July–2 August	10.3-4-71-2	8-2-11-1		2-0-8-0		16-4-49-1		15-2-59-1			21-5-52-5								81.3	254	4	10	
	12.3-3-39-5	32-1-8-0				13-5-38-0		18-6-46-5			9.4-3-33-0								56.3	169	5	10	
v. Kent (Lord's) 13–16 August	35-8-92-2	19-1-64-1		26.2-3-113-2		32-3-119-3				25-3-75-2									137.2	477	14	10	
	6-1-20-1	5.2-1-23-0	1-0-4-0	2-0-18-0		5-1-12-1				5-0-15-0									24.2	96	4	2	
v. Lancashire (Old Trafford) 21–24 August	34-6-124-1	33-5-145-0	11-1-53-0		1-1-0-0	30-5-125-1	29-1-170-2		24-3-96-0										162	734	21	5	1
v. Warwickshire (Edgbaston) 26–29 August	23.5-5-76-3	11-2-28-2		2-0-15-0	22-9-46-2	10-0-43-2				12-0-74-0	15-1-57-4								80.5	290	8	10	1
	25-4-67-4	5-2-8-1			17-5-53-1			2-0-4-0		15-1-57-4									64	198	9	10	
v. Sussex (Hove) 5–8 September	32.2-4-120-4	27-3-101-2			30-7-83-1	35-2-126-3								28-2-100-0					152.2	537	7	10	
	7-2-29-0	5.5-0-23-1			2-0-9-0	7-3-25-2								6-2-20-0					27.5	108	2	3	
v. Nottinghamshire (Lord's) 10–13 September	25-2-105-2	23.2-3-72-2		3-1-8-0	5-1-26-1	28-3-93-1			7-2-5-2	6.4-1-25-1									98	361	17	10	1
	13-2-37-0	23-8-32-1		7-1-23-1	10-0-70-0	11-7-47-1			20-2-71-0		8-0-36-0		5-0-27-1				5-0-19-1	5-0-25-0	109	407	20	5	

	CB Keegan	PN Weekes	EC Joyce	SJ Cook	BL Hutton	JH Dawes	Abdul Razzaq	AA Noffke	JWM Dalrymple	TF Bloomfield	OA Shah	AJ Strauss	Imran Tahir	CT Peploe	TA Hunt	BW Gannon	SG Koenig	DC Nash
Overs	585.4	451.1	56	332.2	83	331.4	202.4	245.4	128	107.4	11	6	59	65	22	23	5	5
Maidens	121	85	7	78	14	58	28	52	16	14	0	0	13	9	4	4	0	0
Runs	1925	1355	219	1048	363	1071	761	754	437	428	55	42	196	239	96	102	19	25
Wickets	63	35	2	27	5	34	16	21	6	8	0	1	1	2	3	0	1	0
Average	30.6	38.7	109.5	38.8	72.6	31.5	47.6	35.9	72.8	53.5	–	42.0	196.0	119.5	32.0	–	19.0	–

FIELDING

45	DC Nash (42 ct, 3st)
20	PN Weekes
17	BL Hutton
11	OA Shah
7	EC Joyce
6	AJ Strauss
5	CB Keegan
5	SJ Cook
3	JWM Dalrymple
?	SG Koenig
3	JH Dawes
2	MJ Brown
2	Abdul Razzaq
2	TF Bloomfield
2	AA Noffke
2	CT Peploe

NORTHAMPTONSHIRE CCC

FIRST–CLASS MATCHES
BATTING

	PA Jaques	MJ Powell	DJG Sales	TMB Bailey	MEK Hussey	JW Cook	A Nel	GP Swann	JF Brown	GL Brophy	TW Roberts	BJ Phillips	MS Panesar	MJ Cawdron	CG Greenidge	DE Paynter	RA White	AJ Shantry	DG Wright	RSG Anderson	AL Penberthy	TB Huggins	JAR Blain	Extras	Total	Wickets	Result	Points
v. Yorkshire	9	0	12	31		74	17	10		2				1		2						1*		25	184	10		
(Headingley) 18-20 April	60	4	1	0		28	8	0		0				9*		0							5	31	146	10	L	2
v. Gloucestershire	14	60	59	38		10	39	1	32		5*			50				13						31	352	10		
(Northampton) 23-26 April	11	13				21*			10*					2										12	69	3	D	9
v. Worcestershire	149*	31	33	12*	45	2			6															34	312	5		
(Worcester) 30 April-3 May																											D	10
v. Cambridge UCCE		64							102*							146	17*	0		45	0			13	387	5		
(Fenner's) 9-11 May		3							45*				28		33*				16	40				9	174	4	L	
v. Yorkshire	222	5	2	7	65	29							3*					32*						37	402	6		
(Northampton) 14-17 May																											D	12
v. Glamorgan	0	55	23	2	39	0	24	0*			23				13	55								28	262	10		
(Northampton) 30 May-1 June	59	15	6	2	14	6	14		12*		16				0	14								14	172	10	L	5
v. Gloucestershire	75	19	46		264	1	0			152*	3			3*	5									54	622	8		
(Gloucester) 4-7 June																											W	22
v. Derbyshire	60	6	20	9	59	10	23*	0	2		4	0												10	203	10		
(Northampton) 27-29 June	57	5	33	40	28	21	23	19	2*		4	1												10	243	10	W	20
v. Hampshire	15	0	6	11	4	0	10	38				48*	24						46					16	218	10		
(Northampton) 2-4 July	0	38*	5*	18	25																			1	87	3	W	18
v. Durham	109	6	33	39	43	18	13	0	9*				11					27						14	322	10		
(Chester-le-Street) 9-11 July	81	7		72*	32*																			14	206	2	W	20
v. Somerset	41	18	38	0	20		22	44	1		83	12				38*								8	325	10		
(Northampton) 23-24 July																											W	20
v. Hampshire	9	31	16		13		5*		0	0	60			6		12	0							24	176	10		
(Southampton) 31 July-3 August	34	47*	75		100			2*	10							27								35	330	5	W	17
v. Somerset	38	3	125	101*	331*	15					45													23	681	5		
(Taunton) 14-17 August																											D	12
v. Derbyshire	123	50	200*	22*	115	85			12															40	647	5		
(Derby) 20-22 August																											W	22
v. Durham	147	10	79	17	187	12	22*	50*	0															14	538	7		
(Northampton) 3-5 September																											W	22
v. Glamorgan	28	3	17	11	147	3	19	0	19*	41				5										26	319	10		
(Cardiff) 10-13 September	0	1	52	7	50	37	42	39	9*	6				1										21	265	10	W	20
v. Worcestershire	29	32	13	4	57	1	6	25	6			6*	4											13	196	10		
(Northampton) 17-19 September	39	29	22	79	31			69	2*	60		0	18											30	379	10	W	16
Matches	16	16	16	14	14	14	9	9	8	7	7	6	5	4	4	3	3	3	2	2	2	1	1					
Innings	25	25	23	19	21	22	13	13	12	12	10	8	7	6	6	6	5	6	3	2	2	3	2					
Not Out	1	2	2	3	2	2	3	1	6	5	0	2	3	0	2	1	0	2	0	0	1	0	1					
Highest Score	222	64	200*	101*	331*	85	42	69	38	152*	83	48*	28	24	13	146	55	38*	46	13	45	40	5					
Runs	1409	494	942	384	1697	517	258	256	91	436	263	119	43	63	32	236	110	55	73	13	93	40	6					
Average	58.71	21.48	44.86	24.00	89.32	25.85	25.80	21.33	15.17	62.29	26.30	19.83	10.75	10.50	8.00	59.00	18.33	55.00	36.50	6.50	46.50	20.00	6.00					
100s	5	0	2	1	6	0	0	0	0	2	0	0	0	0	0	1	0	0	0	0	0	0	0					
50s	6	4	4	0	5	3	0	2	0	1	2	0	0	1	0	1	1	0	0	0	0	0	0					
Catches/Stumpings	9/0	32/0	13/0	29/6	17/0	3/0	4/0	9/0	2/0	14/0	7/0	1/0	3/0	1/0	2/0	0/0	1/0	1/0	1/0	0/0	0/0	0/0	0/0					

Home Ground: Northampton
Address: The County Ground, Wantage Road, Northampton NN1 4TJ
Tel: 01604 514455
Fax: 01604 514488
Email: post@nccc.co.uk (general enquiries) or commercial@nccc.co.uk (commercial enquiries)
Directions: *By rail:* Castle Station, three miles.
By road: M1 to J15, A508 and follow RAC signs. RAC signs from all other areas. Parking on ground when space permits otherwise ample local street parking.
By coach: regular service from Greyfriars coach station.

Capacity: 4,250
Other grounds used: Campbell Park, Milton Keynes.
Year formed: 1878

Chairman: Lynn Wilson
Chief Executive: Stephen Coverdale
Director of Excellence: David Capel
Coach: Kepler Wessels
Captain: Mike Hussey
Coaching contact: Ian Lucas 01604 632917
County colours: Claret and gold

Honours
Benson & Hedges Cup
1980
Gillette Cup/NatWest/C&G Trophy
1976, 1992

Website:
www.nccc.co.uk

NORTHAMPTONSHIRE CCC

FIRST-CLASS MATCHES

BOWLING

Match	JF Brown	A Nel	JW Cook	GP Swann	CG Greenidge	BJ Phillips	MS Panesar	MJ Cawdron	JAR Blain	MEK Hussey	AJ Shantry	DG Wright	RSG Anderson	RA White	PA Jaques	AL Penberthy	TMB Bailey	DE Paynter	DJG Sales	TW Roberts	MJ Powell	Overs	Total	Byes/Leg-byes	Wickets	Run outs
Yorkshire (Headingley) 18-20 April		29-3-120-1	22-3-79-0	26-1-108-1	27-1-164-1			262-3-153-3				4-0-35-1										134.2	673	14	8	1
																						–	–	–	–	–
Gloucestershire (Northampton) 23-26 April		30-7-84-1		21-2-76-2			45-9-135-2					10-1-67-0	1-0-17-0									107	403	24	5	
																						–	–	–	–	
Worcestershire (Worcester) 30 April-3 May			17-7-46-0	8-1-37-1		143-6-45-4	3-0-19-0	15-0-84-5														57.3	236	5	10	
																						–	–	–	–	
Cambridge UCCE (Fenner's) 9-11 May	20-7-37-0			17.1-2-64-2			19-5-45-1	185-2-61-1	15-4-40-1			13-2-47-0		6-1-28-0								103	299	5	5	
	10-1-59-1			8-0-48-0			11-1-65-1	6-2-22-2				7-1-33-2										48	263	8	6	
Yorkshire (Northampton) 14-17 May	46-18-99-4	26-7-84-1		5-2-11-0			31.1-6-113-3	13-0-75-2	3-0-32-0					11-4-26-0						2-0-12-0		127.1	399	2	10	
							1.1-1-0-1	8-0-54-0														19.1	109	–	1	
Glamorgan (Northampton) 30 May-1 June	23-7-52-4	24-4-86-2	8-1-22-1		15-3-65-0	153-7-33-3																85.3	269	11	10	
	7-3-18-1	25-8-57-4	4-1-10-0		12-0-72-2	18-4-59-3																66	220	4	10	
Gloucestershire (Gloucester) 4-7 June	26-8-63-1	261-11-47-5	6-4-10-0			19-1-80-2	13-4-34-1									6-1-26-0						86.1	230	6	10	1
	49-20-106-4	321-6-87-3				14-1-59-1	16-5-32-1															123.1	338	18	10	1
Derbyshire (Northampton) 27-29 June	23-6-39-4	17-1-52-4		15.1-2-33-7			3-1-8-0	10-2-51-1														53	160	10	10	1
	21-5-30-3	6-1-19-0					5-0-19-0															47.1	106	5	10	
Hampshire (Northampton) 2-4 July	15-5-27-1			3.1-0-11-3			6-2-27-1		13-5-25-3			16-6-33-2										53.1	125	2	10	
	15-3-41-1			12-3-24-1			10-6-15-2		19-7-58-3			162-5-38-3										72.2	179	3	10	
Durham (Chester-le-Street) 9-11 July	30-10-53-1		5-2-15-0	13-4-26-0			19-2-58-1		20-3-87-6			273-5-86-2										114.3	327	2	10	
	23.4-3-69-7			13-1-43-2			7-1-29-0		2-0-17-0			14-3-37-0										59.4	199	4	10	1
Somerset (Northampton) 23-24 July	7-3-17-1	13.2-2-51-3		6-0-33-0			11-6-20-2				5-3-8-1											36.2	96	–	10	1
	22.1-7-42-6	16-4-48-1					11-3-21-3				8-2-19-0											63.1	168	5	10	
Hampshire (Southampton) 31 July-3 August	26-7-80-3	21-4-79-2				15-1-74-2				11.4-2-44-3												73.4	278	1	10	
	13-2-58-1	13.2-2-47-1				10-2-53-0				7-2-42-0		3-0-26-0										46.2	227	1	2	
Somerset (Taunton) 14-17 August	31.6-11-82-2	31-10-113-3	18-7-47-1		282-4-111-3			18-3-80-1		5-1-6-0				3-0-8-0			1-0-3-0		1-0-4-0	4-0-4-0		126.2	476	7	10	
	26-6-81-0	18-3-53-0	10-3-28-0		17-2-74-2			11-3-26-2														96	292	5	4	
Derbyshire (Derby) 20-22 August		42-16-60-4	15-5-40-2	15-6-35-4	103-2-33-3					9-2-27-1												49.3	138	3	10	
		20-6-57-1	6-0-33-0	6-0-33-0	174-1-75-3					14-1-41-1												99.4	278	12	9	
Durham (Northampton) 3-5 September	19-4-46-2	15-3-39-2	9.3-2-31-5	4-0-23-0	10-3-41-0				3-1-5-1													60.3	190	5	10	
	34-8-90-5	12-2-52-0	8-2-10-1	243-5-77-3	10-2-26-1																	88.3	263	8	10	
Glamorgan (Cardiff) 10-13 September	24-8-56-2	123-3-24-0	7-2-23-1	16-4-37-5				113-2-58-2														71	203	5	10	
	622-24-100-3	1-0-7-0	20-5-66-4	47-8-116-2				14-3-48-0	3-0-9-0													147.2	361	15	10	1
Worcestershire (Northampton) 17-19 September	11-1-35-0			5-3-8-1		183-5-66-6		17-4-37-1		4-0-22-0												55.3	172	4	8	
	205-1-89-5			6-2-14-0		19-2-86-1		24-2-92-3		7-2-15-1												76.5	311	15	10	

	JF Brown	A Nel	JW Cook	GP Swann	CG Greenidge	BJ Phillips	MS Panesar	MJ Cawdron	JAR Blain	MEK Hussey	AJ Shantry	DG Wright	RSG Anderson	RA White	PA Jaques	AL Penberthy	TMB Bailey	DE Paynter	DJG Sales	TW Roberts	MJ Powell
Overs	647	422.3	162.3	238.2	230.4	149	101.2	142.3	07.1	11	46.4	73.5	30	7	4	17	1	6	1	4	2
Maidens	188	99	46	37	25	47	30	31	7	2	13	19	4	0	0	5	0	1	0	0	0
Runs	1565	1292	479	759	1039	400	557	504	449	52	153	194	147	61	25	54	3	26	4	4	12
Wickets	66	36	19	33	22	21	13	20	13	1	7	7	1	0	0	0	0	0	0	0	0
Average	23.7	35.9	25.2	23.0	47.2	19.0	42.8	25.2	34.5	52.0	21.9	27.7	73.5	61.0	–	–	–	–	–	–	–

FIELDING

TMB Bailey (29 ct, 6st)
MJ Powell
MEK Hussey
GL Brophy
DJG Sales
PA Jaques
GP Swann
TW Roberts
A Nel
JW Cook
MS Panesar
CG Greenidge
JF Brown
DG Wright
RA White
BJ Phillips
AJ Shantry
MJ Cawdron

NOTTINGHAMSHIRE CCC

FIRST–CLASS MATCHES
BATTING

	DJ Bicknell	KP Pietersen	PJ Franks	CMW Read	GJ Smith	CL Cairns	JER Gallian	BM Shafayat	GE Welton	SCG MacGill	CE Shreck	RJ Warren	U Afzaal	AJ Harris	S Elworthy	GD Clough	V Atri	RJ Logan	PJ McMahon	DL Vettori	WM Noon	MN Malik	SR Patel	Extras	Total	Wickets	Result
v. Durham UCCE (Trent Bridge) 12-14 April	62	58	0	94*	4		126	105		0		52	0	20										21	542	9	
	–	–	–	–																				–	–	–	W
v. Warwickshire (Trent Bridge) 18-21 April	61	0	39*	49	35	44	2	97			0	1		4										17	349	10	
	81	54	25*	20*		7	9	1				43		0										24	264	10	W
v. Lancashire (Old Trafford) 23-26 April	30	19	5	57	19	57	0	18				6		16*	30									18	275	10	
	–	–	–	–																				–	–	–	D
v. Surrey (Trent Bridge) 9-11 May	29		0	22	1		112*	8	0		5		16	0	0									18	211	10	
	0	25	26	2		28	10	4		16*		0	3		52									10	176	10	L
v. Sussex (Horsham) 21-24 May	9	166		0	9		36	71	50	4*		35	5		28									8	421	10	
	61	1		42	5*		44	0	12	2		18	1		45									16	247	10	L
v. Essex (Trent Bridge) 30 May-1 June		0		0	1	0	1	1	27			3	4								0	30*		12	79	10	
		18				39	42	21	11	8*		33	4								13	15		11	215	10	L
v. Warwickshire (Edgbaston) 4-7 June		221	62*		0	104	6	11	99	0		72									25	10		36	646	10	
		6	1				6*	8	11			28									0*			7	67	5	D
v. Leicestershire (Leicester) 27-30 June	1	88	123*	2	5	5		41	2			40		3		0								16	326	10	
	38	95	21		41*	5		86				11				1*								20	318	6	D
v. India A (Trent Bridge) 2-4 July	52					6	25						161*			55		10						30	339	5	
	–																							–	–	–	L
v. Kent (Maidstone) 9-11 July	37*	6	0		1	19	51		17			1		0			4		0					20	156	10	
	0	62	45		2	58	106		15			23		0			5*		0					21	337	10	D
v. Sussex (Trent Bridge) 25-28 July	15	139	43	0		1	6		12	0*		42	1		16									21	296	10	
	75	81			7*	0			8			114*												6	291	4	D
v. Middlesex (Trent Bridge) 30 July-2 August	39	67	28	26	27	14		1	5*	1		33				5								8	254	10	
	2	1	0	38	0*	41			69	0	0	9				2								7	169	10	L
v. Surrey (Whitgift) 13-15 August	14	79	8	4	6	26			0	9	0*	76	4											14	240	10	
	3	16	27	93	42	9			0	7	2*	9	5											29	242	10	L
v. Kent (Trent Bridge) 20-21 August	5	100	17	5	0	0		23	7	7*	0					5								8	177	10	
	46	13	5*	0	0	6		0	43	0	0					3								10	126	10	L
v. Leicestershire (Trent Bridge) 26-29 August	59	0	36	16		15		68	60	0	0*	5						1						30	290	10	
	1	16	32*	65		75		13	0			4						13*						22	241	7	D
v. Essex (Chelmsford) 3-5 September	8	2	49*	5		70	65	3		9	19	41							0					13	284	10	
	3	11	23	27		5	79	10		12*	15								1					14	204	10	L
v. Middlesex (Lord's) 10-13 September	35	70	1	16		1	73	5		0	4*	123								7				26	361	10	
	42	68		3*			116	6				113*								30				29	407	5	D
v. Lancashire (Trent Bridge) 17-20 September	75	52	14	9	8*		83	22		4		75											9	25	376	9	
	53	37	100*	2	9		2	26		16*		0											55	19	319	8	W

	DJ Bicknell	KP Pietersen	PJ Franks	CMW Read	GJ Smith	CL Cairns	JER Gallian	BM Shafayat	GE Welton	SCG MacGill	CE Shreck	RJ Warren	U Afzaal	AJ Harris	S Elworthy	GD Clough	V Atri	RJ Logan	PJ McMahon	DL Vettori	WM Noon	MN Malik	SR Patel
Matches	16	16	15	13	13	13	13	13	12	11	10	9	9	8	5	3	2	2	2	2	2	2	1
Innings	29	30	26	23	21	23	24	23	23	18	15	18	15	12	8	4	4	4	4	3	4	3	2
Not Out	1	0	8	3	3	2	2	0	0	6	6	2	1	1	0	1	0	2	0	0	1	1	0
Highest Score	81	221	123*	94*	42	104	126	105	99	27	19	123	161*	16*	52	55	5	13*	30	10	25	30*	55
Runs	936	1546	729	619	172	645	1002	533	572	112	51	734	477	37	179	72	15	23	38	10	38	55	64
Average	33.43	51.53	40.50	30.95	9.56	30.71	45.55	23.17	24.87	9.33	5.67	45.88	34.07	3.36	22.38	24.00	3.75	11.50	9.50	3.33	12.67	27.50	32.00
100s	0	4	2	0	0	1	4	1	0	0	0	3	1	0	0	0	0	0	0	0	0	0	0
50s	9	11	1	4	0	4	5	3	4	0	0	2	2	0	1	1	0	0	0	0	0	0	1
Catches/Stumpings	4/0	17/0	9/0	32/3	4/0	7/0	16/0	3/0	6/0	2/0	1/0	9/2	3/0	2/0	3/0	1/0	3/0	0/0	2/0	1/0	7/0	0/0	1/0

Home Ground: Trent Bridge
Address: Trent Bridge, Nottingham NG2 6AG
Tel: 0115 982 3000
Fax: 0115 945 5730
Ticket line: 0870 168 88 88
Email: administration.notts@ecb.co.uk
Alternative website: www.nottsccc.co.uk
Directions: *By road:* Follow signs from Ring Road, towards city centre.
Capacity: 14,500 (16,000 during Test Matches/ODIs)
Other grounds used: Worksop
Year formed: 1841

Chief Executive: David Collier
Director of Cricket: Mike Newell
Other posts: *Head Groundsman:* Steve Birks;
Sales & Marketing Manager: Lisa Pursehouse;
Academy Director: Chris Tolley
Club Coach: Paul Johnson
Captain: Jason Gallian
County colours: Green and gold

Honours
County Championship
1907, 1929, 1981, 1987
Sunday League/NCL
1991
Benson & Hedges Cup
1976, 1989
Gillette Cup/NatWest/C&G Trophy
1987

Website:
www.nottsccc.co.uk

NOTTINGHAMSHIRE CCC

FIRST-CLASS MATCHES
BOWLING

	PJ Franks	GJ Smith	SCG MacGill	CE Shreck	KP Pietersen	AJ Harris	CL Cairns	BM Shafayat	JER Gallian	S Elworthy	GD Clough	RJ Logan	MN Malik	DL Vettori	PJ McMahon	U Afzaal	SR Patel	DJ Bicknell	Overs	Total	Byes/Leg-byes	Wickets	Run outs
Durham UCCE (Trent Bridge) 12–14 April	8.4-1-33-1 / 11-3-25-2	10-3-22-1		7-0-28-0 / 15-4-54-1	8-3-14-1 / 14.1-5-31-4	10-2-23-4		6-2-22-1	2-0-3-0	14-4-40-3 / 12-1-53-1					4-2-14-0				57.4 / 64.1	165 / 209	5 / 7	10 / 10	1
Warwickshire (Trent Bridge) 18–21 April	17-6-57-2 / 8.2-1-65-1	13-2-55-1 / 26-6-98-5		9.4-1-33-4 / 14-1-76-2	2-0-19-0					19-5-68-3 / 29-0-117-2									58.4 / 79.2	222 / 390	9 / 15	10 / 10	
Lancashire (Old Trafford) 23–26 April	16-1-74-1	19-4-50-3 / 8-4-8-2			9-0-33-1	25-5-87-0 / 4-4-0-20-0	2-0-12-0	7-3-17-0	24.1-6-71-5 / 6-0-13-0										102.1 / 18.4	354 / 41	10 / -	10 / 2	
Surrey (Trent Bridge) 9–11 May		22.1-4-81-4		12-1-81-1		12-1-75-1			5-0-7-1	21-2-136-3									72.1 / -	393 / -	13 / -	10 / -	
Sussex (Horsham) 21–24 May		24-2-97-0	50-12-172-3 / 4-1-13-0		7-0-35-0 / 1-0-9-0	20-2-102-1 / 0-2-0-6-0		4-0-39-0	12-2-45-0	30-3-107-3 / 5-1-22-0									147 / 10.2	619 / 52	22 / 2	7 / -	
Essex (Trent Bridge) 30 May–1 June		18-6-42-5 / 16-2-79-1	13-3-41-2 / 30.2-3-118-5		11-5-17-1	20-2-68-1 / 16-1-75-1		2-1-6-0				15-3-43-0 / 18-3-58-2							68 / 91.2	203 / 359	3 / 12	10 / 10	2
Warwickshire (Edgbaston) 4–7 June	20-2-80-2 / 13-1-57-0	15.3-4-60-4 / 21-4-85-1	28-4-75-1 / 47.4-10-117-6		5-2-19-1 / 29-3-95-3		2-0-8-0					19-1-102-1 / 5-0-24-0							87.3 / 117.4	351 / 405	15 / 19	10 / 10	1
Leicestershire (Leicester) 27–30 June	11-0-47-2	20-8-40-4 / 2-0-3-0	12-2-44-3		1-0-4-0	18-2-64-1 / 1.5-1-2-1					4-0-20-0								66 / 3.5	243 / 5	24 / -	10 / 1	
India A (Trent Bridge) 2–4 July	11-0-48-0			14-2-51-1		9-3-21-1	1-0-3-0			5-0-23-0	14-1-79-0	14-0-104-1					0.3-0-4-0		1 / 68.3	- / 341	- / 7	- / 3	
Kent (Maidstone) 9–11 July	10-0-51-2 / 12-1-53-0	13-0-58-2 / 12-0-55-1		6-0-39-0 / 7-3-0-48-0	9-0-55-1 / 14-4-62-0	3-0-29-0 / 12-2-43-1	3-0-16-0			6-0-48-0		143-2-74-4 / 20-0-124-1							61.3 / 80.3	362 / 418	8 / 17	10 / 3	1
Sussex (Trent Bridge) 25–28 July	19-3-102-2			28-4-109-0	4-0-43-0	28-5-98-2	18-5-63-1			16-0-76-1									113	497	6	6	
Middlesex (Trent Bridge) 30 July–2 August	15-1-36-1 / 3-2-2-0	19.4-6-57-4 / 15-5-37-1	30-8-78-4 / 18.1-4-48-2	16-7-31-0 / 4-1-14-1		18-3-61-1 / 10-1-43-2													98.4 / 50.1	278 / 146	15 / 2	10 / 6	
Surrey (Whitgift) 13–15 August	22-2-01-3	27.3 7 110-3	36-3-196-1	25-4-117-1	4-0-22-0				27-3-133-2										140.3 / -	693 / -	29 / -	10 / -	
Kent (Trent Bridge) 20–21 August	11-2-36-1 / 3-0-20-0	11-1-47-2 / 4-0-21-0	11.3-2-28-2	13-0-55-2 / 23-0-10-1		14-2-59-3 / 4-0-14-0													60.3 / 13.3	242 / 65	17 / -	10 / 1	
Leicestershire (Trent Bridge) 26–29 August	22-2-98-0		27-2-135-2	25-6-100-5		22-1-109-0	1-0-12-0			8-1-46-0									105 / -	523 / -	23 / -	7 / -	
Essex (Chelmsford) 3–5 September	11-5-28-0 / 5-1-21-0		24-3-79-1 / 12-4-47-0	22-9-67-3 / 6-1-21-0		22-4-89-2 / 4-2-11-0							27.5-7-59-4 / 7.1-2-54-1						106.5 / 34.1	335 / 154	13 / -	10 / 1	
Middlesex (Lord's) 10–13 September	12-3-54-2		33-6-98-4	14-5-36-1		30-8-101-3								5-0-29-0					94	326	8	10	
Lancashire (Trent Bridge) 17–20 September	17-7-36-2 / 18-5-02-4	20-7-61-5 / 10.2-3-01-2	14.4-2-52-2 / 22-1 67-1			15-2-59-1 / 6-1-33-0												8-5-10-0	66.4 / 73.2	219 / 243	11 / 10	10 / 10	
Overs	296	356.1	412.2	227.1	108.4	208.5	184	16	31	160.1	25	28	57	48.3	40	4	8	0.3					
Maidens	49	78	73	46	18	31	31	2	6	22	0	2	7	2	9	2	5	0					
Runs	1177	1227	1408	878	428	850	755	96	94	627	119	173	227	302	142	14	10	4					
Wickets	28	51	42	23	11	15	15	1	1	20	1	0	3	6	5	0	0	0					
Average	42.0	24.1	33.5	38.2	38.9	56.7	50.3	96.0	94.0	31.4	119.0	-	75.7	50.3	28.4	-	-	-					

FIELDING

CMW Read (32 ct, 3st)
KP Pietersen
JER Gallian
RJ Warren (9 ct, 2st)
PJ Franks
CL Cairns
WM Noon
GE Welton
GJ Smith
S Elworthy
DJ Bicknell
S Elworthy
BM Shafayat
U Afzaal
V Atri
AJ Harris
PJ McMahon
SCG MacGill
SR Patel
GD Clough
DL Vettori
AC Thomas
CE Shreck

SOMERSET CCC

FIRST–CLASS MATCHES
BATTING

	M Burns	RJ Turner	J Cox	ID Blackwell	JDC Bryant	NAM McLean	MJ Wood	AW Laraman	PD Bowler	RL Johnson	SRG Francis	PS Jones	KP Dutch	T Webley	NJ Edwards	ME Trescothick	GM Andrew	CM Gazzard	PCL Holloway	GM Gilder	KA Parsons	WJ Durston	AV Suppiah	AR Caddick	JC Hildreth	Extras	Total	Wickets	Result
v. Loughborough UCCE	83	88*			109*		21												96							16	413	3	
(Taunton) 12-14 April	118*	139	75*				84																			11	427	1	D
v. Gloucestershire	1	59*	11	31	19		9	0	0	118	34				0											7	289	10	
(Bristol) 18-21 April	25	15	67	0	31		3	23	50	11*	1				10											38	274	10	L
v. Durham	17	27*	0	13	0		1	25	7	0		4			60											17	171	10	
(Taunton) 23-26 April	0		10	51				67*	23*						28											18	197	10	W
v. Derbyshire	40	32*	126	26	15		24	1	1			4			69						1					58	397	10	
(Derby) 30 April-3 May	-																									-	-	-	D
v. Glamorgan	82	32*	29	42	30		61*	92								70										38	476	6	
(Taunton) 14-17 May	-																									-	-	-	W
v. Hampshire	7	11	127*	19	18	16	18		3	0			61				7									21	308	10	
(Southampton) 21-24 May	17	13	8	41*	39*	4																				6	128	4	W
v. Worcestershire	6	23	37	28	28	35*	8			4				17					30	4						18	238	10	
(Bath) 4-7 June	57	10	160	10	12	9*	32			1				1					11	6						58	367	10	L
v. Yorkshire	0	81*	0	19	7	5	16	36	0		44	39														28	275	10	
(Taunton) 27-30 June	39	4	39	23	45	35	1	39*	58		6	0														17	306	10	L
v. Gloucestershire	66	7	69	29		76	10	148*		19			15					2					16			20	477	10	
(Taunton) 2-5 July	6*		28	15	49*													4								13	115	3	D
v. Glamorgan	50	1	24	82	20	0	5	0	5	0*			22													24	233	10	
(Cardiff) 9-12 July	106	9	24	10	7	18	26	21	49	2*			30													11	313	10	L
v. South Africa	35			19	39		55	41*											27		1	8				20	245	7	
(Taunton) 15-17 July				27			9												35*		2	30*				6	109	3	D
v. Northamptonshire	15	10*	22	5	0	0	10	14		8			0							12							96	10	
(Northampton) 23-24 July	55	0	24	40	15	0	6	8		8			7							0*						5	168	10	L
v. Durham	35*	7	29	14	5	0	9	0		25	6										4					5	139	10	
(Chester-le-Street) 30 July-1 August	0	6	1	6	0	14	0		12	9*	0										6					2	56	10	L
v. Northamptonshire	28		30	140	16	30	70					63		32	9			41	7*							10	476	10	
(Taunton) 14-17 August	13		64	38										41*	10											18	292	4	D
v. Worcestershire	89	4	0	21	4*	53	29		24	0			20	45												7	296	10	
(Worcester) 20-22 August	13	26	0	9	7*	6	35		0	25			4	1												21	147	10	L
v. Hampshire	10	67*		189	73		8	52	19				20	59	160											48	705	9	
(Taunton) 26-29 August	-																									-	-	-	D
v. Yorkshire	28	11	11	0	15	3		30		61*			22	7	11											29	228	10	
(Headingley) 3-5 September	34	13	59	48	2	1		14*		15			12	9	90											16	313	10	L
v. Derbyshire	0	16		247*	39	14			25	18			0	10	9										9	22	409	10	
(Taunton) 10-13 September	58	18*		4	0	72			6	4			12	28	0										0	12	214	10	W

	M Burns	RJ Turner	J Cox	ID Blackwell	JDC Bryant	NAM McLean	MJ Wood	AW Laraman	PD Bowler	RL Johnson	SRG Francis	PS Jones	KP Dutch	T Webley	NJ Edwards	ME Trescothick	GM Andrew	CM Gazzard	PCL Holloway	GM Gilder	KA Parsons	WJ Durston	AV Suppiah	AR Caddick	JC Hildreth
Matches	18	16	15	15	14	14	12	12	9	8	8	7	7	6	5	4	3	3	2	2	2	2	1	1	1
Innings	32	26	27	26	24	23	23	18	15	14	13	12	10	11	9	6	5	5	3	3	4	4	1	1	2
Not Out	3	8	2	3	2	4	1	5	1	3	2	2	0	1	0	0	0	1	0	2	0	1	0	0	0
Highest Score	118*	139	160	247*	109*	76	100	148*	92	118	44	63	61	59	160	70	11	41	96	12	6	30*	16	1	9
Runs	1133	641	1087	1160	658	318	536	597	477	290	133	273	161	208	360	237	36	109	137	19	13	48	16	1	9
Average	39.07	35.61	43.48	50.43	29.91	16.74	24.36	45.92	34.07	26.36	12.09	27.30	16.10	20.80	40.00	39.50	7.20	27.25	45.67	19.00	3.25	16.00	16.00	1.00	4.50
100s	2	1	3	3	1	0	1	1	0	1	0	0	0	0	1	0	0	0	0	0	0	0	0	0	0
50s	8	3	5	2	2	1	3	3	5	0	0	2	1	1	1	3	0	0	1	0	0	0	0	0	0
Catches/Stumpings	15/0	65/5	10/0	7/0	8/0	2/0	1/0	5/0	11/0	5/0	2/0	2/0	9/0	3/0	1/0	8/0	2/0	5/0	0/0	1/0	1/0	4/0	0/0	0/0	0/0

Home Ground: Taunton
Address: The Clerical Medical County Ground, Taunton, Somerset TA1 1JT
Tel: 01823 272 946
Fax: 01823 332 395
Centre of Cricketing Excellence: 01823 352266
Email: somerset@ecb.co.uk
Directions: *By road:* M5 junction 25. Follow A358 to town centre. Signposted from there.
Other grounds used: Bath
Year formed: 1875

Chief Executive: Peter Anderson
First XI Coach: Kevin Shine
Captain: Mike Burns
Other posts: *Head Groundsman:* Phil Frost; *Second XI Coach:* Mark Garaway
County colours: Black, white and maroon

Honours
Sunday League/NCL
1979
Benson & Hedges Cup
1981, 1982
Gillette Cup/NatWest/C&G Trophy
1979, 1983, 2001

unofficial Website:
www.somersetcountycc.co.uk

SOMERSET CCC

FIRST-CLASS MATCHES
BOWLING

Match	NAM McLean	ID Blackwell	M Burns	AW Laraman	SRG Francis	RL Johnson	PS Jones	KP Dutch	GM Andrew	NJ Edwards	GM Gilder	KA Parsons	PD Bowler	J Cox	WJ Durston	T Webley	MJ Wood	JDC Bryant	AV Suppiah	AR Caddick	Overs	Total	Byes/Leg-byes	Wickets	Run outs
Loughborough UCCE (aunton) 12-14 April	18-0-91-0	27.4-11-65-5		14-0-82-0	12-4-41-1	20-4-59-2															91.4	345	7	8	
	12-2-49-3	15-6-22-0			14-2-47-4							3-0-6-0	1-0-7-0								45	132	1	7	
Gloucestershire (ristol) 18-21 April	13-1-43-2	1-1-0-0		13-4-54-1	20-7-65-3	13.2-3-27-3															62.2	203	7	10	
	35-9-87-5	19-7-46-1	3-1-5-0	21-7-45-3	22-2-79-0	33-8-84-1															133	368	22	10	
Durham (aunton) 23-26 April	17-4-44-1			11-2-26-1	15-4-49-3	16-1-64-5															59	185	2	10	
	14-4-50-3		6-3-13-0	12.4-3-41-3	19-5-52-4		5-0-20-0														58.4	180	1	10	
Derbyshire (erby) 30 April-3 May	14-5-32-1			6.1-0-38-1	15-4-47-4															17-1-66-4	52.1	190	7	10	
	19-4-66-2			4-0-15-0	10.1-3-25-0			9-1-29-1					1-0-2-0							21-7-44-3	64.1	197	16	6	
Glamorgan (aunton) 14-17 May	17-6-43-5	5-0-19-1		10-2-46-2	14-2-61-1	17-7-23-1															63	200	8	10	
	12-4-38-3			6-2-20-3	12-5-33-1	14-3-36-3															44	133	6	10	
Hampshire (outhampton) 21-24 May	15-7-31-4	10-4-27-0	4-1-11-0		17.5-11-24-3			9-1-30-3													55.5	129	6	10	
	28.5-7-64-4	9-6-19-0	24-5-64-3		30-12-81-2		6-1-16-0	17-5-55-1													114.5	306	7	10	
Worcestershire (ath) 4-7 June	21-1-105-1	45-8-131-4	8-0-25-0		30-5-112-2			15-1-85-1				14.4-3-63-2									133.4	538	17	10	
		3.1-0-28-0			4-0-40-1																7.1	68	-	1	
Yorkshire (aunton) 27-30 June	25-5-87-3	27-6-73-2	3-1-14-0		23-4-82-0	28.2-3-111-3	22-1-135-1														128.2	512	10	10	1
	4-1-22-0					6-2-18-0	3-0-30-0														13	71	1	-	
Gloucestershire (aunton) 2-5 July	16-2-68-3		11.4-4-35-3	18-8-44-3	16-2-73-1																61.4	228	8	10	
	30-2-139-3		31-7-105-1	26-3-102-2	32-2-147-0			28-7-60-2											11-1-44-1		158	611	14	9	
Glamorgan (ardiff) 9-12 July	23.1-4-79-5	35-6-93-3	2-0-8-0	12-4-43-1	5.5-1-20-0				31.1-9-100-1												109.1	349	6	10	
	25-4-84-4	19-6-65-0	18-3-61-2	4.4-0-30-1					16-3-56-3												82.4	307	11	10	
South Africa (aunton) 15-17 July		8-3-26-1		10-2-43-0			13-2-61-1		10-1-54-0		12-2-45-0	8-2-23-1			17-4-60-1						78	326	14	4	
				3-1-8-0			10-1-45-1		11-2-31-0		13-0-56-1	10-0-37-1			15-3-42-1	4-0-26-0					66	245	-	4	
Northamptonshire (orthampton) 23-24 July	15-2-51-1	38-6-96-5		3-0-15-0			17.1-2-61-3	16-3-62-0			4-0-32-0										93.1	325	8	10	1
																					-	-			
Durham (hester-le-Street) 30 July-1 August	22-8-56-3	20-6-33-1	3.1-2-4-1	18-4-45-1				28-0-109-2	22-5-76-2						2-0-7-0						115.1	345	15	10	
	10-2-28-2	3-0-13-0	4-0-19-0	8-2-26-2				4-1-18-0	9.5-2-42-5						6-1-16-1						44.5	168	6	10	
Northamptonshire (aunton) 14-17 August	26-3-99-0	53-4-206-3		18-1-53-1	24-1-91-0			34-3-162-1	8-0-35-0				1-0-8-0		5-1-10-0						169	681	17	5	
Worcestershire (orcester) 20-22 August	21-9-60-1	24.5-6-91-3		4-0-13-0	18-5-49-3			21-7-43-2	15-4-65-1												103.5	331	10	10	
	8-2-29-0	14-3-39-1			3-1-10-0			5-1-15-0	6-2-6-1	2.2-0-14-0											38.2	116	3	2	
Hampshire (aunton) 26-29 August	21-6-68-2	9-5-20-1		4-0-27-0	23-5-71-0			28-9-90-3	21.3-3-102-4												106.3	395	17	10	
	8.3-2-37-2	18-3-48-1		2-0-6-0	6-0-17-0				7-1-31-0		4.3-1-10-0						1-0-16-0	1-0-8-0			48	177	4	3	
Yorkshire (eadingley) 3-5 September	19-1-90-0	14-1-53-0		2-0-21-1	27.4-8-92-3			36-9-98-2			11-2-48-2		1-0-6-0								92.4	410	14	8	
	6-1-21-0				6-0-31-1			6-1-28-0			4-0-36-0		3-0-6-0			1.1-0-6-0					26.1	132	4	1	
Derbyshire (aunton) 10-13 September	27-6-86-2	22-6-58-0	3-1-14-0		23.3-4-94-4	36-9-98-2		12-2-42-1													123.3	400	8	9	
	0.1-0-25-0	27-7-66-4			11.1-1-43-1	11-1-47-0		4-0-14-3													64	196	2	10	
Overs	551.3	466.4	153.5	279.5	328.1	330.1	204.3	126.1	78	18.5	29	32.4	4	2	40	6	5.1	1	11	38					
Maidens	115	111	29	58	72	74	27	25	13	1	2	5	0	0	8	1	0	0	1	8					
Runs	1872	1336	514	979	1179	977	930	428	310	71	133	123	8	15	125	26	32	8	44	110					
Wickets	65	36	13	24	35	36	22	8	10	0	1	4	0	0	3	0	0	0	1	7					
Average	28.8	37.1	39.5	40.8	33.7	27.1	42.3	53.5	31.0	-	133.0	30.8	-	-	41.7	-	-	-	44.0	15.7					

FIELDING

RJ Turner (65 ct, 5st)
M Burns
PD Bowler
J Cox
KP Dutch
JDC Bryant
ME Trescothick
ID Blackwell
AW Laraman
RI Johnson
CM Gazzard
WJ Durston
T Webley
GM Andrew
NAM McLean
SRG Francis
PS Jones
GM Gilder
MJ Wood
KA Parsons
NJ Edwards

SURREY CCC

FIRST–CLASS MATCHES
BATTING

	MR Ramprakash	IJ Ward	AJ Hollioake	IDK Salisbury	Saqlain Mushtaq	AD Brown	J Ormond	GP Thorpe	JN Batty	Azhar Mahmood	R Clarke	MP Bicknell	MA Butcher	AJ Tudor	AJ Stewart	TJ Murtagh	N Shahid	JGE Benning	NC Saker	SA Newman	BJM Scott	PJ Sampson	MJ Todd	J Dernbach	FA Rose	Extras	Total	Wickets	Result
v. Lancashire (The Oval) 18-21 April	50	49	42	18	23	2		15	13		38			9	0*											21	280	10	
	13	158	10		0			35	4		127*			11*												21	379	6	D
v. Loughborough UCCE (The Oval) 23-25 April	205		121*		3	28	15	123	4	0		103*	45				4									12	663	9	
																										-	-	-	D
v. Warwickshire (The Oval) 30 April-3 May	45	2	122	5	2	5*			25			1	64	55	50											14	390	9	
																										-	-	-	D
v. Nottinghamshire (Trent Bridge) 9-11 May	38	3	35		24	9	5		98		33*	0	27	98												23	393	10	
																										-	-	-	W
v. Leicestershire (The Oval) 14-17 May	152	19	41	101*	20*	73			27	0		39		71												17	560	8	
																										-	-	-	D
v. Essex (Chelmsford) 21-24 May	10	0	10	30	30	4	9*	52	7	77			141													6	376	10	
	1	49	51	9*	64			3	168*	16			13													7	381	7	W
v. Sussex (The Oval) 30 May-2 June	37	9	77	45	32	74	1*	156	12	0		11														26	480	10	
	23	135				1*		18*	56																	-	233	3	W
v. Middlesex (Lord's) 27-30 June	110	104	10	17	69			1*	46			10	44	30	87											40	568	10	
																										-	-	-	D
v. Kent (The Oval) 2-5 July	6	33	34*	4	27	15		68				22	144	18	1											29	401	10	
	22				64*			46					90	25*												4	251	3	W
v. Warwickshire (Edgbaston) 9-12 July	18	23	88	0	0	33		30		13		25*	28	74												23	355	10	
	182*	9	30					4		50*		118		45												12	450	5	W
v. India A (The Oval) 15-17 July					0			24	38						12	0		22	5	27	16		6*	3		20	173	10	
								27*									6*									6	39		D
v. Middlesex (Guildford) 23-26 July	33	10	40	61*	8	47		51	2			85	11	27												36	411	10	
	28*	33*						25																		8	94		D
v. Sussex (Hove) 30 July-2 August	104	20	13	1	68		42*	23	12	9	12	42														9	355	10	
	14*	33							65*																	2	114	1	D
v. Nottinghamshire (Whitgift) 13-15 August	279*	17	0	65	50	32		99	17	25	36	9														64	693	10	
																										-	-	-	W
v. Leicestershire (Leicester) 21-24 August	55	59	21	24*	13	0		87	50	30	139				6											17	501	9	
		23						52*	30	3*																9	117	2	D
v. Lancashire (Old Trafford) 26-29 August		10	0	5	11	1		57	154*	63	11				5											20	337	10	
		3	8	0	11	61		7	38	0	8				1	0*										1	138	10	L
v. Kent (Canterbury) 4-6 September	4	2	3	16	2	1			28	26					17*	4									1	21	125	10	
	15	53	6	7	40	32			17	13					12*	1									36	23	255	10	L
v. Essex (The Oval) 17-19 September			14		17			87	4							21	67	18	1	9	58*	3				19	318	10	
			29		0			47		18						0	0	47	0	0	5	32*				16	194	10	L
Matches	15	15	14	14	14	14	13	12	12	11	11	11	7	6	6	6	4	2	2	2	2	1	1	1	1				
Innings	23	24	19	18	15	21	15	19	22	14	16	12	9	7	8	9	6	3	3	4	3	2	1	1	2				
Not Out	4	1	1	4	2	2	5	2	4	1	2	3	0	1	1	4	0	0	0	1	1	1	1	0	0				
Highest Score	279*	158	122	101*	69	74	47	156	168*	98	139	141	144	55	98	21	67	47	5	27	58*	32*	6*	3	36				
Runs	1444	856	688	455	421	484	226	895	968	445	551	421	572	177	451	73	76	87	6	42	79	35	6	3	37				
Average	76.00	37.22	38.22	32.50	32.38	25.47	22.60	52.65	53.78	34.23	39.36	46.78	63.56	29.50	64.43	14.60	12.67	29.00	2.00	14.00	39.50	35.00	6.00	3.00	18.50				
100s	6	3	2	1	0	0	0	1	3	0	2	2	2	0	0	0	0	0	0	0	0	0	0	0	0				
50s	2	2	3	1	4	5	0	6	4	4	1	0	2	1	5	0	1	0	0	0	1	0	0	0	0				
Catches/Stumpings	7/0	8/0	11/0	6/0	4/0	12/0	2/0	8/0	32/2	17/0	10/0	2/0	10/0	0/0	20/0	0/0	2/0	0/0	0/0	2/0	6/0	0/0	0/0	0/0	0/0				

Home Ground: The AMP Oval
Address: The AMP Oval, Kennington, London SE11 5SS
Tel: 020 7582 6660
Fax: 020 7735 7769
Email: enquiries@surreycricket.com
Directions: *By rail:* Vauxhall, SouthWest lines, five minutes' walk away. *By underground:* Northern Line, Oval Tube 100 yds away; Victoria Line, Vauxhall is five minutes away. *By road:* Situated on A202 near junction of A24 and A3 south of Vauxhall Bridge. *By bus:* 36 and 185 from Victoria
Capacity: 16,500

Other grounds used: Guildford Cricket Club, Woodbridge Road, Guildford.
Year formed: 1845

Chief Executive: Paul Sheldon
Chairman: Michael Soper
Coach: Keith Medlycott
Captain: Jonathan Batty
County colours: Brown and silver

Website:
www.surreycricket.com

Honours
County Championship
1890, 1891, 1892, 1894, 1895, 1899, 1914, 1952, 1953, 1954, 1955, 1956, 1957, 1958, 1971, 1999, 2000, 2002
Joint Champions
1950
Sunday League/NCL
1996, 2003
Benson & Hedges Cup
1974, 1997, 2001
Gillette Cup/NatWest/C&G Trophy
1982, 1992
Twenty20 Cup
2003

SURREY CCC

FIRST-CLASS MATCHES
BOWLING

Match	IDK Salisbury	J Ormond	Saqlain Mushtaq	MP Bicknell	Azhar Mahmood	R Clarke	AJ Hollioake	AJ Tudor	TJ Murtagh	MA Butcher	IJ Ward	AD Brown	JGE Benning	MR Ramprakash	NC Saker	N Shahid	GP Thorpe	MJ Todd	SA Newman	PJ Sampson	J Dernbach	FA Rose	AJ Stewart	Overs	Total	Byes/Leg-byes	Wickets	Run outs
Lancashire (The Oval) 18-21 April	42-10-116-4		22-5-78-1		21-0-137-2	8-0-27-0	37-4-137-1	21.4-2-103-1																151.4	599	4	10	1
																								-	-	-	-	-
Loughborough UCCE (The Oval) 23-25 April		14-8-34-6	15-3-58-1	9.3-1-58-1	9-2-42-2	4-2-6-0				2-0-2-0					10-2-31-0		9-2-33-1							53.3	206	6	10	
		12-1-31-1	10-2-30-0	12-3-45-0	7-2-24-1	8-1-29-1																		68	235	12	4	
Warwickshire (The Oval) 30 April-3 May		25.2-4-83-3	26-4-86-1	20-9-62-2	15-3-72-1		3-1-8-0	23-3-92-3		4-0-11-0		8-4-9-0										23-0-23-0		112.2	413	10	10	
		11-3-41-0	19-9-29-3		9-1-34-0			14-2-56-3		9-3-11-1														76.3	221	7	7	
Nottinghamshire (Trent Bridge) 9-11 May		18.4-5-46-5		16-4-41-0	16-4-46-3			16-1-58-1		2-0-8-1														68.4	211	13	10	
		8-0-26-3		25.5-8-83-5	16-3-59-2					1-0-4-0														50.5	176	4	10	
Leicestershire (The Oval) 14-17 May	13-3-33-1		5-3-20-2	17-2-64-1	19-5-78-5	4-2-14-0	6-0-20-2																	51.3	200	4	10	
			15.2-3-46-5	12-5-40-2	14-3-65-0																			54.2	185	1	8	
Essex (Chelmsford) 21-24 May	3.1-1-8-1	19-3-68-3	19-2-65-0	19-5-67-4	11-2-39-2																			71.1	252	5	10	
	22-1-3-2	22-3-82-5	15-6-37-0	12-1-72-1																				62.2	247	11	10	
Sussex (The Oval) 30 May-2 June	14-1-67-1	15.1-2-81-4	21-4-68-2	3-1-9-0	16-1-57-2	4-0-16-0																		73.1	307	9	10	1
	21-5-67-1	19.4-3-65-1	34-15-73-5		21-4-76-3																			95.4	293	12	10	
Middlesex (Lord's) 27-30 June	9-3-21-1	28.2-3-103-3	24-5-66-1	35-7-92-5		4-0-18-0	13-5-43-0			2-0-12-0														115.2	370	15	10	
	17-2-60-1	12-2-53-0	2-1-1-0			6.3-1-15-1	12-2-46-0			0.3-0-1-0														58	218	10	2	
Kent (The Oval) 2-5 July	29-5-111-1	16-4-60-1	23-5-63-1	18-4-65-2				8-1-47-0		1-1-0-0														95	352	6	5	
	54-1-11-3	9-3-23-2	14-5-27-4	11-5-26-0				10-2-26-1																49.4	114	1	10	
Warwickshire (Edgbaston) 9-12 July	6-2-20-1	15-3-57-2	10-0-41-0	21.2-4-62-3	16-4-61-4																			68.2	245	4	10	
	29-2-70-1	17-3-83-1	35.1-3-134-5	11-5-31-1	10-0-53-0	11-2-32-2																		113.1	425	22	10	
India A (The Oval) 15-17 July					18-5-36-2			17.5-0-81-0				2-0-7-0	5-0-42-0		15-1-76-0	9-1-42-0			14-0-92-1	1-0-5-0		13-3-74-1		94.5	462	7	4	
																								-	-	-	-	-
Middlesex (Guildford) 23-26 July	5-0-24-0	26-5-106-4	16-3-33-1	29.3-3-102-4		17-2-74-0		11-4-28-1																104.3	385	18	10	
																								-	-	-	-	-
Sussex (Hove) 30 July-2 August	14-0-42-2	25-6-106-4	36-5-84-1	26-5-94-2	18-5-61-1		7-3-23-0																	126	429	19	10	
	22-1-0-86-1	16.3-1-74-0	26-7-87-2	16-5-54-1	4-1-3-1		0.5-0-11-0																	87.5	302	17	5	
Nottinghamshire (Whitgift) 13-15 August	18-6-44-2		21-4-80-3	15-3-42-5	11-3-32-0	7-0-32-0		8-0-41-1																72	240	10	10	
	11-2-42-1		15-1-49-2	8-2-19-2	9-1-45-4	4-0-22-0																		55	242	24	10	
Leicestershire (Leicester) 21-24 August	13-5-21-1	9-1-30-1	8-4-18-0				16-2-68-3												11-1-73-1					58.1	166	8	10	1
	25-5-92-2	25-5-91-0	26-8-57-0		14-3-37-0	18-3-82-1	18-2-62-0			12-0-64-0														158	636	39	4	
Lancashire (Old Trafford) 26-29 August	19-2-70-3	20-3-70-2	20-2-58-0	24.2-3-76-4	6-0-26-0		5-1-26-1																	94.2	341	15	10	
	5-0-19-1	5-1-25-0	13-3-49-0	7-1-28-1								0.4-0-11-0												30.4	135	3	2	
Kent (Canterbury) 4-6 September	27-4-115-1	10-0-48-0			21-1-95-2			27.2-2-130-4														28-8-101-3		120.2	535	11	10	
																								-	-	-	-	-
Essex (The Oval) 17-19 September	21-1-70-1			20-1-104-3	27-4-89-2									8-1-39-1			16-1-71-1			14.5-1-85-2				106.5	464	6	10	
																	4.1-0-32-0			5-0-16-2				9.1	49	1	2	
Overs	371.1	392.1	471	351.4	283.5	164.1	80.2	144	132.5	14	16.3	11.4	13	18	35.1	18	11	14	1	19.5	13	28	2.3					
Maidens	60	74	100	88	52	22	11	24	13	1	0	3	1	6	2	3	1	0	0	1	3	8	0					
Runs	1224	1428	1364	1111	1097	709	300	532	556	46	76	29	81	40	179	75	73	92	5	101	74	101	23					
Wickets	33	51	41	40	35	17	5	10	11	3	0	1	1	0	1	1	1	1	0	4	1	3	0					
Average	37.1	28.0	33.3	27.8	31.3	41.7	60.0	53.2	50.5	15.3	-	29.0	81.0	-	179.0	75.0	73.0	92.0	-	25.?	74.0	33.7	-					

FIELDING

JN Batty (32 ct, 2st)
AJ Stewart
Azhar Mahmood
AD Brown
AJ Hollioake
R Clarke
MA Butcher
IJ Ward
GP Thorpe
MR Ramprakash
IDK Salisbury
BJ M Scott
Saqlain Mushtaq
J Ormond
SA Newman
MP Bicknell
N Shahid

SUSSEX CCC

FIRST-CLASS MATCHES

BATTING

Match	MW Goodwin	RR Montgomerie	CJ Adams	RSC Martin-Jenkins	MJ Prior	PA Cottey	TR Ambrose	Mushtaq Ahmed	JD Lewry	MJG Davis	RJ Kirtley	KJ Innes	BV Taylor	MH Yardy	PM Hutchison	CD Hopkinson	B Zuiderent	Extras	Total	Wickets	Result
v. Cardiff UCCE	0	116	100	112	25	110	10	19		4*								33	529	6	
(Hove) 18-19 April																		–	–	–	W
v. Middlesex	16	20	26	13	11	0	51	9	45		20*	15						13	239	10	
(Lord's) 23-26 April	23	2	12	50	4	38	35	2	8		25*	1						4	204	10	L
v. Kent	9	22	54	16	40	19	41	37	22		7*	9						3	279	10	
(Hove) 30 April-2 May	96	12	11	34	4	2	10	0	10		14*	1						4	198	10	W
v. Warwickshire	28	41	22	7	84	41	85	2*	1	1	31							24	367	10	
(Edgbaston) 9-12 May	10	0	0	11	5	55	0	7*	0	0	6							12	106	10	L
v. Zimbabwe	49	24									6*				18	7*	50	25	179	4	
(Hove) 15-18 May																		–	–	–	D
v. Nottinghamshire	38	105	9	49	133	58	55	32*				103*						37	619	7	
(Horsham) 21-24 May	23*	25*																4	52	–	W
v. Surrey	60	5	5	61	6	75	41	21	2				4*	0				27	307	10	
(The Oval) 30 May-2 June	26	31	0	88	14	1	36			7	1		0*	69				20	293	10	L
v. Kent	35	13	62	67	23	0	11	43	0*		30			18				9	311	10	
(Tunbridge Wells) 4-7 June	58	0	4	84	45	52	17	9	1*	0	0							16	286	10	W
v. Warwickshire	0	66	31	28	100	188	50	2	6	6	40*							28	545	10	
(Hove) 27-29 June																		–	–	–	W
v. Essex	11	1	20	6	13	107	88	34	22	12	35*							10	359	10	
(Arundel) 9-12 July	18	1	0	21*	98		93*											26	257	4	W
v. Leicestershire	34	52	0	7	96	147	2	21	0	0	14*							43	416	10	
(Leicester) 15-18 July	11	28	16	6*	4*	58	25											18	166	5	W
v. Nottinghamshire	148	32	46	121*	17	53					6*			47				27	497	6	
(Trent Bridge) 25-28 July																		–	–	–	D
v. Surrey	75	90	107	40	0	1	43	26	0	1*					5			41	429	10	
(Hove) 30 July-2 August	29	2	23	45	50*	41	76*											36	302	5	D
v. Lancashire	9	72	140	18	9	18	18	60	3				13*		0			25	385	10	
(Hove) 14-17 August	1	70	190	13	35	0	44	16*										14	383	7	W
v. Essex	210	97	0	10	153*	23	4	0	70	8			3					34	612	10	
(Colchester) 20-22 August																		–	–	–	W
v. Middlesex	14	21	20	8	148	15	12	57	21	168			35*					18	537	10	
(Hove) 5-8 September	4	54*	30	7	11*													2	108	3	W
v. Lancashire	118*	10	1	2	2	40	0	54	2	2			0					20	251	10	
(Old Trafford) 10-13 September	57	2	35	6	10	32	2	16	7*	11			0					2	180	10	L
v. Leicestershire	335*	10	102			56	82											29	614	4	
(Hove) 17-19 September																		–	–	–	W
Matches	18	18	17	16	16	16	16	14	10	10	9	8	5	3	3	1	1				
Innings	30	30	28	26	25	26	27	20	15	13	13	12	7	4	3	1	1				
Not Out	3	2	0	3	3	0	3	2	3	3	7	4	4	0	0	1	0				
Highest Score	335*	116	190	121*	153*	188	93*	60	70	168	40*	103*	35*	69	18	7*	50				
Runs	1545	1024	1066	923	1031	1259	941	475	215	263	207	188	55	134	23	7	50				
Average	57.22	36.57	38.07	40.13	46.86	48.42	39.21	26.39	17.92	26.30	34.50	23.50	18.33	33.50	7.67	7.00	50.00				
100s	4	2	5	2	4	4	0	0	0	1	0	1	0	0	0	0	0				
50s	5	7	2	5	3	7	9	3	1	0	0	0	0	1	0	0	1				
Catches/Stumpings	13/0	27/0	19/0	8/0	30/1	8/0	29/7	3/0	4/0	4/0	3/0	2/0	0/0	4/0	0/0	0/0	1/0				

Home Ground: Hove
Address: County Ground, Eaton Road, Hove, East Sussex BN3 3AN
Tel: 01273 827100
Fax: 01273 771549
Membership: 01273 827133
Scoreline (home games only): 01273 827145
Email: fwatson@btconnect.com
Directions: *By rail:* Hove station is a ten-minute walk. *By road:* Follow AA signs. Street parking at no cost.

Capacity: 5,500
Other grounds used: Eastbourne, Horsham, Arundel
Year formed: 1839

Chief Executive: Hugh Griffiths
Director of Cricket: Peter Moores
Captain: Chris Adams
Vice-captain: James Kirtley
Head Groundsman: Derek Traill
County colours: Dark blue, light blue and gold

Honours

County Championship
2003
Sunday League/NCL
1982
Gillette Cup/NatWest/C&G Trophy
1963, 1964, 1978, 1986

Website: www.sussexcricket.co.uk

SUSSEX CCC

FIRST-CLASS MATCHES
BOWLING

Match	RSC Martin-Jenkins	Mushtaq Ahmed	JD Lewry	MJG Davis	RJ Kirtley	BV Taylor	KJ Innes	PM Hutchison	MH Yardy	PA Cottey	CD Hopkinson	RR Montgomerie	MW Goodwin	CJ Adams	Overs	Total	Byes/Leg-byes	Wickets	Run outs
Cardiff UCCE (Hove) 18-19 April	9-2-21-2	12.2-5-20-6	12-6-34-2	1-1-0-0		9-3-27-0									43.2	116	14	10	1
	1.1-0-4-2	17-6-29-5	9-2-30-0	12-2-18-2		5-1-40-0									44.1	133	12	9	
Middlesex (Lord's) 23-26 April	5-2-10-1	10.3-4-16-3	17-8-34-2		16-3-51-3										48.3	116	5	10	1
	10-2-42-0	28.4-6-97-1	25-4-50-1		33-10-87-4		10-2-35-1								106.4	330	19	7	
Kent (Hove) 30 April-2 May	12-2-31-0	19-3-44-3	13-2-44-2		17-6-41-3		7-1-18-2								68	185	7	10	
	4-2-5-0	13.5-2-42-3	14-1-59-1		15-4-26-6		3-0-14-0								49.5	131	5	10	
Warwickshire (Edgbaston) 9-12 May	6.3-1-46-1	48-7-157-6	11-2-41-0	22-7-58-0	30-4-107-3										117.3	422	13	10	
	13-3-57-3	13-0-69-0	9-1-51-2	9-0-50-2	14-2-48-0										58	285	10	7	
Zimbabwe (Hove) 15-18 May		22-2-98-1		17-4-58-1		30-9-64-2	24-7-57-2	22.5-5-94-4	5-0-10-0		2-0-8-0				122.5	395	6	10	
															–	–	–	–	
Nottinghamshire (Horsham) 21-24 May	17-0-87-1	37.1-3-163-6		7-0-52-0	21-7-85-2	11-3-32-1									93.1	421	2	10	
	6-1-25-0	30-9-81-6		9-1-26-0	24.2-4-74-4	13-3-36-0									82.2	258	5	10	
Surrey (The Oval) 30 May-2 June	23.4-8-86-3	36.5-1-159-3			33-5-122-3	7.2-2-15-1	12-4-59-0		7-1-18-0						119.5	480	21	10	
	19-3-66-0	11-1-47-1			14-3-49-0		14-1-64-2		2-0-7-0						60	233	–	3	
Kent (Tunbridge Wells) 4-7 June	10-3-26-0	17.2-3-70-5	11-4-19-0			21-4-84-4	9-1-28-1	5-0-27-0							73.2	275	21	10	
	7-3-9-3	20.4-7-56-4	11-2-36-3												47.4	131	–	10	
Warwickshire (Hove) 27-29 June	10-1-40-1	22.5-6-55-4	10-2-35-1	2-1-4-0		15-2-57-3									59.5	201	10	10	1
	12-4-38-0	32.4-9-85-7	9-2-41-1	23-6-50-2		16-2-62-0									92.4	285	9	10	
Essex (Arundel) 9-12 July	17-3-44-1	36.5-10-102-2	29-7-72-5	8-0-25-0		24-4-88-2									114.5	340	9	10	
	8-3-19-0	30-4-92-1	19.4-6-52-5	19-3-44-3		17-2-48-0									93.4	274	19	10	1
Leicestershire (Leicester) 15-18 July	13.5-1-66-2	33-4-93-5	6-1-18-0			21-6-68-2	12-1-52-0								85.5	320	23	10	1
	25-9-53-2	41.5-18-96-5				22-7-72-1	7-1-27-1								95.5	258	10	10	1
Nottinghamshire (Trent Bridge) 25-28 July	14-1-60-2	28.5-2-87-2				23-9-60-5		17-5-60-1	5-0-14-0						87.5	296	15	10	
	12-2-43-0	9-2-41-0				11-4-32-2		16-2-66-1	13-2-50-0	9-1-44-0		3-0-9-1			73	291	6	4	
Surrey (Hove) 30 July-2 August	17.3-3-67-3	38-7-123-4		3-0-10-0		28-4-90-2		16-2-58-1							102.3	355	7	10	
	3-0-17-0	6-1-26-0		4-1-18-1		6-1-23-0		7-1-30-0							26	114	2	1	
Lancashire (Hove) 14-17 August	9-1-48-0	48-10-124-6			26-2-86-1	24-8-56-3		14-2-50-0							121	377	13	10	
		33.2-14-49-5			12-6-15-1	26-12-42-4		2-0-20-0							73.2	139	13	10	
Essex (Colchester) 20-22 August	11.5-2-32-1	25-2-87-4	12-4-46-1	12-0-61-2		17-3-52-1									77.5	283	5	9	
	12-4-30-1	28-7-83-3	8-1-28-0	4-1-13-0		16.3-6-50-4									68.3	209	5	9	1
Middlesex (Hove) 5-8 September	14-2-46-1	40-4-145-6	20-6-53-2	11-0-62-1		15-2-66-0									100	392	20	10	
	7-3-12-1	35.2-8-80-4	25-8-73-3	19-4-33-1		10-1-30-1									96.2	250	22	10	
Lancashire (Old Trafford) 10-13 September	23-7-73-1	37-6-99-0			26.3-3-125-3	35-8-114-2									126.3	450	16	6	
															–	–	–	–	
Leicestershire (Hove) 17-19 September	12-6-20-3	24.5-3-71-4	15-4-37-1			18-6-40-2									69.5	179	11	10	
	9.4-0-60-0		24.1-3-106-8	25-9-75-0		21.2-6-84-2				4-0-15-0			3-0-17-0	1-0-1-0	88.1	380	22	10	
Overs	374.1	865.5	358.2	250	430.2	258.1	98	99.5	32	13	2	3	3	1					
Maidens	84	174	81	49	95	73	18	17	3	1	0	0	0	0					
Runs	1283	2588	1182	779	1403	748	354	405	99	59	8	9	17	1					
Wickets	35	114	44	17	49	23	9	7	0	0	0	1	0	0					
Average	36.7	22.7	26.9	45.8	28.6	32.5	39.3	57.9	-	-	-	9.0	-	-					

FIELDING

TR Ambrose (29 ct, 7st)
MJ Prior (30 ct, 1st)
RR Montgomerie
CJ Adams
MW Goodwin
PA Cottey
RSC Martin-Jenkins
JD Lewry
MJG Davis
MH Yardy
Mushtaq Ahmed
RJ Kirtley
KJ Innes
AJ Hodd
B Zuiderent

WARWICKSHIRE CCC

FIRST–CLASS MATCHES

BATTING

	IR Bell	MA Wagh	DR Brown	NV Knight	T Frost	A Richardson	MJ Powell	JO Troughton	IJL Trott	MM Betts	Waqar Younis	AF Giles	NMK Smith	MA Sheikh	DP Ostler	NM Carter	CD Collymore	KJ Piper	CO Obuya	IJ Westwood	GG Wagg	MW Clark	TL Penney	Extras	Total	Wickets	Result
v. Nottinghamshire (Trent Bridge) 18-21 April	32	73	7	1	17	0	16				5	38			0							2*		31	222	10	
	11	14	52	41	0	13	24				56*	94			58							2		25	390	10	L
v. Essex (Edgbaston) 23-26 April	18	32	120	26	59		129*			1			28*	18										15	446	7	
																								–	–	–	D
v. Surrey (The Oval) 30 April-3 May	4	136	8	58	78	20*	17				25	20	14		0									33	413	10	
	13	19	0	103*	5		0				33		4*		25									19	221	10	D
v. Sussex (Edgbaston) 9-12 May	3	43	0	37	47		41		134	20	22			57*	1									17	422	10	
	107	38	0		0			105	5		13*				7									10	285	7	W
v. Cardiff UCCE (Abergavenny) 14-16 May	21				140		69								19			39*		63*				16	367	10	
								40							42*			28*						22	132	1	D
v. Kent (Edgbaston) 21-24 May	31	0	18	6	10*	0	120	9	46				57	5										9	311	10	
	12*	50*					30	31																1	124	2	D
v. Nottinghamshire (Edgbaston) 4-7 June	21	58	40	33	11		0	63	6	15*		13							55					36	351	10	
	64	39	20	146	15		5	28	11	8		8							30*					31	405	10	D
v. Sussex (Hove) 27-29 June	0	39	42*	11	1	0	60		6	21	8								2					11	201	10	
	37	2	20	64	4		0	80	31	15	14								8*					10	285	10	L
v. Leicestershire (Leicester) 2-5 July	0	35	5	66	11	16*	0		23	20	52			4										21	253	10	
	93	138	5	33	17	10	11		9	16*	0			8										21	361	10	D
v. Surrey (Edgbaston) 9-12 July	1	34	61	42	24		27		1		0*			1		20					11			23	245	10	
	71	51	56	8	12		91		51		30*			8		11					4			32	425	10	L
v. Middlesex (Southgate) 15-18 July	31	0	113	11	84	9*	8		37		38	96	30											39	496	10	
																								–	–	–	D
v. Lancashire (Old Trafford) 23-26 July	48	1	52*	27	7	4	28		16		22		10			4								36	255	10	
	28	76*	56	3*	21	4																		23	211	4	D
v. India A (Edgbaston) 30 July-2 August	75			76	68				78	21			42	10	0				36*	19	74			38	537	10	
																								–	–	–	D
v. Leicestershire (Edgbaston) 14-16 August	4	3	56*	0	10	12	28	41					61			30		2						30	277	10	
	7	58		122*		13	55*																	12	267	2	W
v. Middlesex (Edgbaston) 26-29 August	27	62	71	10	0		73	0			0	7					11*	8						21	290	10	
	0	46	0	9	4	1	64				13*	9				1		42						9	198	10	W
v. Lancashire (Edgbaston) 3-6 September	3	20	140*	28	2	0		126	73								0	15					19	23	449	10	
	46	16	44	3	4*	4		43	0								0	6					2	19	187	10	L
v. Essex (Chelmsford) 11-14 September	13	116	77	64	0	30	28	65			45*						1	24						40	503	10	
		23*		24*	10																			4	61	1	W
v. Kent (Canterbury) 17-19 September	54	6	0	25	0		61	26	53						15	0*		3						24	267	10	
	0	0	21	1	7		110	20	7						38	10*		39						4	257	10	L

	IR Bell	MA Wagh	DR Brown	NV Knight	T Frost	A Richardson	MJ Powell	JO Troughton	IJL Trott	MM Betts	Waqar Younis	AF Giles	NMK Smith	MA Sheikh	DP Ostler	NM Carter	CD Collymore	KJ Piper	CO Obuya	IJ Westwood	GG Wagg	MW Clark	TL Penney
Matches	18	16	16	14	13	13	13	12	11	9	8	6	6	6	6	5	5	5	3	2	2	1	1
Innings	31	30	26	26	21	19	24	20	19	14	13	10	8	8	10	7	8	9	5	2	3	2	2
Not Out	1	3	4	3	1	5	0	2	0	2	5	1	0	3	1	0	3	2	3	1	0	1	0
Highest Score	107	138	140*	146	84	47	140	129*	134	73	61	96	57	57*	58	38	11*	42	55	63*	74	2*	19
Runs	875	1228	1028	1012	477	158	934	748	832	348	268	338	138	171	180	118	25	204	131	82	89	4	21
Average	29.17	45.48	46.73	44.00	23.85	11.29	38.92	41.56	43.79	29.00	33.50	37.56	17.25	34.20	20.00	16.86	5.00	29.14	65.50	82.00	29.67	4.00	10.50
100s	1	3	3	3	0	0	2	3	2	0	0	0	0	0	0	0	0	0	0	0	0	0	0
50s	5	7	7	5	4	0	6	2	6	2	2	2	1	1	1	0	0	0	1	1	1	0	0
Catches/Stumpings	5/0	15/0	10/0	11/0	33/2	1/0	6/0	5/0	4/0	2/0	1/0	0/0	2/0	2/0	3/0	1/0	2/0	15/1	2/0	0/0	0/0	0/0	1/0

Home Ground: Edgbaston
Address: County Ground,
Edgbaston, Birmingham, B5 7QU
Tel: 0121 446 4422
Fax: 0121 440 7516
Ticket Hotline: 0121 446 5506
Indoor cricket centre: 0121 446 3633
Email: info@thebears.co.uk
Directions: *By rail:* New Street station, Birmingham
By road: M6 to A38M, to city centre, then follow signs
to County Ground.
Capacity: 20,000

Other grounds used: None
Year formed: 1882

Chairman: MJK Smith OBE
Chief Executive: Dennis Amiss MBE
Director of Coaching: Bob Woolmer
Other posts: *Second XI Coach:* Steve Perryman;
Marketing Manager: Peter Thompson;
Indoor Cricket Centre Coach: RN Abberley
Captain: Nick Knight
County colours: Blue and white

Honours

County Championship
1911, 1951, 1972, 1994, 1995
Sunday League/NCL
1980, 1994, 1997
Benson & Hedges Cup
1994, 2002
Gillette Cup/NatWest/C&G Trophy
1993, 1995

Website:
www.thebears.co.uk

WARWICKSHIRE CCC

FIRST-CLASS MATCHES
BOWLING

	DR Brown	A Richardson	IR Bell	MM Betts	MA Wagh	Waqar Younis	MA Sheikh	NMK Smith	AF Giles	NM Carter	CD Collymore	IJL Trott	CO Obuya	JO Troughton	GG Wagg	MJ Powell	NV Knight	MW Clark	JAS Spires	IJ Westwood	DP Ostler	NA Warren	Overs	Total	Byes/Leg-byes	Wickets	Run outs
Nottinghamshire (Trent Bridge) 18–21 April	19-4-61-3 / 16-1-42-0	22.5-8-85-4 / 24-7-59-1		16-3-76-1 / 16.2-2-48-4				12-1-46-0 / 26-1-59-1									15-2-71-2 / 18-5-39-1						84.5 / 100.2	349 / 264	10 / 16	10 / 7	
Essex (Edgbaston) 23–26 April	7-0-44-0	17-0-70-1	20-2-82-3		18-5-54-1		27.5-3-115-5				2-0-33-0							2-0-33-0					4 / 89.5	66 / 380	– / 15	– / 10	
Surrey (The Oval) 30 April–3 May	27.3-4-96-5	24-4-89-2			23-6-91-2	13-1-53-0	16-2-53-0																103.3	390	8	9	
Sussex (Edgbaston) 9–12 May	23-7-76-1 / 9-4-17-4	29-12-65-1 / 13-6-19-1		23.4-2-83-3 / 13-2-43-5	2-1-2-0		28-11-60-4 / 6-2-15-0		23-5-60-1 / 2-2-0-0														128.4 / 43	367 / 106	21 / 12	10 / 10	
Cardiff UCCE (Abergavenny) 14–16 May		7.5-6-13-4							20-4-61-2			23.3-7-53-1	4.1-1-10-0				7-0-23-2				16-2-74-0	78.3	251	17	10	1
Kent (Edgbaston) 21–24 May	19.5-5-72-5	23-3-91-1	3-0-10-0	15-2-55-1	2-1-3-0		36-4-110-3	8-2-26-0															106.5	376	9	10	
Nottinghamshire (Edgbaston) 4–7 June	25-2-127-0	14.3-1-79-3	4-1-7-1	21-3-93-1 / 1-0-1-0	25-3-84-1 / 6-1-30-4	36-9-94-1 / 4-0-30-1				12-0-54-0	17-1-91-3												154.3 / 11	646 / 67	17 / 6	10 / 5	
Sussex (Hove) 27–29 June	31.1-8-95-3	34-6-92-2	3-0-24-0	20-1-91-0	14-1-40-0	24-2-99-5				2-1-5-0	19-1-89-0												147.1	545	10	10	
Leicestershire (Leicester) 2–5 July	18-3-53-3 / 13-2-47-0	21-6-44-0 / 17-5-29-3	2-1-10-1 / 8-0-33-0	21.2-1-88-4 / 12-2-53-0	22-2-75-1 / 9-1-60-2		4-0-36-0 / 1.3-0-4-0																88.2 / 60.3	328 / 241	22 / 15	10 / 6	1 / 1
Surrey (Edgbaston) 9–12 July	17.2-4-59-2 / 12-0-74-1	3-0-14-0 / 1-0-5-0			17-7-65-1 / 14-1-81-1	7-0-34-0 / 22-1-111-2	17-0-75-5 / 20-3-81-0			18-2-101-2 / 13-0-88-1													79.2 / 82	355 / 450	7 / 10	10 / 5	
Middlesex (Southgate) 15–18 July	5-2-8-1 / 19-5-46-0	19.1-5-37-4 / 12-1-52-0		15-2-63-0 / 12-2-44-2		20-5-47-1	30-7-90-4 / 28-4-78-1						5-0-47-0			4-3-6-0							89.1 / 80	260 / 281	15 / 9	10 / 3	
Lancashire (Old Trafford) 23–26 July	30-7-117-2	29-3-112-0	7-0-23-0		24-5-79-1		15-0-97-1		24-1-133-2														129	575	14	6	
India A (Edgbaston) 30 July–2 August		9-4-12-4 / 9-1-49-0	11-3-34-2 / 15-3-51-0		12.5-4-30-2 / 18-2-69-1		11-4-36-0 / 1.2-3-43-0		12-1-47-0	10-0-06-1		9-2-61-2		3-0-14-0			8-0-57-0						52.5 / 95	181 / 449	8 / 23	10 / 2	
Leicestershire (Edgbaston) 14–16 August	11-4-31-1 / 13-2-37-0	16-3-55-3 / 17-5-34-1	3-0-11-1		15-5-48-1 / 10.4-2-20-4	18-2-52-3 / 13-1-37-4		16-5-53-0 / 8-3-11-1	18-4-71-1 / 10-2-36-0														97 / 71.4	346 / 195	25 / 20	10 / 10	
Middlesex (Edgbaston) 26–29 August	11-2-18-1 / 4-1-14-0	10-1-50-0 / 18-4-40-3	2-0-14-0		3-0-12-1 / 8-1-30-1	18-5-69-4 / 13.5-2-40-5		28-9-69-1 / 6-2-7-0	14-1-42-3 / 15-5-39-1														86 / 64.5	286 / 171	12 / 1	10 / 9	
Lancashire (Edgbaston) 3–6 September		45-8-128-2	16-5-70-0	26-2-151-0	39.5-2-222-7				30-5-99-1	12-0-70-0				6-0-28-0								174.5	781	13	10	
Essex (Chelmsford) 11–14 September	9-3-41-2 / 14-5-20-1	20-6-51-3 / 16-7-25-0		6-1-26-0 / 41-9-111-4	15.2-3-69-2 / 25.1-4-77-5				16-3-60-2 / 11-2-57-0				1-0-4-0										66.2 / 108.1	256 / 302	9 / 8	10 / 10	1
Kent (Canterbury) 17–19 September	24-6-80-1	26-4-87-1	16-3-53-0		30-2-122-1				18-1-90-0	24-2-71-0	11.1-2-39-7			7-0-34-0									156.1	594	18	10	
Overs	377.5	453	104.2	240.2	193.3	244.2	181.5	90.3	198.5	146	138	49.1	77.3	13	44.1	9	6	33	7	8	2	16					
Maidens	81	104	21	30	28	39	43	9	36	24	24	4	9	0	5	0	3	7	0	0	0	2					
Runs	1274	1314	420	970	730	917	553	408	577	583	475	215	329	85	260	42	39	110	23	57	33	74					
Wickets	36	33	13	26	20	39	15	4	13	10	8	7	5	0	5	0	0	3	2	0	0	0					
Average	35.4	39.8	32.3	37.3	36.5	23.5	36.9	102.0	44.4	58.3	59.4	30.7	65.8	–	52.0	–	–	36.7	11.5	–	–	–					

FIELDING

T Frost (33 ct, 2st)
KJ Piper (15 ct, 1st)
MA Wagh
NV Knight
DR Brown
MJ Powell
IR Bell
JO Troughton
IJL Trott
DP Ostler
CO Obuya
MM Betts
MA Sheikh
CD Collymore
NMK Smith
TL Penney
NM Carter
Waqar Younis
A Richardson

WORCESTERSHIRE CCC

FIRST–CLASS MATCHES
BATTING

	BF Smith	SD Peters	GJ Batty	M Hayward	A Singh	VS Solanki	MS Mason	GA Hick	Kabir Ali	SJ Rhodes	Kadeer Ali	AJ Hall	JM Kemp	MA Harrity	DJ Pipe	DA Leatherdale	SC Moore	SA Khalid	SJ Adshead	DH Wigley	Extras	Total	Wickets	Result
v. Hampshire	104	42	12	22	8	22		72	40	22				2*		4					36	386	10	
(Worcester) 18-21 April	82	24	14	6	8	45		4	25	20*				0*		12					24	264	9	D
v. Oxford UCCE	63	87	20*		77	41					27				0*						33	348	5	
(The Parks) 23-25 April																					-	-	-	D
v. Northamptonshire	50	17	0	6	6	79	0*	37	6	4							2				29	236	10	
(Worcester) 30 April-3 May																					-	-	-	D
v. Zimbabwe	53	18	0		14	74	4*	0			10	34	16	15							24	262	10	
(Worcester) 9-12 May	18	63	12		35	5	9	0			14	68	0*	6							17	247	10	T
v. Durham	81	62	18	28	16	52	0	30	84*	1	0										23	395	10	
(Stockton) 14-17 May																					-	-	-	D
v. Gloucestershire	1	8	32*	2	26	34	30	20	0	3		4									15	175	10	
(Worcester) 21-24 May	5	20	0	1	83*	15	29	5	0	9		35									10	212	10	W
v. Derbyshire	0	47	4	1	50	6	4	155	19*	29		0									59	374	10	
(Derby) 30 May-1 June		25*			21			1*													4	51	1	W
v. Somerset	2	165	26	4	105	10		71	0	22		104		2*							27	538	10	
(Bath) 4-7 June					15	20*		29*													4	68	1	W
v. Glamorgan	32	2	49	0*	38		52			15			14			24	13	63			26	328	10	
(Cardiff) 27-30 June	44	32	2		0					53			3			28*		3*			10	175	6	D
v. Durham	73	0	11	2	15	0				35			32		0*	28		5			17	218	10	
(Worcester) 2-4 July	60	0	15	0	8	27				13			5		5*	17		31			17	198	10	W
v. Derbyshire	22	5	37	0	8	28	0	68	81*	18	6										28	301	10	
(Worcester) 15-18 July																					-	-	-	W
v. Gloucestershire	92	14	24	0	50	35	3*	9	34	63		73									42	439	10	
(Cheltenham) 23-26 July																					-	-	-	D
v. Glamorgan	0	29	60	0	30	4	16	1	38*	0						50					9	237	10	
(Worcester) 31 July-3 August	87	56	5	4	10	8	1	6	28*	20						15					17	257	10	W
v. Yorkshire	2	6	5	1*	1	0	25	16	6	10		5									14	91	10	
(Scarborough) 13-14 August	87*	15	54*		41	2	47					23									9	278	5	W
v. Somerset	48	103	52*	0	14	2	13	23		25		32	5								14	331	10	
(Worcester) 20-22 August	2*	54			44			13*													3	116	2	W
v. Hampshire	16	87	1	25		8	0	21	6				90	0	104*						6	364	10	
(Southampton) 3-6 September	11	23	0		77	2*		42	20			79	33	0							26	313	9	W
v. Yorkshire	110	44	34	6*	17			7	0			99	20	10						15	27	389	10	
(Worcester) 12-15 September	57	0	21	7*	14			57	3			21	33	1						8	29	251	10	W
v. Northamptonshire	34	69	1		17	8		0			6					13*	20				4	172	8	
(Northampton) 17-19 September	53	50	20	8*	0	27		4			30					35	61	8			15	311	10	L
Matches	18	18	18	16	16	15	14	13	13	11	8	7	6	6	5	4	2	2	2	1				
Innings	29	30	28	21	27	23	20	23	18	14	14	9	11	9	9	7	4	2	4	2				
Not Out	2	1	4	5	1	1	4	3	4	2	0	0	0	6	3	0	1	0	1	0				
Highest Score	110	165	60	28	105	79	52	155	84*	81*	99	104	90	16	104*	61	28*	13	63	15				
Runs	1289	1167	529	123	754	584	250	670	371	309	426	324	290	30	184	164	97	21	102	23				
Average	47.74	40.24	22.04	7.69	29.00	26.55	15.62	33.50	26.50	25.75	30.43	36.00	26.36	10.00	30.67	23.43	32.33	10.50	34.00	11.50				
100s	2	2	0	0	1	0	0	1	0	0	0	0	1	0	1	0	0	0	0	0				
50s	12	8	3	0	4	4	1	3	2	2	2	2	1	0	0	2	0	0	1	0				
Catches/Stumpings	4/0	15/0	14/0	5/0	6/0	24/0	2/0	19/0	2/0	38/2	2/0	4/0	9/0	0/0	20/2	2/0	2/0	1/0	7/1	0/0				

Home Ground: Worcester
Address: New Road, Worcester WR2 4QQ
Tel: 01905 748474   **Fax:** 01905 748005
Ticket office: 01905 422694
Cricket Development Admin Officer (Allan Scrafton):
01905 429147
Directions: *By rail:* Worcester Foregate Street Station (city centre), half a mile from ground. Worcester Shrub Hill Station, one mile from ground. *By road:* From the north, M5 junction 6 then follow signposted route to Worcester and city centre, then take A44 for New Road. *By bus:* Midland Red West Nos 23–6.

Disabled access: designated viewing area for disabled visitors; free admission for carers; disabled toilet facilities.
Capacity: 4,500
Other grounds used: Kidderminster CC, Chester Road North, Kidderminster
Year formed: 1865
Chairman: John Elliott
Chief Executive: Mark Newton
Director of Cricket: Tom Moody
Second XI Coach: Damian D'Oliveira
Captain: Ben Smith
County colours: Green, black and white

Honours
County Championship
1964, 1965, 1974, 1988, 1989
Sunday League/NCL
1971, 1987, 1988
Benson & Hedges Cup
1991
Gillette Cup/NatWest/C&G Trophy
1994

Website:
www.wccc.co.uk

WORCESTERSHIRE CCC

FIRST-CLASS MATCHES — BOWLING

	GJ Batty	M Hayward	MS Mason	Kabir Ali	AJ Hall	MA Harrity	JM Kemp	DA Leatherdale	SA Khalid	VS Solanki	GA Hick	CG Liptrot	DH Wigley	Overs	Total	Byes/Leg-byes	Wickets	Run outs
Hampshire (Worcester) 18-21 April	25-9-40-1 / 22-4-71-2	31-9-95-4 / 18-2-70-5		26-8-74-4 / 17-1-78-1		24.4-7-90-1 / 12-3-32-0		13-1-47-0 / 5-0-23-1						119.4 / 74	347 / 276	1 / 2	10 / 9	
Oxford UCCE (Parks) 23-25 April	26-9-63-2		16-10-22-3				11-1-31-0		13.5-1-59-2			20-8-47-3		86.5	231	9	10	
Northamptonshire (Worcester) 30 April-3 May	15-2-27-1	19-2-81-0		26-5-80-1	25-6-65-2			9-0-43-0						94	312	16	5	1
Zimbabwe (Worcester) 9-12 May	19.2-8-44-2 / 14-4-32-3		25-10-66-1 / 13-7-18-0	28-8-89-3 / 15-2-48-5	26-7-58-1 / 13-5-38-1		28-7-66-1 / 7-0-29-1							126.2 / 62	334 / 175	11 / 10	9 / 10	1
Durham (Stockton) 14-17 May	11-5-23-1 / 16-6-34-3	10-1-34-2 / 5-0-32-0	8-4-21-0 / 5-0-19-0	9-0-44-0 / 8-0-37-1	3-0-21-0									41 / 40	146 / 151	3 / 3	3 / 19	
Gloucestershire (Worcester) 21-24 May	5-1-11-1	21.1-5-58-4 / 9-3-30-2	22-9-31-2 / 3-1-5-1	14-3-51-3 / 13-5-39-4	10-4-18-0 / 7-1-15-2									72.1 / 32	178 / 98	9 / 9	10 / 10	1
Derbyshire (Derby) 30 May-1 June	9-2-31-0 / 9-1-29-1	16.5-4-53-4 / 14-1-67-4	10-1-27-3 / 19-4-54-1	9-3-35-0 / 11-0-60-3	12-0-28-3 / 10-3-24-1									56.5 / 63	179 / 245	5 / 11	10 / 10	
Somerset (Bath) 4-7 June	22-8-66-3 / 39.1-8-88-6	15-5-56-2 / 15-2-49-0		13.4-1-68-3 / 19-4-75-1	7-1-27-2 / 23-7-63-2	8-3-20-0 / 20-2-69-1								65.4 / 116.1	238 / 367	1 / 19	10 / 10	
Glamorgan (Cardiff) 27-30 June	17-4-47-0 / 30-6-100-1	21.2-4-71-4 / 19-2-74-0	21-7-69-4 / 20-4-69-1					13-2-40-1 / 17-0-48-5	6-0-20-0 / 22-7-54-1					78.2 / 108	270 / 366	23 / 21	10 / 9	1 / 1
Durham (Worcester) 2-4 July	5-1-7-0 / 26-4-78-4	4.5-2-10-1	16-3-48-3 / 30.4-6-68-6				11.1-2-39-4 / 14-1-68-0	8.1-2-15-2 / 15-5-41-0						45.1 / 85.4	120 / 265	1 / 10	10 / 10	
Derbyshire (Worcester) 15-18 July	1-1-0-0	11.2-4-46-2 / 3-0-10-2	14-4-63-5 / 12-7-16-0	7-1-25-1 / 15.4-3-58-8	12-3-38-2					1-0-9-0				44.2 / 32.4	163 / 96	11 / 3	10 / 10	
Gloucestershire (Cheltenham) 23-26 July	8-0-41-2 / 8-1-19-2	17-3-77-3 / 7-2-17-0	16.1-7-48-3 / 8-4-23-0	17-2-64-1 / 12-2-43-2	14-6-29-1 / 6-2-24-1					1-1-0-0				73.1 / 41	271 / 133	12 / 7	10 / 5	
Glamorgan (Worcester) 31 July-3 August	10.1-2-24-1 / 23-3-66-2	11-2-34-2 / 15-1-75-1	12-3-22-3 / 23-6-58-2	13-2-55-2 / 29-6-96-4					5-2-18-2 / 7-3-11-1					51.1 / 97	156 / 324	3 / 18	10 / 10	
Yorkshire (Scarborough) 13-14 August		7.2-2-39-1 / 8.2-0-48-2	8-1-37-1 / 19-6-53-3	16-4-53-8 / 12-2-51-1				18-6-44-4						31.2 / 70.2	130 / 238	1 / 2	10 / 10	
Somerset (Worcester) 20-22 August	24.4-3-111-3 / 6-1-28-1	11-2-53-3 / 13.5-3-46-5	19-1-56-3 / 14-4-31-1				15-5-53-1 / 7-2-26-2	5-0-23-0						74.4 / 40.5	296 / 147	- / 16	10 / 10	1
Hampshire (Southampton) 3-6 September	26-8-77-3 / 34.2-10-94-4	18-4-50-2 / 17-1-69-1	19-5-47-2 / 18-3-66-3	11-1-40-2 / 16-1-60-1			9.4-2-26-0	4-0-11-0 / 3-1-10-0						87 / 88.2	265 / 311	14 / 12	10 / 10	1
Yorkshire (Worcester) 12-15 September	34-10-80-1 / 20-4-57-4	28-10-74-3 / 19-5-37-4		23-2-108-2				12-0-62-2 / 7-1-25-0					19.1-5-56-2 / 10-4-39-1	116.1 / 56	405 / 164	25 / 6	10 / 10	1
Northamptonshire (Northampton) 17-19 September	32-11-63-4 / 24-4-94-2	11.3-0-41-2 / 10-2-37-2	11-3-19-0 / 11.4-3-28-1								21-1-70-3 / 20-5-131-4	7.1-5-6-0		75.3 / 94.4	196 / 379	13 / 26	10 / 10	1 / 1
Overs	574.4	427.3	439.3	379.2	149	166.5	102.1	39	90.5	2	21	20	29.1					
Mdns	142	83	128	67	41	37	17	6	14	1	5	8	9					
Runs	1575	1533	1144	1416	393	549	319	142	334	9	63	47	95					
Wkts	60	67	53	62	19	11	14	4	10	0	0	3	3					
Average	26.2	22.9	21.6	22.8	20.7	49.9	22.8	35.5	33.4	-	-	15.7	31.7					

FIELDING

SJ Rhodes (38 ct, 2st)
VS Solanki
DJ Pipe (20 ct, 2st)
GA Hick
SD Peters
GJ Batty
JM Kemp
SJ Adshead (7 ct, 1st)
A Singh
M Hayward
BF Smith
AJ Hall
Kadeer Ali
SC Moore
CG Liptrot
DA Leatherdale
MS Mason
Kabir Ali
SA Khalid

YORKSHIRE CCC

FIRST–CLASS MATCHES
BATTING

	MJ Wood	MJ Lumb	RJ Blakey	SP Kirby	CEW Silverwood	RKJ Dawson	A McGrath	C White	AKD Gray	RJ Sidebottom	D Gough	SP Fleming	Yuvraj Singh	GM Fellows	SM Guy	VJ Craven	MJ Hoggard	TT Bresnan	CR Taylor	SA Richardson	MP Vaughan	PJ Swanepoel	DR Martyn	GM Hamilton	ND Thornicroft	Extras	Total	Wickets	Result
v. Northamptonshire (Headingley) 18–20 April	157	42	223*		53	38	35		24*	3			30				16									52	673	8	
																										–	–	–	W
v. Hampshire (Southampton) 30 April–3 May	5	115*	24	0	0	10	15	9	72				0								1					42	293	10	
	8*																				10*					5	23		D
v. Derbyshire (Headingley) 9–12 May	9	38	29	0	2	0	61		9								1*	10	47							24	230	10	
	32	86	11	4	2	13	4		4								13*	6	38							27	240	10	L
v. Northamptonshire (Northampton) 14–17 May	15	46	8		77	51		25	0				18				21*	7			103					28	399	10	
	33					0*															64*					12	109	1	D
v. Glamorgan (Headingley) 21–24 May	9	39	1	13*	10	20			28		11	53				3				1						21	209	10	
	73*											25*								50						11	159	1	D
v. Durham (Headingley) 30 May–1 June	0	105	3	0*	0	0				4			56	9					18		17					8	220	10	
	0	9	8	0*	8	21				9			1	4					18		2					13	93	10	L
v. Somerset (Taunton) 27–30 June	207	5	13	0*	22			6	104	16		98	5		16											20	512	10	
	30*											40*														1	71	–	W
v. Derbyshire (Derby) 2–5 July	35	93	0	33			173*	14	2			13	6		0			19								56	444	10	
	21*											42*														5	68	–	W
v. India A (Headingley) 9–11 July	5	65	1				31	15				17		27		52	13				1				1*	18	246	10	
	88	56	20				21*	34*				11		46		4										16	296	6	D
v. Durham (Chester-le-Street) 15–18 July	18	43		17			86	135*	60	12	4	10	7		3											53	448	10	
	10	5		1			3	30	11	18*	0	38	0		7											6	129	10	L
v. Hampshire (Scarborough) 23–26 July	155	64		0	4*			0	30			16	26		13	47										29	384	10	
	43	59							53	0*						38										18	211	4	D
v. Gloucestershire (Cheltenham) 30 July–2 August	15*	37		0	4*			4	23			0			8	7								68		34	226	10	
	33	4*										16				20*										2	75	2	D
v. Worcestershire (Scarborough) 13–14 August	4	0		4	7	42*	11	12	11			31			0	7										1	130	10	
	16	0		15	0*	24	15	54	27			35			26	17										9	238	10	L
v. Glamorgan (Colwyn Bay) 25–28 August	126	5	36	11	9	7	92	48*			12	61	2													13	422	10	
	0	1	0	2*	22		127*	13			16	6														6	193	7	D
v. Somerset (Headingley) 3–5 September	40	2	27			47	0	93			83						3	11*					87			17	410	8	
	53*					67*	8																			4	132	1	W
v. Worcestershire (Worcester) 12–15 September	37	61	3	2	1	60	47	66						45	0*	40										43	405	10	
	14	23	31*	8	6	18	6	9						24	1	14										10	164	10	L
v. Gloucestershire (Headingley) 17–20 September	116	4	9	5	4	48*	28	0		10						2							238			12	476	10	
	25	31	21	7*	5	1	2			2*													17			10	121	7	D
Matches	17	17	13	13	12	12	10	10	9	9	7	7	7	6	6	6	5	4	3	3	3	2	2	1	1				
Innings	33	27	19	18	18	18	18	16	13	11	10	14	12	8	8	11	7	4	5	6	6	3	3	1	1				
Not Out	6	2	2	4	4	2	3	3	2	2	1	2	2	0	0	1	5	0	0	0	2	0	0	0	1				
Highest Score	207	115*	223*	33	53	77	127*	173*	104	28	83	98	56	53	26	47	21*	52	40	50	103	17	238	68	1*				
Runs	1432	1038	468	113	152	467	649	644	415	122	199	469	145	142	73	281	49	81	87	103	263	20	342	68	1				
Average	53.04	41.52	27.53	8.07	10.86	29.19	43.27	49.54	37.73	13.56	22.11	39.08	14.50	17.75	9.12	28.10	24.50	20.25	17.40	17.17	65.75	6.67	114.00	68.00	1.00				
100s	5	2	1	0	0	0	1	2	1	0	0	0	0	0	0	0	0	0	0	0	1	0	1	0	0				
50s	3	7	0	0	1	2	5	3	1	0	2	3	1	1	0	0	0	1	0	1	1	0	1	1	0				
Catches/Stumpings	8/0	7/0	32/1	5/0	2/0	11/0	5/0	4/0	12/0	4/0	2/0	13/0	12/0	1/0	16/2	0/0	2/0	1/0	1/0	3/0	1/0	1/0	1/0	1/0	0/0				

Home Ground: Headingley
Address: Headingley Cricket Ground, Leeds LS6 3BU
Tel: 0113 278 7394
Fax: 0113 278 4099
Ticket Office: 0800 032 6644
Email: cricket@yorkshireccc.org.uk
Other grounds used: Scarborough
Year formed: 1863

Chairman: Michael Ziff

Chief Executive: Colin Graves
Director of Cricket: Geoff Cope
Captain: Anthony McGrath
Youth Development: Arnie Sidebottom and Steve Oldham
County colours: Oxford blue, Cambridge blue and gold

Website:
www.yorkshireccc.org.uk

Honours
County Championship
1893, 1896, 1898, 1900, 1901, 1902, 1905, 1908, 1...
1919, 1922, 1923, 1924, 1925, 1931, 1932, 1933, 1...
1937, 1938, 1939, 1946, 1959, 1960, 1962, 1963, 1...
1967, 1968, 2001
Sunday League/NCL
1983
Benson & Hedges Cup
1987
Gillette Cup/NatWest/C&G Trophy
1965, 1969, 2002

YORKSHIRE CCC

ST-CLASS MATCHES

OWLING

Match	SP Kirby	CEW Silverwood	RKJ Dawson	A McGrath	AKD Gray	RJ Sidebottom	D Gough	MJ Hoggard	VJ Craven	TT Bresnan	Yuvraj Singh	MJ Lumb	GM Fellows	C White	PJ Swanepoel	MJ Wood	MP Vaughan	ND Thornicroft	Overs	Total	Byes/Leg-byes	Wickets	Run outs
orthamptonshire (adingley) 18-20 April		10-2-45-3	4-1-27-1	3-0-10-0		5.1-1-14-2	12-1-40-3	14-3-37-1											48.1	184	11	10	
		13-4-39-4	7-3-9-2			7-1-28-1	11.4-1-41-3					2-0-4-0							40.4	146	25	10	
ampshire (uthampton) 30 April-3 May	11-3-19-3	9-2-34-1	7-2-23-2	4.5-0-19-1		14-3-44-2	14-5-28-0												59.5	175	8	10	1
erbyshire (adingley) 9-12 May	24-4-90-0	23-3-75-0	17.4-3-38-1	10-3-21-1		31-3-97-7		27-4-80-0											132.4	422	21	10	1
	7-0-37-0	6-0-23-0	25.2-4-72-2	6-1-15-0		10-2-24-2		9-2-26-0				1-0-7-0							64.2	214	10	4	
orthamptonshire (rthampton) 14-17 May			27-3-105-0	4-0-22-0	24-4-66-1	23-4-66-2		29-6-74-3		12.2-3-43-0						1-0-5-0			120.2	402	21	6	
lamorgan (adingley) 21-24 May	22-3-89-3	20-4-57-4	10-1-44-0			16-3-51-2				11.4-0-51-1		2-0-3-0							81.4	315	20	10	
urham (adingley) 30 May-1 June	20-4-40-2	21.3-1-80-3	16-7-27-1				23-3-55-2				3-0-15-0	10-1-20-1		18-9-30-1					111.3	280	13	10	
	12-5-29-0	15-2-40-4	2-0-16-1				15-2-36-1				6-0-29-1			16-2-40-2					66	200	10	9	
omerset (nton) 27-30 June	16-1-74-5	14-3-46-3		8-1-34-0		18-3-74-2					2-0-15-0				9-1-21-0				67	275	11	10	
	24.4-5-80-8	15-6-76-1		10-3-22-0		18-3-49-0					11-1-43-1				5-0-27-0				83.4	306	9	10	
erbyshire (by) 2-5 July	12-5-31-3					7-1-25-0		13.4-6-38-6		9-4-14-1	1-0-10-0								42.4	128	10	10	
	30-5-85-3					43-10-125-1		22.3-5-73-3		25-5-63-2	1-1-0-0				7-2-16-0				128.3	383	16	10	1
dia A (adingley) 9-11 July				26-8-64-1					3-0-14-0		21.1-4-88-3	1-0-7-0	5-1-21-1		17-5-59-0	6-0-18-1		14-2-57-0	93.1	336	8	8	2
urham (ester-le-Street) 15-18 July	20-3-93-4		8-3-31-1	9-1-45-2	17-0-67-2	18-2-77-1													72	327	14	10	
	21-5-54-2		11-1-18-0	12-2-30-1		19.3-6-68-1													79.3	251	24	7	1
ampshire (rborough) 23-26 July	16-1-79-2	15-1-86-4		16-0-49-1		11-1-28-2		9-1-38-1											67	289	9	10	
	13-1-59-1	16-3-40-0		26-12-43-3				11-4-25-2		4.4-1-4-0									70.4	180	9	6	
loucestershire (eltenham) 30 July-2 August	24-4-101-6	23-3-81-2		3.5-1-6-1	8-2-22-0				12-5-37-1										69.5	263	16	10	
	13-2-82-4	13-2-48-0		12-0-77-1					1-0-12-0										49	284	6	6	
orcestershire (rborough) 13-14 August	14-5-51-6	10-4-33-3							4-7-6-1										28	91	1	10	
	22.6-7-92-2	18-3-59-1	7-0-17-1	11-2-39-0				14.2-3-52-1	4-1-26-0										76.2	278	6	5	
lamorgan (wyn Bay) 25-28 August	26-1-158-2	19-2-56-4	17-4-70-0	10-2-37-2	18-2-45-1	20-3-73-0						4-1-8-1							114	466	19	10	
	5-0-30-0	9-1-46-0	34-7-119-3	6-0-21-0	2-0-11-0	14-2-33-2						12.5-1-65-1							82.5	336	11	6	
omerset (dingley) 3-5 September	14.5-1-82-1		3-0-35-0			20-8-42-2		22.4-9-49-7	2-0-13-0										62.3	228	7	10	
	13-0-61-2		18-2-59-2	14-2-43-1		19-2-58-2		20.5-2-57-2	12-3-28-0						2-0-4-1				98.5	313	3	10	
orcestershire (cester) 12-15 September	32.3-4-122-5	28-9-56-1	29-12-61-1	7-0-25-0				26-6-85-2	8-1-25-1										130.3	389	15	10	
	28.1-7-62-2	21-7-63-5	6-0-34-0					13-4-41-1	9-1-29-2										77.1	251	22	10	
loucestershire (dingley) 17-20 September	13.5-3-63-0	25.1-7-75-5	3-0-10-0	11.2-2-26-3				22.4-8-83-1	21-3-72-1										96.2	344	15	10	
	8-2-19-1	9-4-19-0		4-1-11-2				10-5-17-1	10-5-26-1										41	93	1	5	

	SP Kirby	CEW Silverwood	RKJ Dawson	A McGrath	AKD Gray	RJ Sidebottom	D Gough	MJ Hoggard	VJ Craven	TT Bresnan	Yuvraj Singh	MJ Lumb	GM Fellows	C White	PJ Swanepoel	MJ Wood	MP Vaughan	ND Thornicroft
Overs	463	351.4	241.5	117.1	233.2	222.2	218.1	192.3	75	70.1	34.3	13	19	21	51	8	1	14
Maidens	80	73	47	20	51	37	46	44	18	16	5	0	2	3	16	0	0	2
Runs	1769	1177	840	347	692	710	651	547	253	259	130	73	48	64	129	22	5	57
Wickets	67	48	17	13	13	35	19	18	8	7	3	1	2	0	3	2	0	0
Average	26.4	24.5	49.4	26.7	53.2	20.3	34.3	30.4	31.6	37.0	43.3	73.0	24.0	-	43.0	11.0	-	-

LDING

RJ Blakey (32 ct, 1st)
SM Guy (16 ct, 2st)
SP Fleming
AKD Gray
Yuvraj Singh
RKJ Dawson
MJ Wood
MJ Lumb
A McGrath
SP Kirby
C White
RJ Sidebottom
SA Richardson
CEW Silverwood
MJ Hoggard
D Gough
TT Bresnan
CR Taylor
PJ Swanepoel
MP Vaughan
GM Fellows
GM Hamilton
DR Martyn